THE 21 MOST

EFFECTIVE

PRAYERS

COLLECTION

THE 21 MOST
EFFECTIVE
PRAYERS
COLLECTION

DAVE EARLEY

BARBOUR
PUBLISHING

Collection © 2014 by David Earley.
The 21 Most Effective Prayers of the Bible © 2005 by David Earley.
The 21 Most Encouraging Promises of the Bible © 2006 by David Earley.
The 21 Most Dangerous Questions of the Bible © 2007 by David Earley.
21 Reasons Bad Things Happen to Good People © 2007 by David Earley.
The 21 Most Amazing Truths about Heaven © 2006 by David Earley.

Print ISBN 978-1-62836-649-5

eBook Editions:
Adobe Digital Edition (.epub) 978-1-63058-087-2
Kindle and MobiPocket Edition (.prc) 978-1-63058-088-9

Bible translations used in each book of this collection are indicated on the reverse of each title page.

The author is represented by literary agent Les Stobbe.

Published by Barbour Books, an imprint of Barbour Publishing, Inc., P.O. Box 719, Uhrichsville, Ohio 44683, www.barbourbooks.com

Our mission is to publish and distribute inspirational products offering exceptional value and biblical encouragement to the masses.

 Member of the
Evangelical Christian
Publishers Association

Printed in the United States of America.

Contents

The 21 Most Effective Prayers of the Bible

Dedication

This book is dedicated in loving memory of
Bob S. Earley.
The last few years of his life
Dad's prayers grew in frequency, fervency, and impact.
He loved praying the prayers of the Bible, and especially,
"God bless me that I might bless others." And God did.

Acknowledgments

No man is an island and no successful book is a solo effort. Many thanks to the team of people who made this project a reality:

- Cathy for loving me, believing in me, and allowing me to serve God in this way
- My boys, Daniel, Andrew, and Luke, for praying for me
- Carol, my favorite sister and the best PR person I could ever imagine
- Susan for all of her help with the details of the church
- The Mighty Men for their prayers
- Paul Muckley, an awesome guy and good friend who went the extra mile to make this project effective
- Ellen Caughey for her editorial expertise, Kelly McIntosh for managing the in-house editorial process, and Glady Dunlap for handling the typesetting
- Rich Nathan, Rhonda Tucker, Roy Mansfeld, and Andy Bullard for allowing me to tell their stories
- Bob and Rusty Russell, Bruce Wilkinson, Henry Blackaby, and David Jeremiah for helping me learn more about prayer

Contents

Introduction

Don't you just love it when a plan comes together? Isn't it awesome when you try something and it actually works?

I have little ability when it comes to fixing things—and, unfortunately, all five of the people in my household are gifted at breaking things. Being the dad, I am the first one called upon, though I'm not sure why. My efforts often end in failure, or I make things worse than they were. But on rare and glorious occasions, the thing-a-ma-jig gets fixed. That's when the band plays, there's dancing in the streets, and all is right with the world.

Through the years one of the true joys in my prayer life has come from praying the actual prayers of the Bible, especially those that worked. I reason that if God answered the petitions of Hannah, David, and Jacob, He might do the same for me—and He has!

Recently I accepted the challenge to narrow the hundreds of prayers in the Bible to twenty-one short, simple petitions that God answered positively. These twenty-one high-impact prayers span thousands of years, come from all classes of people, and were offered for a variety of reasons. Each was particular and direct, expressed with great earnestness, and offered with sincere expectation. They were offered as requests, not demands. They flow in conformity with the life of the requester and were presented with genuine reverence and humility. And they were all wonderfully answered!

They are petitions God enjoyed enough to have recorded as Scripture. They changed the lives of those who prayed them—and they are requests that we can make today. I have found that praying the answered prayers of the Bible gives me confidence that what I am asking is at least close to the will of God.

Learning them is fun.
Remembering them is easy.
Praying them is simple.
Seeing God answer them is exciting.

Praying these petitions will become an adventure that can change your life. However, before you do, let me remind you of some important truths about prayer. I agree with Bob Russell's warning that prayer is not dictation. Prayer is not telling God what to do and then expecting His immediate, positive response. Prayer is cooperating with God so that He can release His power.[1]

Someone said that God answers prayers, "Yes," "No," "Wait," and "You gotta be kidding." Someone else said that if our request is wrong, God says, "No"; if our timing is wrong, God says, "Slow"; if we are wrong, God says, "Grow"; and if our request is right, our timing is right, and we are right, God says, "Go!" However God answers, we know that He is a wise heavenly Father who knows what is best for us, and what is best for others.

When my youngest son, Luke, was three, he began asking me for a pocketknife. Repeatedly, he received the same answer: "Wait until you are old enough so you won't hurt yourself or your brothers." Yet, he kept asking. When he was five and a half, his mother, taken with a genuine Swiss Army knife in a store window, purchased the knife. The end of the story is that Luke ended up needing three stitches in his leg. (That is one of the few times I said to my wife, *I told you so.*)

Even if you do pray the most effective prayers in the Bible, like my son, you may not always get the answer you want when you want it. God's "No" or "Wait" is another way of saying, "I love you and I only give what is best for you." Keep in mind God is not our servant—but we are His. He answers according to *His* plans and purposes, and not ours. Our heavenly Father knows best.

I think you will find that He delights in saying, "Yes." God loves to hear and answer prayers. More often than not, He is the God of "Yes."

Features for More Effective Prayer

This book features three aids to enhance your prayer life:

1. *A Prayer to Remember and to Pray*. Each chapter highlights a short, simple, significant prayer. Most are only four or five words in length. Try to memorize each one so you will always have it available when you need it.

2. *A Chapter to Read*. There are twenty-one chapters in this book. Make a goal to read one chapter every day for the next three weeks. If that is unrealistic, try for one every other day.

3. *Scriptures to Study*. Each prayer is taken from the life of a Bible character. I suggest that you open your Bible to the passage discussed and mark it. These are some of the most fascinating and often overlooked stories in the Bible. You will want to go back to them later.

Suggestions for More Effective Prayer

1. *A Time to Pray.* Try to determine a set time each day when you will read a chapter and pray. It could be first thing in the morning or the last thing at night, or over your lunch hour. The right time is the time that works for you.

2. *An Amount of Time for Prayer*. There are 24 hours in a day, or 1,440 minutes. Setting aside 15, or 30, or 60 minutes a day for study and prayer can become a life-changing experience. Oliver Wendell Holmes said that a mind is like a rubber band—once stretched it never returns to its original size. Pick an amount of time that will stretch you. Even if you can't maintain that schedule after the three weeks is over, you will have experienced significant growth in your prayer life.

3. *A Place for Prayer*. Jesus spoke of a prayer closet. Your place for prayer could be at a desk or the kitchen table or on your bed. I often enjoy taking a prayer walk in the middle of the day. The right place is the place that is right for you.

4. *A Friend with Whom to Pray.* Jesus promised added insight and answers when two or more agree in prayer (Matthew 18:19). Ask a friend to read this book along with you. Gather together face-to-face, or over the phone, and pray together the prayers you are learning.

As a final note, the twenty-one prayers that follow have been ordered as they appear in the Bible. Although there are many ways the prayers could have been presented, I hope God will bless you as you discover the growing spiritual maturity evidenced in this biblical progression.

NOTES

[1]Bob Russell and Rusty Russell, *When God Answers Prayer* (West Monroe, LA: Howard Publishing Company, 2003), pp. 10–14.

1

GIVE ME SUCCESS TODAY:
The Prayer of Eliezer
GENESIS 24:12

Are you due for some success? If so, the prayer of Eliezer is a good place to start.

The story begins with Abraham, a recent widower, arriving at the ripe old age of 140 years. Abraham seriously wanted his son, Isaac, to marry and give him a grandson. Isaac was already forty years old and hopelessly single. So Abraham took action.

Abraham called his chief servant, Eliezer, and sent him on an ancient version of Mission Impossible. He would have to travel 450 rigorous miles by camel to the area where Abraham grew up. There he was to select a suitable bride for Isaac. She would have to be from among Abraham's distant relatives (the custom was to marry a first cousin). After finding such a girl, he would then have to convince her to return with him to marry Isaac, a man she had never met. This would be no walk in the park.

Eliezer gathered a small caravan and made the lengthy trek to Abraham's homeland. His plan was to find the right girl at the central meeting place for desert communities—the well. As he approached the town, he offered a simple prayer:

> *"O LORD, God of my master Abraham, give me success today, and show kindness to my master Abraham. See, I am standing beside this spring, and the daughters of the townspeople are coming out to draw water. May it be that when I say to a girl, 'Please let down your jar that I may have a drink,' and she says, 'Drink, and I'll water your camels too'—let her be the one you have chosen for your servant Isaac. By this I will know that you have shown kindness to my master."*
>
> GENESIS 24:12–14

Give me success today.

Notice the core of his prayer: "Give me success today." This request was simple, specific, and definite in reference to time. He asked God to direct him to the right girl and do it right away. After all, Isaac was not getting any younger. In order to know which girl would be the right one, Eliezer added to his request that she not merely offer to get him a drink but also volunteer to water his camels.

"Give me success today" was a wee, little prayer. Yet it immediately reaped a stupendous, prodigious answer! Look at the glorious results:

> *Before he had finished praying, Rebekah came out with her jar on her shoulder. She was the daughter of Bethuel son of Milcah, who was the wife of Abraham's brother Nahor. The girl was very beautiful, a virgin; no man had ever lain with her. She went down to the spring, filled her jar and came up again. The servant hurried to meet her and said, "Please give me a little water from your jar." "Drink, my lord," she said, and quickly lowered the jar to her hands and gave him a drink. After she had given him a drink, she said, "I'll draw water for your camels too, until they have finished drinking."*
>
> GENESIS 24:15–19

Bingo! God hit the target. He answered Eliezer's prayer and then some. *Before he had finished praying*, God sent the right girl. Rebekah, as it turned out, was a distant relative of Abraham, which meant she was qualified. Not insignificantly, she also happened to be a very beautiful and unattached virgin. To top it off, she not only gave Eliezer a drink, but she also offered to water his camels!

And that's not all. Later we read that Rebekah was willing to leave her family and her home immediately to make the return trip with Eliezer (24:58). The story even has a happy ending—when Isaac met her, he loved her (24:67).

God did not merely answer Eliezer's request with a timid, little "Yes." His answer was a robust, overwhelming "YES!" Yes, a girl offered to give Eliezer water. Yes, she asked to water his camels as well. Yes, she was related to Abraham. Yes, she was beautiful. Yes, she was an available virgin. Yes, she was willing to travel with him all the way back to marry Isaac. And for the two of them, yes, it was love at first sight.

Furthermore, God's "Yes" blessed everyone involved. Abraham had the good fortune of gaining a non-Canaanite daughter-in-law to be the mother of his grandson. Rebekah became an essential part of God's promise to Abraham that he would become the father of many nations. For Rebekah, she received a husband who loved her and a place in the royal line of the Messiah. She moved from a pagan family to a God-fearing one. Isaac's life was changed because he received a very beautiful bride. Rebekah would be the woman he would love and who would bear his sons.

But the greatest windfall came to Eliezer. Prior to this event, Eliezer viewed God solely as Abraham's God. Instead of a personal relationship with the Lord, he had more of a secondhand relationship. But after he experienced the loving and powerful way God answered his prayer, he became a man who worshiped God for himself (Genesis 24:26–27).

Eliezer now had his own story to tell. He eagerly told Rebekah's older brother all that the Lord had done for him (see Genesis 24:34–48). Because of this answered prayer, he had his own testimony to share of how God had worked on his behalf.

Now, the way I figure it, if God would do that for Eliezer when he prayed, "Give me success," He might be willing to do the same for me, and for you.

Making It Personal

One tiny prayer had a tremendous impact on many lives. As we read the story of this ancient prayer, we find several lessons for our lives today.

1. *Prayer is for everyone.* Although we assume the servant was Eliezer, we do not know for sure. Chapter 24 simply calls him "the chief servant of Abraham."[1] But nothing in the Word of God is written the way it is by accident. Eliezer may be intentionally unnamed to remind us that answered prayer is not the privileged domain of the big-name, spiritual elite. It is the heritage of all who call upon the Lord.

2. *God answered a selfish-sounding prayer.* Eliezer prayed, "Give *me* success today"—and God answered in the affirmative. While we may have been convinced it is wrong to pray selfish-sounding prayers, as a result, we are missing many of the blessings God intended.

In the biblical record, God answered some selfish-sounding prayers when they were offered with legitimate motives and for beneficial things. Eliezer's request, while appearing selfish, was also *selfless*, in that he wanted God to answer in order to ultimately serve his master. He was not praying about his own bride but a bride for another man, Isaac. And, if the unnamed servant is indeed Eliezer, then this request was especially unselfish, as Eliezer was sent to get a bride for the man who took his place as Abraham's heir (Genesis 15:2)!

3. *God is very eager to answer prayer.* Notice those first four words in Genesis 24:15: "Before he finished praying." God was already answering *before* Eliezer was finished praying! Rebekah came out with her jar on her shoulder *before* Eliezer had even completed his petition. When we ask for good things with worthy motives, God may respond quickly.

Often we have the misconception that God is reluctant to answer prayer. We think that He must be begged or manipulated or argued into answering. I have come to assume that when it comes to asking in prayer, I have nothing to lose. If mine is not the right request offered at the right time, or if my motives are not quite right, what is the worst that can happen? God can say "No."

But if my request is something to which God can say "Yes," then by asking I may receive a blessing I would not have obtained otherwise. I would rather go to my grave being guilty of asking for more than I received than for missing answers because I did not ask.

4. *When you pray for success, give God a specific target.* Eliezer asked that a very special girl would not only be willing to give him a drink, but that she would also offer to water his camels (24:14). Too often we get vague blessings because we pray vague prayers. If we want specific answers, we need to make specific requests.

I learned the power of specific prayer as a sophomore at a rather strict college. I needed a haircut or I would be in violation of the school hair code. One evening my resident assistant gave me twenty-four hours to get a haircut. I had absolutely no money and no hope of getting a decent haircut for free. (My three roommates had proven to be notorious "butchers" who no sane person would trust with a pair of scissors.)

Later that night I was reading in Luke 11 where Jesus told the story of the persistent friend. The passage encourages specific prayer as the man asks for *three* loaves. So I gave God a specific threefold target: I asked Him for (1) a good haircut, (2) before the next evening ended, and (3) for free. As I prayed, I received a wonderful sense of peace. Soon I dozed off to sleep.

The next day I overslept and ran out to class, forgetting all about my need for a haircut. But God didn't forget. That evening at the dinner table a friend introduced me to a girl I had never met. As we talked, she said that she had graduated from beauty school and her dad had made her attend a liberal arts college for a semester. She said that she really missed cutting hair and was thinking of starting her own business on the side. Then she looked at me and said, "You have a nice head of hair. Hmm, I miss cutting hair so much, I would cut yours for free."

After dinner I could not help but smile as I sat in a chair listening to her whistle and watching the hair drop around my feet. God had heard my simple, specific prayer. He had given me a great haircut, in less than twenty-four hours, for free.

I asked for success and God answered. I had a need and God met it. When given a target to hit, God drilled a bull's-eye.[2]

Need an answer? Can you use some success in a God-directed assignment? Why not give God a target to hit? He might just answer, "Yes!" He might even say, "YES!"

NOTES

[1]The servant's name is not stated in Genesis 24:2. He is simply referred to as "the chief servant of Abraham." Scholars assume that this servant was Eliezer, whom Abraham trusted enough to consider making his heir (Genesis 15). For a more detailed discussion, see note for Genesis 24:2 in John MacArthur, *The MacArthur Study Bible* (Nashville, TN: Word Publishing, 1997), p. 46.

[2]For more on prayer for success, see Dave Earley, *Prayer Odyssey* (Shippensburg, PA: Destiny Image Publishers, 2003), pp. 37–40.

2

Bless Me:
The Prayer of Jacob
Genesis 32:26

As they say where I grew up, Jacob was "in a fix." Years before, he had taken the birthright blessing meant for his older brother, Esau, and Esau had not forgotten. Keep in mind that Esau was a burly, roughhewn, angry man. Not the sort you would want to meet in a dark alley.

Now Esau was bearing down on Jacob with an army of four hundred men. The best plan Jacob could devise was to use Middle Eastern strategy and send Esau a series of carefully selected gifts, even though he had little hope that this would work.

At that point Jacob did what desperate men should do. He prayed (Genesis 32:9–12), but he didn't sound very sincere, apparently even to himself. Thus, he continued to try and wiggle out of sure disaster (Genesis 32:13–24), and ended up finding himself alone and even more desperate (Genesis 32:24).

A man appeared in the dark to Jacob and a battle began. Arms were twisted, legs were seized, and necks were wrenched. All through the night the wrestling war was waged. When it became clear Jacob could not win, he grabbed hold of the stranger and hung on for dear life. Then he uttered a small prayer: "I will not let you go unless you bless me" (Genesis 32:26).

Bless me.

Jacob had taken hold of God—his opponent in the dark—and refused to let go until God had blessed him. Asking for all the blessing he could get was typical of Jacob. He had asked his father to give him the biggest blessing his father could give and now he was asking the same of God.

When I first read this story I was surprised at the boldness, the brashness, and yes, the greediness of Jacob. Come on! I was expecting God to rise up and blast him for making such a request. Instead, God gave Jacob what he asked for. God blessed him with a manifold blessing—one replete with transformation, revelation, direction, protection, and impact.

> *The man asked him, "What is your name?" "Jacob," he answered. Then the man said, "Your name will no longer be Jacob, but Israel, because you have struggled with God and with men and have overcome."*
>
> Genesis 32:27–28

God changed his name from Jacob, meaning "grasper," to Israel, meaning "prince of God." The name change indicated a transformation of heart. There is a positive side to Jacob's personality, and God was obviously impressed with his prevailing perseverance. He had held on, and hung on, until he got what he sought. When he had a chance to get a hold of God, he refused to let go.

> *Jacob said, "Please tell me your name." But he replied, "Why do you ask my name?" Then he blessed him there. So Jacob called the place Peniel, saying, "It is because I saw God face to face, and yet my life was spared." The sun rose above him as he passed Peniel, and he was limping because of his hip. Therefore to this day the Israelites do not*

eat the tendon attached to the socket of the hip, because the socket of Jacob's hip was
touched near the tendon.

GENESIS 32:29–32

When Jacob chose the Hebrew word *Peniel,* which means "the face of God," to com-memorate the site, he was clearly aware that he had been given a rare and glorious opportu-nity. He had a face-to-face encounter with the living God and lived to tell about it. At Peniel, God revealed Himself to Jacob in a life-changing way. God touched his hip and changed the way he walked the rest of his life. More importantly, God touched his heart and changed the way he lived the rest of his life.

Jacob looked up and there was Esau, coming with his four hundred men; so he divid-
ed the children among Leah, Rachel and the two maidservants. He put the maidser-
vants and their children in front, Leah and her children next, and Rachel and Joseph
in the rear. He himself went on ahead and bowed down to the ground seven times as
he approached his brother.

GENESIS 33:1–3

God gave Jacob a plan, one that would require something new for Jacob. He would take the path of humility. When Jacob went and faced his brother, he bowed low before him seven times as an inferior would before a highly honored patron.

But Esau ran to meet Jacob and embraced him; he threw his arms around his neck
and kissed him. And they wept.

GENESIS 33:4

Instead of killing Jacob, Esau embraced him and kissed him. Together they wept. Years of deep bitterness and guilt were erased in a few moments. God had blessed Jacob with protection in the face of sure death.

This little prayer caused lives to be changed! All those with Jacob—his wives, children, servants, and livestock—were spared. Among those was his son, Judah, from whom the Messiah would descend. So, in a sense, Jacob's prayer blessed all of us.

Beyond that, Esau's life was wonderfully altered. He let go of a lifetime of bitterness toward his overly aggressive brother. Instead of killing Jacob, he embraced him.

Yet, the biggest change was seen in the life of Jacob. Jacob not only had a new name, but he had a new heart. Notice how this story ends.

[Esau asked,] "What do you mean by all this company I have met?" And he said, "To
find favor in the sight of my lord." But Esau said, "I have plenty, my brother; let what you
have be your own." Jacob said, "No, please, if I have found favor in your sight, then take
my present from my hand, for I see your face as one sees the face of God, and you have
received me favorably. Please take my gift which has been brought to you, because God has
dealt graciously with me and because I have plenty." Thus he urged him and he took it.

GENESIS 33:8–11 NASB

Can you imagine Jacob begging Esau to "please take my blessing"? Jacob, the one who previously had stolen the blessing, was now eager to give a blessing. He was a new man.

He humbly acknowledged that God had blessed him. Therefore, he desired to bless others.

Making It Personal

1. *God blesses the spiritually aggressive.* The blessing of God does not necessarily rest on the passive or the lax. I think that somewhere along the line we have developed the mistaken notion that Christians are nice, quiet, almost wimpy people.

Nothing could be further from the truth. While we are to be gracious and kind, God wants us to be much more than really nice people. He dreams of His people winning battles, relishing adventures, and enjoying all that He has for us.

One man describes it this way: "Prayer is not a lovely sedan for a sightseeing trip around the city. Prayer is a truck that goes straight to the warehouse, backs up, loads, and comes home with the goods. Too many people rattle their trucks all over town and never back up to the warehouse! They do not go after something when they pray. They do not ask, therefore, they do not receive."[1]

I have to admit that I have a quiet, timid streak. My mother was a Quaker and I was raised to cast a skeptical eye on bold, aggressive people. But timidity must not be confused with humility. God blesses humility, not timidity. He also invites boldness in prayer.[2]

A few years ago we decided to have a special Sunday at our church when everyone would bring unchurched friends to the worship services. The week before that Sunday I had made the bold assertion that I believed if we asked God to bless us, we could see fifty adults giving their hearts to Jesus Christ. Afterward, my wife calmly reminded me how I had stuck my neck out.

In preparation for Sunday, hundreds of our members were fasting and praying. Many of us got alone and wrestled with God. I boldly, and maybe a bit desperately, asked Him to bless us with a record attendance and fifty decisions for Christ.

At that time we had three Sunday services. At the conclusion of the first, a handful of people responded to the opportunity to trust Christ as Savior. The second service concluded with a dozen giving their hearts to Jesus. I was very excited for our new brothers and sisters in the faith, but we would need to have thirty-four decisions in the last service to reach fifty.

The third service was packed and everything went well. I gave the invitation to trust Christ and one by one, dozens of people began to respond. After the service ended one of our other pastors grabbed me. "Fifty," he said with a huge grin. "Can you believe it? I counted a total of fifty adults trusting Christ as Savior today!"

Immediately after that, a handful of men walked up to me with curious looks on their faces. They were the prayer team who had spent the entire service in another part of the building getting hold of God and asking Him to bless that day. They had one question they had to ask: "How many?"

I teased them, "How many what?"

"How many people met Jesus as Savior today?" they asked eagerly. "We felt led to ask God to bless us with fifty," they said. "So how many were there?"

I grinned and said, "You should have asked for fifty-one."

2. *God is willing and able to bless those who ask.* God loves to rain down favors on the lives of His children. He wants to benefit us as much as we can stand. It may not be according to our when, where, or how, but God wants to bless His children! According to Bruce Wilkinson, writing in *The Prayer of Jabez*, "The very nature of God is to have goodness in so much abundance that it overflows into our unworthy lives. If you think about God differently than that, I am asking you to change the way you think. Why not make it a lifelong

commitment to ask God every day to bless you—while He's at it, bless you *a lot.*"[3]

3. *God's blessing is big enough to go beyond us to others.* Jacob asked God to bless him, but he was not the only one blessed. His family, his brother, and ultimately through Messiah, all of us were blessed.

4. *Receiving God's blessing should make us the "blessers" of others.* Being the recipients of God's generous grace should make us graciously generous. God is all about others. Everything He does in us and for us is designed to eventually flow through us to others.

5. *God reveals Himself to those who really want to know Him.* God Himself is the ultimate blessing. Jacob's greatest blessing was not that his brother spared him, but that he got to see God, touch God, and hear God. It doesn't get any better than that!

Here's one final thought on Jacob's prayer: There are no miracles without messes and no need for blessing if we have it all already. So, if there is a blessing you really need or want and could use to bless others, and you believe that God would want you to have it, then don't be shy. Go ahead and ask. God is able and, as we saw with Jacob, He blesses the spiritually aggressive.

NOTES

[1] J. R. Rice, *Prayer: Asking and Receiving* (Murfreesboro, TN: Sword of the Lord, 1942), p. 52.

[2] See Hebrews 4:16.

[3] Bruce Wilkinson, *The Prayer of Jabez* (Sisters, OR: Multnomah Publishers, 2000), pp. 28–29.

3

GO WITH US:
The Prayer of Moses
EXODUS 33:15

Poor guy. Moses faced one of the most difficult leadership challenges in history. He had to lead a million whining slaves out of Egypt, through the desert wilderness, and into the Promised Land. Every time he turned around, his people were either rebelling or griping.

One of the lowest points came when Moses descended from Mount Sinai carrying the Ten Commandments, only to come upon a riotous party at which the people were worshiping dumb idols. God would have annihilated the Hebrew people had Moses not interceded (Exodus 32:9–14).

How was Moses supposed to guide the people safely through the hazards of the desert into the Promised Land without them destroying him or themselves?

In answer, Moses prayed.

> *Now Moses used to take a tent and pitch it outside the camp some distance away, calling it the "tent of meeting."* . . .*As Moses went into the tent, the pillar of cloud would come down and stay at the entrance, while the Lord spoke with Moses. Whenever the people saw the pillar of cloud standing at the entrance to the tent, they all stood and worshiped, each at the entrance to his tent. The Lord would speak to Moses face to face, as a man speaks with his friend.*

> EXODUS 33:7–11

Moses was a man of effective prayer. Moses had a *place* where he met with God—the tent of meeting—far away from the hustle of humanity. When Moses went into the tent to meet God, God came into the tent to meet Moses. Moses understood something we must remember: *God is willing, ready, and available to meet with us when we make time to meet with Him.*

Moses had very personal meetings with God. "The Lord spoke with Moses face to face, as a man speaks with his friend." Nothing was hidden. It was a dear and daily dialogue, as well as a close and consistent conversation. Moses had developed, probably on the backside of the desert during his forty years of exile, a familiar friendship with God. That is the secret of inner strength, and that is the foundation of effective prayer.

Out of this friendship Moses voiced his complaint.

> *Moses said to the LORD, "You have been telling me, 'Lead these people,' but you have not let me know whom you will send with me."*

> EXODUS 33:12

Forty years earlier Moses had tried to deliver Israel in his own strength only to fail miserably. Now he knew that he needed God. Without God, the entire endeavor would be a tragic nightmare. Without God it was hopeless.

Moses needed the presence of God. There was no other way. Yet, he not only recognized his need, he acted on it. Moses was ultimately successful because he asked God for help, praying one of the most effective prayers in the Bible.

"You have said, 'I know you by name and you have found favor with me.' If you are pleased with me, teach me your ways so I may know you and continue to find favor with you. Remember that this nation is your people." The LORD replied, "My Presence will go with you, and I will give you rest." Then Moses said to him, "If your Presence does not go with us, do not send us up from here."

EXODUS 33:12–15

Go with us.

"If your Presence does not go with us, do not send us up from here." In other words, "Your presence is the key to our peace, protection, and prosperity. Go with us. Your presence is the source of our survival and success. Without You there will soon be none of us."

"How will anyone know that you are pleased with me and with your people unless you go with us? What else will distinguish me and your people from all the other people on the face of the earth?"

EXODUS 33:16

Moses prayed, "Go with us." He was saying, "Lord, Your presence is the mark of Your pleasure. Your attendance sets us apart. You are distinctly divine. Without You we are nothing but a tragic troop trampling aimlessly into oblivion."

So Moses asked God to go with them. And God said, "Yes."

And the LORD said to Moses, "I will do the very thing you have asked, because I am pleased with you and I know you by name."

EXODUS 33:17

From that moment, God's presence marked Moses' life. In fact, God was so manifestly with him that Moses' face actually glowed.

When Moses came down from Mount Sinai with the two tablets of the Testimony in his hands, he was not aware that his face was radiant because he had spoken with the LORD.

EXODUS 34:29

Making It Personal

Moses isn't the only one with a dire requirement for the presence of God. If you and I ever hope to fulfill God's plan for our lives, we need God. His presence must accompany us. His being must cover us like a cloud and emanate from us like perfume. He must go with us.

A few years ago as I was reading the Bible, I discovered that embedded in the defining moments of the lives of key people in the Bible is the little phrase, "God was with him." God's presence was the determining factor.

The things we want and need most in life come from God. They are only realized when His presence is manifest with us. Read down through this "grocery list" of the staggering blessings and benefits attending God's people when He accompanies them.

Individual protection and provision—Genesis 28:15, 20
Deliverance and transformation—Acts 7:9
Prosperity in the face of grave adversity—Genesis 39:2

Favor with ungodly authorities—Genesis 39:21
Success—Genesis 39:23; 1 Samuel 18:12,14; 1 Chronicles
    17:2; 2 Kings 18:7
National protection—Numbers 14:8
Blessings—Numbers 23:21
Destruction of fear—Deuteronomy 31:6, 8; Joshua 1:9;
    Psalm 118:6
Godly influence—Joshua 6:27
Courage—Judges 6:12
Victory—Judges 1:19, 22; Isaiah 8:10
Guarantee of God's promises—1 Samuel 3:19
Transformation and power—1 Samuel 10:6–7
Qualification for leadership—1 Samuel 16:18
Greatness—2 Samuel 7:9; 2 Chronicles 1:1; 1 Kings 1:37
Encouragement—1 Chronicles 28:20
Magnetic ability to draw a large following—
    2 Chronicles 15:9
Confidence—Psalm 118:7; 2 Chronicles 13:12; Jeremiah
    20:11; Zechariah 10:5
Evident favor of God—Luke 1:28
Miraculous power—Acts 10:38

I say, sign me up! No wonder Moses prayed, "Go with us."

Moses is not the only one to ask God for His presence. A study of biographies of noted Christians indicates that many have enjoyed this sweet secret of spiritual success and rest. Indeed, the three men who may have had the greatest impact on western Christianity in the eighteenth and nineteenth centuries had one common characteristic: They were indelibly marked by the presence of God.

John Wesley was the father of the great spiritual awakening that shook England and America as well as the founder of the Methodist church. He is surely one of the most influential Christians who ever lived. One of his many biographers noted, "He was a man who sought to keep the glow of God in his life shining at such a white heat that others should recognize it and be led to seek the same transforming power."[1]

Charles Finney was a lawyer who was dramatically converted to Christianity and immediately began to preach in small towns in upstate New York. They say that when Finney entered a town, the presence of God was so thick people either repented or died. Finney and his associates spent hours fervently begging God for powerful manifestations of His presence.

On one occasion, he had been holding a revival at a little place called New York Mills. One morning he was asked to tour the large cotton mill in town. As he walked into the mill, the presence of God became so thick that God began to convict the people there immediately. He entered a large room where the young women working at the looms were laughing and joking. Soon the room grew still. One of the girls looked into his eyes and began to tremble. Her finger began to shake and she broke her thread. One record stated, "She was quite overcome, and sank down, and burst into tears. The impression caught like powder and in a few moments all of the room was in tears. The feeling spread through the factory."[2]

Another biographer has noted, "The owner heard the equipment stopping, and came in to see what was going on. When he saw that the whole room was in tears, he told the superintendent to stop the mill, for it was more important for souls to be saved than for the mill to run. Up to that point Finney had not said a word. The workers assembled in a large room. And in a few days almost all the employees of the mill were saved."[3]

Charles Finney did not have to say a thing! God's presence was so powerful on his life that a mill full of workers repented without him saying a word.

D. L. Moody started a great church, an outstanding college, and is said to have introduced one million souls to Jesus Christ. Early in his ministry he was a highly dedicated man who tirelessly labored to bring souls one by one to Christ. His dear friend, Ira Sankey, described him at this period of his life as "a great hustler; he had a tremendous desire to do something, but he had no real power. He worked very largely in the energy of the flesh."[4]

During a trip to England, Moody's heart was ignited to somehow reach more people for Christ than he was reaching. Yet, he wasn't up to the task. So he began to wrestle with the Lord in prayer. Years later he shared what happened.

> About four years ago I got into a cold state. It did not seem as if there was any unction [power] resting upon my ministry. For four long months God seemed to be just showing me myself. . . . But after four months the anointing came. It came upon me as I was walking in the streets of New York. Many a time I have thought of it since I have been here. At last I had returned to God again, and I was wretched no longer. I almost prayed in my joy, "O stay Thy hand!" I thought this earthen vessel would break. He filled me so full of the Spirit.
>
> If I have not been a different man since, I do not know myself. I think I have accomplished more in the last four years than in all the rest of my life.[5]

Soon afterward God allowed Moody to make global impact and the results of his efforts were incredibly multiplied. The only explanation was the manifest presence of God.

Consider these examples: Wesley sought God for His presence and it marked his life and ministry; Finney and his associates wrestled with God for the manifestation of His presence; Moody deeply and passionately desired God's presence to go with him and consume his life; and Moses refused to go a step farther without the manifest presence of God.

If your life and ministry is lacking the spark of God's power, the favor of the Spirit's anointing, or the aura of divine protection, you need a greater manifestation of the presence of God. Learn to pray Moses' prayer, "Go with me."

NOTES

[1]Basil Miller, *John Wesley* (Minneapolis, MN: Bethany House Publishers, 1969), p. 131.

[2]Idem, *Charles Finney* (Minneapolis, MN: Bethany House Publishers, 1969), p. 55.

[3]Wesley Duewel, *Revival Fires* (Grand Rapids, MI: Zondervan, 1995), p. 103.

[4]R. A. Torrey, *Why God Used D. L. Moody* (Murfreesboro, TN: Sword of the Lord, 2000), p. 29.

[5]Ibid., p. 30.

4

GIVE ME A SIGN:
The Prayer of Gideon
JUDGES 6:17

At certain desperate points in life we all wish we had something—preferably an undeniably clear sign!—to let us know which direction to take. But have you ever needed to know, beyond a shadow of a doubt, that the desires of your heart are God's divine desires for your life?

In Israel around 1200 BC a man named Gideon was minding his own business when God appeared and called him to deliver his nation from an oppressive enemy. How did he know it was God? How was he sure he was hearing God's instructions clearly? Gideon needed answers. He needed a sign.

As happened repeatedly, Israel had wandered from following God, and so God had removed His hand of protection. Consequently, camel raiders freely swooped in on the Israelites and stole their valuables, livestock, and crops. Most of the people of Israel lived in constant fear hiding in caves and dens.

So there was Gideon hiding away threshing grain in a winepress. Grain was usually threshed on the top of a hill so the wind could blow away the chaff. But the situation in Israel was so desperate that he had to thresh it down in a valley, hiding low in a winepress, hoping he would not be seen. Instead of the wind blowing away the chaff, Gideon had to throw it into the air and hope a bit of it would blow away. No doubt such a position of weakness frustrated Gideon.

Then God's messenger appeared.

> When the angel of the LORD appeared to Gideon, he said, "The LORD is with you, mighty warrior."
>
> JUDGES 6:12

Just picture the irony of this: A grown man is hiding in a winepress when an angel of God appears and calls him "mighty warrior"! What was God doing? Bible commentators are divided on this point. Some say Gideon had a reputation as a warrior among the upper class of Israel.[1] Others say this is another example of God's great sense of humor.[2] Still others feel that "warrior" is a prophetic word describing Gideon's destiny.

I think that all three are true. Yes, God does have a wonderful sense of humor, but later events would indicate that Gideon did indeed have a background in battle. At the time Israel had no leader to lead them to rise up and fight. So Gideon was, for the time being, deprived of his destiny.

God's call beckoned to Gideon, showing him what he could and would be. I imagine that while Gideon was threshing grain he was thinking that Israel needed a leader to lead them out of this horrible state of humiliation. In his heart was a passion to be that deliverer. Now God had come to tell him that He wanted him to fulfill his destiny.

However, because the situation in Israel kept getting worse, Gideon was understandably hesitant to accept his mission. Even so, God was insistent. Let's listen in on their conversation.

"But sir," Gideon replied, "if the LORD is with us, why has all this happened to us? Where are all his wonders that our fathers told us about when they said, 'Did not the LORD bring us up out of Egypt?' But now the LORD has abandoned us and put us into the hand of Midian."

The LORD turned to him and said, "Go in the strength you have and save Israel out of Midian's hand. Am I not sending you?"

"But LORD," Gideon asked, "how can I save Israel? My clan is the weakest in Manasseh, and I am the least in my family."

The LORD answered, "I will be with you, and you will strike down all the Midianites together."

JUDGES 6:13–16

God's call was clear: "Go and save Israel. I am sending you!" Gideon was almost convinced, but it is highly unusual to have the angel of the Lord call you to save a nation. He just wasn't sure if God really was calling him to such a big task. Gideon needed more. He needed a clear sign of confirmation.

I am so glad this story is in the Bible. We are a lot like Gideon. We want to hear God, to believe, to step out. But we don't trust ourselves. We just aren't sure. Is it really God? Is this really what God is saying?

This story is in the Bible not because Gideon wrestled with confirmation, but because he used the situation to pray one of the most effective prayers. Here is Gideon's simple prayer.

Gideon replied, "If now I have found favor in your eyes, give me a sign that it is really you talking to me."

JUDGES 6:17

Give me a sign.

He was saying, "Make it clear. There is too much at risk. I am headed for absolute failure unless this is of You. I need confirmation. I have to know that I am not going crazy or having delusions of grandeur or volunteering for certain suicide. So, please, give me a sign."

Although some Bible teachers and pastors frown upon asking God for a sign, I think that there are those rare occasions in everyone's life when it is perfectly appropriate. Like Gideon, you sense God is calling you to something far greater, vastly higher, and much more difficult than you can imagine. You are making the biggest decision of your life. You are mostly convinced that you have heard His voice. But you have to be certain. The stakes are unbelievably high. You need confirmation.

Did God balk at Gideon and tell him that his request was foolish and immature? Let's find out.

"Please do not go away until I come back and bring my offering and set it before you." And the LORD said, "I will wait until you return."

Gideon went in, prepared a young goat, and from an ephah of flour he made bread without yeast. Putting the meat in a basket and its broth in a pot, he brought them out and offered them to him under the oak.

The angel of God said to him, "Take the meat and the unleavened bread, place them on this rock, and pour out the broth." And Gideon did so.

JUDGES 6:18–20

The stage was set for God to give Gideon his needed confirmation.

With the tip of the staff that was in his hand, the angel of the LORD touched the meat and the unleavened bread. Fire flared from the rock, consuming the meat and the bread. And the angel of the LORD disappeared. When Gideon realized that it was the angel of the LORD, he exclaimed, "Ah, Sovereign LORD! I have seen the angel of the LORD face to face!"

But the LORD said to him, "Peace! Do not be afraid. You are not going to die." So Gideon built an altar to the LORD there and called it The LORD is Peace.

JUDGES 6:21–24

Maybe you are facing a high-risk, high-reward venture. It could be that you sense God is speaking, but you aren't certain. You need to know exactly what He is saying. You need confirmation before you launch into this big decision.

Like you, my friend Rich needed such a sign. Here is his encouraging story.

I had been praying for several years about whether the Lord wanted me to leave my job as a business law professor at OSU [the Ohio State University] and begin vocational ministry as the first senior pastor of our new church. I was bi-vocational, preaching many Sundays, leading several small groups, discipling a few men, and so on. In addition, I was a young professor working toward tenure, writing articles in scholarly journals, and authoring a textbook. My wife and I had two small children. Obviously the strain was pretty great.

I went to England to participate on a prayer ministry team at a conference. One Sunday evening I was speaking to a friend about my uncertainty regarding hearing God's voice. I said, "Kevin, I've been praying about whether God is calling me to full-time ministry for a number of years, but I'm no closer to knowing God's will now than I was four years ago. And I'm not interested in simply volunteering for something that God may not be calling me to."

Kevin, said, "Rich, why don't you ask the Lord for a sign?"

I responded, "I used to do that when I was a young Christian, but I think that is an immature way to seek God's will."

Kevin responded and said, "You know, Rich, every pastor in the world kicks poor Gideon around. But God didn't kick Gideon around. God is more than willing to meet you and give you the confirmation you need."

I thought, that's right. God was kind and gracious to Gideon. So that night I prayed, "Lord, if You want me to leave my job at OSU and pursue full-time ministry, please speak to me before Wednesday evening when I call my wife." I didn't prescribe how God was to speak to me, only that God simply would speak to me. I said, "Lord, if You don't speak to me before Wednesday night, I'll assume You are happy with what I'm doing and I just need to cut back on the number of hours that I'm devoting to church work."

Monday and Tuesday I heard nothing. On Wednesday evening I sat down at a two thousand–person conference. The speaker began his talk this way: "I was going to speak about healing tonight, but I feel like the Holy Spirit has instructed me to give a different message. I'm going to speak about 'The Pearl of Great Price.'" He continued, saying, "Some of you tonight are wondering if God is calling you to full-time ministry. You will know it's the Lord when it is the last hour, when there is no more time—then you will know it's God."

    I literally began squeezing the handrails of my chair. I thought, Lord, are You speaking to me? *It was literally the last hour before I was going to talk with my wife, Marlene. In the course of the speaker's talk, he said seven specific things that would happen when you know it's time to move from your job into full-time ministry. All of those things applied to my life.*

    The next day someone walked by me, turned around and walked by again, and then turned around again. He finally looked me in the eye and put his hand on my chest and said, "The Lord is calling you to be a pastor." There were several other remarkable confirmations in the ensuing days that allowed me to know clearly and unmistakably that God had called me to leave my position at Ohio State and go into full-time ministry.[3]

Making It Personal

I don't believe God will or should give us signs about every little aspect of our lives. Before asking, there are several considerations to take into account.

    1. *All of us will probably need a sign of confirmation at one time or another.* The need for a sign occurs rarely in a lifetime. Biblical accounts of people receiving signs of confirmation almost always revolve around a calling to a challenging ministry.

    2. *God's signs often come at desperate times.* Israel was desperate for a deliverer. Gideon was desperate for a change.

    3. *God's signs confirm what God is already doing or has already done in our hearts.* Signs may appear to come out of the blue. But a deeper look almost always reveals that God's callings and confirmations involve dreams and destinies that He has been writing on our hearts for a long time.

    4. *Every sign should be checked against and submitted to the clear teachings of God's Word.* This seems obvious but needs to be stated. God will not give you a sign telling you to divorce your husband, have an affair with your secretary, or plunge your family into backbreaking debt. How do I know? Because the Bible tells me so.

    5. *God can give us confirmation.* God is infinite. He can do whatever needs to be done. If you must have a sign of confirmation, He can give it. When I sensed God's call on my life to go into full-time ministry as a vocation, I had a preaching opportunity and asked God to give me confirmation. When nearly half the audience dedicated their lives to God, I knew that was my sign of confirmation.

    Do you need clear confirmation that the direction you are heading is what God is calling you to do? Do as Gideon did. Ask God to give you a sign.

Notes

[1]Arthur Lewis, *Judges and Ruth* (Chicago, IL: Moody Press, 1979), p. 45.
[2]J. Vernon McGee, *Joshua and Judges* (Nashville: Thomas Nelson Publishers, 1991), p. 151.
[3]Used by permission of Rich Nathan, senior pastor of Vineyard Church, Columbus, Ohio.

5
REMEMBER ME:
The Prayer of Hannah
1 SAMUEL 1:11

Etched into every soul are deep, personal desires and dreams that refuse to go away until they are realized. We may temporarily lose sight of them in the busyness of day-to-day living, but they are always there, crying to be fulfilled. As time goes by, these yearnings take on a painful desperation when the hope of realizing them begins to fade. Nothing we or anyone can do, and no amount of time, can release us from the gnawing hurt of an unfulfilled dream. Doubts and questions disturb our prayers. You wonder, *Has God forgotten me?*

What can we do with these dreams that stubbornly refuse to come true and yet mulishly refuse to go away? We may want to try Hannah's prayer. Like all stories of great answers to prayer, this one begins with a great need. Hannah was a woman who needed nothing less than a miracle.

> *There was a certain man from Ramathaim, a Zuphite from the hill country of Ephraim, whose name was Elkanah son of Jeroham, the son of Elihu, the son of Tohu, the son of Zuph, an Ephraimite. He had two wives; one was called Hannah and the other Peninnah. Peninnah had children, but Hannah had none. Year after year this man went up from his town to worship and sacrifice to the LORD Almighty at Shiloh, where Hophni and Phinehas, the two sons of Eli, were priests of the LORD.*
> 1 SAMUEL 1:1–3

Note the lonely, desperate, painful words at the end of verse two: "Peninnah had children, but Hannah had none." Hannah had no children in a world in which bearing children served as the chief source of a woman's esteem, provision, and protection. Her arms had never felt the trembling joy of holding her own baby. Her lifelong passion to be a mother went unfulfilled year after year.

> *Year after year this man went up from his town to worship and sacrifice to the LORD Almighty at Shiloh, where Hophni and Phinehas, the two sons of Eli, were priests of the LORD. Whenever the day came for Elkanah to sacrifice, he would give portions of the meat to his wife Peninnah and to all her sons and daughters. But to Hannah he gave a double portion because he loved her, and the LORD had closed her womb. And because the LORD had closed her womb, her rival kept provoking her in order to irritate her. This went on year after year. Whenever Hannah went up to the house of the LORD, her rival provoked her till she wept and would not eat. Elkanah her husband would say to her, "Hannah, why are you weeping? Why don't you eat? Why are you downhearted? Don't I mean more to you than ten sons?"*
> 1 SAMUEL 1:3–8

"The Lord had closed her womb." As years passed, Hannah's barrenness caused her to become the object of scorn. And not only that, but she had a husband who totally misunderstood her pain. Like most men, Elkanah failed to understand why he wasn't the alpha and omega of his wife's desires.

Out of her desperation Hannah crafted a prayer, one of the most effective recorded in the Bible.

> *In bitterness of soul Hannah wept much and prayed to the LORD. And she made a vow, saying, "O LORD Almighty, if you will only look upon your servant's misery and remember me, and not forget your servant but give her a son, then I will give him to the LORD for all the days of his life, and no razor will ever be used on his head."*
>
> 1 SAMUEL 1:10–11

Do not miss the urgent simplicity of her prayer. It is summed up in those two anguished words, "Remember me."

Remember me.

This desire to have a child was not a spur-of-the-moment thing. The passion for parenthood grew daily in the womb of Hannah's soul. Undoubtedly, she tried other mothers' suggestions for how to get pregnant but with no success. She was getting older. Her biological clock was running or had run out. She was frantic for some action, some type of answer, a response from God.

Obviously this was not the first time she had prayed about her barrenness. Year after year she had made the trip to Shiloh. Yet her urgency now fused a yearningly specific request: "Remember me, and do not forget your servant, but give her a son." She did not merely seek *any* blessing. She was not even asking for *a* child. Hannah hammered heaven for a *son*.

I don't want to read too much into this prayer, but I sense that Hannah was a woman who wanted to touch a nation. She wanted to restore Israel to a right relationship with God. Her petition for a son was forged over the course of years in the fires of silence and frustration. Now her demand was clear. There was no other way. She had to have a son.

You see, in Hannah's Israel the odds of a woman, especially a barren wife, having such a national impact were slim. But a son, given to God, could grow to exercise prophetic power that could help prod a wayward people back to loving God.

So she cried out for a son. And, finally, God responded.

Making It Personal

Before we look at God's answer, notice a few characteristics of this prayer. These elements could be understood as aids to answered prayers.

1. *Purified Motives.* One benefit of delayed answers is purified motives. The longer our dreams are heated in the flames of frustrating delay, the more the impurities in our motives are burned off. After years of yearning, Hannah's request had been refined to a sheen that God could no longer deny.

Her motives were pure. If or when God should give her a son, she promised to "give him to the Lord." She wanted this to be a God thing. God would be the giver and receiver of the son. The son would come from God and be returned to God. She merely wanted to have a part in the middle.

Yes, there was some "self" involved. Few of our deepest dreams and most passionate prayers are void of self. But while self was acknowledged, God was preeminent.

Hannah's dream was deeper than holding a baby. It reached further than herself, or her family, or even her village. She dreamed of a son, given by God, given back to God, who could be used of God to influence a nation for God.

These are the motives God blesses.

2. *Persistent Faith.*

As she kept on praying to the LORD, Eli observed her mouth.

1 SAMUEL 1:12

Hannah's desperate desire was not merely offered to God once and forgotten. No, her prayer was repeated over and over as she bared her soul before her God.

In this regard, Hannah reminds me of the mistreated widow that Jesus spoke of in the Gospel of Luke.[1] Like Hannah, she had no choice. She was desperate and she was determined. Day after day, she came to the one with power, in this case a judge, and sought relief. She was shameless and stubborn. She was persistent and persevering. And eventually she prevailed. Her shameless and stubborn persistence won out. Jesus said He told this story to teach us that we should always pray and not give up. Then He remarked about the quality of faith displayed by the widow.

Like the widow, Hannah prayed and did not give up. Her faith refused to yield until it was rewarded.

3. *Painful Earnestness.*

Hannah was praying in her heart, and her lips were moving but her voice was not heard. Eli thought she was drunk and said to her, "How long will you keep on getting drunk? Get rid of your wine." "Not so, my lord," Hannah replied, "I am a woman who is deeply troubled. I have not been drinking wine or beer; I was pouring out my soul to the LORD. Do not take your servant for a wicked woman; I have been praying here out of my great anguish and grief."

1 SAMUEL 1:13–16

Hannah described herself as "a woman who is deeply troubled." By this point she was desperate. No one or nothing else but God would do. And the possibility of God not coming through was more than she could bear. So she "poured her soul out to the Lord."

She was not merely pouring out words to the Lord. In fact, so profound was her desire that her voice was not even heard. She was pouring out her very soul. Hers was an extremely deep, highly personal, supremely intimate prayer.

She claimed to be praying "out of great anguish and grief." This prayer erupted from so deep within the depths of her soul that it hurt to let it out. It was born from an intensity that was beyond what words could utter.

There is something painful about exposing the subterranean reaches of our souls to God. To let down the drawbridge and leave our greatest dreams and passions standing naked before God is threatening at best and often agonizing. Even though Hannah was in anguish, she would not retreat. She was in earnest.

4. *Petitions with Fasting.*

Eli answered, "Go in peace, and may the God of Israel grant you what you have asked of him." She said, "May your servant find favor in your eyes." Then she went her way and ate something, and her face was no longer downcast.

1 SAMUEL 1:17–18

Hannah did not eat until she was assured that she had broken through. Obviously, she had been abstaining from food as part of her prayer. She was either so determined that she would not eat or so distraught she could not eat, but either way she was fasting.

There has been much written on fasting in recent years. I know from experience that if a situation or the Holy Spirit dictates abstinence from food as a part of prayer, then it is well worth fasting. Most of the greatest answers to prayer I have ever enjoyed have come out of times of prayer with fasting. And that was the result for Hannah.

Early the next morning they arose and worshiped before the LORD and then went back to their home at Ramah. Elkanah lay with Hannah his wife, and the LORD remembered her. So in the course of time Hannah conceived and gave birth to a son. She named him Samuel, saying, "Because I asked the LORD for him."

1 SAMUEL 1:19–20

Hannah got her answer when God gave her a son. Samuel was dedicated to God and became one of Israel's greatest prophets. He also became a man mighty in prayer. His name, meaning "God heard," was a constant reminder that God had answered a desperate prayer.

About every five years on Mother's Day at my church, we teach Hannah's desperate prayer. As a result, barren women and couples go to a deeper level in their prayers. Soon things start to happen. Women who couldn't get pregnant find themselves "with child." Couples are led to adopt precious babies in need of a home. And prodigal kids come home.

A friend of mine named Rhonda had had no contact with her adult daughter, Megan, for several years. But a few years ago when Rhonda became a part of a church and, after decades of distance, returned to God, she discovered a renewed burden on her heart to connect with her daughter. One Sunday morning she heard a message on the power of prayer and fasting. After all the years of estrangement, Rhonda realized she had nothing to lose.

She began her fast on Monday and sought God with desperate prayer each day. On Thursday evening the telephone rang. It was Megan, calling to say she wanted to get together. God had remembered Rhonda.

But that's not all Rhonda prayed about. She began to pray about Megan's spiritual condition. Soon Megan began coming to church with her and recently accepted Christ as her Savior.[2]

I believe that God wants and is able to give us our deepest, "pure motive" desires. If you're burdened like Rhonda and Hannah, identify the deep, God-sized desire of your heart. Ask God for it persistently, earnestly, and honestly with fasting until you get a response. Of course, if the request is not for the best, God may not answer, or He may let you wait for a long stretch of time until your motives are purified. But if your desire is God given, and God purified, then watch out. You may be given your own "Samuel" to give back to the Lord so that He might bless others.

NOTES

[1] Luke 18:1–7.
[2] Used by permission of Rhonda Tucker.

6

I HAVE SINNED:
The Prayer of David
2 SAMUEL 12:13

You remember what David did. It was ugly. In the midst of his midlife season, bored and weary, he opted out of responsibility (1 Samuel 11:1). And then, with his defenses down, he foolishly initiated an illicit sexual encounter with a married woman named Bathsheba. When she became pregnant (11:2–5), David desperately tried to hide his sin under a blanket of deception. It failed because, ironically, Bathsheba's husband, Uriah, displayed the character and commitment that David lacked (11:6–13). Frantically and decisively, David blatantly misused his power to have Uriah killed in battle (11:14–26). He then married Bathsheba, assuming "no one would ever know." But David knew—and God always knows.

Know that guilt follows sin like a vulture attaches itself to rotten meat. Guilt followed David because he had sinned. His record now carried the heinous stains of adultery, deception, misuse of authority, and murder.

If anyone knew better, it was David. David knew God does not tolerate such behavior. Carefully read these words from the pen of David:

> You are not a God who takes pleasure in evil; with you the wicked cannot dwell.
>
> PSALM 5:4

> God is a righteous judge, a God who expresses his wrath every day.
>
> PSALM 7:11

> The LORD examines the righteous, but the wicked and those who love violence his soul hates. On the wicked he will rain fiery coals and burning sulfur; a scorching wind will be their lot. For the LORD is righteous, he loves justice; upright men will see his face.
>
> PSALM 11:5–7

> LORD, who may dwell in your sanctuary? Who may live on your holy hill? He whose walk is blameless and who does what is righteous, who speaks the truth from his heart and has no slander on his tongue, who does his neighbor no wrong and casts no slur on his fellowman. . .but the Lord laughs at the wicked, for he knows their day is coming. . . the offspring of the wicked will be cut off.
>
> PSALM 15:1–3; 37:13, 28

Earlier, David had even boasted of his blameless living on more than one occasion. How hollow and haunting these words must have been in the face of his guilt!

> Hear, O LORD, my righteous plea; listen to my cry. Give ear to my prayer—it does not rise from deceitful lips. May my vindication come from you; may your eyes see what is right. Though you probe my heart and examine me at night, though you test me, you will find nothing; I have resolved that my mouth will not sin. As for the deeds of men—by the word of your lips I have kept myself from the ways of the

violent. My steps have held to your paths; my feet have not slipped.

PSALM 17:1–5

Vindicate me, O LORD, for I have led a blameless life; I have trusted in the LORD without wavering. . . . I walk continually in your truth. I do not sit with deceitful men.

PSALM 26:1, 3–4

David lived a year under intense and immense guilt. As hell is the expression of the absence of God, and guilt excludes us from the presence of God, David's year was a living hell. David later described the agony of his year of distance through disobedience. Feel the misery contained in these words:

I am faint. . .for my bones are in agony. My soul is in anguish. . .I am worn out from groaning; all night long I flood my bed with weeping and drench my couch with tears.

PSALM 6:2–3, 6

When I kept silent, my bones wasted away through my groaning all day long. For day and night your hand was heavy upon me; my strength was sapped as in the heat of summer.

PSALM 32:3–4

Your arrows have pierced me, and your hand has come down upon me. . . . There is no health in my body; my bones have no soundness because of my sin. My guilt has overwhelmed me like a burden too heavy to bear. My wounds fester and are loathsome because of my sinful folly. I am bowed down and brought very low; all day long I go about mourning. My back is filled with searing pain; there is no health in my body. I am feeble and utterly crushed; I groan in anguish of heart. . . . I am like a deaf man, who cannot hear, like a mute, who cannot open his mouth. . . . For I am about to fall, and my pain is ever with me.

PSALM 38:2–8, 13, 17

Guilt is horrible, hideous, terrible, and terrifying. Yet, God is merciful. He does not abandon us to be swallowed in the cesspool of our guilt. Instead, He pursues us. His Spirit haunts us. His Word hunts us down and speaks to us.

God's love, His Spirit, and words of rebuke chased David down. The messenger's name was Nathan. Nathan told David a story that touched his sense of injustice and provoked him to demand punishment for a thieving sinner (2 Samuel 12:1–6). Then Nathan skillfully turned the tables on David and cut him straight to the heart with four chilling words: "You are the man" (2 Samuel 12:7).

God always convicts in specifics. Satan accuses in generalities. Nathan did not have to be specific with David. God already had done that. David knew exactly what Nathan meant. David was caught. He could hide no longer.

At this point David had three choices: throw Nathan out, deny his guilt, or own it. To his credit, David immediately said the only words that can erase the awful stains of guilt: "I have sinned against the Lord" (2 Samuel 12:23).

I have sinned.

"I have sinned." So states one of the most effective—and one of the most difficult—prayers recorded in the Bible. Pride hates to admit weakness, and arrogance dislikes acknowledging shortcomings. Just ask Adam and Eve. Rather than owning their sin, Adam blamed God and Eve blamed the serpent. But God knew the truth (Genesis 3:8–13).

I have found that when God convicts us of sin, the easiest thing to say is "yes." Silence, excuses, rationalization, and deflection don't work. Forgiveness comes through confession.

After David admitted his sin, grace and mercy were spilled out in his behalf. Immediately, Nathan spoke the best words a guilty soul can ever hear when he said, "The Lord has taken away your sin" (2 Samuel 12:13).

What sweet, glorious, mighty words those were for David, and are to us! The Lord has taken away your guilt. What liberating, life-giving words! Our God is the God who forgives sin and erases guilt.

Slowly read these promises and thank God for His astounding mercy:

"Come now, let us reason together," says the LORD. *"Though your sins are like scarlet, they shall be as white as snow; though they are red as crimson, they shall be like wool."*

ISAIAH 1:18

"I, even I, am he who blots out your transgressions, for my own sake, and remembers your sins no more."

ISAIAH 43:25

Let the wicked forsake his way and the evil man his thoughts. Let him turn to the LORD, *and he will have mercy on him, and to our God, for he will freely pardon.*

ISAIAH 55:7

If we confess our sins, he is faithful and just and will forgive us our sins and purify us from all unrighteousness.

1 JOHN 1:9

Who is a God like you, who pardons sin and forgives the transgression of the remnant of his inheritance? You do not stay angry forever but delight to show mercy. You will again have compassion on us; you will tread our sins underfoot and hurl all our iniquities into the depths of the sea.

MICAH 7:18–19

For as high as the heavens are above the earth, so great is his love for those who fear him; as far as the east is from the west, so far has he removed our transgressions from us.

PSALM 103:11–12

In high school I had a friend who was slow to accept the truth, love, and mercy of God. She said that she had intellectual obstacles to faith. But more importantly, she had an incident of immorality in her past for which she felt guilty and ashamed. She doubted that God would fully forgive her.

Eventually the testimony of spiritually turned-on believers and the persistent pursuit of the love of God wore her down. She relented and ran home to the Father. She found His arms wide open and His mercy to be mighty.

"It felt so very good to be forgiven," she told me the next day. "It was like I was a little girl in a new clean dress dancing in a refreshing spring shower." Her face erupted into a magnificent smile as she gushed, "I have never felt so incredibly clean!"

David knew exactly what she meant. It's no wonder that he wrote these words:

> *Blessed is he whose transgressions are forgiven, whose sins are covered. Blessed is the man whose sin the LORD does not count against him and in whose spirit is no deceit . . . . I acknowledged my sin to you and did not cover up my iniquity. I said, "I will confess my transgressions to the LORD"—and you forgave the guilt of my sin.*
>
> PSALM 32:1–2, 5

After his confession and forgiveness, David's God-given eloquence was unleashed. Read the urgent words of his prayer.

> *Have mercy on me, O God, according to your unfailing love; according to your great compassion blot out my transgressions. Wash away all my iniquity and cleanse me from my sin. . . .*
>
> *Cleanse me with hyssop, and I will be clean; wash me, and I will be whiter than snow. Let me hear joy and gladness; let the bones you have crushed rejoice. Hide your face from my sins and blot out all my iniquity.*
>
> *Create in me a pure heart, O God, and renew a steadfast spirit within me. Do not cast me from your presence or take your Holy Spirit from me. Restore to me the joy of your salvation and grant me a willing spirit, to sustain me.*
>
> *Then I will teach transgressors your ways, and sinners will turn back to you. Save me from bloodguilt, O God, the God who saves me, and my tongue will sing of your righteousness. O Lord, open my lips, and my mouth will declare your praise.*
>
> *You do not delight in sacrifice, or I would bring it; you do not take pleasure in burnt offerings. The sacrifices of God are a broken spirit; a broken and contrite heart, O God, you will not despise.*
>
> PSALM 51:1–2, 7–17

Making It Personal

I don't know what sin or sins you need to confess to God right now. Maybe it's something you said or did. It could be an attitude you have developed or a thought you have had. Maybe it's something you know you should do but haven't, for whatever reason. Don't argue with God. If He is putting His finger on a specific sin or sins in your life, the time to confess is now. Don't wait any longer. Pray the prayer of David, "I have sinned."

7

ENLARGE MY TERRITORY:
The Prayer of Jabez
1 CHRONICLES 4:10

"Surely I was born for more than this."

Sound familiar? Have you ever had a gnawing hunger and restless burden of wanting to do more and be more for God? If so, you are not alone. You were created with the craving to do your part to create a better world.

God is the fulfiller of dreams. I believe that at conception He begins writing dreams on each of our hearts. These deep dreams perfectly wed His purposes on the planet with the passion of our souls. In your heart today are the seeds of great imaginings of a future you hope for, long for, and dream of either consciously or subconsciously. God planted them there. They are the secret of your fulfillment.

One man took a risk and acted on his ambition. His name was Jabez, and his story has been widely publicized recently in Christian circles. Interestingly, the Bible record of Jabez is condensed into four short sentences found in two simple verses.

> *Jabez was more honorable than his brothers. His mother had named him Jabez, saying, "I gave birth to him in pain." Jabez cried out to the God of Israel, "Oh, that you would bless me and enlarge my territory! Let your hand be with me, and keep me from harm so that I will be free from pain." And God granted his request.*
>
> 1 CHRONICLES 4:9–10

God summarized the entire life of Jabez into four facts: (1) Jabez was more honorable than his brothers; (2) he received his name, Jabez, because his mother gave birth to him in pain; (3) he asked God to give him his dream of enlarged territory; and (4) God answered, "Yes!" Jabez's prayer is one of the most effective prayers in the Bible. We are not told *how* God answered, but we are clearly told *that* God granted his request.

Likewise, Jabez's request was fourfold: (1) Bless me; (2) enlarge my territory; (3) let Your hand be with me; and (4) keep me from harm so that I will be free from pain.

Of the four requests made by Jabez, the one I find most compelling is "enlarge my territory," because I find myself yearning for the same thing. But is it selfish or arrogant to ask God for that? The first time I read this verse, I assumed that God would say, "You have got to be kidding!"

But God took the sincere cry of Jabez's heart seriously. So, I figure, if God would do such a thing for Jabez, He might do it for me. And He has.

Enlarge my territory.

Asking God to enlarge our territory is not something we should feel guilty about. It can leave a powerful testimony with the world, according to Henry Blackaby.

> *God is interested in the world coming to know him. The only way people will know him is when they see him at work. Whenever God involves you in his activity, the assignment will have God-like dimensions to it. Some people say, "God will never ask me to do something I can't do." I have come to the place in my life that, if the assign-*

ment I sense God is giving me is something I can handle, I know it probably is not from God. The kind of assignments God gives. . .are always beyond what people can do because he wants to demonstrate his nature, his strength, his provision, and his kindness to his people and to a watching world. That is the only way the world will come to know him. . . . When God's people and the world see something happen that only God can do, they come to know Him.[1]

When we ask God to enlarge our territory, we are asking God to increase our sphere of influence for His kingdom. Bruce Wilkinson helps us understand how this prayer works.

If Jabez had worked on Wall Street, he might have prayed, "Lord, increase the value of my investments/portfolios." When I talk to presidents of companies, I often talk to them in terms of this particular mind-set. When Christian executives ask me, "Is it right for me to ask for more business?" my response is, "Absolutely!" If you're doing business God's way, it's not only right to ask for more, but He is waiting for you to ask. Your business is God's territory that God has entrusted to you. He wants you to accept it as a significant opportunity to touch individual lives, the business community, and the world for His glory. Asking Him to enlarge that opportunity brings Him only delight.[2]

When we ask for more territory we are tapping into the heart of Jesus, whose heart was so large it encompassed the whole world. Among His final words to His followers was to "make disciples of *all* nations" (Matthew 28:19); to "preach the good news to *all* creation" (Mark 16:15); that "repentance and forgiveness of sins be preached in his name to *all* nations" (Luke 24:47); and for His followers to be His "witnesses in Jerusalem, and in *all* Judea and Samaria, and to the ends of the earth" (Acts 1:8) [all italics are mine]. Notice the word "all" in each reference. Part of the world was not enough. Some of the people won't do. He wanted His kingdom, His territory, to extend to *all* the people in the world.

When we ask God to expand our territory we are standing on the shoulders of spiritual giants. At the age of eighty-five Joshua's visionary buddy Caleb was not ready to retire, nor was he content with the status quo. He asked for greater territory.

"So here I am today, eighty-five years old! I am still as strong today as the day Moses sent me out; I'm just as vigorous to go out to battle now as I was then. Now give me this hill country that the LORD promised me that day."

JOSHUA 14:10–12

Enlarge my territory is a prayer God loves to answer. John Knox, the great fifteenth-century Scottish reformer, prayed, "Give me Scotland or I will die!" He almost succeeded. Even though he was unsuccessful in his attempt to win Mary, Queen of Scots, to Christ, she is reputed to have said, "I fear the prayers of John Knox more than all the assembled armies of Europe."

Likewise, Henrietta Mears was a big dreamer. At the age of thirty-eight she took the position of director of Christian education at the First Presbyterian Church in Hollywood, California. "God doesn't call us to sit on the sidelines and watch. He calls us to be on the field, playing the games," said Ms. Mears. Knowing Christ intimately and telling others about Him was her first and foremost objective.

Three years after her arrival at the church, Sunday school attendance grew from four hundred to four thousand. During her tenure over four hundred young people entered full-time Christian service. One of them was Bill Bright, founder of Campus Crusade for Christ.

God kept expanding her territory. Frustrated with the material being taught in the Sunday school when she arrived, she began to write lessons that would honor Christ and be faithful to the Bible. It wasn't long before her efforts gained results and requests for copies of her material came in from all across the country. Her office staff worked many long hours mimeographing and mailing the lessons. When the demand became too great, Mears and a group of businesspeople established Gospel Light Publications, one of the first publishers in the Christian education field.

For years, Mears searched for a retreat area where she could take her high-school and college-aged students. She asked God to provide for her dream. Soon, a privately owned resort in the San Bernardino Mountains was available, but the price was too high. For a moment, the dream appeared impossible. Mears called a group of people together for prayer. She insisted that they should "dream big whenever God was involved" and trust Him for His blessing at the right time. After a miraculous intervention, Forest Home, valued at $350,000, was purchased in 1938 for the unheard of price of $30,000.

God expanded her territory into unique realms. Initially, Mears had been drawn to California for the opportunity to witness to those in the entertainment industry. God provided an open door into this area through the Hollywood Christian Group, which began meeting in her home. Many entertainment professionals came to know Christ as a result of her ministry. Dozens of Christian leaders acknowledge her as well, including Billy Graham who said of her, "I doubt if any other woman outside my wife and mother has had such a marked influence [on my life]."[3]

And the stories of such trust in God continue!

In 1931 a young man decided to pray two hours a day every morning for forty days before he went to work. He took a map with him as he lay on his face before God in prayer in the Sierra Nevada Mountains of California. By the end of a few weeks he was asking God to extend his spiritual influence to every state in the United States. As his burden and his faith grew, he was asking for continents he could touch by "training trainers of men."

God heard his cry. By the beginning of World War II, the young man, Dawson Trotman, and his resulting organization, The Navigators, had raised up "key men" for every ship in the United States Navy. Because of the war, Trotman's ministry was extending around the world.

A few years later, Trotman died the way he had lived—saving others. At the age of fifty he went home to be with the Lord after rescuing someone from a cold lake. At his funeral Billy Graham said, "I think he touched more lives than any man I have ever known. We today represent thousands of people touched by this great man."

Graham continued, "Dawson was a man of vision. When our God is small, the world looks big; but when our God is big, the world looks small. And Dawson saw the world as conquerable for Christ. To Dawson, God was big and the world was little. The day he went to be with the Lord some of his men arrived from Africa. One of his great visions was to open Africa. He was always dreaming, planning, and scheming about new ways and means of reaching people."

Trotman was constantly asking God for new ground. He surely was a student and practitioner of the prayer of Jabez when he effectively asked God to "enlarge my territory." The ministry he started, The Navigators, is guiding tens of thousands of people worldwide to come to know and grow in Jesus Christ. Internationally, more than 3,800 Navigators of 62 nationalities serve in more than 100 countries.[4]

Making It Personal

What is the dream God has etched into your soul? Is it seeing your children become great Christians? Starting your own business? Becoming a nurse? Building a great church? Training teens? Writing a Christian bestseller? Winning your family to Christ? If God could expand the territory of Jabez, He can expand yours.

NOTES

[1] Henry Blackaby and Claude King, *Experiencing God* (Nashville, TN: Broadman and Holman, 1995), p. 138. Used by permission.

[2] Bruce Wilkinson, *The Prayer of Jabez* (Sisters, OR: Multnomah Publishers, 2000), pp. 31–32.

[3] "Henrietta Mears: Dream Big," In Touch Ministries, www.intouch.org/myintouch/mighty/portraits/henrietta mears 213642.

[4] "Dawson Trotman: The Disciplined Life," In Touch Ministries, www.intouch.org/myintouch/mighty/portraits/dawson trotman 213713.

8
GIVE ME WISDOM:
The Prayer of Solomon
2 CHRONICLES 1:10

What if God gave you the sweetest deal of the century? Maybe the best offer in the millennium? Suppose God said to you, "Ask Me for whatever you want and I will give it to you."

Can you imagine? "Ask Me for *whatever* you want—anything at all, nothing is too big—*and I will,* not might, or could, but I will *give it to you.*"

What would you ask for? Would it be truckloads of money (not to be used selfishly, of course)? Would you want to be able to pay off your bills, help out some friends, secure your children's future, help your church, support a bunch of missionaries, and pay for finding a cure for cancer or AIDS? It may cross your mind that having a new house and luxury car might be a way to let people know that God is not a stingy God. After all, it's okay to have money as long as it doesn't have you.

Or would you go for an ultimate makeover? Would you want a younger, sleeker, stronger, healthier model? Maybe you desire a tall, blond, and beautiful version, or would you ask for the tall, dark, and handsome edition? Of course, the reason you would want this wonder body would be so you could share your faith more confidently and serve the Lord more effectively.

Or, you might ask for some super powers. Think of all the people you could help if you could heal crowds of sick people as Jesus did. Raising the dead certainly could glorify God. Feeding thousands with a small boy's lunch is a beneficial ability.

Hearing God tell you that He would gladly give you anything you asked would be a mind-boggling prospect. Impossible, you say? Not so. Nearly three thousand years ago, God gave that exact opportunity to a man named Solomon (1 Chronicles 1:7).

Solomon had his hands full. As the second son of the fateful David and Bathsheba union, he was born with a stain on his record. His home life wasn't easy with five stepmothers and some wild half-brothers. One half-brother, Amnon, raped his half-sister, Tamar. Her brother, Absalom, then sought revenge and murdered Amnon (2 Samuel 13). Later, Absalom made a violent, and ultimately suicidal, play for the throne (2 Samuel 14–18).

Yet, Solomon was to be given the reins of the kingdom of his father, King David. David was the action superhero of 1000 BC. He was good-looking, dashing, intelligent, hugely talented, and a larger-than-life living legend. He was a man's man and a ladies' man, and yet he was a man after God's own heart. David's résumé reads like a fantasy. He was a boy shepherd, military hero, gifted songwriter, folk legend, national spiritual leader, and king. He had killed Goliath, eluded Saul's army, recruited a band of merry men, become the king, led a tiny nation to become a world power, written many Psalms, created the "Bathsheba-gate" scandal, survived an ugly military coup plotted by his own son, and he planned to build God a great temple.

When David died, the weight of a young nation rested on the untested shoulders of his son, Solomon. He had to step up and take David's place as king. Talk about big shoes to fill!

Yet, God knows when we are facing more than we can handle, and He knows just what we need. So God appeared to Solomon in a dream and made him the unconditional proposal: "Ask Me for whatever you want and I will give it to you." To his credit, Solomon knew what to ask for.

That night God appeared to Solomon and said to him, "Ask for whatever you want me to give you." Solomon answered God, "You have shown great kindness to David my father and have made me king in his place. Now, LORD God, let your promise to my father David be confirmed, for you have made me king over a people who are as numerous as the dust of the earth. Give me wisdom and knowledge, that I may lead this people, for who is able to govern this great people of yours?"

2 CHRONICLES 1:7–10

Give me wisdom.

Solomon asked for what he believed to be the most important gift anyone can receive—wisdom. He ranked wisdom ahead of money or looks or miracle powers.

Solomon was a diligent student and he used his time growing up in the court of a king to study from the greatest minds of his land. He accumulated the teachings of the ages and collected the parables of the sages. It was his conclusion that the road to blessing leads through the doorway of wisdom. In his book, Proverbs, he wrote the following:

Blessed is the man who finds wisdom, the man who gains understanding, for she is more profitable than silver and yields better returns than gold. She is more precious than rubies; nothing you desire can compare with her. Long life is in her right hand; in her left hand are riches and honor. Her ways are pleasant ways, and all her paths are peace. She is a tree of life to those who embrace her; those who lay hold of her will be blessed.

PROVERBS 3:13–18

To Solomon, if you can only acquire a single gift, the gift to get is wisdom.

Get wisdom, get understanding; do not forget my words or swerve from them. Do not forsake wisdom, and she will protect you; love her, and she will watch over you.

PROVERBS 4:5–6

In his mind, wisdom was life's most valuable pursuit.

Wisdom is supreme; therefore get wisdom. Though it cost all you have, get understanding. Esteem her, and she will exalt you; embrace her, and she will honor you. She will set a garland of grace on your head and present you with a crown of splendor.

PROVERBS 4:7–9

A careful study of the book of Proverbs reveals wisdom to be the diligently acquired art of skillful living. It is the careful cultivation of a God-centered, Christ-like, character-driven, commonsense way of living. Wisdom is the path that leads to God. It is characterized by righteousness, mercy, tact, humility, discipline, respect for authority, "teachability," and honesty.

So, when given the opportunity to ask God for anything, Solomon asked for wisdom. "Give me wisdom" is one of the most effective prayers found in the pages of Scripture, and one God loves to answer. The Book of 1 Kings records God's response.

The Lord was pleased that Solomon had asked for this. So God said to him, "Since you have asked for this and not for long life or wealth for yourself, nor have asked for the death of your enemies but for discernment in administering justice, I will do what you have asked. I will give you a wise and discerning heart, so that there will never have been anyone like you, nor will there ever be."

1 KINGS 3:10–12

In 2 Chronicles we read this record of the Lord's answer:

God said to Solomon, "Since this is your heart's desire and you have not asked for wealth, riches or honor, nor for the death of your enemies, and since you have not asked for a long life but for wisdom and knowledge to govern my people over whom I have made you king, therefore wisdom and knowledge will be given you. And I will also give you wealth, riches and honor, such as no king who was before you ever had and none after you will have."

2 CHRONICLES 1:11–12

Soon after, Solomon's wisdom was put on display. Two harlots came to Solomon for a verdict. They both lived in the same house and both were mothers of newborn children. Woman number one claimed that woman number two's baby died in the night so woman number two switched babies while woman number one was still asleep. Woman number two denied it. It was up to Solomon to decide who was right.

Shrewdly he ordered a man to cut the living baby in half and give each woman a half. The first woman cried out, "Give her the baby. Don't kill him!" The second woman said, "Neither of us will have a living baby. Cut him in two."

The ploy worked perfectly. Solomon ordered, "Don't kill that baby. Give him to the first woman. She obviously is the real mother."[1] Not surprisingly, Solomon's reputation for unusual wisdom spread throughout the nation.

Solomon asked for wisdom and God said, "Yes." In the Book of 1 Kings we can read a summary of the amazing way God answered Solomon's prayer for wisdom.

God gave Solomon wisdom and very great insight, and a breadth of understanding as measureless as the sand on the seashore. Solomon's wisdom was greater than the wisdom of all the men of the East, and greater than all the wisdom of Egypt. He was wiser than any other man, including Ethan the Ezrahite—wiser than Heman, Calcol and Darda, the sons of Mahol. And his fame spread to all the surrounding nations. He spoke three thousand proverbs and his songs numbered a thousand and five. He described plant life, from the cedar of Lebanon to the hyssop that grows out of walls. He also taught about animals and birds, reptiles and fish. Men of all nations came to listen to Solomon's wisdom, sent by all the kings of the world, who had heard of his wisdom.

1 KINGS 4:29–33

Solomon became known as one of the wisest and richest men who ever lived. The "wisdom" books of the Bible—Proverbs, Song of Solomon, and Ecclesiastes—came from his divinely inspired pen. It was God who answered his prayer for wisdom.

Like Solomon, Jesus' adolescence and young adult years were characterized by progress in wisdom (Luke 2:52). If Jesus as a mortal being needed to grow in wisdom, how much more do you and I?

Making It Personal

Asking God for wisdom and receiving it is not a one-time deal that only Solomon was able to cash in on. "Give me wisdom" is a prayer all of us can pray with confidence. The New Testament book of James gives us the encouragement to ask for wisdom with this promise: "If any of you lacks wisdom, he should ask God, who gives generously to all without finding fault, and *it will be given to him*" (James 1:5).

Of the twenty-one most effective prayers, the one I use most often is "Give me wisdom." I have three teenage sons and I lead a church. There is always a need to make an important decision or give someone necessary advice. I have learned to ask for wisdom and God is faithful to answer.

With what decisions are you currently wrestling? Do you need wisdom to carry out your ministry more effectively? Are you trying to figure out how to lead your family? Do you need insight into a relationship? Do your job responsibilities require you to make decisions that affect the livelihoods of other people? Are there other areas where you need wisdom?

When Solomon prayed, "Give me wisdom," God answered "Yes!" Pause right now and ask God to give you wisdom for every decision you are encountering and every situation you face today.

NOTE

[1]See 1 Kings 3:16–28.

9

Answer Me:
The Prayer of Elijah
1 Kings 18:37

Elijah needed a miracle. There are many times when what we need is an answer to prayer. And then there are those rare, probably once-in-a-lifetime moments when we have to have a miracle. The Old Testament prophet did not need a nice, run-of-the-mill, easily explainable answer to prayer. The situation demanded an outright, jaw-dropping, undeniable, superceding-the-laws-of-nature, impressive, verifiable miracle! Without it, Elijah would be killed and God's chosen people would drift into pagan oblivion.

As Charles Dickens would say, it was the worst of times. King Ahab and Queen Jezebel had steered the nation of Israel down a road leading away from the Lord and then stepped on the accelerator—and woe to anyone who caused a traffic jam! Ahab was a man whose wickedness was exceeded only by that of his wife, Jezebel. Everything about that woman dripped iniquity and emanated evil. Together, they publicly promoted the worship of the pagan god Baal.

In order to shock the nation back from its dangerous path, the Lord sent a drought. This was not just a seasonal sign but a heaven-sent plague that lasted for three long years. The lack of rain was an obvious slap in the face of the supposed rain god, Baal.

After three years without rain, the people stood precariously with one foot on either side, partially following the false god and sort of following the Lord. Not a good place to be.

Into this boiling cauldron of chaos, God sent His man, Elijah, the roughhewn prophet. He was a wild, eccentric, bold messenger of the Almighty God. Risking death, Elijah faced Ahab and challenged him to gather the people for a power duel of deities.

When the day of decision dawned, Elijah stood alone on Mt. Carmel facing 450 prophets of Baal and 400 prophets of the goddess Asherah before the gathered nation of Israel. The odds were 950 to 1. It looked like a mismatch. As it turned out, it was.

Sidestepping political correctness, Elijah confronted the people with a challenge: "Quit sitting on the fence! If the Lord is the real God, follow Him. If Baal is the one, follow him" (1 Kings 18:21, paraphrased).

The people sat in stunned silence as he continued, "Let's have a duel between the deities. We will both offer an ox on the altar. The Baal prophets will pray to their God, and I will pray to mine. The god who answers with fire will prove to be the real God. The winner takes all" (1 Kings 18:22–24, paraphrased).

Since Baal was supposedly able to control lightning, thunder, and rain, everyone agreed. Humans love to watch car wrecks. The show would be highly entertaining.

The Baal prophets went first. They prayed all morning, "Baal, answer us." The only response they received was a wall of absolute silence. When Elijah began to taunt them, they prayed louder, harder, and more passionately. They did anything they could think of to provoke a response from their deity. Yet, there was not even a flicker of a reply. They prayed all afternoon. Nothing. Nada. Zippo. Baal had failed (see 1 Kings 18:27–29).

Then it was Elijah's turn. First, he repaired the altar the other prophets had knocked down in their feeble attempts to attract the attention of Baal. He dug a trench around the altar and then put wood on it and another ox. Then he did an absolutely outrageous thing.

Elijah had the altar drenched in water, time after time, until the excess water filled the trench. He had to be crazy. If 950 prophets' prayers could not get their god to send a spark, how did he think one man could get his God to consume a water-soaked sacrifice?

Standing in front of the altar before an entire nation and the hundreds of false prophets and King Ahab, Elijah needed a miracle. If he failed, they would kill him, and the Lord would be squeezed out of the nation through Ahab's political clout.

So Elijah did the only thing a man in desperate need of an impossible miracle does. He prayed. How big is God? Big enough! So Elijah offered one of the most effective prayers recorded in the Bible and asked God for a really big thing:

> At the time of sacrifice, the prophet Elijah stepped forward and prayed: "O LORD, God of Abraham, Isaac and Israel, let it be known today that you are God in Israel and that I am your servant and have done all these things at your command. Answer me, O LORD, answer me, so these people will know that you, O LORD, are God, and that you are turning their hearts back again."
>
> 1 KINGS 18:36–37

Answer me.

Elijah offered a simple, two-word request, "Answer me." And God did.

> Then the fire of the LORD fell and burned up the sacrifice, the wood, the stones and the soil, and also licked up the water in the trench.
>
> I KINGS 18:38

I read this story to my boys when they were little. One gasped in glee and another looked around and said, "Whoa!" The third one smiled and said, "Cool."

I would have loved to see the fire of the Lord shoot down from heaven. Wouldn't it have been awesome to see the looks on the faces of the people? What a blast to witness the humiliation and total embarrassment of the false prophets! Wouldn't it have been sheer delight to see the frustrated anger on the wicked king's face?

Elijah's petition was powerful. The prophets of Baal prayed all day and Baal couldn't even make a spark to light dry kindling wood. Then Elijah prayed for less than a minute and God sent fire from heaven that was so mighty it ignited a soaking wet sacrifice and burned up the wet wood, saturated stones, and soil. And if that wasn't enough, the blaze consumed all the water in the trench.

I say, "Wow!" And so did the people who witnessed the miracle.

> When all the people saw this, they fell prostrate and cried, "The LORD—he is God! The LORD—he is God!"
>
> I KINGS 18:39

How big is God? Big enough!

The spiritual direction of an entire nation was turned back to God all because one man was not afraid to confront the enemy and ask God for a miracle. Elijah lived in the largeness of God, and miracles were the result. He prayed, "Answer me!" and God did. He prayed, "Answer me!" and many people were steered back on course. He asked for a victory-producing miracle, and the enemy was crushed.

Twenty-five years ago I had the privilege of hearing a wonderful woman speak. Helen Roseveare was a missionary doctor who spent twenty years ministering in the Congo. This was one of the awesome stories she told:

One night I had worked hard to help a mother in the labor ward; but in spite of all we could do she died leaving us with a tiny premature baby and a crying two-year-old daughter. We would have difficulty keeping the baby alive, as we had no incubator. (We had no electricity to run an incubator.) We also had no special feeding facilities.

Although we lived on the equator, nights were often chilly with treacherous drafts. One student midwife went for the box we had for such babies and the cotton wool the baby would be wrapped in. Another went to stoke up the fire and fill a hot water bottle. She came back shortly in distress to tell me that in filling the bottle, it had burst. Rubber perishes easily in tropical climates. "And it is our last hot water bottle!" she exclaimed.

As in the West, it is no good crying over spilled milk, so in Central Africa it might be considered no good crying over burst water bottles. They do not grow on trees, and there are no drugstores down forest pathways.

"All right," I said, "put the baby as near the fire as you safely can, and sleep between the baby and the door to keep it free from drafts. Your job is to keep the baby warm."

The following noon, as I did most days, I went to have prayers with any of the orphanage children who chose to gather with me. I gave the youngsters various suggestions of things to pray about and told them about the tiny baby. I explained our problem about keeping the baby warm enough, mentioning the hot water bottle. The baby could so easily die if it got chills. I also told them of the two-year-old sister, crying because her mother had died. During the prayer time, one ten-year-old girl, Ruth, prayed with the usual blunt conciseness of our African children. "Please, God," she prayed, "send us a water bottle. It'll be no good tomorrow, God, as the baby will be dead, so please send it this afternoon."

While I gasped inwardly at the audacity of the prayer, she added by way of a corollary, "And while You are about it, would You please send a doll for the little girl so she'll know You really love her?"

As often with children's prayers, I was put on the spot. Could I honestly say, "Amen"? I just did not believe that God could do this. Oh, yes, I know that He can do everything. The Bible says so. But there are limits, aren't there? The only way God could answer this particular prayer would be by sending me a parcel from the homeland. I had been in Africa for almost four years at that time, and I had never, ever received a parcel from home. Anyway, if anyone did send me a parcel, who would put in a hot water bottle? I lived on the equator!

Halfway through the afternoon, while I was teaching in the nurses' training school, a message was sent that there was a car at my front door. By the time I reached home, the car had gone, but there, on the verandah, was a large twenty-two-pound parcel. I felt tears pricking my eyes. I could not open the parcel alone, so I sent for the orphanage children. Together we pulled off the string, carefully undoing each knot. We folded the paper, taking care not to tear it unduly.

Excitement was mounting. Some thirty or forty pairs of eyes were focused on the large cardboard box. From the top, I lifted out brightly colored, knitted jerseys. Eyes sparkled as I gave them out. Then there were the knitted bandages for the leprosy patients, and the children looked a little bored. Then came a box of mixed raisins and sultanas—that would make a nice batch of buns for the weekend.

Then, as I put my hand in again, I felt. . .could it really be? I grasped it and pulled it out. Yes, it was, a brand-new, rubber hot water bottle!

I cried. I had not asked God to send it; I had not truly believed that He could. Ruth was in the front row of the children. She rushed forward, crying out, "If God has sent the bottle, He must have sent the doll, too!"

Rummaging down to the bottom of the box, she pulled out the small, beautifully dressed dolly. Her eyes shone! She had never doubted. Looking up at me, she asked: "Can I go over with you, Mummy, and give this doll to that little girl, so she'll know that Jesus really loves her?"

That parcel had been on the way for five whole months. Packed up by my former Sunday school class, whose leader had heard and obeyed God's prompting to send a hot water bottle, even to the equator. And one of the girls had put in a doll for an African child—five months before—in answer to the believing prayer of a ten-year-old to bring it that afternoon! "Before they call, I will answer!" (Isaiah 65:24).[1]

Making It Personal

I read stories like this and they remind me that God truly is amazing. He can do miracles. He can do anything. Nothing is too big, too hard, or too complicated for Him. He is the God over all. He can send fire from heaven in answer to prayer. He can deliver a hot-water bottle and doll to the Congo on exactly the right day.

How big is God? Big enough! I could tell story after story of how God worked in amazing ways as the result of desperate prayer. But you don't need to hear someone else's story. You need your own story.

What is your impossible situation? Where do you need a miracle? Why not tell God? Ask Him to answer so you can give Him the glory!

NOTE

[1] Helen Roseveare, a missionary from England to Zaire, Africa, told this as it had happened to her in Africa. She shared it in her testimony on a Wednesday night at Thomas Road Baptist Church. It is also found in her book, *Living Faith*, published by WEC International, P.O. Box 1707, Fort Washington, PA 19034. Used by permission.

10

DELIVER US:
The Prayer of Hezekiah
2 KINGS 19:19

Poor King Hezekiah faced a fate worse than his own death. The nightmare had the name Sennacherib, the undefeated king of Assyria. Sennacherib had a massive army and, in the literal sense, cutting-edge chariots. Sennacherib had already crushed all of the nations around Judah from Lebanon in the north to Egypt in the south. And now he was poised to ride his mighty war chariots right through Judah.

In order to intimidate Hezekiah, Sennacherib sent a message reminding Judah of his complete destruction of nine city-states that had opposed him. His message was clear. He intended to make Judah number ten unless they unconditionally put up a white flag and surrendered, then became slaves that were taken captive back to Assyria.

Hezekiah faced a deadly dilemma. Option A was to watch his nation get crushed by a superior force under the wheels of thundering chariots. Option B was to see his people shackled and led away to Assyria to be slaves. What could he do? What would you do?

Hezekiah chose Option C. He did what we all should do when we face extreme pressure and ferocious enemy attack. He prayed.

> *Hezekiah received the letter from the messengers and read it. Then he went up to the temple of the LORD and spread it out before the LORD. And Hezekiah prayed to the LORD: "O LORD, God of Israel, enthroned between the cherubim, you alone are God over all the kingdoms of the earth. You have made heaven and earth. Give ear, O LORD, and hear; open your eyes, O LORD, and see; listen to the words Sennacherib has sent to insult the living God.*
>
> *"It is true, O LORD, that the Assyrian kings have laid waste these nations and their lands. They have thrown their gods into the fire and destroyed them, for they were not gods but only wood and stone, fashioned by men's hands. Now, O LORD our God, deliver us from his hand, so that all kingdoms on earth may know that you alone, O LORD, are God."*
>
> 2 KINGS 19:14–19

Deliver us.

Notice carefully the sentence "Now, O LORD our God, deliver us from his hand, so that all kingdoms on earth may know that you alone, O LORD, are God." This was the expression of Hezekiah's heart and the heart of his prayer. Hezekiah prayed a very simple prayer. The essence of it is captured in those two little words, "Deliver us." What else is there to say at times like that?

It turns out Option C was a great idea. Look at what happened.

> *That night the angel of the LORD went out and put to death a hundred and eighty-five thousand men in the Assyrian camp. When the people got up the next morning— there were all the dead bodies!*
>
> 2 KINGS 19:35

Hezekiah was in a battle he had no shot at winning. Yet, God fought the battle for him. In the dark of night the angel of the Lord went out and killed such a massive number of the enemy that Sennacherib got God's message. Sennacherib was so shaken that he and his army packed up and marched straight home. They did not pass "Go" or collect $200.00. They didn't harass anyone else. They ran home like scared dogs.

God had not been impressed with the arrogance of Sennacherib, but God did like Hezekiah's prayer. Hezekiah's soldiers did not even have to fight! All Hezekiah's soldiers had to do was collect the booty that the Assyrians left in their haste. Hezekiah turned the problem over to God and God fought the battle and won.

Isn't it great serving a God who is both able and willing to deliver us when we ask? That is the promise of Psalm 91. Read it slowly.

> He who dwells in the shelter of the Most High will rest in the shadow of the Almighty. I will say of the LORD, "He is my refuge and my fortress, my God, in whom I trust." Surely he will save you from the fowler's snare and from the deadly pestilence. He will cover you with his feathers, and under his wings you will find refuge; his faithfulness will be your shield and rampart. You will not fear the terror of night, nor the arrow that flies by day, nor the pestilence that stalks in the darkness, nor the plague that destroys at midday. A thousand may fall at your side, ten thousand at your right hand, but it will not come near you. You will only observe with your eyes and see the punishment of the wicked. If you make the Most High your dwelling— even the LORD, who is my refuge—then no harm will befall you, no disaster will come near your tent. For he will command his angels concerning you to guard you in all your ways; they will lift you up in their hands, so that you will not strike your foot against a stone. You will tread upon the lion and the cobra; you will trample the great lion and the serpent. "Because he loves me," says the LORD, "I will rescue him; I will protect him, for he acknowledges my name. He will call upon me, and I will answer him; I will be with him in trouble, I will deliver him and honor him. With long life will I satisfy him and show him my salvation."

What an awesome promise is this: "He will call upon me, and I will answer him; I will be with him in trouble, I will deliver him." In preparing this chapter, I came across many modern-day stories of God's people calling out to Him and God answering and delivering them. I don't have room to tell them all, but let me summarize a few.

Nebio, a man who came to Christ in Ecuador, and two missionary evangelists were caught in an ambush by angry villagers. Within minutes the attackers ran away. When Nebio returned to the village, one man explained, "When they saw all those soldiers on the ridge, they ran for their lives!"

Nebio used his experience to lead his entire family to the Lord. Today there's a Christian church in that community with many coming to Christ.[1]

Corrie Ten Boom told of an event during the Jeunesse Rebellion in the Congo. An army of rebels approached a school where children of missionaries lived. As the army of hundreds advanced, the children and their teachers huddled in prayer. Suddenly, the rebel force stopped and retreated. This happened again the next day. Then the rebels left to fight elsewhere.

Later one of them was injured and was brought to the missionary school for treatment. The doctor asked him, "Why didn't you break into the school as you planned?"

"We couldn't do it," the soldier said, "When we saw the hundreds of soldiers in white uniforms, we became scared."[2]

Joan Wester Anderson records the story of Steve and Phil, two Christian plain-clothed police officers assigned to discover the source of the drugs ruining the community of Nutley, New Jersey. After prayer, they successfully found the hideout to be a cave. One night they chased a group of young adults to the cave. Praying Psalm 91, they found the cave held a dozen violent young adults, including their leader, Mr. Big, the drug dealer himself.

Unarmed but filled with courage, they went in and calmly apprehended Mr. Big and the rest. As they led their prisoners out, a police van pulled up to take them back to the station.

They asked Mr. Big, "Why didn't you or any of the others try to attack us when we came in?"

"You think I am crazy or something? There were at least twenty guys in blue uniforms."

"Twenty? No, there were just two of us," the officers replied.

"Hey, Belinda," Mr. Big called to another young prisoner, "how many cops came into the cave?"

Belinda shrugged, "At least twenty-five."[3]

In 2002 the Rodeo-Chediski forest fire consumed nearly half a million acres, roaring through much of Arizona. Firefighters labored valiantly to save the American Indian Christian Mission, but they were forced to leave when the blaze became too dangerous. Prayers from thousands of people were mingled with those of the children who asked God to deliver the mission.

It looked as though God had not heard their cries for deliverance when the blaze roared up to within a few feet of the mission school on three sides. But God came through. Not one building was touched.

Interestingly, three crosses stood near the entrance to the school. In the inferno, only one was burned. It was the one in the middle. To those in the mission, that lone burned cross was a powerful reminder that Jesus Christ had saved the mission just as He has saved our souls, by being the one who is consumed.[4]

Myra worked for Teen Challenge in a very rough neighborhood in Philadelphia. A gang ruled the street outside the ministry center, harassing any young people who wanted to come to the center for help. One night when the gang appeared, Myra suddenly felt inspired to tell them about Jesus. She opened the door and walked outside. Instead of listening to her, the gang shouted threats of drowning her in the nearby river. Myra breathed a prayer to Jesus. "Lord, let Your angels come with me and protect me," she murmured.

Then she opened the door and was about to speak when the gang members suddenly stopped their shouting, turned to look at one another, and left silently and quickly. Myra was surprised. Why had they gone?

The gang did not return for several days. Then one afternoon, to the surprise of everyone, they entered the center in an orderly fashion. Much later, after a relationship had been built with them, they were asked what had made them leave so peacefully that night.

One young man said, "We wouldn't dare touch her after her boyfriend showed up. That dude had to be seven feet tall."

"I didn't know Myra had a boyfriend," they were told. "But at any rate, she was here alone that night."

"No, we saw him," insisted another gang member. "He was right behind her. He was big as life in his classy white suit."[5]

Making It Personal

Asking God for deliverance from evil is definitely a prayer God delights to answer. We don't have to be facing urgent danger to use it. You may recall that when Jesus gave us the sample prayer, He taught us to regularly pray, "Deliver us from evil or from the evil one" (Matthew 6:13).

Only God knows what evil awaits you today. You don't need to face it alone. God fights many battles for us, especially when we ask Him to deliver us. Make "Deliver us" one of your daily prayers. When you get to heaven, you will be able to see "behind the veil" of how many times God answered, even times when you did not ask for His help.

NOTES

[1] Dr. Ron Cline, "Protecting Angels," a message given at HCJB World Radio, Tuesday, May 18, 2004.

[2] Corrie Ten Boom, *Marching Orders for the End Battle* (Fort Washington, PA: Christian Literature Crusade, 1969), pp. 89–90.

[3] Joan Wester Anderson, *Where Angels Walk* (New York, NY: Ballantine Books, 1992), pp. 216–18.

[4] Rachel Clark, "Arizona Fire Leaves Long Term Burden," *Disaster News Network* (www.disasternews.net), September 2002.

[5] Betty Malz, *Angels Watching Over Me* (Old Tappan, NJ: Chosen Books, 1986), pp. 97–98.

11

Help Us:
The Prayer of Asa
2 Chronicles 14:11

If you haven't been there yet, you will be. Mark it down. There will be those times when there is nothing else you can do. There is nowhere else to turn. You need big-time help and you need it now. You need God.

Maybe you read that first paragraph and nodded your head. When despair, helplessness, and hopelessness are mentioned, they resonate deep within. You understand what it means to be swept up in that current and somehow live to tell about it. You know exactly what I am writing about. You have been there and done that. And guess what? Times like that will probably happen again.

Maybe you don't think such crises will ever happen to you. Just ask Asa.

All was going great for Asa. He was the golden boy. As the king of Judah, he seemed to be doing everything right. During his first ten years in office, he radically cleaned up and significantly built up the nation.

> And Abijah rested with his fathers and was buried in the City of David. Asa his son succeeded him as king, and in his days the country was at peace for ten years. Asa did what was good and right in the eyes of the Lord his God. He removed the foreign altars and the high places, smashed the sacred stones and cut down the Asherah poles. He commanded Judah to seek the Lord, the God of their fathers, and to obey his laws and commands. He removed the high places and incense altars in every town in Judah, and the kingdom was at peace under him. He built up the fortified cities of Judah, since the land was at peace. No one was at war with him during those years, for the Lord gave him rest. "Let us build up these towns," he said to Judah, "and put walls around them, with towers, gates and bars. The land is still ours, because we have sought the Lord our God; we sought him and he has given us rest on every side." So they built and prospered. Asa had an army of three hundred thousand men from Judah, equipped with large shields and with spears, and two hundred and eighty thousand from Benjamin, armed with small shields and with bows. All these were brave fighting men.
>
> 2 Chronicles 14:1–8

That was a highly impressive decade as Asa did what was right in the eyes of God. He tore down the tools of pagan worship. He led his people to seek God and obey His commands. He strengthened the fortified cities and assembled a large, well-equipped army. He had every reason to assume his good fortune would continue and peace would perpetuate.

He was woefully wrong.

> Zerah the Cushite marched out against them with a vast army and three hundred chariots, and came as far as Mareshah. Asa went out to meet him, and they took up battle positions in the Valley of Zephathah near Mareshah.
>
> 2 Chronicles 14:9–10

All was sweet and joyful in Judah until one decisive day when a dark cloud rolled up from Egypt. In the eye of the terrible tempest was Zerah, leading a massive war machine of one million Ethiopians and three hundred gleaming chariots. Asa would have to face a skilled opponent who had him outnumbered by over four hundred thousand troops, which was bad enough. But what made it worse were those three hundred war wagons. Judah had no defense against the awesome speed and power of the best modern weapons of mass destruction on the planet in 900 BC. It would be one of the most massive massacres in history.

How would you handle the horrible hopelessness of facing definite defeat and destruction? What do you usually do when things are bleak?

Asa did the right thing. He prayed one of the most effective prayers recorded in the Bible.

> Then Asa called to the LORD his God and said, "LORD, there is no one like you to help the powerless against the mighty. Help us, O LORD our God, for we rely on you, and in your name we have come against this vast army. O LORD, you are our God; do not let man prevail against you."
>
> 1 CHRONICLES 14:11

Help us, O Lord our God.

What an excellent pattern for effective prayer! The prayer is short—only twenty-seven words in Hebrew—and complete. Moreover, Asa's simple petition consists of three outstanding components of effective prayer:

1. *He opened with appropriate words of praise:* "Lord, there is no one like you to help the powerless against the mighty." Praise positions us to pray.

2. *He stated the petition clearly and succinctly:* "Help us, O LORD our God."

3. *He gave God the reasons he expected Him to answer*—in his case, four reasons. First, Judah was depending on God, not on themselves or anyone else: "for we rely on you." Second, Judah was representing God in this cause: "in your name we have come against this vast army." Third, Israel belonged to and was allied with God: "O LORD, you are our God." Fourth, ultimately the battle was the Lord's: "do not let man prevail against you."

It worked, and then some. God heard Asa's prayer and gave him a miraculous answer, exceedingly and abundantly above all he asked or thought.

> The LORD struck down the Cushites before Asa and Judah. The Cushites fled, and Asa and his army pursued them as far as Gerar. Such a great number of Cushites fell that they could not recover; they were crushed before the LORD and his forces. The men of Judah carried off a large amount of plunder. They destroyed all the villages around Gerar, for the terror of the LORD had fallen upon them. They plundered all these villages, since there was much booty there. They also attacked the camps of the herdsmen and carried off droves of sheep and goats and camels. Then they returned to Jerusalem.
>
> 1 CHRONICLES 14:12–15

God sent such a holy terror upon the Cushites that they ran away in fear before the battle began. Exactly how God did it, the Bible does not say. That'll be something we find out in heaven when we watch the movie in the "You Were There Theater." Maybe He sent a host of glimmering angels who blinded them in the early morning sunrise. Maybe He spoke in a thunderous voice. Maybe He painted a million different images of their secret nightmares across the canvas of their minds. It will be fun to find out.

They were too scared to fight and were routed by Judah's army. All Asa and his men had to do was chase them. Amazingly, the huge Ethiopian force had been completely conquered by Asa's smaller army.

Yet, God not only gave them a victory, but He gave them prodigious plunder. Judah grabbed up what the fleeing Cushites left behind as well as pillaged the Philistine villages that made the costly error of housing those Cushites. On top of that, Judah was able to defeat and fleece the rich camps of the pesty nomadic herdsmen who had been following the Cushite army selling them sheep, goats, and camels.

Can you imagine how excited and happy everyone was when the victorious troops marched back into Jerusalem with the precious prizes and bountiful booty? Not only were they spared probable annihilation and certain slavery, they were free. The margin of victory was not even close. They totally crushed the opponent.

Asa's prayer was more than effective. It was miraculously, powerfully, liberatingly, wealth-producingly potent.

Help us, O Lord our God.

Making It Personal

1. *You can tap in to the overlooked power of God by crying out for help.* Consider the story of the prophet Jonah, who was running from God. When he was thrown from a ship in the midst of a terrible storm, he had two choices: drown or pray. He prayed and asked God for help: "In my distress I called to the LORD, and he answered me. From the depths of the grave I called for help, and you listened to my cry" (Jonah 2:2).

God sent a great fish to swallow Jonah. The fish saved Jonah's life and delivered him to where he was supposed to have gone in the first place, the evil city of Nineveh.

> From inside the fish, Jonah prayed to the LORD his God. He said: "In my distress I called to the LORD, and he answered me. From the depths of the grave I called for help, and you listened to my cry. . . ." And the LORD commanded the fish, and it vomited Jonah onto dry land.
>
> JONAH 2:1, 10

Riding through the sea inside a fish couldn't have been the most luxurious mode of travel, and being vomited out is not the most fashionable way to make an entrance. But for a man who should have been dead it wasn't bad. Tap in to the power of God and be saved!

2. *Praying Asa's prayer may result in an answer exceedingly and abundantly above all you could ask or think.* Think of Daniel the prophet, who spent most of his life as an exile in Babylon. When Daniel discovered that his commitment to God would lead to being thrown into the lions' den, he asked God for help: "Then these men went as a group and found Daniel praying and asking God for help" (Daniel 6:11).

God answered Daniel's prayer for help and gave Daniel multi-layered blessings as a result. First, though, Daniel was miraculously protected from the lions. He told the king, "My God sent his angel, and he shut the mouths of the lions. They have not hurt me, because I was found innocent in his sight" (Daniel 6:22). Beyond that, Daniel's enemies were removed and the pagan king Darius glorified the Lord by telling Daniel's testimony to the nation.

"May you prosper greatly! I issue a decree that in every part of my kingdom people must fear and reverence the God of Daniel. For he is the living God and he endures forever; his kingdom will not be destroyed, his dominion will never end. He rescues and he saves; he performs signs and wonders in the heavens and on the earth. He has rescued Daniel from the power of the lions."

So Daniel prospered during the reign of Darius.

DANIEL 6:25–28

3. *If you need help today, God is listening.* The Psalms are full of examples of survival prayer. Notice the word "help" in each of these passages.

God is our refuge and strength, an ever-present help in trouble. Therefore we will not fear, though the earth give way and the mountains fall into the heart of the sea.

PSALM 46:1–2

I lift up my eyes to the hills—where does my help come from? My help comes from the LORD, the Maker of heaven and earth.

PSALM 121:1–2

Come quickly to help me, O Lord my Savior.

PSALM 38:22

Be pleased, O LORD, to save me; O LORD, come quickly to help me.

PSALM 40:13

Then my enemies will turn back when I call for help. By this I will know that God is for me.

PSALM 56:9

Hasten, O God, to save me; O LORD, come quickly to help me.

PSALM 70:1

Yet I am poor and needy; come quickly to me, O God. You are my help and my deliverer; O LORD, do not delay.

PSALM 70:5

Help us, O God our Savior, for the glory of your name; deliver us and forgive our sins for your name's sake.

PSALM 79:9

Our help is in the name of the LORD, the Maker of heaven and earth.

PSALM 124:8

Do you need help today? Ask God. He's listening, He's able, and He's willing.

12

Grant Me Favor:
The Prayer of Nehemiah
Nehemiah 1:11

Maybe you know exactly what you need to happen and where you need God to work. Yet, God first might work through someone in authority over you. That person could be a government official, teacher, or pastor or maybe even your boss, coach, parent, or spouse! But in order to get what you need, God has to move their hearts on your behalf.

As the cupbearer for King Artaxerxes, Nehemiah held a very responsible position, yet he longed to be eight hundred miles away, back with his people in the destroyed city of Jerusalem. They were facing possible annihilation and Nehemiah needed to return to rebuild the city walls. More specifically, he needed three years off from his job and enough supplies to rebuild a wall around the entire city of Jerusalem! First, though, a huge change had to happen in the heart of the man in authority, that is, King Artaxerxes. Nehemiah's superior, an unbeliever, had a nasty reputation for cutting the heads off subordinates who upset him. For Nehemiah to march into the king's oval office and demand time off and building materials would be signing his own death warrant. So what could he do?

If you read the story of Nehemiah, you find a man who consistently turned his problems into prayer. He lived by the advice, "Pray when troubles trouble you." We find him turning his problems into prayer in almost every one of the twelve chapters in the book bearing his name (Nehemiah 1:5–11; 2:5; 4:4–5, 9; 5:19; 6:9–14; 9:32; 13:14, 22, 29, 31). So when the need in Jerusalem was brought to his attention, he did as he always did. He brought the matter to the Lord. His prayer, one of the most effective in the Bible, is a tutorial on how to pray. Let's see what we can learn from him.

Nehemiah opened with words of praise and perspective. God's address is praise. Praise and thanksgiving are gateways into the presence of God (see Psalm 100:4). He also mentions the perspective that the God he is addressing is the one who keeps His covenant. The importance of this will become clear as the prayer develops.

> *Then I said: "O LORD, God of heaven, the great and awesome God, who keeps his covenant of love with those who love him and obey his commands."*
>
> Nehemiah 1:5

Nehemiah did not pray once and quit. He brought his burden to God repeatedly, day and night. It may have been weeks or even months from when he first began to pray about the plight of Jerusalem until God granted his request.

Jesus made a promise when He said, "keep on asking and it shall be given unto you" (a literal translation of Matthew 7:7). He also encouraged us to be as persistent in our prayers as the friend at midnight (Luke 11:5–10) and the widow who beseeched the unjust judge (Luke 18:1–8).

> *"Let your ear be attentive and your eyes open to hear the prayer your servant is praying before you day and night for your servants, the people of Israel."*
>
> Nehemiah 1:6

Nehemiah then moved to a season of assessment and confession of sins. Because sin creates a barrier between God and us (Isaiah 59:1–2), it removes God's obligation to hear and answer prayer (Psalm 66:18). So Nehemiah confessed his sins.

> *"I confess the sins we Israelites, including myself and my father's house, have committed against you. We have acted very wickedly toward you. We have not obeyed the commands, decrees and laws you gave your servant Moses."*
>
> NEHEMIAH 1:6–7

Note that Nehemiah confesses not only his own sins but also those of his people. The big request he is going to make is not all about Nehemiah. Should God say "Yes" to Nehemiah's petition, the answer will bless all of God's people.

Nehemiah reminded God of the promise He made through Moses. God had promised that the people would be scattered through disobedience and they were. He also promised that they would be returned through obedience. This was the key to Nehemiah's expectation: that God would act on his behalf, and that God had a soft spot for His people in whom He had already invested so much.

> *"Remember the instruction you gave your servant Moses, saying, 'If you are unfaithful, I will scatter you among the nations, but if you return to me and obey my commands, then even if your exiled people are at the farthest horizon, I will gather them from there and bring them to the place I have chosen as a dwelling for my Name.' They are your servants and your people, whom you redeemed by your great strength and your mighty hand."*
>
> NEHEMIAH 1:8–10

Those skilled in the art of intercession apply the importance of the timely use of God's promises. There are hundreds of promises in the Bible, one for every need. Claiming them in prayer and reminding God of His promises gives us boldness in prayer.

When the Israelites escaped Egypt and wandered in the wilderness, they rebelled against God. God told Moses that He would destroy them (Exodus 32:7–10). Yet, Moses pleaded the promises God had made to Abraham, Isaac, and Israel (Exodus 32:11–13). Moses' appeal worked! God relented and spared the entire nation (Exodus 32:14; Psalm 106:23).

Nehemiah got down to business and offered his petition:

> *"O Lord, let your ear be attentive to the prayer of this your servant and to the prayer of your servants who delight in revering your name. Give your servant success today by granting him favor in the presence of this man."* I was cupbearer to the king.
>
> NEHEMIAH 1:11

Grant favor.

Nehemiah must have been familiar with the book of Genesis and with the prayer of Abraham's servant, "Give me success today." But he did not stop there. He told God specifically how he needed success: "Give your servant success today by *granting him favor* in the presence of this man." "This man" was none other than Nehemiah's boss, the most powerful man on the planet, King Artaxerxes. Nehemiah's petition was that God would touch the king's heart in such a way as to give favor to Nehemiah and give him what he needed. Nehemiah was going to ask the king to send him off with his blessing to rebuild the walls *and* for the resources to pay for it!

The nature, size, and scope of Nehemiah's request were such that the odds of Artaxerxes saying "Yes" were slim. That's why Nehemiah went to God first. God would have to touch the king's heart before he would ever agree to Nehemiah's petition.

And He did, but not without a little nail biting. See for yourself:

> *In the month of Nisan in the twentieth year of King Artaxerxes, when wine was brought for him, I took the wine and gave it to the king. I had not been sad in his presence before; so the king asked me, "Why does your face look so sad when you are not ill? This can be nothing but sadness of heart." I was very much afraid.*
>
> NEHEMIAH 2:1–2

Of course he was afraid! It was a capital offense to appear in the king's presence with an unhappy face. He was hoping that his prayer would hold up. What else could he do?

Nehemiah acted on the belief that God would answer. There is a time for prayer and there is a time for action. Now was the time to act.

> *But I said to the king, "May the king live forever! Why should my face not look sad when the city where my fathers are buried lies in ruins, and its gates have been destroyed by fire?" The king said to me, "What is it you want?"*
>
> NEHEMIAH 2:3–4

This was the big moment. If Nehemiah did not have the king's favor, asking for such an outlandish thing would be fatal. If he did have the king's favor for such a huge request, it would be a miracle. God had to come through. So he reminded God of his request.

Nehemiah kept praying until the answer arrived.

> *Then I prayed to the God of heaven, and I answered the king, "If it pleases the king and if your servant has found favor in his sight, let him send me to the city in Judah where my fathers are buried so that I can rebuild it."*
>
> NEHEMIAH 2:4–5

Gulp. Nehemiah's fate, the fate of Jerusalem, and the fate of the Israelites rested on the response of the king.

> *Then the king, with the queen sitting beside him, asked me, "How long will your journey take, and when will you get back?" It pleased the king to send me; so I set a time.*
>
> NEHEMIAH 2:6

Did you see it? He said, "It pleased the king to send me." Unbelievable, impossible, amazing! God came through. Nehemiah was on a roll. Instead of quitting while he was ahead, he pressed on.

Nehemiah did not give up until he received all he needed.

I also said to him, "If it pleases the king, may I have letters to the governors of Trans-Euphrates, so that they will provide me safe-conduct until I arrive in Judah? And may I have a letter to Asaph, keeper of the king's forest, so he will give me timber to make beams for the gates of the citadel by the temple and for the city wall and for the residence I will occupy?"

NEHEMIAH 2:7–8

First, God worked so the king would let him go. Now, Nehemiah was asking the king to pay for safe conduct and supplies. Did he go too far?

And because the gracious hand of my God was upon me, the king granted my requests. So I went to the governors of Trans-Euphrates and gave them the king's letters. The king had also sent army officers and cavalry with me.

NEHEMIAH 2:8–9

The king gave Nehemiah all he asked for plus an army escort! Coincidence? No way. Nehemiah knew why the king showed him such incredible favor. He said it was because the gracious hand of his God was upon him.

Gaining the favor of Artaxerxes was a big obstacle to Nehemiah, but the power of Nehemiah's God dwarfed it. The king's heart was putty in God's hands. Nehemiah received exceedingly and abundantly more than he had asked or thought.

Making It Personal

God *is* able to change the hearts of those in authority. A friend who serves as an associate pastor recently told me how discouraged he had been by the refusal of his church's leadership to allow him to make necessary changes in the way the church did ministry. After the friend patiently prayed for favor, God touched their hearts and the changes are taking place. On top of that, he received a promotion and a raise!

God is able to change hearts, and I have seen that most recently in my own life. After weeks of prayer, God granted my son favor with his school's superintendent concerning a very challenging and difficult decision. God's favor cleared the way for a positive response toward my son.

Who needs to grant you favor if you are to carry out your ministry? With whom do you need favor if you are going to be able to follow God's heart? "Grant me favor" is one prayer we may need to use often. Start praying it now, and see what God can do for you.

13

Strengthen My Hands:
The Prayer of Nehemiah
Nehemiah 6:9

Weary and tottering on the brink of despair, Nehemiah had been working for brutally long days week after week. He was attempting the impossible. His task was to lead a remnant of God's people in the impossible task of rebuilding the walls of Jerusalem.

All during the weeks of work, a strong enemy named Sanballat and his friends had attempted to discourage Nehemiah and his workers by laughing at their vision (Nehemiah 2:19) and later criticizing and belittling their efforts (4:1–3). When that failed, they gathered a coalition force to frighten and intimidate the workers with the threat of a surprise attack (4:7–12). On top of that, there was division in the ranks of Nehemiah's workforce (5:1–13). Yet, through it all, Nehemiah's integrity, courage, and God-focused encouragement kept the work moving ahead until the walls were nearly completed.

At that point, Nehemiah desperately needed some relief and rest. Instead, things got worse. Before he could catch his breath, his cunning nemesis Sanballat tried a new approach. Repeatedly, he requested meetings with Nehemiah. Yet, Nehemiah wisely refused each request, sensing that Sanballat wanted, at the very least, to distract him from the task. Most probably, Sanballat wanted to lure Nehemiah away so he could kidnap or kill him.

After four refusals, Sanballat launched a devious new scheme. He cleverly misrepresented Nehemiah's motives, character, and methods in an open letter. In it, Sanballat even stated that Nehemiah was rebuilding the wall to make himself rich and powerful. These unsubstantiated and inaccurate rumors were designed to undercut Nehemiah's authority (see Nehemiah 6:5–7).

Oh, the ruinous nature of rumors! They pierce deeply, as did Sanballat's carefully crafted lies about Nehemiah. Yet, Nehemiah would not quit.

Note that God does not make it easy on His people. Just because we are trying to do as God wants does not mean that we will be immune to problems, frustrations, and attacks. Just the opposite is true.

Yet, Nehemiah fought on by fighting from his knees. He turned his problems into prayer. This was not a new thing for Nehemiah. Prayer was part of his lifestyle. Looking over the book that bears his name reveals his relentless reliance on prayer. First, Nehemiah turned his burden for the broken-down walls into prayer (Nehemiah 1:5–11). Then he turned the potential disaster of his appointment with the king into prayer (2:4). As he began building the walls, he prayed his way out of Sanballat's early assaults (4:4–5). Now as he faced back-breaking weariness and undeserved attack, Nehemiah turned again to prayer:

> *They were all trying to frighten us, thinking, "Their hands will get too weak for the work, and it will not be completed." But I prayed, "Now strengthen my hands."*
> Nehemiah 6:9

Strengthen my hands.
Nehemiah did not ask God to wipe out his enemies, as I might have done. He did not ask God to give this daunting responsibility to someone else, which I almost surely would have.

He did not even ask for the walls to be miraculously built by legions of angels overnight, which I would at least have tried. Instead, he prayed, "Strengthen my hands."

Sometimes God prefers to do the miracle *in* us.

"Strengthen my hands." And God responded, as is revealed in the first five words of verse 15: "So the wall was completed on the twenty-fifth of Elul, in fifty-two days" (Nehemiah 6:15).

The wall was completed in a mere fifty-two days. No one would have believed it possible. Engineers are still marveling at the accomplishment. Mission Impossible became Mission Accomplished!

And make no mistake: This material structure was the result of spiritual activity. Prayer guided, fueled, forced, and completed the impossible. Nehemiah refused to quit, and God did not fail to bless. Yet, that's not all. When God gave Nehemiah strength to complete the project, his enemies became so discouraged that they were led to acknowledge that the rebuilding of the walls was the work of God!

> *When all our enemies heard about this, all the surrounding nations were afraid and lost their self-confidence, because they realized that this work had been done with the help of our God.*
>
> NEHEMIAH 6:16

Charles Swindoll has written, "That has to be the most thrilling experience in the world—to watch God come to the rescue when you have been helpless. In the middle of the incessant assault of the enemy, in spite of endless verbal barrage, the wall was built! While the enemy blasts, God builds."[1]

Making It Personal

1. *Nehemiah was not the first to find God as his source of strength.* From the Psalms we read:

> *The LORD is the strength of his people, a fortress of salvation for his anointed one.*
>
> PSALM 28:8

> *God is our refuge and strength, an ever-present help in trouble.*
>
> PSALM 46:1

> *My flesh and my heart may fail, but God is the strength of my heart and my portion forever.*
>
> PSALM 73:26

> *Sing for joy to God our strength; shout aloud to the God of Jacob!*
>
> PSALM 81:1

2. *Nehemiah also was not the only one to ask God for strength.* The Psalmist prayed, "My soul is weary with sorrow; strengthen me according to your word" (Psalm 119:28). The prophet Isaiah prayed, "O LORD, be gracious to us; we long for you. Be our strength every morning, our salvation in time of distress" (Isaiah 33:2).

Samson, the world's strongest man, forfeited his strength when he lost his connection to God, courtesy of his fateful haircut in Delilah's beauty salon (Judges 16:4–21), which then led to his blinding and imprisonment. You might not recall the rest of the story. The

Philistines were having a party in honor of their god, Dagon, and they brought Samson out to entertain the guests. After he was finished, they chained him between the pillars of the great temple to Dagon. Then Samson did something he should have been doing all along (Judges 16:23–27):

> Then Samson prayed to the LORD, "O Sovereign LORD, remember me. O God, please strengthen me just once more, and let me with one blow get revenge on the Philistines for my two eyes."

JUDGES 16:28

Sadly, Samson's death was his greatest triumph. He had finally learned the frailty of human strength and the necessity of divine power. He prayed, "Strengthen me." And God did.

"Strengthen me." I find this prayer to be one I use often. Life will wear us out and responsibility will wear us down. The added pressure of the attacks of an "enemy" rapidly erodes our strength.

Many pastors are a little like Nehemiah when it comes to building projects. I have helped lead our church through four major building projects, and every one was riddled with its own unique challenges, opponents, and frustrations. I have learned to ask God to strengthen my hands, and He has come through on every occasion.

3. *God can give you enough strength today for whatever challenge you are facing.* The greater the obstacles, the greater His strength. One man found this out in a miraculous fashion.

Stanley got up early on September 11, 2001, and left for work in the World Trade Center Tower Two where he was the assistant vice-president of loans for a bank. That morning in his quiet time with God, Stanley felt an unusual need to ask God for strength and protection.

Later, as he sat in his office talking on the phone, he looked up to see what he would later know was United Airlines Flight 175 heading straight toward him. "All I can see is this big gray plane, with red letters on the wing and on the tail, bearing down on me." It seemed like it was happening in slow motion. All he could do was pray, "Lord, You take control, I can't help myself here."

Just before the plane hit, Stanley dove under his desk. Immediately the plane tore into the side of the building and exploded. Flaming rubble filled the room.

Somehow, Stanley was unhurt. But from under the desk he could see the flaming wing of the plane blocking his doorway. He knew he had to get out of his office, but how? He was trapped in debris as high as his shoulders.

"Lord, You take control, this is Your problem now," he prayed. Later he said, the Lord "gave me so much power and strength in my body that I was able to shake everything off. I felt like the strongest man alive."

Stanley's office resembled a war zone, with walls flattened into dusty heaps, office furniture strewn violently around, flames dancing menacingly, and heavy rubble everywhere. He would somehow have to get through it all to escape.

"Everything I'm trying to climb on [to get out] is collapsing," he recalled. "I was getting cuts and bruises, but I'm saying, 'Lord, I have to go home to my loved ones, I have to make it. You have to help me.' " In other words, "Give me strength."

His heart sank when he came to a wall. He could not go back into the flames and he could not go on through the wall. Again, he prayed for strength. "I got up, and I felt as if a power came over me," he said. "I felt goose bumps all over my body and I'm trembling, and

I said to the wall, 'You're going to be no match for me and my Lord.' " Then he punched through the wall.

On the other side was a man named Brian who desperately needed help. To get out alive they had to somehow get down eighty-one flights of rubble-filled steps trapped in the heart of a burning building. Praying for strength, they descended step after step, flight by flight. Finally, they reached the concourse. The only people there were firefighters.

The weary men now faced a wall of flames. They soaked themselves in the building sprinkler system to run through the flames. Praying all the way, they burst through the flames, out of the building, and to the safety of a church two blocks away. "As soon as I held on to the gate of that church, the building [World Trade Center Tower Two] collapsed," Stanley recalled.

Hours later, cut and bloody, with clothes tattered and wearing a borrowed shirt, Stanley Praimnath made it home to his wife, Jennifer, and his two girls, Stephanie, 8, and Caitlin, 4. "I held my wife and my two children and we cried," Stanley said. Then they thanked God.[2]

If God can give Nehemiah, Samson, and Stanley strength, He certainly can give you the strength you need. Ask Him.

NOTES

[1] Charles Swindoll, *Hand Me Another Brick* (Nashville, TN: Thomas Nelson, 1978), p. 137.
[2] Adapted from Dan Van Veen, "Surviving the 81st Floor of World Trade Tower Two," Assemblies of God News Service, September 14, 2001. Copyright © 2002 The General Council of the Assemblies of God, 1445 North Boonville Ave., Springfield, MO 65802. Used by permission of Stanley Praimnath.

14

SEND ME:
Isaiah's Response to God's Call
ISAIAH 6:8

What do you usually say when God comes calling? What should you say?

The way you answer can change your life. . .and the lives of many others. Let me explain, using the life of an Israelite named Isaiah.

In 739 BC, Isaiah was a restless young man in a seething nation. The last good king had died, leaving the Israelites hanging in the balance between prosperity and destruction. As a righteous and sensitive young man, Isaiah felt his country's pain and ached to do something about it. As a God seeker, he longed for a more intimate relationship with God. And God obliged both passions. Let's read how it happened.

> *In the year that King Uzziah died, I saw the Lord seated on a throne, high and exalted, and the train of his robe filled the temple. Above him were seraphs, each with six wings: With two wings they covered their faces, with two they covered their feet, and with two they were flying. And they were calling to one another: "Holy, holy, holy is the LORD Almighty; the whole earth is full of his glory." At the sound of their voices the doorposts and thresholds shook and the temple was filled with smoke. "Woe to me!" I cried. "I am ruined! For I am a man of unclean lips, and I live among a people of unclean lips, and my eyes have seen the King, the LORD Almighty." Then one of the seraphs flew to me with a live coal in his hand, which he had taken with tongs from the altar. With it he touched my mouth and said, "See, this has touched your lips; your guilt is taken away and your sin atoned for." Then I heard the voice of the Lord saying, "Whom shall I send? And who will go for us?" And I said, "Here am I. Send me!"*
>
> ISAIAH 6:1–8

Isaiah was one of the few persons still living on earth that was privileged to peer into heaven. Can you imagine seeing the Lord? Isaiah's vision of the throne room put God in perspective. He is vastly unlike all others. God is majestic, seated on a throne. He is supreme, high, and exalted. But above all, He is holy, very holy.

We know God is holy because He is the only being in the universe worshiped by seraphs. The Hebrew word *seraph* means "burning." We may hope that God is a big, soft, teddy bear, but the Bible tells us that God is a consuming fire (Hebrews 12:29). Seraphs are unique angels who fly constantly around the throne of God. These asbestos-like wonders experience spontaneous and eternal combustion without consumption because they are so near to God.

God's holiness is made clear from the antiphonal calls of the seraphs. They perpetually cry out, "Holy, holy, holy is the LORD Almighty; the whole earth is full of His glory." God has many attributes, but those closest to Him recognize that His dominant one is His surpassing holiness. It is so overpoweringly pervasive that all the seraphs can do is repeat over and over to each other, "Holy, holy, holy," in an eternal symphony to Him.

Thirdly, Isaiah's response to God signifies His incredible holiness. When Isaiah saw God up close and personal, he did not sit down and chat, or stand up and cheer, or kick back and relax. He fell down and repented. "Woe is me," he cried. "I am ruined." A literal translation might read, "I am condemned guilty of sin and am melting away in the oven-blast brilliancy of God's holiness."

In His mercy God did not leave Isaiah in the misery of condemnation. Instead, He saw that Isaiah was cleansed. Yet, what is especially striking to me is that God not only cleansed Isaiah, but He called him. Both Isaiah and God were keenly aware of Israel's need for a new prophet. In Isaiah, God had found one. Humble and clean vessels are what God is seeking to pour Himself through. When Isaiah became clean, God called, "Whom shall I send? And who will go for us?"

This call resonated deep within Isaiah. It must have been tied to something God had written on Isaiah's heart before he was born. Maybe Isaiah had been aware of it before, or maybe this was the first moment of recognition. Either way, Isaiah did not hesitate to respond. He could not wait, so he said, "Here am I. Send me!"

Send me.

"Send me." This effective prayer caused God to respond by sending Isaiah to his own people to deliver message after message of necessary and convicting warning. And God also sent Isaiah to us, as he would record his messages in what would become sixty-six chapters in the book bearing his name.

Isaiah is one of the most amazing books ever written. The promises found in it, especially in chapters 40 and later, are some of my favorites. Yet, beyond the promises are the incredible prophecies. There are prophecies about Israel and her neighboring nations that came true during Isaiah's own lifetime, as well as dozens of predictions about the Messiah seven hundred years before Jesus was born. They all came true with outlandish accuracy. Beyond that, his many eschatological prophecies give us great insight into the end times and the coming kingdom of God.

"Send me" is one prayer God delights to answer. I know from experience.

I woke up that day just like every other day. I read a few chapters of my Bible and briefly prayed about the day. The only thing out of the ordinary was that I did something I had only done on a few other occasions. I happened to specifically pray a "send me" prayer. I told God to send me to make a difference in someone's life for His sake. Then I forgot about it and went off to work.

All morning long I had a gnawing thought. I need a haircut. I ought to go to the mall and get it. I am a thrifty (some might even say cheap) person. I had never gone to the salon in the mall for a haircut before. I usually saved money by having some student on campus do it for a few bucks. But over and over I kept getting the thought that I needed to go to the mall for a haircut.

Just before lunch I remembered that I had prayed the "send me" prayer that morning. It hit me like a thunderbolt. "It must be God!" I realized. "But why is He sending me to the mall? What could He want me to do for Him by getting a haircut?"

Yet when the thought immediately returned, I got up, grabbed my coat, and headed for my car. I must confess that I was grumbling as I drove the short distance to the mall. I wonder how much this haircut is going to cost? How will I explain to Cathy my sudden urge for extravagance? Why would God want me to go to the mall? Why couldn't God give me a more glamorous assignment?

I walked into the hair salon and was given the only open chair. A young woman put a sheet around my neck and asked me how I wanted my hair cut. Then we engaged in small talk. As we did, she asked me where I worked. I told her that I was the campus pastor of the Christian university down the road.

"Oh my God!" she gasped. (I became worried at this point because she was holding scissors and I was unarmed.) "I don't believe this!" she said as she started to cry. "This morning as I got ready for work, I told God I would give Him one last chance. If He did not send me a Christian to talk to today, I was going to end it all tonight."

Now I understood why I was sent to the mall to get a haircut. As a result of our conversation, she got her life back on track with God. And I gained a deeper appreciation for the power of "send me" prayers.[1]

When Christian author Henry Blackaby pastored Faith Baptist Church in Saskatoon, Saskatchewan, he began to sense God leading the congregation to an outreach ministry on the college campus. Neither he nor the church had worked with students, and furthermore, for two years the church had tried to start a Bible study in the dorms without success. One Sunday they decided to ask God what His will was for the congregation and to use them. Read how God responded:

On Wednesday one of the girls reported, "Oh, Pastor, a girl who had been in class with me for two years came to me after class today. She said, 'I think you might be a Christian. I need to talk to you.' I remembered what you had said. I had a class, but I missed it. We went to the cafeteria to talk. She said, 'Eleven of us girls in the dorm have been studying the Bible, and none of us are Christians. Do you know someone who can lead us in a Bible study?'" As a result of that contact we started three Bible studies in the women's dorms and two in the men's dorm. Over the following years many of those students trusted Christ as Savior and Lord. Many of those surrendered to full-time ministry and are now serving as pastors and missionaries all over the world.[2]

After telling this story, Blackaby gave a wise word of caution and encouragement.

When the love relationship [with God] is right, He is free to give you assignments at His initiative. Whenever you do not seem to be receiving assignments from God, focus on the love relationship and stay there until the assignment comes.[3]

Bruce Wilkinson tells of God's quick and specific response to his wife's request to be used of God. "A neighbor we hardly knew came knocking on our door. 'Ma'am,' she said through tears. 'My husband is dying, and I have no one to talk to. Can you help me?'"[4]

In speaking about the adventure of asking God to use us, Wilkinson writes, "People will show up at your doorstep or at the table next to you. They will start saying things that surprise even them. They'll ask for something—they are not sure what—and wait for your reply."[5]

Making It Personal

I am always amazed that whenever God answers the "send me" prayer, He has also made sure the person He is sending is uniquely qualified to fulfill the assignment. God has shaped you to serve through your experiences, education, gifts, personality, passions, and relationships. God has people and situations that you are divinely prepared to touch.

I wonder what God has in store for you *today*. I am curious as to what adventure He may want to send you on, if you are willing to go. Ask God to send you today, and be ready for an adventure that will make a difference in people's lives.

NOTES

[1] Adapted from Dave Earley, *Prayer Odyssey* (Shippensburg, PA; Destiny Image, 2004), p. 14.

[2] Henry Blackaby and Claude King, *Experiencing God* (Nashville, TN: Broadman and Holman, 1994), pp. 44–45. Used by permission.

[3] Ibid., pp. 45–46.

[4] Bruce Wilkinson, *The Prayer of Jabez* (Sisters, OR: Multnomah Publishers, 2000), p. 42.

[5] Ibid., p. 36.

15

SAVE US:
The Prayer of the Disciples
MATTHEW 8:25

Sandy and Joe were sailing in the Gulf of Mexico when they were caught in an unexpected storm. The wind blew them far out to open sea. When the storm subsided, they drifted helplessly for two days, baking in the hot sun. Their water supply dwindled away. They knew their lives were in danger.

The couple prayed to God for help, but no help came.

Then Sandy prayed one more time. "Oh, Lord, You are our only hope. Please save us."

As she finished, she looked up and saw in the distance what appeared to be a cross coming toward them. She thought she must be hallucinating and blinked to clear her vision but there was indeed a cross on the horizon. She awakened her husband, Joe. He also could make out a cross moving in their direction.

As the cross drew closer, they could see that it was actually the masthead of a large yacht—and it was definitely coming their way! The couple stood up, waving their arms to attract attention.

When they were safely on deck, Sandy said, "It's incredible that you found us! We thought we'd never be rescued!" But what the yacht owner explained next convinced Joe and Sandy that their rescue was no coincidence. The yacht had been traveling on automatic pilot for several hours, but inexplicably the boat ended up traveling ten miles off its intended course.[1]

"Save us." You can be sailing along through life, making progress and enjoying the trip, when out of nowhere a storm arises. In seconds you are overwhelmed. Huge waves pound and then launch you mercilessly into the air. Water pours relentlessly into your boat faster than you can bail it out. Howling winds whip you around and drive you far off course. You lose your bearings and your hope. The gaping jaws of doom start to shut around you.

No one is immune to the storms of life. Even if you are doing all the right things and headed in the right direction, storms will find you. The question is not *if* you will face them, but *how* you will respond.

One of the most effective prayers in the Bible came from the disciples as they sailed across the Sea of Galilee. At the time, the ministry of Jesus was in high gear. The disciples were sailing away from the crowds to get a rest when a storm arose. Matthew recorded the event:

> *Then he got into the boat and his disciples followed him. Without warning, a furious storm came up on the lake, so that the waves swept over the boat. But Jesus was sleeping. The disciples went and woke him, saying, "Lord, save us! We're going to drown!"*
> MATTHEW 8:23–25

When they realized that the storm was too big for them, they did not even try to deal with it on their own. It was already way beyond their ability to handle. So they went to Jesus

Lord, save us!

When they came to Jesus they were able to say it all in three words: "Lord, save us!" There was no time for flowery speeches. This was not the occasion for sounding impressive by offering profound thoughts or multi-syllable words. This prayer had to be like an arrow, lean and pointed, directed to the heart of the matter.

They did not tell Jesus all the details about the storm. In fact, they did not even mention the storm. He already knew.

They did not tell Jesus how to save them. It was beyond them. They did not need Him to help them with their bailing or with lowering the sails. They needed Him to do something and do it now!

They just asked Him to save them.

> He replied, "You of little faith, why are you so afraid?" Then he got up and rebuked the winds and the waves, and it was completely calm. The men were amazed and asked, "What kind of man is this? Even the winds and the waves obey him!"
>
> MATTHEW 8:26–27

Making It Personal

There are several simple lessons we can take away from this story.

1. *Storms are inevitable.* Storms aren't reserved for the wicked. These disciples were not men who were out on a whiskey-soaked gambling cruise. They were not out in the boat cheating on their wives. They had not just robbed a bank and were fleeing from the authorities. They were not pirates raiding hapless vessels. They were the disciples of Jesus Christ.

You will face storms. They may be storms of discipline or storms of development, but they will come. Even God's greatest people in the Bible faced storms. Adam and Eve had a rebellious son. Noah faced a global flood and later his own failure. Joseph was thrown into a pit, sold as a slave, and then unjustly cast into prison. Moses lost his temper and murdered a man. Later he had the responsibility of leading a horde of immature whiners. David was forced to run for his life when his father-in-law, the king, grew jealous of his success. Nehemiah had a strong enemy. After his conversion, Paul was repeatedly beaten, imprisoned, and persecuted.

2. *Sometimes following Jesus leads us into storms.* The men in the boat were not Jonahs out on the sea, trying vainly to sail away from God's plan for their lives. They were not even out on the water fishing for fun or profit. They were only in the boat because they had followed Jesus there. It was Jesus who got into the boat in the first place.

There is a mistaken notion that following Jesus leads to immediate prosperity and peace. Not necessarily. Certainly, the way of the cross leads to life eternal and the glories of heaven. There is a day coming when there will be no more sickness or sorrow. But in the meantime, we will experience some mean times.

3. *Storms are tests of faith.* Before calming the storm, Jesus made the point that the presence of fear was an indication of the absence of faith. Faith is the prime necessity for pleasing God (Hebrews 11:6). Faith overcomes the world (1 John 4:4). Faith is the fuel of righteous living (Habakkuk 2:4).

Sometimes when storms hit I wonder if God really loves me. My life is being tossed by several storms as I write these words. I am ashamed to confess that I have been overwhelmed by my grief and stupidly said, "God, I thought You loved me."

The thinking is that if God really loved me, He would protect me from storms. But that clearly is not the case. Jesus loved these disciples, yet they found themselves in the midst of a deadly storm. God the Father loves God the Son, yet Jesus, the Son of God, was in a boat that was about to be swallowed by angry waves.

4. *Jesus goes with us through the storms.* Jesus was right there in the boat. On another occasion when the disciples encountered a storm at sea, Jesus came to them walking on the water. If Jesus did not go with us through the storms, then we would have good reason to be afraid. But He goes.

5. *Jesus can handle the storms.* No storm is too big, no wind too fierce, no wave too high. Jesus can handle all of it. Jesus was so unafraid of this storm that He was sleeping through it. Yet, He had the power to calm the waves with just a word.

I don't know what storms you are facing. Maybe the loss of your job, a serious illness, or the death of a loved one is sending you reeling. One of your children is in trouble or was in an accident or is in jail. You could be in the throes of a divorce. Just as Jesus was there for the disciples, and for countless others, He will be there for you. The solution may not be quick or painless, but Jesus can work it all for good. You know He can. Trust Him.

6. *We need to ask.* The disciples did not wait until the boat was capsized and they were hopelessly adrift in the dangers of the deep. They went to Jesus and asked Him to save them before waiting too long. Asking in prayer was often advocated by Jesus. Here are some of my favorite requests:

Matthew 7:7: "Ask and it will be given to you."

Matthew 7:11: "How much more will your Father in heaven give good gifts to those who ask him!"

John 14:14: "You may *ask* me for anything in my name."

John 15:7: "If you remain in me and my words remain in you, *ask* whatever you wish, and it will be given you."

John 15:16: "Then the Father will give you whatever you *ask* in my name."

John 16:24: "Until now you have not asked for anything in my name. Ask and you will receive, and your joy will be complete."

James 1:5: "If any of you lacks wisdom, he should ask God, who gives generously to all without finding fault, and it will be given to him."

James 4:2: "You do not have, because you do not ask God."

If you find yourself in a storm right now, don't be afraid to ask God to save you.

NOTE

[1]Bob Russell and Rusty Russell, *When God Answers Prayer* (West Monroe, LA: Howard Publishing Company, 2003), pp. 98–100.

16
Have Mercy on Us:
The Prayer of the Blind Men
Matthew 9:27

It is such a short tale that most people overlook it. In fact, the whole scene is played out in a mere five verses and less than one hundred words. Yet for two men it was the biggest, grandest, greatest, most beautiful event in their lifetimes. We don't even know their names, but we do know that these men prayed one of the most effective prayers in the Bible. Here's their story:

> As Jesus went on from there, two blind men followed him, calling out, "Have mercy on us, Son of David!" When he had gone indoors, the blind men came to him, and he asked them, "Do you believe that I am able to do this?" "Yes, Lord," they replied.
> Then he touched their eyes and said, "According to your faith will it be done to you"; and their sight was restored. Jesus warned them sternly, "See that no one knows about this." But they went out and spread the news about him all over that region.
>
> Matthew 9:27–31

They had most likely been born blind. Most probably they had never experienced the inexpressible joy of seeing a sunset or watching the leaves on a tree blow in the wind. Instead of witnessing a rainbow arching across humid sky, they had only seen blackness. Twenty-four hours a day, seven days a week, 365 days a year, nothing but darkness. They had no hope of ever being freed from their prison of endless night.

Beyond the physical frustration of being blind, they had to face monumental social pressure. In their world, blind men were not considered to be whole. They did not marry and had difficulty getting a job. They were excluded from the synagogue as "unclean," based on the faulty belief that their sin was the cause of their handicap. They were doomed to a life with only the tiniest of joys and slimmest of blessings.

Yet, they had heard about Jesus. The local buzz was that this itinerant, unlicensed rabbi could heal the sick. He had been healing all around the area. Maybe, just maybe, He could heal them.

So out of their desperation they hunted this healer. Stumbling along in pained pursuit, they followed Him. To follow Jesus was to track the miraculous. Lame children walked. Demon-possessed folks were freed. A dead girl was even raised to life. Surely He could heal them. They had no other hope and no other plan.

Finally, one day they heard that He was just down the street within earshot. Raw excitement, anticipation, fear, desperation, pain, and joy overcame them. Shouting into the dark, they began yelling, "Have mercy on us, Son of David!" Again and again they cried out. A lifetime of blindness, years of living life as social outcasts, and dozens of dashed dreams prodded them on. "Have mercy on us, Son of David!"

Have mercy.

Jesus heard them and paused. Eagerly, cautiously, yet irresistibly, they came to Him. Calmly He asked, "Do you believe that I am able to do this?"

We don't know if they paused and added up their faith or if they just blurted out their answer. All we know is that they said, "Yes, Lord."

All the time they had been on His trail, they had thought up long speeches as to why He must heal them. Yet, in the crisis of decision all they had been able to say was "Have mercy on us" and "Yes, Lord."

But those words were enough. "Then he touched their eyes and said, 'According to your faith will it be done to you'; and their sight was restored."

A little prayer yielded a great big answer. The Bible record is so subtle and matter of fact. All it says is that their sight was restored. These wonderful words are not in all capital letters. They are not in rainbow colors. There is not even an exclamation point.

But you had better believe that as far as these two men were concerned, fireworks were going off. Cannons were booming. Meteors were shooting through the sky. Bands were playing. Dancers were dancing. Banners were flying. And they couldn't take it all in. I can hear them now, "Oh my, look at that! I can't believe it is so beautiful! Look over here. Did you see this?"

Then Jesus did something that tells me He has a wonderful sense of humor. The Bible says, "Jesus warned them sternly, 'See that no one knows about this.' "

Right! He had to be kidding. These men had been blind. They were without sight. They had spent a near eternity visually impaired. And with a simple touch He had totally, radically, wonderfully changed their worlds. Jesus must have had a smile on His face when He said it because it would be a greater miracle for them to keep quiet than it was for Him to heal them.

And they couldn't. Their story ends with these words: "But they went out and spread the news about him all over that region."

"Have mercy." Just two little words, yet they are so wonderfully powerful. And they still work today. Roy Mansfield is the dynamic young pastor of the Manhattan Bible Church in New York City. On Sunday, January 25, 2003, he had six strokes in one day and, for all practical purposes, should have died. Below are a few of the e-mails he sent his congregation and prayer partners.

February 2, 2003
My dear friends,

As many of you are aware, one week ago last Sunday I had 6 strokes, and the next day I almost died in the ICU of Columbia Presbyterian Hospital. By Monday I am told there were probably 10,000–20,000 of God's people interceding for me. I am a living, breathing, talking, typing, and even sometimes walking miracle. Even the doctors and nurses acknowledged God's healing in my life, as they watched person after person come into my room and pray for me. If you had not heard of my condition I am sorry to shock you, but I'm sure that many of you had heard of my condition and had prayed for me. I thought I would share with you every day or two a bit of how God had answered your prayers on my behalf.

I have been on the supernatural, super-accelerated Jesus recovery plan. If you continue to pray for me and I continue on this recovery plan, I am hoping to attend church on Sunday and greet our people in the English and Spanish ministry. By God's grace, I hope to preach a week from Sunday (March 2nd). Thank you for your continued prayers.

February 9, 2003
Dear friends,

    Thank you for you continued prayers. Two weeks ago I was having 6 strokes in St. Joseph's emergency room. Today I went to church and lifted my hands in praise (which I should not be able to do) and greeted our Spanish and English congregations. Please keep praying for me.

Roy

February 10, 2003
My dear friends,

    [Mansfield begins by describing what happened the day after his six strokes. Then he tells the following story.] I had lots of visitors, and I seemed to be steadily improving. A very close friend told me that morning that God had led her to pray that He would "pour on the water" before the fire fell to bring Him glory. She was referring to Elijah's encounter with the prophets of Baal. Elijah poured water on the sacrifice before God sent His fire to consume it. Through this God's glory was magnified even more. I didn't really understand the implications of what God had led her to pray at the time. In essence she was praying that God would make things worse before He made them better, so that His glory would be magnified even more.

    It became obvious that God had led her to pray in this way because about 1:00 a.m. I began to feel my entire right side go numb. Immediately a whole team of doctors rushed into the room and began working furiously on me. They began trying to run I.V.s and lines into every imaginable (and even unimaginable) part of my body. Again I was paralyzed but could see and hear and (unfortunately) feel everything that happened. They tipped my bed for my head to hang down so everything would rush to my head. I remember thinking, "Hey, this is just like on TV." Everyone was rushing frantically around me except for one doctor. I remember the doctor in charge standing motionless in all the frenzied activity, staring at me for several seconds. He soon disappeared, and I later found he went to talk to Natalie. He told her that they were doing everything they could, but the stroke kept progressing. He told her that it was possible for them to attempt a very high-risk procedure that had not been tried before on any patient in I.E. He said if they tried the procedure there was a great risk that I could die. If they did not, it was probable that I would spend the rest of my life unable to move any part of my body but my eyes.

    Let me say that Natalie is not by nature a decision maker. When she has to decide on skim milk or 2% she relies heavily on the multitude of counsel. She was surrounded by church members, but nobody was saying anything. That's understandable. Who wants to make the decision that kills the pastor? Can you imagine, "And this is elder so-and-so, who killed our last pastor." Finally, one of our elders, Charles Delph, asked the doctor what he would do if it were one of his loved ones. He said that he would opt for the procedure. By that time there were probably 10,000–15,000 people praying for me. I understand God had led Victoria, from our church, to pray specifically that the doctors would be willing to try something new. I believe God took all those prayers and converged them in that room at that one climactic moment, and Natalie told the doctor to begin the procedure that God would use to save my life.

By this time I had stopped breathing and they had put a tube down into my lungs and put me on a respirator. I think I had the world's record for most stuff stuck in my body. . . .

After two hours the doctors were able to stabilize me. The lead doctor came back a couple of hours later and began to run the neurological tests on me. After each test he said one word, "Unbelievable."

I'll continue the story of God's grace in a day or two. If there is someone you know prayed for me, please thank them and feel free to forward this to them so they are able to rejoice with us in God's gracious answer to their prayers.

Thank you for your continued prayers,

Roy[1]

God had healing mercy on Roy Mansfield. Today he has resumed his high-energy, high-intensity ministry. He is a walking miracle and living testimony of the power of God.

Making It Personal

When it comes to physical affliction and healing, there are several truths we know:

- God is able to heal any and all afflictions, including the ultimate affliction, death.
- Sometimes He uses modern medicine. Other times He circumvents medicine and heals without it.
- There are times when we ask and God says "No" to our healing because He has a higher purpose to accomplish. Instead of giving us healing mercy, He provides us with enduring grace.
- There are also occasions when His answer is "Wait."
- One day all of God's children will experience complete and permanent healing in heaven.
- It doesn't hurt to ask for mercy. The blind men chased Jesus down and asked for healing mercy. Roy Mansfield had thousands praying for him.

I don't know the nature or extent of your physical affliction. But I do know that God can't answer your prayer if you don't pray. Go ahead and ask. Pray, "Have mercy on me." Give God a chance to answer. And when He does, give Him the glory.

NOTE

[1]Used by permission of Roy Mansfield, pastor of Manhattan Bible Church, New York, New York.

17

LORD, TEACH US TO PRAY:
The Prayer of the Disciples
LUKE 11:1

"I'm just too busy."

"Even though I'm trying to go faster, I keep getting further behind."

"I am going as hard as I can, but I am not sure where it's getting me."

"I want to care about all the needs around me, but I just don't have enough strength."

Ever feel like any of the above? Wish you knew what to do?

At another time and in another place, twelve tired men wrestled with many of those gnawing frustrations. They were trying desperately to keep up with Jesus as He rolled through the daily onslaught of highly needy people and deeply challenging situations. Overwhelming dilemmas and staggering burdens flew at Jesus at a dizzying pace. Yet, He seamlessly flowed through each encounter with astounding grace, poise, and power. What was His secret? Where did He get His stunning inner strength and wonderfully winsome wisdom?

After careful observation the answer became clear. This Man had an exceptional prayer life. S. D. Gordon has summarized the central role prayer held in the life of Jesus:

> *How much prayer meant to Jesus! It was not only His regular habit, but His resort in every emergency, however slight or serious. When perplexed He prayed. When hard pressed by work He prayed. When hungry for fellowship He found it in prayer. He chose His associates and received His messages upon His knees. If tempted, He prayed. If criticized, He prayed. If fatigued in body or wearied in spirit, He had recourse to His one unfailing habit of prayer. Prayer brought Him unmeasured power at the beginning, and kept the flow unbroken and undiminished. There was no emergency, no difficulty, no necessity, no temptation that would not yield to prayer, as He practiced it. . . . He prayed so much and so often that it became to Him like breathing—involuntary.*[1]

The disciples, noting the authority by which Jesus spoke, the compassion He showed the hurting, and His miraculous power, observed that all of it flowed from His prayer life. So when they had an opportunity to ask Him anything they wanted, they made this request: "Lord, teach us to pray." Luke's Gospel records the incident.

> *One day Jesus was praying in a certain place. When he finished, one of his disciples said to him, "Lord, teach us to pray, just as John taught his disciples."*

LUKE 11:1

Somewhat innocently and inadvertently, the disciples stumbled onto one of the most effective prayers written in the Bible, "Lord, teach us to pray." This prayer could be considered the foundation from which all other requests are formed.

The disciples' request is supremely significant for several reasons. First, it was answered. Second, the answer changed their lives. Third, we can pray the same request today.

Jesus did not deny, ignore, or delay to answer their request. His affirmative response was immediate. That is because "Teach us to pray" is a prayer God loves to answer for several reasons. First, God delights in our prayers. Too often we wrongly assume that God tolerates our prayers when, in reality, He revels in them. In fact, they are so precious to Him that He collects them as beautiful bowls of incense perfuming His throne (Revelation 5:8). Because our prayers end up in heaven, they are some of a tiny handful of things that are eternal in nature. (The others are God, the Word of God, and the souls of people.)

God also wants to teach us to pray because prayer is conversing with God, and He loves to spend time with us. As people get older they can gain great insight and wisdom. I remember being with my mentor, Elmer Towns, on his sixtieth birthday. I asked him what was important to him at that age. Without a moment's hesitation he said, "Relationships—I have learned that relationships are the most important part of life." God already knows this and greatly prizes our prayers as they build our relationship with Him and Him with us.

Moreover, God is willing to teach us to pray because He has an immense Father's heart that loves us and wants to meet our needs. Prayer touches His heart and, therefore, is the key to everything else. Everything we need is at the disposal of prayer. Pastor David Jeremiah has written, "I scoured the New Testament some time ago, looking for things God does in ministry that are not prompted by prayer. Do you know what I found? Nothing. I don't mean I had trouble finding an item or two: I mean I found *nothing*. Everything God does in the work of ministry, He does through prayer. Consider:

Prayer is the way you defeat the devil (Luke 22:23; James 4:7).
Prayer is the way you get the lost saved (Luke 18:13).
Prayer is the way you acquire wisdom (James 1:5).
Prayer is the way a backslider gets restored (James 5:16–20).
Prayer is how saints get strengthened (Jude 20; Matthew 26:41).
Prayer is the way to get laborers out to the mission field (Matthew 9:38).
Prayer is how we cure the sick (James 5:13–15).
Prayer is how we accomplish the impossible (Mark 11:23–24).

. . .everything God wants to do in your life He has subjugated to one thing: Prayer."[2]

When the disciples prayed, "Lord, teach us to pray," Jesus answered by giving them what has become the most popular pattern for prayer ever uttered. Often called the Lord's Prayer, this sample prayer provides amazing and timeless insights into the hows and whys of prayer.

> He said to them, "When you pray, say: 'Father, hallowed be your name, your kingdom come. Give us each day our daily bread. Forgive us our sins, for we also forgive everyone who sins against us. And lead us not into temptation.' "

> LUKE 11:2–4

This is a wonderful, simple, eloquent, robust, rich little treasure of a prayer. Most scholars agree that this is not merely a prayer to be prayed verbatim by rote. This prayer serves as a road map for prayer, providing an outline of the key elements of prayer. This model prayer has six primary points:

Adoration: "Father, hallowed be Your name."
Submission: "Your kingdom come."
Petition: "Give us each day our daily bread."
Confession: "Forgive us our sins."
Forgiveness: "Forgive everyone who sins against us."
Protection: "Lead us not into temptation."

Several years ago I made it my habit to take a prayer walk every morning using this prayer as my outline. The moment I walk out the door and down the driveway, I begin, "Our Father in heaven, hallowed be Your name." At that point I launch into a season of adoration, such as "I praise and worship You today because there is none like You, You are creative and make all things beautiful in Your time, You are mighty beyond compare," and so on. Many great prayer warriors have used this prayer as their guide.

Note carefully the exact words of the disciples' request. They said, "Teach us *to* pray." They did not ask, "Teach us *how* to pray." They recognized that the key *to* praying is found *in* praying.

The deepest secrets and greatest experiences of prayer cannot be revealed in books or lectures. Indeed, the most personal and powerful experiences are when we are on our knees, in our prayer closets, at the throne of God. Chester Toleson and Harold Koenig have written, "We don't really need to know a lot about prayer or prayer techniques. What we need to do is practice it. The more we pray the more we understand it and prosper from it."[3] Bible scholar Andrew Murray said, "Reading a book about prayer, listening to lectures, and talking about it is very good, but won't teach you to pray. You get nothing without exercise, without practice."[4]

Also note that the disciples did not say, "Teach us to preach, pastor, sing, serve, do miracles, or testify." They said, "Lord, teach us to *pray*." They recognized the great importance of prayer. As Oswald Chambers has reminded us, "Prayer does not fit us for the greater works; prayer is the greater work."[5]

And did the disciples pray! When Jesus ascended into heaven, they immediately convened a ten-day prayer meeting (Acts 1:14, 24). When the church was born, they transcribed prayer into its DNA (Acts 2:42). In the face of persecution they fell to their knees in prayer (Acts 4:24–31). As administrative responsibilities increased, they refused to be sucked into the tyranny of the urgent and instead reprioritized prayer as the most important task (Acts 6:4). Difficult decisions were made as the result of prayer (Acts 1:24, 6:6). When deadly opposition grew intense, prayer became more intense (Acts 12:5). If nothing else, and driving all else, the disciples were men of prayer.

Making It Personal

"Lord, teach us to pray" is the foundation on which our prayer lives can be built. It acknowledges that God is the teacher and prayer is the course. Once we start praying, we can begin to experience the riches of prayer as well. And make no mistake, there are untold treasures awaiting you in the place of prayer. Success, blessing, direction, fulfilled dreams, forgiveness, wisdom, and miracles are available. The treasures of strength, deliverance, expanded ministry influence, help in raising children, mercy, healing, faith, and freedom from the prison of resentment have been discussed through the pages of this book and are experienced in the place of prayer.

Here are some additional "prayer helps."

1. *A time to pray.* Try to determine a set time each day when you will read a chapter of this book and pray. It could be first thing in the morning or the last thing at night or even over your lunch hour.

2. *An amount of time for prayer.* There are 24 hours in a day or 1440 minutes. Setting aside 15, or 20, or 30 minutes a day for study and prayer can become a life-changing experience.

3. *A place for prayer.* Jesus spoke of a prayer closet. Your place could be at a desk or the kitchen table or on your bed, or you could take a "prayer walk."

4. *A friend to pray with.* Jesus promised added insight and answers when two or more agree in prayer (Matthew 18:19). Ask a friend to read this book along with you. Gather together face-to-face, over the phone, or by e-mail, and pray together through the prayers you are learning.

One last piece of advice. . .don't wait any longer. Determine that you won't put off prayer one more day. In fact, why don't you begin by praying the disciples' prayer, "Lord, teach me to pray"? Spend some time in prayer asking God to help you do your part so you can grow as much as possible as a person of prayer.

Notes

[1] S. D. Gordon, *Quiet Talks on Prayer* (Grand Rapids, MI: Baker Book House, 1980), pp. 209, 233.

[2] David Jeremiah, *Prayer: The Great Adventure* (Sisters, OR: Multnomah Publishers, 1997), pp. 40–41.

[3] Chester Toleson and Harold Koenig, *The Healing Power of Prayer* (Grand Rapids, MI: Baker Book House, 2003), p. 66.

[4] Donald S. Whitney, quoting Andrew Murray, *Spiritual Disciplines for the Christian Life* (Colorado Springs, CO: NavPress, 1991), p. 66.

[5] Oswald Chambers, *Prayer—A Holy Occupation* (Grand Rapids, MI: Discovery House, 1992), p. 7.

18

LORD, HELP ME:
The Prayer of a Desperate Mother
MATTHEW 15:25

No one on earth has the power to break your heart like your own child. Seeing them hurt and watching them struggle is a gut-wrenching, soul-shaking experience. You feel their pain. They have the power in a split second to bring tears to your eyes. When they make you proud, joy explodes in your heart that cannot be contained. When they disappoint you, it is like a knife jabbed deep into your heart. When they are treated unjustly, righteous indignation overwhelms your common sense. And when they hurt, you would do anything you could to take their place.

As I write this, I have three boys in high school. From the hospital, to the awards banquet, to the church platform, to the police station, to the prom, and yes, to the emergency room, Cathy and I have ridden the emotional roller coaster of parenting. I have cried, laughed, prayed, worried, lost sleep, and made more sacrifices as a parent than in any other role in life.

Among the many prayers I pray as a dad have been "Give me wisdom," "Give me success," and "Strengthen my hands." I have asked God to protect my children, bless them, grow them, and use them. But as parents sometimes the need is greater than our resources.

In Matthew 15, we find the very special prayer that is the cry of a desperate parent. As Jesus was resting from His heavy schedule in a non-Jewish region east of the Mediterranean Sea, He encountered a desperate mom.

> *A Canaanite woman from that vicinity came to him, crying out, "Lord, Son of David, have mercy on me! My daughter is suffering terribly from demon-possession."*
>
> MATTHEW 15:22

There is much we don't fully understand about demon possession. We do know that it has ugly, physical results and emotional expressions. We recognize that those possessed by the evil one are in extreme pain. We see that while human medicines may relieve symptoms, they are ineffective to produce lasting cures. We can appreciate the challenge that modern psychology faces in adequately understanding, explaining, or dealing with such a curse.

Most of all, we can confidently affirm that it was overwhelming to this mother to see her daughter experience such anguish of the soul. But when this mother cried out to Jesus for mercy, He did not answer.

> *Jesus did not answer a word.*
>
> MATTHEW 15:23

As a follower of Jesus, I find it most difficult to deal with the unexplained silences of God. You have been there. You have a legitimate need. You have come to the right source for help. You ask for mercy but all you get in response is the thundering silence of God. Most people would quit at this point.

This woman, a Canaanite, was used to the unresponsiveness of her gods. This was not new to her. She could have easily marked Jesus down as just as uncaring or impotent.

But she didn't.

So his disciples came to him and urged him, "Send her away, for she keeps crying out after us."

MATTHEW 15:23

Still, she badgered them for help. She kept coming for relief. Her pain was greater than her pride. After she persisted, Jesus answered.

He answered, "I was sent only to the lost sheep of Israel."

MATTHEW 15:24

Thanks a lot! He didn't even speak directly to her. He made this comment to His disciples. It was not what she wanted to hear.

She knew that she had no right to ask a Jewish man to help her. She knew that she had no basis for expecting Him to respond. But she had heard that He was mighty and compassionate. And she was desperate. So she pressed the issue ahead.

The woman came and knelt before him. "Lord, help me!" she said.

MATTHEW 15:25

Lord, help me.

What a simple prayer! "Lord help me." What a powerful prayer!

With all of her faith, all of her emotions, and all of her love for her daughter, she prayed. The weight of her need, every ounce of her hurt, and the totality of her helplessness were embodied in those three little words, "Lord, help me."

What do you say when you have nothing else to say? What words can better express the burden of the brokenhearted parent? "Lord, help me."

What is your pressure point of pain today? What about your child's situation is overwhelming you? What burden is completely beyond your control? Where do you need help?

"Lord, help me." Say the words slowly. See the suffering soul of your beloved child. See your own empty hands. See the all-sufficient Savior. Bow before Him and speak your heart.

Jesus was moved to act on her behalf.

He replied, "It is not right to take the children's bread and toss it to their dogs."
"Yes, Lord," she said, "but even the dogs eat the crumbs that fall from their masters' table." Then Jesus answered, "Woman, you have great faith! Your request is granted." And her daughter was healed from that very hour.

MATTHEW 15:26–28

Read verse 28 again. First, Jesus commends her faith. Then He promises that her request is granted. Her little prayer had produced a big answer and her daughter was healed.

Making It Personal

What can we learn from this desperate mom?

Prayer needs all the faith we have.

Jesus said, "Woman, you have great faith!" A look back through this passage gives us some insights into the type of faith she displayed. As a Canaanite, non-Jew, and not yet a devoted follower of Jesus, she had great faith. Her faith was great for the little amount of truth and light she had been given. She had not had the privilege of growing up hearing about the powerful love of the God of the Bible. This was a new venture for her. She had to turn from pagan deities in order to trust in Jesus to help her. She was way out of her comfort zone. Coming to Jesus, persistently asking and not giving up until she was helped, took all of the faith she had.

1. *Prayer needs faith that refuses to quit.* We don't fully understand the ways of God. We do know that sometimes God holds off answers in order to allow our faith to blossom fully. This desperate mother did not give up, even when she initially got no answer. She did not quit asking until the disciples again asked Jesus to do something. She continued asking even after He said "No." Her love for her daughter and her confidence in Jesus' ability to heal would not let her give up.

2. *Prayer needs faith that is humbly dependent.* Her faith was great because it was not based on her sense of worth but on her conviction that Jesus must eventually respond to those in need. If a master would give crumbs to dogs, then Jesus must surely answer the prayer of a Canaanite.

3. *Prayer works.*

> Then Jesus answered, "Woman, you have great faith! Your request is granted." And her daughter was healed from that very hour.
>
> MATTHEW 15:28

Her prayer worked. God heard her heart, saw persistent faith, honored her humble dependence, and touched her daughter. I can only imagine the joy that exploded in her heart. I bet she danced all the way home. She probably had a huge smile on her face for years to come.

It is a wonderful thing when God answers the prayers of desperate parents. And all parents get desperate at one time or another. Among many painful concerns, we wonder if they are well physically, who they are involved with, what college they will choose, or will choose them, and what career they will pursue.

Desperation takes over when children begin to take the path of prodigal living. One of my good friends and a fantastic worship leader, Andy Bullard, is the son of a dear pastor and his wife. In college, Andy went through a period of prodigal living. This is his story of how his father's love and prayer helped him realize that living for God is the only way.

> I grew up in a pastor's home. My parents loved God with all their hearts and were great parents! During the last two years of high school and the first two years of college, I slowly fell into a bad lifestyle of ignoring the Holy Spirit's conviction in my heart. I chose to get heavily involved with alcohol and partying.
>
> One lonely night when I was twenty years old, I had been drinking and hanging out at a party. Someone came in and told me my dad was outside. It was about 2 a.m. I immediately felt this huge lump in my throat, and I walked outside. Ashamed, I approached my father, who calmly looked at me and said, "Son, the Holy Spirit woke me up a little while ago and I felt Him telling me to go take a drive. He told me, 'Your son is in trouble and needs you.' That's how I found you here. Andy, I believe God has a plan and design for your life and wants to use you for His glory,

but if you keep on living like this, you're going to miss out on all of it. I love you—I'll see you at home."

That same weekend I was on my face before God, weeping and repenting for the way I had been living. I felt so dirty inside and decided, from that moment on, I would acknowledge God's greatness. I would fear Him and let Him change my life. By God's glory, I have not lived that kind of lifestyle since then. I know that God used my father and my mother and their prayers, love, and loving rebuke to draw me back to the Lord! I am so thankful for honest, praying, and loving parents![1]

I recently spoke at a missionary training conference and had a wonderful time of fellowship with these pioneer servants of God. A mom who had heard me speak in previous years stopped me after my second day of teaching. The year before, she had told me of the difficult transition her children were having upon returning to the States from the mission field.

Then she said, "The first time we heard you speak, we were convicted to fast and pray for our children one day a week. But we did not do it. They had a very frustrating year that year. The next year we made a commitment to fast and pray for them one day a week. My husband and I would pray together over lunch. It was not easy," she said, pausing, with tears welling up in her eyes, "but it sure made a difference."

God loves our kids because He is their Father. He wants to give us all the help He can in raising them.

As I write this, my three teenage sons are all in high school at the same time. None of them is a shrinking violet or wallflower. They all seem to be gifted at getting themselves in a variety of complex situations. Like all pastors' kids and second or third generation Christians, they struggle to find their own faith relationship with God. As very human young men, they are not immune to temptation, trials, or troubles. Parenting three teenagers, while often a great deal of fun, is also very challenging. Parenting "just ain't easy." Almost daily I pray the prayer of the desperate woman, "Lord help me."

If you are a parent, this chapter has probably resonated with you on several levels. Learn to pray the prayer of the desperate mother for her daughter, "Lord, help me." If you do not yet have children, begin now to pray for the children that you may have in your future. Ask God to help you. Or pray for your nieces and nephews. Ask God to help them and their parents.

If you are past the point of having children, that's all right. Pray for Cathy, me, and our three boys. We need all the prayer we can get.

NOTE

[1] Used by permission of Andy Bullard.

19

INCREASE OUR FAITH:
The Prayer of the Disciples
LUKE 17:5

I appreciate the disciples. Their bald humanness shines out again and again. They repeatedly ended up with egg on their face or a foot in their mouth. Fear, doubt, ignorance, confusion, arrogance, and thick-headedness—they unwittingly displayed all of these and more. Reading about them in the Gospels never ceases to give me hope. If these guys could make it as disciples, then I have a chance.

One day Jesus was telling them about the need to repeatedly forgive repentant sinners. The disciples came back with a sincere yet comical response. Read it for yourself.

> [Jesus said,] "So watch yourselves. If your brother sins, rebuke him, and if he repents, forgive him. If he sins against you seven times in a day, and seven times comes back to you and says, 'I repent,' forgive him." The apostles said to the Lord, "Increase our faith!"
>
> LUKE 17:3–5

Don't you just love it? Jesus told them to offer forgiveness seven times a day if necessary. The very thought of such "radical forgiveness" seemed so beyond them that all they could say was "Increase our faith."

Somewhat innocently and inadvertently, the disciples again stumbled onto one of the most effective prayers written in the Bible, "Increase our faith." They could not have prayed a better prayer.

The Bible persistently points to the priceless personality of faith. Faith is portrayed as the requirement for pleasing God (Hebrews 11:6). It is to be central in our lives (Romans 1:17; Galatians 3:11; Hebrews 10:38). It is the means of salvation unto eternal life (John 3:16; Acts 16:31). Faith is the activity that leads to a right standing before God (Galatians 2:16) and pure hearts with God (Acts 15:9). Faith helps us walk in the light (John 12:36, 46) and experience spiritual life (John 20:31). It is the victory that overcomes the world (1 John 5:4).

Jesus continually exemplified and addressed the ability of faith in God to accomplish amazing things. The disciples heard Him commend the centurion for his great faith and then heal his servant without even seeing him in person (Matthew 8:5–13). They saw Jesus heal a paralyzed man because of the faith of his friends (Matthew 9:2). They witnessed Him heal a woman who had the faith to reach out and touch the hem of His garment (Matthew 9:23), blind men who had the faith to ask Him for mercy (Matthew 9:29), and a demon-possessed girl because of the persistent faith of her mother (Matthew 15:28).

They heard Jesus say that faith has the power to move mountains and uproot mulberry trees (Luke 17:6; Matthew 17:18–21; Mark 11:22–24). He also said that all things are possible to the person with faith (Mark 9:23). Later, He told them that faith was a key to answered prayer (Mark 11:24). He demonstrated the potential of faith to heal disease, cast out demons, and release the miraculous (Matthew 8:2–3, 8, 13; 9:20–22; Mark 9:21–26).

The one thing Jesus repeatedly rebuked His disciples for and warned them about was being of little faith (Matthew 6:30; 8:26; 14:31; 16:8; 17:20; Luke 12:28). The disciples cowered in the boat as the storm raged because they lacked faith (Matthew 8:23–27). After successfully walking on the water, Peter sank when he lost his faith (Matthew 14:22–33). The disciples were incapable of grasping spiritual truth when they lacked faith (Matthew 16:5–12). Likewise, they failed to cast out a demon (Matthew 17:14–21).

It would seem that the major lesson Jesus wanted them to learn from His ministry was to trust God. And they finally got it. After repeated bouts of fear and failure, they realized what they needed was faith, and lots of it. So when Jesus again challenged their level of spirituality by calling them to radical forgiveness, the light bulb went on. The "aha" moment arrived at last and they offered a short, sweet, powerful prayer.

Increase our faith.

An initial reading of the rest of the chapter might lead you to believe that Jesus ignored their request. Not so. The answer to their prayer is not found in the rest of the chapter or even Luke's Gospel. To see how Jesus answered, you need to look at the book of Acts, Luke's follow-up to his Gospel. It is a book that could well be titled "The Acts of the Holy Spirit through the Apostles."

The great faith of the disciples is on display in every page of the first half of the book of Acts. While the word *faith* is not always used, the concept is demonstrated through every event described.

In chapter one the disciples' faith had grown enough to pray down the outpouring of the Holy Spirit on the day of Pentecost, ushering in the birth of the church. In chapter two Peter's fearless faith was front and center as the previous coward stood before thousands and boldly proclaimed the Resurrection of Jesus. His courageous faith led to the conversion of three thousand!

In chapter three the strong faith of Peter and John led to the miraculous healing of a lame man. Peter explained it this way:

> *By faith in the name of Jesus, this man whom you see and know was made strong. It is Jesus' name and the faith that comes through him that has given this complete healing to him, as you can all see.*

> ACTS 3:16

Later, faith spurred Peter to preach to another huge crowd about the crucifixion and resurrection of Jesus.

Chapter four shows Peter and John being arrested for their brave preaching. By faith they fearlessly proclaimed the resurrected Christ in the face of stern opposition and refused to be silenced. After their release, the other disciples joined them in a faith-saturated prayer for greater boldness in the face of greater persecution, not deliverance from it.

Chapter five is the dramatic account of Ananias and Sapphira being exposed by Peter for lying to the Holy Spirit and the consequences of such an act. It also shows the powerful faith of the apostles as they did many signs and wonders and were even thrown in jail for their Christian witness. Subsequently, they were released by an angel and walked away, only to be brought before the authorities again. Their daring faith led to a beating but also shook the Jewish leaders to the point of letting them go.

Chapter six opens with wisdom-producing faith as the disciples develop a plan and select personnel to meet a logistical nightmare. They selected their ministry assistants on the basis of their faith (Acts 6:5). Chapters six and seven tell how one of their disciples, Stephen, a man "full of faith and power" (Acts 6:7), had been deeply challenged by the contagious faith of the apostles to preach Jesus so boldly that he was killed, becoming the first Christian martyr.

As the flames of fierce persecution swelled, the faith of the disciples became evident in the lives of *their* disciples. Chapter eight tells how they began to spread the gospel out from Jerusalem to Samaria and beyond. Both an influential sorcerer and an Ethiopian eunuch came to saving faith through their testimony.

In chapter ten the gospel jumped across racial and ethnic divides to reach the Gentiles. The instrument was Peter, the man whose faith had failed the night Jesus was arrested.

In chapter twelve the faith of the early church is severely tested. James, the brother of John, was arrested and executed. Herod, sensing a public relations bonanza, arrested Peter and put him under the guard of sixteen men who watched him four at a time, in four-hour shifts. During that time he was chained between two of the soldiers while the others guarded the door.

The church turned this problem into prayer and faced the battle on their knees. God heard and sent an angel, who suddenly appeared by Peter's side. Immediately the chains fell from his wrists. Unnoticed, Peter walked past the guards and the guard posts to freedom. Peter went looking for his friends and ended up being the surprise guest at his own prayer meeting!

The disciples prayed, "Increase our faith," and God did. These men, who had been guilty of being of little faith, ended up as men of outstanding faith. They had enough faith to launch the church less than two months after seeing Jesus brutally executed in Jerusalem. They had enough faith to continue preaching in the face of withering persecution. All would face torture and horrible deaths.

Church history is rich in describing the martyrdom of the church's founders. Church historian Gottlieb Schumacher researched the lives of the apostles. He discovered that Matthew suffered martyrdom in Ethiopia, killed by a sword wound. John faced martyrdom when he was boiled in a huge basin of boiling oil during a wave of persecution in Rome. Miraculously delivered from death, he was then sentenced to the mines on the prison island of Patmos.

Peter was crucified upside down on an X-shaped cross because he told his tormentors that he felt unworthy to die in the same way that Jesus Christ had. James the Just, the leader of the church in Jerusalem, was thrown a hundred feet down from the southeast pinnacle of the temple when he refused to deny his faith in Christ. When they discovered that he survived the fall, his enemies beat him to death with a fuller's club.

Bartholomew, also known as Nathaniel, was a missionary to Asia. He witnessed to our Lord in present-day Turkey. Bartholomew was martyred for his preaching in Armenia when he was flayed to death by a whip.

Andrew was crucified on an X-shaped cross in Patras, Greece. After being whipped severely by seven soldiers, they tied his body to the cross with cords to prolong his agony. His followers reported that when he was led toward the cross, Andrew saluted it in these words: "I have long desired and expected this happy hour. The cross has been consecrated by the body of Christ hanging on it." He continued to preach to his tormentors for two days until he expired.

The apostle Thomas was stabbed with a spear in India during one of his missionary trips to establish the church in the subcontinent. Matthias, the apostle chosen to replace the traitor Judas Iscariot, was stoned and then beheaded.

James the Greater, a son of Zebedee, was ultimately beheaded at Jerusalem. The Roman officer who guarded James watched amazed as James defended his faith at his trial. Later, the officer walked beside James to the place of execution. Overcome by conviction, he declared his new faith to the judge and knelt beside James to accept beheading as a Christian.[1]

Making It Personal

1. *Big requests may take a while to be fully answered.* After asking Jesus to increase their faith, the disciples were not immediately men rich in faith. They were afraid to stand for Christ. Peter denied Jesus, Thomas doubted, and, except for John, the others abandoned Him. Their faith did not blossom until after the resurrection.

Although God is able to give us big answers instantly, we may not be ready to handle them. After asking for increased faith, the disciples had to grow through character-building experiences. God is always believable and trustworthy, but we have to grow into the type of people who can fully trust Him.

2. *We are the key to the answer of some of our prayers.* Faith is a choice. God can provide the reasons to believe, but belief is ultimately our choice.

3. *God delights in faith and is willing to answer our request for more.* Of all the things we can ask for, faith is one that God is always ready to give. So why not ask?

NOTE

[1]Grant R. Jeffrey, *The Signature of God* (Toronto, Canada: Frontier Research Publications, Inc., 1996), pp. 254–57.

Note that the details of the martyrdoms of the disciples and apostles are found in traditional early church sources. These traditions were recounted in the writings of the church fathers and the first official church history written by the historian Eusebius in AD 325. Although we cannot at this time verify every detail historically, the universal belief of the early Christian writers was that each of the apostles faced martyrdom faithfully without denying their faith in the resurrection of Jesus Christ.

20

GOD, HAVE MERCY ON ME, A SINNER:
The Prayer of the Tax Collector

How do you know if God is really listening to your prayer? How can you be sure that your request is the type of petition that He likes to answer? What sort of demeanor impresses God?

Jesus wanted to help us understand the answers to these questions. Being the world's best teacher, He told a tale of two men that answers these questions and more.

> *To some who were confident of their own righteousness and looked down on every-body else, Jesus told this parable: "Two men went up to the temple to pray, one a Pharisee and the other a tax collector. The Pharisee stood up and prayed about him-self: 'God, I thank you that I am not like other men—robbers, evildoers, adulterers— or even like this tax collector. I fast twice a week and give a tenth of all I get.' But the tax collector stood at a distance. He would not even look up to heaven, but beat his breast and said, 'God, have mercy on me, a sinner.' I tell you that this man, rather than the other, went home justified before God. For everyone who exalts himself will be humbled, and he who humbles himself will be exalted."*

LUKE 18:9–14

This short parable contains a diminutive prayer that produced a dynamic answer. But before we can fully appreciate the prayer, we need to understand the context.

1. *The Audience*. Jesus, in the presence of His disciples, was specifically addressing "some who were confident of their own righteousness and looked down on everybody else." These were probably the Pharisees, since one of the two characters in the story was a Pharisee. The Pharisees, a Jewish sect, were strict observers of the Mosaic law of the Old Testament. They loved the external, detailed aspects of the law and, when it was not specific enough, they added their own traditions—hundreds of them. Unfortunately, these overzealous rule-keepers valued the outward keeping of their rules above all else. As a group, because they had become exceedingly self-righteous, they looked down on anyone who was not in their sect.

2. *The Setting*. The two men Jesus told about in the little story had one similarity and many differences. Their similarity was that both "went up to the temple to pray." For a Jew living during the time of Jesus, the temple was the prime place of prayer. When Solomon dedicated the first temple, his prayer was that God's eyes would be open to the temple day and night. It was to be the place where God would hear prayers and forgive (see 2 Chronicles 6:20–21).

Jews still view the temple in Jerusalem as the supreme location for prayer. Today in modern Jerusalem you can see Jews gathered at the Western Wall of the remains of Solomon's temple. This sacred place is often called the Wailing Wall and was believed to be the back wall of the Holy of Holies on the temple mount. Three times a day, for thousands of years, Jewish prayers from around the world have been directed toward the Western Wall.

Jewish mystical tradition teaches that all prayers from around the world ascend to the Western Wall, and from there, to heaven. The Talmud says, "If someone is praying outside the Land of Israel, he should direct his heart in the direction of Israel. If the person is praying in Israel, he should direct his heart toward Jerusalem. Those in Jerusalem should direct their hearts to the Temple."[1]

3. *The Main Characters.* In Jesus' story, one man was a Pharisee and the other, a tax collector. Jesus, no doubt, used these two types of men because they represented the extremes of the culture. The Pharisees represented the superficially upright, externally moral, legalistic, self-righteous, ultra-right wing of Judaism. The tax collectors signified the bad boys.

Because Israel was under Roman occupation, the Jews were saddled with a heavy tax burden. Tax collectors were Jews who collected taxes from their Jewish brothers and sisters for the Romans. This made them traitors in the eyes of their people. To make matters worse, often they were found to be guilty of extortion as well as associating with prostitutes and other "dregs of society."

You have to love it!

4. *The Ineffective Prayer of the Pharisee*

"The Pharisee stood up and prayed about himself: 'God, I thank you that I am not like other men—robbers, evildoers, adulterers—or even like this tax collector. I fast twice a week and give a tenth of all I get.' "

LUKE 18:11–12

Good storytellers follow the axiom, "Show but don't tell." Skillfully Jesus shows us five reasons why God refused to respond to the Pharisee's prayer.

(a) He prayed from a position of self-promotion. When he prayed, he "stood up." It was customary for men to stand when they prayed at the temple. But this Pharisee was standing with an attitude. An amplified study of the language reveals that he took his stand ostentatiously. The posture of the prayer may say much about the nature of the prayer and the one praying. Proud men stand in order to be noticed, especially when they pray. The Pharisee's prayer was pretentious and showy—and God was not impressed.

(b) The Pharisee was self-centered. He "prayed *about* himself" [italics mine]. The King James Version says that he "prayed with himself." The New American Standard Version states that he "prayed to himself." His prayer was self-absorbed. It was to himself, with himself, and about himself. Self-centered people focus their conversations and prayers on themselves. God's heart is all about selflessness.

(c) The Pharisee was self-righteous. He prayed, "God, I thank You that I am not like other men—robbers, evildoers, adulterers—or even like this tax collector." He is telling God all the bad things he is too good to do. This Pharisee views himself as too righteous to rob, do evil, or commit adultery. He saw himself as above such lowly behavior. Self-righteous persons love to point out and criticize the shortcomings of others. God does not need our help in seeing others' shortcomings.

(d) The Pharisee was self-absorbed. He prayed, "I fast twice a week and give a tenth of all I get." He not only told God what he wouldn't do, but also what he did do that set him apart from ordinary sinful men. This man fit the description of Jesus' hearers—those "who were confident of their own righteousness and looked down on everybody else" (verse 9). Self-absorbed men like to speak of the good they do. The awesome God is not awed by our deeds of righteousness.

Rabbi Simeon, the son of Jochai, exemplified this kind of pride:

If there were only thirty righteous persons in the world, I and my son would make two of them; but if there were but twenty, I and my son would be of the number; and if there were but ten, *I and my son would be of the number; and if there were but* five, *I and my son would be of the five; and if there were but* two, *I and my son would be those two; and if there were but* one, *myself should be that* one.[2]

(e) Prayer is often a wonderful revealer of the heart. The Pharisee had a proud, self-promoting, self-centered, self-righteous, self-absorbed heart. But the main cause of his inefficiency in prayer was his *self-sufficiency*. He did not feel the need to ask God for anything. He had it all together and under control. The biggest problem with legalistic religion is that it quickly digresses to the point where God is no longer needed. For the Pharisee, prayer had become little more than a chance to brag.

5. *The Effective Prayer of the Tax Collector*

"But the tax collector stood at a distance. He would not even look up to heaven, but beat his breast and said, 'God, have mercy on me, a sinner.' "

LUKE 18:13

Jesus began with the word "but," signifying that in every way the tax collector was a contrast to the Pharisee. As a result, the tax collector's prayer was highly effective. There are several reasons why his prayer succeeded.

First, the tax collector was without pretense. He stood at a distance. He did not consider himself worthy of a front-and-center place at the temple. Instead of standing where he could be easily seen, he was entirely unassuming.

The tax collector was also humble. Instead of staring confidently into heaven, he prayed with a bowed head. Modest people bow their heads in deference to those they consider above them.

Further, he did not judge or condemn. He did not tell God how much better he was than someone else. Instead of picking at the splinter in the eye of another, his vision was overwhelmed with the beam in his own.

Rather than tout his own righteousness, he simply called himself a sinner. The tax collector knew better than to try and bluff God or deny the obvious. He knew what he was—a sinner. Unlike the Pharisee, he was dependent. He did not think he had it all together or could handle it. He knew he was insufficient. He knew his need and who could meet it. So he asked God to supply.

When someone approaches God with the humble, dependent, unpretentious attitude of the tax collector, his or her heart is attuned to real needs and right directions. The tax collector's prayer was right on target. He not only asked *for* something, he asked for *the right thing*.

God wants to answer our prayers, but so often we ask for the wrong things. We pray about nonessentials and miss the real needs of our hearts. This tax collector nailed the request, just as Solomon did when he asked for wisdom, and the disciples when they wanted to be taught to pray. The tax collector asked God for mercy. He offered one of the most effective prayers found in the Bible.

Have mercy on me, a sinner.

Our relationship with God is founded upon God's mercy. As Isaiah witnessed, God is absolutely holy, without sin in any way, shape, or form. His level of holiness is so intense that the seraphim literally burn in the brilliant flame of His holiness.

We are not holy in any way, shape, or form. We are sinners by nature and deed, attitude and act. The wages of sin is death, and we deserve severe punishment for our continued sin. The best our righteousness merits is total and eternal banishment from God's presence and from blessing of any type.

Yet, God is merciful. He can rightfully withhold our punishment because His mercy drove Jesus to the cross in our place. The Father can spare us because He refused to spare Jesus. Jesus took our penalty. He died in our place. We can be saved.

Living in this consumer-centered, commercial-filled world, we are constantly being told that we have a *right* for more and better. Such a message may make for an effective advertisement, but it spells poor theology. The tax collector knew what he deserved, and it was not more or better. It was eternal separation from God in outer darkness. So instead of telling God that He must give him the great riches that were his right, he asked God for mercy so he would not receive the judgment he truly did deserve.

The word used here for mercy is *hilaskomai*, which is actually the word for an atoning sacrifice. In the fullest sense, the tax collector is saying, "God, be merciful to me through Your atoning sacrifice for sins, because I am a sinner."

The tax collector understood what too many miss. He knew that he could not merit a relationship with God through his own righteousness or good works. Paul summarized this reality:

> *For it is by grace you have been saved, through faith—and this not from yourselves, it is the gift of God—not by works, so that no one can boast.*
>
> EPHESIANS 2:8–9

Making It Personal

If you never have before, now is the time to say to God the words uttered by the tax collector, "God be merciful to *me*, a sinner" [italics mine]. If you mean it, this can be a soul-saving, life-changing prayer. It was for the tax collector and it has been for untold others. Praying this is our part in being justified or made right with God.

> *"I tell you that this man, rather than the other, went home justified before God."*
>
> LUKE 18:14

Learn to pray as the tax collector, not the Pharisee. Lose any trace of arrogance, pretense, self-righteousness, self-centeredness, and self-sufficiency as you approach life in general and prayer in particular. Live and pray with humility, honesty, and modesty. Come dependently to God in prayer. Learn to tell Him what you really need.

> *"For everyone who exalts himself will be humbled, and he who humbles himself will be exalted."*
>
> LUKE 18:14

NOTES

[1] b. Berachot 30a.
[2] Adam Clarke, *Adam Clarke's Commentary on the Bible* (Nashville, TN: Abingdon Press, 1977), p. 401.

21
FATHER, FORGIVE THEM:
The Prayer of Jesus
LUKE 23:34

It may have been the most difficult request ever made. It certainly was one of the most powerful.

I know you have heard this story before, but let me ask you to read through these facts as though they were contained in the lead story of today's newspaper.

In the previous twenty-four hours, Jesus had been through an emotional hell. A close follower selfishly betrayed Him so that Jesus would be unjustly arrested. One of His best friends denied knowing Him on three separate occasions. His other friends and followers deserted Him.

Alone, Jesus faced the most powerful men in His nation who had been plotting His death. They paraded Jesus through a ludicrous series of illegal trials. The savage soldiers who held Him decided to have some wicked fun, so they mocked and spit upon Him. The man who was judging His case turned Him over to these ruthless soldiers in order to have Jesus nearly flogged to death. Sadistic and brutal, they placed a crown of thorns on His head and then spit on Him.

A judge then brought Jesus before a bloodthirsty mob and let them decide His fate. Spurred on by the religious leaders, the people mercilessly cried out for His public execution. Afterward, forced to carry a cross up a hill through the center of town, the already half-dead Jesus was unable to make it on His own. Another man had to help.

At a place known as Skull Hill, Jesus' hands and feet were spiked into the wood of the cross with long metal stakes. There He was hung before the murderous mob, on the center cross between two convicted criminals. There He was left to fight for air while pulling His weight up and down against the metal spikes. The pain must have been excruciating.

Below Him the circus of the absurd continued. Religious leaders sneered at Him, and a cruel crowd scoffed. The whole scene was so hideous, so horrible, and so heinous that God the Father had to turn His back on His beloved Son. A dark cloud swallowed the hilltop as the afternoon sun refused to shine.

Yet, in the midst of the betrayal, denial, and desertion; despite the brutality, lies, and injustice; and in the middle of the murderous mayhem; Jesus said three of the most powerful words ever spoken.

Father, forgive them.

How He did it, I cannot guess. It would have been totally unexpected and unnatural from anyone else. But Jesus, the victim in this awful passion play, was ever the victor.

"Father, forgive them." Three simple words powerfully summed up the reason for His life on earth. The bridge from God to man was paved with His blood and built on the foundation of forgiveness. His birth in Bethlehem, childhood in Nazareth, baptism in the Jordan, His miracles and teachings, and the Last Supper with His disciples were all scenes leading up to this moment. They all built steadily and relentlessly to this climax.

"Father, forgive them."

Jesus' prayer was powerfully answered. Dozens of those gathered around Jesus when He said those words found forgiveness. One of the thieves crucified with Jesus was pardoned with the promise of a home in paradise with Him. The Roman centurion who had overseen the crucifixion found forgiveness as he confessed Jesus to be the Son of God. Peter was forgiven for his denial, as were the other disciples for their desertion. Later, the debt of guilt owed by the priests in pursuing, or for some at least condoning, Jesus' death was cancelled for those who believed. Many members of that cutthroat crowd who cried for His crucifixion no doubt found forgiveness on the day of Pentecost or soon after.

Beyond the people who were in Jerusalem during Jesus' prayer, many others were to be forgiven as well. Three thousand from around the world found forgiveness on the day of Pentecost. Later, the message of forgiveness was taken to cities all over the known world of the first century.

Jesus' prayer of forgiveness has continued to echo throughout the centuries, as those of every tribe, tongue, and nation have experienced the cleansing joy of having their sins washed white as snow and cast into the depths of the deepest sea. God has been answering Jesus' prayer ever since it was uttered two thousand years ago.

I have been a recipient of the forgiveness Jesus prayed for on the cross. You see, my sins were part of what nailed Him to the cross. When He said, "Father, forgive them," He included *me*. And He included *you,* too.

When Jesus prayed, "Father, forgive them," He set us free from the prison of our sin. When we pray, "Father, forgive them," we set ourselves free from the prison of bitterness. Jesus described this prison in a story He told, which goes something like this.

Once upon a time long ago and far away, a man owed a king a massive, multibillion-dollar debt. But the king mercifully forgave him the entire amount.

Instead of celebrating his wonderfully good fortune, the forgiven man immediately went after a poor guy who owed him only a few thousand dollars. The poor guy couldn't pay, so the forgiven man had him locked up in debtors' prison. When the king heard what had happened, he was so upset that he restored the previously forgiven man's debt and threw him into the dungeon to be tortured.

This story reminds us that God has forgiven us a gigantic debt caused by our sin. Such forgiveness should prompt us to forgive others of the much smaller debts we feel owed to us because of offenses they may have caused. And it tells us that failing to forgive hurts us more than the other person. It locks us into a dungeon of torture and a prison of bitterness.

Although this prison does not have visible bars, chains, and torture chambers, they are every bit as real. When I am harboring bitterness in my heart toward another, I have unwittingly become a prisoner to them. Just the mention of their name can flood my mind with powerful and ugly thoughts. Seeing them elevates my heart rate and blood pressure. Hearing their voice can make me wince and cringe. Even when they are not around, I cannot get them out of my mind. I am their prisoner and my bitterness toward them tortures me.

There is only one way out of the horrible prison of harbored hurts. There is only one key that turns the lock of freedom from the jail cell of resentment. It is the prayer Jesus prayed two thousand years ago, "Father, forgive them."

Praying this prayer is not optional for a healthy Christian—it is mandatory. As long as we live on earth, we will be hurt and offended by other people. We must learn to liberate them and set ourselves free in the process.

Lack of forgiveness is devastatingly powerful. It produces the awful fruit of resentment, bitterness, anger, hatred, strife, and jealousy. When we have unresolved hurts, we will find ourselves responding with insults, attacks, broken relationships, betrayal, and distance from God. Lack of forgiveness rips apart families, divides marriages, splits churches, and poisons friendships.

Recent studies have found wonderful physical healing and power in learning to forgive and great danger in not doing so. "Carrying around a load of bitterness and anger at how unfairly you were treated is very toxic," says Fred Luskin, Ph.D., director of Stanford University's Forgiveness Project. His researchers found that letting go of a grudge can slash one's stress level up to 50 percent. Volunteers in the study showed improvements in energy, mood, sleep quality, and overall physical vitality. Another study has shown that giving up grudges can reduce chronic back pain. And yet another experiment found practicing forgiveness limited relapses among women battling substance abuse.[1]

Physically, anger and resentment produce a steady stream of stress hormones, which then turn into toxins. According to Bruce McEwen, Ph.D., director of the neurological lab at Rockefeller University in New York City, these wear down the brain, leading to cell atrophy and memory loss. Stress also raises blood sugar, hardens arteries, and leads to heart disease. Yet, forgiveness stops these hormones from flowing. In a separate study of thirty-six men who had coronary heart disease and a history of painful hurts, half were given forgiveness training and half were not. The ones who forgave showed greater blood flow to their hearts.[2]

Forgiveness is not only beneficial for our physical and emotional well-being, it is tremendously powerful spiritually. John Bevere recounts the story of a burly middle-aged man standing before a church in Naples, Florida, telling his story.

> "All my life I have felt like there was a wall between me and God. I would attend meetings where others sensed God's presence and I watch detached and numb. Even when I prayed there was no release or presence."
>
> The man went on to tell how he realized that his problem was a lack of forgiveness. He continued, "I hated my mother for abandoning me when I was six months old. I realized that I had to go to her and forgive her. I called and spoke with her for only the second time in thirty-six years. I cried, 'Mom, I have held unforgiveness toward you all my life for giving me away.' She began to weep and said, 'Son, I hated myself for the last thirty-six years for leaving you.'" He continued, "I forgave her, and she forgave herself; now we are reconciled. Now the wall that separated me from God's presence is gone!"
>
> Then the man began to weep so strongly he could barely get the next sentence out. "Now I cry in the presence of God like a baby."[3]

Making It Personal

Odds are good that there is someone who has inadvertently taken you prisoner because you have not forgiven their offense. Life is too short to be shackled with the ball and chain of an unforgiving heart. Our response to an offense determines our future. There are too many wonderful opportunities awaiting us when we take the way of escape from the dungeon of resentment.

Picture those who need your forgiveness and their offenses clearly in your mind. Make the choice Jesus made. Choose to forgive by praying one of the most powerful prayers in the world, "Father, forgive them."

NOTES

Lisa Collier Cool, "The Power of Forgiving," *Reader's Digest*, May 2004, p. 54.
Ibid., p. 54.
Adapted from *The Bait of Satan* by John Bevere, p. ix. Used by permission of Charisma House. Copyright 2004 by Strang Communications Co., USA. All rights reserved.

FINAL THOUGHTS

After having read the twenty-one most effective personal prayers in the Bible, prayers that worked because God answered them positively, we should spend some time considering what we should do if God does not answer the way we had hoped. Or, what do we do when He does not seem to answer at all?

One reason God may be silent is sin. Sin can keep God from responding to our prayers.

If I had cherished sin in my heart, the Lord would not have listened; but God has surely listened and heard my voice in prayer.

PSALM 66:18–19

Sometimes God is silent because the request is too selfish.

What causes fights and quarrels among you? Don't they come from your desires that battle within you? You want something but don't get it. You kill and covet, but you cannot have what you want. You quarrel and fight. You do not have, because you do not ask God. When you ask, you do not receive, because you ask with wrong motives, that you may spend what you get on your pleasures.

JAMES 4:1–3

And at other times, God may not be responding because He is giving another message. He is saying, "Wait." Russell Kelfer's story illustrates this well.

Because Russell had always loved the written word, he decided to pursue a journalism degree at the University of Texas. However, after sustaining a sports injury to his eye, he was unable to complete the required reading. So he gave up his dream and joined the family business, Kelfer Tire Company. He took his place as the third generation of Kelfers to run the business.

Nearly twenty years later, Russell found himself teaching a home Bible study to single adults. As the group grew in number from 20 to 150, a local church asked him to teach the same material on Sunday mornings. What was to be a six-week Sunday commitment lasted the rest of his life. From those first classes, he developed a series of lessons, stories, poems, and audio and video tapes that would comprise his counseling and mentoring ministry. Today, Russell Kelfer's Discipleship Tape Ministry helps people around the world.

The boy who couldn't finish college because it required too much reading became the man God enabled to read, study, and write prolifically. Although Russell possessed no formal credentials for teaching, writing, or ministering, God gently led him into a ministry that used all of those skills. Russell often said, "I didn't have sense enough to be frightened."

From experience, he learned that God often answers our most passionate prayers with the frustrating response of "Wait." Russell's best-loved poem has ministered to thousands for the past twenty years because it speaks to our human desire to hear God's plan for our lives and our subsequent frustration when we feel we are met with His silence. What we often hear as God's "No," however, is often God's "Wait." God wants us to wait to "grow" our character, develop our faith, and thus fulfill His larger scheme.

Wait
by Russell Kelfer

Desperately, helplessly, longingly, I cried;
Quietly, patiently, lovingly, God replied.
I pled and I wept for a clue to my fate. . .
And the Master so gently said, "Wait."

"Wait? You say wait?" my indignant reply.
"Lord, I need answers, I need to know why!
Is Your hand shortened? Or have You not heard?
By faith I have asked, and I'm claiming Your Word.

"My future and all to which I relate
Hangs in the balance, and You tell me to wait?
I'm needing a 'yes', a go-ahead sign,
Or even a 'no' to which I can resign.

"You promised, dear Lord, that if we believe,
We need but to ask, and we shall receive.
And Lord, I've been asking, and this is my cry·
I'm weary of asking! I need a reply."

Then quietly, softly, I learned of my fate,
As my Master replied again, "Wait."
So I slumped in my chair, defeated and taut,
And grumbled to God, "So, I'm waiting for what?"
He seemed then to kneel, and His eyes met with mine. . .
and He tenderly said, "I could give you a sign.
I could shake the heavens and darken the sun.
I could raise the dead and cause mountains to run.

"I could give all you seek and pleased you would be.
You'd have what you want, but you wouldn't know Me.
You'd not know the depth of My love for each saint.
You'd not know the power that I give to the faint.

"You'd not learn to see through clouds of despair;
You'd not learn to trust just by knowing I'm there.
You'd not know the joy of resting in Me
When darkness and silence are all you can see.

"You'd never experience the fullness of love
When the peace of My spirit descends like a dove.
You would know that I give, and I save, for a start,
But you'd not know the depth of the beat of My heart.

"The glow of My comfort late into the night,
The faith that I give when you walk without sight.
The depth that's beyond getting just what you ask
From an infinite God who makes what you have last.

"You'd never know, should your pain quickly flee,
What it means that My grace is sufficient for thee.
Yes, your dearest dreams overnight would come true,
But, oh, the loss, if you missed what I'm doing in you.

"So, be silent, my child, and in time you will see
That the greatest of gifts is to truly know Me.
And though oft My answers seem terribly late,
My most precious answer of all is still. . .Wait."[1]

When the silence from God is not the result of sin and not a call to wait, it may be God's way of giving us a better answer. Prayers that appear to be unanswered may in reality be answered very well. If we think we are not getting results from our prayers, we should look again.

Too often we pray with the idea of "*my* will be done." We need to remember that we are part of the larger fabric of life. There are times when, instead of praying for relief from an affliction, it may be more important to pray for strength to accept and overcome the trouble. Then we will have grown in courage and patience and wisdom. The following poem by Francis of Assisi captures this insight.

I asked God for strength, that I might achieve;
I was given health, that I might learn to obey.
I asked for riches, that I might be happy;
I was given poverty, that I might be wise.
I asked for power, that I might have the praise of men;
I was given weakness, that I might feel the need of God.
I asked for all things, that I might enjoy life;
I was given life, that I might enjoy all things.
I received nothing that I had asked for—
Everything I had hoped for.
My prayers were answered.

Remember, prayer is not dictation. Prayer is not telling God what to do and His immediately doing it. Prayer is cooperating with God so that He can accomplish His will. Don't be discouraged when God says "Wait," or when He gives you something other than what you asked. Remember, Father always knows best.

Note

The 21 Most Encouraging Promises of the Bible

Acknowledgments

*T*ogether *E*veryone *A*ccomplishes *M*ore. My gratitude to the team that made this project a reality, including:

- Cathy, for your wise and wonderful wifely editing skills.

- My boys, Daniel, Andrew, and Luke, for liking all my books (or at least saying that you do).

- Carol and Sandy, my favorite sisters and PR persons.

- Susan Chittum, for your amazing ability to proofread what I write.

- The Mighty Men, for your prayers.

- Paul Muckley, for your passion for God and zeal to make this project a reality.

- Kelly McIntosh, for managing the in-house editorial process.

- Catherine Thompson, for handling the typesetting.

- Elmer Towns, Jamal Jivanjee, and the Arthur DeMoss family, for allowing me to tell your stories.

Contents

Introduction

Imagine that you have discovered a well-worn, leather-bound book. You slowly open it to find that it contains twenty-one checks. But unlike any other checkbook you have ever seen, each of these checks is already written. You become deeply puzzled when you read the "pay to the order of" line on the checks. Your name is already clearly written on each one.

Then your eyes fall on the "amount" section. Curious goose bumps burst out all over your arms when you see what is written there. The first one says, "Escape from Temptation"; the next, "Victory over Fear"; the check after that says, "Divine Guidance"; the next says, "A Blessed Life"; another reads, "Bad Turning into Good." You find that all twenty-one checks are made out to you. Each one offers an amazing blessing for your emotional and spiritual life.

"This must be a joke," you think. "This cannot be true." Slowly, fearfully, your eyes move down to the lower right-hand corner of the top check. Who signed these checks guaranteeing you so many promised blessings?

The signature line has one short word inscribed on it. You read this word and it staggers you. This is no joke. The payer's name is God.

I know what you are thinking. "Cute story, Dave. But I don't live in a fantasyland. Life is tough. Tell me something that will help me here and now in the real world."

I am about to tell you that very thing.

Today could be one of the most important days of your life. I say this because my story is not a joke. Figuratively speaking, God has given each of us an amazing checkbook written on the pages of the Bible. The book you are now reading highlights twenty-one amazing biblical checks and shows you the way to cash them.

How It All Began

It was an exciting but uncertain time in my life. Newly married, I was trying to clearly discern God's future plans for my wife and me. I needed provision, protection, and peace. Plus, I knew I needed more faith because I seemed to be easily swamped by fear.

At that time, as director of discipleship for Liberty University, I wrote a self-study Bible course entitled "Standing on the Promises." It was a simple survey of some of the 7,487 promises of God. I don't know how much this study helped the students, but it certainly encouraged me.

As I wrote that Bible study, I learned that each biblical promise tells us something of God and His love for His people. I found that His promises are faith-building guarantees from God Himself and that God is able to fulfill these promises.

It was thrilling to discover that God made promises that applied to all areas of my life and every event I encountered. Studying them brought me desperately needed inspiration, comfort, and challenge.

It's rather humbling, yet quite exciting, to realize that in some ways I'm back where I started when I was first married. I have gone full circle in my spiritual life and have returned to the place where I first stepped out in faith trusting the promises of God. The verses that were so precious to me twenty years ago are alive for me today in fresh, new ways. I am discovering how to be truly "rich" by trusting in the promises of God.

In this book I will share with you some of the most exciting, encouraging, and enriching promises in the Bible. As I do, I will dust off several colorful Bible characters who lived the promises. Their experiences will instruct, inspire, and meet your need as you cash each check in the checkbook of God's promises.

Many of the promises I will share with you are familiar. Most will be wonderfully comforting. All are extremely powerful.

As you study them, you will deepen your relationship with God as you intensify your faith and confidence in Him. These promises will breathe calm and peace into your hectic life. They have the power to lift you out of horizontal, temporal thinking into a vertical, eternal perspective of God's purposes. You will find your life enriched with renewed inner courage to bravely and boldly face the challenges of your life.

You Must Have Faith

I must confess, the concept of God's Word as a checkbook full of promises is not unique to me. About 130 years ago, a wise man named Charles H. Spurgeon wrote a little book called *Faith's Checkbook*. In it he said:

> *A promise from God may very instructively be compared to a check payable to order. It is given to the believer with the view of bestowing upon him some good thing. It is not meant that he should read it over comfortably, and then have done with it. No, he is to treat the promise as a reality, as a man treats a check. He is to take the promise and endorse it with his own name by personally receiving it as true. He is by faith to accept it as his own.* [1]

Wouldn't it be a tragedy if you left God's rich promises in the bank because you failed to believe that the checks were really made out to you? But such neglect occurs every day. Everyone who owns a Bible has access to hundreds of promises. But these promises only encourage and enrich those who accept them by faith. For the rest, faith's checkbook lies unused and the owner unblessed.

You Must Cash the Checks

Years ago I read the account of a widow who, after her husband's death, barely had money to buy food and couldn't pay her bills. Her son, a successful businessman, heard reports of her stunning poverty and called her on the telephone:

"Mother, I hear that you don't have enough money to pay your bills."

"That's right," she said sadly.

"But how can that be? Don't you get my letters every month?"

"Yes, I get your letters," she sighed.

"Then what do you do with the money?" he asked. "I always send more than enough to cover all of your needs."

"What money?" she huffed. "All you ever send are those pretty slips of paper with your name scrawled on the bottom! I keep them in the desk drawer in case you might want them."

As it turned out, thousands of dollars of uncashed checks lay in her desk drawer. She lived in poverty even though she had more than enough money to meet all of her needs. If only she would have cashed those checks!

Before you are too hard on this poor widow, think about your situation. God has given you promises to cover your every need, but they do you no good until you cash them.

Spurgeon's little book *Faith's Checkbook* tells us that once we have accepted a promise as our own by faith, we "must present the promise to the Lord, as a man presents a check at the counter of a bank. He must plead it by prayer, expecting to have it fulfilled."[2]

Believe me, God can pay up on anything He promised. He alone possesses unlimited strength, infinite power, and matchless wisdom! He can be trusted. It would be foolish and a great waste to possess a checkbook full of awesome blessings and not attempt to cash them because you don't believe that the check writer can pay.

Be Patient

Maybe you are reading this and thinking, "Yeah, that sounds good, but I claimed one of God's promises by faith in prayer once, and nothing happened."

I understand. But let's not forget the big picture.

There is only one true God in the universe—and it's not you. God is our heavenly Father who loves to bless His children. He is the guarantor of many amazing promises that only He can fulfill. But God is also the supremely wise and absolute ruler of the universe. This means that although He longs to bless you, He may not do it when or how you want. He is entitled to fulfill His promises exactly when and how He wants. Often He knows it is not best if we get what we want when we want it. Often it is best for us to wait. In His wisdom, God may choose that we do without small blessings now so He can pour out huge blessings later.

The Twenty-One Most Encouraging Promises of the Bible

Studying the promises of God can be like trying to drink out of a fire hydrant. They are so powerful and there are so many of them that they may knock us off our feet. We might come away wet but not refreshed. So I will focus on just twenty-one promises that share these characteristics:

1.   *Most are conditional.* This means that before God will do His part, we have to do our part.
2.   *All are evident in the life of a Bible character or characters.* Bible personalities bring God's promises to life.
3.   *Each is especially encouraging.* Life can be hard and discouraging. These promises will breathe courage into your life and hope into your heart.
4.   *All of the promises are universal.* They are as applicable in your twenty-first-century situation as when they were written.

Suggestions for Getting the Most Out of This Book

1.   *Study each chapter with a prayerful heart.*
2.   *Memorize the verse(s) containing the promise.*
3.   *Share what you are learning with someone else.*
4.   *Better still, study this book with a friend or a small group.*
5.   *Reread chapters that especially apply to your needs.*
6.   *Claim each promise in prayer.*
7.   *Live what you learn.*

My Favorite Quotes about the Promises of God

Every promise of God is made for me.
MARTIN LUTHER

The future is as bright as the promises of God.
PIONEER MISSIONARY ADONIRAM JUDSON (when asked about the
prospects of taking the gospel to the nation of Burma)

A promise by God is a pledge by God. It provides the warrant
and forms the basis of the prayer of faith.
J. O. SANDERS

God has always intended that His people should share His wealth and He has written a
book to tell us so. The book contains the title deeds.
W. T. H. RICHARDS

God's promises are never broken by leaning upon them.
HOWARD HENDRICKS

It is the prerogative of every believer to enter the inexhaustible mine of divine wealth, to
search the sacred veins, to gather up the beautiful treasure that will enrich them. There is no
excuse for spiritual poverty when we are invited to come and partake freely. Our inheritance
is there to be taken and enjoyed.
W. T. H. RICHARDS

NOTES

1. Charles H. Spurgeon, *Faith's Checkbook* (Chicago: Moody Press, n.d.), ii.
2. Ibid., ii.

1

God's Promise of Escape from Temptation

1 CORINTHIANS 10:13

A deadly predator is out to get you. This marauder is cunning and shrewd. One moment its advance is subtle and apparently innocent. The next, it rises up and assaults with overwhelming force. This soul seducer can present itself as a harmless lamb, but it has the bite of a viper. It is both too beautiful to resist and too powerful to deny. This wicked shape-shifter will take any form necessary in order to persuade you to yield to its power.

You cannot let up, because your assailant won't. This relentless raider is always on the attack, never takes a break, never goes on vacation, and never takes a day off.

Be aware. Like a cagey boxer, this adversary will size you up quickly, diagnose your weaknesses, wait for an opening, or fake you into letting down your guard. Then, *bam!* It will drop you with an unexpected blow.

Temptation is a fierce foe—and it's after you. That's the bad news. The good news is that no matter how severe the temptation, you don't have to give in to it.

The Example of Joseph

If anyone ever had an excuse for giving in, it was Joseph. A powerful, "unattainable" woman, his master, Potiphar's wife, was freely offering herself to him. And Joseph was a healthy, red-blooded young man. And as they say, "Young men have needs." Surely, Joseph had his share of hormones. Besides that, he was far from home and had gone through a horrible ordeal. Certainly he was due a little pleasure. Plus, no one would know. And as his master's wife, this woman was Joseph's boss. How could he refuse her? On top of that, she had the power to significantly improve his life. Everything inside him said, "Go for it."

But Joseph firmly said, "No" (Genesis 39:7–9).

Unfortunately, the temptation didn't go away easily. Undaunted by his rebuff, Joseph's master's wife intensified her efforts to seduce him. Day after day, she made her appeal. Again and again, she enticed, she persuaded, she coaxed, she pleaded. Yet repeatedly Joseph resisted, refused, and rejected her advances (v. 10).

But just as he refused to give in, she stubbornly refused to give up.

One day her pride and lust would not go unfulfilled any longer. No one else was around. Desperately, she reached out for Joseph, grabbed his cloak, and pulled him down next to her. No man would resist such pressure.

But Joseph did. He jerked back so hard his cloak was left in her hands as he ran out of the room (vv. 11–15). This angered Potiphar's wife so severely she accused him of rape and had him thrown in prison (vv. 16–20). But the Lord was with Joseph and showed him His love (v. 21). So Joseph modeled faith in a promise that we can also claim.

You Are Not Alone in Temptation

No temptation has seized you except what is common to man. And God is faithful; he will not let you be tempted beyond what you can bear. But when you are tempted, he will also provide a way out so that you can stand up under it.

1 CORINTHIANS 10:13

"No temptation has seized you except what is common to man." When we are tempted, we may think that we are the only one facing temptation. But that simply is not true. Humans have been facing temptation since the Garden of Eden. We all face it. Even Jesus faced temptation. It is part and parcel of the human condition.

Temptation is no respecter of persons. It pursues children and adults, men and women, the lost and the saved, the spiritually young and the spiritually mature. Pastors and missionaries face temptations as often as anyone else. When you battle temptation, you are not alone.

We also may assume that we are the only person who has ever faced a certain type or level of temptation. Again, this is not true. Every sin imaginable has existed as long as there have been people around to commit it. Certainly, you are a unique person. But you are not facing unique or special temptation.

A survey in *Discipleship Journal* ranked its readers' greatest spiritual challenges. They included the following:

1. Materialism
2. Pride
3. Self-centeredness
4. Laziness
5. Anger/bitterness tied with sexual lust
7. Envy
8. Gluttony
9. Lying[1]

I don't know about you, but I have wrestled with all of these and more. I could easily add selfish ambition, disobedience, doubt, distraction, rebellion, gossip, slander, worry, covetousness/greed, idolatry, and dishonesty to the list. I am sure there are many more that I have overlooked. The array of sins we are tempted to commit is more varied and numerous than the colors of the rainbow.

It's Not Irresistible

"God is faithful; he will not let you be tempted beyond what you can bear." This is the promise. No temptation is irresistible. Let me repeat that: No temptation is irresistible. God will not allow any temptation to be unbearable.

Note carefully that the basis for the ability to bear temptation is not our strength, wisdom, or willpower. Rather, it is God's faithfulness. Through this we can bear up under temptation just as Joseph did.

Note that the promise is not that we won't be tempted. We will. Count on it. Until we get to heaven, we will be tempted. It is a fact of life. Rather, the promise is that we won't face any temptation that is more than we can handle.

Let me clarify this. Temptation, in and of itself, is not sin. Temptation is the appeal to sin. It is possible to be tempted and not sin. The thought of sin is not sin until it is entertained and acted on. Alone in the wilderness, Jesus Himself, the holy Son of God, was tempted three times. Yet all three times He refused the temptation (Matthew 4:1–11). Likewise, God gives us the power to resist temptation. He who resisted temptation gives us victory over temptation.

The Great Escape

"But when you are tempted, he will also provide a way out so that you can stand up under it." A child of God has no excuse for sin. There is always a way to avoid it, because God is faithful to provide a way to avoid it or the power to resist it. That is His promise. But while it is God's responsibility to give us a way out, it is our responsibility to take the escape route.

Temptation came to Joseph several times in a variety of ways. Each time Potiphar's wife tried to seduce him, Joseph took an appropriate way of escape. Her first approach was a direct, surprise solicitation.

> *Now Joseph was well-built and handsome, and after a while his master's wife took notice of Joseph and said, "Come to bed with me!" But he refused. "With me in charge," he told her, "my master does not concern himself with anything in the house; everything he owns he has entrusted to my care. No one is greater in this house than I am. My master has withheld nothing from me except you, because you are his wife. How then could I do such a wicked thing and sin against God?"*
>
> GENESIS 39:6–9

Note that Joseph's first escape route was *firm refusal*. His strong sense of responsibility and accountability to his master and his steadfast reluctance to sin against God gave him the power to refuse and the way of escape.

Yet temptation is relentless. So Potiphar's lusty wife switched tactics to tempt Joseph by persistent appeal.

> *And though she spoke to Joseph day after day, he refused to go to bed with her or even be with her.*
>
> GENESIS 39:10

Joseph countered this constant insistence with *enduring denials*. But she would not take no for an answer.

> *One day he went into the house to attend to his duties, and none of the household servants was inside. She caught him by his cloak and said, "Come to bed with me!" But he left his cloak in her hand and ran out of the house.*
>
> GENESIS 39:11–12

When resistance and refusals are not enough, there is another way of escape, a literal one. *"Run for it."* That is exactly what Joseph did, leaving his jacket in her clutching fingers.

God is faithful to help us avoid temptation and can be quite creative in helping us run from it.

God Has a Sense of Humor

During my last year in high school, I dated a very attractive young lady. One warm evening we were driving around and pulled off the side of the road to talk in a secluded section of a quiet neighborhood. As a newly committed Christian, I was convicted about maintaining a high level of purity in my relationships with girls. Yet I had foolishly put myself in a place of temptation. When there was a pause in the conversation, she scooted over on the bench seat, began to stroke the hair on the back of my head, and smiled knowingly.

I don't need to tell you that my hormones were hopping out of my skin. Silently, I shot a prayer up to God: "Lord, please get me out of this before we do something we'll later regret."

She began to lean in closer. I gulped as my heart began to pound. Then her eyes got as big as saucers, and she pointed over my shoulder as she screamed, "What is that?"

I turned my head and found myself eyeball-to-eyeball with a huge dog. I jerked back, scared that the monster dog would bite my face off. But the gentle giant was content to just look at us.

"Shoo!" I said hoarsely, trying to sound brave. Colossus the Canine just blinked happily. We looked out of the windows and found that a posse of seven or eight dogs of all shapes, sizes, and colors surrounded us. There were little fat ones and medium-sized, sleek ones. Most were well groomed, but some were scruffy mutts.

"Get!" I said even more loudly. Then, mustering as much authority as I could, I said, "Get outta here!"

With that, the enormous beast pulled his head out of the car window and began to lumber off. His motley crew of mutts followed in a happy pack, looking for mischief. My date and I just laughed. "I guess it's time to get you home," I said, relieved that I had been rescued by a bunch of neighborhood dogs out for a night on the town.

Who would have believed it? What were the odds of a Great Dane being loose in that neighborhood at that time? It was a chance in a million that he would stick his big head into an open car window at exactly the moment a weak child of God desperately needed a way of escape. What can I say except God uses whatever means are at hand in order to keep His promises.

A Final Encouragement

You do not have to be defeated by temptation. You can win by taking the way of escape. God will be faithful to provide one. Joseph used several escape routes, and so can you.

NOTE

1. Stanley J. Grenz, "Don't Take the Bait! The Best Time to Fight Temptation Is Before It Strikes," *Discipleship Journal*, November/December, 1992, http://www.navpress.com/EPubs/DisplayArticle/1/1.72.3.html.

2

God's Promise of Victory over Fear
ISAIAH 43:1–2

I used to be fearless, with the emphasis on *used to be*. After a few untimely setbacks occurred and some huge obstacles arose, a major dose of reality knocked the edge off my overconfidence. I imagine you might be the same. Adversaries loom large on the horizon. Potential defeat hangs in the air like a dark cloud. Uncertainty about the unknown makes it tough to stride boldly into the fog of the future.

Fear can be an unwelcome companion and a paralyzing partner. It zaps our strength, runs off with our joy, murders our peace, and stomps the spring out of our step. Yet God promises that no matter how hot the fire or how high the flood, we can face it without fear.

A Fearful Fire

Heat resonated off the giant furnace so intensely it created visual ripples in the air. Huge slippery drops of sweat rolled off the guards as they pushed the three tightly bound young men up the stairs to the awful agony of the excruciating execution. Massive, menacing flames danced merrily up to the sky. Billows of smoke swirled above the furnace in a hungry, wicked grin. All other noise was sucked out of the stifling air by the roaring bellow of the ravenous blaze.

Shadrach, Meshach, and Abednego were going to die and die ugly. Soon smoke would pour into their lungs and choke them mercilessly. The heat of the fire would char their skin black before melting the flesh from their bones—all because they would not worship the king of Babylon.

An Idolatrous King

King Nebuchadnezzar was the most powerful man in the greatest nation on earth. His capital, Babylon, was unrivaled in wealth and beauty. "In addition to its size," wrote Herodotus, a historian in 450 BC, "Babylon surpasses in splendor any city in the known world."[1] Rising above the city was the famous temple to the god Marduk that seemed to reach to the heavens.

During his long reign, King Nebuchadnezzar had constructed an astonishing array of temples, streets, palaces, walls, and gardens. His mountainous terraced trophies, the Hanging Gardens, were so stunning in beauty and amazing in architecture that they have been acclaimed as one of the Seven Wonders of the Ancient World.

When Nebuchadnezzar decided that he had achieved the lofty status of god, he had a giant gold statue made in his likeness. It stood ninety feet high and proudly proclaimed the glory of the king. Nebuchadnezzar ordered all of the important officials in his kingdom to come and bow before his image—or die. Included in this order were three young Hebrew men. They had been taken captive from Jerusalem, raised in the culture of the Babylonians, and given positions in the king's cabinet. With the privilege came the responsibility of unquestioned obedience to the mighty rule of Nebuchadnezzar.

Jealous conspirators used the king's order as an opportunity to corner and accuse these three Jews. Gleefully, they told the king of Shadrach, Meshach, and Abednego's failure to bow and worship at the feet of the golden statue. This infuriated the king, so he ordered them to be brought before him.

Normal men quivered in the presence of this most powerful man on earth. Many were those who suffered torture and death for making him upset. The three young men had good reason to fear.

But they didn't.

Three Courageous Believers

The king threatened to kill them. But Shadrach, Meshach, and Abednego were fearless and resolute.

> *Shadrach, Meshach and Abednego replied to the king, "O Nebuchadnezzar, we do not need to defend ourselves before you in this matter. If we are thrown into the blazing furnace, the God we serve is able to save us from it, and he will rescue us from your hand, O king. But even if he does not, we want you to know, O king, that we will not serve your gods or worship the image of gold you have set up."*
>
> DANIEL 3:16–18

What confidence! "God is able to save us. He will rescue us."

What courage! "Even if He does not, we will not serve your gods or worship your image."

What insanity! Nebuchadnezzar was no one to tease or trifle with. They had better be ready to back up their boldness with commitment.

Obviously, Nebuchadnezzar did not want to hear such bold declarations. Incensed, he ordered the execution furnace heated to seven times its normal temperature. It was so incredibly hot that the guards who dropped them into it died carrying out their orders. The three Hebrews would catch fire like dry kindling and be consumed in minutes.

A Fourth Man in the Fire

Eagerly, Nebuchadnezzar peered into the furnace. He was not expecting what he saw. Shocked and stunned, he turned to his advisers and asked,

> *"Weren't there three men that we tied up and threw into the fire?" They replied, "Certainly, O king." He said, "Look! I see four men walking around in the fire, unbound and unharmed, and the fourth looks like a son of the gods."*
>
> DANIEL 3:24–25

He got it all right except the last part. Yes, Shadrach, Meshach, and Abednego were all alive. Yes, they were now unbound. Yes, they were unharmed. Yes, there was a fourth figure in the fire, but the fourth was not merely "*like* a son of the gods." He *was* the Son of God!

Jesus went through the fire with Shadrach, Meshach, and Abednego. And He'll do the same for you.

Shadrach, Meshach, and Abednego not only walked out unharmed, but they did not even smell of smoke (Daniel 3:27)! Nebuchadnezzar was impressed.

> *Then Nebuchadnezzar said, "Praise be to the God of Shadrach, Meshach and Abednego, who has sent his angel and rescued his servants! They trusted in him and defied the king's command and were willing to give up their lives rather than serve or worship any god except their own God. Therefore I decree that the people of any nation or language who say anything against the God of Shadrach, Meshach and Abednego be cut into pieces and their houses be turned into piles of rubble, for no other god can save in this way." Then the king promoted Shadrach, Meshach and Abednego in the province of Babylon.*
>
> DANIEL 3:28–30

What an awesome story of divine protection and human courage! They lived through the fire. They were so completely unharmed by it, they did not even smell of smoke. Their testimony was told throughout the nation. And they got a promotion! All this happened because Shadrach, Meshach, and Abednego had the courage to face their fire with the Lord.

We must ask several questions. Where did they get such courage? How could they face execution unafraid? Is it possible for us to be as fearless and bold as they?

The answers are found in a promise.

A Faithful Promise

Prior to the Babylonian captivity, Isaiah, a Hebrew prophet, ministered in Jerusalem. Isaiah recorded a promise that sounds eerily applicable to their situation.

> *But now, this is what the LORD says—he who created you, O Jacob, he who formed you, O Israel: "Fear not, for I have redeemed you; I have summoned you by name; you are mine. When you pass through the waters, I will be with you; and when you pass through the rivers, they will not sweep over you. When you walk through the fire, you will not be burned; the flames will not set you ablaze."*
>
> ISAIAH 43:1–2

Notice the last sentence: "When you walk through the fire, you will not be burned; the flames will not set you ablaze." Not only were they unburned; they did not even smell of smoke.

We all face fires in our lives. By "fires" I mean those dangerous, painful, terrifying situations and seasons when it seems there is no possible way to survive. Maybe it's a divorce, a very sick child, the death of a loved one, a lost job, a lawsuit, or a health issue. A fire can be anything that threatens to consume us.

Perhaps Isaiah's image of a flood is more appropriate for your situation. Like a flood, the pressure in your life builds higher and higher. It threatens to wash away everything you love or carry you away. It feels overwhelming.

Whether fires or floods, the Lord promises not to protect us *from* them but to protect us *in* them. We need not fear.

Fear Not, God Is with You in the Fire

Reading Isaiah's promise, I find special comfort in the phrase, "I will be with you." It is important to know that Jesus did not keep Shadrach, Meshach, and Abednego from going into the fire. They were thrown into it. But when they went into the fire, He went through it with them. They were not alone. And neither are you alone in your personal fires and floods.

Certainly, fires and floods have a way of making us feel isolated. The terrifying nature of out-of-control events leaves us feeling afraid and very alone. But God is there with us. This is His promise.

Fear Not, God Will Help You

The encouragement to "fear not" and the promise of God's presence in fearful events are reiterated elsewhere by Isaiah:

> *Do not fear, for I am with you; do not be dismayed, for I am your God. I will strengthen you and help you; I will uphold you with my righteous right hand.*
>
> ISAIAH 41:10

Here God does not merely promise to be with us but goes further by guaranteeing to help us. When the flames blaze or the floodwaters swirl, we definitely need His help. And He will help us.

Fear Not, I Will Hold You by the Hand

When the flames are crackling hungrily or the floodwaters are swirling crazily, it is easy to lose your sense of direction. Confusion reigns, compounding fear. This is when you need someone to hold your hand and walk you through the danger. Even better, the divine Someone will take you by the hand and guide you.

> For I am the LORD, your God, who takes hold of your right hand and says to you, Do not fear; I will help you.
>
> ISAIAH 41:13

Twenty-First-Century Supernatural Courage

She had lived in her apartment only two days. She got out of the car and walked to the door. Ashley Smith felt fear well up inside as a man came up out of the shadows behind her, stuck a gun to her head, and forced her inside.

The fear spread more deeply when she realized that she was the hostage of accused rapist and murderer Brian Nichols. Hours earlier, Nichols had escaped from an Atlanta courthouse, leaving a trail of blood and four dead in his wake. He just happened to show up at her door.

Smith, a twenty-six-year-old widow, was newly involved in a Celebrate Recovery group at a local church. There she sought help to overcome her battle with drug and alcohol addiction. Fearing rape and murder, Smith looked to God for courage.

As the night passed, she slowly won Nichols's confidence. Eventually she told him he needed to turn himself in and stop hurting people. She said that he needed to go to prison and share the Word of God with the prisoners.

The next morning, as Ashley Smith calmly served him pancakes, the murderer-rapist Brian Nichols looked at her and said that he believed she was an angel sent from God. He was lost and needed her to tell him to stop hurting people. Eventually he allowed her to leave. Shortly after, he surrendered to the police.

Newspapers across America reported that God gave Ashley Smith supernatural courage to overcome her fear in order to minister in an abnormally dangerous and unusual situation. She said, "I believe God brought him to my door so he would not hurt anyone else."[2]

A Final Encouragement

God can give you all you need to overcome your fear. If God can do it for Shadrach, Meshach, Abednego, and Ashley Smith, He can do it for you. That is His promise. Trust Him.

NOTES

[1] "The Hanging Gardens of Babylon," http://www.unmuseum.org/hangg.htm (June 13, 2005).

[2] "I Felt Really, Really Scared," CNN, March 15, 2005, http://www.cnn.com/2005/LAW/03/14/atlanta.hostage.

3

God's Promise of Divine Guidance
PROVERBS 3:5–6

Decisions—life is full of decisions. This reality starts to hit home near the end of high school when everyone begins to ask what you are planning to do after graduation. Unfortunately, if you answer, "Go to college," that just brings more questions. What college? What are you going to major in? And how are you going to pay for it?

A few years out of high school, the interrogations shift to career and marriage decisions. Then the questions revolve around having children and educating them. As we move along through life, we face constant career choices, housing options, church alternatives, ministry opportunities, and more. How do we decide?

Who you are today is the product of the decisions you have made in the past. Who you become tomorrow will be the result of the decisions you make today. How do you know whether you are making the right decisions? What do you do when you need direction? Fortunately, God's Word gives simple, clear, encouraging directions. It is all found in one of the most encouraging promises in the Bible:

> *Trust in the LORD with all your heart, and lean not on your own understanding; in all your ways acknowledge Him, and He shall direct your paths.*
>
> PROVERBS 3:5–6 NKJV

And He Shall Direct Your Paths

I love the last six words of this promise. They clearly and confidently proclaim that God will do His part. He *will* direct your paths, make your next step clear, and keep you on track. What a relief! It is possible to be in step with God, follow His plan, make the right decision, and know the next step. We do not have to fear that we will make a bad decision, miss what God has for us, and end up ruining our life.

When we feel overwhelmed by decisions, it is encouraging to know that God will do His part. But we have to do ours.

> *Trust in the LORD with all your heart, and lean not on your own understanding; in all your ways acknowledge Him.*

God's promise of direction is contingent upon our relationship with Him. We need to trust in, depend upon, and confide in Him from the bottom of our hearts. We can't go halfway. We must go the distance in relying on Him and not ourselves.

I am a big believer in getting good information and informed advice. When facing major decisions, I usually make a chart of pros and cons. But trusting in the Lord must supersede this. It must come ahead of our own understanding. Once we have gathered all the facts, sorted through all the advice, and examined our own hearts, we need to give it all over to God and follow Him, no matter what.

When we trust the Lord, He may lead us in paths that don't make much sense from a human perspective. We can't always figure it all out on our own. Remember, He is God and we are not. He can see further and more clearly into the future than we can. We may not accurately discern the next step, but He can see the whole path and process. We may not see upcoming potholes and land mines. We do not even fully understand our own deepest desires, but He does.

According to the promise, our responsibility in securing divine guidance includes knowing, recognizing, and acknowledging Him in all our ways. The Lord must be our focal point in the decision-making process. We must keep our ears open to His voice as we surrender our plans, priorities, dreams, and desires to Him. We must trust Him even if it doesn't immediately make sense to do so.

Trusting When It Doesn't Make Sense

My mentor, Dr. Elmer Towns, has had a long and fruitful career as a Christian leader and author. One day he had to trust God for direction when doing so didn't make sense. He had resigned his job as a teacher at a small Bible college in order to take a more prestigious job traveling and speaking to diverse denominations and at various conventions. In his mind, this was the perfect job—travel, influence, ministry to many churches, and national recognition. He saw it as a golden opportunity, but God had a different plan.

Dr. Towns wrote about his experience later:

I woke up violently in the middle of a black night. Something was wrong. I began to sweat all over.

"Lord, what is it?"

The Lord was in the room, not physically, nor did I see a vision, nor did I hear an audible voice; but I knew that the Lord was standing by my bed to warn me of something.... I prayed several times, "Lord, what are You trying to tell me?"

Then the Lord spoke to my heart, telling me not to take the new job I had just accepted...."Don't take the job," God kept saying.

As I wrestled with God, I reviewed my long-range priorities. I asked myself what those priorities were. I also considered my strongest gifts, and how I could make the greatest contribution with my life. I confessed to the Lord that I was ego driven. Ever since I was a freshman in Bible college, I wanted to be a Bible-college president. I had rationalized that the fame I would get from the new position of traveling for Sunday school would open up a door into a Bible college somewhere, sometime. But every time I talked to God, I got the same message: "Don't take the Sunday school job."

After a couple of hours of praying, I surrendered before the Lord. I told Him that fame was not important. I surrendered my reputation and even said, "God, if I never become a Bible-college president, Thy will be done!" [1]

By faith Elmer put God's will above his own even though it did not make sense. As he did this, he said that he felt God saying, "Don't take the Sunday school job. . .but within a year I will give you a college presidency." Elmer resigned the new prestigious position and continued teaching at the small Bible college. He also continued to trust in the Lord with all his heart and acknowledge His voice. And God did not forget His promise.

Six months later Elmer decided to drive home the long way, past his church. Seeing his pastor's car, he stopped and went in to chat. Soon into the conversation, he blurted out his heart's desire. "Someday, I want to be a Bible-college president."

While his pastor confirmed this dream as valid, based on Elmer Towns's drive and abilities, the phone rang. On the other end was a friend of the pastor. Oddly, the man asked, "Do you know where we can find a young man to be president of Winnipeg Bible College?"

The pastor grinned at Towns and said, "Your man is sitting right here."[2]
Later Towns wrote:

I could hear the voice of God whispering in my other ear, "See. . .I told you that if you wouldn't take the Sunday school job, I'd have a college presidency for you within a year."[3]

What had happened? Elmer Towns, a young Bible-college professor, had faced a decision. He made what he thought was a good decision to take a prestigious job traveling and speaking. God said, "No." Elmer surrendered his dreams to God, trusting God from the bottom of his heart. He obeyed God's voice even when it did not make sense. The Lord directed his paths and gave him the desire of his heart.

The Desires of Your Heart

Delight yourself also in the LORD, and He shall give you the desires of your heart.
Commit your way to the LORD, trust also in Him, and He shall bring it to pass.
                                                                    PSALM 37:4–5 NKJV

I believe that God gives us the desires of our hearts in a two-fold fashion. First, He writes them into our hearts—sometimes so deeply that we don't fully realize them. He gives us a burden, a passion, a vision of some good thing that we want to see occur in our lives in the future. He later makes them become a reality.

Long before Elmer's experience, God had etched into his heart the deep desire to be a Bible-college president. When the timing was right, God made it a reality. Between the promise and the fulfillment, Elmer did his part. He delighted himself in the Lord and committed his way to Him. He made the Lord his highest desire. He surrendered his future into God's hands, even when it did not make sense. And then God put all the pieces together to make it a wonderful reality. It all worked out according to God's plan for Elmer's future.

A Future and a Hope

"I know the plans I have for you," declares the LORD, "plans to prosper you and not to harm you, plans to give you hope and a future. Then you will call upon me and come and pray to me, and I will listen to you. You will seek me and find me when you seek me with all your heart."
                                                                    JEREMIAH 29:11–13

It is encouraging to know that God does not forget or abandon us. He has plans for us. His plans are positive and even include true prosperity. He promises to take care of us and not abandon us. He gives us hope and a future.

But in order to experience God's plans, we must call on Him and seek Him with all of our hearts. He must be the priority of our thoughts and the object of our trust. We need to make the Lord the focal point of our decision-making process.

A Final Encouragement

I do not know what decisions you are facing today, but the Lord does. He has not forgotten you. Your future is important to Him; He just wants to be trusted. He desires that you seek

Him and His will above all else. He may not wake you up in the middle of the night, but if you really trust Him, He will direct your path.

NOTES

[1] Elmer Towns, *God Encounters* (Ventura, CA: Regal Books), 2000, 16. Used by permission.
[2] Ibid., 17.
[3] Ibid., 18.

4

God's Promise of a Blessed Life
PSALM 1:1–3

What if you were promised true happiness? What if someone guaranteed you a stable life? What if they gave you the assurance of a productive, fruitful life and pledged that you would become strong and resilient through the dry seasons? What if they even promised prosperity on top of all the rest?

Would you believe it?

You should, because Someone has made such a promise and can deliver on it. But before we get to the promise, let me first tell you about a man who experienced it. His name was Ezra.

The Story of a Blessed Life

Ezra was a Jewish man living in Persia nearly five hundred years before the birth of Jesus. The Jews were in Persia because the Babylonian army had taken them captive years earlier and brought them to Babylon as slaves.

Ezra's heritage was that of a Hebrew priest. His job was to serve in the royal archives of the Persian Empire. As a scribe, he had access to the Word of God. Eventually his Bible study fanned into flame a burden for his people and a desire to return to Jerusalem.

Because Ezra's heart was aligned with God's Word and his passion linked with God's heart, God poured His blessing out on Ezra. Amazingly, when Ezra asked the pagan king to allow him to take a contingent of Jews back to Jerusalem, the king agreed. When Ezra asked the king to pay the bill for this journey, the king said yes. Even when Ezra asked to rebuild the Jewish temple and restore the Jewish community, the king supported him.

So Ezra led his band of pilgrims on the long and perilous five-month journey back to Jerusalem. In spite of the great odds against them, they arrived in Jerusalem safe and sound. There, Ezra succeeded in his massive undertakings to restore the community and rebuild the temple. He also helped Nehemiah rebuild the walls around the city. On top of that, he led the people in a time of revived obedience and renewed relationships with God. And if that was not enough, he wrote several books of the Bible.

The Jewish nation could have easily been assimilated into the pagan Persian culture if Ezra had not come on the scene. He gave his people back their city, their temple, their religion, and their distinctiveness. Humanly speaking, Jerusalem would have remained in shambles without the incredibly successful and visionary efforts of Ezra. He was a man who prospered on every level. By all accounts, he lived a blessed life.

One phrase repeatedly appears in the autobiographic story of Ezra's life. "The hand of the LORD my God was on me" (Ezra 7:6, 28; 8:18, 22, 31). Ezra knew that God richly blessed everything he did. He also knew why.

The Secret of a Blessed Life

While Ezra was writing the official records of the Jewish people, he revealed the secret of his success. Sometimes Ezra wrote about himself in the third person. Note carefully what he said.

> *The gracious hand of his God was on him. For Ezra had devoted himself to the study and observance of the Law of the LORD, and to teaching its decrees and laws in Israel.*
> EZRA 7:9–10

God blessed Ezra's life so richly because Ezra based his life so completely on God's Word. The secret of Ezra's success was the fact that he lived a Scripture-centered life.

Prior to returning to Jerusalem, restoring the Jewish community, and rebuilding the Jewish temple, Ezra had access to the Word of God. He had an opportunity few others enjoyed at that time; he could personally examine the Hebrew law and the records of the Hebrew kings. Ezra had access to all of the Word of God that had been written by that time. He did not take this privilege lightly. He devoted himself to the lifelong habit of studying, living, and teaching the Word of God.

Others had the same access to God's Word as Ezra enjoyed, but their names are long forgotten by history. Ezra did not just have access to the Word of God; he committed himself to it. He put his whole heart into it. It shaped him, including his values, decisions, attitudes, and actions. He invested his time, energy, and effort into studying, living, and teaching the Word of God. It was the secret of his success.

A Man Who Knew the Secret of Blessing

I had the privilege of attending college with Mark DeMoss. One day in chapel, Mark's father, Arthur DeMoss, was the guest speaker. Art and his wife, Nancy, were known for hosting evangelistic dinner parties to reach executives with the gospel of Jesus. A devoted Christian father and highly successful businessman, Art had founded a large insurance company.

He passed away a few years later, but his influence remains. The Arthur S. DeMoss Foundation supports evangelism through the *Power for Living* television commercials and book distributions. The foundation is also one of the largest philanthropic organizations in the country. DeMoss led a thriving Christian family that continues to make an impact for Christ. By any measure, Art DeMoss was a blessed, prosperous, successful man.

This plain, lively, straightforward Greek gentleman full of common sense and biblical advice immediately connected with the audience of students that day in chapel. During his talk, Art gave the threefold secret of his success, and I have never forgotten what he said. He told how, as a struggling young businessman, he discovered God's secret of success. His secret was his commitment to give God the first hour of every day, the first day of every week, and the first dime of every dollar. Soon he was out of debt and his business took off. More important, his family flourished and his ministry to executives was launched.

A decade later, Nancy Leigh DeMoss, Art's daughter and a bestselling Christian author in her own right, had this to say about her dad:

> As I look back on my dad's life, I see several reasons for the blessing of God on his life. First, he put God first above everything else. He believed that the greatest wealth was in knowing God. This priority was evident as he gave the first hour of every day to the study of God's Word and prayer. In the twenty-eight years that he knew Christ, there was not a single day when anything else came before that hour alone with God. He put God first in his business, in spite of the prevailing opinion that biblical ethics cannot be applied in the business world. God proved that His way works! [1]

Art DeMoss was incredibly blessed because he gave God the first hour of every day by studying God's Word and praying. He then spent the rest of the day trying to live and share what he had learned in the morning. Just like Ezra, he lived a life devoted to the Word of God, studying, living, and teaching it. And God blessed him for it.

Ezra's Secret of a Blessed Life

It is likely that Ezra collected the Psalms as we know them today. Of all 150 psalms, Ezra chose one in particular to lead the collection. It is foundational to the rest. I also believe that it was his personal favorite, because he obviously patterned his life after it. It contains God's promise of prosperity.

> Blessed is the man who does not walk in the counsel of the wicked or stand in the way of sinners or sit in the seat of mockers. But his delight is in the law of the LORD, and on his law he meditates day and night. He is like a tree planted by streams of water, which yields its fruit in season and whose leaf does not wither. Whatever he does prospers.
>
> PSALM 1:1–3

Computer geeks used to talk about GIGO. GIGO stands for garbage in, garbage out. Input is everything. A computer is a neutral tool. It does not create good or bad; it only spits out what has been entered.

In many ways, our minds are like computers. Input is everything. Our minds cannot produce good thoughts, feelings, or actions if they have not received good data. Psalm 1 promises blessing on the one who deliberately decides to monitor the data entering his or her mind. Here are ways to do this:

- *Limit Negative Input*

> Blessed is the man who does not walk in the counsel of the wicked or stand in the way of sinners or sit in the seat of mockers.
>
> PSALM 1:1

> How well God must like you—you don't hang out at Sin Saloon, you don't slink along Dead-End Road, you don't go to Smart-Mouth College.
>
> PSALM 1:1 THE MESSAGE

> Blessed (happy, fortunate, prosperous, and enviable) is the man who walks and lives not in the counsel of the ungodly [following their advice, their plans and purposes], nor stands [submissive and inactive] in the path where sinners walk, nor sits down [to relax and rest] where the scornful [and the mockers] gather.
>
> PSALM 1:1 AMPLIFIED

The word *blessed* describes a life of rich happiness and deep satisfaction. This blessed life begins when we accept responsibility to monitor what goes into our minds. We need to be keenly aware of the amount of negative, ungodly, or even neutral data we take in. We must carefully consider the people we spend time with, the music we listen to, the movies and television shows we watch, the books and magazine we read, and the Web sites we visit. The secret of the blessed life begins by restricting the amount of nonbiblical information we receive.

- *Love Positive Input*

But his delight is in the law of the LORD, and on his law he meditates day and night.
PSALM 1:2

Instead you thrill to GOD'S Word, you chew on Scripture day and night.
PSALM 1:2 THE MESSAGE

But his delight and desire are in the law of the Lord, and on His law (the precepts, the instructions, the teachings of God) he habitually meditates (ponders and studies) by day and by night.
PSALM 1:2 AMPLIFIED

The blessed life is built on the choice to fill our thoughts with the truth of God's Word. As God's Word saturates our minds, it will enhance our attitudes and guide our actions. The result will be the kind of life that God cannot help but bless.

Notice that the ones who are blessed not only delight in the Word; they act on their desire. They meditate on Scripture. They think it over, ponder its meaning, pray it out, study it more deeply, recall it often, and consider how to apply it. God's Word is the controlling lens by which everything else is viewed, the standard by which everything else is judged, the foundation on which everything else is added, and the compass by which every decision is made.

Blessed Prosperity

He is like a tree planted by streams of water, which yields its fruit in season and whose leaf does not wither. Whatever he does prospers.
PSALM 1:3

When a person truly lives a Scripture-centered life, he or she is like a tree planted by rivers of water—vital, stable, fruitful, durable, and successful.

A Final Encouragement
Ezra, Art DeMoss, and many others found that the secret to a blessed life is daily dedication to the Word of God. God's promise will work for you if you, too, will make a serious commitment to the Word of God.

NOTE

[1]Taken from *A Legacy of Giving: Lessons from the Life of a Father* by Nancy Leigh DeMoss, © 2003. Used by permission of Revive Our Hearts, www.reviveourhearts.com.

5

God's Promise of Bad Turning into Good
ROMANS 8:28

"I went to sleep with gum in my mouth and now there's gum in my hair and when I got out of bed this morning I tripped on the skateboard and by mistake I dropped my sweater in the sink while the water was running and I could tell it was going to be a terrible, horrible, no good, very bad day."

So begin the trials and tribulations of the irascible Alexander, as told by Judith Viorst in her book *Alexander and the Terrible, Horrible, No Good, Very Bad Day*. As poor Alexander's day progresses, he faces a barrage of bummers worthy of a bad country-and-western song. Alexander offers us a cranky retelling of that awful day of seemingly endless mishaps and misfortunes, including getting crushed in the middle seat of the car, a lunch sack with no dessert, a cavity at the dentist's office, sneakers with no stripes, lima beans for supper, nothing but kissing on television, being forced to sleep in the dreaded railroad-train pajamas, and the final indignity of being rejected by the cat that wants to sleep with his brother, Anthony, not with him. Alexander's conclusion is that it would be best to move to Australia.

The reason this book has remained a popular classic with children and adults for over thirty years is because we all have days like Alexander's, and we can't buy a break. Too often, such terrible, horrible, no good, very bad days pile up into awful, horrendous, rotten weeks. Too many of those dreadful weeks can leave us buried under an avalanche of discouragement and despair.

Bad things happen to all of us, even when we are trying to be good. Sometimes when we are living our best, we experience the worst. That's bad news. But the good news is that God is big enough to turn every tad of bad into good.

Unlike Alexander, we have a better option than moving to Australia. We have a wonderful book called the Bible filled with promises that inject high-octane encouragement into our deflated souls. Joseph experienced one of these promises. His life makes Alexander's terrible, horrible, no good, very bad day look like a picnic in paradise.

A Dream Turns into a Nightmare

Upside down. Suddenly, violently, unexpectedly, awfully, Joseph's life turned upside down. God reached down and, in one ugly event, jerked him out of his comfortable existence filled with bright potential and stuffed him into a coffin of slavery. Here's what happened:

Seventeen-year-old Joseph awoke one morning both excited and scared. God had given him a dream of becoming a leader. He had been given a glimpse of his destiny. Yet in his excitement and enthusiasm while sharing his dream, Joseph unwittingly offended his jealous older brothers. This was not good.

Soon, events turned ugly. Joseph was doing what his father had asked as he went to get a report on how his brothers were getting along grazing the family flocks. Little did Joseph suspect that their jealousy would lead them to kidnap him, throw him into an empty well, and sell him to slave traders headed for Egypt (see Genesis 37:1–28).

That is how his dream turned into a nightmare. It must have felt like a punch to the gut when Joseph, formerly the favorite son of a wealthy shepherd, woke to find himself a slave in Egypt.

But slowly his life got better—temporarily better, that is. Joseph's hard work and skill as a leader eventually elevated his status until he was put in charge of managing the household of Potiphar, Pharaoh's captain of the guard. Things were looking up when it all came crashing down.

A Slave Becomes a Convict

As I mentioned earlier, Potiphar's lonely wife made a series of unsuccessful passes at Joseph. Yet Joseph loved God and felt too much responsibility to his master to give in to her temptations. She was embarrassed and angry that he refused her advances, so she accused him of rape. The next thing he knew, Joseph was in prison and life looked uglier. Yet it got worse (see Genesis 39:1–20).

At first, his situation in prison contained a thread of promise. Joseph was again given an opportunity to develop as a leader. He also got to associate with some very intelligent and formerly high-ranking political prisoners (39:21–40:4). While in prison, Joseph had the unusual opportunity of predicting that the king's cupbearer would be restored to his former position. When he made this prediction, Joseph hoped that the cupbearer would air his unjust plight and plead his case to Pharaoh.

But when the cupbearer was restored to his position, he forgot Joseph (40:5–23).

Years went by.

Rejected by his family, sold into slavery, cast into prison, and now forgotten and left to rot behind bars, Joseph had one bad experience after another. But God promises to work all things—even very bad things—for the good of those who love Him and are called according to His purpose. That's just what happened to Joseph.

From Prisoner to Prime Minister

Two years after the cupbearer resumed his post, Pharaoh awoke in a cold sweat from a night of unusual dreams. None of his advisers could interpret these dreams. Eventually the cupbearer remembered Joseph and told Pharaoh about him. Pharaoh called for the prisoner, told him the dream, and waited. Skillfully, Joseph interpreted the dream and laid out a plan for dealing with its implications. Pharaoh was so impressed that he made Joseph the prime minister of the entire nation. From his position, Joseph prepared for the coming famine and saved the lives of many people, including his own family (41:1–57).

Joseph had traveled down a deep, difficult, and lonely road of kidnapping, slavery, and prison. Yet the boy with a dream of leading his family now led the number-one nation in the world! God had taken all of the bad events in Joseph's life and skillfully put them together like pieces in a puzzle to create a beautiful picture. Consider the following:

- Joseph learned more about leadership in Potiphar's house and as a prisoner than he would have learned in the comfort of his father's home. God had worked much that was bad to produce a greater good.

- Because he was in prison, Joseph met some royal officials and was thus strategically placed to be able to explain Pharaoh's dream. God again took something bad and used it to accomplish good.

- Because this all happened in Egypt, Joseph was able to serve in the most influential nation on earth. Yet again God turned much bad into more good.

None of the good things in Joseph's life could have happened without the bad. Like a skilled weaver, God used ugly events, evil people, unjust treatment, and long imprisonment to weave a beautiful tapestry. Like an elite chef, He cooked up a delicious stew out of the leftovers languishing in the pantry of Joseph's life. God turned horrendous bad into great good.

God Turns Harm into Good

Several years later Joseph confronted his guilty brothers. Most men in his position would have had them imprisoned or killed. They were deathly afraid of him, with good reason. But fortunately for them, Joseph saw the bigger picture and understood the ways of God.

> *His brothers then came and threw themselves down before him. "We are your slaves,"*
> *they said. But Joseph said to them, "Don't be afraid. Am I in the place of God? You*
> *intended to harm me, but God intended it for good to accomplish what is now being*
> *done, the saving of many lives."*
>
> GENESIS 50:18–20

Joseph was not bitter toward his brothers, because he saw that what they intended for bad God worked out for good for him, for them, and for the whole world. Multiplied good came out of misguided bad, Joseph was living the promise of Romans 8:28 two thousand years before it was written!

Bad into Good

> *And we know that in all things God works for the good of those who love him, who*
> *have been called according to his purpose.*
>
> ROMANS 8:28

This verse imparts confidence to us when things appear to be utterly awful. It tells us of the comprehensive power of God to work every detail in our lives, even the ugly ones, into something beautiful. It also encourages each of us to build a deep love life with God. After all, He has given us this promise.

We Need to Love Him

This promise is unbounded as to what God can use for good. But it is limited as to whom He'll bless in this way. His responsibility is to change trials into triumphs. Our responsibility is to be people who qualify for this promise. The promise of changing bad things into good is given only to those who love God.

Whole books have been written on what it means to love God. This is not the focus of this book. Remember, however, that when trouble comes, it is a reminder to reexamine your love relationship with God. It helps to realign our priorities, motives, and attitudes.

Advancing the Gospel

The apostle Paul recorded the promise of Romans 8:28. He certainly loved God. He also had plenty of bad experiences in his life. On one occasion, he and his missionary partner, Silas, were evangelizing the city of Philippi. After they set free a demon-possessed girl, authorities had Paul and Silas thrown in jail. The enemy certainly meant this for evil. But God used it for good. Through a divinely sanctioned earthquake, Paul and Silas were released, and the jailer and his entire household were converted to Christianity.

On several other occasions, Paul was persecuted. Because he saw the big picture of God's purpose and so understood that God can turn bad into good, he never whined. Instead, he repeatedly turned his persecutions into opportunities to share the gospel. While he was in shackles, Paul told the truth to a lynch mob, the leading Jewish religious body in Jerusalem, two Roman governors, and a king. None of these good opportunities would have happened without the bad event of his imprisonment. Also, as a prisoner Paul had the time to write several epistles he might not have written otherwise (Philippians, Ephesians, Colossians, Philemon, 2 Timothy, and Titus). On top of that, he led many of his guards to Christ.

Because the unique position of imprisonment enabled him to share the gospel, Paul actually rejoiced that good had come out of bad. From prison, he wrote to the Philippians the following:

> Now I want you to know, brothers, that what has happened to me has really served to advance the gospel.
>
> PHILIPPIANS 1:12

Paul understood that imprisonment is bad. But God used it for great good not only for him or the first-century believers, but also for the whole world. No wonder he recorded Romans 8:28, a great promise of God's ability to turn bad into good.

Bad to Good in the Twenty-First Century

It was early in the morning when Pastor Jamal's phone began to ring. Everyone had the same questions and the same bad news. Had he seen the sidewalks? Did he know what had happened? Did he have any idea who did it?

His young church was only a little over a year and a half old and was still working hard to be a positive voice for Christ on campus. Now this happened: Someone had taken chalk and written all over the sidewalks of the campus of Ohio State University the condemning words, "New Life Church Hates Gays!"

What do you do when falsely accused and helpless to do anything about it? You pray. So Jamal and others turned their problems into prayers, and God quickly turned evil into good. Whoever wrote the lying words must have been infuriated when they learned what soon happened.

First, in a feature article in the weekly student newspaper, the church was given the opportunity to set the record straight. No, they had not written that message on the sidewalk. The truth was they loved all people. They did not condone homosexuality, but they did not hate gays. They existed to help students find deeper meaning in life through a personal relationship with God.

Second, because their church name was smeared on the sidewalks, the church was featured in the school newspaper. This created a buzz in the student body and afforded New Life Church a presence on campus that would have taken them years to attain otherwise. Now everyone knew there was a new church on campus.

Third, the publicity drew a reporter with a camera to the church's service the following Sunday. There the pastor addressed the issue in a gracious and loving way, and guests witnessed vibrant Christianity in action.

Fourth, it rained the next day, washing the sidewalks clean. But this did not happen before God had turned evil into great good. Yay, God![1]

A Final Encouragement

If God could turn Joseph's big mess into greater good, He can do it for you. If He could turn Paul's imprisonment to something positive, He will do it for you. You don't have to be perfect or one of the spiritual superelite. You just need to love God. That's the promise.

Note

[1] Story used by permission of Jamal Jivanjee. Jamal is the lead pastor of Newlife–OSU, an exciting young church on the campus of the Ohio State University.

6
God's Promise of Providential Provision

We all have material needs. Food, shelter, and clothing are right there at the top of the list. Following close behind are things like furniture, drapes, sheets, blankets, and towels. It's great to have a job and a means of transportation to get there. Gas money and car insurance are important. Money for books, an occasional meal out, and a few toys for the kids is very nice. Health insurance is a big one. So is money for retirement. On and on the list goes.

I don't know what you really need or what you can live without, but God does, and He promises to provide all of your needs.

> *And my God will meet all your needs according to his glorious riches in Christ Jesus.*
> PHILIPPIANS 4:19

God promises to provide us with the necessities of life. This is a reassuring promise, because God is a reliable source. We need not worry if He can come through. He promises to provide for our needs according to His riches in glory.

Now, if I promised to meet all your needs according to my glorious riches, it would not be such a great promise. This is because I have limited riches, and the ones I have are not all that glorious. If your need exceeded the amount of money in my checking account, my promise would mean little and you'd be in trouble.

But God's promise to meet your needs is an awesome encouragement. God can meet your needs and everyone else's, because He has infinite riches in Christ Jesus. Money is no obstacle to God. If He wanted, He could snap his fingers and bury you in hundred-dollar bills (which sounds like a lot of fun)! He could blink His eyes and surround you with gold, silver, and diamonds (also fun). Believe me, God is able to supply all of your needs.

The Condition for God's Provision
Paul promised the Philippians that God would meet their needs because of their previous generosity to those in God's service. The promise of Philippians 4:19 follows on the heels of his thanking them in verses 14–18 for giving to his needs. They had sent a care package to him when he was in a prison in Rome.

They were not wealthy people giving out of their abundance. They were persecuted Christians, living in a town in the midst of an economic depression. Yet when the opportunity was presented to give to Paul, they did it.

God wants to pull our eyes off ourselves and focus them on others. We must not forget that others need us. When we meet the needs of others, God assumes the obligation to meet our needs. The point is this: The key to receiving is giving.

The Key to Receiving Is Giving
Philippians 4 is not the only place God promises to provide the needs of those who give to others. A few of my favorite promises include these:

> *He who gives to the poor will lack nothing.*
> PROVERBS 28:27

"Give, and it will be given to you. A good measure, pressed down, shaken together and running over, will be poured into your lap. For with the measure you use, it will be measured to you."

LUKE 6:38

He who is kind to the poor lends to the LORD, and he will reward him for what he has done.

PROVERBS 19:17

Seventeenth-Century Generosity

In the latter part of the seventeenth century, August H. Francke founded an orphanage to care for homeless children. One day, when Francke desperately needed funds to carry on his work, a destitute Christian widow came to his door begging for a gold coin. Because of his financial situation, he politely but regretfully told her he couldn't help her.

Disheartened, the woman began to weep. Moved by her tears, Francke asked her to wait while he went to his room to pray. After seeking God's guidance, he felt that the Holy Spirit wanted him to change his mind. Trusting the Lord to meet his own needs, he gave her the money.

Two mornings later, he received a letter of thanks from the widow. She explained that because of his generosity she had asked the Lord to shower the orphanage with gifts.

That same day Francke received twelve gold coins from a wealthy lady and two more from a friend in Sweden. He thought he had been amply rewarded for helping the widow, but he was soon informed that the orphanage was to receive five hundred gold pieces from the estate of Prince Lodewyk Van Wurtenburg! Francke found that God meets the needs of those who meet the needs of others.

A Twenty-First-Century Provision

I love stories about God providing for His believers; I could tell dozens of them. However, as I was writing this chapter, I was convicted that I had recently been lax in living by faith. Apart from tithing, I had not given much away lately and very little to the poor. As I was thinking about my lack of extra-generous giving, my phone rang. On the other end was a young man who had come to America from Africa for an education and a job. Yet things had not worked out for him. He had no work visa and was in desperate straits. His only income came from singing in churches. He told me the next day he was hoping to meet with a lawyer who, for a small fee, would help him get his visa.

Without thinking, I said, "I can't talk now; I'm late for an appointment. But I'll drop by and see you tonight. I have some money for you." Excitedly, he gave me his address and said he'd be waiting. When I hung up the phone, a wave of regret swept over me.

"Uh-oh," I thought. "What money will I give him?" I had just left a meeting where I took a 50 percent pay cut because I believed God wanted me to follow a new direction in my ministry. I have three teenage boys. They are expensive just to feed, let alone provide everything else they require. I would need all the money I could get. Besides, I had been on the go nonstop for two weeks, and that night was to be my first night home in a long time. Then I remembered that the week before I had earned a couple of hundred dollars by selling my books at a pastors' conference. I thought, "I'll give him that money."

As the time approached to visit him, I felt more and more exhausted. I thought of several good excuses for not going, but no legitimate reasons. So I dragged myself out the door and drove across town toward the apartment complex where the young man was staying with friends.

I got lost several times trying to find the right apartment building in the dark. Eventually I found the building but did not have a key to get through the secured door. I did not know the name of the person he was staying with, and I had forgotten his phone number.

I went back to my car and prayed. "Lord, if You want me to see this man and give him the money, I need to get into the building. If You don't provide me a way within the next five minutes, I am going home and going to bed."

After a few minutes, a beat-up car pulled up near the door of the building. A scraggly young man carrying a case of beer got out. I jumped out of my car and walked to the entrance. I hoped to nonchalantly walk to the door and get inside before it could swing closed in my face.

I missed it by a tenth of a second.

"Lord, help me," I whispered as I banged on the door.

The young man turned and saw me. He shook his head no.

"Wait," I said, "I need your help."

He just smirked.

"I am a pastor, and I need to visit a man on the third floor. He is from Africa, and I don't think he understands how these security systems work."

He glared into my eyes. Then he opened the door for me and walked off, shaking his head.

I bolted up the stairs and banged on the door. My friend met me and let me in. He began to tell me how glad he was to see me and again recounted all he had gone through. After a while, I couldn't keep my eyes open. So I stood up and handed him the two hundred dollars. He hugged me, danced around, and walked me to my car. I went home and went to bed. I was glad I had been able to give the money to someone who needed it more than I did.

The next morning my phone rang. A pastor who had been at the conference the week before was on the line. He had bought my book and had read it. Now he wanted to order a copy for each of his church leaders. He said that above my costs, he'd send me two hundred dollars.

$943.00!

As a pastor, I am obligated to teach the Word of God, even the parts I do not necessarily like. A few years ago when my children were small and money was quite tight, I was struggling to write a Sunday morning teaching on the subject of giving to God.

Later that week I received a letter in the mail from a Virginia bank in a town where my wife and I had lived when we first got married. It stated that they were closing my old account and sending me the money. Enclosed with the letter was a check. I was certain I had closed all my accounts with that bank when we had moved to Ohio. So I called the bank, and they said that the money was definitely mine.

I jumped up, ran into my study, and yanked down our home budget book. My heart pounded. I was eager to see exactly how much we had given above our tithe that year. We had given $943.00.

Slowly I turned the check over to read the amount. It was $943.00!

A Final Encouragement

The key to receiving is giving. God can and will meet your needs. He has promised to do this and many believers have found it to be true. You can, too.

7

God's Promise of Eternal Life
JOHN 3:16

If you died today, are you sure you would go to heaven? What would you say if God were to ask you, "Why should I allow you into heaven?" You would want to be confident you had the right answers to those two questions.

Wrestling with Doubt

If you had asked Thomas those questions, he probably would have been stumped. With the high-powered mind of an engineer, Thomas wrestled with doubt. He would never think of committing to something lightly. He needed evidence. He needed to be sure.

This man enjoyed the rare privilege of being one of Jesus Christ's twelve closest traveling companions. With his own eyes, Thomas had seen Jesus do what no other man had ever done. He witnessed Jesus miraculously healing the sick, feeding the hungry, freeing the demonized, calming the storm, and even raising the dead. Such displays of deity kept Thomas's doubts at bay. He was starting to truly believe that Jesus was Messiah. However, his confidence was violently crushed one dark afternoon.

Jesus, the man who claimed to be the Messiah, had been arrested, beaten, and tried. Beyond that, Jesus had appeared to helplessly allow evil men to drive spikes through His hands and feet into a cross.

Thomas's mind could not accept the data. It did not make sense.

"If Jesus really was God, why was He powerless to stop this brutal injustice? No God would allow mere men to take His life. So maybe Jesus really wasn't Messiah. Maybe it was some sort of magic."

Thomas's old friend Doubt dogged his thoughts and flooded his heart. He began to wonder why he had wasted those three years following a fake. Then some of Thomas's friends claimed to have seen Jesus resurrected from the dead.

"Right," Thomas thought. "I'll believe that when I see it for myself and not a second before. Actually, seeing it is not enough. I'll believe it when I literally stick my fingers in those nail marks in His hands. I will not be fooled."

Thomas Accepts Reality

One week later, Thomas was eating with some of his friends. They had kept the door locked because they were afraid that the same people who had arrested and killed Jesus might do the same to them. Suddenly the bizarre occurred. Jesus walked right into the room through the closed, locked door as though it was nothing out of the ordinary. He even smiled and greeted them. Then Jesus went to Thomas and said:

> "Put your finger here; see my hands. Reach out your hand and put it into my side. Stop doubting and believe."

JOHN 20:27

That was more than enough for Thomas. All his doubt was gone when he touched those nail-pierced hands of Jesus. He looked at Jesus and said, "My Lord and my God!"

Then Jesus told him:

"Because you have seen me, you have believed; blessed are those who have not seen and yet have believed."

JOHN 20:29

Your Greatest Need

Your greatest need is for eternal life. It is not just your greatest spiritual need; it is your greatest need, period. Whether one thousand years from now or this very second, the most significant issue in your life is whether you have eternal life.

"For God so loved the world that He gave His only begotten Son, that whoever believes in Him should not perish but have everlasting life."

JOHN 3:16 NKJV

God really loves you. You are more than a random gathering of highly evolved atoms. You are a person God loves and for whom Jesus died. You are someone God wants to spend eternity with. You are a candidate for the gift of eternal life.

The Bad News about the Good News

The good news is that God wants to give you eternal life. The bad news is that without it you are in big trouble. The Bible is very clear about our condition without God.

Fact: We have all committed sins and fallen short of God's glory.

For all have sinned and fall short of the glory of God.

ROMANS 3:23

The word used for "sinned" in Romans 6:23 means to miss the mark. It was a first-century archery term that described failing to hit the bull's-eye. The moral, spiritual bull's-eye is God's glory. It is perfect holiness. Unfortunately, none of us are perfect, none holy. Somewhere along the way we have lied, or stolen, or cheated, or sworn, or failed to treat someone with love, or lost our temper, or gossiped, or slandered. We have been greedy, or jealous, or envious, or lustful, or lazy. Even when we try hard to be good, we just can't consistently pull it off.

Let's say that getting into heaven requires that we hit the bull's-eye of righteousness. Now, maybe you have lived a better life than I have and the arrow of your morality hits closer to the bull's-eye than mine. But the bottom line is this: Unless you are perfect, you have sinned; you have missed the bull's-eye.

Fact: Sin has a steep price tag.

For the wages of sin is death.

ROMANS 6:23

The price tag of sin is death. When the Bible uses the term *death* here, the concept is separation. Physical death is the separation of one's soul from the body. Spiritual death is the separation of the soul from God. Eternal death is separation of a soul from God forever.

If we don't have eternal life, we look forward to eternal death. We face an eternity of separation from God. God is perfectly holy. We are not. Our sin creates a great chasm separating us from God. On our own, we have no hope of bridging the chasm to get to God and eternal life.

But Jesus did it for us.

The Good News about the Bad News

Fact: Jesus never sinned.

This fact makes Jesus unique in all of history and in the entire universe. As the Son of God, He is sinless. Only Jesus lived a perfectly moral, righteous, holy life. Only Jesus hit the bull's-eye of righteousness. Only Jesus fulfilled the glory of God. Only Jesus never sinned. Only Jesus did not deserve to die.

Fact: Jesus died to pay for our sins.

I am a Christian and would never consider being a Muslim, a Buddhist, or anything else because Jesus provides the only way to get to God. When Jesus died for my sins, He bridged the gap between God and me, thereby making it possible for me to receive eternal life.

I deserve to experience death. He did not deserve to experience death. Yet because God loves me, Jesus died for me. Now I have eternal life—a new spiritual relationship in God's family that begins at the moment of salvation. Here are the facts about eternal life:

- *It's new.* Jesus also called it being "born again" or "born anew."
- *It's spiritual.* It is not a physical birth, but a birth of the spirit.
- *It's a relationship.* Prior to salvation, our relationship with God is distant because of sin. He is under no obligation to bless us or hear our prayers. We are called enemies of God. Our sin is viewed as a barrier between God and us. Yet after we are saved, the barrier is torn down. We are born anew into God's family. He is no longer our judge declaring us guilty but our Father declaring us loved.
- *It begins at the moment of saving faith.* The clock of eternity does not begin the moment we die; it begins the moment we believe. The clock of eternal life begins the moment we are saved, born again, not the moment we die physically.

"You Gotta Believe"

The condition for receiving eternal life is belief in Christ. We believe *in* Him, not facts *about* Him. It is not enough to believe there was a man named Jesus who once lived in Israel, or that Jesus was a good man, or that Jesus was the Son of God, or even that Jesus was the Son of God who died on the cross to pay for sins. We must believe *in* Him. Many people believe things *about* Jesus but do not have eternal life. James 2:19 states that even demons believe and tremble, but they certainly do not have eternal life. In order to have eternal life, you must believe *in* Christ. What does this mean? The following story will help make it clear.

You Must Get in the Wheelbarrow

One summer vacation, our family visited Niagara Falls. The falls span 1,060 feet and stand at a height of 176 feet. 150,000 gallons of water pour over the falls every second. They are so large you can hear the water pounding over them several miles away.

Across one of the main streets of Niagara is a statue of a man on a tightrope. His name was Jean Francois Gravelet, the great Blondin. He was a professional artist and showman trained in the great tradition of the European circus. At age thirty-one, he came to America and announced that he would cross the gorge of the Niagara River on a tightrope.

On June 30, 1859, Blondin became the first man to walk across Niagara Falls on a tightrope. But he did more than that. He eventually crossed the falls several times in a variety of ways: blindfolded, on a bicycle, with his hands and feet manacled, and even with his manager on his back.

Yet none of these stunts compares with Blondin's greatest feat. One day Blondin put a wheelbarrow on his tightrope and asked the crowd if they believed he could wheel it across. They yelled, "We believe!"

He wheeled it across and back. Then he called out, "Who believes I can put a man in my wheelbarrow and wheel him across?"

The excited crowd yelled, "We believe."

So he looked into the faces of that crowd and said, "Who will be first?"[1]

Blondin was not asking the crowd what they believed *about* him and his wheelbarrow. He was asking if they believed *in* him. Eternal life is not a matter of standing on the sidelines with nice beliefs *about* Jesus. It is a matter of believing *in* Him. You will never cross over into eternal life until you get in the wheelbarrow.

If you were in the crowd that day, you could cross the Niagara by having the faith to get in the wheelbarrow. In the same way, you receive eternal life by having the faith to get in Jesus' wheelbarrow. That is, you must have faith in Him as the complete payment for your sins.

I wonder, have you ever really believed *in* Jesus? God loves you so much that He sent His Son to bridge the gorge to provide the only way for you to experience eternal life.

A Final Encouragement

If you died today, are you sure you would experience eternal life in heaven? If not, you can be. Do you need to get into Jesus' wheelbarrow? If so, it is a matter of faith. Would you express your faith right now by calling upon Jesus to be your Savior? You can do it by honestly praying this simple prayer:

> *Dear Jesus,*
>   *I admit that I am not perfect. I have sinned. Forgive me. I do not deserve eternal life. I have fallen short of Your standard of righteousness. I admit I need a Savior. I believe that You took my place and died for my sin. Now I personally commit myself to You. I'm getting in the wheelbarrow. I trust You and You alone as my Savior.*

NOTE

[1]"The First Tightrope Walker, Jean Francois Blondin" by the Niagara Parks Commission in Niagara, http://www.niagara-info.com/historic. htm#Section1c (August 25, 2005).

8

God's Promise of Sufficient Grace
2 Corinthians 12:9

On August 18, 1991, I woke up with a horrible case of the flu, and it never completely went away. I lost eighteen pounds in three weeks. I felt continual pain in my joints and muscles. Any inkling of cold air made it all the worse.

Then there was the giant headache that refused to go away. Also, I found that I was suddenly allergic to all sorts of new things. Catching a whiff of perfume was like getting hit in the head by a two-by-four. The smell of freshly cut grass made me feel awful all over.

Frustratingly, my cognitive capacities would randomly short-circuit. I could form words in my mind but had great difficulty getting them to come out of my mouth. This is not a good thing for a pastor who speaks in four services every weekend.

Strangely, about five o'clock every evening, I would get a sore throat and begin to feel waves of despair crashing on the beach of my soul. Because I ached so much, it was difficult to sleep for more than a few hours at a time.

Yet I gladly would have kept all of those maladies to be rid of the constant, devastating fatigue. Formerly a morning person, I woke up exhausted every day, and this only got worse as the day wore on. There were times when the highlight of my day was to crawl down the hall to the bathroom. Many nights I'd lie in bed concentrating all my strength just to turn over.

At that same time, my three boys were all under the age of five. They could not understand why Dad would not play with them like he used to, why he could not go out and make a snowman.

Meanwhile, my church needed my leadership. Yet I barely had the energy to get to the office, let alone provide significant leadership.

Worst of all was the guilt. My wife needed me to help around the house and with the children. Yet it was all I could do to take care of myself and try to keep working. I hated to see my exhaustion wearing her out.

I suffered like this for ten months before I sought help. I kept thinking that I'd wake up the next day feeling better, but I never did. I went through a wearisome battery of tests, doctors, and diagnoses.

Eventually I was diagnosed with chronic fatigue immunodeficiency syndrome—CFIDS—an illness few people understood and no one was sure how to treat.

I was frustrated at being the slave of my pain and fatigue. I was a goal-oriented person not able to pursue any goal beyond survival. I was perturbed and sad because I did not have the strength to get off the couch to play with my boys. I was so disappointed to see how my fatigue was exhausting my wife.

I hate to admit that my frustration was focused on the Lord. Day after day, I asked for deliverance, for an explanation, for a time frame for my agony. Yet day after day, week after week, month after month, the only response I received from God was silence—deafening silence.

I am glad that I did not quit reading my Bible or praying. Several encouraging Bible promises and personalities kept me going. I wore out the book of Job, finding some comfort that his adversity was greater than mine and that his story had a happy ending. I practically memorized the story of Joseph's shocking kidnapping, enslavement, and false imprisonment.

I found strength reading of innocent David, running for his life from Saul and eventually becoming king. I read his journal, the book of Psalms, over and over again.

However, I was especially encouraged by the words of the apostle Paul. Even though he experienced extreme sufferings, he only benefited from them. He never let his pain distort his perspective or steal his joy. He obviously had discovered a secret I needed to learn, a promise I needed to apply.

Paul's Battle with a Thorn

Near the end of his second letter to the church at Corinth, Paul pulls back the veil and gives us a wonderful glimpse into his interior life. In doing so, he reveals his battle with what he refers to as a thorn in the flesh.

> *To keep me from becoming conceited because of these surpassingly great revelations, there was given me a thorn in my flesh, a messenger of Satan, to torment me. Three times I pleaded with the Lord to take it away from me. But he said to me, "My grace is sufficient for you, for my power is made perfect in weakness." Therefore I will boast all the more gladly about my weaknesses, so that Christ's power may rest on me. That is why, for Christ's sake, I delight in weaknesses, in insults, in hardships, in persecutions, in difficulties. For when I am weak, then I am strong.*
>
> 2 CORINTHIANS 12:7–10

There is much for the soul in these four verses of Scripture. I was encouraged by several discoveries.

Even Paul experienced "a thorn in [his] flesh, a messenger of Satan" (12:7). No one is exempt from suffering. It is an unavoidable aspect of the human condition.

God can use such thorns to restrain us from pride (12:7). Since pride blocks our relationship with God (James 4:6), anything that blunts the edge of pride is beneficial.

Even a spiritual giant like Paul received unanswered prayers (12:8). You and I may have thorns, but this does not necessarily mean we are not spiritual.

Such thorns remind us that life ultimately is not about us (12:9). Life is about the Lord, His grace, and His power.

Thorns help us boast in and depend upon God (12:10). They also help us find our strength in the Lord (2 Corinthians 12:9).

The fact that the nature of Paul's thorn is unspecified makes his experience applicable to each of us at our point of pain. Scholars love to debate what Paul was talking about when he spoke of his thorn in the flesh. Was it a physical problem with his eyes? Was it a demon? Was it a divorce by an unbelieving wife?

We don't know the answer to this, because the Bible does not say. We are not supposed to know. Whether our battle is physical, spiritual, or relational in nature is not the issue. The issue is that God's grace is sufficient. His grace is sufficient for any and every thorn in anyone's flesh.

Grace Is Found in Weakness

> *"My grace is sufficient for you, for my power is made perfect in weakness."*
>
> 2 CORINTHIANS 12:9

Paul asked God to remove the thorn. God said, "No." Paul asked again. God said, "No." The third time Paul received the same answer, "No." Why is this?

God said, "No," because God wanted Paul to learn that His grace was sufficient *even when* Paul suffered with a thorn in the flesh. God's grace is not just available on the easy days. It is especially real when it is needed the most. God wanted Paul and countless others through Paul's words to realize the reality of God's grace. It runs deeper, reaches higher, stretches broader, and lasts longer than any thorn Satan can ever send our way.

Our defining moment as unbelievers occurred when we understood that God's grace is greater than any sin. Our joyous breakthrough as Christians occurs when we understand that God's grace is greater than any thorn.

I have served as a pastor of God's flock for many years and have had the privilege of ministering to people when they had great need, severe pain, and deep sorrow. Many times I have walked out of a hospital room, a funeral home, a cemetery, or even a police station and thought, "Wow. A normal person would be knocked out cold by this agony. I have just left the presence of a saint who has discovered God's secret of sufficient grace."

A Final Encouragement

I don't know specifically why God is allowing that unremoved thorn in your life. However, I do know that His grace is sufficient to see you through. I also know that His grace is able to use the pain and suffering caused by your thorn to wonderfully bless your life. Trust Him.

9

God's Promise of Supernatural Support
2 CHRONICLES 16:9

There are times when waves of problems threaten to capsize our small boat. Or, to use another image, there are times when troubles hound us like a pack of angry dogs. These are times when we face an impossible set of circumstances and need supreme strength; otherwise, we are not going to make it.

I have three quick questions for you to consider at such times:

1. How big is God? The answer: Big enough!
2. How strong is God? The answer: Strong enough!
3. How do you get God to show His might on your behalf? The answer: It is a matter of the heart.

Just ask Asa.

Holding Back on God

Asa was a prince, the son of Abijah, king of Judah. In his father, Asa saw a man who struggled to give the Lord all of his heart. At times Abijah did well. He rebuked those in idolatry and refused to turn his back on God. When he faced a battle, he completely depended on the Lord, and God blessed him for it (2 Chronicles 13:6–18). Yet on other occasions he was a disloyal, halfhearted follower of the Lord who kept idols in the land and held back on God. Eventually God withheld His support, and Abijah's reign was filled with war (1 Kings 15:3). In a sense, he was one man with two hearts. Most of us can identify with him.

All Out for God

After observing his father's struggles, Asa launched his reign as king with a wholehearted commitment to the Lord. Beyond merely rebuking those with idols, he tore down altars to foreign gods and cut down their images. He commanded his people to worship and obey the Lord. When the Ethiopian army came to invade his land, Asa turned his problem into prayer. God liked what He saw in Asa's heart and supported him with a glorious, miraculous triumph (2 Chronicles 14:11–13).

The Lord promised to continue His supernatural support of Asa as long as Asa maintained his wholehearted devotion to the Lord (2 Chronicles 15:2, 7). And Asa did this. He destroyed idols, rebuilt altars, gave gifts, and made sacrifices. He also led his people to pledge their wholehearted allegiance to the Lord. So the Lord protected them.

> They entered into a covenant to seek the LORD, the God of their fathers, with all their heart and soul. . . . They took an oath to the LORD with loud acclamation, with shouting and with trumpets and horns. All Judah rejoiced about the oath because they had sworn it wholeheartedly. They sought God eagerly, and he was found by them. So the LORD gave them rest on every side. . . . Asa's heart was fully committed to the LORD all his life.
>
> 2 CHRONICLES 15:12–17

Asa gave God his whole heart, and God gave Asa His full support. It was a sweet arrangement as long as it lasted.

Wholehearted No More

It was simple, really. As long as Asa was totally committed, the Lord blessed him with supernatural support and he experienced victory, peace, and prosperity. But as time went by, Asa let his defenses down and allowed outside pressure to push him to drop his all-out commitment to God.

This is how it happened. Judah, Asa's kingdom, lived in constant military threat by Israel—a part of the Jewish nation that had turned from God years earlier. Instead of living in wholehearted dependence on the Lord, Asa came up with a scheme. He would persuade the nation to the north of Israel, Aram, to attack Israel for him, thereby drawing their attention from Judah. So he sent the king of Aram money to attack Israel. Initially, Asa's plot worked. But God was not pleased. He sent a sobering message to Asa:

> "Because you relied on the king of Aram and not on the LORD your God, the army of the king of Aram has escaped from your hand. . . . When you relied on the LORD, he delivered them into your hand."
>
> 2 CHRONICLES 16:7–8

God told him that the small success of his scheme had cost him the opportunity to do away with his enemies once and for all. God also reminded him that when he previously relied on the Lord, he won great victories. Now the hand of the Lord's protection and peace would be removed, and Judah would have to contend with both Israel and Aram.

Then God made a piercing observation and a stunning promise. Read this carefully in the translations given:

> "For the eyes of the LORD range throughout the earth to strengthen those whose hearts are fully committed to him. You have done a foolish thing, and from now on you will be at war."
>
> 2 CHRONICLES 16:9

> "For the eyes of the LORD move to and fro throughout the earth that He may strongly support those whose heart is completely His."
>
> 2 CHRONICLES 16:9 NASB

> "For the eyes of the LORD run to and fro throughout the whole earth, to show Himself strong on behalf of those whose heart is loyal to Him. In this you have done foolishly; therefore from now on you shall have wars."
>
> 2 CHRONICLES 16:9 NKJV

Good News: Strength on Our Behalf

The promise is this: God will strongly support, strengthen, and show Himself strong for those whose hearts are wholly committed to Him. Wow! That is good news. Simply put, God's promise to us is that His supernatural strength will work on our behalf.

Since nothing is too big for God, and nothing is too complicated for Him to understand, then no problem is outside His capabilities to resolve. Think of it. The almighty, all-knowing, awesome God is on our side. He will help us. He will hold us up. He will roll up His sleeves and flex His muscles on our behalf. It does not get any better than that!

No problem you are facing is too big for Him. No situation you are in is too complex. He is big enough. He can handle it. He is God. He will give you His full support.

What a relief! This promise is such an encouragement. It lifts our burdens.

There have been times in my life when the Lord was obviously supporting me. Knotted issues, massive problems, and impossible situations were resolved because God was clearing the way. I also have experienced times when I was trying to handle it all in my strength and wisdom. There was no powerful hand pushing the obstacles aside. There was no all-knowing mind solving the problem. The results were not pretty.

Anytime He chooses, God can accomplish everything and anything better, bigger, and faster than we can. He is God. We are not. We need Him. The extent to which we trust in, depend on, and commit to Him is the extent to which we see His strength working on our behalf.

There's a Catch

Look again at the promise: "The eyes of the LORD range throughout the earth to strengthen those whose hearts are fully committed to him."

Such a sensational promise has a stringent requirement. God's full support of us is dependent on our full commitment to Him. The promise is that the Lord God is looking to strongly support those whose hearts are fully committed, completely devoted, and absolutely loyal to Him. He will do His part *if* we do our part. This means we must have no other gods crowding our hearts. We cannot put our ultimate reliance on persons or things other than God. And we cannot hold back any portion of our hearts from Him.

Yet sometimes our commitment to Him wavers. As a result, His strong support on our behalf disappears. Then trouble comes. Just ask Asa.

God's Support Will Abandon the Heart That Abandons Him

> *"For the eyes of the LORD range throughout the earth to strengthen those whose hearts are fully committed to him. You have done a foolish thing, and from now on you will be at war."*

> 2 CHRONICLES 16:9

Instead of seeking the Lord's aid, Asa had given his trust to the king of Aram. This was foolish. No king, especially the king of Aram, could possibly surpass, let alone compare to, God. Foolishly, Asa acted as though he did not need God, so God left him alone. Without the protecting hand of God, peace was forfeited and problems set in. Unlike the early days of Asa's reign, the last years of his reign were marked with war (16:9). He was full of anger (16:10). And his feet were afflicted with disease (16:11). But it need not be that way for us.

Supernatural Support Today

The other day my good friend Pastor Chris Brown told me how God proved Himself strong on his behalf as he launched a brand-new church. This is his story:

On the first day of July of 1999, two committed staff members, a core group of twenty-five adults, and myself were planning to plant New Life Community Church. Our plan was to meet in a local elementary school, and we were discussing an interesting dilemma. How do we transport all the equipment and materials for a church worship gathering each week, fifty-two weeks a year?

The answer was found in an ingenious system that included a twenty-four-foot trailer, fifteen cases, and a Suburban truck. Wonderful! Not quite. We needed forty-five thousand dollars for the system, of which twelve thousand dollars was due as a deposit by the first week of July. Great. . .we only had two thousand dollars in the bank.

After some discussion, our entire group agreed: this wasn't a want, it was a need, and we needed to order the system. So we did the only logical thing—we dropped to our knees and prayed, asking God for ten thousand dollars by the end of the week.

We ended the gathering and I started the drive home, trying to figure out a way to ask my wealthiest friends for money. But God had His own plans.

The first clue came when I stopped by the post office box and discovered a check for one thousand dollars. "Okay," I thought, "we're on the way, but what about the rest? We still need nine thousand dollars." Sunday night I returned home to find an envelope with my name on it. As I opened the envelope, it contained nothing but a single check. No note, no explanation, just a check. . .for nine thousand dollars!

I gave thanks to God. I knew New Life was God's church from that day forward, and that the Lord was with us and would strongly support us. We simply needed to remain committed to and dependent upon Him.[1]

A Final Encouragement

When we commit everything of ourselves to God, He commits all of Himself to us. This is a great deal! He will strongly support those who are dedicated to Him. He did it for Asa, Chris Brown, New Life Community Church, and countless others. He will do it for you.

NOTE

[1] Used by permission of Chris Brown. Chris is the lead pastor of New Life Community Church, an outstanding young church in Canal Winchester, Ohio.

10

God's Promise of Full Forgiveness
1 JOHN 1:9

It's an all-too-familiar story. Israel's King David was in his midlife crisis. After years of working hard to follow God and to establish the kingdom of Israel, David let down his defenses. Like too many leaders, he began to believe his press clippings. He did not think he needed to be accountable to anyone or obey the same rules as everyone else. Predictably, such arrogance set him up for a downfall.

David, as king, should have been out leading his nation. Instead, he stayed home. Bored and restless, he wandered on the terrace of the roof of his palace one night. There temptation awaited him in the shapely form of another man's wife. Arrogance and desire welled up within him. Lust overpowered his heart, and he took steps to commit adultery with Bathsheba.

But it did not stop there. Pride took the upper hand, and David attempted to cover his sin by having Bathsheba's husband killed. After that, he denied his sin by going on as though nothing had happened.

But something had happened—something big, bad, and significant.

David had sinned.

Guilt and shame don't just go away on their own. For David, they grew stronger day by day. His inner anger and disappointment with himself bred deep depression. Unresolved guilt hung over him like a black cloud. His once-passionate relationship with God was only a shell. Silently, David was drowning in a dark sea of guilt and shame. Later he recalled that draining, dreadful, painful period with these words:

> *When I kept silent, my bones wasted away through my groaning all day long. For day and night your hand was heavy upon me; my strength was sapped as in the heat of summer.*
>
> PSALM 32:3–4

You Are the Man

Finally, God stopped waiting for David to act and took things into His own hands. In His great mercy and grace, the Lord sent Nathan, a prophet, to confront David about his sins. I imagine that Nathan fully expected to be killed for his obedience. After all, if David had Bathsheba's husband killed, what would he do to a man who confronted him with his sin?

Nathan was very wise in his approach. Rather than sticking his bony prophet's finger in David's face, he told David a story of a poor man who owned just one beloved lamb and of a rich man who had many sheep. When a guest dropped in to visit, the rich man wanted to feed him well. But rather than use one of his lambs to feed the man, he took the poor man's lamb.

Fortunately, the story struck a chord deep in David's heart. Filled with righteous indignation, David immediately condemned the rich man to death.

Now Nathan had David where he wanted him. Turning to face David, Nathan confronted him with his sin.

> *"You are the man! This is what the LORD, the God of Israel, says: 'I anointed you king over Israel, and I delivered you from the hand of Saul. I gave your master's house to you, and your master's wives into your arms. I gave you the house of Israel*

and Judah. And if all this had been too little, I would have given you even more. Why did you despise the word of the LORD by doing what is evil in his eyes? You struck down Uriah the Hittite with the sword and took his wife to be your own. You killed him with the sword of the Ammonites."

2 SAMUEL 12:7–9

At that moment, David had three options. He could blow up in anger at Nathan, and at God, for declaring him guilty and pestering him about his sin. He could give up and melt away in depression and defeat. Or he could own up to his sin and seek to make things right with God.

Fortunately, for himself and for us, David did the latter. He admitted his sin and found forgiveness.

Lord, Have Mercy

Later David reviewed that defining moment. His thoughts and prayer are found in Psalm 51. Read slowly through the beginning of this psalm, and note carefully the caption.

A psalm of David. When the prophet Nathan came to him after David had committed adultery with Bathsheba.

Have mercy on me, O God, according to your unfailing love; according to your great compassion blot out my transgressions. Wash away all my iniquity and cleanse me from my sin. For I know my transgressions, and my sin is always before me. Against you, you only, have I sinned and done what is evil in your sight, so that you are proved right when you speak and justified when you judge. . . . Cleanse me with hyssop, and I will be clean; wash me, and I will be whiter than snow. Let me hear joy and gladness; let the bones you have crushed rejoice. Hide your face from my sins and blot out all my iniquity. Create in me a pure heart, O God, and renew a steadfast spirit within me.

PSALM 51:1–10

The bad news is that David and his family would deal with the deep scars of that great sin for the rest of their lives (see 2 Samuel 12:10–19). The good news is that God heard him, forgave him, and restored him. Later David recorded the tremendous happiness that was unleashed in his heart when his sin was forgiven. His resulting song of experienced joy is Psalm 32. Eugene Petersen in *The Message* renders this psalm with these words:

Count yourself lucky, how happy you must be—you get a fresh start, your slate's wiped clean. Count yourself lucky—GOD holds nothing against you and you're holding nothing back from him. When I kept it all inside, my bones turned to powder, my words became daylong groans. The pressure never let up; all the juices of my life dried up. Then I let it all out; I said, "I'll make a clean breast of my failures to GOD." Suddenly the pressure was gone—my guilt dissolved, my sin disappeared.

PSALM 32:1–5 THE MESSAGE

David's story and the corresponding psalms are a great example of God's encouraging promise of forgiveness. The apostle John recorded it succinctly with these words:

If we confess our sins, he is faithful and just and will forgive us our sins and purify us from all unrighteousness.

1 JOHN 1:9

If We Confess Our Sins

The word *confess* means "to say the same thing," which means that we say the same thing about our sin that God says. When we confess our sin, we don't call it a mistake, a mess-up, an error, or misbehavior. We call it what it is, sin. We agree that it is wrong. We concur with the fact that it must be forgiven, it needs to be washed off our record, and it has to be purified from our hearts.

David was forgiven because he was truly sorry for his sin and meant business with God about being cleansed of it. He was not merely sorry that he had been caught or that he would be punished. He was sorry that he had disobeyed and hurt God.

All sin hurts God, not merely adultery and murder. Worry, doubt, laziness, lust, greed, jealousy, envy, bitterness, resentment, lying, cheating, deceit, gossip, slander, hatred, harshness, arrogance, and pride all break the heart of God.

Look back at Psalm 51. Notice the way David heaped up his brokenhearted requests as he confessed his sin. Hear the sorrow in his voice as he cried, "Have mercy on me. . . ; blot out my transgressions. Wash away all my iniquity and cleanse me from my sin. . . . ; cleanse me with hyssop. . . . ; wash me. . . . ; hide your face from my sins and blot out all my iniquity." David was truly sorry for his sin, and God took notice.

God Will Forgive Us Our Sins

Such serious sorrow over sin does not go without reward. It produces forgiveness. The idea of the word *forgiveness* is that of a bookkeeper stamping a bill "Paid in Full." It is the idea of a king declaring a condemned murderer fully pardoned. It is as if a spreadsheet detailing our sins were deleted. Imagine yourself saying, "Lord, do You remember that sin I committed last week?" and God saying, "No, I don't remember it." That is forgiveness.

I know all of that sounds too good to be true, but I am not making this up. Listen to what God promises:

"I, even I, am he who blots out your transgressions, for my own sake, and remembers your sins no more."

ISAIAH 43:25

"For I will forgive their wickedness and will remember their sins no more."

JEREMIAH 31:34

Late in his life, the mighty hand of God wonderfully healed King Hezekiah. In his prayer of thanks, he said, "You have put all my sins behind your back" (Isaiah 38:17).

In writing of his vision of a better future, the prophet Micah said, "You will again have compassion on us; you will tread our sins underfoot and hurl all our iniquities into the depths of the sea" (Micah 7:19).

God Will Purify Us of All Unrighteousness

God not only cancels our sin. He cleans us up from the inside out. That feels awesome.

In high school, a good friend believed the promise of John 3:16 and trusted Jesus Christ as her Savior. She also acted on the promise of 1 John 1:9 and confessed her sins. When she was telling me about it the next day, I asked her, "How did it feel?"

She gave me a huge smile and said, "Amazing! For the first time since I was a little girl, I felt really, truly clean. . .clean on the inside. I felt like a little girl dancing in the fresh, gentle rain of a spring shower. I have never felt this good before!"

He Loves You

One of my favorite Bible verses is Revelation 1:5. It says, "To Him who loved us and washed us from our sins in His own blood. . ." (NKJV). What I like about this verse is that God loves us *before* He washes us.

When my son Andrew was a toddler, our happy family was out walking by a pond one afternoon. The pond was pretty, but the section we were near happened to be covered with a layer of pea-green scum.

We had stopped by the side of the pond as his older brother, Daniel, threw a rock in the pond. Andrew had to do everything his older brother did, so he picked up a stone. But he was still unsteady on his feet. The force of throwing the stone into the water propelled him into the scum-covered pond, face-first. The pond was shallow around the edges, but he was totally submerged. All that was showing were the bottoms of his tennis shoes, which stuck out through the green scum.

Alarmed, my wife, Cathy, cried, "Dave, get him out!" Being a brave dad, I reached in and pulled him up by his ankles. Andrew, of course, was scared and crying. He also was completely covered in stinky, pea-green pond scum.

Then Cathy called out, "Give him a hug."

I was torn. I desperately love my son. But I absolutely detest reeking pond scum. It gives me the creeps. While I paused to count the cost, Cathy, a true mom, sprang into action. She grabbed him up in both arms and hugged him close.

I felt a bit embarrassed.

Reflecting back on that moment, I was so glad that God loves us before He forgives us and washes us. In fact, His great love is the reason He is willing to forgive us and wash us. That is encouraging!

A Final Encouragement

If God could forgive David's big sin, He certainly can forgive you of any sin in your life. You don't have to be perfect or one of the spiritual superelite. You just need to be truly sorry. You need to confess your sin and ask for forgiveness. The Lord will forgive your sins and cleanse your heart. That's God's promise.

11

God's Promise of Godly Confidence
PHILIPPIANS 1:6

Do you lack confidence? What do you do when your faith is wavering? How do you respond when you are faced with a gnawing awareness that your faith is too small? How will you deal with those times when you doubt your ability to make a difference? What do you do when you feel like you can't get through? If you are not sure of how to answer those questions, you are not alone.

Crisis of Faith
A young man named Billy was once at a crisis of faith and confidence. He realized that his wavering faith could not enable him to minister to others effectively. Despairingly, he went out into the woods to pray and think. There he found this promise:

> *Being confident of this, that he who began a good work in you will carry it on to completion until the day of Christ Jesus.*
>
> PHILIPPIANS 1:6

As he read those words, God spoke to his need. Later he wrote, "From that day to this [God] has never stopped giving and performing that which He has begun."[1]

With that promise, Billy was able to launch out as an evangelist. Maybe you have heard of him. His name is Billy Graham, one of the most influential Christians of the twentieth century. He has preached the gospel to more people in live audiences than anyone else in history—over 210 million people in more than 185 countries and territories. Hundreds of millions more have been reached through television, video, film, and webcasts. He has led hundreds of thousands of individuals to Christ, which is the main thrust of his ministry. Dr. Graham has preached in remote African villages and in the heart of New York City. Those to whom he has ministered have ranged from heads of state to the simple-living Aborigines of Australia and the wandering tribes of Africa. Since 1977 Billy has conducted preaching missions in virtually every country of the former Eastern Bloc, including Russia. Mr. Graham has written twenty-four books, many of which have become top sellers.

Wow! Think of it. One little promise rekindled the faith and relaunched the ministry of Billy Graham. Let's go back and look at that Scripture more deeply.

> *Being confident of this, that he who began a good work in you will carry it on to completion until the day of Christ Jesus.*
>
> PHILIPPIANS 1:6

This promise, like the others, has two sides to it—the human and the divine. The human prerequisite is to be confident in God. We are responsible for believing God's Word, trusting God's ability, and having faith in God's timing. This is not easy. We often can't see God's work. Much of His best work is done underground, invisible to the human eye.

Being confident is not always easy. Sometimes it involves great patience. God doesn't work according to our time frame. He does things according to His schedule, not ours. Often

He is much more patient than we are. He is content to allow a situation to go on for weeks, months, years, and even decades, seemingly with no divine activity. For example, Joseph spent over a dozen years in slavery and in prison before God's work became evident and Joseph was released to become prime minister of Egypt. But that's nothing. Moses spent forty years in the desert before God showed up to set him on his course for delivering Israel. And then he spent another forty years leading a group of whiny people through the wilderness before they reached the Promised Land.

Confident faith is especially tough when things get worse before they get better. A friend of mine recently remodeled his house. The house was old and worn. The first thing the crew did was tear everything up and make a huge mess. Believe me, the house looked much better *before* the remodeling started. But little by little, progress was made, and eventually it looked better and was structurally stronger.

When my friend showed me the finished product, he said, "The outcome was worth the mess. Several times I wished we had just left things as they were and never even started, but now I am so glad we did not quit on the process."

It is so with us. God goes to work, and things actually look much worse than before. But if we stay with it, we'll be very well pleased with the finished product.

Staying confident can be difficult. But confidence in God to do as He has promised and finish the work He has begun in you is powerful. It releases Him to complete it.

God Promises to Do It

The promise of Philippians 1:6 was written by Paul as he sat in a Roman prison chained to guards 24/7. As he reflected on his life in God and his ministry to others, Paul no doubt realized how often and firmly he had stood on God's promise. From the beginning of his life in Christ, Paul knew that it would be tough. God's plan for Paul was big and difficult. In order to see it become a reality, he would need great faith. As God was calling Paul, this is what God said:

> *"This man is my chosen instrument to carry my name before the Gentiles and their kings and before the people of Israel. I will show him how much he must suffer for my name."*
> ACTS 9:15–16

This all came true. Paul brought the gospel to the Israelites. He took the gospel to the Gentiles and shared it with their leaders. He agonized for the sake of the name of Jesus Christ. Now, as he sat suffering in jail, he was on the verge of sharing Jesus with the emperor of the world, Caesar himself.

Inwardly, Paul wrestled with a lack of confidence. Often he asked his friends to pray that he would be bold (Colossians 4:3; Ephesians 6:18–19; 1 Thessalonians 5:25). God responded to these prayers. With powerful boldness, Paul launched his vast ministry and faced persecution and suffering. He fearlessly shared Jesus Christ before angry crowds, indignant judges, and skeptical kings. He confidently gave directions, took risks, and made decisions. He was the picture of confidence.

Paul lived with an abiding, contagious confidence that God would fulfill what He had promised. Summarizing his experience, Paul wrote, "The one who calls you is faithful and he will do it" (1 Thessalonians 5:24).

God Is Able

Too many times I have said, "I am absolutely overwhelmed," or "I am too busy," or "I need more time," or "I don't understand," or "I am so tired."

Unlike me, God has never said any of those words. That's because, unlike any of us, God has no limits. He is eternal and unbounded by time. In fact, He dwells outside the realm of space and time. He is omniscient—all knowing. He is omnipotent—almighty. He has unlimited strength and power. God has all the time, wisdom, and strength to keep His promises. So if He says that He will do something, you'd better believe He is able to carry it out.

Trust Him

Paul did not become so bold through his own strength. Even though he was an extremely intelligent and gifted man, he said that his ministry was not based on his intellect or eloquence but was the result of God's power (1 Corinthians 1:16; 2:1–5). The secret of his great success was that he relied on God.

$\left(\textit{I can do everything through him who gives me strength.} \right)$

PHILIPPIANS 4:13

Billy Graham did not become a powerhouse preacher and leader on his own. God did it while Graham trusted. He has testified that from time to time he knew God was providing him with special strength for a certain task. "Sometimes," Dr. Graham said, "as I have lain awake at night the quiet assurance has come that I was being filled with the Spirit for the task that lay ahead."[2]

I Can't. You Can. Please Do.

I have worked hard to develop a life of prayer, but I am not eloquent. Much of my praying is the offering of simple prayers. One simple prayer I find myself saying to God often is this: "I can't. You can. Please do."

That prayer says much more than six words. When I pray it, here is what I am saying to God:

1. "I can't." I acknowledge my inability to meet the challenge. I am not big enough, smart enough, or strong enough to do it. If it is totally up to me, it won't happen.
2. "You can." I am expressing my faith in God. I communicate my confidence in God to be sufficient for the task. I rest on the fact that He is big enough, smart enough, and strong enough for anything at hand.
3. "Please do." I ask Him to act. I expect Him to fulfill His promise.

A Final Encouragement

God has begun a good work in you. He is not finished with you yet. He will complete it. He did it for Billy Graham. He did it for Paul. He has done it for countless others, and He will do it for you. Be confident in Him.

NOTES

[1]Hubert A. Elliot, ed. *Bible Words That Have Helped Me* (New York: Grosset and Dunlop, 1963), 84.
[2]Billy Graham, quoted in Elmer Towns, *Understanding the Deeper Life* (Old Tappan, NJ: Revell, 1988), 214–215.

12

God's Promise of Inner Strength
ISAIAH 40:28–31

Who says the Bible is dull? How can people generalize that godly people are boring? Anyone who says or thinks that living for God is mundane never met Elijah.

When Elijah blew out of the desert onto the pages of the Scriptures, he stuck his bony prophet's finger in the face of wicked King Ahab and declared that there would be no rain in Israel until he said so (1 Kings 17:1). That was a bold and reckless act. Ahab was notorious for executing prophets for much less brashness than that. However, Elijah not only lived; his word came true. It did not rain in Israel for three years.

Later we read of Elijah's providing a starving widow with daily food through a perpetually replenishing jar of flour and jug of oil (1 Kings 17:7–16). Then, when the widow's son died, Elijah raised him from the dead (1 Kings 17:17–24)!

But those feats were nothing compared to his next display. Imagine one man fearlessly standing alone in a valley in view of hundreds of thousands of people surrounding him on the hillsides. Imagine Elijah facing 850 prophets of the false god Baal. Then picture Elijah challenging them to a public duel to prove which god was the true God, Baal or Jehovah.

See the 850 priests of Baal begin the morning by praying and pleading for Baal, the lightning god, to come down and ignite their sacrifice with fire. Watch as Elijah taunts them. Watch the frustrated pagan prophets continue late into the afternoon shadows, desperately shouting out and cutting themselves before Baal, trying to persuade him to respond. See their efforts meet with nothing but disappointing silence.

Hear the crowd gasp as Elijah brazenly soaks his sacrifice with barrel after barrel of water until the trench around the altar is full. Listen as he simply prays:

> *"O LORD, God of Abraham, Isaac and Israel, let it be known today that you are God in Israel and that I am your servant and have done all these things at your command. Answer me, O LORD, answer me, so these people will know that you, O LORD, are God, and that you are turning their hearts back again."*
>
> 1 KINGS 18:36–37

Stand amazed as a bolt of fire shoots down out of heaven and explodes in the sopping-wet sacrifice. Remain speechless as the wet sacrifice bursts into flames. Watch the flames spread until they have consumed not only the bull but also the wood, the rocks of the altar, and all the water in the trench surrounding the altar. Join the frightened, humbled, excited crowd as you dive on your face, shouting, "The LORD—he is God! The LORD—he is God!" (1 Kings 18:39).

Ordinary Man, Extraordinary Strength

Elijah was an unusual man with rare boldness and incredible spiritual power. Yet the Scriptures remind us that he was just as human as you and me. His amazing strength was not his own. Elijah's outstanding quality was his extraordinary ability to draw his strength and power from God.

> *Elijah was a man just like us. He prayed earnestly that it would not rain, and it did not rain on the land for three and a half years. Again he prayed, and the heavens gave rain, and the earth produced its crops.*
>
> JAMES 5:17–18

The Secret of His Strength

When I study the sketch of Elijah's life recorded in the sacred Scriptures, I find it easy to overlook an event that was the core and foundation of his remarkable strength and power. It occurred right after he predicted the three-year drought and before he performed the miracles with the widow and called down fire on the sacrifice.

> *Then the word of the LORD came to Elijah: "Leave here, turn eastward and hide in the Kerith Ravine, east of the Jordan. You will drink from the brook, and I have ordered the ravens to feed you there." So he did what the LORD had told him. He went to the Kerith Ravine, east of the Jordan, and stayed there.*
>
> 1 KINGS 17:2–5

This tiny vignette reveals why Elijah was able to be so mighty *for* the Lord. He spent time alone *with* the Lord. He hid himself from people in order to nourish himself in the Lord.

Later in his life, when the pressure of fleeing the wrath of Ahab was too intense, Elijah again went into the desert alone and was refreshed (1 Kings 19:3–90). There he met the Lord in an intense and personal way (1 Kings 19:10–18).

Different Man, Same Secret

Jesus is the Son of God. He is fully God, yet He is also fully man. He got hungry and thirsty. He got tired and took naps. When Jesus' ministry began, the load of His daily duties was staggering. On one particular Sabbath, as He was teaching in the synagogue, He was confronted by a demonized man. Jesus cast out the demon (Mark 1:21–27).

Leaving the synagogue with some friends, Jesus went to Peter's house. There Peter's mother-in-law was sick in bed with a fever. Jesus went in and healed her. She got up and helped fix lunch (Mark 1:29–31).

Later that evening the entire town gathered outside the door, gawking as Jesus healed the sick and liberated the demonized. This continued late into the night (Mark 1:32–34).

What an exhausting day!

Any normal man would have been worn out by half as much activity. But the next day, Jesus launched out in a multiple-city preaching and deliverance tour (Mark 1:36–39).

How did He do it? Where did He get His strength? What was his secret?

The Secret of His Strength

Tucked in the middle of this account in Mark's gospel is a golden gem of life-changing insight. Read it carefully:

> *Very early in the morning, while it was still dark, Jesus got up, left the house and went off to a solitary place, where he prayed.*
>
> MARK 1:35

How did Jesus combat the fatigue of a draining day of ministry? The same way we should. He took time away from others so He could trust God in prayer. Notice carefully what He did:

"Very early in the morning, while it was still dark"—Jesus chose a solitary time.

"Jesus got up, left the house"—Jesus distanced Himself from people for a time.

". . .went off to a solitary place"—Jesus chose a solitary place.

". . .where He prayed."

Like Elijah, Jesus found the source of His strength in the Father and the secret of His strength in prayer.

Jesus got away *from* others so He could get away *with* the Father. He sought physical solitude in order to address His spiritual needs. He not only got still before God; He got alone with God. He practiced solitary prayer.

This was Jesus' secret for staying fresh, sharp, full, centered, and on track. During His three-and-a-half years of intense ministry, He practiced waiting on the Father in solitude to keep His spiritual tank full and His emotional battery charged.

Don't we need to learn to do the same? If the Son of God needed to pray, how much more do you and I? If the Son of God rose early and went to a solitary place to pray, shouldn't you and I?"

The sad reality is that most of us are too busy, too crowded, and too cluttered to stay spiritually sharp. Our lives are filled with too much activity, too much noise, and too many relationships, so we have little time for God. Our lives are so full of stuff—good stuff, perhaps, but still stuff—that there is little room for God.[1]

A Promise to Weary People

As we go through life, it is easy to get inwardly worn down. Consistently choosing to do good can empty our emotional reservoir. We also go through rib-rocking blows that can crush us. Without great strength, we can crumble under the weight of it all. It is not that we need more physical strength. We usually need more emotional strength, increased mental toughness, and greater spiritual fortitude. In other words, we need inner strength.

Isaiah is written to people facing tremendous trials: war, famine, persecution, and corruption, to name a few. To such weary people, Isaiah pointed to a wonderful promise:

> *Have you not known? Have you not heard? The everlasting God, the LORD, the Creator of the ends of the earth, neither faints nor is weary. His understanding is unsearchable. He gives power to the weak, and to those who have no might He increases strength. Even the youths shall faint and be weary, and the young men shall utterly fall, but those who wait on the LORD shall renew their strength; they shall mount up with wings like eagles, they shall run and not be weary, they shall walk and not faint.*
>
> ISAIAH 40:28–31 NKJV

This sounds almost too good to be true—renewed strength, wings like those of eagles, strong legs to keep going, and spiritual stamina to not quit. Often that's exactly what we need. The question is, how do we get it? Look again at verse 31: "But those who *wait on the LORD* shall renew their strength."

The Way to Inner Strength Is Waiting on the Lord

The picture is clear. If I do not *wait* on God, I will be *weighted* down by life. What does it mean to wait on the Lord?

1. *Waiting on the Lord means taking time with God.*

Waiting is a time-oriented word. It implies spending a quantity of quality time with the Lord.

The story is told of an American on a trip to Africa many years ago. His entourage hiked for six days. On the seventh day, he awoke the men and was ready to push on. The leader of the men carrying his cargo said, "We will not be going today."

The man was exasperated. Why wouldn't they go? He'd pay them extra. He was in a hurry to get where he was going. They had to press on.

"No," the leader said.

"Why?" the man cried.

"We walked fast and far all week. Today we must wait for our souls to catch up with us."

I have a suspicion that many of us have left our souls back in the dust somewhere. It would not hurt us to slow down and wait for them to catch up. How much time did you spend this week with God? How much unhurried quality time did you spend with the God who can renew your waning strength?

2. *Waiting on the Lord requires trusting Him.*

The word translated "wait" in the above verse can also be translated "hope in." It means "to rely upon." I think we often are tired because we are weighed down from carrying things we have no business carrying. Mentally and emotionally, we carry loads of responsibility that grind us down. We must learn to take on less and trust God with the rest. We need to realize that He is big enough to shoulder the load. We need to trust Him.

Then He'll give us strength.

3. *Waiting on the Lord requires talking it out with God in prayer.*

Both Elijah (James 5:17–18) and Jesus (Mark 1:35) gained renewal and refreshment from the Lord in prayer. Prayer is talking with God. It is telling Him how you feel and what you need.

Prayer is verbally looking at life from God's perspective. It is receiving the relief of seeing the bigger picture and tracing the easily unnoticed hand of the Father.

A Final Encouragement

We need inner strength. What should we do? We should do the same thing Elijah, Jesus, and countless others have done. Live by a promise. The condition for inner strength is waiting on the Lord.

NOTE

[1]For more on solitude in prayer, see Dave Earley, *Prayer Odyssey* (Shippensburg, PA: Destiny Image, 2004), 25–28.

13

God's Promise of Answered Prayer
MATTHEW 7:7–11

A missionary in the Andes of Ecuador was deathly sick with typhus. His young wife dyed her wedding dress black. His friends purchased a coffin. He was "so far out into the River of Death that [he] was closer to the other side than to this." Utterly incapacitated, he knew he would very soon be in eternity.

At the same time, in faraway New England, believers gathered at a Bible conference. Their study was interrupted by a deep and heavy burden for this very missionary. And so they knelt and prayed with such agony of spirit that they were unaware that mealtime had come and gone. They did not know that the man in Ecuador was delirious and at death's door, that his bride's wedding dress had become a widow's garment. By midafternoon, the burden in their spirits lifted and they had heavenly assurance that their prayers were answered.

That missionary was the late Raymond Edman, president of Wheaton College. He later testified that in those hours as strangers prayed for him, he "experienced a sweet sense of the love of God in Christ such as I had never known before in all the years of my life." After two weeks, he returned to the land of the living.[1]

What amazes me about Dr. Edman's story is the power of the prayers of people thousands of miles away from him. It reminds me of one of the most encouraging promises in the Bible:

> *"Ask and it will be given to you; seek and you will find; knock and the door will be opened to you. For everyone who asks receives; he who seeks finds; and to him who knocks, the door will be opened. Which of you, if his son asks for bread, will give him a stone? Or if he asks for a fish, will give him a snake? If you, then, though you are evil, know how to give good gifts to your children, how much more will your Father in heaven give good gifts to those who ask him!"*

MATTHEW 7:7–11

What do you need? Is it wisdom, strength, food?

What do you need? Do you need guidance, forgiveness, healing, help with a troubled child?

What do you need? Is it money, a job, empowerment to minister, favor with a superior, a promotion?

Do you need a miracle?

God's response to your need is one little word.

Ask.

Ask is a simple word describing a simple act. In its raw sense, it means to use words to express desires. It conveys the concept of recognizing need and seeking the ability of another to meet it. Such an act requires humility.

When used of prayer, *ask* is very much a two-sided word. On one side is our insufficiency, and on the other lies God's all-sufficiency; on one side is our weakness, on the other, God's strength; our dependency rests on one side, and God's dependability on the other. The act of asking is what stretches between the two, connecting them. For us it is a powerful connection. Without it, God's infinite ability to act on our behalf is untapped, wasted, and useless.

By definition, prayer is talking with God. In practice, prayer is asking and receiving.

The words used most often for prayer in both the Old and New Testaments mainly mean "ask." In its purest sense, prayer is asking. You have not really prayed until you have asked God for something that is needed.

Someone once said, "God answers prayers in four ways: 'Yes,' 'No,' 'Wait,' and 'You gotta be kidding.' " Someone else said, "If our request is wrong, God says 'No'; if our timing is wrong, God says 'Slow'; if we are wrong, God says 'Grow.' If our request is right, our timing is right, and we are right, God says 'Go!' " But Jesus said, "Ask and it shall be given to you."

Prayer Is Asking

When Jesus taught His disciples to pray, He taught them to ask the Father for things. John R. Rice, the great country evangelist of the first part of the twentieth century, wrote, "Asking is prayer and prayer is asking. So when God invites us to pray, He invites us to ask things of Him."[2]

Have you ever noticed that when people prayed in the Bible, they asked God for things? Notice the short, simple prayers of these people in the Bible:

Listen to Peter out on the Sea of Galilee sinking into the waves after walking on the water with Jesus: "Lord, save me!" (Matthew 14:30).

Pay attention to the blind man: "Jesus, Son of David, have mercy on me!" (Mark 10:47). "Rabbi, I want to see" (Mark 10:51).

Eavesdrop on the prayer of the thief on the cross: "Jesus, remember me when you come into your kingdom" (Luke 23:42).

Hear the heartbroken mother: "Lord, Son of David, have mercy on me! My daughter is suffering terribly from demon-possession" (Matthew 15:22). "Lord, help me!" (Matthew 15:25).

Think about this: The only prayer Jesus ever held up as errant was one that asked nothing.

> *"Two men went up to the temple to pray, one a Pharisee and the other a tax collector. The Pharisee stood up and prayed about himself: 'God, I thank you that I am not like other men—robbers, evildoers, adulterers—or even like this tax collector. I fast twice a week and give a tenth of all I get.' "*
>
> LUKE 18:10–12

When I first got married and my wife and I went shopping, I began to notice how different men and women could be. For my wife and me, shopping meant two completely different things. She had never had much money, so to her shopping meant "looking." She could look all day. I grew up working a paper route, so I always had some cash but not much time. To me shopping meant "buying"—walking in, seeing what I wanted, buying it, and leaving. The whole process may take ten to fifteen minutes, tops. I figured, if you are not going to buy, why shop?

God has promised that the storehouse of heavenly blessings is opened at the sound of genuine requests. We do not have to merely look. We have the power to ask for exactly what we need. And God wants to give it to us.

If It Is Good to Have, It Is Good to Ask For

I think many of us will get to heaven and find that God wanted to give us so much more, if only we had asked for it. I would rather ask for something and have God refuse than not get it because I failed to ask. If you really want something, and it would not be an embarrassment for God to give it to you, ask.

Anything you have a right to want, you have a right to ask for. Every Christian should take every desire to God in prayer. But if you cannot honestly pray for something, it is a sin to desire it. Ask God to remove a desire if it is wrong. If the desire itself is not wrong, however, then you should ask God to fulfill it![3]

Keep Asking

The verbs in Matthew 7:7, "ask," "seek," and "knock," carry the sense of persistence. Because of the verb tense, you could translate these words in this way: *Keep on* asking, *keep on* seeking, *keep on* knocking. For a variety of reasons, we may not receive what we desire the first time we ask for it. But from Matthew 7:7 and the parable of the persistent widow in Luke 18:1–8, we know that in prayer, persistence pays.

Persistent Prayer Pays

George Mueller modeled persistent prayer. He would pray until he felt he knew God's will about a matter and then keep bringing this to God in prayer until he got his answer. Mueller claimed that he saw over ten thousand immediate answers to prayer. His secret? He asked.

For example, he wrote in his autobiography:

> In November 1844 I began to pray daily for the conversion of five individuals. I prayed every day without a single intermission. . . . Eighteen months elapsed before the first of the five was converted. I thanked God and prayed on for the others. Five years elapsed, and the second was converted. I thanked God for the second and prayed on for the other three. Day by day, I continued to pray for them, and six years passed before the third was converted. I thanked God for the three and went on praying for the other two.
>
> [I have] been praying day-by-day for thirty-six years for the conversion of these individuals, and yet they remain unconverted. I hope in God, I pray on, and look yet for the answer. They are not converted yet, but they will be.[4]

He kept praying for these two individuals for a total of fifty-two years. One was saved at Mueller's funeral and the other one a few weeks later!

Once Mueller needed a new orphan house for three hundred needy children. After ninety-three days of asking God to provide land, a landowner called him. The man said he'd been awakened at 3:00 a.m. and couldn't get the idea of selling to Mueller out of his mind. So he wanted to know if Mueller would buy it at about roughly half the price he'd been asking. Next, God provided the money for the land and the building!

A Final Encouragement

If you have a need, your first step should be to seek the Lord in prayer. He will answer if we will ask. That's His promise.

Notes

V. Raymond Edman, *They Found the Secret* (Grand Rapids, MI: Zondervan, 1984), 143–146.

J. R. Rice, *Prayer: Asking and Receiving* (Chicago: Moody Press, 1961), 130.

Ibid.

George Mueller, quoted in Basil Miller, *George Muller* (Minneapolis: Bethany Fellowship, 1943), 146.

14

God's Promise of Invincible Love
ROMANS 8:38–39

I am not necessarily a "huggy" person, but there are days when I really need a hug. You know what I mean. Life is not playing fair; things are not turning your way; everything is uphill, harder than you ever expected; deep down inside you wonder if God really loves you.

He does. It's the promise of Romans 8:38–39.

> *For I am convinced that neither death nor life, neither angels nor demons, neither the present nor the future, nor any powers, nor neither height nor depth, nor anything else in all creation, will be able to separate us from the love of God that is in Christ Jesus our Lord.*
>
> ROMANS 8:38–39

The Desperado

How could anyone not love this promise? It encourages us that God's love is so invincible that it overcomes death, demons, past failures, present problems, future fears, and anything else we could imagine. It tells us that God loves us even if we may not feel like He loves us, if we see ourselves as unlovable, if life seems unfair. The Lord loves us even if He has been silent and our prayers have gone unanswered. God loves us even when everyone else appears to be doing better than we are, when we feel like we have hurt God, when we have run from Him.

Two thousand years ago, Jesus told the story of a desperado who ran away from home only to find out that everything he was desperately looking for was back home with his father. The boy is commonly referred to as the prodigal son.

I love this story because I have been a desperado. My desperado days were those when I desperately tried to run from God, came to my senses, and returned to find His arms still open.

The story of this first-century desperado reminds us of the invincible power of God's love. It shows us that in God's heart, there is always a fire in the fireplace and a place for us at the table.

Running from Love

> *There was a man who had two sons. The younger one said to his father, "Father, give me my share of the estate." So he divided his property between them.*
>
> LUKE 15:11–12

Two unusual things occurred at the very start of this story. First, the younger son asked for his inheritance while his father was still alive and in good health. In that culture, this was an unthinkably selfish act and the ultimate insult to a father. The father would be expected to refuse such a request.

This leads us to the second unusual occurrence. The father divided the inheritance! His dividing of the inheritance would have been public knowledge, and the family would have been shamed before the entire community. This is the first of several times in this story the father goes against tradition. The rest of the story makes it clear that the son's share of the estate was substantial.

Not long after that, the younger son got together all he had, set off for a distant country and there squandered his wealth in wild living.

LUKE 15:13

When the younger son got together all he had, he sold his part of the family estate. This would have further shamed the family, because Jewish law did not permit a child to sell his inheritance until after the father died. Yet the self-centered son didn't care.

Then it got worse. The absolute unpardonable sin for a Jewish son was to lose his family's inheritance to non-Jews. In ancient days, if any violator of this law ever came home, villagers would take a large earthenware jar, fill it with burned nuts and corn, and dramatically break it in front of the guilty individual. While doing this the people would shout, "This man is now cut off from his people!" From that point on, no one in the village would have any contact with the offender. Yet the desperado did not care. He persisted in partying all his money away.

Ruining His Life

After he had spent everything, there was a severe famine in that whole country, and he began to be in need.

LUKE 15:14

Normally a son in need would simply return home. This desperado had burned his bridges and so closed the door on a return. He had publicly disgraced his father and family. He couldn't return now, after losing his money to non-Jewish people in a far country. The first villagers to see him would call for the excommunication ceremony, and he would be publicly cut off from his people. Therefore, the desperado came up with a plan.

So he went and hired himself out to a citizen of that country, who sent him to his fields to feed pigs. He longed to fill his stomach with the pods that the pigs were eating, but no one gave him anything.

LUKE 15:15–16

To come home, he had to earn the money back. Yet as a pig herder, he received a place to sleep but no money. So he was in a hopeless situation.

Returning Home to the Father's Love

When he came to his senses, he said, "How many of my father's hired men have food to spare, and here I am starving to death! I will set out and go back to my father and say to him: Father, I have sinned against heaven and against you. I am no longer worthy to be called your son; make me like one of your hired men." So he got up and went to his father.

LUKE 15:17–20

This entire story shows the desperado doing dumb things. Then he finally did something smart. He returned home.

He came to his senses. "Aha! Eating good food with the guys who work at my dad's farm is better than eating pig slop. Being around a family is better than being alone. Being close to my father is better than being far away. It would be better to be a hired servant at home than a free man far away."

He remembered that life was always better at his father's house. And for us, life is always better with our heavenly Father. There is no guilt, no shame, and no emptiness in the Father's house. There is belonging and acceptance, dignity and destiny. There is mercy, grace, truth, meaning, fulfillment, and forgiveness in the Father's house. Invincible love reigns in the Father's house.

Receiving the Father's Invincible Love

> *But while he was still a long way off, his father saw him and was filled with compassion for him; he ran to his son, threw his arms around him and kissed him.*
>
> LUKE 15:20

The son deserved the ceremony of rejection. Instead, he was given an undeserved, warm reception. The father's four loving actions blow my mind!

First, the father saw his son. The fact that the father saw the son implies that the father was on the lookout for the son. The son was gone a long time, yet throughout that period the father kept looking for the son to return. The father never gave up.

Wow! It reminds me that our heavenly Father does not quit on us. He is patiently watching and awaiting our return.

Second, the father felt compassion for his son. He was not filled with hurt. He was not filled with wounded pride. He was filled with love.

It is the same with our heavenly Father. He does not view us through the distorted lens of a bruised ego. He is full of love for us.

Third, the father ran to his son. If the father saw him first, he had every right to call for the ceremony of rejection. After all, he was the one who had been disgraced. Or if he did not call for the ceremony of rejection, he could have seen the son, made sure the son saw him, turned his back, and let another family member be the first to speak to the son. But he did not.

I am so glad that my heavenly Father does not hold back. Often in the past God has pursued me, and still He pursues me on my desperado days.

Fourth, the father hugged and kissed his son. No folded arms. No stiff handshake. No questions. No words of anger, frustration, or rebuke. Just a simple, big, deep, heartfelt hug.

There is nothing like that unmistakable, indescribable, supernatural sense of being drawn back into the arms of the heavenly Father. Nothing compares with the warm favor of His renewed affection.

The Restoring Power of Love

> *The son said to him, "Father, I have sinned against heaven and against you. I am no longer worthy to be called your son." But the father said to his servants, "Quick! Bring the best robe and put it on him. Put a ring on his finger and sandals on his feet. Bring the fattened calf and kill it. Let's have a feast and celebrate. For this son of mine was dead and is alive again; he was lost and is found." So they began to celebrate.*
>
> LUKE 15:21–24

The son deserved the ceremony of rejection. The father had every right to hoist a jar of burnt nuts and corn high over his head and then smash it dramatically in the desperado's face.

But the father did not disown him or make him a servant. He restored him as his son! He gave him an elaborate and expensive party! He presented to him the best robe. He put a ring on his finger. He invited a big crowd of people and served a fatted calf (it would take a lot of people a long time to eat a fatted calf). The father gave his wayward son a big-time celebration. This is a picture of powerful, invincible love!

Twenty-First-Century Desperados

Every word of this story is a portrait of God's invincible love for desperados. Make no mistake about it. We are all desperados, desperately seeking love as we wrestle with loneliness, hopelessness, frustration, and emptiness. We all seek a love that provides us with genuine acceptance, lasting hope, deep meaning, and ultimate destiny. Each of us thirsts for a truly triumphant love that will reach through our pride and rebellion to love us.

Such an invincible love is available. God, our Father, has promised it to us. But like the first-century desperado, we twenty-first-century desperados must come to our senses, stop running from the Father, and hurry home to His outstretched arms. He is waiting.

A Final Encouragement

You can never run so far that you can't get back home. The Father is watching and waiting for you to return. He won't scold or condemn. He will forgive and restore. He'll even throw a party. But you have to run home.

15

God's Promise of Timely Promotion
PSALM 75:6–7

Does your heart ever burn for a higher status in life? Do you live with a gnawing sense that you're meant for more? Maybe you, like me, long for a greater position of influence in order to touch more people for God. Maybe you are worn out from dreaming and scheming of how to get there. God has a promise for you, but first a story.

Bad News for the Jews

Esther was an extremely beautiful young Jewish woman. Her cousin, Mordecai, was a very good and noble man. However, the king's highest official, Haman, was a viciously evil man with more power than he could handle. Nearly twenty-five hundred years ago in the land of Persia, their three lives were woven together to tell a fascinating story of God's principles of promotion.

One day the Persian king Xerxes ordered all of his servants to bow down before Haman in order to honor him. But a Jewish man named Mordecai refused. He would only bow before the true God, and Haman did not qualify. When he discovered Mordecai's unwillingness to bow down to him, Haman hatched a plot.

"Why kill one Jew when I can annihilate them all?" he reasoned. So he offered to pay the bill for the extinction of the Jews throughout Xerxes' vast kingdom, which ranged from India to Ethiopia. He reasoned that by plundering the Jews he could collect the millions of dollars it would take to kill them. Haman presented a prejudiced case against the Jews to the king and obtained Xerxes' permission to carry out his plan.

The Divinely Positioned Person of Influence

Not long before this, the king had become disillusioned with his wife and wanted a new one. So a special beauty contest was held to find the king a new queen. Esther was selected for the contest. The king fell deeply in love with her and made her the next queen. No one in the palace knew that Esther was a Jew or that Mordecai was her relative. Of course, all of this was according to God's sovereign plan.

When Mordecai heard that Haman was planning to wipe out the Jews, he went to Esther seeking her help. In those days, even a queen was forbidden to approach the king uninvited. To do so could mean death. So Esther asked Mordecai to call all of the Jews to fast on her behalf before she approached the king.

Their fasting made a difference. When Esther entered King Xerxes' presence, he was so happy to see her that he blurted out that he'd gladly give her anything she wanted. But Esther had more than just a pretty face and a shapely figure. She was wise and patient. So she invited the king to return the next night with Haman for a special banquet.

The king so enjoyed the meal that he again offered to give Esther anything she wanted. But she knew that he was not yet ready to grant her huge request. So she again invited Xerxes and Haman to return the next night for another magnificent feast.

After the feast, Haman went home full of himself. He had been invited to eat two meals in a row with the king and queen. Heady with power and angered over Mordecai's seeming disrespect, he ordered the building of a gallows. The next day he planned to ask the king to authorize the execution of the Jew Mordecai.

Timely Bedtime Reading

Back at the palace, God's sovereign plan continued. The king was restless and unable to fall asleep. He ordered the record of the daily events of his palace read to him. The reader read of an event involving Mordecai the Jew. It seemed that some time earlier Mordecai had uncovered a plot to assassinate the king. As a result, the king's life was spared, but Mordecai had somehow gone unrewarded. The king wondered what should be done to honor this unsung hero.

Bad Timing by Haman

As the sun rose over Persia, Haman boldly knocked on the king's door. He hoped to receive permission to execute his nemesis, the faithful Jew Mordecai. But the king had another plan for Mordecai.

King Xerxes brought Haman in and asked him what he suggested should be done for someone the king would like to honor. Haman arrogantly assumed the king was referring to him, so he gushed that the man should be given one of the king's robes, placed on one of the king's horses, and led through the city square, proclaimed as a hero.

The king loved the idea. So he ordered Haman to do this for Mordecai the Jew! Haman had to watch as the man he was hoping to execute was given one of the king's robes, placed on the king's horse, and recognized as a hero!

Don't you love the divine irony?

Haman's Horrible Day

When Mordecai returned from his victory lap, the palace aides arrived to take Haman to dinner. But by then he was losing his appetite.

Unlike Haman, the king greatly enjoyed the meal and once again told Esther that he'd gladly give her anything she asked. Buoyed by her faith in God and driven by the dire situation awaiting her and her people, Esther humbly yet boldly made her request:

> *"If I have found favor with you, O king, and if it pleases your majesty, grant me my life—this is my petition. And spare my people—this is my request. For I and my people have been sold for destruction and slaughter and annihilation. If we had merely been sold as male and female slaves, I would have kept quiet, because no such distress would justify disturbing the king."*
>
> ESTHER 7:3–4

Then she must have held her breath. But instead of being angry with her, the king was livid against her adversary. He demanded to know the name of the wicked fool who wanted to kill her and her people. To Haman's horror, she was only too happy to oblige the king's request and said, "The adversary and enemy is this vile Haman" (Esther 7:6).

Furious, the king stomped out. Ironically, pathetically, and almost comically, Haman begged Esther for his life. This was a poor choice and bad timing on Haman's part.

Just as the king returned from the palace garden to the banquet hall, Haman was groveling at the couch where Esther was reclining—a bad decision.

> *The king exclaimed, "Will he even molest the queen while she is with me in the house?" As soon as the word left the king's mouth, they covered Haman's face. Then Harbona, one of the eunuchs attending the king, said, "A gallows seventy-five feet*

*high stands by Haman's house. He had it made for Mordecai, who spoke up to help
the king." The king said, "Hang him on it!" So they hanged Haman on the gallows
he had prepared for Mordecai. Then the king's fury subsided.*

ESTHER 7:8–10

And They Lived Happily Ever After

These were incredible happenings. Instead of killing all the Jews starting with Mordecai,
Haman was forced to honor Mordecai. Then Haman was executed on the very gallows he
had built to kill Mordecai!

What happened next would have been utterly impossible a few days earlier. Instead of
being killed for her brashness, Esther was given her own palace, which just so happened to
be Haman's former estate!

On top of that, she was given the power to spare the Jews. Plus, her people were given
the authority to kill those who had persecuted them and to confiscate their property. As a
result, many non-Jews decided to become Jews!

But the divine icing on the cake is reserved for Mordecai. Instead of being the first Jew
killed, he was promoted to Haman's position as the king's highest-ranking official. Wow!

Yay, God!

Esther is the only book of the Bible that does not mention God, although its story has God's
fingerprints all over it.

Who else but God led Mordecai to uncover the plot to kill the king? Obviously, the
Lord was the One who allowed Esther to become the queen. God kept the king awake that
night. The Lord directed the royal reader to expound the account of Mordecai's valor and
point out that it had gone unrewarded. God gave Esther favor with the king so he'd grant her
every request. And God arranged to bless Esther, spare the Jews, destroy their enemies, and
take evil Haman down while lifting honorable Mordecai up.

Yay, God!

Promotion by Preparation and Providence

*No one from the east or the west or from the desert can exalt a man. But it is God
who judges: He brings one down, he exalts another.*

PSALM 75:6–7

Human nature dreams and schemes for promotion, thinking it comes as the result of
luck or knowing the right people. But for God's people, promotion is the result of preparation
and providence. When all is said and done, God gives the demotions and promotions
according to His purpose and plan. He is the ultimate ruler over the universe. Just ask Esther,
Mordecai, and Haman. They teach us several lessons about divine promotion.

- *Promotion Ultimately Comes from God*

Ultimately, Mordecai's promotion came from the Lord, not from the king. This was not
the only time God gave supernatural promotions in a single day. God exalted Joseph from
prisoner to prime minister in a day. God promoted David from shepherd boy to military hero
in a day. God lifted Daniel from the ranks of plebe on probation to a position in the king's
cabinet in a day.

- *Promotion Comes according to God's Timing, Not Ours*

No doubt, Mordecai would have loved to receive his promotion at the time he uncovered the assassination plot against the king. But if he had been promoted then, Haman would have been his boss and would have been able to hold him back or kill him. However, because the promotion came according to God's timing, it was to a higher position and a better situation. Certainly, God's ways and God's timing are best.

- *Promotion Is Given to Those the Lord Deems Promotable*

Before his promotion, Mordecai was viewed as a good and honorable man. He already held a position in the king's court. He proved himself to be loyal to the king. He was definitely loyal to his people. He refused to worship anyone other than the Lord. He was obviously a man with strong character and good capabilities. And God knew it. Clearly, Mordecai was prepared and ready.

A Twenty-First-Century Promotion

The atmosphere at work was tense on a good day, downright fearful on the others. Dread hung like a black cloud since the company had been bought out. Rumor had it that seventy-five of the staff would be let go.

Debbie had labored under a miserable, vulgar, ungodly woman for three years. Maybe being laid off wouldn't be so bad, at least for a while. But Debbie was a single mom with two teenage daughters, and she desperately needed the income. Her boss hated everything about Debbie's Christianity. She mocked Debbie's ever-positive attitude, disliked her unwillingness to lie, and was very jealous of Debbie's relationship with her daughters. Everyone knew that Debbie would be the first her boss would release if given the opportunity.

The situation cleared some when word was sent down that only 25 percent of the total workforce would be let go. Unfortunately, everyone in Debbie's department was to be released or reassigned.

Debbie was enjoying her day because her boss wasn't around. Everyone assumed she was out sick. Then Debbie's phone rang. She gulped when the vice president's secretary requested that she come up to his office right away. She had always respected the vice president, because he was known around the company as a man of strong ethics and genuine concern for those who worked most closely with him. The other people working in her department avoided making eye contact with her as she made her way to the elevator. Cautiously she sat down in the vice president's office.

He entered briskly through the side door and sat down. "Let's not beat around the bush here," he said. "Your department is being phased out, and most of the people are being let go, including your boss. But I have received permission to keep the best and the brightest, and that's you. I have been watching you, and you have what it takes. My assistant is retiring at the end of the month, and I want you to take her place. It will mean more responsibility, but . . ." He paused, looking at a paper. Then he smiled and said, "But you'll get a 10 percent raise immediately and a 5 percent increase at the end of the year. What do you think?"

A Final Encouragement

Often we want to get ahead of God's timing. Often we want things to follow our plans. But the Father knows best. It is more productive to focus on being better prepared than to scheme how to get a better job.

When God knows you are ready, when His timing is right, and when it will best advance His purposes, then your promotion will come.

God's Promise of Comfort for the Brokenhearted
PSALM 34:18

Betrayed, forsaken, misunderstood, cheated, exhausted, confused. If you have ever wrestled with such feelings and the heartbreaking emotions they bring, you are not alone. King David felt them all at the same time, on a major scale. Though he was forced to flee, he couldn't run from his problems.

Man on the Run

Sneaking through the wilderness, David was a fugitive in the biggest manhunt in the history of Israel. Imagine the thoughts that must have flooded his mind every time he stopped to catch his breath:

> *How did this happen to me? What did I do to deserve this? When will I wake up and find this nightmare over?*
>
> *One day I was anointed the new king. The next thing I knew, I'd killed Goliath. God had used me to save the nation. Immediately, I became the general of the king's army, the husband of the king's daughter, and the darling of the king's people. I was loyal, faithful, successful, secure, and happy.*
>
> *Then—wham!—the king went crazy with jealousy and tried to kill me. He declared me an outlaw and led his army out after me. I had to leave my wife, my career, my friends, my reputation, and all I have ever loved to run for my life.*
>
> *I tried to hide in the last place he'd think of looking for me with the Philistines. But they were still very upset about the Goliath incident, so I had to grovel and slobber and act like a deranged lunatic to escape.*
>
> *Now King Saul has jumped off the cliff of sanity and gone violently berserk. He murdered eighty-five priests in cold blood just because they had helped me. Saul and his soldiers will not rest until he's cut off my head and fed my carcass to the birds. They are out there, coming after me.*
>
> *What is going on? What did I do wrong? Why is this happening to me? When will this nightmare end?*

The Antidote for an Achy-Breaky Heart

Unexpected, undeserved, unexplainable adversity—it happens to all of us, and David found himself neck-deep in it. It broke his heart.

David found that nothing hurts as profoundly as a broken heart. It steals our strength, robs our joy, and takes away our peace. It keeps us awake through the night and exhausted through the day.

Yet just as David knew the agony of a crushed spirit, somewhere in that lonely desert he also experienced the universal antidote in a marvelous little promise. Fortunately, he wrote it down in his journal. This three-thousand-year-old promise still holds true today:

> *The LORD is close to the brokenhearted and saves those who are crushed in spirit.*
>
> PSALM 34:18

This promise opens with these key words: "The LORD." He is the prescription for a broken heart. When we ache in inner agony, what we desperately need are love, light, joy, peace, and perspective. God is the source of these and more. Like rays of light and heat that radiate from the sun, God brings health and healing to our aching hurts and deflated spirits. Everything our hurting hearts need flows from the heart of God.

This brings us back to David. He was called a "man after God's own heart" because he learned how to beat a path to God when his spirit was crushed. The psalm in which this promise is found is a four-part primer on the art and science of getting to God when you have a broken heart.

- *Turn Your Pain into Praise*

I will extol the LORD at all times; his praise will always be on my lips. My soul will boast in the LORD; let the afflicted hear and rejoice. Glorify the LORD with me; let us exalt his name together.

PSALM 34:1–3

It seems like an outrageous impossibility—praising God when your heart is broken. But it is very possible. And it does make a huge difference. David determined that God was worthy of praise no matter what. He decided that he would live a life of praise regardless of his circumstances. He practiced praise when times were good, so it was less difficult to praise when all went awry. He turned his pain into praise and found a path to God. Many others have done the same.

Job's heart was pounded and pulverized even more severely than David's was. In one awful day he was stripped of his wealth, business, career, and employees. Then he was told that all of his children were dead. I cannot imagine the immense weight of grief that crushed his soul. Such pressing sorrow could have driven a normal man to insanity. But Job knew the path to God. He acknowledged his burden and then turned his pain into praise.

At this, Job got up and tore his robe and shaved his head. Then he fell to the ground in worship and said: "Naked I came from my mother's womb, and naked I will depart. The LORD gave and the LORD has taken away; may the name of the LORD be praised."

JOB 1:20–21

Paul and Silas were serving God with everything they had. They were trying to capture Philippi for Christ. But the powers in Philippi captured them, beat them, and threw them into prison. This would have disillusioned and discouraged most people, but not Paul and Silas. They knew the path to God. They turned their pain into praise.

About midnight Paul and Silas were praying and singing hymns to God, and the other prisoners were listening to them.

ACTS 16:25

In the case of Paul and Silas, their praise not only brought them to God but brought God to them in a big way.

> *Suddenly there was such a violent earthquake that the foundations of the prison were shaken. At once all the prison doors flew open, and everybody's chains came loose.*
>
> ACTS 16:26

God sent an earthquake to His imprisoned praisers. You may know the rest of the story. The jailer and his family were saved (Acts 16:31), and Paul and Silas were set free (16:35). Never underestimate the power of praise and thanksgiving. It is the path to God and the prescription for a broken heart.

• *Make Your Grief a Motive for Prayer*

David not only blessed God when life was cursing him; he also turned his problems into prayer, and God answered.

> *I sought the LORD, and he answered me; he delivered me from all my fears. Those who look to him are radiant; their faces are never covered with shame. This poor man called, and the LORD heard him; he saved him out of all his troubles. The angel of the LORD encamps around those who fear him, and he delivers them.*
>
> PSALM 34:4–7

It is important to notice that David did not say that his prayers kept him from experiencing trouble. He said that his prayers saved him out of his troubles. The bad news is that as long as we are on this planet, we will experience heartbreaking trouble. The good news is that prayer allows God to deliver us out of it.

We may feel as though our hearts are so heavy or so angry that we cannot pray. But it is at these times we must pray. We must choose to make the effort to talk with the One who can make things better.

• *Pursue God Even When It Hurts*

What sets David apart from so many others is that His fervent passion for God was undaunted by the fierce problems he faced. He allowed his difficulties to drive him to God, not away from God. Provision and inner healing were the result.

> *Taste and see that the LORD is good; blessed is the man who takes refuge in him. Fear the LORD, you his saints, for those who fear him lack nothing. The lions may grow weak and hungry, but those who seek the LORD lack no good thing.*
>
> PSALM 34:8–10

Periods of intense, piercing pain are defining moments for the followers of God. They can either force us far from God or draw us amazingly close to Him. It is up to us. If we let our difficulties drive us from God, our heartache will only grow. But if we decide to let our pain press us toward God, we will find a level of soul satisfaction previously unattained and unimagined.

• *Practice Good Living and God-Centered Choices*

When my heart is broken, it pulls my focus off God and onto me. I forget that life is ultimately all about Him, and I begin to live as though it's all about me. I see and hear everything around me through the skewed lens of me. Such a distorted outlook leads to hurt feelings and bad decisions and only makes me more miserable.

Also, when my heart is broken, the enemy loves to whisper through the cracks and tempt me to sin. He will tell me that God failed me and I have an excuse for sin. My old nature gladly accepts any reason to get relief or distraction from the pain. Yet toleration of sin only leads to guilt, and guilt does not heal the brokenhearted. David understood this. Hence, he stepped up his commitment to practice righteous living and make God-centered choices.

Come, my children, listen to me; I will teach you the fear of the LORD. Whoever of you loves life and desires to see many good days, keep your tongue from evil and your lips from speaking lies. Turn from evil and do good; seek peace and pursue it. The eyes of the LORD are on the righteous and his ears are attentive to their cry; the face of the LORD is against those who do evil, to cut off the memory of them from the earth. The righteous cry out, and the LORD hears them; he delivers them from all their troubles.

PSALM 34:11–17

A Final Encouragement

He heals the brokenhearted and binds up their wounds.

PSALM 147:3

God has the ability and desire to heal broken hearts. He did it for David, and He has done it for countless others. He can do it for you. Do your part to get to Him, and He'll do His part to mend your heart.

God's Promise of Maturity through Adversity
JAMES 1:2–4

He knew adversity. His brother had been illegally arrested, unjustly tried, and violently executed. Now everyone close to him was in jeopardy.

James, the son of Joseph and Mary, the half brother of Jesus, went from skeptic to believer after seeing his brother Jesus resurrected from the dead. At that moment, James's half brother became his Lord and his God. At that moment, Jesus' enemies became James's enemies. He and the others who followed Jesus became targets of persecution.

James began to care for Jesus' followers as a shepherd cares for sheep. All the believers who lived in Jerusalem looked to him for special spiritual care and leadership. The Romans and the Jews focused their abuse on Christians. The Romans taxed them mercilessly and treated them as glorified slaves. The Jews booted them from their families, fired them from their jobs, and accused them of heresy. Soon, Jews and Romans joined forces to throw the Jerusalem Christians in jail and kill their leaders.

The ferocity of the persecution that James's spiritual flock faced was so intense that many fled for their lives and scattered all over the earth. James must have been heartbroken. Beyond that, he saw many of his colleagues imprisoned and killed.

Out of his suffering and sorrow, James penned a powerful letter to his scattered sheep. In it he gave them one of the most encouraging promises in the Bible:

> *Consider it pure joy, my brothers, whenever you face trials of many kinds, because you know that the testing of your faith develops perseverance. Perseverance must finish its work so that you may be mature and complete, not lacking anything.*
>
> JAMES 1:2–4

These sentences are two sticks of dynamite packed with encouragement. In them, God promises to develop our maturity through adversity. This is very important, because the Lord does not promise to exempt us from adversity.

Some of us struggle because we have the mistaken notion that if God really loved us, He would protect us from problems. This is simply not true. It is *because* God loves us that He allows us to experience adversity. He allows our trials because they produce growth and maturity. The loving God values our growth more than our comfort. He allows our discomfort with good cause.

Many believers accept the myth that Christians don't have problems. Ridiculous! When James records God's promise of maturity through adversity, he is addressing Christians, saying, "my brothers." Many of these people were experiencing problems only because they were Christians. They were forced to abandon their jobs, flee their homes, and run for their lives because they had identified themselves as followers of Jesus.

Sometimes I need to remind myself that I am not home yet. Heaven will be perfect, but I am not there. So I should not be surprised by problems. I should expect them.

Bad Things Do Happen to Good People

Far too often, I catch myself thinking, "Why is this trouble happening to me? I am living for God and doing all the good I can. I live right, so why I am experiencing wrong?" The truth is, bad things happen to good people.

Again I say, some would have us believe that so-called spiritual Christians never face adversity. Absurd! In the first century, the higher someone was positioned in spiritual leadership, the greater the persecution they faced. Godly people face adversity. They always have and always will. Remember, most of the apostles died as martyrs.

Walk through the Bible with me and note the adversity God's people endured. Adam and Eve had a rebellious, murderous son. Sarah was barren until she was ninety years old. Then she had to chase a toddler around!

Job lost his sheep, cattle, oxen, servants, children, and health. Joseph went through slavery and prison. Moses had to deal with Pharaoh, and then he had to lead some of history's all-time greatest whiners. Joshua faced one battle after another. Hannah was barren and had to deal with a cruel adversary.

David was totally innocent, yet he was nearly murdered twice and had to run for his life like a fugitive. Daniel faced a den of hungry lions. Shadrach, Meshach, and Abednego were thrown into a flaming furnace.

Mary watched her son be executed unjustly. Paul was repeatedly beaten and thrown into jail. And James died as a martyr.

Problems are a universal reality of life on this groaning planet—even for Christians!

Choose Joy

> *Consider it pure joy. . .*
>
> JAMES 1:2

A quick study of this opening line of the promise brings several insights. The promise begins with the command, "Consider it pure joy, my brothers, whenever you face trials of many kinds." The fact that this is a command means that we have the option of obeying it or not. It is our choice. This is powerful. We do not have to live as the helpless victims of our circumstances. We can be victors. It is our choice.

Victor, Not Victim

Victor Frankl was a true victor in the midst of awful adversity. He was a Jew in Nazi Germany during World War II and was thrown into the Auschwitz prison camp. Conditions there were unbearable. He experienced extreme suffering from hunger, cold, and brutality. He lived under the threat of imminent extermination. His father, mother, brother, and wife had died in concentration camps. His every possession was lost, every valuable destroyed. Such losses broke most men, and they gave up and died. But Frankl survived, even thrived, and came to understand something we all should know:

> *Everything can be taken from a man but. . .the last of the human freedoms—to choose one's attitude in any given set of circumstances, to choose one's own way.*[1]

We don't have to be victims. Like Victor Frankl, we can be victors. It is our choice.

Problems Produce Perseverance

> *The testing of your faith develops perseverance.*
>
> JAMES 1:3

This promise gives us good reason to choose joy in the midst of adversity. The reason is that adversity produces maturity. Look again at the promise. "Consider it pure joy, my brothers, whenever you face trials of many kinds, *because* you know that the testing of your faith develops perseverance" (emphasis added).

Perseverance is an awesome word that is overlooked and under-used in today's vernacular. Don't take it lightly. It is the ability to press through adversity until you come out on the other side.

Run through the Pain

When I was a student, I ran track. My legs were (and still are) short, and I was (and still am) not very fast. But I wanted to earn a varsity letter. So I ran the least popular races. These happened to be the longest races. In the eighth grade, the longest race available was the mile. So that became my specialty, even though I was not all that special.

One day, at the end of a hard practice, the coach asked several of my teammates and me to run a mile race. We were tired, but we agreed.

Somewhere around the three-quarter-mile mark, I hit the wall. My legs turned to lead. My lungs burned. A sharp cramp dug into my rib cage. The finish line appeared to be miles away. The track seemed to be going uphill. Everything inside cried out, "Stop. Lie down. This is too much. You cannot go on."

Then I heard my coach's voice ringing through the air.

"Run *through* the pain," he yelled. "You can do it, Earley. Run *through* the pain."

So I did. His encouragement was what I needed. I found reserves I did not realize I had. As a result, I turned in a better time than anyone expected. I also learned that I could do more than I realized.

Too often when adversity hits, we feel tired and weary. We run *to* the pain. But then we want to quit. God promises to give us what we need to run *through* the pain. He gives us the grace to persevere.

You may have hit a wall of pain in the race of your life. Let me encourage you not to quit. Run through the pain.

No Pain, No Gain

> *Perseverance must finish its work so that you may be mature and complete, not lacking anything.*

> JAMES 1:4

I also participated in wrestling. Part of wrestling conditioning is weight lifting. I will never forget my first day in the weight room. I was a skinny ninety-eight-pound freshman surrounded by a horde of mammoth football players. I had lifted weights a little at home, but somehow the weights seemed much heavier in the weight room with everyone watching. I was so sore the next day I could hardly move.

There was a sign on the wall of the weight room that I have never forgotten. Its words are the essence of James 1:4. It said, "No pain. No gain."

I learned the truth of this message. If you lift until your muscles begin to ache and then stop, you will make little or no progress. But lifting through the pain is what makes your muscles grow. Pain produces gain.

Trials can be troubling and terribly painful. Remember, the pain is a tool that produces gain in the development of our character and our spiritual maturity.

Perseverance Produces Maturity

I have three boys, all teenagers. All of them are fully capable of walking on their own and have been since they were a little over a year old. When each boy was about a year old, he took his first steps. After that first staggering attempt to walk, he crashed mightily and cried.

My wife and I had a choice. We could have said, "We love this cute little boy so much that we don't want him to get hurt anymore. From now on one of us will carry him around on a golden pillow. No more painful falling down for our precious little boy."

Today all of our sons are the same size as I am and bigger than their mom. To carry them around on a golden pillow would be impossible. Plus, they would resent us for never allowing them to learn to walk. Such protection would have kept them from maturing.

Instead of pursuing the shortsighted scheme of protecting them from pain, we let them go through it. We let them try to learn to walk. Every time they fell, we'd pick them up, wipe away their tears, and let them go at it again. And they did.

God treats us the same way. His goal is to develop our maturity more than to cater to our comfort. So He allows us to experience adversity and encourages us to press through it. By doing so, we mature.

A Final Encouragement

You will face adversity. As you choose joy in the midst of your adversity and persevere through it, God promises to give you maturity. Don't quit. Run through the pain, and you will grow. That is His promise.

NOTE

[1]Victor Frankl, quoted in Jone Johnson Lewis, "Attitude Quotes" from *Wisdom Quotes: Quotations to Inspire and Challenge,* http://www.wisdomquotes.com/cat_attitude.html (August 25, 2005).

God's Promise of Peace Instead of Worry
PHILIPPIANS 4:6–7

Are you a worrier? Do troubling thoughts about what could happen drive you to distraction? Are you skilled at focusing on what could go wrong? Do uncertain situations make you anxious? I understand. Being a worrier at heart, I am always impressed with people who win over worry in the worst situations.

Paul lived a life of victory over anxiety. As an elderly man, he was taken to Rome and held in strict custody in the Praetorium, that is, the barracks of the Praetorian guards attached to the palace of Nero in Rome (Philippians 1:13; 4:22).[1] There he spent two years chained to Roman guards (Philippians 1:12).[2]

If that was not enough to make a man worry, Paul faced probable execution at the hands of the maniacal emperor, Nero, and his newly installed prefect, Tigellinus, whom history calls "a monster in wickedness."[3] Paul's letter, although radiating joy and peace, also reveals his awareness of the possibility of his execution (Philippians 2:17; 3:11).

If I had been in his situation, I would have been tempted to whine and worry. Thoughts of "This is not fair," "Why did this happen to me?" and "What is going to happen next?" would have flooded my mind. But these were not Paul's thoughts. When he sat down to write a letter to his friends at Philippi, not a whiff of worry, fear, or self-pity slipped out. Amazingly, the tone is so worry-free and optimistic that his letter to the Philippians is often called the "Epistle of Joy"!

Where did Paul get this ability to be at peace in the midst of prison? How could he manifest such joy from jail? What was his secret? How did he do it?

Fortunately for us, Paul did not keep his path to peace to himself. When he penned his letter to the Philippians, he shared the following promise:

> *Do not be anxious about anything, but in everything, by prayer and petition, with thanksgiving, present your requests to God. And the peace of God, which transcends all under-standing, will guard your hearts and your minds in Christ Jesus.*
>
> PHILIPPIANS 4:6–7

It is a privilege to possess more than one spiritual gift. I have always joked that as a pastor my two greatest gifts are delegation and irritation. But I have to confess that I also possess the non-spiritual gift of "tending toward anxiety." I am highly analytical. When I cannot figure out how something will work out, I struggle to find peace with it. Unresolved situations and uncertain circumstances drive me to distraction. Once anxious thoughts start running through my mind, it is as though a dam has broken and apprehension flows in such torrents that I struggle mightily to make them stop.

Therefore, I am eternally grateful for the promise of Philippians 4:6–7. It worked for Paul, it works for me, and it will work for you. Let's examine it more closely.

Do Not Worry about Anything
Paul opened the promise with a strong, inclusive directive: "Do not be anxious about anything." Peace won't flow when anxiety clogs the pipe. Worry must be recognized and refused. Anxiety must be flushed out before peace can run freely through the pipes of our minds and souls.

If you are like me, you ask, "How can I stop being anxious? It feels like an involuntary emotion. What is strong enough to turn it off and flush it out?" The answer is found in the next part of the promise.

Pray about Everything ✕

"Do not be anxious about anything, but in everything, by prayer and petition, with thanksgiving, present your requests to God." Notice the last phrase of the above sentence. The only way to stop negative emotions is to replace them with positive actions. The only way to stop greed is to trade it for generosity. The only way to stop bitterness is to substitute forgiveness and love. The only way to defeat fear is to exchange it with faith. And the only way to win over worry is to replace it with grateful prayer. Let's look a little more deeply at exactly how to replace worry with thankful prayer.

Stay Focused on God

Worry has a way of dominating our focus. This is dangerous, because once we become focused on worry, our worries seem to get steadily larger and more complex. In order to defeat anxiety, we must stay fixed on God. He needs to be foremost in our thinking, primary in our conversations, and central in our deeds. As we concentrate on God, we will see Him for who He is—the One who is bigger than anything we could worry about.

Turn Pressures into Prayers

The term *petition* speaks of "making specific requests to God." Just as we are tempted to worry over specific problems, we need to practice definite petitioning in prayer.

To keep from being eaten by anxiety, I have learned that I must turn my pressures into prayers. Every morning I take whatever I am worried about and write it down in my prayer journal. The list usually contains four to eight worries, though one day I had fifty-seven! This is how I pray about everything. I take each item on my list and give it to God. I turn my pressure list into my prayer list. One by one I cast all my cares on Him. By doing this, I replace worry with prayer.

When I do this, simple but wonderful things occur. My pressures turn to peace. My concerns turn into confidence. My burdens are lifted. My hope is renewed, and I feel better. More important, God works on my problems as I ask Him to act.

The Perspective of Thankfulness

Pressures and problems are powerful forces that can easily pull our thinking off track. We lose perspective. Little troubles or problems that have a vague chance of becoming reality can look so massive that they crowd out God's blessings. We get so focused on a little bad that we fail to see the abundant good we have been given.

My eldest son is now in college. So I appreciate one of my favorite stories on perspective even more. It involves a daughter's letter written to her parents from college.

> *Dear Mom and Dad,*
>
> *Just thought I'd drop you a note to clue you in on my plans. I've fallen in love with a guy named Jim. He quit high school in the eleventh grade to get married. It didn't work out, and he's been divorced now about a year. Jim and I have been going together for a few months, and we plan to get married in the fall. Until then, I decided to move into his apartment.*
>
> *I hate to admit it, but I am having a problem with drugs. By the way, I think I*

am pregnant. At any rate, I dropped out of school last week, although I would like to finish college sometime in the future.

The young woman's parents anxiously turned over the letter to page two.

Mom and Dad, I want you to know that everything I have written so far is false. None of it is true. But it is true that I got a C– in French and that I failed a math test. I just wanted to put things in perspective.

Anxiety has a devious way of causing us to see only negatives. We tend to think about negatives from our past, are overwhelmed by the negatives currently confronting us, and are staggered by the potential negatives looming on the horizon. Gratitude has the power to shrink negatives down to size.

I have a friend named Sandy. Seizures have made her unable to work and have put her in the hospital on many occasions. Yet every time I talk to her, she gushes with gratitude. The last time we spoke, she told me her most recent seizure blocked her verbal abilities for a time. If I were in her shoes, I would be worried about what further losses I might experience, but not Sandy. She uses the power of thanksgiving to replace worry and usher in peace.

When I talked with her about her health issues, she smiled broadly and said, "But it's a blessing." Then she really floored me. She said, "I am thankful for it because it helped me be a better listener."

As she spoke, her face shone. Her eyes sparkled with joy, and her smile radiated peace. Sandy is less than five feet tall, but I could tell I was in the presence of a spiritual giant, a very powerful person. Sandy has learned to tap fully in to the power of thanksgiving. Never underestimate the power of thanksgiving, because it is the cure for worry.

I have a few lists in the back of my journal enumerating things I am thankful for. When I get anxious or down, I simply refer to these lists. This lifts me up. I generally walk away humming and thinking, "I have it better than I thought. God has been good to me."

We cannot be full of gratitude and full of worry at the same time. The only way to change strong emotions is to replace them with ones that are more powerful. The apostle Paul learned that thanksgiving has the power to eradicate worry.

Peace in the Place of Worry

The apostle Paul said, "The peace of God, which transcends all understanding, will guard your hearts and your minds in Christ Jesus" (Philippians 4:7). God promises that His peace has the power to replace our anxiety. When we give our problems to God, who is greater than our problems, we find peace that is greater than our problems. Could it be that when we fail to experience such peace, we have failed to give our problems to God in prayer?

But the beauty of prayer is not seen in how it makes us feel. The beauty of prayer is in what it does. Prayer invites God into our situation. It turns the problem over to the One who is big enough to handle it. And He handles it with peace.

I sometimes revisit my daily prayer list late at night or first thing the next morning. I do this because I often forget the worries I had listed the pervious morning. Often I find that God has already worked them out. I love to put checks by all my answered prayers. And there are many answered prayers. Some of my concerns never materialize. Some do, and God defeats them that very day. In other areas of concern, I do not see the answer, but I do see God working.

A Final Encouragement

Are you facing some difficult decisions, anxious situations, or tough adversaries? Stop worrying and start praying. Write down your worries. Spread them out before the Lord. Ask Him to take care of them. Then leave them with Him and go off into victory.

NOTES

[1] Commentary by A. R. Fausett in Jamieson, Fausett & Brown: The Epistle of Paul the Apostle to the Philippians, Blue Letter Bible, www.blueletter bible.org/tmpdir/c/1120182378-5162.html (June 30, 2005).

[2] Courson, The Epistle to the Philippians: Philippians One, Blue Letter Bible, www.blueletterbible.org/tmp_dir/c/1120183548-1988.html (June 30, 2005).

[3] A. R. Fausett in Blue Letter Bible, www.blueletterbible.org/tmp_dir/c/1120182785-5695.htm (June 30, 2005).

[4] Courson, in The Blue Letter Bible, www.blueletterbible.org/tmp_dir/c/1120222581-229.html (July 1, 2005).

19

God's Promise of Spiritual Revival
ISAIAH 55:17

Do you ever feel spiritually lifeless? How about inwardly empty? Are you less than hot in your love relationship with God? Do you ever wish that the guilt that is keeping you from really experiencing God were wiped completely away?

Would you like to know that you are as close to God as you can be?

Years ago, an entire nation was wrestling with these sort of questions. The answers led them to experience God's promise of revival.

The Water Gate Revival

To my generation, the name Watergate dredges up memories of an ugly bruise on our nation's conscience. Many of us recall the painful period of intense national scrutiny, intrigue, and shame. Watergate is the name of a Washington, DC, hotel, the site of a crime that led to the downfall of President Nixon. For America, Watergate signifies a national loss of confidence in its leaders.

Hundreds of years before this, an actual gate served as the backdrop for a national spiritual awakening. Around 450 BC, Nehemiah led a group of Jews from Babylon back to Jerusalem. This remnant left the confines of captivity to rebuild the city's walls. One of the twelve gates was on the east side of Jerusalem near the Gihon Spring. People carried water into the city from the spring through that gate, so it became known as the Water Gate.

The walls and buildings of the city of Jerusalem had lain in ruins for several generations because of the ineffective attempts to defend the city against foreign invaders. In spite of long odds, dangerous opposition, and constant frustration, Nehemiah and his crew successfully rebuilt the walls surrounding the city. This made it safe for the captured Hebrew remnant to begin to return and rebuild their nation.

After the walls were complete, Nehemiah gathered all of the people together in front of the Water Gate. They were excited to be safely together in the holy city. That day was especially significant because Ezra did something that had not been done for seventy years—he read the Law of God aloud to the people of God (Nehemiah 8:1–3).

It must have been an awesome scene. Ezra, the wise man of God, walked out on a raised platform carrying the law of God; carefully, lovingly, deliberately, he unrolled the scroll. A holy hush descended on the people, and with quiet spontaneity all stood as one in profound reverence to the Word of God (Nehemiah 8:4–5).

I can almost hear Ezra excitedly clear his throat, then lift his voice and bless the Lord, hailing Him as the great God. I can see the people soberly nodding and answering, "Amen! Amen!" as they bow their faces to the ground in deep humility and worship (Nehemiah 8:6).

All morning Ezra read the Law. The sound of God's Word cascaded over the people, some of it vaguely familiar. Although most of them had never heard it read aloud, some may have heard bits and pieces of it from their parents or grandparents. The pointed and powerful words from the Lord cut deep into the people's hearts as Ezra and other priests explained and applied them (Nehemiah 8:8).

The words of God's Law were crystal clear and convicting. The people became aware that individually and as a nation, they had disobeyed the Law. Yet the Lord had been good to them. He kept them intact during the captivity. He restored them to their homeland. He gave them back their city.

Soon, sniffling was heard throughout the gathering. Men, women, boys, and girls wiped their eyes as hot tears raced down their dusty cheeks. Sobs and weeping punctuated the scene (Nehemiah 8:9).

Those were tears of gratitude and guilt. Ezra, Nehemiah, and the other leaders cried out, "This day is sacred to the LORD your God. Do not mourn or weep" (Nehemiah 8:9). Then Ezra sent them home to get something to eat, saying, "Go and enjoy choice food and sweet drinks, and send some to those who have nothing prepared. . . . Do not grieve, for the joy of the LORD is your strength" (8:10).

The next day, as they read the Law of the Lord, they discovered that they were supposed to have been celebrating three annual weeklong feasts. These weeks were to be set apart for God. Since it was fall, they dedicated the next seven days to celebrate the Feast of Ingathering, also called the Feast of Tabernacles (Nehemiah 8:13–18; Exodus 23:16; Leviticus 23:33–36). The people celebrated with great joy (Nehemiah 8:17). Each day they continued to listen eagerly as Ezra read the Law (8:18).

The weeklong feast culminated in a sacred assembly for the confession of sins. They spent a quarter of the day listening to the Law and the next quarter confessing their sins and worshiping the Lord (Nehemiah 9:1–3). The day of confession of sins, mixed with praise and worship, culminated in all of the leaders and the people signing a covenant of strict obedience to the Law (9:38–10:39). The decisions and commitments made during this nine-day revival blessed and carried the nation of Israel for years to come.

Revival

The word *revival* is a compound word combining the prefix *re-* and the Latin word *vive*. *Re-* means "new" or "again," and *vive* means *life*. So, *revival* is "new life" or "renewed life."

English Bibles use *revive* several times in the Old Testament. "Revive" is the translation of the Hebrew word *hayah,* which comes from the root *hay,* meaning "life." The prefix *ya* denotes "again" or "renewed."

A spiritual revival is a renewal of life to the spiritually dead. It is a return of people who are spiritually distant; a renewal of obedience to the Lord; a rekindling of a relationship with God. Years before the days of Ezra and the revival at the Water Gate, the prophet Isaiah recorded a promise of revival that applies to every generation:

> For thus says the High and Lofty One who inhabits eternity, whose name is Holy: "I dwell in the high and holy place, with him who has a contrite and humble spirit, to revive the spirit of the humble, and to revive the heart of the contrite ones.
>
> ISAIAH 57:15 NKJV

The Source of Revival Is God

The Lord's promise is that when we dwell with Him we will experience revival. Revival is a good thing. Even more, it is a *God thing*. Revival is the return of spiritual life, and God is the Spirit of life. When we experience God, we experience His life. When we lack God, we lack life.

God is the creator of life (Genesis 1:1). Jesus declared that He is the way, the truth, and the life (John 14:6). Since God is the source of life, He is the source of revival. As Isaiah 57:15 reminds us, revival comes from the "High and Lofty One who inhabits eternity, whose name is Holy." We cannot grit our teeth and become spiritually alive. Revival comes from God. The closer we get to God, the more alive we become.

In other words, God's part in revival is simply to be himself. Since He is life, when we get close to Him, we experience renewed spiritual life.

The Key to Revival Is Spiritual Brokenness

God is the source of revival. So how do we access that source? Look again at this promise. Note the words that are repeated there:

> *For thus says the* High *and* Lofty *One who inhabits eternity, whose name is* Holy: *"I dwell in the* high *and* holy *place, with him who has a* contrite *and* humble *spirit, to revive the spirit of the* humble, *And to revive the heart of the* contrite *ones."* *(emphasis added)*

The keys to this promise are found in the concepts of highness, holiness, humility, and contrition. God is high and lofty. He lives on a higher plane than anyone else. He also is holy. He dwells in the holy place. We experience Him as we humble ourselves before His highness and His holiness. In other words, the door to God is opened with the key of brokenness.

The New Testament author James wrote as though he was very familiar with Isaiah 55:17. Note carefully his clarion call to humility in light of God's loftiness.

> *"God opposes the proud but gives grace to the humble." Submit yourselves, then, to God. Resist the devil, and he will flee from you. Come near to God and he will come near to you. Wash your hands, you sinners, and purify your hearts, you double-minded. Grieve, mourn and wail. Change your laughter to mourning and your joy to gloom. Humble yourselves before the Lord, and he will lift you up."*
>
> JAMES 4:6–10

Spiritual brokenness becomes evident as we humble ourselves and admit that we are not God, we are insufficient, we are not holy, and we need God. Then we yield to God and confess our sin, and revival is the result.

For example, the disciple Peter, after denying Jesus, returned to God with great power and preached the greatest sermon ever given. But this did not occur until after he was first broken and honest about his failure to be loyal to Christ (John 21:15–19). Next, he spent a week in the upper room, praying with 120 other believers (Acts 1:12–26). Then he was revived and stood in Jerusalem preaching the gospel to Israel (2:1–36).

The prodigal son returned to the blessed life of his father's house. But not until he came to his senses and admitted his foolishness, confessing his sin in leaving the father in the first place (Luke 15:11–24).

Paul lived in a continual state of revival because he was spiritually broken. On one hand, he knew that without Christ he was the chief of sinners (1 Timothy 1:15). On the other, he could do all things through Christ (Philippians 4:13)

Remember, when we finally come to the end of ourselves, we come to the beginning of God. Spiritual brokenness is the key that opens the door to God's revival.

A Final Encouragement

Have you grown tired of what you can do? Are you weary with the status quo? Are you worn out by business as usual? Are you sick of human-sized things? Do you hunger for some

God-sized things? Do you long to see God do in seconds what you have failed to do over years? Is good enough no longer good enough? If you have reached this place of humble honesty, you are on the verge of revival.

God cannot resist the spiritually broken. He gives them spiritual revival. He has done it for many others, and He'll gladly do it for you.

God's Promise of Divine Protection
PSALM 91:1–2

Have you ever felt a strange heaviness of spirit or oppression in your mind that made prayer impossible? For sure, prayer can be difficult sometimes. But have you ever felt as if your prayers were shut up in a box, strangely thwarted, going nowhere, unheard? At such times, you may find that wicked, even vile thoughts rise up from nowhere. Sleep is difficult. Suicide may come to mind.

Well, you are not alone.

Chuck Swindoll says that these are "subtle yet distinct hints that evil forces are at work." He testifies, "My wife and I have often talked about how we can sense the invisible presence of the adversary."[1]

Please take note: Some weird wacko didn't say this. Chuck Swindoll is the former president of the Dallas Theological Seminary and a bestselling author. Plus, I have experienced the same things on more than one occasion. I know what it is like to come under spiritual attack. And you do, too, although maybe you may not realize what it is or know what to do about it.

When I first began to pursue God, Satan came after me. I began to experience spiritual attack, not unlike what Swindoll described. I thought I was the only one experiencing this. I wondered if I was crazy. Eventually I discovered that it is not unusual for the enemy to attack us when we step out for God. But back then I had no idea what it was or what to do about it. In fact, I was so intimidated that I drew back from my pursuit of God and postponed getting radical in my walk with God. The enemy was successful. His attacks were effective. I was defeated.

Under Attack in AD 1500

Martin Luther was a monk, a theologian, and one of the most influential people in history. His insistence on salvation by grace sparked a movement called the Protestant Reformation and led to the rise of Protestantism. His love of music and hymns brought a renaissance to church music. His ideologies helped shape several European governments. He may have done more for God than anyone else in his day, and the enemy did not like it.

Luther believed in a literal devil and the attack of evil spirits. He freely spoke of being pestered by devils, evil spirits, and demons throughout his life. These attacks increased in frequency and intensity when he went into hiding in Wartburg Castle. There Luther, a fugitive for his faith, spent his time translating the Bible into the language of his people, German.

God's enemy was aware of the power that would be unleashed when the Bible became available in the language of the masses. Satan did not like this and kept attacking Luther. One night the attacks hit a climax. Luther sensed the presence of the enemy in his room. Exasperated by the close and constant hounding, Martin whirled and heaved his inkwell at the devil. The ink stain on the wall in Wartburg Castle was visible for centuries.

I am not sure how effective his inkwell was in defeating the devil, but I do know that Luther's usual practice of praising, praying, and trusting in God's promises is effective. Later in life, Luther put into practice God's promise of deliverance when under attack. He penned a song. I am sure you have sung this hymn, but I bet you probably never noticed how clearly the words speak to those under enemy attack.

A mighty fortress is our God,
A bulwark never failing;
Our helper He, amid the flood
Of mortal ills prevailing.
For still our ancient foe
Doth seek to work us woe;
His craft and pow'r are great,
And, armed with cruel hate,
On earth is not his equal.

Did we in our own strength confide,
Our striving would be losing;
Were not the right Man on our side,
The man of God's own choosing.
Dost ask who that may be?
Christ Jesus, it is He;
Lord Sabaoth His name,
From age to age the same,
And He must win the battle.

And though this world, with devils filled,
Should threaten to undo us,
We will not fear, for God hath willed
His truth to triumph through us.
The Prince of Darkness grim,
We tremble not for him;
His rage we can endure,
For lo, his doom is sure;
One little word shall fell him.[2]

Under Attack in 1990

When we first started our church, I was ignorant of the enemy's schemes, and the enemy took advantage of that. Every Saturday evening was miserable at my house, especially if a big crowd was expected on Sunday morning. The kids would be healthy all week, but wake up vomiting in the middle of Saturday night. Or they would be good all week, but get in arguments and fights with each other on Saturday night. Or my wife and I would get along great all week and find ourselves getting upset with each other over some insignificant thing on Saturday night. Also, at about 12:30 a.m. every Saturday night, after we had fallen asleep, the phone would ring. It would be either a wrong number or a drunk.

I may seem a little slow, but after a few years of this, I began to see a pattern. So I took action. First, I made an effort to read my Bible and pray aloud before retiring on Saturday night. Second, swallowing my pride one Sunday night, I explained to my congregation what was going on and asked them to pray for me every Saturday night. The next Saturday night was heaven in my home. The kids were good and healthy; Cathy and I got along great; the phone did not ring; I slept like a baby; and that Sunday I preached better than ever.

I have shared this story at pastors' conferences and have had many pastors and their wives tell me afterward, often with tears in their eyes, how they, too, have had to battle the enemy on Saturday nights. Many of them wanted me to know that they had discovered God's promise of deliverance:

> He who dwells in the shelter of the Most High will rest in the shadow of the Almighty. I will say of the LORD, "He is my refuge and my fortress, my God, in whom I trust."
>
> PSALM 91:1–2

God is a supernaturally strong shelter. He is a formidable fortress and a haven of true rest. We do not have to fear when the enemy assaults us. We can be protected. We also don't have to fight back, and we don't need to surrender to defeat. We need to learn to dwell in the shelter of the Most High and rest in the shadow of the Almighty.

The Lord is described in this promise as "the Most High" and "the Almighty." This means that He is higher, bigger, smarter, and stronger than the enemy and so able to defeat him. The name "Most High" (in Hebrew, *El Elyon*) means "the God above all gods." If anyone has the authority to keep promises, God does. The name "Almighty" (in Hebrew, *El Shaddai*), means "the God who sees and provides." God knows when we are attacked and is able to rescue us from it. He is willing and able to protect us from enemy assault. He is greater than our foe. As the apostle John wrote, "You, dear children, are from God and have overcome them, because the one who is in you is greater than the one who is in the world" (1 John 4:4).

Accessing Divine Deliverance

God will, of course, do His part. But we must learn to do ours. Psalm 91 points to several doors of entry to the fortress of our Father God.

- *Make Yourself at Home in God*

> He who *dwells in the shelter of the Most High* will rest in the shadow of the Almighty.
>
> PSALM 91:1 (EMPHASIS ADDED)

We must make ourselves at home in God, and God will make Himself at home in us. Protection is within a relationship with God. You need to get in God and dwell there.

- *Trust the Lord Actively*

> I will say of the LORD, "He is my refuge and my fortress, my God, in whom I trust."
>
> PSALM 91:2 (EMPHASIS ADDED)

We must have faith not only that He'll one day take us to heaven. We need to rely on Him to protect us from enemy attack. We cannot defeat the enemy or handle the attack on our own. We must depend on the Lord.

Every time the enemy begins to assault you with worrisome thoughts, tell God that He is your refuge. When you are hit with floods of fear, declare that God is your fortress. When troubles come, proclaim your trust in God.

- *Love the Lord Loyally*

"Because he loves me," says the LORD, "I will rescue him; I will protect him, for he acknowledges my name."

PSALM 91:14

The path to protection lies in the power of our personal relationship with the all-powerful God. If the enemy sees you using his attacks as an excuse to draw closer to God, he will be foolish to persist. Every time Satan hits you with an attack, respond by sending up praise to God.

Our hearts and minds need to be so full of God that the enemy has no room to attack and no basis of operation. The more our lives are under His authority, the less power the enemy will have to harass us.

- *Call upon the Lord Dependently*

He will call upon me, and I will answer him; I will be with him in trouble, I will deliver him and honor him.

PSALM 91:15

When you sense the enemy striking out at you, cry out to God, pray, and ask Him to protect you. Before you go to bed, call on God. When you wake up with a nightmare, call on God. When you find yourself in an argument that is becoming unreasonable, call on God. When you are oppressed with despair, call on God. When you are overwhelmed with suicidal thoughts, call on God. When temptation is all around, call on God. When evil thoughts are flooding your mind, call on God. When circumstances are eerily against you or when the atmosphere is strangely tense, call on God.

One day a dad was picking up his little girl from Sunday school. He asked her what she had learned that day. The small child gave a very insightful response: "I learned that there is a devil. When he knocks on my door, I need to ask Jesus to answer it."

A Final Encouragement

It's inevitable—the enemy will try to knock you off stride. But have no fear, because God is near and will deliver you. He has done it many times for many others; you can count on Him to do it for you.

NOTES

[1]Charles Swindoll, *Living Beyond the Daily Grind, Book 2: Reflections on the Songs and Sayings in Scripture* (Nashville: W Publishing Group, 1989), 260.
[2]Martin Luther, "A Mighty Fortress Is Our God."

5-8-18

God's Promise of Heavenly Help
PSALM 46:1

A prayer to be said
when the world has gotten you down,
and you feel rotten,
and you're too doggone tired to pray,
and you're in a big hurry,
and besides, you're mad at everyone. . .
Help!

Ah, poster theology. Sometimes nothing says it any better. I try to be a man of prayer. Many days I pray for more than an hour at a time. I have even written a few books on prayer. But the prayer I pray most often is that one simple word, "Help!"

Many times I need divine assistance, angelic aid, real-life relief, and heavenly help. You do, too. Thankfully, there is a source for surefire supernatural support. It is expressed in Psalm 46:1, one of the most encouraging and oft-repeated promises in the Bible:

> *God is our refuge and strength, an ever-present* help *in trouble.*
> PSALM 46:1 (EMPHASIS ADDED)

God is a safe place to hide. He is always ready to help us. He is an ever-present, willing source of strength. He promises mercy and grace to help in time of need. Wow! Those are very encouraging promises.

When I am in seasons of severe hardship, I need all the mercy, grace, and help I can get. Thank God for His promises—like this one:

> *Let us then approach the throne of grace with confidence, so that we may receive* mercy *and find grace to* help *us in our time of need.*
> HEBREWS 4:16 (EMPHASIS ADDED)

Notice that at the beginning of Hebrews 4:16, God's help comes because we confidently approach His throne of grace and ask for it. In other words, God doesn't help those who help themselves. He helps those who ask for it.

David Asked for Help and Got It

Like you and me, David needed help many times. When his failures opened the door to inner turmoil and enemy attack, he prayed, "Come quickly to help me, O Lord my Savior" (Psalm 38:22). When swallowed by his circumstances as though in a muddy pit, he cried, "Be pleased, O LORD, to save me; O LORD, come quickly to help me" (40:13). When captured by his enemies, he prayed, "Hasten, O God, to save me; O LORD, come quickly to help me" (70:1). Later he testified, "My enemies will turn back when I call for help. By this I will know that God is for me" (56:9).

In his twilight years, David looked back on the importance of the Lord's help. A rousing song was the result:

If the LORD had not been on our side—let Israel say—if the LORD had not been on our side when men attacked us, when their anger flared against us, they would have swallowed us alive; the flood would have engulfed us, the torrent would have swept over us, the raging waters would have swept us away. Praise be to the LORD, who has not let us be torn by their teeth. We have escaped like a bird out of the fowler's snare; the snare has been broken, and we have escaped. Our help is in the name of the LORD, the Maker of heaven and earth.

PSALM 124:1–8 (EMPHASIS ADDED)

Jonah Asked for Help and Got It

Sometimes we need help because of our own ignorant rebellion. God told Jonah to go to Nineveh to preach a message of repentance. But Jonah didn't like the people of Nineveh and refused to go. Instead, he jumped on a ship headed in the opposite direction. As we know, you can run from God, but you cannot hide.

The Lord sent a ferocious storm. Jonah knew that as long as he stayed on the boat, the crew was in danger. So he had them throw him in the angry waves. As the furious sea swallowed him, Jonah asked for help, and God had an answer. Later he recalled his prayer and God's answer:

In my distress I called to the LORD, and he answered me. From the depths of the grave I called for help, and you listened to my cry. You hurled me into the deep, into the very heart of the seas, and the currents swirled about me; all your waves and breakers swept over me. . . . The engulfing waters threatened me, the deep surrounded me; seaweed was wrapped around my head. To the roots of the mountains I sank down; the earth beneath barred me in forever. But you brought my life up from the pit, O LORD my God.

JONAH 2:1–6 (EMPHASIS ADDED)

God promises to help His people when they ask for it. The Lord helped Jonah before he drowned by sending a giant fish to swallow him. The fish vomited the repentant prophet on the beach. Jonah immediately journeyed to Nineveh and preached to the people. Gloriously, the entire population of the city turned to the Lord.

Daniel Asked for Help and Got It

The elderly prophet Daniel was a wise, godly man in an ungodly environment. Jealous underlings were aware that Daniel regularly prayed to the Lord. They were jealous of Daniel's position of authority over them, so they set a trap for him. They tricked the king into signing a petition stating that for a thirty-day period, anyone found praying to any god other than the king would be executed in a den of lions. No exceptions were allowed. Then they waited and watched Daniel's house (see Daniel 6:1–28).

Daniel was unmoved by the new law. He knelt down and prayed to the Lord as he had always done. The conspirators caught him. But not before he asked the Lord for help.

Then these men went as a group and found Daniel praying and asking God for help.

DANIEL 6:11 (EMPHASIS ADDED)

The Lord answers when people ask for help. God heard Daniel's prayer and sprang to the rescue, sparing him from the lions. Later Daniel described the event, saying,

> *"My God sent his angel, and he shut the mouths of the lions. They have not hurt me, because I was found innocent in his sight. Nor have I ever done any wrong before you, O king."*
>
> DANIEL 6:22

The king, relieved by this miraculous display of heavenly help, removed Daniel from the lethal lions' den. Daniel did not suffer even a scratch from the deadly man-eaters. Then the king had Daniel's conspirators thrown into the lions' den to see how they'd fair. Unfortunately for them, their gods were not as helpful as Daniel's had been.

> *And before they reached the floor of the den, the lions overpowered them and crushed all their bones.*
>
> DANIEL 6:24

But that's not all. God's supernatural support continued flowing on behalf of Daniel and his cause.

> *Then King Darius wrote to all the peoples, nations and men of every language throughout the land: "May you prosper greatly! I issue a decree that in every part of my kingdom people must fear and reverence the God of Daniel. For he is the living God and he endures forever; his kingdom will not be destroyed, his dominion will never end. He rescues and he saves; he performs signs and wonders in the heavens and on the earth. He has rescued Daniel from the power of the lions." So Daniel prospered during the reign of Darius.*
>
> DANIEL 6:25–28

I guess so! God not only helped Daniel by sparing him from the lions but also aided him by eradicating his jealous conspirators. On top of that, the Lord used the king to give a tremendous testimony to the nation and to protect His people's freedom to worship Him.

Asa Asked for Help and Got It

Asa was the righteous king of Judah. God blessed his obedience, and the nation prospered. Then one dark day Zerah, a fierce warrior, marched oh Judah, leading an army of one million Ethiopians and three hundred gleaming chariots. Asa faced a skilled opponent who had him outnumbered by over four hundred thousand troops *and* three hundred chariots! Judah had no defense against the awesome speed and power of the best weapons of mass destruction on the planet in 900 BC. This could have been one of the most massive massacres in history.

Asa did the right thing. He asked for help, resting on God's promise.

> *Then Asa called to the LORD his God and said, "LORD, there is no one like you to* help *the powerless against the mighty. Help us, O LORD our God, for we rely on you, and in your name we have come against this vast army. O LORD, you are our God; do not let man prevail against you."*
>
> 2 CHRONICLES 14:11 (EMPHASIS ADDED)

God keeps His promises. The Lord heard Asa's prayer and gave him a miraculou answer:

The LORD struck down the Cushites before Asa and Judah. The Cushites fled, and Asa and his army pursued them as far as Gerar. Such a great number of Cushites fell that they could not recover; they were crushed before the LORD and his forces. The men of Judah carried off a large amount of plunder. They destroyed all the villages around Gerar, for the terror of the LORD had fallen upon them. They plundered all these villages, since there was much booty there. They also attacked the camps of the herdsmen and carried off droves of sheep and goats and camels. Then they returned to Jerusalem.

1 CHRONICLES 14:12–15

Don't miss all that the Lord did in helping Asa and His people. First, God sent a supernatural dread upon Zerah's army, the Cushites. We do not know how He did it, but we know that He did. They fled in fear before the battle began. As a result, all Asa and his men had to do was chase them down. Miraculously, the huge Ethiopian war machine was completely conquered by Asa's smaller army.

But beyond this, Asa's men gathered sensational spoils. As they hunted down the fleeing Ethiopians, they pillaged the Philistine villages that had aided them as they ran away. On top of that, they defeated and robbed the camps of the nomadic herdsmen who had been supplying the Cushite army with sheep, goats, and camels. So Asa and Judah not only did not get crushed; they won the battle without losing a man and got an incredible amount of plunder in the process! Yay, God!

A Final Encouragement

You are human, so you will always need help. God is the best source of the best help. He helped David, Jonah, Daniel, Asa, and countless others. And if you ask, He has promised to help you.

Final Thoughts

A mother came home from shopping and found her freshly baked pie dug out crudely in the center. A gooey spoon lay in the sink, and crumbs were scattered over the kitchen counter and floor.

She called her son into the kitchen. "Son," she said sternly, "you promised me you wouldn't touch that pie before dinner."

The boy hung his head.

"And I promised you I'd spank you if you did," she continued.

Her son's face brightened. "Now that I've broken my promise," he offered, "it's okay with me if you break yours, too!"

Maybe you have read this book with skepticism. You are thinking, "I have asked, but I have not received. I believed God was working all for good, but things just keep getting worse. I cried out to God for help, but there is no help in sight."

I know exactly how you are feeling. As a student of the promises, I have discovered a few truths that apply to those rare occasions when God seems silent.

- *God is not merely a machinelike "blessing dispenser."* He is our heavenly Father. He deeply desires to build a relationship with us. His desire is that His blessings build up and flow out of our relationship with Him.

- *God is always more committed to His cause and our character than to our comfort or convenience.* He will often trade our immediate pleasure for our long-term profit and His kingdom's progress. He is very willing to suspend our relief in order to test and deepen our belief.

- *Just as it takes faith to claim a promise, it requires faith to hang on to it when it seems to be ineffective.* God richly honors such resilient faith. If you need to be convinced about this, read Hebrews 11:35–40.

- *God is very patient.* He will frequently withhold a small blessing today in order to prepare us to receive a larger blessing tomorrow. He will not give us pretty good blessings now in lieu of really great blessings later.

- *God's ways are not necessarily our ways.* Some events will only make sense years from now. Some situations will remain foggy until we can see with heavenly eyes.

- *The Lord is the sovereign God.* He has the authority and power to do whatever He wants, however, whenever, and wherever He wants to do it.

- *God is always faithful, even when we are faithless.*

- *Ultimately, you can never go wrong by trusting God.*

A Promise Kept

A year ago, I was working on the first book in this series. It is called *The 21 Most Effective Prayers in the Bible*. As I wrote that book, I consistently applied the thirteenth promise in this book, God's promise of answered prayer. I asked specifically that God would bless that book in larger ways than I envisioned. I prayed that it would encourage thousands of people to become more effective in prayer.

I believed that the Lord would answer my prayer and keep His promise, unless He had a good reason not to. Then, in the busyness of life, I forgot about it.

A few weeks ago, I walked into one of the largest bookstore chains in the nation. As I usually do, I headed toward the Christian Inspiration section. I began to look through books according to their alphabetical listing. What I often do is try to picture a book with my name on it sitting on the shelves. I read over the books written by people with last names beginning with the letters *A*, *B*, *C*, and *D*. I wondered if I would ever have a book in such a large bookstore chain.

Then I came to the *E*s and was stunned. Leading off the *E* section was a book by Dave Earley. I gasped and then smiled. Pulling the cell phone out of my pocket, I dialed my wife.

"Hello, Cathy," I said as calmly as possible. "Guess where I am."

"I have no idea," she said. "Where are you?"

"I am in the bookstore. Guess what I'm looking at?"

"A book?" she asked wisely. "I don't know," she continued, "what are you looking at?"

"I am looking at *my* book! *The 21 Most Effective Prayers in the Bible* is on the shelf."

"Are you going to buy it?" she asked.

"No," I said. "Then I wouldn't have a book in this bookstore, and besides, I already have a copy."

As I hung up, I sensed God speaking to my heart. "Why are you so surprised?" He asked. "Didn't you expect Me to keep My promise?"

A Final Encouragement

There are over seven thousand promises in God's Word. We've looked at twenty-one of the most encouraging ones. I am sure that you can grab hold of a few of these and claim them as your own. God is big enough to keep every one of His promises. He loves you and longs to bless you. Keep your eyes on Him and continue to trust Him to keep His Word. Then when He answers your prayers, He'll be able to ask you as He did me, "Didn't you expect Me to keep My promise?"

The *21* Most Dangerous Questions *of the* Bible

Acknowledgments

Teamwork is the fuel that allows common people to attain uncommon results. If this book attains extraordinary results it will be because of the efforts of a capable and qualified team.

- Cathy, you are my very best friend. Thank you for being such an encouragement, and for praying over, editing, critiquing, and proofing every word.

- Carol, for your consistent encouragement.

- Sandy, for modeling grace under fire.

- Steve, for being my favorite brother.

- Dave Wheeler, Rebecca Autry, Neil Grobler, David Brinkley, Chip Stallings, Becky Mahle, and Julie Moore—you are wonderful LCMT teammates.

- Elmer Towns—you set the pace.

- The Barbour team, for asking me to write this book.

- Paul Muckley, you are a joy to work with.

- Les Stobbe, for opening the door.

- Kelly McIntosh and Annie Tipton, for managing the in-house processes, and Sharon Dean, for handling the typesetting.

Contents

Introduction

We had known each other a year and a half. Cathy had just spent a summer in Virginia working and teaching Sunday school. I had spent the summer in New York City doing evangelism and discipleship. For months, I had fasted one day a week, praying about whether or not she was the girl I should marry. I was 99 percent sure.

When I returned from New York, Cathy fixed me a great spaghetti dinner. She looked gorgeous as the joy of the Lord shone through her face. During dinner a dangerous question kept running through my head. Before I knew what had happened, I blurted out, "I need to ask you something."

"What?" She smiled.

"Would you. . ."

"Yes?" she asked.

". . .um. . .pass me the salt?" I said with a sigh.

After dinner we sat on the couch talking. I made the mistake of looking into her sparkling green eyes. Everything got misty. It was as if time stopped—or at least shifted into slow motion. My head swam, and I heard an indistinguishable tune floating through my mind. The dangerous question kept popping into my brain. My heart pounded.

I couldn't take it for another second. I had to ask the question. Suddenly, I grabbed her shoulders.

"I need to ask you a question." I swallowed.

"What?" she smiled, confused by my sudden seriousness.

"Would you. . ."

"Yes?" she responded, now frowning at me like I was an idiot.

I took a deep breath. "Cathy," I said with great gravity. "Will you. . ." I gulped. The words were literally choking me.

"Yes?" she said, a smile slowly forming on her lips. She leaned closer, now aware of what I was about to ask.

"Will you. . ." I gulped again, ". . .marry me?"

More Dangerous Questions

The book you hold in your hands is a simple study of what I consider the twenty-one riskiest questions in the Bible. It considers nearly two dozen questions that created defining moments in the lives of significant Bible figures. These timeless questions can be life changing for you, too, as you ask them of yourself and wrestle to a response.

When you first saw the title *The 21 Most Dangerous Questions of the Bible*, you may have asked yourself, "Dangerous for whom or for what?" That depends on how you answer these twenty-one questions. Respond one way, and you'll create grave hazards for the status quo—and the kingdom of darkness. Answer in the opposite, and you'll bring about peril for yourself and the world around you.

We also thought of calling this book *The 21 Most Important Questions* or *The 21 Most Defining Questions* or *The 21 Major Watershed Questions* or *The 21 Tipping Point Questions of the Bible*. Each question covered is that significant and potentially powerful.

Let me say that if you are thoroughly content with your life as it is and the direction the world is heading, *don't* read this book and consider these questions. If you are happy to have an unexamined faith, this probably is not the book for you. But if you long for change and yearn to make a difference—if you are willing to risk everything with the hope of coming out better on the other side—then, please, read on.

This is an unsafe book. I hope at times to make you a little uncomfortable. My intent is not so much to *inform* as to *transform*.

These questions will force you to evaluate what you really believe about God and His Word. They will challenge the level of your faith and commitment. Hopefully, they will change your life for the better.

1

What Is Man That You Are Mindful of Him?
PSALM 8:4

It's always one of the highlights of my day. At ten o'clock each evening, I pull on a jacket and get the dog's leash from the closet. Then Rocky, our miniature schnauzer, and I walk out into the night.

Most evenings, when the sky is clear, I can't keep myself from looking up. I can't help gawking at the incredible display in the heavens. We live in the country where there is less ambient light, so the stars, moon, and planets are gloriously apparent in the heavens. The sight is truly breathtaking. By the time I return home, I usually have a kink in my neck from stargazing.

Recently, for my birthday, Cathy got me a telescope. Now, on warm nights, I can gaze to my heart's content at the silver diamond stars gleaming on their black velvet background.

Of course, I'm not the first person to be mesmerized by the stars. Three thousand years ago, a young shepherd was also awestruck by the nightly display that quietly occurs in the heavens. What David saw and how it made him feel ended up as a song. I don't know if you've sung it before, but I'll bet you've read it. Embedded in that song is a potentially dangerous question.

> O LORD, our Lord, how majestic is your name in all the earth! You have set your glory above the heavens. From the lips of children and infants you have ordained praise because of your enemies, to silence the foe and the avenger.
>
> When I consider your heavens, the work of your fingers, the moon and the stars, which you have set in place, what is man that you are mindful of him, the son of man that you care for him?
>
> You made him a little lower than the heavenly beings and crowned him with glory and honor. You made him ruler over the works of your hands; you put everything under his feet: all flocks and herds, and the beasts of the field, the birds of the air, and the fish of the sea, all that swim the paths of the seas.
>
> PSALM 8:1–8

As he gazed into the sky, David was enthralled by the vast glory of the heavens—the heavens that the Lord God made and owns. Deep within David's heart, a question arose: "What is man that you are mindful of him, the son of man that you care for him?" (Psalm 8:4). David was awed by the amazing heavens, yet he was more astounded that the Lord, who can make such immense works of art, would have any interest in the human race. His question and its answer led him to a profound sense of significance.

The Heavens Are Amazing

When I look at the stars, I'm floored to remember that they are so incredibly far away that the distance has to be measured in light-*years*. The speed of light is almost beyond comprehension—186,000 miles per second. Therefore a light-year equals 5.87 *trillion* miles!

The distance around the earth is about twenty-five thousand miles. So a "particle" of light traveling at the speed of light can zip around the earth about seven or eight times in just one second. Yet our own galaxy is so vast that we measure the distance to stars within the Milky Way in light-years—the distance light travels in a year.

I am also impressed with the incredible *number* of stars visible on a clear night. Consider that the total number of individual stars visible to the naked eye in both the northern and the southern celestial hemispheres is about six thousand. Therefore, if I took the time to count, I could see at most about three thousand stars at the same time. Yet our Milky Way galaxy has been found to contain two hundred thousand *million* stars! If somebody could count three stars per second, after one hundred years he would have counted less than 5 percent of this number.

Scientists now estimate that the total number of stars in the observable universe is 10^{25} (1 followed by 25 zeros). Using an extremely fast computer, making ten thousand million calculations per second, it would still require thirty million years of nonstop counting to number those stars![1]

Wow!

Yet God knows each star by name:

He determines the number of the stars and calls them each by name.

PSALM 147:4

No wonder stargazing brought David to worship, saying, "O LORD, our Lord, how majestic is your name in all the earth! You have set your glory above the heavens" (Psalm 8:1). No wonder David was compelled to ask, "What is man that you are mindful of him, the son of man that you care for him?" (Psalm 8:4).

What Is Man?

David asked, "What is man?" If we allow science to answer this dangerous question, we're told that man (and woman) is an animal, the highest form of life, a bipedal primate belonging to the mammalian species, *Homo sapiens,* the product of millions of years of evolution, a tiny creature in an immense universe. Such sterile answers, coupled with the massive vastness of the universe, can bring people to the dangerous brink of despair, drowning in their own insignificance.

Yet when David asked the question some three thousand years ago, he was swept away by awe. He responded in worship, sharing a prayer, writing a hymn, and uttering a strong statement of praise. Instead of feeling lost as a meaningless speck in an immeasurable universe, David was thrilled to realize that the same Lord who made the heavens made him. The same God, who knows countless stars by name, knew *his* name!

David discovered that the same God who is big enough to create gigantic galaxies is small enough to be vitally involved in the day-to-day dealings of individual people. The innate dignity of humanity lies not in who *we* are, but rather in who *God* is. The issue is not who do *I* say I am, but instead, who does *God* say I am?

In an article on the Internet Infidels Web site titled "Death and the Meaning of Life," Keith Augustine makes a game attempt to argue that atheists can find meaning in life. Yet when he answers the question, "What is man?" he comes up empty. The writer states that death is inevitable and leads to "a dreamless sleep from which we will never awake, our consciousness snuffed out forever." He continues by saying, "As far as science can tell, there is no greater purpose for our lives." Yet he also argues that life can be meaningful.[2] To which I say, "You've got to be kidding!"

David, on the other hand, was able to ask a dangerous question and come through with a meaningful answer. Instead of saying, "There is no God," David saw everything through the lens of God. When he asked, "What is man that you are mindful of him?" his God-centered understanding of the universe led him to a strong sense of personal identity, a marvelous dignity, a deep significance, and a God-given purpose. Reread his grateful words of praise:

You made him a little lower than the heavenly beings and crowned him with glory and honor. You made him ruler over the works of your hands; you put everything under his feet: all flocks and herds, and the beasts of the field, the birds of the air, and the fish of the sea, all that swim the paths of the seas.

PSALM 8:5–8

Look at those words more closely. "You made him a little lower than the heavenly beings and crowned him with glory and honor." Humanity has dignity because we are *not* the product of chance; we are the masterwork of the sovereign Creator.

God made us. Not only that, He dignified us by placing us "a little lower than the heavenly beings," crowning us with glory. And beyond that, He elevated us to the position of "ruler" over the works of His hands. He put *everything* under our feet, including "all flocks and herds, and the beasts of the field, the birds of the air, and the fish of the sea, all that swim the paths of the seas."

David may have only been a poor shepherd, but his clear understanding of his identity as a creation of God gave him the confidence to face a giant. Because David recognized that the God who made the heavens also knew his name, he was able to lead armies to victory and wear the crown of a king.

Who Are You?

According to Psalm 8, you are much more than an animal or the random product of millions of years of evolution. You are the unique handiwork of the most intelligent and powerful being imaginable. God, the Creator and Sustainer of the vast heavens, made you and gave you an important status on this planet. You were given dominion and dignity, position and privilege.

There is no reason to feel insignificant or that life is without meaning. You were made on purpose, with purpose. Your life matters. You can make a difference. What happens to you is important. Someone is watching, and He does care.

NOTES

[1]Distances and measurements were primarily taken from the article "Counting the Stars: The Vastness of the Universe Is Cause for Joy, not Loneliness," by Werner Gitt, Answers in Genesis, http://www.answersingenesis.org/creation/v19/i2/stars.asp (accessed June 18, 2007).

[2]Keith Augustine, "Death and the Meaning of Life," The Secular Web, http://www.infidels.org/library/modern/features/2000/augustine1.html#F2 (accessed June 18, 2007).

2

Who Do You Say I Am?
Matthew 16:15

Who is Jesus?

Is He a great teacher, a good man, a gifted prophet—or something more? Is He legend, liar, lunatic—or someone else? These are dangerous questions. How we answer them has important ramifications because the identity of Jesus Christ is the foundation of Christianity. As John Stott has noted,

> *Essentially Christianity is Christ. The person and work of Christ are the rock upon which the Christian religion is built. If he is not who he said he was and did not do what he said he came to do, the foundation is undermined and the whole superstructure will collapse. Take Christ from Christianity, and you disembowel it; there is practically nothing left. Christ is the [center] of Christianity; all else is circumference.*[1]

Even more importantly, the identity of Jesus Christ is the basis of the salvation of a soul from sin and its punishment. Belief in Jesus is the only way to experience eternal life.

> *"Salvation is found in no one else, for there is no other name under heaven given to men by which we must be saved."*
>
> Acts 4:12

> *"Whoever believes in the Son has eternal life, but who-ever rejects the Son will not see life, for God's wrath remains on him."*
>
> John 3:36

"Who Do You Say I Am?"

Peter and the other disciples had been following Jesus for over three years. They had seen Him do things no other man had ever done and heard Him say things no one had ever said. Jesus knew that His time on earth was drawing to a close. He wanted Peter and the others to have one fact firmly fixed in their minds—His identity. In order to withstand all that lay ahead, they would need to understand exactly who Jesus really was. In order to clarify their convictions, Jesus asked them a dangerous question.

> *When Jesus came to the region of Caesarea Philippi, he asked his disciples, "Who do people say the Son of Man is?"*
> *They replied, "Some say John the Baptist; others say Elijah; and still others, Jeremiah or one of the prophets."*
> *"But what about you?" he asked. "Who do you say I am?"*
>
> Matthew 16:13–15

The answer to Jesus' question had been forming in Peter's mind and heart for several years. Hearing all he had heard and seeing all he had seen had solidified his convictions.

Confidently, he gave a succinct answer, voicing one of the most significant statements ever made.

> Simon Peter answered, "You are the Christ, the Son of the living God."
> Jesus replied, "Blessed are you, Simon son of Jonah, for this was not revealed to you by man, but by my Father in heaven."

MATTHEW 16:16–17

"You Are the Christ"

When Peter announced that Jesus was "the Christ," he was speaking of the long-awaited Anointed One. "The Christ," or "Messiah," was the One set apart by the Father and anointed with the Holy Spirit to be the Chief Priest of His people (see Deuteronomy 18:15–18; Isaiah 55:4; Luke 24:19; Acts 3:22, 7:37).

Peter and the others had seen how Jesus uniquely fulfilled the prophecies about the Messiah. His birth, life, death, and resurrection were described in amazing detail hundreds and, in some instances thousands, of years prior to their occurrence.

The name of His great-great-great-grandfather was predicted. The place of His birth was predicted. So was the visit by the wise men, the gifts the wise men brought, the appearance of the Christmas star, and Herod's attempt to kill Him. Jesus' trip to Egypt to avoid Herod was predicted. Those are merely a few of the fulfilled prophecies about Jesus' birth.

In observing the unique and astounding reality of the impressive prophecies fulfilled by the birth and life of Jesus, my friend and internationally recognized Bible scholar, H. L. Wilmington, poses the question:

> Can any other founder of a known religion point to a similar written record of his life already in existence hundreds of years before his birth? . . . The answer is no.[2]

In the Old Testament, there are as many as 332 distinct predictions that are literally fulfilled in Christ.[3] Astronomer and mathematician Peter Stoner, in his book *Science Speaks*, offers an analysis showing that it is impossible for the precise statements about the Messiah to be fulfilled in a single person by mere coincidence. He estimates that the chance of only *eight* of these prophecies being fulfilled in the life of one man is only 1 in 10 to the 17th power.[4] That is the number one followed by seventeen zeroes, or one chance in 100,000,000,000,000,000! (Compare this to winning the lottery, with odds of "one in a million" as one followed by only six zeroes.)

In order to understand how amazing it is that one man fulfilled just eight of the prophecies Jesus fulfilled, consider this example:

> Take 100,000,000,000,000,000 silver dollars and lay them on the face of Texas [with its approximate land area of 262,000 square miles]. They will cover all of the state two feet deep. Now mark one of these silver dollars and stir the whole mass thoroughly, all over the state. Blindfold a man and tell him that he can travel as far as he wishes, but he must pick up one silver dollar and say that this is the right one. What chance would he have of getting the right one? Just the same chance that the prophets would have had of writing these eight prophecies and having them all come true in any one man.[5]

That is one man fulfilling only *eight* of the prophecies regarding the Messiah. Yet Jesus fulfilled 332!

Say it with me, "Wow!" Jesus fulfilled the prophecies as only the Messiah could.

"The Son of the Living God"

Peter also called Jesus "the son of the living God." The title "the living God" was a name reserved for Jehovah Himself (see Deuteronomy 5:26; Joshua 3:10; 1 Samuel 17:26, 36; 2 Kings 19:4, 16; Psalm 42:2, 84:2; Daniel 6:26; Hosea 1:10). For Peter to call Jesus by this name was to clearly state his belief that Jesus was no mere man—He was God. Why would Peter believe that?

1. Jesus did things only God can do.

Jesus walked on a stormy sea (Matthew 14:25). He rebuked the wind and it obeyed Him (Luke 8:24; note that He did not ask God to calm the sea; He accomplished that by Himself). Jesus turned water into wine (John 2:6–11) and cured a centurion's servant without any contact with the ill man (Matthew 8:5–13). He fed massive crowds with as little as a boy's lunch (Matthew 14:15–21, 15:34–38). At the pool of Bethesda in Jerusalem, Jesus healed a man who had been unable to walk for thirty-eight years (John 5:1–9). He cast out demons (Matthew 17:14–20, 15:22–28; Mark 1:23–28, 5:1–19), healed the sick (Matthew 8:14–16, 9:20–22; Mark 7:32–37), cured the leprous (Matthew 8:2–4; Luke 17:11–19), mended the lame (Matthew 9:2–8), and gave sight to the blind (Matthew 12:22; Mark 8:22–26). Jesus even raised the dead (Matthew 9:18–26; Luke 7:12–16; John 11:1–46)!

2. Jesus accepted worship.

Even though He clearly knew that only God was to be worshiped, Jesus accepted worship on several occasions. He did not refuse the worship offered by a leper (Matthew 8:2–3), His own disciples (Matthew 14:33), a Canaanite woman (Matthew 15:25), and a man born blind (John 9:38).

3. Jesus displayed characteristics or attributes that can only be true of God.

Jesus not only had power over disease, death, demons, wind, and waves, He also displayed omniscience in that He knew people's lives, even their secret histories (John 4:16–19). He knew the inner thoughts of people, knew all people, and what was in people (Mark 2:8; Luke 5:22; John 2:24–25). He essentially knew everything (John 16:30).

4. Jesus made claims that only God can make.

When He claimed to have the authority to forgive sins, He backed it up by healing a lame man (Mark 2:1–12).

> *"Why are you thinking these things? Which is easier: to say to the paralytic, 'Your sins are forgiven,' or to say, 'Get up, take your mat and walk'? But that you may know that the Son of Man has authority on earth to forgive sins. . . ." He said to the paralytic, "I tell you, get up, take your mat and go home." He got up, took his mat and walked out in full view of them all.*
>
> MARK 2:8–12

Jesus claimed to be able to give life (John 5:21) and to be the source of life (John 14:6). He further claimed to have the divine authority and responsibility for eternal judgment.

*"Moreover, the Father judges no one, but has entrusted all judgment to the Son. . . .
I tell you the truth, a time is coming and has now come when the dead will hear the voice
of the Son of God and those who hear will live. For as the Father has life in himself, so
he has granted the Son to have life in himself. And he has given him authority to judge
because he is the Son of Man. Do not be amazed at this, for a time is coming when all who
are in their graves will hear his voice and come out—those who have done good will rise to
live, and those who have done evil will rise to be condemned."*

JOHN 5:22, 25–29

5. *Jesus equated a response to Him with a response to God.*

He said that to know Him was to know God (John 8:19, 14:7); to believe in Him was to
believe in God (John 12:44); to see Him was to see God (John 12:45, 14:9); to hate Him was
to hate God (John 15:23); and to honor Him was to honor God (John 5:22–23).

Jesus' claims of divinity were so obvious that the Jews wanted to stone Him for
blasphemy.

"I and the Father are one."
      *Again the Jews picked up stones to stone him, but Jesus said to them, "I have
shown you many great miracles from the Father. For which of these do you stone me?"*
      *"We are not stoning you for any of these," replied the Jews, "but for blasphemy,
because you, a mere man, claim to be God."*

JOHN 10:30–33

*Jesus said to them, "My Father is always at his work to this very day, and I, too, am
working." For this reason the Jews tried all the harder to kill him; not only was he
breaking the Sabbath, but he was even calling God his own Father, making himself
equal with God.*

JOHN 5:17–18

His bold claims reached the pinnacle when He claimed to be Jehovah, the great "I AM"
described in Exodus 3:13–14.

*"I tell you the truth," Jesus answered, "before Abraham was born, I am!" At this, they
picked up stones to stone him.*

JOHN 8:58–59

Who Is Jesus?

Jesus claimed to be God. You and I are faced with a question: Who is Jesus, really?

In his famous book, *Mere Christianity*, Oxford professor and former skeptic C. S. Lewis
made this statement:

*A man who was merely a man and said the sort of things Jesus said would not be
a great moral teacher. He would either be a lunatic—on the level with a man who
says he is a poached egg—or he would be the devil of hell. You must take your choice.
Either this was, and is, the Son of God, or else a madman or something worse. You
can shut him up for a fool or you can fall at his feet and call him Lord and God. But
let us not come with any patronizing nonsense about his being a great human teacher.*

He has not left that open to us.[6]

After studying the facts for himself, Lewis concluded that Jesus was indeed God. He spent the rest of his life using his gift for writing to tell the world about Jesus.

Who is Jesus? Peter believed that Jesus is Lord and God. He became the leading spokesman for the Christian faith and died as a martyr for that faith.

So let me ask you: Who is Jesus?

Do you believe that He is God?

Will you put Him above everything else in your life?

Will you make Him the focal point of your day?

Will you make Him central in your decisions about the future?

Will the rest of your life reveal your faith in Him?

NOTES

[1]John R. W. Stott, *Basic Christianity* (Downers Grove, IL: Intervarsity Press, 1958), 21.

[2]H. L. Wilmington, quote taken from a lecture given by Dr. Wilmington at Liberty Bible Institute, Lynchburg, VA, on Oct. 21, 1982.

[3]Floyd Hamilton, *The Basis of Christian Faith* (New York: Harper and Row, 1964), 160.

[4]Peter Stoner, *Science Speaks* (Chicago: Moody Press, 1963), 100.

[5]Ibid. 107.

[6]C. S. Lewis, *Mere Christianity* (New York: The MacMillan Company, 1952), 41.

3

Do You Love Me?
JOHN 21:15–17

Serving Jesus is often not easy. Each month, as many as two thousand pastors and their families leave the ministry never to return.[1] Only God knows how many good church members drop out of ministry each year and stop serving in their churches.

The apostle Peter knew the desire to quit. One minute he had boasted that he would follow Jesus to prison or even death (Luke 22:33). The next thing he knew, he had denied Jesus three times (Luke 22:54–62). He wanted to quit, run away, and hide. Discouraged, Peter and several of the disciples went back to what they did before they were called—fishing.

Yet God is a God of the second chance. Jesus, the resurrected Christ, surprised His disciples as they were fishing on the Sea of Galilee. In their encounter, Jesus asked Peter one of the most significant and penetrating—in fact, one of the most dangerous—questions ever asked.

Do You Love Me?

> When they had finished eating, Jesus said to Simon Peter, "Simon son of John, do you
>   truly love me more than these?"
> "Yes, Lord," he said, "you know that I love you."
> Jesus said, "Feed my lambs."
> Again Jesus said, "Simon son of John, do you truly love me?"
> He answered, "Yes, Lord, you know that I love you."
> Jesus said, "Take care of my sheep."
> The third time he said to him, "Simon son of John, do you love me?"
> Peter was hurt because Jesus asked him the third time, "Do you love me?" He
>   said, "Lord, you know all things; you know that I love you."
> Jesus said, "Feed my sheep."
>
> JOHN 21:15–17

Three times Jesus asked Peter, "Do you love Me?"

Three times Peter answered, "You know that I love You."

Three times Jesus responded by giving Peter a responsibility: "Feed My lambs; shepherd My sheep; feed My sheep."

This scenario, summarized by John in three little verses, shows us that the essence of effective ministry will always be an overflow of our love relationship with Jesus. If Peter hoped to accomplish anything good in the future, it would only be because of His love for Jesus.

Initially, this pointed question hurt Peter. But his life was wonderfully changed as a result of Jesus' query. Oswald Chambers writes:

> The Lord's questions always reveal the true me to myself. . . . Rarely, but probably once
> in each of our lives, He will back us into a corner where He will hurt us with His
> piercing questions. Then we will realize that we do love Him far more deeply than our
> words can ever say.[2]

Do You Love Me?

Jesus might have asked Peter all kinds of questions that day. If I had been in Jesus' position, I might have asked, "Why did you deny Me?" or "What were you thinking?" or "What do you have to say for yourself?" But that's not the angle Jesus took. He asked, "Do you love Me?"

I don't think the question implies that Peter lacked love for Jesus. Instead, the Lord penetrated to the core of what a life of dynamic discipleship is all about. As Jesus taught, the greatest command is, "Love the Lord your God with all your heart and with all your soul and with all your mind" (Matthew 22:37). Christianity is a relationship, not a religion.

Note also that Jesus did not ask Peter if he was a gifted speaker, a talented leader, or even a person of sound character. Jesus didn't inquire about Peter's seminary training or Bible knowledge. Those things are important, but they're not *the* issue. *The* issue is quite simple. The one basic qualification for lasting ministry is found in Jesus' question, "Do you love Me?" Love for Jesus is the only motive for ministry that will endure the test.

I find it interesting that Jesus didn't even ask Peter, "Do you love *people?*" Loving people is important for ministering. But loving Jesus is more important. Pastor Richard Tow writes:

> *Ministry does not begin with a love for people. It begins with a love for God and that love overflows to people. If we minister only out of a humanistic love for people we will be people-pleasers rather than God-pleasers. We ultimately will not help them nor serve the purposes of God. But if everything begins with a holy love toward the Lord we will love people and we will serve their best interest—not always their whims and desires but always their best interest. Nothing will keep ministry on course like a deep love for the Lord. Nothing will carry us through the hard times like a sincere devotion to Christ.*[3]

Nothing Is More Important Than Our Relationship with Jesus

Three times Jesus asked Peter, "Do you love Me?" Notice that He asked this question *before* giving Peter the commission to shepherd His sheep. Why?

Jesus wanted Peter (and us, for that matter) never to forget that the chief criteria of enduring, effective ministry is loving Him above all else. Love of Christ is central; all else is peripheral.

Too often we assume that the prime prerequisite for serving Jesus well is great giftedness, immense talent, or impressive academic credentials. But Peter and most of the other disciples were ordinary fisherman from a backward part of the country. They were nobodies until Jesus called them.

The main requirement for making a difference *for* Jesus is being in love *with* Jesus. Jesus repeated the question three times because He wanted the concept to be crystal clear: Nothing is more important than our relationship with Jesus.

A Most Dangerous Disciple

When Peter realized the gravity of Jesus' question, and when he was able to respond positively, his life changed significantly. He became a most dangerous disciple. Just a few weeks later, the former coward, a denier of Jesus, stood before thousands of people, boldly preaching Christ. Amazingly, three thousand people gave their lives to the Lord and the Christian church was born (Acts 2:1–41). Beyond that, Peter was used of God to open the door of salvation to non-Jews (Acts 10:34–48).

What made Peter so positively dangerous? He discovered his passion for Jesus and continued to build the relationship. Before he and the other disciples launched their ministry, they held an intense prayer meeting (Acts 1:12–14). He was careful to maintain a regular hour of prayer (Acts 3:1). He, along with the other disciples, made a conscious decision to give their attention to prayer and the ministry of the Word (Acts 6:4).

Real Ministry for Jesus Flows Out of Our Relationship with Jesus

What we do *for* God is only a reflection of the relationship we have *with* God. If we want to be able to do great things, we need to have a great relationship. If we want to have a ministry that is strong, our relationship must be strong.

Oswald Chambers was a man others recognized as being abandoned to God. He was a Scottish itinerant preacher and Bible college founder. In his early forties he died of a ruptured appendix far from home in Egypt while ministering to British troops during World War I. His meditations on the Christian life, collected in the daily devotional classic *My Utmost for His Highest*, have enriched millions. Chambers deeply understood the essential nature of our relationship with Jesus.

> *The main thing about Christianity is not the work we do, but the relationship we maintain, and the atmosphere produced by that relationship. That is all God asks us to look after, and it is the one thing that is being continually assailed.*[4]

The Love-Slave

Samuel Logan Brengle was a Salvation Army preacher. While street preaching in a very rough section of Boston, he was severely injured when a drunk threw a brick at him. His writings are powerfully pungent with the aroma of a man who knew that real ministry flowed from a red-hot relationship with Jesus.

Using the imagery of the apostle Paul, Brengle viewed his relationship with Jesus as that of voluntary servitude fueled by love.

> *The love-slave is altogether at his Master's service. He is all eyes for his master. He watches. He is all ears for his master. He listens. His mind is willing. His hands are ready. His feet are swift. To sit at the master's feet and look into his loved face; to listen to his voice and catch his words; to run on his errands; to do his bidding; to share his privations and sorrows; to watch at his door; to guard his honor; to praise his name; to defend his person; to seek and promote his interests, and, if needs be, to die for his dear sake, this is the joy of the slave of love, and this he counts his perfect freedom.*[5]

The Disciple Jesus Loved

As Jesus asked Peter the probing question, "Do you love Me?", the young apostle John eavesdropped. He watched, he listened, and he learned. Later, he wrote of the event in his Gospel. But he also wrote it into his life.

John lived an amazing life of enduring, effective ministry. He was co-pastor of the thriving church of Jerusalem. He wrote one of the four Gospel accounts of Jesus' life as well as three epistles, and he was privileged to be given the Revelation that concludes our Bible. In spite of persistent heartache and persecution, he kept going strong up through his nineties. What was his secret? Rather than identifying himself as "John, the pastor of First Church in Jerusalem," or "John, the author of the Revelation," or "John, the apostle," he only identified himself as "the disciple whom Jesus loved."

Now there was leaning on Jesus' bosom one of his disciples, whom Jesus loved.

JOHN 13:23 KJV

When Jesus saw his mother there, and the disciple whom he loved standing nearby, he said to his mother, "Dear woman, here is your son."

JOHN 19:26

So she [Mary Magdalene] came running to Simon Peter and the other disciple, the one Jesus loved, and said, "They have taken the Lord out of the tomb, and we don't know where they have put him!"

JOHN 20:2

Peter turned and saw that the disciple whom Jesus loved was following them.

JOHN 21:20

Obviously Jesus loved all the disciples, but John was the most aware and appreciative. John lived by this principle: First we receive God's love for us, then out will flow our love for God and others.

NOTES

[1] Global Pastors Network newsletter, August 3, 2004.
[2] Oswald Chambers, *My Utmost for His Highest, Updated Edition* (Grand Rapids, MI: Discovery House Publishers, 1992), March 2 entry.
[3] Richard Tow, "Ministry Essentials: Fortifying the Foundation #47," http://www.sermoncentral.com/sermon.asp?SermonID=83277&ContributorID=10438 (accessed June 19, 2007).
[4] Oswald Chambers, *My Utmost for His Highest* (Uhrichsville, OH: Barbour Publishing, Inc., 1999) August 4 entry.
[5] Samuel Logan Brengle, *Love-Slaves* (London: Salvationist Publishing and Supplies, Ltd., 1929), http://wesley.nnu.edu/wesleyctr/books/0001-0100/HDM0021.PDF accessed February 12, 2007, p. 4.

4

Jesus I Know, and I Know About Paul, but Who Are You?
ACTS 19:15

Reality television shows find a limitless supply of people who will eat insects, lie in a bathtub of snakes, or humiliate themselves trying to sing, dance, or answer trivia questions. Why? They want to be noticed. They want, like the characters in the 1980 movie *Fame*, for you to "remember my name."

A desire for fame and influence is nothing new. Paul encountered the same passion for popularity and power nearly two thousand years ago in Ephesus.

> *While Apollos was at Corinth, Paul took the road through the interior and arrived at Ephesus. . . . Some Jews who went around driving out evil spirits tried to invoke the name of the Lord Jesus over those who were demon-possessed. They would say, "In the name of Jesus, whom Paul preaches, I command you to come out."*
>
> ACTS 19:1, 13

These men who were casting out demons in the name of Jesus did not *know* Jesus. They had only *heard* of Him—and they soon discovered that a secondhand relationship with Jesus is not sufficient when encountering the dark spirits of the devil. Merely saying the words, "In the name of Jesus, whom Paul preaches, I command you to come out," was not enough.

> *Seven sons of Sceva, a Jewish chief priest, were doing this. One day the evil spirit answered them, "Jesus I know, and I know about Paul, but who are you?" Then the man who had the evil spirit jumped on them and overpowered them all. He gave them such a beating that they ran out of the house naked and bleeding.*
>
> ACTS 19:14–16

Ouch! Dealing with the devil is not fun and games. It is serious business that requires a mature relationship with Jesus Christ. It also demands that we ask ourselves a very dangerous question.

Look again at Acts 19:15. Before provoking the severe beating of the sons of Sceva, one of the evil spirits asked a profound question.

> *"Jesus I know, and I know about Paul, but who are you?"*
>
> ACTS 19:15

"Jesus I Know"

One of the evil spirits declared, "Jesus I know!" The name of Jesus was, and is, certainly well known in hell.

The name of Jesus was well known to Satan. It was Jesus whom Satan tried to have killed as an infant in Bethlehem (Matthew 2:13–18). It was Jesus whom Satan personally tried to tempt in the wilderness (Luke 4:1–13). It was Jesus whom the devil tried to have thrown over a cliff at the beginning of His ministry (Luke 4:28–30). Of course, it was Jesus whom Satan prompted Judas to betray to be crucified (John 13:27–30; 18:1ff).

The identity of Jesus was also well known to demons.

Whenever the evil spirits saw him, they fell down before him and cried out, "You are the Son of God."

MARK 3:11

Moreover, demons came out of many people, shouting, "You are the Son of God!" But he rebuked them and would not allow them to speak, because they knew he was the Christ.

LUKE 4:41

Demons were cast out in the name of Jesus.

Finally Paul became so troubled that he turned around and said to the spirit, "In the name of Jesus Christ I command you to come out of her!" At that moment the spirit left her.

ACTS 16:18

"Paul I Know"

The name of Paul was also well known in hell. Before the evil spirits prompted the possessed man to beat the sons of Sceva, one of them declared, "I know about Paul."

When Paul, the leading persecutor of the church, switched sides and converted to Christ, the news was received coldly in hell (Acts 8:1–3, 9:1–22). Hell certainly noted with anger that Paul's preaching to the Gentiles was so powerful he was accused of turning the world upside down (Acts 17:6 KJV)! While in Ephesus, prior to the beating of the sons of Sceva, Paul had developed quite a ministry and reputation. Others wanted the power he had.

God did extraordinary miracles through Paul, so that even handkerchiefs and aprons that had touched him were taken to the sick, and their illnesses were cured and the evil spirits left them. Some Jews who went around driving out evil spirits tried to invoke the name of the Lord Jesus over those who were demon-possessed. They would say, "In the name of Jesus, whom Paul preaches, I command you to come out."

ACTS 19:11–13

Merely mouthing words didn't work—just ask the sons of Sceva. There needed to be a dangerous life supporting those words—a life like Paul's, that was dangerous to hell.

In his classic book *Why Revival Tarries*, Leonard Ravenhill explained why Paul was well known in hell. Building on the theme of Paul viewing himself as crucified with Christ, Ravenhill writes,

He had no ambitions—and so had nothing to be jealous about. He had no reputation—and so had nothing to fight about. He had no possessions—and therefore nothing to worry about. He had no "rights"—so therefore he could not suffer wrong. He was already broken—so no one could break him. He was "dead"—so none could kill him. He was less than the least of the least—so who could humble him? He had suffered the loss of all things—so who could defraud him? Does this throw any light on why the demon said, "Paul I know"? Over this God-intoxicated man, hell suffered headaches.[1]

"Who Are You?"

Our discussion circles back to the main issue. The demons asked the sons of Sceva one of the most dangerous questions that can be asked:

> *"Jesus I know, and I know about Paul, but who are you?"*

"Who are you?" In other words, "We've never heard of you. Your faces don't hang on the walls of hell's post office. There's no 'Wanted' poster saying 'Approach carefully—considered armed and very dangerous.'"

Clearly, the sons of Sceva had no answer to the demons' question. As we have read, the lone man possessed by the demons beat up Sceva's boys and sent them running for their lives (Acts 19:14–16).

Does the Devil Know Your Name?

I don't claim the amazing authority of the Lord Jesus Christ or the apostle Paul. But I believe I can live a positively dangerous life. I hope to live so completely for God's kingdom that I am known by those in the kingdom of darkness. I want to give hell a headache.

What about you? If an evil spirit questioned your identity, what would you say? How would you answer? Are you becoming a dangerous Christian? Are you famous in hell? Do demons shudder at the mention of your name?

How would you respond if a demon asked you the same question? "Jesus I know, and I know about Paul, *but who are you?*"

Prayer Is the Battle

> *For our struggle is not against flesh and blood, but against the rulers, against the authorities, against the powers of this dark world and against the spiritual forces of evil in the heavenly realms.*
>
> EPHESIANS 6:12

We are seeing an increased level of satanic activity in North America. We hear more and more accounts of church members and churches bound by demonic oppression. As the occult has become part of mainstream culture in America, the strongholds of the enemy have increased and multiplied.

We must pray in order to take ground. On our own, we are less powerful than the enemy, but when we pray, we can fight him successfully. We can march forward on our knees. The weapon he fears most is the weapon of prayer—which we should use "without ceasing" (1 Thessalonians 5:17 KJV).

Missionary statesman S. D. Gordon traveled to many of Satan's strongholds and gained a deep understanding of the vital power of prayer in spiritual warfare. He wrote,

> *In its simplest meaning, prayer has to do with conflict. Rightly understood it is the deciding factor in a spirit conflict. . . . Prayer is man giving God a footing on the contested territory of this earth.*[2]

Dick Eastman sees the importance of prayer in spiritual conflict as central. He writes, "Prayer is not so much another weapon on our list of weaponry as it is the actual battle."[3]

The Word Is the Sword

The Word of God gives us the strength to fight the devil in our personal lives. Remember that when Jesus was tempted by the devil, He fought him off by persistently quoting the Word of God (Matthew 4:1–11). The apostle John said the Word of God is what gives us strength to conquer.

> *I write to you, young men, because you are strong, and the word of God lives in you, and you have overcome the evil one.*
>
> 1 JOHN 2:14

Paul had trained himself to use the scriptures as an offensive weapon. He knew that nothing makes demons tremble like the sword of the Spirit, the Word of God.

> *Take the helmet of salvation and the sword of the Spirit, which is the word of God.*
>
> EPHESIANS 6:17

Daily Boot Camp

You cannot become a soldier without training. Learn to use your weapons. Every day set aside time to read, study, memorize, and apply the Word of God. Take time to pray urgent, faith-filled, passionate prayers. Become skilled in hearing and following the commands of your heavenly Commander. Surrender your cause for God's cause. As you do these things, you'll be known by the devil and his demons. You will give hell a headache.

NOTES

[1]Leonard Ravenhill, *Why Revival Tarries* (Minneapolis, MN: Bethany House Publishers, 1986), 186.
[2]S. D. Gordon, *Quiet Talks on Prayer* (Grand Rapids, MI: Baker Book House, reprinted 1980), 31–38.
[3]Dick Eastman, *Love on Its Knees* (Tarrytown, NY: Fleming Revel, 1989), p. 65.

5

Who Is My Neighbor?
Luke 10:29

Where are the Good Samaritans? I asked myself this question some time back when a newspaper blared this shocking headline: DETROIT CROWD CHEERS AS TRIO CHASE WOMAN TO HER DEATH. The story said,

> As dozens of people looked on, and some cheered, three men pulled a woman from her car, ripped off her clothes, and chased her as she jumped or was forced off a bridge to her death. . . . None of the 40 or so passersby tried to help Deletha Word during the confrontation.

The story went on to say that though nearly fifty people watched the awful events, "many of them were laughing about the men beating the woman." One person had a cellular phone, but would not call police. One witness said, "It seemed like people did not care."[1]

Lest we think a lack of compassion is a recent development, Jesus addressed the issue two thousand years ago. The Lord's words came in response to one man's dangerous question:

> On one occasion an expert in the law stood up to test Jesus. "Teacher," he asked, "what must I do to inherit eternal life?"
>
> "What is written in the Law?" he replied. "How do you read it?"
>
> He answered: " 'Love the Lord your God with all your heart and with all your soul and with all your strength and with all your mind'; and, 'Love your neighbor as yourself.' "
>
> "You have answered correctly," Jesus replied. "Do this and you will live."
>
> But he wanted to justify himself, so he asked Jesus, "And who is my neighbor?"
>
> Luke 10:25–29

Who Is My Neighbor?

This religious leader was obviously rather selective in whom he chose to love, so he asked, "Who is my neighbor?" Jesus, a wonderful teacher, did not answer the question directly, but rather told a story—a story that more than answered the man's question.

> "A man was going down from Jerusalem to Jericho, when he fell into the hands of robbers. They stripped him of his clothes, beat him and went away, leaving him half dead. A priest happened to be going down the same road, and when he saw the man, he passed by on the other side. So too, a Levite, when he came to the place and saw him, passed by on the other side. But a Samaritan, as he traveled, came where the man was; and when he saw him, he took pity on him. He went to him and bandaged his wounds, pouring on oil and wine. Then he put the man on his own donkey, took him to an inn and took care of him. The next day he took out two silver coins and gave them to the innkeeper. 'Look after him,' he said, 'and when I return, I will reimburse you for any extra expense you may have.'
>
> "Which of these three do you think was a neighbor to the man who fell into the hands of robbers?"

> *The expert in the law replied, "The one who had mercy on him."*
> *Jesus told him, "Go and do likewise."*

LUKE 10:30–37

The Priest

The first person who had a chance to help was not your ordinary Joe—or should I say, Joseph. He was a priest, of all people. Yet he passed by on the other side? That's bad.

But maybe the guy was busy. Maybe he was running late for a meeting. Maybe he passed by because his plate was already full of problems, and he didn't need another one right then. This half-dead man would be a big problem. He'd need time and attention, money and emotional energy.

Or maybe the priest was just playing it safe. He might have sensed a trap. The wounded man could be a decoy with hidden thieves nearby just waiting to pounce.

We don't know why he refused to help. We just know he didn't help.

The Levite

It's interesting that the guy who asked the question about loving our neighbors was a lawyer, possibly a Levite himself. Levites were priests' assistants and were sometimes called *lawyers*. From our modern perspective, we would think a lawyer would certainly stop, if for no other reason than to file a claim. "Sue the crooks who did this. Sue the people who built this road in such a dangerous place. Sue the police for never being there when you need them. This could be worth several million bucks."

But two thousand years ago in Israel, Levites and lawyers didn't concern themselves with civil, but religious, law. They saw that the rules of the Jews were explained and enforced. Certainly he'd stop, right?

Wrong.

The Samaritan

A Samaritan was a person from Samaria. They were racially mixed—half Jewish and half non-Jewish. Samaritans dated back to about 700 BC, around the time the Assyrian Empire overran Israel. The conquered Israelites forfeited their Jewish heritage, adopted some pagan worship practices, and intermarried with Gentiles who were sent into Samaria to repopulate the area. As such, the Samaritans were despised by the Jews.

No one would ever expect a Samaritan to stop to help a Jew. That would be like asking a runaway slave to help an injured slave owner in Mississippi in 1850. But the Samaritan of Jesus' story did something truly shocking:

> *"He took pity on him. He went to him and bandaged his wounds, pouring on oil and wine. Then he put the man on his own donkey, took him to an inn and took care of him. The next day he took out two silver coins and gave them to the innkeeper. 'Look after him,' he said, 'and when I return, I will reimburse you for any extra expense you may have.' "*

LUKE 10:33–35

The Samaritan crossed racial and religious barriers to help the Jewish man. He took risks. He risked not only getting mugged himself, he risked having the victim reject his help because it came from a hated Samaritan. He risked his reputation with his Samaritan friends, who would probably take offense at him for helping a Jew.

The Samaritan gave up his time. How long do you think it took to stop, bandage the wounded Jew, and take him to an inn? The Samaritan inconvenienced himself. Who wants a dirty, bloody man messing up the back of his nice, clean donkey? Who wants to walk while a half-dead Jew rides his animal? Who wants to go that far out of his way for someone else?

Even beyond that, the Samaritan paid for the other man's stay and care at the inn. Those two silver coins weren't fifty cent pieces—they would be equivalent to about 250 dollars each. Imagine spending five hundred dollars to help a person you'd never even met.

The Samaritan could have said, "I've gone to all this cost and trouble, and I'll go no further. This is my limit." But no, he went as far as was needed. He volunteered to pay any extra expense necessary.

Wow! Put a big *S* on his chest for Superfriend.

Then, as He always did, Jesus asked the self-righteous lawyer a dangerous little question of His own.

> *"Which of these three do you think was a neighbor to the man who fell into the hands of robbers?"*
> *The expert in the law replied, "The one who had mercy on him."*
> *Jesus told him, "Go and do likewise."*

LUKE 10:36–37

My Good Samaritan

I have a nasty little secret I need to confess. I don't like this story.

I think I've always had an aversion to the Good Samaritan. That guy is just too much. We're supposed to be like him, yet I often feel more like the priest or Levite. When it comes to that kind of compassion, I feel like a loser, a love bozo.

One night after everyone else in the house went to bed, I got honest with God. I said, "God, I hate this story. I've tried and I can never be like the Good Samaritan. What's wrong with me?"

It seemed like God was saying, "I know you don't quite live up to the profile of the Good Samaritan."

That's for sure, I thought.

"But you don't exactly fit the profile of the priest and Levite either. I've seen you get involved with hurting people. I've seen the time, the tears, and the money you've given to people in need."

Then it seemed like God was prompting me to look at the characters in this story again.

"Okay. There is the Samaritan, the priest, and the Levite."

"And. . . ?"

"And. . .there's the guy who got robbed and left for dead."

Then it hit me. I *am* in this story. Not so much as the priest or scribe, or even the Samaritan. I began to laugh. "I'm the half-dead guy."

Then I wondered, *Who's the Good Samaritan? No one has ever loved me like that? No one. . .*

It was as though God cleared His throat.

Then I understood. "No one ever loved me like that, except. . .Jesus. Jesus is the Good Samaritan. Jesus is *my* Good Samaritan."

Was I really half dead? According to the Bible, before we meet Jesus, we are all dead in our sins (Ephesians 2:1). Our spirits are dead to God and the things of God.

Was I really that needy? The Bible describes us as being spiritually destitute (Revelation 3:17).

Was I really dirty? According to the scriptures, before being saved, we are unclean and all our righteousness is as filthy rags (Isaiah 64:6).

Was I really a foreigner? Prior to being adopted into God's forever family, we are aliens (Ephesians 2:19).

Was I really helpless and hopeless? According to the Bible, that is truly our spiritual condition apart from Christ (Ephesians 2:12).

I am that half-dead guy, beaten and dirty, left to die by the side of the road.

And so are you.

Religion can't help us. When we really need help most, religion will just walk on by. We need someone who is both willing and able to save us. We need a Good Samaritan, and God the Father sent one. Actually, something even better.

Like the Samaritan, Jesus crossed barriers. God became a man.

Like the Samaritan, He came to us when we could not get up to Him.

Like the Samaritan, He risked our rejection in order to meet our needs.

Like the Samaritan, He paid a great price for us. Unlike the Samaritan, the price He paid is not measurable in dollars and cents—He paid with His own life. He died to save us. He died loving us. He died to be our friend.

Better than the Samaritan, He didn't just bandage us up, He made us brand-new. He's not merely taking us to an inn, but one day He'll take us all the way home to His Father's mansion.

Instead of getting discouraged because you struggle to *be* the Good Samaritan, be thankful that you *have* a Good Samaritan. You say, "But doesn't God want us to love like the Good Samaritan?" Absolutely! But be encouraged.

We can only begin to love *like* the Good Samaritan when we realize how much we have been loved *by* the Good Samaritan. We must continually grow in our awareness and appreciation of God's self-sacrificing love for us. As we do, we can become more and more like the Good Samaritan, and ultimately more like Jesus.

NOTE

[1] I read the article "Detroit Crowd Cheers as Trio Chase Woman to Her Death," in *The Columbus Dispatch*, August 22, 1995. More extensive coverage was available in an article by David Grant, "40 Watched Attackers Chase Woman to Her Death," *Detroit News*, August 21, 1995.

6

Why Have You Forsaken Me?
MATTHEW 27:46

I don't know what shadows may currently darken your life, but I want to remind you that Jesus is the light of the world. Maybe it feels as though you walk down a dark tunnel, but Jesus is the light at the end of the tunnel. Perhaps you're in a period of midnight gloom, but with Jesus, joy comes in the morning. He knows all about the darkness, and He knows all about *your* darkness.

Please walk back with me two thousand years.

Jesus and His disciples had finished their last meal together that fateful Thursday evening. During that special supper in the upper room, Jesus instituted the memorial meal commemorating His coming death on the cross for our sins. After dinner, the men quietly descended the stairs and made their way across the small Kidron Valley. Out of the city, they climbed the Mount of Olives to the dark Garden of Gethsemane.

Ironically, the name *Gethsemane* means "the crush"—as olives were crushed there to release their oil. It was in that garden the old olive trees witnessed Jesus being crushed by the weight of all that lay ahead. Here He gazed into the cup of His coming suffering and crucifixion. What He saw squeezed Him so brutally that His forehead erupted into rivulets of blood. Here Jesus sought His heavenly Father for the strength to continue in the awful, yet awesome, plan to redeem a sinful world.

As Jesus finished His prayer, the hillside suddenly blazed with torchlight. The serene silence was shattered by rough and anxious voices. Crowded around Jesus were the angry faces of soldiers, temple guards, and Jewish leaders, as well as the troubled visage of the betrayer, Judas himself. To them Jesus raised a question.

The Hour When Darkness Reigns

> "Am I leading a rebellion, that you have come with swords and clubs? Every day I
> was with you in the temple courts, and you did not lay a hand on me. But this is your
> hour—when darkness reigns."

> LUKE 22:52–53

Notice that last sentence: *But this is your hour—when darkness reigns.* What a sinister, yet lyrical, word picture. *The hour darkness reigns.* From the utterance of those words, an unstoppable series of history-making events was unleashed. Jesus was arrested and dragged through a series of illegal trials and kangaroo courts. He was brutally whipped, beaten, mocked, and rejected. All of that was merely the shadow leading up to the true darkness that was to come.

When Jesus allowed Himself to be nailed on the cross, He made a choice that produced the greatest darkness a single soul would ever know. It was as He hung on the cross that darkness ruled supreme.

Remember that Jesus did not begin in Bethlehem. He is God—and as God He has always existed in fellowship with His Father.

> In the beginning was the Word, and the Word was with God, and the Word was God.
> He was with God in the beginning.

> JOHN 1:1–2

Yet when Jesus went to the cross, He took all of our sins with Him. So the sinless Son of God became sin. God is holy—totally separate from all sin. His nature demands that He must judge and turn His back on sin. So when our sin was poured out on the Son, the Father had to turn away. Imagine the anguish He felt. God had to turn His back on His own Son, Jesus Christ. When God, who is light, turned His back on Jesus, it created a darkness so severe it literally affected the earth.

From the sixth hour until the ninth hour darkness came over all the land.

MATTHEW 27:45

The sixth hour on the Hebrew clock is noon; the ninth hour would be three p.m. I have been in Jerusalem at that time and the sun is blazingly bright. The sandstone buildings are alive with sunlight.

But not that day!

That afternoon, darkness reigned. Heavy shadows spread like a thick curtain over the land. When the Father turned His back on the Son, the sun refused to shine. For three awful hours, the Son of God was separated from God the Father. He experienced hell for each of us as He bore our sins and received our judgment.

This was one of the most significant, history-altering, powerful moments the Earth ever witnessed. It was the hour darkness reigned.

At this defining moment, Jesus uttered one of the most amazing, important, agonizing, and dangerous questions ever spoken.

My God, My God, Why Have You Forsaken Me?

About the ninth hour Jesus cried out in a loud voice, "Eloi, Eloi, lama sabachthani?"—which means, "My God, my God, why have you forsaken me?"

MATTHEW 27:46

Sadder words were never spoken.

Jesus was racked by physical anguish. He hung suspended between earth and space—alone, dying, betrayed by Judas, denied by Peter, forsaken by His disciples, mocked by the crowd, and attacked by demons. It was horrific.

All of which He could bear.

But now, as He hung in darkness, dying on the cross, He faced the only unbearable thing in the world—His Father had turned His back on Jesus.

On the cross, Christ became our sacrificial Lamb. God the Father placed all the sin of all the people who had lived, were living, or would ever live on Jesus Christ. Sin was poured out on Him like raw sewage. His pure and innocent soul was darkened—Jesus became sin for us.

God made him who had no sin to be sin for us, so that in him we might become the righteousness of God.

2 CORINTHIANS 5:21

In an amazing, grotesque way, the sinless Son of God became the greatest sinner of all time. With that sin came the price of separation.

But your iniquities have separated you from your God; your sins have hidden his face from you, so that he will not hear.

ISAIAH 59:2

At that moment, as darkness reigned, Jesus was truly alone in the universe—more alone than any man has ever been. Not merely rejected by the crowds, betrayed by a disciple, denied by a friend, and abandoned by His students; Jesus was forsaken by God.

Read those last three words again slowly—*forsaken by God*. Those haunting, piercing words stand alone as the bleakest conceivable indictment. In those awful hours when darkness reigned, God the Father was forced to turn His back on God the Son. Eternal communion was broken. Eons of unbroken fellowship were severed.

Deep within His soul, Jesus cried out the most dramatic, the most desperate question ever uttered by human lips, "My God, My God, why have You forsaken Me?" Imagine, for the only time in all of eternity, Jesus could not even call God His Father. The best He could say was "My God."

My God, My God, why have You forsaken Me?
What has happened?
Where are You, God?

In a sense, this question was actually a realization, a stunning statement, an astounding declaration, a shocking discovery, a desperate plea—

My God, I am separated from You!
It is too much. I cannot bear this.
This darkness of separation is too much.

It Was the Lord's Will to Crush Him

Seven hundred years earlier, this ghastly moment was predicted by the prophet Isaiah. He wrote:

We all, like sheep, have gone astray, each of us has turned to his own way; and the Lord has laid on him the iniquity of us all.

ISAIAH 53:6

Yet it was the Lord's will to crush him and cause him to suffer.

ISAIAH 53:10

It is one thing to suffer at the hands of wicked men.
It is worse to be betrayed and abandoned by friends.
It is terrible to suffer at the hands of Satan.
But it is an entirely different thing to suffer at the hands of your God. . .and Father.

At that moment on the cross, when Jesus asked, "Why have You forsaken Me?", God the Father was crushing His Son. The intensity, severity, and agony of such pain would have been incalculable.

The author of Hebrews reminds us of a supremely somber reality.

It is a dreadful thing to fall into the hands of the living God.

HEBREWS 10:31

Never before had darkness reigned over the earth in such a great way.
Never before had darkness ruled over one soul in such a great way.
God the Father allowed darkness to have dominion over the soul of God the Son.
Why?
Why did God allow darkness to reign?
Why did God allow Jesus to fall into the hands of dark-hearted men?
Why did God allow Jesus to be attacked by Satan?
Why did God allow Jesus to be separated from Himself?
Why did God forsake His Son?
Why?

Darkness Was Allowed to Reign Briefly in Order That Light May Reign Eternally

Read these verses slowly and seriously. Drink in the depth of love they proclaim.

For Christ died for sins once for all, the righteous for the unrighteous, to bring you to God.

1 PETER 3:18

"For God so loved the world that he gave his one and only Son, that whoever believes in him shall not perish but have eternal life."

JOHN 3:16

"I am the light of the world."

JOHN 8:12

Remember, darkness reigned for hours; light reigns for eternity.

That Friday afternoon was shrouded in deep darkness. But three days later, life erupted from the grave, and the light of the world shone brilliantly.

Yes, the horrors of hell won briefly, but only in order that the gates of heaven could be opened wide. The devil claimed a victory that afternoon, but only so Jesus could win victory forever. Sin stood as champion over one so salvation could come to all. Death was king for a moment so life could be offered eternally.

Jesus experienced the greatest levels of darkness so we can experience the greatest levels of light.

Darkness only lasts through the night, but joy comes in the morning.

Jesus understands your pain.

Jesus Understands Your Pain and Has Defeated Your Darkness

Maybe it feels as though God has forsaken you. Maybe you are experiencing the frightening loneliness of a seemingly passive silence from the sovereign God.

Maybe the vultures of darkness are circling your soul. The terrors of terrible trials have ravaged your faith.

Maybe you feel lost in a wilderness of darkness and wonder when, if ever, you will find the way out.

Are you struggling with some dark situation in your life? Maybe a loved one is in the hospital—or has died. Maybe it's a personal health issue. It could be a job. There might be an unexplained, unresolved hurt. Possibly there is a dark cloud turning everything you see to gloom.

Cry out to Jesus.

He understands.

He cares.

Come to the Lord of Light. He can chase all your darkness away.

7
How Can a Man Be Born When He Is Old?
John 3:4

"Lose Your Religion!"

A few years ago, my church mailed out ten thousand postcards emblazoned with the words, "Lose Your Religion!" On the back of the card, I paraphrased the words of Jesus, "If all you have is religion, you will never see the kingdom of heaven" (John 3:3). I also paraphrased the words of the apostle Paul, who said that "religion is dung" (Philippians 3:3–10).

As I had expected, we received some very interesting e-mails that week. People wanted to know how I, as the pastor of a well-known church, could be so dead-set against religion.

My point was simple: Religion by itself is not enough. Religion will not get anyone to heaven. Real Christianity is a *relationship*. It is a relationship into which you must be spiritually born. You must be born again.

Nic at Night

Nicodemus hoped his clandestine meeting would go unnoticed in the clamor of the Passover celebration. Power, position, prestige—he potentially had much to lose. Meeting with Jesus, the unsanctioned teacher, could cost Nicodemus dearly.

Nicodemus was not merely a Pharisee. He was a member of the Sanhedrin, the elite group of seventy men who ruled Israel in all matters regarding religion. Religion—that's what had raised his curiosity about Jesus. It seems Jesus was more committed to talking about a relationship with God than about keeping religious rituals and rules. The miracles Jesus had performed had piqued Nicodemus's interest to see if this man really was who some said He was—the Messiah.

So Nicodemus came at night and sat down across from Jesus. Peter, James, and John probably sat in the background, joined by a few of Nicodemus's assistants. They may have been surprised by the unthreatening manner with which Nicodemus approached Jesus. But Nicodemus was soul thirsty. Jesus wisely whetted his appetite and drew from his lips a most dangerous question.

> Now there was a man of the Pharisees named Nicodemus, a member of the Jewish ruling council. He came to Jesus at night and said, "Rabbi, we know you are a teacher who has come from God. For no one could perform the miraculous signs you are doing if God were not with him."
>
> In reply Jesus declared, "I tell you the truth, no one can see the kingdom of God unless he is born again."
>
> "How can a man be born when he is old?" Nicodemus asked. "Surely he cannot enter a second time into his mother's womb to be born!"
>
> John 3:1–4

"How Can a Man Be Born When He Is Old?"

Jesus had said no one could even *see* heaven without being born again. But Nicodemus wasn't sure what it meant to be "born again." He knew that a second physical birth made no sense. So Jesus explained.

Jesus answered, "I tell you the truth, no one can enter the kingdom of God unless he is born of water and the Spirit. Flesh gives birth to flesh, but the Spirit gives birth to spirit. You should not be surprised at my saying, 'You must be born again.' The wind blows wherever it pleases. You hear its sound, but you cannot tell where it comes from or where it is going. So it is with everyone born of the Spirit."

JOHN 3:5–8

Religion Is Not Good Enough

Sometimes it's easier to understand what a person is saying by first determining what he or she is *not* saying. Clearly, Jesus was not saying that people needed to be very religious to enter the kingdom of heaven. Nicodemus did not need to become religious because he already was very religious. As we read in John 3:1, he was "a member of the Jewish ruling council."

In order to be on that select council of seventy, one had to be a Pharisee. Pharisees were the most religious of the Jews. Their whole life was religion. The word *Pharisee* is from a word meaning "separate." The Pharisees were noted as those who kept away from anyone or anything they considered to be religiously unclean. They fasted two days every week and never missed synagogue. The Pharisees felt the Old Testament had too *few* religious rules in it, so they added hundreds of their own.

But Nicodemus was more than a Pharisee—he was a leader of the Pharisees! He was a part of the ruling council known as the Sanhedrin. These seventy men were the most religious of the Pharisees.

If anyone was religious, it was Nicodemus. Yet his religion was not good enough. Jesus looked Nicodemus in the eye and told him that he had to be born again. That must have been a little unnerving for Nicodemus—if his religion wasn't good enough, whose would be? Would yours?

Recently I asked a man this question: "If you died today, are you certain you would be welcomed into heaven?"

He said, "I guess so."

I asked him, "On what basis would God let you in?"

He replied, "Well, I go to church."

I asked, "If I sat in a garage a few hours every week, would it make me a car?"

He laughed and said, "Of course not."

So I replied, "Sitting in a garage will no more make you a car than attending a church will make you a Christian. Jesus said that you need to be born again."

Being Good Is Not Good Enough

Not long ago, I asked a young lady the question, "If you died today, are you certain you would be welcomed into heaven?", and the follow-up question, "On what basis would God let you into heaven?"

She answered, "I'm a pretty good person."

"But are you good enough?" I asked.

She didn't care much for that question, answering with a certain amount of pride, "Well, I'm better than most."

"But is that good enough?" I pressed. "Is your righteousness good enough to get you into heaven?"

She answered, "I hope so. . .I don't know. What *is* good enough?"

"According to the Bible," I replied, "the only righteousness that is good enough for heaven is perfection. Are you perfect?"

"No."

"Then maybe your righteousness is not good enough. Jesus said that you need to be born again."

The Bible teaches that there has been only one person in history who was "good enough." Only one person hit the bull's-eye of the righteousness required by God. That person is Jesus Christ. He is the only one who earned a relationship with a perfect God by living a sinless life. Yet He died in our place on the cross and rose again from the dead. So our relationship with God is not the result of the religion we have or good works we do. It is the result of believing in what Jesus has *done*. It is not something we earn. It's a gift we receive.

You see, if we could get to heaven by being really religious or really good, why did Jesus have to die for sin? No matter how good we are, we are not perfect. No matter how much good we do, we can't erase the stain of our past sins.

A Second Birth

Being born again is not something you do. It's something you experience. Jesus was crystal clear: You will not experience the kingdom of God unless you experience a second birth.

I asked a gentleman if he was born again. He told me, "Sure, I've been a Christian all my life." That's not what Jesus was saying. He said we need a *second* birth. We need to be born *again*.

A Spiritual Birth

Nicodemus was thinking in physical terms when he asked:

> *"How can a man be born when he is old? . . .Surely he cannot enter a second time into his mother's womb to be born!"*

JOHN 3:4

Jesus responded that being "born again" is experiencing a *spiritual* birth.

> *Jesus answered, "I tell you the truth, no one can enter the kingdom of God unless he is born of water and the Spirit. Flesh gives birth to flesh, but the Spirit gives birth to spirit."*

JOHN 3:5–6

By describing births of both water *and* the Spirit, Jesus contrasted physical birth with spiritual birth. He said we need both.

It was the physical birth Jesus described in verse 5 when he said "born of water." When a woman is pregnant, a sack of water protects the baby inside her. She knows the baby is ready to come when the water breaks. When the baby is born, it's all wet—because the physical birth involves being "born of water."

By saying, "Flesh gives birth to flesh," Jesus was further referring to physical birth. When we are born physically, we mark the event with a certificate that gives the date, time, and place of our arrival. Note carefully that Jesus said the physical birth alone will not get us into the kingdom of God. We need a spiritual birth. We need to be "born of water *and* the Spirit" (John 3:5).

The First Birth Is Not Good Enough

I once saw a bumper sticker that said, "Born once. It was good enough." I thought, *Not according to Jesus.* Jesus taught the first birth is insufficient. Our first birth is corrupted by our sin nature, called "the flesh."

> *"The Spirit gives life; the flesh counts for nothing."*
>
> John 6:63

> *I know that nothing good lives in me, that is, in my sinful nature. For I have the desire to do what is good, but I cannot carry it out.*
>
> Romans 7:18

"So, How Do I Get Born Again?"

One day, a lady became upset with me because I had mentioned the fact that we are all sinners.

"Sinner?" she said. "That is such a strong term. I resent being called a sinner."

I asked her, "How many murders does it take to be a murderer?"

"One," she replied. "It only takes one."

"So," I continued, "how many sins does it take to be a sinner?"

"Oh," she said. "Now I see what you mean. So, how do I get born again?"

The answer is given later in Jesus' discussion with Nicodemus.

> *"For God so loved the world that he gave his one and only Son, that whoever believes in him shall not perish but have eternal life."*
>
> John 3:16

John's Gospel also says,

> *Yet to all who received him [Jesus], to those who believed in his name, he gave the right to become children of God [i.e., be born again].*
>
> John 1:12

We are born again when, by faith, we receive Jesus Christ as our savior.

Let me ask several vitally important questions:

1. Do you know the date, time, and place of your spiritual birth?
2. Do you know for sure that you have been born again?
3. If you are not absolutely certain that you have been born again, will you respond to God and be born again today, on this date, at this time, at this place? This is a chance to make sure.

On the next page is a simple prayer hundreds have prayed when they were serious about turning their lives over to Jesus Christ. Read through it. If you mean it, you can say it to God.

Dear God,

I admit that I have sinned. I admit that my religion alone is not going to give me a relationship with You. I admit that my goodness is not good enough. I admit that I need to be born again.

I believe that Jesus is God's Son. I believe that Jesus never sinned. I believe that Jesus died to pay for my sins. I believe that Jesus rose from the dead to give me eternal life.

Right now, I call upon the name of the Lord Jesus to save me. I ask the Holy Spirit to come into my heart and make me a new person. I ask that I may be born again as a child of God. I surrender the throne of my heart to You. I ask to experience Your love and power.

I am willing to do anything You tell me to do. I am willing to stop doing anything that displeases You. I ask for the power to follow You all the days of my life. In Jesus' name, amen.

If you said that prayer to God and meant it, you might want to fill out the spiritual birth certificate below. Also, please send me an e-mail (dbearley@liberty.edu) so I can rejoice with you and pray for you.

MY SPIRITUAL BIRTH CERTIFICATE

On _____ _____, 20___,

I, _____ _____,

was born again by responding to God's Word
and called upon the name of the Lord to save me.
I am now born again as I have admitted my sin,
believed in Jesus Christ to pay for my sin,
and committed my life to Him.

8

Which Is the Greatest Commandment?
MATTHEW 22:36

What really matters? What are the most important things in life?

One way to choose your top priorities is to consider what you want people to say about you at your funeral. Epitaphs are brief statements commemorating or epitomizing a deceased person. They can be spoken or written. Some are serious; others are not. In years past, they were often written on gravestones. Following are some of the best I've either seen or read about.

In a Uniontown, Pennsylvania, cemetery, one gravestone tells the story of an accident:

Here lies the body
of Jonathan Blake.
Stepped on the gas
instead of the brake.

A headstone in a Silver City, Nevada, cemetery tells of a gun battle:

Here lays Butch,
We planted him raw.
He was quick on the trigger,
But slow on the draw.

In the Boot Hill Cemetery in Tombstone, Arizona:

Here lies Lester Moore
Four slugs from a .44
No Les No More

Anna Hopewell's gravestone in Enosburg Falls, Vermont, is amusing:

Here lies the body of our Anna,
Done to death by a banana.
It wasn't the fruit that laid her low,
But the skin of the thing that made her go.

Some epitaphs don't rhyme. On Margaret Daniels's grave at Hollywood Cemetery in Richmond, Virginia, we read:

She always said her feet were killing her
But nobody believed her.

A headstone in a London cemetery reads,

Here lies Ann Mann,
Who lived an old maid
But died an old Mann.
Dec. 8, 1767

In a Thurmont, Maryland, cemetery is this thought-provoker:

Here lies an Atheist
All dressed up
And no place to go.

My favorite was one we saw on vacation at a cemetery in Key West, Florida. It simply says:

I Told You I Was Sick

Those are all pretty funny. But the very best headstone I'm aware of honored a man whose life made a positive difference. Dr. John Geddie went to the Pacific island of Aneiteum in 1848 as a missionary and worked there for God for twenty-four years. On the tablet erected to his memory, these words were inscribed:

When he landed, in 1848, there were no Christians.
When he left, in 1872, there were no heathen.[1]

What would the epitaph of your life be? Several years ago, a friend of mine was diagnosed with cancer. When he died soon thereafter, his family held a service celebrating his life. Relatives and friends shared the positive impact he had had on their lives. They talked about his unswerving commitment to God, his deep love of his family, and his effect on others. After that night, I determined to make sure I knew what was most important—and to spend the rest of my life living for what mattered most.

A Dangerous Question for Jesus

Jesus had become an annoying irritant and potentially large threat to the business-as-usual religion of the Pharisees. His teachings and lifestyle exposed the superficial character of their legalistic rituals and manmade rules. He spoke of life and love. He talked about a genuine relationship with God. He was refreshingly authentic and had a passionate depth and compassionate heart that drew people to Him.

Since their religion was built on words and rules, the Pharisees tried to discredit Jesus by trapping Him in the web of questions and theoretical dilemmas. They asked, "Is it right for a Jew to pay taxes?" and "In the resurrection who will be the husband of a remarried widow?" But Jesus was no fool. He repeatedly avoided their rhetorical knots and tied them up in their own questions.

Finally, they came at Him with an apparently unsolvable dilemma. The question was simple, presumably unanswerable, and designed to discredit Jesus. It went like this: "Out of the 613 commands given in the Old Testament law, which was the greatest?" The Pharisees figured that if Jesus named one command as greater than another, He would be disparaging the rest. Then they would nail Him for dealing irreverently with the Word of God.

> *Hearing that Jesus had silenced the Sadducees, the Pharisees got together. One of them, an expert in the law, tested him with this question:*
>
> *"Teacher, which is the greatest commandment in the Law?"*
>
> MATTHEW 22:34–36

This attempted trap serves as one of the most dangerous questions in the Bible. It was potentially dangerous then, as to answer incorrectly would discredit Jesus as a teacher. It is dangerous now, as the way we answer it and what we do with it will change our lives.

Notice the amazing wisdom of Jesus as He skillfully answered their dilemma.

> *Jesus replied: " 'Love the Lord your God with all your heart and with all your soul and with all your mind.' This is the first and greatest commandment. And the second is like it: 'Love your neighbor as yourself.' All the Law and the Prophets hang on these two commandments."*
>
> MATTHEW 22:37–40

Jesus' reply is marvelous. He cut to the main point of the commandments by quoting two passages, one from the sixth chapter of Deuteronomy, the other from an obscure corner of Leviticus 19. That concisely, Jesus summarized the 613 commands of the Old Testament law (plus those of the rest of the entire Bible) and simplified all of life at the same time. His answer? "Love God and love people—everything else hangs off those two pegs."

Do you see the brilliance of Jesus' answer? Instead of giving the Pharisees a loophole that allowed them to obey one commandment while ignoring another, He gave them one commandment that contained all the commandments of God in two simple sentences: "Love the Lord" and "Love your neighbor."

Priorities

Priority can be defined as "something given precedence of rank in terms of time, energy, thought, finances, etc." A priority is something that is valued or deemed as important. We often state what is important to us by how we spend our time and money. I have learned there are several truths regarding priorities:

1. Not everything can be a priority.

You cannot have it all. The commercials say you can, but don't believe them. We are not infinite beings. None of us can have it all or do it all. When we try to do so, we become overloaded and overwhelmed.

2. Not everything should be a priority.

Not all things are created equal. Not every activity is the best choice possible. We must choose when it comes to priorities. Some activities and investments are more important than others.

3. Fulfilling two commands must become our priorities.

Jesus summarized life's most important priorities and simplified life for us into one awesome statement—love God and love people. Notice what Jesus did *not* give as being of primary importance: things, achievements, careers, and money. He did not list possessions, power, popularity, pets, pleasure, comfort, convenience, entertainment, or recreation as having chief importance, either.

Loving God

Loving God is a choice. The verse Jesus quoted, "Love the LORD your God" (Deuteronomy 6:5), was originally written in Hebrew. The Hebrew term translated "love" describes an act of the will characterized by dedication and commitment of choice. Matthew's Gospel was written in Greek. The Greek term used here for "love" is the verb of intelligent, purposeful, committed love. Both languages make it clear that loving God is a choice. This is also evident by the fact that loving God is used as an imperative (or command) in this verse. Loving God is more than a random feeling or an innate urge. It is a choice that must be made.

Choosing to Love God Above Everything Else

Early in high school, I felt I could balance my life by segregating parts of it into separate boxes. I had a big box for sports, a container for friends, and a section for school. I had separate boxes for art, music, my paper route, family, and God. *I* was central in my life and my boxes revolved around me.

God was definitely part of my life, but only in His own box. I went to church on Sunday, and I helped a friend with a ministry to poor children. I got my "God box" out if something really bad happened. But besides that, I kept God in His box. I was reluctant to allow Him to affect the other areas of my life. I really loved God with only half a heart—or less.

I was miserable.

For a couple of years, I disobeyed the Great Commandment as I battled to be the center of my own life, keeping God in His own box. Eventually, I tired of the mess I was making. I felt so empty. My friends who loved God with all of their hearts were full of joy. They seemed so much more happy and satisfied. I thirsted for that type of relationship with God.

One Sunday morning, I delivered my newspapers and went to church. As usual, I went to the very last row of the balcony, to the corner farthest from the platform. Normally, when the sermon would start, I would fall asleep. But that Sunday was different. Someone had handed me a bulletin on the way in, and that piece of paper had a large boxed quote that read:

> *Commitment to God is simply giving all you know of yourself to all you know of God.*

I was intrigued. *I can do that,* I thought. *I can't be perfect or spiritual on my own. I have tried so many times and failed miserably. I have tried the overly emotional route, and that did not last. But I can choose to give all I know of myself to all I know of God.*

I have no recollection of that day's sermon. All I could think about was, "Commitment to God is simply giving all you know of yourself to all you know of God."

Later that night, at the invitation of a friend, I attended a student gathering held in a large house. As dozens of teens sang praise to God and gave testimonies of His work in their lives, I could only think of one thing: "Commitment to God is simply giving all you know of yourself to all you know of God."

At home that night, I went straight to my room and got down on my knees. My prayer was simple.

> *God, I believe You are real.*
> *I am very sorry for my sins and the mess I have been making of my life.*
> *As of this moment, by an act of my will, I choose to give all I know of me to all I know of You.*
> *From this moment on I choose to put You ahead of sports, friends, school, art,*

music, my paper route, and my family. No more boxes. You can have all of me—past, present, and future.

> *I want to put You first and love You most.*
> *Amen.*

I did not hear thunder or see lightning. But for the first time in a long time, I experienced inner fullness, deep peace, and an especially rich joy. I felt clean and whole, loved and accepted.

Choosing to love God above all else is a commitment I must return to consistently. Sometimes it's easy—because I know that God is perfect, wise, powerful, and good. But other times, choosing to love God is excruciatingly difficult. My own desires can draw me away. God's discipline is sometimes hard to accept. At times, He seems silent. But my priority is to love Him.

Choosing to Really Love People

The second half of the great command is loving people as much as we love ourselves. That can be a challenge—because people are flawed, imperfect, needy beings. Loving people is hard when they can't (or worse, they refuse) to return our love. It's hard when they hurt us.

But we must remember this: Loving people is a choice to be made and a command to be obeyed before it becomes a feeling to be felt. The feeling may come or it might never come. But we must still act in love.

Jesus elaborated on what He meant by "loving our neighbors" when He gave His famous teaching on the mountainside. Slowly read His words below. As you do, realize that the only way you can love this way is by focusing on the love God has already given you.

> *"To you who are ready for the truth, I say this: Love your enemies. Let them bring out the best in you, not the worst. When someone gives you a hard time, respond with the energies of prayer for that person. If someone slaps you in the face, stand there and take it. If someone grabs your shirt, giftwrap your best coat and make a present of it. If someone takes unfair advantage of you, use the occasion to practice the servant life. No more tit-for-tat stuff. Live generously.*
>
> *"Here is a simple rule of thumb for behavior: Ask yourself what you want people to do for you; then grab the initiative and do it for them! If you only love the lovable, do you expect a pat on the back? Run-of-the-mill sinners do that. If you only help those who help you, do you expect a medal? Garden-variety sinners do that. If you only give for what you hope to get out of it, do you think that's charity? The stingiest of pawnbrokers does that.*
>
> *"I tell you, love your enemies. Help and give without expecting a return. You'll never—I promise—regret it. Live out this God-created identity the way our Father lives toward us, generously and graciously, even when we're at our worst. Our Father is kind; you be kind.*
>
> *"Don't pick on people, jump on their failures, criticize their faults—unless, of course, you want the same treatment. Don't condemn those who are down; that hardness can boomerang. Be easy on people; you'll find life a lot easier. Give away your life; you'll find life given back, but not merely given back—given back with bonus and blessing. Giving, not getting, is the way. Generosity begets generosity."*
>
> LUKE 6:27–38 THE MESSAGE

Thank God that He has consistently loved you with this type of love. Ask God to help you love the people you will meet today in the same ways He has loved you.

NOTE

[1]"Influence," Sermon Illustrations.com, http://www.sermonillustrations.com/a-z/i/influence.htm (accessed June 20, 2007).

9

Will You Really Lay Down Your Life for Me?

JOHN 13:38

It was an important night in Jerusalem. The disciples were gathered together with Jesus in an upper room for a meal. It would be the last supper they would share before Jesus would be arrested, tried, beaten, crucified, and resurrected. Judas had just left to set into motion the ugly events that rested ominously on the horizon. Jesus commented that He would be with the disciples only a little longer. He also said that they could not come where He was going (John 13:33). Peter, feeling secure in his role as lead disciple, began to ask Jesus questions. Unknowingly, it would lead Jesus to ask him, and the rest of us, a most dangerous question.

Will You Really Lay Down Your Life for Me?

> Simon Peter asked him, "Lord, where are you going?"
> Jesus replied, "Where I am going, you cannot follow now, but you will follow later."
> Peter asked, "Lord, why can't I follow you now? I will lay down my life for you."
> Then Jesus answered, "Will you really lay down your life for me?"
>
> JOHN 13:36–38

Following the way of Jesus was (and is) radically serious business. It is a path littered with life-and-death implications. Knowing His death was imminent, Jesus had given strong hints that true discipleship was a difficult road leading to sacrifice—even death.

> "If anyone would come after me, he must deny himself and take up his cross daily and follow me. For whoever wants to save his life will lose it, but whoever loses his life for me will save it."
>
> LUKE 9:23–24

> "If anyone comes to me and does not hate his father and mother, his wife and children, his brothers and sisters—yes, even his own life—he cannot be my disciple. And anyone who does not carry his cross and follow me cannot be my disciple."
>
> LUKE 14:26–27

Earlier that very week, Jesus had clearly said that His life was to be like a seed that must die in the ground before bearing much fruit. His way was leading to His death. To follow Him was to take the same path with the same outcome:

> "I tell you the truth, unless a kernel of wheat falls to the ground and dies, it remains only a single seed. But if it dies, it produces many seeds. The man who loves his life will lose it, while the man who hates his life in this world will keep it for eternal life. Whoever serves me must follow me; and where I am, my servant also will be. My Father will honor the one who serves me."
>
> JOHN 12:24–26

Peter was quite confident that he could handle the painful path of sacrifice Jesus was leading them down. Boldly he declared, "I will lay down my life for you" (John 13:37).

But Jesus knew Peter. Without truly coming to the end of himself, he would never learn how to rely on Jesus when facing the option of denial or death. So Jesus asked Peter a most dangerous question, followed by a disheartening prediction.

> *"Will you really lay down your life for me? I tell you the truth, before the rooster crows, you will disown me three times!"*
>
> JOHN 13:38

As we know, Jesus was right. Later that awful night, Peter did deny Jesus three times (Luke 22:54–61). Peter's failure broke his heart. He lost his arrogance and his pride died. When he realized what he had done, he wept bitter tears of remorse (Luke 22:62). Fortunately for Peter, God gives second chances and new life. Fortunately for Peter, he allowed his failure to create in him greater dependence upon Christ. He became the bold preacher of Pentecost (Acts 2) and a man willing to face imprisonment and beating for Jesus (Acts 4, 12).

Would Peter really lay down his life for Jesus? History tells us that he ultimately answered yes. Rather than deny Jesus, Peter died with a glorious testimony as he was crucified upside down because of his faith in Christ.

He Said No

As we also know, one of Jesus' disciples refused to take the narrow way of sacrifice. When faced with the question of whether he would lay down his life for Christ, Judas answered no. Judas betrayed Jesus to the authorities for a bag of money. Later, instead of repentance, he felt only a depressing remorse. Ironically, by trying to save his life, he died inside. Judas's guilt and shame ultimately led to his suicide.

They Answered Yes

Here are Jesus' last words before ascending into heaven:

> *"But you will receive power when the Holy Spirit comes on you; and you will be my witnesses in Jerusalem, and in all Judea and Samaria, and to the ends of the earth."*
>
> ACTS 1:8

It is interesting to note that the word *witness* is the same Greek word from which we get our word *martyr*. Jesus knew that taking the gospel to the world would be costly and that many would pay the ultimate price.

He was right.

Peter was not the only Christ-follower required to answer the question, "Will you really lay down your life for Me?" History tells us that many said yes. Thousands died for their faith during the early years of the church.

A deacon named Stephen was preaching the gospel in Jerusalem on the Passover after Christ's crucifixion. He was cast out of the city and stoned to death (Acts 6–8). James, the son of Zebedee and the elder brother of John, was killed when Herod Agrippa I arrived as governor of Judea (Acts 12). History tells us that Philip suffered martyrdom at Hierapolis in Phrygia. He was scourged, thrown into prison, and afterward crucified around AD 54.

Matthew, the tax collector from Capernaum who wrote a Gospel in Hebrew, was preaching in Ethiopia when he suffered martyrdom by the sword around AD 60. Andrew, the brother of Peter, preached the gospel throughout Asia. On his arrival at Edessa, he was arrested and crucified on a cross, two ends of which were fixed transversely in the ground (thus the term *St. Andrew's cross*). Bartholomew translated the Gospel of Matthew in India. He was cruelly beaten and crucified. Thomas, the one-time doubter of Christ, preached in Parthia and India. He was martyred with a spear.

James, the half brother of Jesus, led the church in Jerusalem and was the author of a book in the Bible. At the age of ninety-four he was beaten and stoned, and finally had his brains bashed out with a fuller's club. Matthias was the apostle who filled the vacant place of Judas. He was stoned at Jerusalem and then beheaded. Mark was converted to Christianity by Peter and then transcribed Peter's account of Jesus in his Gospel. Mark was dragged to pieces by the people of Alexandria in front of Serapis, their pagan idol.[1]

They Also Said Yes

Others with names less familiar were also martyred by heathen emperors, governors, and judges for refusing to denounce Jesus Christ. In his *Ecclesiastical History*, Eusebius tells of numerous martyrs in the Christian church prior to AD 324.[2]

They did not receive proper trials. Many were tortured before being put to death. Even as they suffered such abuse, they refused to deny Jesus. Picture the fearless faith in Christ of these few:

A man named Alpheus was scourged, scraped with iron hooks, and tortured on the rack, and eventually was beheaded.

A woman named Ennathas was scourged with thongs of hide. She endured the torture cheerfully, and when returned to the judge was condemned to the flames.

Metra was an old man who refused to deny Christ. His tormentors beat his aged body with clubs then led him out of town where they stoned him to death.

Sanctus suffered unimaginable abuse. He was beaten, had hot brass plates attached to parts of his body, was scourged with a whip, and dragged down a road. When he survived the attacks of wild animals, his persecutors strapped him into an iron chair and roasted his body.

Still Saying Yes

The accounts of Christian martyrdom are not merely stories from antiquity. Tens of thousands die for Jesus each year. Many of their stories are untold, but here are two:

Three teenage girls in Poso, Central Sulawesi, Indonesia, all members of a Christian high school, were beheaded on October 29, 2005, by machete-wielding men dressed in black. One of the severed heads was placed in front of a church.[3]

In south India, Pastor Daniel and his wife, Hephzibah, started a Christian church in the Hyderabad area by distributing tracts. He was opposed and beaten several times, and finally on May 19, 2005, he disappeared, only to be found murdered a few days later. When Hephzibah went to identify Daniel's body, she could only recognize him by the clothes he'd been wearing. Acid had been poured over his body.[4]

She Said Yes

On Tuesday, April 20, 1999, seventeen-year-old Cassie Bernall was reading her Bible in the Columbine school library when two students burst in with guns. According to a witness, one of the killers pointed his weapon at Cassie and asked, "Do you believe in God?"

Another student in the library recalled what happened next:

*She paused, like she didn't know what she was going to answer. . .then she said "yes."
She must have been scared, but her voice didn't sound shaky. It was strong. Then they
asked her why, though they didn't give her a chance to respond. They just blew her
away.*[5]

Will I Really Lay Down My Life for Christ?

This is a dangerous life-and-death question. I find it intensely challenging and deeply convicting. I read the accounts of these martyrs, and I ask myself, "Could I die for the One who died for me?" I don't know for sure. I hope I'd say yes. I like to believe He will give me the grace I will need if I ever face that awesome choice.

One thing I know for sure: If you and I are not living all of our lives for God now, we probably wouldn't die for Him then.

Notes

[1]"Christian Persecution: Dramatic Evidence," All About Following Jesus, http://www.allaboutfollowingjesus.org/christian-persecution.htm (accessed June 20, 2007).

[2]Eusebius, *Ecclesiastical History,* http://www.innvista.com/culture/religion/earlmart.htm (accessed June 20, 2007).

[3]*Witness Magazine,* July 2006, "Pray That God Would Restrain Militants," http://www.releaseinternational.org/media/download_gallery/wit29web.pdf (accessed June 20, 2007).

[4]*Witness Magazine,* July 2006, "On the March," http://www.releaseinternational.org/media/Witness/wit32web.pdf (accessed June 20, 2007).

[5]Misty Bernall, *She Said Yes!* (New York: Pocket Books, 1999), 14. The so-called myth of Cassie's shooting is debunked in the *Christianity Today* article, "Cassie Said Yes, They Said No" by Wendy Murray Zoba, http://ctlibrary.com/14911, November 1, 1999 (accessed June 20, 2007).

10

Did God Really Say. . .?

Have you ever been less-than-convinced of something God has said in His Word? Have you ever had questions about the validity, reliability, and authority of God's Word? Have you ever used your skepticism as an excuse for disobedience? If so, you are not the first.

Did God Really Say. . . ?

The story of the Bible opens with what may be the most dangerous question of them all. It is a question that can potentially render the rest of the Bible meaningless.

In the beginning, God did not give Adam hundreds of pages of rules. In fact, there was only one very simple rule: *Don't eat the fruit of the tree of the knowledge of good and evil.* Other than that, Adam, do as you please.

> *And the Lord God commanded the man, "You are free to eat from any tree in the garden; but you must not eat from the tree of the knowledge of good and evil, for when you eat of it you will surely die."*
>
> GENESIS 2:16–17

It was a simple enough command: "Don't eat the fruit of this one tree." The consequences were clearly explained: "If you disobey, you will die." It should have been easy enough to obey. The garden was loaded with plenty of trees bearing an abundant supply of wonderful fruit. Adam and Eve would not need to eat from the forbidden tree. No problem.

But then a cloud appeared on the horizon. It was the cloud of doubt surrounding one of the most dangerous questions ever asked. You know the story:

> *Now the serpent was more crafty than any of the wild animals the Lord God had made. He said to the woman, "Did God really say, 'You must not eat from any tree in the garden'?"*
>
> GENESIS 3:1

Sure, on the surface it seems like a simple enough question. It opens with four apparently innocent words: "Did God really say?" But underneath the serpent's slick smile and false ignorance lies sinister intent. Those four words raise dangerous uncertainty about the authority of the Word of God. Suspicion is aroused about the goodness of God. The command of God is questioned. Most damaging is that the question "smuggles in the assumption that God's word is subject to our judgment."[1]

The rest of the story is familiar. Adam and Eve doubted the Word of God, and as a result, they disregarded God's one simple command (Genesis 3:2–6). It was not only a watershed moment in *their* lives, it was also one of the defining moments in all human history. Adam and Eve's disobedience led to disastrous results and dragged the entire planet down with them. Doubt can be dangerous to us and damaging to others when we give in and disregard the Word of God. But doubt can also be dangerous to the enemy when it leads us to greater faith.

Is the Bible the Word of God?

I put the question on the search engine Google. The very first article listed was from a Web site hosted by the "Internet Infidels" who arrogantly describe themselves as "a drop of reason in a pool of confusion."[2] An article about the Bible concluded by saying:

> *The greatest obstacle to our peace and survival is the foolish, irrational delusion that the Bible is "the word of God." If we are to save our children and our world we must accept the fact that the Bible is not the word of God.*[3]

I found the bloated article full of false ideas stated in pompous terms. After reading it, I realized something—Satan is still asking the dangerous question, "Did God really say. . .?"

Why Believe the Bible Is the Word of God?

I've had times in my life when there was ample opportunity to doubt the goodness of God and the truthfulness of His Word. Yet I have invested my life in teaching and applying that Word of God. I wanted to be certain that the book I base my life upon is trustworthy, so several years ago I began to study various evidences of its reliability and validity. I was stunned to discover that there are so many.

Now, I proudly state that no one who believes in the Bible commits intellectual suicide. I believe there are solid intellectual reasons for believing, reading, and obeying the Bible. I do not believe the Bible *in spite of* the facts, but *because of* the facts.

Entire books have been written on this issue. Allow me to briefly discuss four compelling reasons for believing the Bible is the trustworthy Word of God.

The Bible Is Indestructible

You would expect that the words of God would have supernatural indestructibility. Isaiah said as much when he wrote, "The grass withers and the flowers fall, but the word of our God stands forever" (Isaiah 40:8). Jesus promised:

> *"I tell you the truth, until heaven and earth disappear, not the smallest letter, not the least stroke of a pen, will by any means disappear from the Law until everything is accomplished."*
>
> MATTHEW 5:18

Throughout history, Satan has used many means and men to attack the Bible. They have all failed.

The Roman emperor Diocletian fiercely attacked the Bible. He killed so many Christians and burned so many Bibles that in AD 303 he erected a pillar inscribed, "The name of Christians has been extinguished."

I don't think so.

Twenty years later, the new Roman emperor, Constantine, saw a vision of the cross and was, amazingly, converted. He not only became a Christian himself, he made Christianity the official religion of Rome. When he asked for a copy of the Bible, the book Diocletian had supposedly wiped out, he was stunned that fifty copies were delivered to him within twenty-four hours. Where had they come from? Each one had been hidden in Diocletian's own palace!

Two hundred years ago, the French atheist Voltaire declared, "Fifty years from now the world will hear no more of the Bible."

I don't think so.

In fact, fifty years after his death, the Geneva Bible Society bought Voltaire's house and his printing press in order to create even more Bibles. In 1933, the same year a first edition copy of Voltaire's book was selling for eight cents in Paris bookshops, the British Museum bought a copy of the New Testament from Russia for a half million dollars. Two hundred years after Voltaire's death, the Bible exceeded a half billion copies in print![4]

I could tell you one true story after another. Make no mistake about it. The Bible is the indestructible Word of God!

The Bible Is Scientifically Accurate

Some have said they cannot believe the Bible because of apparent contradictions with science. I have come to believe "apparent contradictions with science" are some of the best reasons *for* believing the Bible. Let me explain: The Bible, written over a period of fifteen hundred years by nearly forty different men, is an ancient book that demonstrates astounding scientific accuracy.

Let's look at four facts about science and the Bible:

1. Although it is not a science book, the Bible speaks accurately on scientific subjects. God is truth. Therefore, God cannot lie. The Bible is the Word of God. Therefore, it cannot lie. When it speaks, it speaks truth. When it speaks on scientific matters, it speaks accurately.

2. Because the Bible is an ancient book written thousands of years ago, the authors, although speaking accurately, were limited to expressing themselves in the language of their day. They do not say God superintends "hydrology: the water cycle," but they explain it.[5]

3. Through the ages, the Bible has contradicted some scientific theories. Yet, as science has developed, science has also contradicted itself! Ninety-nine percent of science books are considered out-of-date in a few years. The world's largest museum, the Louvre in Paris, has three miles of out-of-date science books.[6]

4. Therefore, when science and the Bible contradict, relax. Give science a few hundred years or so, and it will catch up. A scientist named Henry Morris has written:

   One of the most arresting evidences for the inspiration of the Bible is the great number of scientific truths that have lain hidden within its pages for thirty centuries or more, only to be discovered by man's enterprise within the last few centuries or even [the last few] years.[7]

Here are a few examples of how the Bible contradicted science until science later caught up:

1. Until AD 1400, science taught that the world was flat. Columbus proved otherwise in 1492. Yet the Bible, in Isaiah 40:22 (written about 700 BC), states that the earth is a circle! Luke 17:30–35, written around AD 60, indicates that people are experiencing both day and night on the earth at the same time. It only took science two thousand years to catch up with what the Bible said in 700 BC!

2. Since its early history, science held that the world was resting on pillars (or even the back of a turtle) until Sir Isaac Newton discovered the law of gravity in 1687. Yet the Bible, in Job 26:7, described the world as hanging in space. Job was written well over three thousand years ago!

3. In the seventeenth century, Galileo discovered that the winds traveled in circuitous patterns and had weight. Yet, Ecclesiastes 1:6, written in 900 BC, describes the circuits of winds. Job 28:25, written around 1500 BC, tells us that the wind has weight. It only took science three thousand years to catch up with the Bible![8]

The Bible Is a Book of Fulfilled Prophecy

> *"I am the Lord; that is my name! I will not give my glory to another or my praise to idols. See, the former things have taken place, and new things I declare; before they spring into being I announce them to you."*
>
> ISAIAH 42:8–9

God states that His existence can be proved because He tells us what will happen *before* it happens. We know the Bible is the Word of God because it has told us, on hundreds of occasions, what would happen before it happened.

The Bible is the only ancient book with detailed predictive prophecies. If just a few of these prophecies came true, it would be impressive—but you need to understand that *hundreds* of predictive prophecies have come true. Many of these prophecies came true hundreds, and in some cases, thousands of years after they were made! This is an overwhelming reason to believe the Bible.

In the Bible, we have many examples of God predicting the destruction of cities, the rise of leaders and nations, and the details of certain people's lives. We will see, in a later chapter, incredible details about the birth, life, death, and resurrection of the Messiah that were predicted in the Bible hundreds of years before those events transpired. In the Bible, God has described the end-times world events in detail. We are starting to see them occur before our very eyes, thousands of years after the prophecies were made.

"He Changed My Life"

These words summarize the story of a skeptic named Josh. As a practical young man, he says he "chucked religion." But God put some real Christians in Josh's life. They had something he knew he lacked, and he was curious. They challenged him to examine the claims of Christ for himself. Yet, Josh was skeptical.

> *I thought it was a farce. In fact, I thought most Christians were walking idiots. . . . I imagined that if a Christian had a brain cell it would die of loneliness.*[9]

But Josh's friends kept challenging him, and eventually he accepted their dare to thoroughly investigate the Bible. He writes:

> *Finally, out of pride, I accepted their challenge. I did it to refute them. I didn't know there were facts. I didn't know that there was evidence that a person could evaluate.*[10]

Josh was determined to win the argument and silence the Christians. He thought it would be easy. He was wrong.

I set out to refute Christianity. When I couldn't, I ended up becoming a Christian. I have spent fifteen years documenting why I believe faith in Jesus Christ is intellectually feasible.[11]

Josh McDowell is one of the multitudes who trust the words of the Bible because it has positively changed their lives. What other book has had such a powerful effect on so many people?

Did God Really Say. . . ?
Is the Bible really the Word of God? You'd better believe it. It is indestructible. It is scientifically accurate. The Bible is full of detailed predictions that have come true, and it changes lives. It has changed mine. It will change yours. Trust it, study it, live it, and share it.

NOTES
[1] Derek Kidner, *Genesis* (London: Tyndale Press, 1967), p. 67.

[2] http://www.infidels.org/ (accessed June 20, 2007).

[3] "Word of God Debate," Internet Infidels, http://www.infidels.org/library/modern/emmett_fields/word_of_god_debate.html (accessed June 20, 2007).

[4] H. L. Wilmington, *The Manuscript from Outer Space* (Lynchburg, VA: self-published textbook, 1974), pp. 92–93.

[5] John Macarthur, *Why I Trust the Bible* (Wheaton, IL: Victor Books, 1983), 88.

[6] H. L. Wilmington, p. 110.

[7] Henry M. Morris, *The Bible and Modern Science* (Chicago, IL: Moody Press, 1951), p. 7

[8] H. L. Wilmington, pp. 100–102.

[9] Josh McDowell, *Evidence That Demands a Verdict* (San Bernardino, CA: Here's Life Publishers, 1979), p.16.

[10] Ibid.

[11] Ibid.

11

Is There Any God Besides Me?
ISAIAH 44:8

Several years ago, I was out of town taking a doctoral studies course. One evening after a long day of study, I went to the local YMCA where I exercised, showered, then lowered my tired, aching body into a hot tub. Soon, a big, red-haired fellow joined me, and before long, we struck up a conversation. He was a fascinating man, having served around the world in various military and business capacities. He enjoyed talking about himself and fancied himself an authority on many things. I found much of what he said quite interesting.

After a while, as I often do, I attempted to bring Jesus into the conversation. The man had been talkative before, but now became positively enthusiastic in telling me of his religious odyssey. He had studied all of the major religions, he said, and indicated he was an expert in all of them. His journey had led him to conclude that all religions were comparable and that his own brand of New Age religion—with himself as god—was best. In defending this Eastern model of faith, he used an old Indian tale of blind men who tried to describe an elephant. The story goes like this:

> Once upon a time, a king gathered a few men who were born blind. They were asked to describe an elephant, but each one was presented with only a certain part of the animal. One man was positioned near the head of the elephant, another near the trunk, one by an ear, another by a leg, one next to the body, another near the tail, and the last by the tuft of the tail.
>
> The man near the head said: "The elephant is like a pot!" The one by the trunk answered, "The elephant is like a hose." The one who touched only the ears thought that the elephant was a fan. The others said that it was a pillar, a wall, a rope, or a brush, depending on the part of the elephant they encountered.
>
> Then they quarreled among themselves, each thinking that he was right and the others wrong. The obvious truth is that the elephant is a unity of many parts, a unity that the men could not grasp in their limited knowledge.

My new friend used this story to show that, when put together, all world religions form a unity. Then, in a very patronizing tone, he informed me that, "Only this unity provides the right perspective on ultimate truth."

I could agree that the elephant tale was indeed a fine story. But I pointed out one fatal flaw in the man's analogy—the God of the Bible is not an elephant!

Is There Any God Besides Me?

Seven hundred years before Jesus, the nation of Judah was, spiritually speaking, like a wife cheating on her husband. In her empty religious ritualism, she played a sham with her husband—the Lord—while at the same time committing spiritual adultery by worshiping idols. The nation hung in the balance of decision.

Was the Lord God of the Bible just another god or was He something more? The Lord Himself posed a dangerous question through His prophet Isaiah.

> *"This is what the Lord says—Israel's King and Redeemer, the Lord Almighty: I am the first and I am the last; apart from me there is no God. Who then is like me? Let him proclaim it. Let him declare and lay out before me what has happened since I established my ancient people, and what is yet to come—yes, let him foretell what will come. Do not tremble, do not be afraid. Did I not proclaim this and foretell it long ago? You are my witnesses. Is there any God besides me? No, there is no other Rock; I know not one."*
>
> ISAIAH 44:6–8

No Comparison!

Are all gods created equal? Not according to the God of the Bible. Using Isaiah as His messenger, God repeatedly and boldly claimed to be unique and superior, incomparably the only true God—and, therefore, worthy alone of our worship.

> *"I, even I, am the Lord, and apart from me there is no savior."*
>
> ISAIAH 43:11

> *"I am the Lord, and there is no other; apart from me there is no God. . . . There is none besides me. I am the Lord, and there is no other."*
>
> ISAIAH 45:5–6

> *"There is no God apart from me, a righteous God and a Savior; there is none but me. Turn to me and be saved, all you ends of the earth; for I am God, and there is no other."*
>
> ISAIAH 45:21–22

> *"To whom will you compare me or count me equal? To whom will you liken me that we may be compared?"*
>
> ISAIAH 46:5

> *"I am God, and there is no other; I am God, and there is none like me."*
>
> ISAIAH 46:9

What basis does God have for such bold assertions? In Isaiah, He verifies His claims based on His unique ability to forecast the future.

The God of the Bible Accurately Predicts the Future

When God spoke through His prophet Isaiah, He revealed His displeasure with the defection of many Israelites from the true worship of Himself to the worthless worship of manmade gods and nature deities. God argued that He had the right to demand their worship because He was able to accurately tell the future. He challenged the people's false gods to do the same.

> *"Present your case," says the Lord. "Set forth your arguments," says Jacob's King. "Bring in your idols to tell us what is going to happen. Tell us what the former things were, so that we may consider them and know their final outcome. Or declare to us the things to come, tell us what the future holds, so we may know that you are gods.*

Do something, whether good or bad, so that we will be dismayed and filled with fear."

ISAIAH 41:21–23

Accurately predicting the future presumes at least one of two abilities: 1) the power to cause history to unfold in a certain way, and 2) the power to step outside of the constraints of time.[1] The God of the Bible could do both. Read what He said:

"This is what the Lord says—Israel's King and Redeemer, the Lord Almighty: I am the first and I am the last; apart from me there is no God. Who then is like me? Let him proclaim it. Let him declare and lay out before me what has happened since I established my ancient people, and what is yet to come—yes, let him foretell what will come. Do not tremble, do not be afraid. Did I not proclaim this and foretell it long ago? You are my witnesses. Is there any God besides me? No, there is no other Rock; I know not one."

ISAIAH 44:6–8

"Remember the former things, those of long ago; I am God, and there is no other; I am God, and there is none like me. I make known the end from the beginning, from ancient times, what is still to come. I say: My purpose will stand, and I will do all that I please."

ISAIAH 46:9–10

"Gather together and come; assemble, you fugitives from the nations. Ignorant are those who carry about idols of wood, who pray to gods that cannot save. Declare what is to be, present it—let them take counsel together. Who foretold this long ago, who declared it from the distant past? Was it not I, the Lord? And there is no God apart from me, a righteous God and a Savior; there is none but me. Turn to me and be saved, all you ends of the earth; for I am God, and there is no other."

ISAIAH 45:20–22

"I foretold the former things long ago, my mouth announced them and I made them known; then suddenly I acted, and they came to pass. For I knew how stubborn you were; the sinews of your neck were iron, your forehead was bronze. Therefore I told you these things long ago; before they happened I announced them to you so that you could not say, 'My idols did them; my wooden image and metal god ordained them.' You have heard these things; look at them all. Will you not admit them? From now on I will tell you of new things, of hidden things unknown to you. They are created now, and not long ago; you have not heard of them before today. So you cannot say, 'Yes, I knew of them.' "

ISAIAH 48:3–7

God showed boldness, even audacity, in predicting the future, but also wisdom in having each prediction carefully recorded, accurately copied, and widely distributed *prior to* the happening of the event. This record is found in the Bible, a book unlike other religious literature, as it contains the written record of the prophetic messages of God, some recorded hundreds of years in advance of the happenings. Each is fulfilled in minute detail and proves that He indeed is the only true God.

It is beyond the scope of this book to detail all the amazing predictions God made and their detailed fulfillment. But allow me to mention a few of my favorite examples.

Cyrus

Around 700 BC, Isaiah recorded God's prediction that a man named Cyrus would rebuild the temple of Jerusalem (Isaiah 44:28, 45:13). At the time the prediction was made, the temple in Jerusalem had not been destroyed. But, sure enough, about 120 years later the city and temple were destroyed by the Babylonian king, Nebuchadnezzar. Shortly after that, the Babylonians were conquered by the Persians. Several years later, 160 years after the prophecy of Isaiah, a Persian king, who happened to be named *Cyrus*, gave the order to rebuild the temple (Ezra 1:1–4)!

Tyre and Sidon

The prophet Ezekiel recorded a stunningly detailed prophecy of judgment against the powerful ancient city of Tyre (Ezekiel 26). God specifically said: 1) Nebuchadnezzar would destroy the mainland of Tyre; 2) many nations would come against it; 3) she would be flattened like a table rock; 4) fisherman would spread their nets over the place the city once stood; 5) the debris of the city would be thrown into the water; 6) she would never be rebuilt; and 7) she would never be found again. Over the course of hundreds of years, each of these seven events has occurred. Mathematician Peter Stoner evaluated the miracle with this conclusion.

> *If Ezekiel had looked at Tyre in his day and had made these seven predictions in human wisdom, these estimates mean that there would have been only one chance in 75,000,000 of coming true. These all came true in the minutest detail.*[2]

Ezekiel also records a prediction regarding Tyre's sister city, Sidon (Ezekiel 28). Unlike Tyre, she would not be destroyed but would suffer a relentless series of bloody conquests and battles. Exactly as predicted, Sidon has suffered ongoing bloodshed, having been captured again and again, especially during the Crusades. Yet the city of Sidon is still standing today.

The Jewish People

Four thousand years ago, God predicted that a man named Abram would father a great nation, become a blessing to all nations, and have a land that would forever belong to his descendants (Genesis 12:2–3, 13:14–16). Seven hundred years later, a nation of millions arose and moved into their own land (Joshua 1 and following). When they disobeyed God, He allowed them to be taken captive and carried away from their land. They returned for a short time, but were expelled again by the Romans in AD 70.

Seemingly, God's promise had failed. The Jewish people wandered the earth experiencing persecution on every side—culminating in Adolf Hitler's Holocaust of World War II, when six million European Jews were murdered. Amazingly, though, unlike other people groups throughout history, Abram's nation never lost its corporate identity. Against all odds, after 1,878 years in exile, on May 14, 1948, the nation-state of Israel was reborn!

Jesus

As I've already mentioned, Jesus didn't fulfill only one or two Bible prophecies. Instead, there are upwards of 332 distinct predictions fulfilled by the lineage, birth, life, death, and resurrection of Jesus Christ![3] Incredible details about Him were written hundreds of years before they occurred. Through David (Psalm 22) and Isaiah (Isaiah 53), God describes details of the Messiah's death on the cross, an instrument of execution not even invented until years after the prophecies were recorded!

Doubt Quencher

Is there any God besides the Lord God of the Bible? Should we ever wonder if He is the only true God?

When doubts arise in my mind, I quickly quench them by reminding myself of the hundreds of distinct, detailed predictions about future events that God has literally fulfilled. The odds of such "coincidences" make doubt an absolute impossibility. The God of the Bible is unique, incomparable, and superior to all others. Worship Him!

Place God where He belongs in your life. Elevate Him above all else that clamors to be God of your life. Exalt Him above every hobby, job, career, possession, title, position, ministry, and relationship. Put Him ahead of yourself.

He alone is God. There is no other!

NOTES

[1]Dennis McCallum, *Christianity, the Faith That Makes Sense* (Wheaton, IL: Tyndale House, 1992), 61.
[2]Peter Stoner, *Science Speaks* (Chicago: Moody Press, 1963), 80.
[3]Floyd Hamilton, *The Basis of Christian Faith* (New York: Harper and Row, 1964), 160.

12

Is There Not a Cause?

1 SAMUEL 17:29 KJV

It was the worst of times. The Philistines had brought all their ferocious armies together to attack Judah. King Saul and the men of Israel faced them on the other side of the valley of Elah. The Philistines sent out their champion, Goliath the giant, to challenge Israel's strongest man to a winner-take-all, man-to-man rumble.

But Israel had no champion—at least none willing to fight the Philistine monster. Standing over nine feet tall, strong enough to wear a 125-pound coat of mail, one look at Goliath made the men of Israel, including King Saul, shrink back in fear (1 Samuel 17:1–11). After forty days of Goliath's twice-daily challenges and taunts, the entire Israelite army cowered in despair.

But one Israelite saw the battle from a different perspective. A teenager named David had left his flock to attend to three older brothers who were members of the army (1 Samuel 17:12–22). When David saw the arrogant Goliath, something snapped inside him. A holy passion erupted from deep within. He turned to the soldiers around him and asked:

> *"What will be done for the man who kills this Philistine and removes this disgrace from Israel? Who is this un-circumcised Philistine that he should defy the armies of the living God?"*
>
> 1 SAMUEL 17:26

The teen's bravado did not play well in the Israelite camp, especially within David's own family. When his brother, Eliab, heard David's response, he mocked and belittled his young sibling. But David saw the battle from God's perspective—and his outlook would ultimately determine its outcome. David's godly ardor was aroused, and he was unable to resist blurting out a very dangerous question.

> *What have I now done? Is there not a cause?*
>
> 1 SAMUEL 17:29 KJV

"Is There Not a Cause?"

David saw what no one else did: the big picture, the divine point of view. He realized that this battle was not merely between two men, or even two armies. When Goliath taunted the Israelites, he was mocking God—and David saw that someone needed to stand for the Lord's cause!

Surely, he knew that he alone, a scrawny youth, would be no match for a giant warrior, a veteran soldier and experienced killer. But David's hope wasn't in himself. God had gone with him before, and God could be counted on to go with him again. When questioned, he explained to Israel's King Saul:

> *"Your servant has been keeping his father's sheep. When a lion or a bear came and carried off a sheep from the flock, I went after it, struck it and rescued the sheep from its mouth. When it turned on me, I seized it by its hair, struck it and killed it. Your servant has killed both the lion and the bear; this uncircumcised Philistine will be*

like one of them, because he has defied the armies of the living God. The Lord who delivered me from the paw of the lion and the paw of the bear will deliver me from the hand of this Philistine."

1 SAMUEL 17:34–37

"The Lord who delivered me. . .will deliver me." David's bold self-confidence was rooted in a deep God-reliance. The Lord was David's hope—and only hope—for victory. Would the Lord be enough? Let's see.

The Battle Is the Lord's

David refused Saul's unfamiliar armor and instead entered combat with the staff and sling-shot he had successfully used as a shepherd. When he approached Goliath, the giant warrior scorned him for his puny size, tender age, and general inexperience. Goliath "cursed David by his gods" (1 Samuel 17:43) and mocked him by saying, "Come here. . .and I'll give your flesh to the birds of the air and the beasts of the field!" (17:44).

At this point, most intelligent men would have turned and run as fast as they could—but not David, because he was directed by the cause of God. Goliath had crossed the line. He had gone too far. He was going down because David was fighting for the name of the Lord.

David said to the Philistine, "You come against me with sword and spear and javelin, but I come against you in the name of the Lord Almighty, the God of the armies of Israel, whom you have defied. This day the Lord will hand you over to me, and I'll strike you down and cut off your head. Today I will give the carcasses of the Philistine army to the birds of the air and the beasts of the earth, and the whole world will know that there is a God in Israel. All those gathered here will know that it is not by sword or spear that the Lord saves; for the battle is the Lord's, and he will give all of you into our hands."

1 SAMUEL 17:45–47

I love David's courageous confidence. He believed that the Lord is bigger than any giant—especially this pagan blasphemer—and that it would be no contest. David was certain that God could wipe out this enemy without his help. He understood that he was merely the tool God was using to bring about Goliath's and the Philistines' defeat. So instead of running away, he ran *toward* Goliath in full attack mode.

As the Philistine moved closer to attack him, David ran quickly toward the battle line to meet him. Reaching into his bag and taking out a stone, he slung it and struck the Philistine on the forehead. The stone sank into his forehead, and he fell facedown on the ground.

So David triumphed over the Philistine with a sling and a stone; without a sword in his hand he struck down the Philistine and killed him.

David ran and stood over him. He took hold of the Philistine's sword and drew it from the scabbard. After he killed him, he cut off his head with the sword.

1 SAMUEL 17:48–51

That didn't take long! One God-directed stone from a slingshot and the enemy was down—and quickly decapitated. One boy plus God proved to be a clear majority, an army that was more than Goliath could handle.

But Goliath wasn't the only loser that day.

> *When the Philistines saw that their hero was dead, they turned and ran. Then the men of Israel and Judah surged forward with a shout and pursued the Philistines to the entrance of Gath and to the gates of Ekron. Their dead were strewn along the Shaaraim road to Gath and Ekron. When the Israelites returned from chasing the Philistines, they plundered their camp.*

> 1 SAMUEL 17:51–53

David changed history because he lived for a cause larger than himself. He wasn't the only one. Many have changed the world when they answered the question, "Is there not a cause?"

Wilberforce's Cause

William Wilberforce was elected to Parliament as a twenty-one-year-old student in 1780. A few years later, he experienced what he later called the "Great Change" as Christ became the center of his life. Wilberforce briefly considered abandoning Parliament to enter the clergy, but supporters persuaded him that he could serve God more effectively in public life. He knew that his new commitment might cost him friends and influence, but he was determined to act on what he now believed.

Wilberforce said that God gave him two great causes, including the "renewal of society." He led an attack on vices such as drinking and gambling that afflicted and demoralized the poor. He called on the upper classes to introduce true Christian values into their lives. He contributed to a Sunday school program that provided children with regular education in reading, personal hygiene, and religion.

His second great cause was the primary area of his activism: a lifelong, lonely, and unpopular battle to abolish slavery in England. Nearly fifty years of uphill effort paid off when, three days before his death in 1833, Wilberforce heard that the House of Commons had passed a law emancipating all slaves in Britain's colonies. A major motion picture in 2007, *Amazing Grace*, commemorated his courageous battle against human bondage.

Find Your Cause and Go for It

Ordinary people can make an extraordinary difference if they sell out to God's cause. David fought a giant and saved a nation. William Wilberforce abolished slavery in England, starting a process that ended the practice in the United States, too. I challenge you to ask yourself:

What has God uniquely gifted, trained, and prepared me to do?

What need breaks my heart?

What sight makes my blood boil?

What cause will I spend the rest of my life for?

What would I die for?

13

Who Knows but That You Have Come. . . for Such a Time as This?

ESTHER 4:14

Have you ever wondered why you are where you are right now? Are you in a particular job or ministry or personal relationship by accident? Is your life merely the result of random decisions and consequences?

I doubt it. That certainly wasn't the case for a girl named Esther.

Bad News for the Jews

Nearly twenty-five hundred years ago in the land of Persia, a high government official had way too much power. Haman, the king's second-in-command, hoped to use his status to elevate himself and eradicate God's people, the Jews.

One day, Haman's boss, King Xerxes, ordered all his servants to show honor to Haman by bowing before him. But one man refused—the good and godly Jew, Mordecai. He would only bow before the true God, and Haman simply didn't qualify.

When Haman discovered Mordecai's attitude, he was incensed and hatched a sinister plot: He would get back at Mordecai by annihilating every Jew in the kingdom. Haman obtained Xerxes' approval for his plan by dishonestly telling the king of a people "whose customs are different from those of all other people and who do not obey the king's laws" (Esther 3:8). Haman even offered to pay for the program, figuring the plunder of all the Jews in the vast Persian kingdom would generate the millions of dollars it would take to kill them.

All looked grim for the Jews. But there is more to this story.

The Dangerous Question

"Coincidentally," not long before, the king had become disillusioned with his wife and sought out a new one. A nationwide beauty contest was held to find a new queen for Xerxes. A beautiful girl named Esther caught the king's eye and won the tiara. Xerxes fell deeply in love with Esther and made her queen of the realm. "It just so happened" that Esther was Jewish—and Mordecai was her cousin.

When Mordecai learned that Haman was planning to wipe out the Jews, he told Esther's bodyguard of the terrible tragedy awaiting their people. But Esther felt powerless to help. In Persia, at that time, a queen couldn't approach a king uninvited. To do so could incur the death penalty. But at that point, Mordecai asked Esther a most dangerous question.

> *"Do not think that because you are in the king's house you alone of all the Jews will escape. For if you remain silent at this time, relief and deliverance for the Jews will arise from another place, but you and your father's family will perish. And who knows but that you have come to royal position for such a time as this?"*

> ESTHER 4:13–14

"For Such a Time as This?"

This question put Esther between the proverbial rock and a hard place. No matter how she responded, she could die. To act would surely risk her life with the king. To fail to act would be to condemn all Jews—including herself—to certain death.

But Mordecai was wise in his approach and choice of words. "Look," he basically said, "here you are—a Jewish girl—in the king's palace, living large as the favored wife of the most powerful man on earth. You have no business being there apart from the sovereign workings of God. Surely, He's put you here for a higher purpose." In Esther's unique position, she was one of very few people with intimate access to the king. Her people needed her. No one else could help. She was their only hope.

"If I Perish, I Perish"

What did Esther do? Play it safe and avoid the issue? Or take a risk and get involved? She didn't waste much time pondering her options:

> *Then Esther sent this reply to Mordecai: "Go, gather together all the Jews who are in Susa, and fast for me. Do not eat or drink for three days, night or day. I and my maids will fast as you do. When this is done, I will go to the king, even though it is against the law. And if I perish, I perish."*
>
> ESTHER 4:15–16

I love Esther's fearlessness as she put it all on the line. I agree with Erwin McManus who wrote,

> *I am convinced that the great tragedy is not the sins that we commit, but the life that we fail to live. You cannot follow God in neutral. God created you to do something.*[1]

Henry Blackaby writes, "You cannot continue life as usual or stay where you are, and go with God at the same time."[2] It's true throughout scripture—God calls us to take risks.

Noah could not continue life as usual and build an ark at the same time—he had to risk looking foolish. Moses could not stay in the desert herding sheep and fearlessly stand before Pharaoh at the same time—he had to risk facing his past.

Joshua took a risk when he followed God's command to step into the Jordan River, believing it would open to allow his army to cross it. He took a risk marching around the walls of Jericho seven times.

Ruth risked the familiar to strike out with her mother-in-law. Gideon took a risk to face an army of thousands with only three hundred men. David embraced a huge risk by facing Goliath with only a slingshot. Elijah took a risk when he challenged a wicked king and queen and 850 false prophets to a spiritual duel.

Peter, Andrew, James, and John left the security of their fishing business to follow Jesus. Matthew left his lucrative tax booth to become Jesus' disciple. Paul risked his life repeatedly to take the gospel to the Gentiles.

Esther Took the Risk

The people fasted as the queen had requested. Then Esther, buoyed by the knowledge that she was not queen by accident, bravely approached Xerxes. When Esther came before the king, he didn't order her execution. Instead, he was so pleased to see her he blurted, "What is your request? Even up to half the kingdom, it will be given you" (Esther 5:3).

Esther waited to answer, patiently asking her husband to come the next night, along with Haman, for a banquet. Twenty-four hours later, the king enjoyed a special meal and offered once again to give Esther anything she desired, up to half his kingdom. But again she delayed, knowing the king wasn't yet ready to grant her huge request. Esther simply invited Xerxes and Haman back the next night for another feast.

Viewing the two royal dinner invitations as good fortune, Haman figured he could now do whatever he wanted. So he ordered the construction of a monstrous, seventy-five-foot-tall gallows. He planned to ask the king the next day to order the execution of Mordecai.

God Was at Work Behind the Scenes

That evening, the king was strangely restless. He couldn't fall asleep, so he ordered a record of the daily events of his reign read to him. An interesting item was mentioned, one that the king had somehow forgotten or perhaps never heard about. Some time earlier, Mordecai had uncovered a plot to assassinate the king. His good citizenship spared the king's life. But Mordecai had inadvertently gone unrewarded.

Early the next morning, Haman arrived at the king's chamber to ask permission to execute his nemesis, Mordecai. But before he could make his request, Xerxes asked Haman what could be done to honor someone special to the king. Blinded by his own arrogance, Haman assumed the king was talking about him—and Haman poured out a lavish plan involving a royal robe, the king's horse, and an official court crier to shout, "This is what is done for the man the king delights to honor!" (Esther 6:9).

The king loved the idea and ordered Haman to carry it out—for Mordecai!

Later that night, the king and Haman dined at Esther's table. Again, Xerxes gushed that he'd gladly give Esther up to half of his kingdom. Now was the time. God had brought Esther to the palace for such a time as this. So she said,

> *"If I have found favor with you, O king, and if it pleases your majesty, grant me my life—this is my petition. And spare my people—this is my request."*
>
> ESTHER 7:3

I imagine Esther gulping after making her request. But the king had no anger toward her—he was livid against her adversary, demanding to know the villain's name. To Haman's horror, she boldly pointed him out and said, "The adversary and enemy is this vile Haman" (Esther 7:6).

In fury, the king stomped out of the room.

Then Haman made his final mistake. Groveling at the couch where Esther reclined, begging for his life, he got a little too close to the queen. When Xerxes returned, he saw Haman hovering awkwardly over Esther and asked incredulously, "Will he even molest the queen while she is with me in the house?" (Esther 7:8).

> *Then Harbona, one of the eunuchs attending the king, said, "A gallows seventy-five feet high stands by Haman's house. He had it made for Mordecai, who spoke up to help the king."*
>
> *The king said, "Hang him on it!" So they hanged Haman on the gallows he had prepared for Mordecai. Then the king's fury subsided.*
>
> ESTHER 7:9–10

Add It Up

Esther answered her dangerous question appropriately. As a result, though things looked dicey for a while, the good guys staged a rally and crushed the villains. God won a great victory

Add up the score:

1. Bad guy Haman threatens to kill all Jews, starting with Mordecai. Good Guys 0, Bad Guys 1.
2. But instead of killing all the Jews, Haman is forced to honor Mordecai. Good Guys 1, Bad Guys 1.
3. Haman is hanged on the gallows he built to kill Mordecai. But that's not all—the rest of the story would have been considered absolutely impossible just a few days earlier. Good Guys 2, Bad Guys 1.
4. Instead of the death penalty for approaching the king, Esther receives her own palace—Haman's former estate! Good Guys 3, Bad Guys 1.
5. Esther is given the power to spare all the Jews. Good Guys 4, Bad Guys 1.
6. Beyond that, the Jews are given authority to kill those who had persecuted them and to confiscate their property. Good Guys 5, Bad Guys 1.
7. As a result, many non-Jews decide to become Jews! Good Guys 6, Bad Guys 1.
8. If that's not enough, Mordecai, instead of being the first Jew killed, is honored as a hero *and* is given Haman's position as the king's highest-ranking official. Good Guys 7, Bad Guys 1!

All of these victories came after Esther faced a dangerous question and risked giving the right answer.

I wonder: Are you currently facing a tough situation or decision? Why does God have you in the position you're in? Will you trust that He hasn't made a mistake? Will you take a risk in order to really follow Him?

Notes

[1] Erwin McManus, *Seizing Your Divine Moment* (Nashville: Thomas Nelson, Inc., 2002), 34–35.

[2] Henry Blackaby, *Experiencing God* (Nashville: Broadman & Holman Publishers, 1994), 234.

14

Does Job Fear God for Nothing?
JOB 1:9

Why do you worship God? Out of fear or love or gratitude? To receive blessings from the Lord? To impress others? Is guilt your motivation?

Do you love God only when blessings flow? Do you draw back from God when things don't go your way? Does your situation determine your motivation for serving Him?

These are dangerous questions indeed.

Why Do You Worship the Lord?
One day long ago, Satan asked a question that profoundly affected the life of one man, his family, his employees, and probably his entire community. The question still has the power to dynamically change lives today.

The Scene

> In the land of Uz there lived a man whose name was Job. This man was blameless
> and upright; he feared God and shunned evil. He had seven sons and three daughters,
> and he owned seven thousand sheep, three thousand camels, five hundred yoke of oxen
> and five hundred donkeys, and had a large number of servants. He was the greatest
> man among all the people of the East.
>
> JOB 1:1–3

The opening scene seems harmless enough. A good man named Job is blessed with a great family and a prosperous business. But behind the scenes, something sinister lurks.

The Unseen Scene
As you may know, God and Satan are locked in a cosmic battle for loyalty and allegiance. Sometimes *we* are the battleground. Job couldn't hear the dangerous question that would suddenly change his entire life.

> Then the Lord said to Satan, "Have you considered my servant Job? There is no one on
> earth like him; he is blameless and upright, a man who fears God and shuns evil."
>
> "Does Job fear God for nothing?" Satan replied. "Have you not put a hedge
> around him and his household and everything he has? You have blessed the work of his
> hands, so that his flocks and herds are spread throughout the land. But stretch out your
> hand and strike everything he has, and he will surely curse you to your face."
>
> The Lord said to Satan, "Very well, then, everything he has is in your hands, but
> on the man himself do not lay a finger."
>
> Then Satan went out from the presence of the Lord.
>
> JOB 1:8–12

Notice carefully Satan's question. It is one of the most dangerous ever uttered: "Does Job fear God for nothing?"

In other words, "Will a man continue to loyally follow God even when he is overwhelmed by unexpected, unprovoked, inexplicable evil? Is God really worth it? Does He merit such loyalty?"

Satan knew that *he* didn't merit loyalty in spite of adversity. No one would follow him unless he bribed them. He simply isn't worth it. But blinded by his own arrogance and jealousy, Satan refused to believe that God is worth such allegiance. So, based on one dangerous question, he proposed a high-stakes chess game with poor Job serving as a pawn.

Surprisingly, God played along.

Disaster Strikes

Satan wasted no time in ambushing Job. He struck and struck quickly, thoroughly, and very, very hard.

> One day when Job's sons and daughters were feasting and drinking wine at the oldest brother's house, a messenger came to Job and said, "The oxen were plowing and the donkeys were grazing nearby, and the Sabeans attacked and carried them off. They put the servants to the sword, and I am the only one who has escaped to tell you!"
>
> While he was still speaking, another messenger came and said, "The fire of God fell from the sky and burned up the sheep and the servants, and I am the only one who has escaped to tell you!"
>
> While he was still speaking, another messenger came and said, "The Chaldeans formed three raiding parties and swept down on your camels and carried them off. They put the servants to the sword, and I am the only one who has escaped to tell you!"
>
> While he was still speaking, yet another messenger came and said, "Your sons and daughters were feasting and drinking wine at the oldest brother's house, when suddenly a mighty wind swept in from the desert and struck the four corners of the house. It collapsed on them and they are dead, and I am the only one who has escaped to tell you!"

JOB 1:13–19

"Does Job Fear God for Nothing?"

This is a very dangerous question on several levels. First, because it led to devastating tragedy, it was dangerous for Job. He lost his children, his employees, his property, and his reputation. Second, it was potentially dangerous for God. If Job turned his back, it would be an affront to the Lord's intrinsic worth. Third, it was risky for the devil. If Job remained true to God, it would be a major victory for the Lord.

How did Job answer the question? Did he truly believe God was worthy of worship even when everything was taken away?

After the last terrible report that his children had all been killed by a tornado, Job gave his answer.

> At this, Job got up and tore his robe and shaved his head. Then he fell to the ground in worship and said: "Naked I came from my mother's womb, and naked I will depart. The Lord gave and the Lord has taken away; may the name of the Lord be praised." In all this, Job did not sin by charging God with wrongdoing.

JOB 1:20–22

What an answer! Crushed, broken, aching, and numb, Job refused to turn on God. He even used his grief over his loss as an opportunity for worship.

Did Job fear God for nothing? His answer was loud and clear. "No!" Job feared God for *something*—the intrinsic worth of God demands worship no matter what!

Suddenly, the cosmic question became very dangerous for Satan. The devil had hoped to bring God's worth into question. But Job's response was so heroically clear that, instead, the amazing worth of God's character was reaffirmed.

The Unseen Scene, Part 2

Satan didn't quit. His stubborn resiliency and persistence are impressive, so he moved on to plan B.

> *Then the Lord said to Satan, "Have you considered my servant Job? There is no one on earth like him; he is blameless and upright, a man who fears God and shuns evil. And he still maintains his integrity, though you incited me against him to ruin him without any reason."*
>
> *"Skin for skin!" Satan replied. "A man will give all he has for his own life. But stretch out your hand and strike his flesh and bones, and he will surely curse you to your face."*
>
> JOB 2:3–5

Again, Satan questioned God's integrity by attacking Job's. He asked permission to attack the suffering man's health. God agreed and Job got blindsided. . .again.

> *The Lord said to Satan, "Very well, then, he is in your hands; but you must spare his life."*
>
> *So Satan went out from the presence of the Lord and afflicted Job with painful sores from the soles of his feet to the top of his head. Then Job took a piece of broken pottery and scraped himself with it as he sat among the ashes.*
>
> JOB 2:6–8

I have had boils. They're brutal. They are ugly, swollen, angry red sores that have to be lanced to bring even the slightest relief. One boil is sheer misery. Being covered from head to toe with them would be off-the-charts, relentless agony. If his emotional grief wasn't bad enough, Job now had to endure severe physical suffering. No wonder his already grief-stricken wife gave him such sour advice.

> *His wife said to him, "Are you still holding on to your integrity? Curse God and die!"*
>
> JOB 2:9

"Does Job Fear God for Nothing?" Part 2

> *He replied, "You are talking like a foolish woman. Shall we accept good from God, and not trouble?"*
>
> *In all this, Job did not sin in what he said.*
>
> JOB 2:10

Agony piled upon agony, torment heaped upon torment, sorrow loaded upon sorrow—yet Job remained loyal to the Lord. He refused to turn on God. In spite of the severity of his suffering, Job worshiped God.

Satan's great gamble blew up in his face.

God's risk proved worth it.

Job answered the dangerous question heroically.

Satan was shamed and silenced. Nowhere is he mentioned in the final forty chapters of the book of Job!

Do You Fear God for Nothing?

I wonder, what would have happened if you'd been in Job's situation? Or me? How would we have responded to such extreme loss? Would you have worshiped Him no matter what? What would it take for you or me to turn our backs on God?

The suffering we face in life might have nothing to do with us but everything to do with God's plan to silence Satan's pride, to shut his boastful mouth. Maybe a dangerous question, with us as the subject, has been asked. Perhaps two entire kingdoms—of darkness and of God—are watching to see how we handle our pain. Will our lives prove that God is truly worthy?[1]

NOTE

[1]For a practical, encouraging, and detailed study of the question of suffering and evil, see Dave Earley, *The 21 Reasons Bad Things Happen to Good People* (Uhrichsville, OH: Barbour Publishing, 2007).

15

Have You Any Right to Be Angry?
JONAH 4:4

What is your biggest obstacle?

On two separate occasions, five years apart, I asked the members of my church about the areas where they faced the greatest struggles. The overwhelming response in both surveys was the same: That thing we all struggled with, as growing followers of Jesus, was anger.

Anger is part of human nature. Most flows out of perceived injustice. It's born from the feeling that you're being mistreated—or that someone you care about is being wronged.

It's easy to sin in our anger, but it's also possible to be angry without sin. That's up to us, since anger as an emotion is neutral. What causes our anger and how we handle it is what determines its sinfulness.

As I reviewed every example of anger in the Bible, I was surprised to find so many. There were at least four times as many examples of destructive anger than constructive. I think that's pretty accurate in my own life: I find myself angry over the wrong things, in the wrong way, for the wrong reasons much more often than I feel anger over the right things, in the right way, for the right reasons. Are you like that?

Jealousy may cause our anger (read about Cain in Genesis 4, and Saul in 1 Samuel 18). It could be the self-centered desire to be in control (read about Balak in Numbers 22–24). But the inappropriate cause of anger I wrestle with most often is a desire to claim "my rights." I struggle with a disproportionate sense of entitlement. I get mad when I feel like someone or something is infringing on my right to be listened to, respected, understood, appreciated, recognized, and rewarded the way I want. If you are an entitlement, rights-centered person, you are an angry person.

More than two thousand years ago, one of God's leading men had an anger problem. God asked him a dangerous question that can serve as the key to overcoming inappropriate anger.

Jonah Goes to Nineveh

You probably know the story of Jonah, the wayward prophet. God basically told him, "I want you to go to Nineveh and tell the people there they've got forty days to repent." Nineveh was a wicked, brutal, pagan city. Yet God loved its people and graciously gave them a chance to turn from their sin before judgment fell. Jonah, however, didn't care about Nineveh. He wanted to preach where he wanted to preach. He wanted to preach to the people he wanted to preach to. So he boarded a boat going the opposite direction.

God's response to Jonah's disobedience was, "Hold on, now." The Lord caused a devastating storm to rock Jonah's ship, with wind and waves so severe they frightened the professional sailors on board. To spare his fellow travelers, Jonah came clean, admitting that he was the cause of the storm. At his request, the sailors eventually threw Jonah overboard.

Even now, God was gracious—and provided a big fish to swallow Jonah (Jonah 1:17). If that doesn't sound very gracious, consider this: Jonah was kept alive inside the fish and had time to repent of his selfish rebellion (Jonah 2). You probably would, too, at that point.

Three days later, the fish spits Jonah out, and God restates His command: "Go to the great city of Nineveh and proclaim to it the message I give you" (3:2). This time, Jonah obeys—perhaps grudgingly, but he does what he's told—preaching a message of repentance. And, wonder of wonders, the Ninevites take his message to heart (Jonah 3).

You probably already knew that much of the story. What you might not know is the rest of the story.

Blinded by His Rights

Jonah's message to Nineveh was one of the most influential sermons ever preached. In a city where the people were likely to ignore or even kill Jonah, the miraculous happened. Over one hundred thousand people repented. A large and powerful city was spared judgment. Shouldn't Jonah be dancing for joy?

> *But Jonah was greatly displeased and became angry. He prayed to the Lord, "O Lord, is this not what I said when I was still at home? That is why I was so quick to flee to Tarshish. I knew that you are a gracious and compassionate God, slow to anger and abounding in love, a God who relents from sending calamity. Now, O Lord, take away my life, for it is better for me to die than to live."*
>
> JONAH 4:1–3

Jonah felt he had a right *not* to go to Nineveh. He felt he had the right to preach judgment—and to see judgment fall. All he could see were his rights, and he wanted things to go his way. Jonah completely missed the awesome work of God he had just witnessed. Blinded by his "rights," Jonah held them so tightly that when he didn't get what he wanted, he fell into a suicidal depression.

The Dangerous Question

Cutting through the dark fog of selfish entitlement, God asked a dangerous question.

> *But the Lord replied, "Have you any right to be angry?"*
>
> JONAH 4:4

One little question—seven simple words—and the key to unlocking a cause and cure of our selfish anger is revealed. *Have you any right to be angry?* This question has the power to expose our hearts, diagnose our anger, and put us on the road to freedom. But before we delve further into that, let's see how Jonah responded.

Silenced by Self-Pity

What did Jonah do when God asked him this question? Nothing. Jonah was so immersed in self-pity that he didn't even reply. He just wandered off in the vague hope that maybe those pagans from Nineveh weren't sincere, and that God would end up zapping them anyway.

> *Jonah went out and sat down at a place east of the city. There he made himself a shelter, sat in its shade and waited to see what would happen to the city. Then the Lord God provided a vine and made it grow up over Jonah to give shade for his head to ease his discomfort, and Jonah was very happy about the vine.*
>
> JONAH 4:5–6

God loved Jonah and blessed him by sending a cooling plant to cheer him. But Jonah sat in the shade, still full of self-pity. He enjoyed his new plant perhaps too much. His heart was still selfish.

God loved Jonah too much to allow him to stay in his self-pitying funk. So God moved on to plan B.

> But at dawn the next day God provided a worm, which chewed the vine so that it withered. When the sun rose, God provided a scorching east wind, and the sun blazed on Jonah's head so that he grew faint. He wanted to die, and said, "It would be better for me to die than to live."
>
> JONAH 4:7–8

Some people just don't get it. God was up to big, beautiful things in the lives of people, but Jonah was so selfish he was oblivious to them. All he could see were his rights, his comfort, and his plant.

The Dangerous Question, Part 2

Once again, God cut through Jonah's gloom by asking a similar question.

> But God said to Jonah, "Do you have a right to be angry about the vine?"
>
> JONAH 4:9

At this point, we would hope Jonah would drop to his knees and say something like this:

> "Lord, I am so sorry. Please forgive me for my selfish grasping at rights. Thank You for calling me to come here. Thank You for giving me a second chance when I ran the first time. Thanks for sending the storm to get my attention. Thank You for sending the big fish to save my life. Thank You for letting me preach to these people. Thank You that they listened and repented. Thanks for sending the plant for even a little while.
> "I don't deserve any of these blessings. I deserve death and hell. I should be the one You destroy."

But sadly, Jonah still didn't get it. Read his response to God's question:

> But God said to Jonah, "Do you have a right to be angry about the vine?"
> "I do," he said. "I am angry enough to die."
>
> JONAH 4:9

Poor Jonah, I say with some sarcasm. All he could see were the violations of his supposed rights. In his eyes, God had sent him where he did not want to go. The Lord had given him a message he did not want to deliver. The people had responded in a way he had hoped they wouldn't. God had given mercy to people whom Jonah did not think deserved it. Then the Lord took his vine. In Jonah's mind, he had every right to be angry—so angry he wanted to die.

The Bigger Picture

> But the Lord said, "You have been concerned about this vine, though you did not tend it or make it grow. It sprang up overnight and died overnight. But Nineveh has more than a hundred and twenty thousand people who cannot tell their right hand from their left, and many cattle as well. Should I not be concerned about that great city?"

God wanted Jonah to see the bigger picture. If the conversation is about rights, Jonah needed to acknowledge God's right to spare and love 120,000 pagans. Those ignorant pagans had the right to hear the truth before they were destroyed.

"I Just Want What I Deserve"

I was sitting across my desk from a couple struggling in marriage. The angry partner leaned forward, looked at me, and said, "Pastor, I just want what I deserve out of this relationship, and I am upset because I am not getting it." That's what Jonah was saying.

Have you ever thought or said something like that? "I just want what I deserve. I've got my rights."

I have.

What if you went to God Almighty and said, "God, right this second I want exactly and entirely every single thing I deserve. Because You are a just God I want You to give me exactly what I deserve this moment." It's not a good idea.

I don't think you would like what you'd get. The scriptures tell us that the wages of sin is death (Romans 6:23). Scriptures say that death and hell will be cast into the lake of fire (Revelation 20:14). In one sense, if a just God gave you or me everything we really deserved right now, that would mean immediate death and hell.

Thank God that He treats us with mercy! You know, with that outlook, life is a lot easier. Who cares if I have to go to Nineveh when I should be going to hell? How can I worry about a plant when I should be forever separated from God?

Sinful Anger Ceases When Selfish Rights Are Yielded

How did Jesus avoid being trapped by inappropriate anger? If ever a person had a right to be ticked off by imperfect people, disappointing situations, and violations of rights, it would have been Jesus. Before coming to earth He lived in heaven. He was served by angels. He literally had it all. But note the response of Jesus:

> *Your attitude should be the same as that of Christ Jesus: Who, being in very nature God, did not consider equality with God something to be grasped.*
>
> PHILIPPIANS 2:5–6

Let go of your selfish rights, and you can say good-bye to most of your anger and depression. Let me give you a suggestion that works: When I find self-pity and anger growing inside, I make two lists. First, I jot down everything I'm claiming as a "right." Then, one item at a time, I say, "God, I surrender this to You. I yield this to You. I let go of this right." Then I list everything I have to be thankful for. It is a list of undeserved blessings—more than a hundred at a time, sometimes. And I thank God for every undeserved blessing on the list.

The combination of surrendered rights and active gratitude is powerful. Try it for yourself.

16

Do You Believe That I Am Able?

MATTHEW 9:28

We all have moments in our lives when we need a miracle. We all face situations that are more than we could possibly handle on our own. We all have needs—financial, spiritual, emotional, physical, familial—that can become overwhelming.

Maybe your issue is not so much a bad thing in your life as it is the absence of something good. You have a dream that is unfulfilled, a desire that is unmet. Maybe it's the need for direction. Sometimes, nothing less than a miracle will do.

Two thousand years ago, two blind men needed a miracle. Matthew tells their story, and in it we will find a dangerous question.

> As Jesus went on from there, two blind men followed him, calling out, "Have mercy on us, Son of David!"
>
> When he had gone indoors, the blind men came to him, and he asked them, "Do you believe that I am able to do this?"
>
> "Yes, Lord," they replied.
>
> Then he touched their eyes and said, "According to your faith will it be done to you"; and their sight was restored.
>
> MATTHEW 9:27–30

The Need: Two Blind Men Want Sight

In Jesus' time, the blind were societal outcasts. Many people thought they had been judged unworthy by God Himself. Robbed of sight, they lived in a world that robbed them of worth. The Pharisees even taught that people were blind because of sin—either they or their parents, it was assumed, had been wicked.

Probably blind from birth, these two men had never enjoyed the thrill of seeing a sunset or a flower. Jobless and homeless, they usually owned nothing more than discarded junk. They lived on scraps and charity handouts. Their world had always been dark and lonely. Apart from each other, they really had nothing. Life was a fearful battle for survival.

They were desperate.

They couldn't take it any longer.

They needed help.

These blind men went beyond the fact of admitting their need to the point of doing something about it. What did they do? They sought Jesus.

Following Jesus, they cried out for help. Just a year before in their town, Jesus had healed a number of people, including a leper. Undoubtedly, they were thinking, "If He would heal a leper then maybe, just maybe, He'll heal us."

As I picture these two men in my mind, I imagine one as more skeptical and jaded than the other. I can see him shaking his head and mumbling, "What can this Jesus do for us? We're blind, remember? God is punishing us. And you want us to go out in the crowd and make a spectacle of ourselves? I don't know what's gotten into you. Why seek a miracle from a stranger? Don't you know the Pharisees don't like this Jesus?"

But I imagine his friend is different. He responds, "So the Pharisees don't like Him? That's one point in His favor! Look, I think Jesus is someone special. You heard Him yourself the other day near the synagogue. His voice was so clear and powerful—it wasn't the voice of an ordinary man. I believe He can help us. It's worth a try. I'm going to go whether you come or not. I've got to find Jesus."

With that, I see the man getting up to seek out Jesus. His friend doesn't want to be left behind, so he follows. Before long, they approach the center of town and hear the noise of a crowd. It's time to do something desperate.

"Let's call for Him," the first man says. With that, the pair begins to shout out from their darkness, "Jesus, Son of David, have mercy on us."

The Question: Do You Believe That I Am Able to Do This?

When he had gone indoors, the blind men came to him, and he asked them, "Do you believe that I am able to do this?"

MATTHEW 9:28

It was a dangerous question for the blind men. If they said no, they doomed themselves to the deepening despair of darkness. If they said yes, they risked additional public embarrassment if Jesus couldn't come through with their miracle. Or, perhaps just as frightening, they faced the threat that He might actually heal them—in which case, they would be responsible for living their lives without any excuses.

So what did they do? How did they answer the question?

Yes, Lord!

They had come too far to turn back.

They had sought out Jesus, crying to Him in the crowd. They had followed Him indoors. They had made it this far. This close, they had nothing to lose and everything to gain. So when Jesus asked if the two men believed, a concise answer sprang simultaneously from both sets of lips. They are the words of faith: "Yes, Lord."

They didn't hesitate. They didn't waver. They plunged in. "Yes, Lord."

One thing that distinguishes these blind men from other needy people at that time is the element of *active* faith. What is faith anyway? We could define it as "a conviction that God can and the confident assurance that He will."

These men had a huge, hopeless, overwhelming need, and they wisely added faith to need. Not just "faith in faith," but "faith in Jesus."

Their Sight Was Restored

Then he touched their eyes and said, "According to your faith will it be done to you"; and their sight was restored.

MATTHEW 9:29–30

Faith is one thing God finds irresistible. When He sees it, He's pleased—and He acts.

And without faith it is impossible to please God, because anyone who comes to him must believe that he exists and that he rewards those who earnestly seek him.

HEBREWS 11:6

In this story, we see a pattern that is repeated throughout the Gospels. You could call it a formula for miracles:

$$\text{NEED} + \text{FAITH} + \text{JESUS} = \text{MIRACLES}$$

Jesus is the key to any miracle. He is the third part of this equation, the most important part. Faith alone does not get the job done. The faith must have the right subject. His name is Jesus.

When you read the Gospels, you see extremely needy people taking a variety of approaches to get to Jesus. A desperate father walked deliberately up to Jesus (Matthew 9:18–19, 23–26). A suffering woman sneaked up behind Him (Matthew 9:20–22). A leper knelt at His feet (Matthew 8:1–3). As we've seen in this chapter, two men literally chased blindly after the Lord. Each one made it to Jesus. Each one had faith. Each one received a miracle.

Let me be perfectly clear: It doesn't matter *how* you come to Jesus, it matters *that* you come to Jesus.

You can take a plane, a bus, or a bicycle. Who cares? What matters is that you get to Jesus. He is the only One who can ultimately meet your need.

Do You Believe?

Do you have a need you can't meet alone? Are you facing a problem that is bigger than you? Is it a relationship, a financial issue, a physical situation? Do you need a miracle today?

Do you have the faith to seek out Jesus? Do you have the faith to pray and turn the matter over to Him? Do you have the faith to step out and do what you know He is telling you to do?

Do you believe He is able?

17

Whom Shall I Send? And Who Will Go for Us?
ISAIAH 6:8

Many, many years ago, God asked a young man the same dangerous question He's still asking today.

In 739 BC, Isaiah was brokenhearted, burdened for the state of his nation. Israel had developed commercially and militarily, yet she was rotting spiritually. She was cancerously corrupt and riddled with the putrefying sores of sexual immorality, idolatry, and religion without relationship.

Isaiah loved God passionately and longed to make a difference. Since God knows our hearts, He gave this young man his greatest desire—a glimpse of heaven.

I Saw the Lord

In the year that King Uzziah died, I saw the Lord seated on a throne, high and exalted, and the train of his robe filled the temple.

ISAIAH 6:1

Stop—don't miss those four words: "I saw the Lord." This young man was given a vision only a handful of humans had ever seen. He saw the Lord. He was taken into the throne room of Almighty God.

Isaiah didn't even try to describe God. He is indescribable. He truly is beyond words. God is infinite, so when we use adjectives like awesome, glorious, majestic, powerful, kind, wise, and compassionate, we are only giving a tiny glimpse of the real thing. We can only guess at what Isaiah saw. In those visionary moments, Isaiah's mind must have exploded with images of the raging fire of holiness, the laser light of purity, the flowing river of wisdom, the roaring ocean of love, the powerful torrent of truth.

The young prophet saw the Lord "seated on a throne." We know from elsewhere in scripture that the throne of God is covered in jewels, radiating rainbows of colors, surrounded in glorious light.

"And the train of his robe filled the temple." Imagine a gigantic, majestic, regal robe of rich red and deep purple so huge that it fills the temple.

Above him were seraphs, each with six wings: With two wings they covered their faces, with two they covered their feet, and with two they were flying.

ISAIAH 6:2

"Above him were seraphs." The beings closest to God are a special type of angel called *seraphim*. That's a Hebrew word meaning "burning ones." Why burning ones? God's holiness is a consuming fire. These seraphim are asbestos angels, burning constantly through eternity in the presence of a holy God.

Holy, Holy, Holy

> *And they were calling to one another: "Holy, holy, holy is the Lord Almighty; the whole earth is full of his glory." At the sound of their voices the doorposts and thresholds shook and the temple was filled with smoke.*
>
> ISAIAH 6:3–4

These glorious angel beings not only burn continuously in the presence of God, they also worship unceasingly in the presence of God. Their praise takes the form of a declaration they can't help but make. The essence of the One before them is so intense that the words flow irresistibly from their lips: "Holy, holy, holy is the Lord Almighty; the whole earth is full of his glory."

Imagine that. Minute after minute, hour after hour, day after day, year after year, decade after decade, century after century, millennium after millennium, these glorious angels sing and shout one word over and over: *Holy, holy, holy.*

Survey American evangelicals to ask what God's primary attribute is and most would probably say, "Love. God is love."

It's true that God is love. But love without holiness is meaningless. The angels closest to God know that the primary attribute of God is *holiness,* a word that means "separation." God is absolutely separate from any and all sin. Through all eternity, the only moment sin and God ever came together was on the cross. Jesus Christ wore our sin as He died for us. It is God's holiness that gives God's love content and strength.

Woe Is Me!

In seeing the Lord, Isaiah was confronted with an astounding awareness of the absolute holiness of God. . .and it terrified him.

> *"Woe to me!" I cried. "I am ruined! For I am a man of unclean lips, and I live among a people of unclean lips, and my eyes have seen the King, the Lord Almighty."*
>
> ISAIAH 6:5

I have often heard people talk about the questions they'd like to ask God when they see Him. Comedians joke about the smart-mouthed things they would say if they were ever in God's presence. But if any of us were to see the Lord today, it would at best be through our fingers—as we cover our faces from His glory, majesty, power, and blazing holiness.

When Isaiah said, "Woe to me," he was acknowledging his sin. He was literally saying, "I am damned, guilty, and condemned to hell." When he said, "I am ruined," he was saying, "I am melting." God is a consuming fire (Hebrews 12:29). When Isaiah saw the undisguised holiness of Almighty God, he knew he deserved eternal punishment in hell. . .and he was crushed.

"Your Guilt Is Taken Away"

> *Then one of the seraphs flew to me with a live coal in his hand, which he had taken with tongs from the altar. With it he touched my mouth and said, "See, this has touched your lips; your guilt is taken away and your sin atoned for."*
>
> ISAIAH 6:6–7

Fire can do two things. It can burn and consume, or it can cleanse and purify. The angel took a burning coal from the altar and placed it upon Isaiah's trembling lips. Instead of burning and consuming him, it purified him. What a gracious, merciful, compassionate God we have, one who is willing to cleanse us of our sins!

Isaiah's cleansing occurred more than seven hundred years before the coming of Christ—and provided a temporary relief. When you and I come to God with brokenhearted sorrow and repentance, we are washed with the permanent cleansing of blood, the blood of the Lamb slain for our sins.

"Who Will Go?"

Now that Isaiah was clean before God, he was ready to hear from God. When we are ready to hear, God is ready to speak. Note carefully the dangerous question the Lord asked Isaiah:

> *Then I heard the voice of the Lord saying, "Whom shall I send? And who will go for us?"*
>
> ISAIAH 6:8

In 739 BC, God saw what Isaiah saw in His nation, Israel. He saw the sin, the spiritual charades, the cancerous corruption, the religion without relationship. . .and it broke His heart.

The Lord sees the needs of our world today. . .and it still breaks His heart.

He sees the billions of people who do not know Christ and His heart aches. He sees the hungry and homeless and His heart breaks. He sees the villages that have no church. He sees too many Christians wasting their lives on meaningless things and He cries, "Whom shall I send? And who will go for us?"

We must remember that "God so loved *the world*" (John 3:16). The Great Commission is global in scale, as Jesus charged His followers to go *"into all the world"* (Mark 16:15), to "go and make disciples of *all nations"* (Matthew 28:19), *and "*be my witnesses in Jerusalem, and in all Judea and Samaria, and *to the ends of the earth"* (Acts 1:8). The commission was not to be limited by geography, culture, language, or people. God's heart aches for lost people everywhere, all over the world.

God's Plan

> *"Everyone who calls on the name of the Lord will be saved."*
> *How, then, can they call on the one they have not believed in? And how can they believe in the one of whom they have not heard? And how can they hear without someone preaching to them? And how can they preach unless they are sent? As it is written, "How beautiful are the feet of those who bring good news!"*
>
> ROMANS 10:13–15

God's plan for mankind *is* mankind. He does not use angels or special writing in the clouds to spread the gospel. He uses men and women totally committed to Him. He uses young men and women willing to die for Him—and willing to live for Him.

God doesn't see only the world's needs. He's also looking for solutions to those needs. At this very moment, He sees you as a potential answer to the needs of this world. He is asking you a most dangerous question: "Will you go?"

I believe that, just as the angels are perpetually crying out "Holy, holy, holy" because they can't help it, God is constantly crying out, "Who will go?" He can't help it, either.

Here Am I. Send Me!

When you read Isaiah's story, you get a picture of God in His throne room, and you also see His holy angels. As far as we know, the only human present was Isaiah. I find it amusing and insightful that God apparently looked around the room, saw only Isaiah, and yet asked the question,

> *"Whom shall I send? And who will go for us?"*
>
> ISAIAH 6:8

Isaiah must have sensed all the angels looking expectantly at him. I imagine he gulped and raised his hand like an excited first grader saying, "Here am I. Send me!"

Isaiah already had a burden. He already had a passion. He was just waiting for his calling. When it came he responded, "Here am I. Send me."

He was saying, "Lord, here, take all of me. Here is my past, my present, my future. I give You all of me—my dreams, my hopes, my aspirations. Here I am. Send me. I'm available. Use me. Send me to turn Judah back to You. Send me to my people. Send me."

God didn't hesitate.

Go Tell

> *He said, "Go and tell this people."*
>
> ISAIAH 6:9

God's message to Isaiah wasn't particularly happy. But the Lord has a strategy for winning the world back to Himself—and He does that by *sending* men and women who will *go*. It is interesting that the last words of Jesus are:

> *"As the Father has sent me, I am sending you."*
>
> JOHN 20:21

> *"Go and make disciples of all nations."*
>
> MATTHEW 28:19

> *"Go into all the world and preach the good news to all creation."*
>
> MARK 16:15

Want to make a difference in the world? Often, we are the answer to our own prayers. I know of three things that are vitally true of every person reading this book: 1) we need God; 2) we need each other; and 3) *others need us.* Jesus' hands are you and I. The Word of God will only come to the hurting, needy people of this world through our mouths.

When God called me to be saved, I was sitting in a church. When God called me to full-time ministry, I was sitting in a bathtub. When God called me to plant a church, I was sitting on church steps reading a book. When God calls some of you, it may be as you read this book.

Today God is calling His people to ministry. Maybe you are hearing God's call right now. Will you answer His dangerous question by saying, "Yes, Lord. I will go. Here am I, send me"?

18

What Will Be the Sign of Your Coming?
MATTHEW 24:3

One of my favorite stories concerns a college freshman who was really enjoying his first year away from Mom and Dad. His first semester was so much fun that he hadn't studied at all. Prior to Parents Weekend, he e-mailed his mother:

Having a great time.
Flunking all my classes.
Prepare Pop.

Mom e-mailed back:

Pop prepared.
Prepare yourself!

Like our careless scholar, we also need to be prepared—for the soon return of Jesus Christ. Let me explain.

The Dangerous Question
It had been a whirlwind week. First, Jesus had ridden a donkey into Jerusalem, symbolizing His Messiahship. He had cleansed the temple in an act of righteous indignation. Angry religious leaders had tried to trap and expose Jesus with rhetorical dilemmas. But He had repeatedly tied up His questioners in the cords of their own words.

As Jesus and His disciples left the temple area, the Lord made a stunning prediction. Indicating the grand worship center, He said,

> *"Do you see all these things?" he asked. "I tell you the truth, not one stone here will be left on another; every one will be thrown down."*
>
> MATTHEW 24:2

The disciples' minds probably ran to various Old Testament teachings on the end times. So they asked Jesus a dangerous question:

> *As Jesus was sitting on the Mount of Olives, the disciples came to him privately. "Tell us," they said, "when will this happen, and what will be the sign of your coming and of the end of the age?"*
>
> MATTHEW 24:3

What Will Be the Sign of Your Coming?
Are we seeing signs of the end times? Is the end really near? How close are we to the Tribulation and Armageddon? How can we know?

These are dangerous questions. How we answer them affects how we live our lives today.

Recently, for six weeks, I took the challenge of reading the front section of a large daily newspaper through the lens of Bible prophecy. I was stunned. Every day I found at least one article that had a potential bearing on the last days.

Just as highway signs provide information, give direction, and offer warning, prophetic signs prepare us for the future. Many of them involve the seven years of the Tribulation period. We are told what reality will be *then*. Our challenge is to see what's happening *now* and decide if that indeed is a birth pang of the end. If so, those events and conditions can be considered "signs of the times."

The disciples asked, "What will be the sign of Your coming and of the end of the age?" In doing so, they gave Jesus the opportunity to describe several signs of the times. In the rest of this chapter, let's look at some of the major indicators that we are living in the last days.

Major Signs of the End Times

1. *Increasing Natural Disasters.* Jesus answered His disciples' question by describing some of what will happen during the Tribulation as it relates to Israel:

> *"Watch out that no one deceives you. For many will come in my name, claiming, 'I am the Christ,' and will deceive many. You will hear of wars and rumors of wars, but see to it that you are not alarmed. Such things must happen, but the end is still to come. Nation will rise against nation, and kingdom against kingdom. There will be famines and earthquakes in various places. All these are the beginning of birth pains."*
>
> MATTHEW 24:4–8

Note the phrases "famines and earthquakes" and "the beginning of birth pains." One major sign of the end times will be an increase in natural disasters. Jesus mentioned two specifically, saying they will be the "beginning" of birth pains. Birth pains begin weakly and infrequently; an increase in occurrence and intensity leads up to the big event—the birth of a baby. Similarly, a steady increase in natural disasters points to a big (the biggest) event—the second coming of Christ and the time of the end.

What other disasters might herald the end times? The book of Revelation indicates that the third horseman of the apocalypse carries famine (Revelation 6:5–6). Today, we are seeing some of the worst famines in history. In the early 1980s, millions of Africans died of starvation caused by what some news sources called a "famine of biblical proportions." Today, two decades later, twice as many are dying of starvation.[1]

In recent years we've seen record numbers killed by tornadoes, typhoons, and other severe storms. Think of the giant tsunami that killed nearly two hundred thousand people in Indonesia or Hurricane Katrina, which was one of the deadliest storms in United States history.

2. *Moral Disintegration.* Note carefully what the apostle Paul wrote to Timothy, nineteen hundred years ago:

> *But mark this: There will be terrible times in the last days. People will be lovers of themselves, lovers of money, boastful, proud, abusive, disobedient to their parents, ungrateful, unholy, without love, unforgiving, slanderous, without self-control, brutal, not lovers of the good, treacherous, rash, conceited, lovers of pleasure rather than lovers of God—having a form of godliness but denying its power. Have nothing to do with them.*
>
> 2 TIMOTHY 3:1–5

The Bible predicts that, in the last days, moral dis-integration will create perilous times. Pockets of moral meltdown have always occurred in societies, but many see a larger, more widespread problem on the rise. Bible scholar Tim LaHaye, speaking on the end times, has said, "List the eighteen conditions the prophet foretells for the last days. Then examine your daily newspaper, and you will agree: They are already here."[2]

3. *Geo-Political Positioning.* Certain geographic and political events are indicators of the end times. First is the rebirth of Israel, the most amazing nation on earth. With a population less than that of Los Angeles and a landmass less than that of Massachusetts, Israel annually receives the third most media attention of all the nations of the world. Little wonder, since it has the highest per capita number of news correspondents in the world.[3]

The Bible predicted Israel would be scattered and the Holy Land under Gentile control until the last days, when Israel would be regathered to her homeland (Luke 21:24; Ezekiel 38:8, 39:27–28; Jeremiah 23:7–8). Astoundingly, in 1948, Israel became a nation—and since 1948, Jews have been migrating to Israel from all over the world.

Twenty-five hundred years ago, the prophet Daniel wrote that, at the beginning of the Tribulation, the antichrist would sign a peace treaty with Israel (Daniel 9:27). In order for this to occur, Israel had to be a nation and war had to be a threat. Israel has been a nation for some sixty years, and is under a continual threat from her Islamic neighbors, who have a stated goal of wiping the Jewish nation off the face of the earth. They tried in 1967 and in 1973, but both times God miraculously intervened to preserve the grossly outmanned Jews against Arab aggression.

Due to the growing power of her enemies and concessions forced on her regarding the Palestinians, Israel has become a battle zone of suicide bombers, rocket attacks, and other means of violence. Israelis awaken each morning with the possibility of all-out war. Many long for a peace treaty.

Meanwhile, the Bible indicates that in the last days, Europe will be united in a multinational confederacy under the ultimate leadership of the antichrist. He will use this platform to pursue the establishment of a one-world government, a one-world economy, and a one-world military (Daniel 7; Revelation 13).

Twenty years ago, such unity was considered impossible—because European nations had such a history of fighting amongst themselves. Yet, in 1989, the Berlin Wall came down, and in 1993 the seemingly impossible happened: Nations of the European Common Market agreed to create a single economic market. United Europe now rivals the United States, with 345 million people from twelve nations engaging in unrestricted trade with a common currency. That currency, the Euro, gives Europe complete economic unity for the first time in seventeen hundred years—since the Romans ruled the world. The Western European Union is already positioned to be the single European military machine.[4]

4. *Technological Advances and an Information Explosion.* Writing two thousand to twenty-five hundred years ago, biblical prophets were limited to the language and understanding of their times. Gunpowder, airplanes, television, satellites, computers, helicopters, tanks, missiles, space travel, and nuclear bombs had yet to be invented. But today, for the first time in human history, the technology needed to fulfill the Bible's prophetic predictions is well in place. For example, the Bible speaks of:

a) *Huge numbers killed in the battles of Armageddon* (Revelation 9:13–19,14:17–20, 16:12–16, 19:17–18; Ezekiel 39:1–9). Since 1945, with the invention of the nuclear bomb, this has been entirely possible.

b) *A universal identifying "mark of the beast" on people's hands or heads by which cashless banking is transacted* (Revelation 13:15–18). This seemed bizarre until recently. But the technology is now in place for a single card that contains all the information and identification a person could ever need: medical history, credit card and banking information, photo identification, etc.

Biochips, the size of a piece of uncooked rice, have been created to track lost pets, and, more recently, lost children. These devices can bounce a signal off a satellite onto a police department computer screen, helping officers find a missing child. Laws have been proposed to install such chips in soldiers to carry their medical and financial information and in criminals and terrorists to allow authorities to track them anywhere in the world. Do you see where this is heading?

With such technology, it is now possible for a world dictator to impose complete tyranny. There would be no way to fight back. The birth pains of the rise of antichrist are happening before our very eyes.

c) *The whole world seeing the dead bodies of God's witnesses in Jerusalem* (Revelation 11:7–10). Until recent years, this was not possible. But satellite technology now allows us to see what is happening around the world live, as it occurs, without leaving our own living rooms.

d) *An information explosion* (Daniel 12:4). "Many will go here and there to increase knowledge," Daniel predicted. Through computers and the Internet, each of us now has access to more information than we could possibly ever use.

Are You Ready?

I believe the prophetic end-times clock, after almost two thousand years of silence, began ticking in 1948. It's been ticking louder and faster ever since. The birth pains are coming closer and closer together. The scene is set.

How near are we to the end? No one knows for sure. But we definitely need to be ready.

NOTES

[1]"Ethiopia: More Aid, More Hunger Still," BBC News, Famine in Africa, http://news.bbc.co.uk/1/hi/in_depth/africa/2002/famine_in_africa/default.stm (accessed June 25, 2007).
[2]Tim LaHaye, October 2, 2005, at Thomas Road Baptist Church's annual Super Conference.
[3]Ed Hindson, *Final Signs* (Eugene, OR: Harvest House, 1996), pp. 105, 106.
[4]Ibid.

19

Who Is It You Are Looking For?

A man once told me that for him to become a genuine follower of Jesus Christ, he would need to leave his brain at the door. Christianity, he said, is an irrational, anti-intellectual, sentimental, and purely emotional leap in the dark.

I strongly disagree. Some of the greatest minds in history have been devoted followers of Jesus Christ. Christianity is the only belief system that is both logically sensible and spiritually powerful.

It is not intellectual suicide to place faith in Jesus Christ. He died to take away our sins, not our brains.

Some have defined faith as "believing in spite of the facts." I have found true faith to be "believing *because* of the facts." And I'm not the only one. Some of the first to believe *because* of the facts were Peter, John, and Mary Magdalene.

"Who Is It You Are Looking For?"

> Early on the first day of the week, while it was still dark, Mary Magdalene went to the tomb and saw that the stone had been removed from the entrance. So she came running to Simon Peter and the other disciple, the one Jesus loved, and said, "They have taken the Lord out of the tomb, and we don't know where they have put him!" So Peter and the other disciple started for the tomb. Both were running, but the other disciple outran Peter and reached the tomb first. He bent over and looked in at the strips of linen lying there but did not go in. Then Simon Peter, who was behind him, arrived and went into the tomb. He saw the strips of linen lying there, as well as the burial cloth that had been around Jesus' head. The cloth was folded up by itself, separate from the linen. Finally the other disciple, who had reached the tomb first, also went inside. He saw and believed.
>
> John 20:1–8

Seeing the empty tomb, and especially the unique way the graveclothes were laid, was enough for John ("the other disciple, the one Jesus loved"). Peter was still processing the scene (Luke 24:12). Mary also needed some convincing.

> Mary stood outside the tomb crying. As she wept, she bent over to look into the tomb and saw two angels in white, seated where Jesus' body had been, one at the head and the other at the foot.
>
> They asked her, "Woman, why are you crying?"
>
> "They have taken my Lord away," she said, "and I don't know where they have put him." At this, she turned around and saw Jesus standing there, but she did not realize that it was Jesus.
>
> "Woman," he said, "why are you crying? Who is it you are looking for?"
>
> John 20:11–15

Mary was stunned by the disappearance of Jesus' body from its tomb. Even the sight of angels failed to convince her of the Lord's resurrection. But then Jesus Himself stood before her and, I believe, playfully asked her a dangerous question: "Who is it you are looking for?"

> *Thinking he was the gardener, she said, "Sir, if you have carried him away, tell me where you have put him, and I will get him."*
>
> *Jesus said to her, "Mary."*
>
> *She turned toward him and cried out in Aramaic, "Rabboni!" (which means Teacher).*
>
> *Jesus said, "Do not hold on to me, for I have not yet returned to the Father. Go instead to my brothers and tell them, 'I am returning to my Father and your Father, to my God and your God.'"*
>
> *Mary Magdalene went to the disciples with the news: "I have seen the Lord!" And she told them that he had said these things to her.*

JOHN 20:15–18

Those who sincerely look for Jesus will find Him. Many are the skeptics who've come to faith when confronted with the facts of Jesus' resurrection. No one has ever successfully denied or disproved the empty tomb. They've tried, but their explanations don't stand up to the primary proofs of the resurrection.

The Testimony of the Empty Tomb

One of the primary proofs of the resurrection is that shortly after Jesus was crucified and buried, His tomb was found to be vacant. There was no body. How could that be?

1) *Did He Swoon?* Some skeptics say Jesus didn't really rise from the dead, because He never died in the first place. He merely "swooned" on the cross and revived in the cool of the tomb.

But the facts make this theory impossible to believe. Jesus was definitely dead on the cross. He had been scourged prior to the crucifixion (Matthew 27:26–28). Historically, a scourging stopped at thirty-nine lashes, as forty were considered fatal. So Jesus was more than half dead even before being placed on the cross.

Shortly before the crucifixion, Jesus had sweat blood (Luke 22:44), had a crown of thorns smashed on his head (Matthew 27:27–29), and was beaten on the head with a stick (Matthew 27:30).

On the cross, Jesus uttered a death cry: "It is finished" (John 19:30). When a Roman soldier stuck a spear in Jesus' side, blood and water flowed out (John 19:34). Blood and water do not separate unless a person is dead.

The Romans were convinced Jesus was dead. Crucifixion is a hideously slow and painful style of execution, as victims expired from lack of air. Spiked to the cross, they fought for every breath, pushing and pulling, working their way up and down for oxygen. When they no longer had strength or will to push against the spikes, they would suffocate. With the Jewish Sabbath beginning Friday at sunset, the Romans would hasten the criminals' deaths and remove them from their crosses. Soldiers broke the legs of the two thieves (John 19:31–32) so they could no longer push up and therefore no longer breathe. But when they came to Jesus, the soldiers didn't need to break His legs (John 19:33–34). Why? The answer is evident—Jesus was already dead.

After Jesus was taken off the cross, His body was wrapped in linen soaked with spices (John 19:38–40). The aromatic scents were poured into each layer of the linen grave wrappings and could weigh up to a hundred pounds. Jesus' friends wouldn't have done this if He wasn't already dead.

Finally, here's a good question: "How could a man who had been beaten nearly to death, who had been hanging on a cross for six hours, and who had been wrapped in very heavy grave clothes get up by himself, work his way out of his wrappings, move the large stone from the grave entrance, and overpower the guards stationed there?" The answer is simple: He could not. The evidence is clear—Jesus did not swoon. He was dead.

Only the resurrection explains the empty tomb.

2) *Did the Disciples Go to the Wrong Tomb?* Some try to explain the empty tomb by another theory: On Sunday morning, the women and the disciples went to another tomb that just happened to be empty. But this theory has holes, too. Remember, those women were there when Jesus was placed in the tomb (Luke 23:55)—they knew which tomb it was. Plus, the tomb had a Roman seal and a Roman guard (Matthew 27:62–66). No other tomb would have that.

But suppose the women and the disciples somehow did go to the wrong tomb. Why would the Jewish leaders and Roman soldiers then invent a story that the body had been stolen (Matthew 28:11–15)? In order to silence the disciples, Jesus' enemies could simply lead all the disciples to the right tomb, open it, and show them the dead body of Jesus Christ.

3) *Was the Body Stolen?* Some doubters argue that Jesus' body was stolen either by His disciples (to create an appearance of resurrection) or by His enemies (so his disciples couldn't steal the body).

But the facts tell us the disciples did nothing of the sort. They didn't even believe the resurrection themselves, as they were scared and hiding (John 20:19). Roman soldiers, the most professional, best trained on earth, were there to keep anyone from stealing anything. There is no way a group of common men and women could have taken the body.

Beyond that, the disciples would not steal Jesus' body only to face certain persecution and death for a known lie. Most of the disciples died ugly martyrs' deaths for preaching the resurrection of Jesus Christ. Let me ask you: Would you die for a lie? Would you die for a lie you *knew* was a lie? Of course not—and neither did they.

As for the idea of Jesus' enemies stealing the body, it makes no sense. First, they had no motive. Second, if they had His body, why not simply produce it to silence the disciples who began to preach Jesus' resurrection? They produced no body *because* they had no body. They had no body *because* Jesus rose from the dead.

The Testimony of Eyewitnesses

Many people saw Jesus after He rose from the dead. One legitimate eyewitness can turn a legal trial upside down—but the eyewitness testimony regarding Jesus' resurrection dwarfs that. Jesus was seen on more than a dozen occasions by more than five hundred people. He was seen in the city and in the country, inside and outside, during the day and at night. He was seen by a variety of people. Some of them had been His followers prior to His resurrection, but others had not.

More impressive is the way the lives of those eyewitnesses changed as a result of what they saw. The disciples went from cowards to crusaders, from hiding in fear to preaching in public. Peter, Andrew, Philip, Simon the zealous, James the son of Alphaeus, and Bartholomew were all later crucified. Peter was crucified upside down. Matthew and James, the brother of John, were beheaded. Thaddeus was shot to death by archers.

Even more compelling is the change in those who had doubted. Two of the most amazing eyewitnesses were Jesus' half brothers, Jude and James. Neither believed that Jesus was the Christ prior to His resurrection (John 7:5). In fact, they thought He was crazy (Mark 3:21). But after they saw Jesus crucified and resurrected, they became believers and leaders in the church. Both wrote letters in our New Testament bearing their names. James was later stoned to death for preaching the resurrection of Jesus. Let me ask you again: Do you really think these men would die for a lie?

Thomas, the doubter, met the resurrected Jesus and fell to his knees crying, "My Lord and my God" (John 20:28). Paul, the Christian-killer, got on his face and called Jesus "Lord" (Acts 9:5). Paul spent the rest of his life spreading the word of the living Lord Jesus to the world and ended up beheaded for his belief in the resurrected Jesus Christ.

He's Alive!

Christianity is no dead religion. It's not a set of legalistic rules, dull routines, or lifeless rituals. It is a vital relationship with a living, loving God.

Jesus is alive. The empty tomb proves it. The eyewitnesses and their changed lives verify it.

Jesus is alive. He still changes lives today. He still empowers disciples to change the world. He still heals broken hearts.

Who is it you are looking for? Jesus is everything you need.

20

Who Shall Separate Us from the Love of Christ?
ROMANS 8:35

Does God really love you?

Have your circumstances ever pressed you to doubt His love? Have you ever heard a voice in your head whispering notions such as:

God must not really love you.
If God really loved you, He would not have let this happen to you.
God may love you, but not as much as He loves other people.
You don't deserve God's love.
Why should God love someone like you?

If ever a man had reason to question God's love, it would be the apostle Paul. He devoted his life to serving Christ, yet most of what he got in return was deep frustration and violent adversity. Draining work, difficult travel, sleepless nights, raw injustice, and ugly betrayal filled his résumé, Frequent trips to jail, plentiful beatings, even visits to death's door were part of his portfolio. Paul's sorrows were so numerous he had reason to wonder if he was truly the undisputed champion of pain (see 2 Corinthians 11:23–27). Such severe sufferings prompted Paul to ask a series of questions, culminating in the most dangerous of all:

What, then, shall we say in response to this?
> *If God is for us, who can be against us?*
> *He who did not spare his own Son, but gave him up for us all—how will he not also, along with him, graciously give us all things?*
> *Who will bring any charge against those whom God has chosen? . . .*
> *Who is he that condemns? . . .*
> *Who shall separate us from the love of Christ?*

ROMANS 8:31–35

Nothing Shall Separate Us from the Love of Christ

What would make you doubt God's love? Relentless troubles or hurtful hard times? Facing hatred, hunger, or homelessness? What about painful persecution, betrayal by friends or family, or, worse yet, your own awful sins? What is so severe as to strangle the flow of God's love into your life? In other words, "What can separate you from God's love?"

The answer is *nothing*! There is not one thing evil enough, ugly enough, heinous enough, deep enough, or powerful enough to stop God from loving you. Nothing anyone could possibly do to you can sever that connection. Nothing you could ever do to yourself can dam the unstoppable love of God.

Who can separate you from the love of God? A fierce persecutor? A past abuser? Does a supernatural power—an angel, devil, or demon—have that power? Can you separate yourself from the love of God? No. Absolutely nothing can separate you from God's love!

They kill us in cold blood because they hate you.
We're sitting ducks; they pick us off one by one. None of this fazes us because Jesus

loves us. I'm absolutely convinced that nothing—nothing living or dead, angelic or demonic, today or tomorrow, high or low, thinkable or unthinkable—absolutely nothing can get between us and God's love because of the way that Jesus our Master has embraced us.

ROMANS 8:37–39 THE MESSAGE

In other words, there "ain't nothin' or nobody" big enough, bad enough, dark enough, or strong enough to keep God from loving you. His love for you is unimaginable, unconditional, undeniable, and immeasurable. It is unrelenting, unceasing, and unstoppable.

Love Greater Than Horrible Loss

On September 11, 2001, Lisa Beamer's husband, Todd, was killed opposing terrorists on United Airlines Flight 93. Days after the loss, she stood firm in the love of God.

God knew the terrible choices the terrorists would make and that Todd Beamer would die as a result. He knew my children would be left without a father and me without a husband. . . .Yet in His sovereignty and in His perspective on the big picture, He knew it was better to allow the events to unfold as they did rather than redirect Todd's plans to avoid death. . . . I can't see all the reasons He might have allowed this when I know He could have stopped it. . . . I don't like how His plan looks from my perspective right now, but knowing that He loves me and can see the world from start to finish helps me say, "It's OK." [1]

Love Greater Than Sin

You know the story: King David made the mistake of growing complacent in his spiritual and professional life. When he should have been leading his troops into battle, he was back at home, restless and bored. When temptation came in the form of the shapely Bathsheba, he did not resist. Before he awoke from his spiritual stupor, he had committed adultery—and murder. The bodies of a betrayed soldier and a wrongly conceived baby were left in the wake of the king's quest for pleasure. It took the piercing rebuke of the prophet Nathan to bring David back to his senses.

Then David found the awful weight of his guilt to be a crushing reality. In extreme contrition, he finally owned up to his sin and went to God who, instead of handing down burning judgment, offered the cool, refreshing waters of mercy and forgiveness. David discovered that nothing—not even his own heinous sin—could separate him from God's love.

Several psalms record David's journey to cleansing and the amazing power of God's love. Here are parts of two:

Generous in love—God, give grace! Huge in mercy—wipe out my bad record. Scrub away my guilt, soak out my sins in your laundry. I know how bad I've been; my sins are staring me down.

PSALM 51:1–3 THE MESSAGE

Count yourself lucky, how happy you must be—you get a fresh start, your slate's wiped clean. Count yourself lucky—God holds nothing against you and you're holding nothing back from him.
When I kept it all inside, my bones turned to powder, my words became daylong

groans. The pressure never let up; all the juices of my life dried up. Then I let it all out; I said, "I'll make a clean breast of my failures to God." Suddenly the pressure was gone—my guilt dissolved, my sin disappeared.

PSALM 32:1–5 THE MESSAGE

God's love is so vast it surpasses our greatest sins.

Love, No Matter What

To show the Pharisees that God values all people, including the worst of sinners, Jesus told stories of a lost coin, a lost sheep, and a lost son (Luke 15).

The lost boy is well known as the "prodigal son." In the epitome of disrespectfulness, this young man asked for his inheritance while his father was still living. To make matters worse, he left home and promptly squandered the money in wild living. When his cash disappeared, so did his friends—and he was reduced to feeding pigs to make a meager living.

When his hunger and humiliation became too much, the young man came to his senses, deciding he would return home and beg for the chance to eat at his father's table as a hired man. But the boy underestimated the power of his father's love. No amount of personal pain and public shame was great enough to separate the prodigal son from the love of his father. As the boy shuffled home, broken and empty, his waiting father saw him coming.

"But while he was still a long way off, his father saw him and was filled with compassion for him; he ran to his son, threw his arms around him and kissed him."

LUKE 15:20

Amazing! The father had every right to disown the boy—but this father had no such intention. We might expect him, at best, to let the boy eat with the servants—but this father went far beyond that. We could imagine the father perhaps biting his tongue and greeting the boy with folded arms and a disappointed sneer—but not this father. He *ran* to his son. He threw his arms around him and kissed him. That is inseparable love.

But the father didn't even stop there. When the son tried to grovel, the man would have none of it.

"The father said to his servants, 'Quick! Bring the best robe and put it on him. Put a ring on his finger and sandals on his feet. Bring the fattened calf and kill it. Let's have a feast and celebrate. For this son of mine was dead and is alive again; he was lost and is found.' So they began to celebrate."

LUKE 15:22–24

The father in the story, of course, is God Himself. His love is so immense it overwhelms our selfish rebellion.

More Love Than You Can Imagine

More than a thousand years ago, a Jewish poet penned a stunning poem, a stanza of which was later found scrawled on the cold stone wall of an insane asylum. That poem, converted into a Christian hymn by Frederick M. Lehman in 1917, bears dramatic testimony to the fact that nothing can separate us from the love of God.

Could we with ink the ocean fill,
And were the skies of parchment made,
Were every stalk on earth a quill,
And every man a scribe by trade,
To write the love of God above,
Would drain the ocean dry.
Nor could the scroll contain the whole,
Though stretched from sky to sky.[2]

Nothing can separate us from the love of God. Not the stone walls of an asylum. Not even the challenges of mental illness.

I have no idea what threatens your sense of God's love. I can't say what is attempting to come between you and God. But I know one thing for sure: There is nothing that can separate you from the love of God.

NOTES

[1] Lisa Beamer, quoted in Ann Henderson Hart, "Finding Hope Beyond the Ruins: An Interview with Lisa Beamer," *Modern Reformation*, Vol. 11, No. 5, September/October 2002, pp. 24–25.

[2] "History of the Song, '*The Love of God*,' " 200 Amazing Hymn Stories, http://www.tanbible.com/tol_sng/theloveofgod.htm (accessed June 26, 2007).

21

Who Is Worthy?
REVELATION 5:2

Let me tell you a story about an aged pastor named John. In his younger days, John's spiritual zeal was easily recognized, and he was given a leadership role in his church. Eventually, he became an influential pastor and writer.

Late in his life, John's nation went through political turmoil and spiritual unrest. He was persecuted for his faith. Pulled away from his home and church, John faced his twilight years mostly alone and forgotten.

But God never forgets His servants.

One Sunday, as John was having his special time with the Lord, everything changed. The old man was stunned by the presence of an angel, one that took John on an amazing journey. John stepped out of the ordinary and into the extraordinary—leaving earth for the wonders of heaven, the "here and now" for the yet-to-come. What he saw and heard was beyond the experience of any other mortal.

Before him was a stunning throne, encircled by the most amazing array of color any human had ever seen. Lightning flashed and thunder roared from the throne, shaking the old man's bones.

Anchoring the four corners of the throne were giant angelic beings. Each was a glorious symphony of the familiar—a lion, an ox, an eagle, a man—and the unfamiliar—with six wings and eyes all around. They sang in beautiful antiphonal praise, "Holy, holy, holy is the Lord God Almighty, who was, and is, and is to come" (Revelation 4:8).

John noticed others around the throne—elders, church leaders, saints. All were wearing pure white robes. Each wore a golden crown. Each was stretched out on his or her face, overwhelmed by the majestic, magnificent glory of the amazing One who sat on the throne.

Before long, a single voice broke through with the most dangerous question of all.

Then I saw in the right hand of him who sat on the throne a scroll with writing on both sides and sealed with seven seals. And I saw a mighty angel proclaiming in a loud voice, "Who is worthy to break the seals and open the scroll?"

REVELATION 5:1–2

Who Is Worthy?

Some of the most important questions we can ask include these: Who deserves my heart, mind, soul, and strength? Who merits my love—and my life? Who is worthy of my worship?

Two thousand years ago, the apostle John experienced those questions firsthand in the throne room of heaven. He heard the angel shout, "Who is worthy to break the seals and open the scroll?" He saw the reaction of the assembled multitude.

As I imagine it, John's eyes searched the faces of the human heroes gathered around God's throne. Some in the countless crowd may have pointed to Abraham, the father of God's chosen people. Others put forward Moses the deliverer, or David the shepherd king, or Elijah the prophet, or Daniel the statesman.

Some suggested Mary, the mother of Jesus. Others James, the first martyr, Peter the apostle, or Paul, the genius church planter and author of much of the New Testament. But each of them shrank back in humility and declared themselves, "Unworthy."

No one on earth is worthy.

"Who is worthy?" the angel will cry.

John might look at his own angel guide. Angels are incredibly strong, brilliantly white, servants of God from ages past. *Are you worthy?* John's eyes ask as they meet the eyes of the angel. *No.* The angel shakes his head. *Unworthy.*

"Who is worthy?" the angel cries.

I can even imagine Satan, in his proud, arrogant, defiant way, attempting to take the scroll. But the pretender prince completely misjudges its incredible weight, which drives him to his knees, then flattens him on his back. The color rushes from Satan's face as he fights for breath.

Casually, the One on the throne reaches down and lifts the scroll off Satan's chest.

"Unworthy," the giant angel whispers into the face of the dark prince.

We know that John is weeping, saddened by the complete unworthiness of all who are above the earth, on the earth, or under the earth (Revelation 5:3–4). The harsh reality is this: *No one is worthy.*

The Lion of the Tribe of Judah

But then I imagine a hand gently touching John's arm.

> *Then one of the elders said to me, "Do not weep! See, the Lion of the tribe of Judah, the Root of David, has triumphed. He is able to open the scroll and its seven seals."*
>
> Revelation 5:5

Lifting his face from his hands, John scans the horizon, eagerly searching for a glorious king—regal, royal, majestic, and magnificent—a lionlike Lord with a golden crown and giant scepter.

But what John sees next stuns him. At center stage, on the throne, surrounded by the angels and the elders is no powerful lion.

> *Then I saw a Lamb, looking as if it had been slain, standing in the center of the throne.*
>
> Revelation 5:6

John notices the Lamb had at one time been wonderfully white, pure, innocent, and holy. But now its coat is covered in blood. Beaten and bruised, a crown of thorns hangs on its head.

The Lamb that John sees, which we will one day see, is *the* Lamb of God who takes away the sin of the world. He is the One wounded for our transgressions, bruised for our iniquities, sacrificed for our sins.

Slowly, joyfully, mightily, triumphantly the Lamb will hoist the weighty scroll over His head. As He does, I envision a transformation: He becomes the true Lion King John had expected.

> *And when he had taken [the scroll], the four living creatures and the twenty-four elders fell down before the Lamb. Each one had a harp and they were holding golden bowls full of incense, which are the prayers of the saints. And they sang a new song:*
>   *"You are worthy."*
>
> Revelation 5:8–9

I believe the crowd will spontaneously drop, as if cut at the knees by a giant sword. Rows of men and women from every age, nation, and tribe will be joined by row after row of bright, strong, proud angels.

A thunderous silence descends on the crowd as each one gasps in a holy hush of acknowledgment. They don't bow—they dive on their faces. They spread out their arms, open their hands, and lay bare their hearts. Tears pour from each eye, sobs piercing the cloud of awful silence.

Then slowly, sweetly, like incense, a song rises from the crowd.

> *"You are worthy to take the scroll and to open its seals, because you were slain, and with your blood you purchased men for God from every tribe and language and people and nation."*

REVELATION 5:9

Though the crowd contains people from every time, place, and language, the swelling song blends as a symphony, a beautiful, harmonic, spontaneous offering of praise.

Because You Were Slain

When the word *slain* is sung, I imagine John recalling himself as a young man—seeing an angry crowd drag Jesus up the hill called Golgotha, helplessly watching the Messiah hang suspended between earth and space. Hanging alone, the sinless Lamb wore the disgusting sins of the whole world—including John's.

> *You are worthy!*
> *You are worthy!*
> *You are worthy because You were slain.*

The song turns from broken to jubilant; mourning is transformed into dancing and sorrow is turned into joy. Every creature in heaven, on earth, and under the earth cries out in unison:

> *"Worthy is the Lamb, who was slain, to receive power and wealth and wisdom and strength and honor and glory and praise! . . . To him who sits on the throne and to the Lamb be praise and honor and glory and power, for ever and ever!"*

REVELATION 5:12–13

Who Is Worthy?

Everything John saw and wrote in the book we call the Revelation points to one dangerous question. It may be the most important question ever asked. It may be the most life- and destiny-defining question ever posed.

It is the question asked by the angel before the throne, the question asked in one form or fashion by every thinking person through the ages. That question is this:

> *Who is worthy?*
> Who is worthy of my allegiance?
> Who is worthy of my affection?
> Who is worthy of my devotion?

Who is worthy of my faith?
Who is worthy of my time, money, and possessions?
Who is worthy of my dreams, hopes, and future?
Who is worthy of my hands, feet, mind, and heart?

Who is worthy?
Who is worthy of my giving?
Who is worthy of my Sunday mornings?
Who is worthy of my purity?
Who is worthy of my living with integrity?
Who is worthy of sharing with friends and strangers?
Who is worthy of my complete trust?

Who is worthy?
Who is worth living for?
Who is worth going to jail for?
Who is worth dying for?

The vote is in. Every precinct has reported.
All the votes are counted. It is unanimous.

"Worthy is the Lamb, who was slain, to receive power and wealth and wisdom and strength and honor and glory and praise!"

REVELATION 5:12

What if you lived every day, for the rest of your life, as the answer to the angel's question?

Final Thoughts

Every few months, after so many miles, wise car owners take their vehicles to the shop for a checkup. Fluid levels, seals, belts, hoses, tires, and brakes are inspected, in hopes of catching small problems before they become big ones. Neglect in this area can result in costly repairs or even dangerous situations.

In a similar way, people should have a physical checkup each year. Doctors give tests and ask pertinent questions:

"Do you use tobacco?"
"Do you consume alcohol?"
"Have you noticed any changes in your eyesight?"
"Have you had trouble sleeping?"
"How has your energy level been?"

Having a safe and dependable vehicle is important. Our physical health is significant. But far more important is our spiritual state. It affects everything else—and even impacts eternity. So it's essential that we undertake periodic spiritual examinations.

In the previous twenty-one chapters, we have discussed the most dangerous questions in the Bible. These queries could also be described as the most important questions Christ-followers could ask themselves. Read through the following list slowly and thoughtfully, honestly examining yourself in light of each question. Carefully note those for which you are unable to answer yes.

1. Does it amaze you that the God who created the universe is intimately concerned about you? (Psalm 8)
2. Do you believe Jesus is God? (Matthew 16)
3. Do you really love Jesus, more than anything else? (John 21)
4. Is your name known in hell? (Acts 19)
5. Are you loving your neighbors? (Luke 10)
6. Have you allowed the death and resurrection of Jesus to be your bridge to God? (Matthew 27)
7. Have you been born again? (John 3)
8. Do you love God with all of your heart, soul, mind, and strength? (Matthew 22)
9. Would you die for Jesus? (John 13)
10. Do you believe the Bible is the Word of God? (Genesis 3)
11. Do you worship the only true God? (Isaiah 44)
12. Are you living for God's cause? (1 Samuel 17)
13. Are you seizing your God-given opportunities to make a difference for Him? (Esther 4)
14. Will you still serve God even if the blessings go away? (Job 1)
15. Have you moved past a selfish focus on your own personal "rights"? (Jonah 4)
16. Are you trusting God for God-sized things? (Matthew 9)
17. Will you go where God leads? (Isaiah 6)
18. Are you prepared for the return of Jesus Christ? (Matthew 24)
19. Do you know whom you're really looking for? (John 20)

20. Are you clinging to God's love no matter what? (Romans 8)
21. Are you living each day as though you truly believe Jesus is worth it? (Revelation 21)

How did you do? Are you a dynamically dangerous disciple of Jesus? Are you a terror to the kingdom of darkness?

How does your response to these questions make you feel:

- Ready to charge hell for Jesus?
- Pleasantly surprised that you did so well?
- Spiritually challenged to make some changes?
- Deeply troubled?

Turn your feelings into prayers. Go to the Lord over your responses. Pursue Him for those areas in which you sense Him wanting you to grow.

Be dangerous for God. It's really the safest way to live.

21
Reasons
Bad Things
Happen *to*
Good People

Acknowledgments

Thanks to the great team of people who made this project a joy:

- Cathy, for being my traveling companion these past twenty-six years, for being such an encouragement, and for praying over, editing, and proofing every word.
- Luke, Andrew, and Daniel, for letting me tell some of your stories and for making me proud.
- Carol, for your amazing prayers and support.
- Sandy, for modeling perseverance in affliction.
- Steve, for being my favorite brother.
- Rod Bradley, Dave Jackson, Paul Coppel, and the other mighty men, for your prayers and encouragement.
- Terry Faulkenberry, Dave Martin, and Frank Carl, you have helped pastor us in our transition.
- Jim, Joan Angus, Dan Mitchell, Matt Chittum, Sujo John, and Saint Bert, for permitting me to tell your stories.
- Dave Wheeler, Rebecca Autry, Neil Grobler, Juan Dugan, David Brinkley, Becky Mahle, Julie Moore, Allen Anjo, and Chelsea Burkhalter, you are wonderful LCMT teammates.
- Elmer Towns, one day I might catch up with you.
- Paul Muckley, you are a joy to work with.
- Les Stobbe, for opening the door.
- Kelly McIntosh, for managing the in-house process, and Yolanda Chumney, for handling the typesetting.

Contents

Introduction: Why?

"I haven't prayed in over a year. . . . Every time I try to pray, I run headfirst into the same big, black wall: 'Why? Why did God let this happen?' "

A senior at a Christian college, I was also the supervisor for a dorm of young men. As the new school year began, we had joined together with a girls' dorm for a coed hall meeting. You need to understand that this was a fairly strict Christian college, so a coed hall meeting was an exciting event. The guys saw it as a low-key way to meet a lot of girls.

Afterward, all the guys were energized, especially the freshmen. That is, all the guys were excited but one. His name was Jim. He was in tears. I sat down next to him and asked, "What's wrong?"

"Nothing," he said, trying to brush back the tears.

"Something's wrong," I said. "Tell me."

He began to choke on tears as he answered, "I prayed tonight."

I was thinking, *Why is praying such a momentous event? This is a* Christian *college, and we did have* everyone *say a prayer as part of the program.* "So, we all did," I said.

"Yeah," he answered. "But that's the first time I've prayed in over a year."

Jim went on to tell me his story. He had grown up in a strong Christian family and had previously done well spiritually, praying daily. He had come to a Christian college because he wanted to become a pastor. Yet for the past year he had had no relationship with God. He had no faith. He had nothing inside but empty, hollow bitterness and doubt. Every time he tried to pray, one big ugly word blocked it out. *Why? Why? Why?*

What had happened to turn him from God?

"My older sister is the best person I have ever known. She loved God, was involved in everything at church. She never did anything wrong," he explained.

"A little more than a year ago, some man got ahold of her. He beat her up and viciously raped her," Jim said through clenched teeth.

"She is the best person and the best Christian I know," he sobbed. Then he gulped on tears and looked at me. "Why did God allow this to happen? Why does God allow such terrible things to happen to good people?"

I have to admit I really did not know what to say. How would you answer his question? What do you say in the face of such pain?

Why *do* bad things happen to good people? It's a question we all ask. Every day in the newspaper we read the tragic tales of suffering, pain, and evil on planet Earth. Horribly bad things happen to very good people. Men with large families and women who are single moms lose their jobs. People get cancer. There are devastating floods and fires, hurricanes and tornadoes. Babies die or are born with crippling diseases. People are robbed, mugged, raped, abused, and murdered. In some parts of the world, Christians are tortured for their faith.

Why do such bad things happen to good people? It is a question that easily can become a great source of bitterness in our lives or in the lives of people we love.

Pain, suffering, and evil are relentless realities that will not go away until we are in heaven. Until then, what are we to do and think when bad things happen to good people?

This book is an attempt to answer Jim's question, "Why does God allow bad things to happen to good people?" It is a biblical study of potential benefits that come into our lives through suffering. It discusses twenty-one possible reasons bad things happen to good people. It is designed to be informative, inspiring, and encouraging. I hope reading it will nourish your faith so you can face the inevitable distress, the despair, the doubts, and the darkness that will confront your soul when you are hit with devastating hardship. But before we begin, let me frame our discussion by reminding you of several important truths.

1. *God is under no obligation to give us an explanation for suffering.*

Some say they don't want to believe in a god unless they can figure him out. But I have discovered that a god I can completely comprehend is no God at all. I am glad that the God I worship, the God I serve, the God I trust in the midst of suffering, pain, and evil is bigger than I can totally understand.

How big is our God? Our God is bigger than we can figure out and therefore big enough to see us through. He is a God who is beyond simple explanation. He is big enough for us to trust.

We don't want to hear it, but it's true. God is under no obligation to answer our questions. In this life, we may never see or fully understand why many things happen. That's what faith is about. It is trusting God *in the midst of*, trusting God *in spite of*, trusting God not only when we can see, but also *when we cannot see.*

2. *God has given us plenty of explanation if we will only look for it and accept it.*

The Bible gives many principles and examples to point us toward potentially productive reasons bad things happen to good people. The stories of Christians who have battled severe suffering show that God is able to produce much good from the bad we encounter. This book discusses many possible positive benefits that come into the life of the Christian through suffering.

3. *God can do more than one good thing through the bad things that happen to us.*

Have you ever had the delight of dropping a heavy rock into a still pond and seeing the many round ripples radiate out from the center? So it is with our episodes of suffering. They often drop like a weighty stone in a calm body of water and many good purposes may emanate from that point. We may not know the exact reason why bad things are happening to us, but we can know that good does come out—often many areas of good—radiating from one bad event.

4. *God knows what it is to suffer, and He knows how to help us in our suffering.*

Sometimes when we are hurting, we feel all alone and that, of all people, God has no idea what we are experiencing. This is a lie. Two thousand years ago, God stepped out of paradise so that He could experience our pain. He not only saw our suffering, but He tasted it, He wore it, He lived it, and He died as a result of it.

The ultimate and only pure picture of a bad thing happening to a good person is the cross. Jesus Christ was the only sinless person who ever lived. He is the Son of God and God the Son. Yet He experienced the ultimate in bad. Pain, suffering, sorrow, and evil resulting from sin filled the cup that Jesus drank in full measure.

The ultimate case of a bad thing happening to a truly good person was when the only truly good person, Jesus, was crucified for our sins.

Are you struggling with emotional anguish? Many of the people Jesus had lovingly healed and fed called for His crucifixion. His friend betrayed Him, His best friend denied Him, and His followers abandoned Him. He was spit upon and mocked. Jesus knows about emotional pain.

Are you frustrated by injustice? The witnesses at the trial of Jesus lied about Him. The courts operated illegally to convict Him. Even the governor, after plainly stating, "I find no fault with this man," condemned Him to death.

Are you in physical pain? Remember that Jesus was beaten. He was whipped nearly to death with a whip designed to shred and rip the skin off His body. He experienced crucifixion—the most painful type of execution the Romans could imagine. Jesus died gasping for air, pulling against spikes in His wrists and feet, writhing for hours in front of a vicious crowd.

Is your battle against spiritual torment? The eternally innocent One, Jesus, had the filth of our sins dumped on Him. His own Father had to turn His back on His sin-covered Son. Darkness, torment, and hell filled the cup He drank down for us.

Imagine the excruciating agony of the heavenly Father, after an eternity in union with His Son, being forced to turn away at His Son's greatest point of need. Imagine having the power to remove all the pain from His Son but knowing that to do so would leave the world cursed by sin.

Does God know anything about pain? You have got to be kidding. On a much higher, deeper, broader level than we can possibly imagine, God experienced exactly what it is to have bad things happen to a good person. He knows what it is to suffer, and He knows how to help us in our suffering.

Are you in deep anguish? Battling bitterness? Staring at a thick wall of doubts and questions? Worn out by your pain?

You need God. Take your pain and turn it into prayer. Talk with God. Tell Him that you hurt. Tell Him you need encouragement.

He is there.

1

The Reason No One Wants to Hear

Maybe you are ready to dive in to this book and read a collection of encouraging principles and uplifting stories of God bringing good to pass in the midst of very bad situations. I don't blame you. Suffering can be incredibly discouraging. When we hurt, we need every drop of encouragement we can get. So go for it. I suggest that you skip this chapter and go straight to chapter 2. You will find twenty soul-bracing chapters. Be stretched and see God being His awesome self and bringing plenty of positives for the negatives He allows His children to endure.

But if you are not in quite such a big hurry, I suggest that you slow down and read this chapter. It will become a big frame that is helpful in understanding the issue of why God allows bad things to happen to good people. But let me warn you: This chapter is the one no one wants to hear. Before we begin, it is important to understand that when we ask, "Why do bad things happen to good people?" there are assumptions behind why we even ask such a question.

The Assumptions behind the Question

When we ask, "Why would a good God allow bad things to happen to good people?" we ask this question based on three logical assumptions.

1. The world is full of suffering and evil.
2. God created the world.
3. Therefore, God is the one to blame!

1. "The world is full of suffering and evil." No doubt about that. Pain and suffering season the news every day of our lives. We live in a hurting world.

2. "God created the world." The Bible is very clear about God being the Creator of the universe (Genesis 1:1). This intricate universe had to come from somewhere. This effect had to be caused. Christians know that God is the ultimate Uncaused Cause who caused this universe to come into existence.

3. "Therefore, God is the one to blame!" We assume that if God is so good, then He would prevent bad things from happening. But He doesn't stop it. So, either God is not all that good or He is not powerful enough to stop evil from happening.

A Biblical Response to the Assumptions

The Bible gives one clear response to blaming God for suffering and evil: No, God is not the one to blame. Consider these five biblical truths:

1. God created the world good.

In the beginning God created the heavens and the earth. . . . God saw all that he had made, and it was very good.

GENESIS 1:1, 31

Yes, God created the world. But notice those last four words from Genesis 1:31: "it was very good." The word "good" used here means "admirable, suitable, pleasing, fully approved." When God created the world, there were no earthquakes, hurricanes, floods, droughts, sickness, murder, suicide, or crime. The world God made was very good. It was Paradise.

2.   *God created people with the ability to choose.*

So God created man in his own image, in the image of God he created him; male and female he created them.

GENESIS 1:27

Being made in the image of God is what sets people apart from animals. Animals do not have a God-consciousness and cannot make moral choices. Humans can. God gave people the power to choose for several reasons.

First, choice is the essence of love. God let us choose because God loves us and wants us to choose to love Him back. Paul Little has written:

But many ask, "Why didn't God make man so he couldn't sin?" To be sure, He could have, but let's remember that if He had done so we would no longer be human beings, we would be machines. How would you like to be married to a chatty doll? Every morning and every night you could pull the string and get the beautiful words, "I love you." There would never be any hot words, never any conflict, never anything said or done that would make you sad! But who would want that? There would never be any love, either. Love is voluntary. God could have made us like robots, but we would have ceased to be [human]. God apparently thought it worth the risk of creating us as we are.[1]

Second, choice is always a risk. When God let us choose, He let us take a risk. J. B. Phillips says, "Evil is inherent in the risky gift of free will."[2] He is right.

When our boys were younger, we gave them what we called "The Summer Challenge." We usually asked them to complete a project over the course of the summer, and if they did it, they would get a reward of their choice.

One of the first years we tried this, we challenged them to memorize and recite the eight verses called "the Beatitudes" (Matthew 5:3–12). They were to learn one a week. At the end of the summer, they could pick out any toy they wanted, up to a certain price, from Children's Palace. I turned them loose in the store and gave them thirty minutes to make their selection. My wife, Cathy, was certain they would choose something very educational. I wasn't so sure.

What do you think they selected? Educational games? No way. They chose instruments of destruction—toy rifles! We should have known. They are boys, and boys like guns. Giving them a choice was a risk.

3.   *People chose evil.*

And the Lord God commanded the man, "You are free to eat from any tree in the garden; but you must not eat from the tree of the knowledge of good and evil, for when you eat of it you will surely die."

GENESIS 2:16–17

> *When the woman saw that the fruit of the tree was good for food and pleasing to the eye, and also desirable for gaining wisdom, she took some and ate it. She also gave some to her husband, who was with her, and he ate it.*
>
> GENESIS 3:6

God gave Adam and Eve a choice. What did they choose? They chose to disobey. They chose evil.

4. *Their choice brought evil into the world.*

> *Therefore, just as sin entered the world through one man, and death through sin, and in this way death came to all men, because all sinned.*
>
> ROMANS 5:12

Phillips writes, "Exercise of free choice in the direction of evil. . .is the basic reason for evil and suffering in the world."[3] When we think of blaming God for the evil in this world, we need to stop and remember that humans introduced evil into the world. Not God.

5. *Their choice has had lasting consequences.*

Since the Garden of Eden, the choice of Adam and Eve has had lasting implications. First, the world is no longer good.

> *For the creation was subjected to frustration, not by its own choice, but by the will of the one who subjected it, in hope that the creation itself will be liberated from its bondage to decay and brought into the glorious freedom of the children of God. We know that the whole creation has been groaning as in the pains of childbirth right up to the present time.*
>
> ROMANS 8:20–22

> *The Bible teaches that there is not always a one-to-one correspondence between sin and suffering. When we human beings told God to shove off, He partially honored our request. Nature began to revolt. The earth was cursed. Genetic breakdown and disease began. Pain and death became part of the human experience. The good creation was marred. We live in an unjust world. We are born into a world made chaotic and unfair by a humanity in revolt against its Creator.*[4]

Why are there earthquakes? The answer is that we live in a sin-cursed world that has subterranean faults. Why did you get sick? The answer is because we live in a world with germs. We no longer live in Paradise. The world now is abnormal. The world is no longer good. It is flawed, as is everything in it, including us.

People are no longer "good." Romans 3:10 says, "There is no one righteous, not even one." We need to remember that the blame for the majority of human evil and suffering lies at the feet of human irresponsibility.

How can you blame God for starving babies in Ethiopia when the best-selling books in the United States are on dieting, on how to take the extra fat off? It is not God's fault people are starving today. The earth produces enough right now to give every person 3,000 calories a day. The problem is that some of us hoard so others go to bed hungry. It is a cop-out to blame God for human irresponsibility. If a person gets drunk, drives his car across the median, and sends your friend to an early grave, will you blame God? Do you blame God for Hitler's seven million murders? That would be escapism. The vast majority of human evil and suffering is the direct result of human irresponsibility.[5]

Drunker Than Skunks

The world is no longer good, and people are not perfectly good. I'm not sure I believed that until I had kids. I knew I was not good, but it seemed that there had to be some purely good people out there. Then we had kids. Cathy and I have three amazing sons, but I have found that I didn't have to go out of my way to teach them how to be *bad*. They have a way of picking that up on their own. I had to go out of my way to teach them to be *good*.

When my sons were much younger, we watched an old movie together, *The Adventures of Huck Finn*. Then I put them in the bathtub, attempting to give them a bath. The phone rang, so I left the bathroom for just a minute or two. Soon I heard a wild ruckus coming from the bathroom. I rushed in to see them laughing and acting crazy.

I put my hands on my hips and did my best "intimidating dad" routine, saying, "What is wrong with you boys?"

Four-year-old Daniel piped up, "We're drunk."

"Drunker than skunks," two-year-old Andrew added merrily.

"What?" I said, shocked by their response. "You guys have never seen any drunk people. Where did you get this idea?"

Daniel looked at me proudly and replied, "Huck Finn's dad. He was drunk."

"Drunker than a skunk," Andrew chimed in.

I could not believe it. We had watched a clean, classic, two-hour movie, and what had they learned? How to get drunk!

The next night it was Luke's turn. Luke was a cooperative, well-behaved toddler. He was easygoing, generally quick to please and obey. When he was about eighteen months old, we had pizza for supper. We tried to feed him a piece, but a defiant look rose in his eye. He did not want *this* piece; he had to have *that* piece. Then he did not want *that* piece; he had to have *another* piece. He did not want *those* pieces; he had to have *my* piece.

Exasperated, Cathy looked at me and said, "What's wrong with him?"

Then I had an epiphany.

I looked at her and said, "Well, theologically speaking. . .he's a sinner."

So were Adam and Eve. So are you and I. God gave us the ability to choose between right and wrong. We sometimes choose wrong. We have proven that if it had been us in the Garden of Eden, we would have made the same choice. We are sinners by nature.

I once had a guy come up to me in the grocery store. He was eager to tell me a big, dark secret. "Pastor, there's something you need to know about your church," he said.

"Really, what's that?" I asked.

"I hate to break it to you, but you have some *sinners* going to your church."

"What!" I looked at him and said, "Sir, if there were no *sinners* in my church, there would be no *people* in my church."

Why?

We ask, "Why do bad things happen to good people?" But if we really want to be honest, we have to reword the question. Considering this issue, we can conclude that instead of asking why so many bad things happen to good people, we should ask ourselves why so many good things happen to bad people.

Instead of being bitter over the hardships we face, we must be thankful for all the blessings we enjoy. We can anticipate the perfect, pain-free life we will enjoy in heaven. We also need to learn that our God produces many good things from the bad.

NOTES

[1]Paul Little, *Know Why You Believe* (Downers Grove, IL: InterVarsity, 1988), 132.
[2]J. B. Phillips, *God Our Contemporary* (New York: Macmillan, 1960), 88.
[3]Ibid.
[4]Cliffe Knechtle, *Give Me an Answer That Satisfies My Heart and Mind* (Downers Grove, IL: InterVarsity, 1986), 54.
[5]Ibid.

To Win an Unseen Victory
JOB 1–2

The fact that you are reading this book tells me that, at least at some level, you are confronting adversity and the inevitable questions evoked by suffering. Maybe someone you love has had his or her world racked by excruciating pain. Possibly you are the one standing toe to toe with untold agony. Overrun by adversity and ransacked by sorrow, answers are sought and encouragement is required. You are not alone on the road of suffering. Although often very lonely, it is heavily traveled and has been since the earliest days of history. Although your situation seems unique and extreme, rest assured, others have also drunk deeply from the cup of sorrow. One man's massive misery makes even my most severe seasons of suffering seem almost tame and tiny. He is the poster boy of pain. His name is Job.

Life Was Very, Very Good

> Job was. . .honest inside and out, a man of his word, who was totally devoted to
> God and hated evil with a passion. He had seven sons and three daughters. He
> was also very wealthy—seven thousand head of sheep, three thousand camels, five
> hundred teams of oxen, five hundred donkeys, and a huge staff of servants—the most
> influential man in all the East!
>
> JOB 1:1–3 THE MESSAGE

In the thumbnail sketch drawn by those three verses, we know several important facts about Job's life. First, he was a good man. In fact, he was about as good a man as could be found.

Second, he was a family man who enjoyed his seven sons and three daughters. Elsewhere in Job chapter 1, we find that he regularly prayed for his children (v. 5).

Third, Job had it made! One of the richest, most influential men in his part of the world, he had huge flocks and herds, and a large staff to care for them.

The envy of all, Job could truly look around and say, "Life is good!"

Life Turned Very, Very Bad

> While Job's children were having one of their parties at the home of the oldest son, a
> messenger came to Job and said, "The oxen were plowing and the donkeys grazing in
> the field next to us when Sabeans attacked. They stole the animals and killed the field
> hands. I'm the only one to get out alive and tell you what happened."
>
> While he was still talking, another messenger arrived and said, "Bolts of
> lightning struck the sheep and the shepherds and fried them—burned them to a crisp.
> I'm the only one to get out alive and tell you what happened."
>
> While he was still talking, another messenger arrived and said, "Chaldeans
> coming from three directions raided the camels and massacred the camel drivers. I'm
> the only one to get out alive and tell you what happened."
>
> While he was still talking, another messenger arrived and said, "Your children
> were having a party at the home of the oldest brother when a tornado swept in off the

desert and struck the house. It collapsed on the young people and they died. I'm the only one to get out alive and tell you what happened."

JOB 1:13–19 THE MESSAGE

I can't possibly imagine! In one day, one single day, every nightmare and every unspoken fear that had ever sneaked like a thief into the corners of Job's mind exploded into reality and hit him like a train wreck. With no warning, Job's family and fortune were swept away in a landslide of loss. In one day, his job, his employees, his property, his income, his retirement, and his life work were all totally, terrifyingly taken away. All he had worked for, all he had dreamed of, all he had owned was gone.

In one day, the precious ones who proudly bore his image and carried his name, the ones he had joyfully watched take their very first steps, the ones he diligently prayed for, were cruelly killed, their promising lives prematurely snuffed out. I can't imagine losing one child, but ten! All at the same time! All gone! Oh, the agony!

Numb? Crushed? Flattened? What words can possibly describe what he must have felt? Job's mountainous good fortune had suddenly become a gaping crater of what used to be. His very, very good life had turned violently and vilely bad.

Why would a good God possibly allow one of His most faithful servants to suffer so unjustly? What was God thinking? Why didn't He protect Job? Why did He allow it to happen?

The Scene behind the Scenes

God and Satan are locked in a cosmic battle for loyalty and allegiance, and often, we are the battleground. What Job was not able to see was that his sorrow was birthed out of an intriguing conversation Satan had with God.

> *God said to Satan, "Have you noticed my friend Job? There's no one quite like him—honest and true to his word, totally devoted to God and hating evil."*
>
> *Satan retorted, "So do you think Job does all that out of the sheer goodness of his heart? Why, no one ever had it so good! You pamper him like a pet, make sure nothing bad ever happens to him or his family or his possessions, bless everything he does—he can't lose!*
>
> *"But what do you think would happen if you reached down and took away everything that is his? He'd curse you right to your face, that's what."*
>
> *God replied, "We'll see. Go ahead—do what you want with all that is his. Just don't hurt him." Then Satan left the presence of God.*

JOB 1:8–12 THE MESSAGE

As we have already discussed, Satan left God and proceeded to have Job's livestock, his servants, and his children killed. Yet this situation extended far beyond Job, his animals, his employees, or his children. The unjust, unprovoked suffering of one single man standing alone in the entire universe struck at the very heart of the greatest conflict in the complete scope of human history. That is a stunning reality.

The question of evil and suffering on planet Earth must be understood as a spiritual battleground. There is more at stake than the comfort or heartache of a single sufferer. Monumental issues may be at stake. Massive questions may be hanging on the response of a lone individual.

"Will a man continue to loyally follow God even when he is overwhelmed by unexpected, unprovoked, inexplicable evil?"

"Is God worth it?"

"Does He merit such loyalty?"

Satan knew that no one with his or her eyes wide open to the facts would fully follow him if he did not bribe that person with forbidden powers and pleasures. He knew that his intrinsic nature does not merit such loyalty. He is not worth it. Out of blind arrogance and jealousy, he refused to believe that God is worth such allegiance. So he staged a high-stakes chess game with God, and poor Job served as the pawn. Surprisingly, God played along.

Job's Response

So, how did Job respond when struck by a tsunami of suffering? Did Job's reaction prove Satan to be right or God to be worthy? After getting the last report that his children had all been killed in a tornado, note carefully Job's next step.

> *Job got to his feet, ripped his robe, shaved his head, then fell to the ground and worshiped: Naked I came from my mother's womb, naked I'll return to the womb of the earth. God gives, God takes. God's name be ever blessed.*
> *Not once through all this did Job sin; not once did he blame God.*
>
> JOB 1:20–22 THE MESSAGE

Yeah, Job! Crushed, broken, aching, and numb, Job still worshiped God. Job's response to suffering proved that he believed God to be worthy of worship even when everything was taken away and life turned horribly, terribly ugly. God won! Satan lost! Yeah, God!

Bad Turned Worse

Before Job had a chance to catch his breath or get his feet back under him, before his aching heart could begin to heal, bad turned worse—much, much worse.

> *Satan. . .struck Job with terrible sores. Job was ulcers and scabs from head to foot. They itched and oozed so badly that he took a piece of broken pottery to scrape himself, then went and sat on a trash heap, among the ashes.*
>
> JOB 2:7–8 THE MESSAGE

If the inner agony caused by loss of family and fortune was not enough, now Job had the outer anguish of boils. Why would a good God possibly allow one of His most faithful servants to suffer so unjustly? What was God thinking? Why didn't He protect Job? Why did He allow it to happen?

The Scene behind the Scenes, Part 2

Satan did not give up easily. His ability to "take a lickin' and keep on tickin' " is impressive. After Job initially responded to his loss by worshiping God anyway, Satan pulled himself off the mat to fight round two.

> *Then God said to Satan, "Have you noticed my friend Job? There's no one quite like him, is there—honest and true to his word, totally devoted to God and hating evil?*

> *He still has a firm grip on his integrity! You tried to trick me into destroying him, but it didn't work."*
>
> *Satan answered, "A human would do anything to save his life. But what do you think would happen if you reached down and took away his health? He'd curse you to your face, that's what."*
>
> *God said, "All right. Go ahead—you can do what you like with him. But mind you, don't kill him."*
>
> JOB 2:3–6 THE MESSAGE

Satan again challenged God's integrity by attacking Job's. He said that even if Job had not given in and given up on God after losing everything, Job would certainly throw in the towel if God allowed Satan to attack his health.

Ever secure in the knowledge of His incredible worth, and confident in the depth of Job's character and loyalty, God said, "Yes." So, as we read earlier, Satan raced out and coated Job with ugly, aching, pus-oozing boils.

Job's Response, Part 2

> *His wife said, "Still holding on to your precious integrity, are you? Curse God and be done with it!"*
>
> *He told her, "You're talking like an empty-headed fool. We take the good days from God—why not also the bad days?"*
>
> *Not once through all this did Job sin. He said nothing against God.*
>
> JOB 2:9–10 THE MESSAGE

Yeah, Job. . .again! Anguish piled upon anguish, sorrow heaped upon sorrow, grief loaded upon grief, yet Job still worshiped God. Job's response to suffering proved that he believed God to be worthy of worship even when suffering the zenith of emotional *and* physical pain. God won again! Satan lost again! Yeah, God—again!

A Reason Bad Things Happen to Good People

Let me stretch your thinking for just a few moments. This is an amazing thought. Maybe some of our suffering has little or nothing to do with us and everything to do with God's plan to silence Satan's pride, to shut Satan's mouth. Satan wants to be worshiped like God, but he knows he is not worth it. If his followers were put in the same position in which Job was placed, they would turn on him very quickly.

Yet, when one of God's followers, in this case Job, lost everything, he refused to turn. God was worth it. And Satan was shut up.

There are forty more chapters in the book of Job, and do you know how many times Satan is mentioned after chapter 2? None, nada, zero, zip! Why? Satan is no longer mentioned because Satan was thoroughly silenced by the stunning worthiness of God as seen in the extraordinary integrity of Job. He was shut out, soundly defeated. God had won and Satan had lost, so he slunk off in embarrassed silence.

I love it!

Wow! One little human who suffered so triumphantly had the power to shut the mouth of the prince of darkness! He did not bind the enemy with some well-worded prayer. He did not call down fire from heaven to burn up the enemy. He just remained loyal to God even though bad things were crashing in all around him. He was faithful in spite of a heart broken by grief and a body broken by pain. Job did not realize it at the time, but he was winning an unseen victory. Wow!

Friend, maybe the bad things that are happening to you right now really don't have to do with you so much as with the titanic struggle of the universe. Maybe the entire kingdom of darkness and the entire kingdom of God are watching to see how you handle your pain, in order to know if your life proves that God is truly worthy.

Edith Schaeffer, in her book *Affliction*, takes this concept to a higher level when she proposes that this scenario has been reenacted over and over throughout history. She imagines a conversation similar to one in which Satan says to God, "Okay, so Job kept trusting You, but what if a woman had five sons die in the war? She would not continue trusting You." God replies, "Look at Mrs. So and So, whose five sons died in the Civil War and she kept trusting Me." Satan comes back the next day and says, "Okay, so she trusted You, but what if a man lost his wife and baby in a fire? He would not continue trusting You." God replies, "Well, Joe So and So lost his wife and baby in a fire and he kept on trusting Me."[1]

The idea is that by the time Jesus comes and ends history as we know it, every conceivable type of affliction will have been courageously faced by one of us making Satan's defeat and silence complete. His big mouth will be permanently shut and he will have to get on his knees and declare that Jesus is Lord (Philippians 2:9–11).

Schaeffer writes, "There is titanic meaning and purpose in our individual afflictions, since the particular one Satan is hitting us with today has not been lived through before at any time in history—nor will it be again."[2] Each of us faces unique and individual sets of suffering. Therefore, our afflictions and responses truly matter to God, and our response may impact history!

> *This to me is the fabulous "discovery of all discoveries"—that God is so fair that He enables us each to have the opportunity to have outstanding things to do in His total history of victory through the ages. . . . We cannot know which [affliction] will turn out to be the most important moment in our lives. Its arrival won't be announced with a blast of silver horns or blare of an orchestra's full crescendo. Our most important moment can come when no one but God and Satan are aware of it, when our response to the Lord is one which at once wins a battle [against our unseen foe].*[3]

Why?

So why do bad things happen to good people? What good can come from the bad? It could be that there is an unseen victory to be won. Maybe we don't realize it now, but we may be players in an unseen battle. Our response to suffering may give God greater glory and get Satan to shut up.

Wow!

NOTES

[1] Edith Schaeffer, *Affliction* (Old Tappan, NJ: Revell, 1978), 76.
[2] Ibid., 77.
[3] Ibid., 78–79.

3

To Expand Our Perspective of God
JOB 42:1–2

August 18, 1991, is a day I will never forget. I woke up that morning with a raging case of the flu that never quite went away. I dropped from 140 pounds to 122 pounds in three weeks. There was a persistent pain in my joints and muscles that grew steadily more intense through the day. Mysteriously, the slightest bit of cold air made it all the worse. My head felt like it was trapped in a vise as I carried around a sharp headache that refused to go away. Suddenly, I was allergic to all sorts of things. A whiff of grass, perfume, leaves, pets, or any of a number of other things would make my eyes water, throat tighten, and head ache even more.

Frustratingly, my cognitive capacities would short-circuit. I could see words in my head but found myself incapable of getting them smoothly out of my mouth—not a good thing when you are a pastor. I could not sleep for more than a few hours at a time. Without fail, about five o'clock every night, I would get a terrible sore throat and an ugly, dark cloud of despair would fill my soul.

But the greatest aggravation was the incredible crushing fatigue that weighed me down as if I were encased in cement and trying to run underwater. Day after day after day, I woke up aching and tired and grew more exhausted as the day wore on. Night after night, I'd lie in bed and have to concentrate on mustering all of my strength just so I could turn over by myself. I had been an athlete in college, yet now I had days when the big adventure was trying to crawl down the hall to the bathroom by myself.

Making it worse was the fact that my three sons were all under the age of five. My little boys had a hard time understanding why I couldn't get off the couch to play with them like I used to or why I could not go out to make a snowman.

Beyond that, my church was going through a difficult period of transition. As the senior pastor, it was important that I invest additional energy in helping navigate the church through the challenging waters it faced. Yet I did not have any extra energy.

Topping it all off was the awful guilt. With three little boys, my wife really needed me to help out around the house and with the children. Yet I was overwhelmed with trying to take care of myself and trying to continue to lead a church. It was horrible to see how my exhaustion was wearing her out.

After months of seeing multiple doctors and specialists, I was eventually diagnosed with chronic fatigue immune deficiency syndrome. (My male ego was bruised to find that it is an illness contracted most frequently by overachieving females.) CFIDS, at that time, was an illness few people understood.

It was awful being a POW to my pain and fatigue. I had always been such a driven, goal-oriented person, and now I was unable to pursue any goal beyond daily survival.

But more than anything, I was deeply disappointed in God. The only response He gave was silence—blank, empty, hollow, deafening silence. Day after day I asked for deliverance, yet nothing happened. Then I began to ask for at least some sort of explanation or, at the very minimum, a time frame for my agony.

I read and reread the book of Job, searching for a time frame. How long did Job suffer? I even asked some of the best Bible scholars in the country that question, and they all had the same infuriating answer: "The Bible does not say."

Day after day, week after week, month after month, God said nothing. My illness continued and months stretched into years, yet God refused to answer me.

I was determined to get His attention, so I prayed diligently for an hour a day. I fasted. Yet God was still silent.

It felt like He had abandoned me, and I had no idea why. I was not living in sin. I was serving Him diligently.

Why would He allow this to happen?

Why did He not intervene?

Why didn't He at least give me some explanation?

Why wouldn't He tell me when it would end?

Yet, God remained silent.[1]

No Explanation Given

Although my suffering was small compared to Job's, it was just as real. Therefore, I think I can understand some of the frustration Job felt as he looked up from the devastation that had been his life and cried out to God for an explanation yet heard nothing from God. Through much of his story, Job wanted a chance to defend his cause before God and receive some type of clarification as to why he was forced to suffer such severe sorrow. Yet chapter after chapter, all Job received from God was the deafening cacophony of absolute silence. Note the keen note of frustration in his voice.

> *"If I have sinned, what have I done to you, O watcher of men? Why have you made me your target? Have I become a burden to you?"*
>
> JOB 7:20

> *"Though one wished to dispute with him, he could not answer him one time out of a thousand."*
>
> JOB 9:3

> *"Even if I summoned him and he responded, I do not believe he would give me a hearing."*
>
> JOB 9:16

> *"He is not a man like me that I might answer him, that we might confront each other in court. If only there were someone to arbitrate between us, to lay his hand upon us both."*
>
> JOB 9:32–33

> *"I will say to God: Do not condemn me, but tell me what charges you have against me."*
>
> JOB 10:2

> *"I desire to speak to the Almighty and to argue my case with God."*
>
> JOB 13:3

As you read the book of Job, you find that for 36 chapters (chapters 3–38), Job honestly bemoaned his fate and defended himself against the criticisms of his self-righteous friends. For 36 chapters, he sought God for an explanation. For 36 chapters, possibly spanning months or even longer, God did not answer.

No Explanation Needed

Finally, in chapter 38, God miraculously stepped to the stage. The Lord honored Job by addressing him from out of a storm. But instead of giving Job answers, the Lord took Job on a tour of creation. Instead of answering Job's questions, the Lord grilled Job with a flurry of rhetorical questions revealing the immense gulf between God, the infinite Creator, and Job, the insignificant creation. The entire scene is designed to put the matter of Job's suffering and loss into a much bigger perspective.

No Explanation Necessary

Through his loss and grief, Job came to a much deeper realization of the immense and sovereign personhood of God.

> *Then Job replied to the Lord: "I know that you can do all things; no plan of yours can be thwarted."*

> JOB 42:1–2

Note the conviction in Job's voice. He now "knew" that God can do all things. He understood that God is, well, God, and is answerable to no one. No one can be higher than the Highest or mightier than the Almighty. The Lord is so exceedingly before, above, and beyond humanity that it is ridiculous to think we could possibly pull Him down to our level by demanding answers, reasons, and explanations. God does not have to explain Himself to us or anyone else. He owes us no answers. He can and will do what He deems right. Job observed:

> *"In his hand is the life of every creature and the breath of all mankind. . . . To God belong wisdom and power; counsel and understanding are his. What he tears down cannot be rebuilt; the man he imprisons cannot be released. If he holds back the waters, there is drought; if he lets them loose, they devastate the land. To him belong strength and victory; both deceived and deceiver are his. . . . He makes nations great, and destroys them; he enlarges nations, and disperses them."*

> JOB 12:10, 13–16, 23

God may be doing things that are bigger than we can imagine and, as in the case of Job, our suffering may be part of something much bigger than we. What He is up to may be beyond the realm of our comprehension (Isaiah 55:8). Job saw that God is the absolute ruler of all creation. He did not know everything about God, but he knew enough to trust God in the things he did not know.

Possessing a bigger, more accurate view of God is a very valuable gift. A. W. Tozer writes, "What comes to mind when we think of God is the most important thing about us."[2]

What would be the best thing you or I could ever possess? The best answer is "God," as every good and perfect gift comes from Him and is found in Him. When it comes to God, what would be the best thing you or I could obtain? The answer is "an accurate view of the immense size of our infinite God." To our detriment, we too easily forget how infinitely big, intelligent, powerful, and good is our God. As Tozer notes,

The [one] who comes to a right belief about God is relieved of ten thousand temporal problems, for he sees at once that these have to do with matters which at the most cannot concern him for very long.[3]

A Bigger Perspective of God

Why did God allow Job to suffer? Why did God initially respond to Job with thunderous silence? Why did God give Job a lesson in His power instead of an answer to Job's questions?

One of the good things that may come from bad things is a sense of clearer, bigger perspective. Ultimately we need God far more than we need explanations. Sometimes we need to get a larger view of God and of life.

The Terrible, Wonderful Fire

There is a Norwegian folktale about a fisherman who, with his two sons, went out on their daily fishing run. Their catch was good, but by midafternoon a sudden and severe storm blotted out the shoreline, leaving the men groping for the slightest sight of home. Meanwhile, a ferocious fire broke out in the kitchen of their home. Before it could be extinguished, it had destroyed everything.

Finally, the sons and their father were able to row to shore. The man's wife was awaiting him with the tragic news of the fire.

"Karl," she sobbed, "a terrible fire has destroyed everything. We have nothing left."

Yet he was unfazed.

"Didn't you hear me?" she pleaded. "The house is gone."

"Yes, I heard you," he said calmly.

"How can you be so calm?" she pleaded.

"You don't understand. A few hours ago we were completely lost at sea. I was sure we would perish." He continued, "Then something happened. I saw a strange golden glow. It grew larger and larger. We decided to steer toward that light."

Then grabbing her shoulders and looking into her eyes, he said, "Don't you see? The terrible fire that destroyed our house was the wonderful fire that saved our lives. God had it under control. God is a big God."

Sometimes houses and health seem to be so very important, but suffering has a way of adjusting our perspective—especially our view of God.

Why?

Why did God allow Job to suffer? Why did God initially respond to Job with thunderous silence? Why did God give Job a lesson in His power instead of an answer to Job's questions? One of the many good things that can come from very bad things is a clearer, bigger perspective. More important than knowing exactly why we are suffering is the knowledge gained of God through our suffering. More significant than receiving an explanation for our pain is embracing a bigger view of God through our pain.

Allow your questions, doubts, and pain to press you closer to God than ever before.

NOTES

[1] This story is adapted from Dave Earley, *Prayer Odyssey* (Shippensburg, PA: Destiny-Image Publishers, 2001), 167–68, and used by permission.

[2] A. W. Tozer, *The Knowledge of the Holy* (New York: Harper and Row, 1961), 9.

[3] Ibid., 10.

To Deepen Our Humility Before God
JOB 42:3

Peeling the Onion

The last few months of my dad's life were a tough time for both of us. He had been a very healthy, capable, sharp, bright, lively, witty, successful businessman deep into his seventies. Even in the years after he retired, he was independent in every way. But weakened by the ravages of the final stages of bone cancer, he became dependent on people and needed help.

He could not drive, do his laundry, or shop for his groceries. He was too weak to even write out checks to pay his bills. He needed help getting to the bathroom. He was unable to bathe or dress himself.

His transition to dependence was extremely hard on both of us. He had always been so abundantly capable that it was humiliating to need the help of his son. I was the one who had always depended on him. He was a rock, a foundation, the one person I could always trust. But roles were eerily reversed. The father had become the child and the child the parent, and neither of us liked it.

One day as he lay in bed, he had an unexpected bowel movement, and I was the only one around to clean it up. The thought of me cleaning him up made us both very tense, uncomfortable, and embarrassed. We avoided making eye contact. We both wanted to get it cleaned up and to move on as quickly as possible. But with an emaciated eighty-two-year-old man and an inexperienced forty-five-year-old son, cleaning up the mess was not quick or easy. Uncharacteristically, he barked at me, and I barked back. He did not want to be seen like this, and neither did I.

After the ordeal was over and he was safely back in bed, in clean clothes, lying on clean sheets, I noticed tears filling his eyes. At least that is what I thought I saw. It was hard to be sure because I was looking out of my own tear-filled eyes. I wish I could write that he cracked a joke and we both broke into a laugh, but I can't. His cancer was breaking us both. It was revealing levels of pride neither of us had known existed. The whole process was incredibly hard. Pride is a rock that is uneasily broken.

Someone once described the process of true examination as peeling an onion, in that the exposure of each new layer brings a fresh set of tears. One of the extremely good benefits of suffering is that it uncovers and unwraps layers of inner pride, independence, arrogance, self-will, self-centeredness, and selfishness that would be exposed no other way. This exposure is very painful but also essential. Through hopeless brokenness comes the amazingly beautiful and liberating virtue called humility.

He Humbled Himself

Apart from selfless love, no virtue is more Christian than humility. Everything Jesus accomplished for us as the Son of God flowed from His humility. In the great passage theologians refer to as "the kenosis of the Christ," the apostle Paul shows us the deep extent and marvelous fruit of the humility of Jesus.

> *Think of yourselves the way Christ Jesus thought of himself. He had equal status with God but didn't think so much of himself that he had to cling to the advantages of that*

status no matter what. Not at all. When the time came, he set aside the privileges
of deity and took on the status of a slave, became human! Having become human,
he stayed human. It was an incredibly humbling process. He didn't claim special
privileges. Instead, he lived a selfless, obedient life and then died a selfless, obedient
death—and the worst kind of death at that: a crucifixion.

Because of that obedience, God lifted him high and honored him far beyond
anyone or anything, ever, so that all created beings in heaven and on earth—even
those long ago dead and buried—will bow in worship before this Jesus Christ, and
call out in praise that he is the Master of all, to the glorious honor of God the Father.
PHILIPPIANS 2:5–11 THE MESSAGE (EMPHASIS ADDED)

"It was an incredibly humbling process." I guess so! Think about it. Jesus willingly let go of more than we can ever possibly imagine. No one ever experienced the level of humility Jesus willingly endured. He endured the humility of no longer having free access to infinite riches, but instead became totally dependent on others. Jesus experienced what it means to leave a glorious dwelling in a breathtakingly beautiful place and take up residence in a borrowed barn. He underwent the frustration of no longer being able to walk or feed Himself, because long ago, He became a helpless baby.

Instead of being treated as God, He became a member of a despised nation of slaves. No longer served by legions of angels, He instead became the servant of all. Rather than closely associating with mighty angels, His new companions became the hurting, the helpless, and the broken. Instead of being worshiped as God, He was called a bastard, a liar, and a lunatic. Beyond that, He was beaten, spit upon, scourged, and executed.

Because Jesus humbled Himself, justice was treated unjustly. Love was betrayed, abandoned, and rejected. Truth was mocked.

King became slave. God became man. The Ancient of Days became infant.

Jesus knows humility.

I do not know what flavor of humility it is that adversity is forcing down your throat, but I do know that Jesus has already drunk at the same well. In every conceivable way a man could be humbled, Jesus Christ was humbled. Because of it, we call Him Lord, Master of all, and King of kings.

Nothing makes us more like Jesus than pure humility. Nothing is as honored by God as true humility.

A Humbled Man

Job was the richest, most highly esteemed man around—until adversity hit. His entire life's work was gone in a day. His income, job, career, and retirement were wiped out in a few dreadful hours. His prestige was removed. Instead of being honored by those he had never even met, he was mocked by strangers. Instead of being envied and feared, he was scorned.

Job believed he could endure all of that if only God would give him an audience, if only he could defend himself before the Almighty. Yet, when it finally happened, it did not turn out as he hoped. Instead of impressing God with the justice of his cause, Job was left dumbfounded by the immense power and sovereign authority of the Creator and God of the universe. Job felt stupid for even imagining that he could somehow straighten God out and show Him a thing or two.

Nevertheless, good came from the bad.

One sweet fruit of Job's heinous suffering was the flower of deeper humility blooming more brightly in his life. His testimony is that the experience left him a changed man. Instead of being the one with all the answers, he had nothing much to say.

> *"You asked, 'Who is this that obscures my counsel without knowledge?' Surely I spoke*
> *of things I did not understand, things too wonderful for me to know."*
>
> JOB 42:3

Adversity has a way of reminding us that we are not the center of the universe. Pain has the power to point out our insufficiency. It reminds us, often brutally, of our naked insecurity, broken vulnerability, often overlooked mortality, and immense dependency. It forces us to depend on others and turn to God. When suffering has thrown us flat on our back and we have nowhere to look but up, it is only then that we truly see God.

Rudy

I am a sucker for underdog, feel-good movies. One of my favorites is *Rudy*, the story of the too short, too slow, too dumb kid who longed to play big-time football at Notre Dame University. After doing his all-out best and receiving yet another severe setback, he went to see his priest. The old man gave him a wonderful word of advice when he said, "After a lifetime of theological studies, I have discovered but two indisputable truths—there is a God and I am not He."

We are not God. Yet we are upset when life does not come under our control and play out as we planned. Suffering is never in our plans, and facing it humbles us. Humility is an accurate assessment of oneself and of God. It is only through setbacks, suffering, and sorrows that we really understand who we are, who we aren't, and even more important, who He really is. This sense of deeper humility is one of the great benefits of affliction.

Humility Is a Magnet

> *For this is what the high and lofty One says—he who lives forever, whose name is*
> *holy: "I live in a high and holy place, but also with him who is contrite and lowly in*
> *spirit, to revive the spirit of the lowly and to revive the heart of the contrite."*
>
> ISAIAH 57:15

This verse is an amazing promise. The Lord, who is above and beyond anyone and all else, pledges to be with the hurting, helpless, hopeless, and humble. When difficulties knock us down, God will reach down and pick us up. When trouble draws near, God draws nearer. True heartbroken humility is like a magnet that attracts the God who is hopelessly in love with the hopeless.

God Is No Fan of Self-Sufficient Pride

> *"God opposes the proud but gives grace to the humble."*
>
> JAMES 4:6

> *"For whoever exalts himself will be humbled, and whoever humbles himself will be*
> *exalted."*
>
> MATTHEW 23:12

All of you, clothe yourselves with humility toward one another, because, "God opposes the proud but gives grace to the humble."

1 PETER 5:5

God opposes the proud. He stiff-arms the self-sufficient. God is nauseated by conceit and sickened by smugness. After all, He is God. Nothing we do, say, think, have, or are can impress Him. He made us from dust. He has seen it all, owns it all, and can do it all. In the light of who He is, human pride, arrogance, and boasting are ridiculous and odious. He simply stiff-arms them out of His way, or He graciously allows them to be broken.

Because affliction deepens our humility, it draws us nearer to God than we would be otherwise. This is a marvelous blessing that comes through buffeting.

Why?

So why does a good God allow bad things to happen to good people? Often it is to bring us to a deeper level of humility. Humility is a virtue that opens the door to many true blessings and is a place where God can meet us. Allow the suffering you are experiencing to produce a deeper level of humility in your life.

5

To Produce Greater Intimacy with God
JOB 42:5

When someone else is hurting, we wrestle with the theoretic "problem of evil." We ask, "Why does a good God allow bad things happen to good people?" However, when we are the one who is suffering, the question often changes. We no longer are as interested in a philosophical argument. Our pain pushes us to ask much more personal questions. What we really want to know is:

> Does God really care when bad things happen to me?
> Does He still love me?
> Does He even see what I am going through?
> Has God somehow forgotten me?
> Does He have any idea how much I hurt?

The answer to all those questions is yes. The answer is undeniably, unequivocally, unceasingly, *yes.*

Read the next five sentences carefully.

> God does care when bad things happen to you.
> He still loves you.
> He sees and feels your pain.
> He has not forgotten you.
> He knows more about suffering than you can imagine.

Remember, Jesus Knows Suffering

Read the description of the sufferings of our Savior slowly. Note the variety and intensity of the pain He endured.

> *He was despised and rejected by men, a man of sorrows, and familiar with suffering. Like one from whom men hide their faces he was despised, and we esteemed him not. Surely he took up our infirmities and carried our sorrows, yet we considered him stricken by God, smitten by him, and afflicted. But he was pierced for our transgressions, he was crushed for our iniquities; the punishment that brought us peace was upon him, and by his wounds we are healed. . . . He was oppressed and afflicted, yet he did not open his mouth; he was led like a lamb to the slaughter. . . . By oppression and judgment he was taken away. And who can speak of his descendants? For he was cut off from the land of the living; for the transgression of my people he was stricken. . . . Yet it was the Lord's will to crush him and cause him to suffer. . . . After the suffering of his soul, he will see the light of life and be satisfied; by his knowledge my righteous servant will justify many, and he will bear their iniquities.*
>
> ISAIAH 53:3–11

What are you experiencing that Jesus hasn't? Look again at those words: *infirmities, sorrows, stricken, smitten, afflicted, pierced, crushed, punishment, wounds, oppressed, afflicted, slaughter, oppression, cut off, stricken, crush, suffer,* and *suffering of his soul.* Jesus knows suffering. The only One who did not deserve to suffer indeed suffered the uttermost to save us. In speaking of the sufferings of Jesus, the Bible says:

> For we do not have a high priest who is unable to sympathize with our weaknesses,
> but we have one who has been tempted in every way, just as we are—yet was without
> sin. Let us then approach the throne of grace with confidence, so that we may receive
> mercy and find grace to help us in our time of need.
>
> HEBREWS 4:15–16

Jesus understands the sufferings we experience. This makes Him an infinitely approachable deity and is yet another reminder that our God desires an intimate relationship with us.

My Eyes Have Seen You

Possibly nothing is as difficult for a parent as burying his or her child. Imagine—Job buried *ten* children at the same time. His heart was cruelly crushed by his immense grief. Yet, instead of lying in the dust and crying for himself, Job cried out to God. As you read his story, you encounter a man who sincerely bared his soul to God. It wasn't always pretty. His emotions were raw, his words angry. He yelled *at* God and he yelled *to* God. He questioned God.

But make no mistake: Job did not allow his pain to push him *from* God. Instead, he let it press him *to* God. Job came to God, and although He didn't do so immediately, God came to him (Job 38:1). God came in power, provision, affirmation, consolation, and ultimately blessing.

In Job's journey through the tunnel of adversity, he ended up confronting the fact that God's goal in allowing him to suffer was not the revelation of a rationale for Job's agony, but rather the revelation of God Himself. After avoiding Job for thirty-six chapters, as Job defended himself and requested an audience, when God finally did show up to speak with Job, He didn't give Job a list of reasons for the suffering. Instead, He gave Job a tour of His person and His power.

Seeing God through the lens of suffering gave Job a different, and ultimately closer, perspective of God. As I studied the book of Job, I was confronted and comforted with the fact that God's goal in suffering is not the revelation of reasons or explanations, but rather the revelation of Himself. Job wrote,

> "My ears had heard of you but now my eyes have seen you."
>
> JOB 42:5

Job went from having a hearsay relationship with God ("my ears had heard of you") to a face-to-face encounter ("but now my eyes have seen you"). Through suffering he went from a secondhand faith to a firsthand relationship.

So often when things are going well, we are too busy or too distracted to really see God. But when suffering narrows our options, the blinders of pain can force us to truly look at God. It is not until suffering throws us on our backs that we finally look up and see God.

Many of us would testify that we met God when we were pressed to Him through pain. Although raised in a God-fearing home, taken to church from birth, and sent to a Christian school, my mom did not meet God personally until she nearly died of pneumonia as a teenager. Suffering brought her closer to God.

God Comes to the Brokenhearted

God does not always come to every brokenhearted seeker in the same way, but He always comes. To Elijah, God came as a still, small voice. To Jonah, God came through a vine and a voice. To Shadrach, Meshach, and Abednego, God came and stood with them in the furnace of fire. To the disciples, Jesus came walking on the waves in the middle of a storm. God can't keep from coming to brokenhearted seekers.

David recognized this when he was unjustly forced to live the life of a fugitive. He found himself the target of the biggest manhunt in Israel's history, as jealous King Saul led an entire army out to chase him down. He lost his home, job, career, friends, wife, and future. Constantly on the move, unsure of whom to trust, hiding in caves, running for his life, narrowly escaping death, David had to have wrestled with doubts of God's love. Nevertheless, he came to God, and God came to him at his lowest point. As a result, David proclaimed a precious promise.

> *The Lord is close to the brokenhearted and saves those who are crushed in spirit.*
>
> PSALM 34:18

This verse seems rather sweet and pleasant when you are not suffering. But when you are staring in disbelief at the smashed pieces of your broken heart or when you are enduring the helpless feeling of being crushed by sorrow, these words can be transformed into something of great comfort and tangible power. To you, this promise can be a lifeline, an anchor, and a foundation. As you are suffering, remember these four truths:

1. God does not abandon us when we suffer, although it often feels as if He does. No. He has been with us, will be with us, and is always with us. But He is closest to us when we hurt.
2. The presence of hardship does not mark the absence of God. A broken heart is irresistible to Him. God comes to the brokenhearted because He cannot help Himself. A crushed spirit is a magnet drawing Him close.
3. God does not promise to protect us from all problems, but He does promise to be with us through our problems.
4. It is really up to you. Adversity will either come between you and God or it will push you closer to God—it's your choice.

Companionship in the Ruins

Christian celebrity Sheila Walsh admitted herself as a patient to the psychiatric unit of a hospital in Washington, DC. She was extremely afraid she would end up like her father who died in his thirties in a bleak psychiatric hospital in Scotland. With the sensitivity that is only learned in the school of severe suffering, she writes:

> *I did not understand that God's most precious gifts come in boxes that make your hands bleed when you open them. Inside is what you have been looking for all of your*

life. Only God can do that. Only His love is as fierce and relentless as our deepest pain and unspoken fears. . . . I longed for rescue; He gave me relationship. I wanted deliverance; He gave me companionship in the ruins.[1]

"Companionship in the ruins"—what a beautiful thought. Sounds reminiscent of the apostle Paul when he wrote, "That I may know Him, and the power of His resurrection, and *the fellowship of His sufferings*" (Philippians 3:10 NKJV, emphasis added). It also reminds me of the words of author Oswald Chambers when he prayed, "Pierce a hole in the darkness so that I can behold the face of God."

He Came So Near

In the mid-1800s, over one hundred thousand pioneers loaded all their possessions into covered wagons and ventured west. Walking fifteen miles a day, they attempted to travel the two thousand miles from Missouri to the Pacific Coast via the Oregon Trail. The journey west was extremely hard, and many turned back or did not survive.

Hardships were plentiful, from lack of good water to food shortages to real dangers. Crossing rivers was a constant headache to the pioneers. Many people drowned in the Kansas, North Platte, and Columbia rivers. Some died when they fell under the massive wheels of a wagon. Indians, outlaws, and cholera were also constant threats.

After a life-threatening trial on the trail, one pioneer wrote in her diary:

I had known what it was to believe in God, but now He came so near that I no longer simply believed in Him but knew His presence there. . . . That calm strength, that certainty of One near and all-sufficient, hushed and cheered.[2]

"He came so near." Her words are echoed by many of us who have walked the path of pain.

Why?

So why does God allow bad things to happen to good people? One reason is that we often experience the nearness of God more in trial than in triumph. God is near to the brokenhearted.

NOTES

[1] Sheila Walsh, "A Winter's Tale," in *The Desert Experience: Personal Reflections on Finding God's Presence and Promise in Hard Times* (Nashville: Nelson, 2001), 172, 176.
[2] From the diary of the mother of Josiah Royce, quoted in Donald Morgan, *How to Get It Together When Your World Is Coming Apart* (Grand Rapids: Revell, 1988), 18.

To Prepare Us to Receive Far Greater Blessings
Job 42

In his book *The Dream Giver*, Bruce Wilkinson tells of the time he and his wife, Darlene Marie, launched a magazine by faith, obeying God at great personal cost. For five months he asked God to provide, and for five months God seemingly did nothing. Finding themselves in debt more than five years' salary, they called a meeting to shut down the magazine. For Wilkinson it was a crucifixion, the death of a dream. Later he describes what he called his "WasteLand" experience with these painful words:

> *It felt like God had watched from the sidelines while we went down in flames. It was one of the most disillusioning seasons of my life. . . . Before long, I felt adrift in anger and confusion.*[1]

Yet painful loss can lead to plentiful gain. Bruce observed:

> *It wasn't until years later that I could look back on that season and see that God had been faithfully at work. What we couldn't know then was that He had plans for a different kind of magazine,* The Daily Walk, *and He was preparing us to accomplish it. Today* Walk Thru the Bible *publishes ten magazines every month. . . . One hundred million devotional magazines later, it's clear God didn't let us down. God just had a bigger dream than we could have achieved or even imagined at the time.*[2]

Bruce became the publisher and executive editor of ten monthly magazines with distribution numbering over 120 million. Later he wrote a little book called *The Prayer of Jabez*. That book is the only book in history to win Evangelical Christian Publishers Association's "Book of the Year" two years in a row. *Publisher's Weekly* reported *The Prayer of Jabez* as the "fastest-selling book of all time" in 2001.[3]

Why does God allow bad things to happen to good people? Sometimes it is to position and prepare them for greater blessings.

Twice as Much after Prior Pain

I have read the book of Job dozens of times. My favorite chapter is the last. As you recall, the first two chapters tell us that Job, one of the richest men in the East, underwent one of the worst seasons of loss any individual has ever endured. He lost seven thousand head of sheep, three thousand camels, five hundred teams of oxen, five hundred donkeys, and a huge staff of servants. He also lost his ten children. So as a businessman and as a father, Job lost it all.

Thankfully for Job, the story did not end there. In the middle of the last chapter, God stretches a rainbow over the storm, and the sun bursts through the clouds. Notice carefully the second half of this verse.

After Job had prayed for his friends, the Lord made him prosperous again and gave him twice as much as he had before.

JOB 42:10

Do you see what happened? The Lord did not merely return everything back to Job. No. The Lord gave Job *twice as much as he had before!* Why does God allow bad things to happen? Sometimes He seems to be preparing us for a greater blessing.

What is interesting is that when the Bible says that Job received *twice* as much, it means literally *twice* as much. Look at the rest of the chapter.

The Lord blessed the latter part of Job's life more than the first. He had fourteen thousand sheep, six thousand camels, a thousand yoke of oxen and a thousand donkeys.

JOB 42:12

Prior to suffering, Job had seven thousand head of sheep; he ended up with fourteen thousand. He had three thousand camels; he ended up with six thousand. He had five hundred teams of oxen; after suffering, he had one thousand. He had five hundred donkeys; he finished with one thousand. But there was more.

And he also had seven sons and three daughters. . . . Nowhere in all the land were there found women as beautiful as Job's daughters.

JOB 42:13, 15

You may be thinking, *But I thought Job had ten children prior to the tragedy. Why did the Lord not give him twice as many, which would be twenty kids?* The answer is that the loss of Job's first ten children was only temporary. He was to be reunited with the first ten in heaven.

Oh, by the way, Job also received twice the life span of an ordinary man added on to his life. Instead of living the normal seventy years, the Bible says, "After this, Job lived a hundred and forty years; he saw his children and their children to the fourth generation" (Job 42:16).

Because Job's response to suffering was relentless worship, the results of his suffering were such amazing gains as a bigger perspective of God, greater intimacy with God, and deeper humility before God. Also, God was able to bless Job with twice the number of earthly blessings he had before. Sometimes God may be allowing bad things into your life to prepare you to handle greater blessings.

Are You Really Ready for Success?

Most of us have dreamed of having amazing wealth and incredible influence, but we need to be reminded that vast amounts of money and power ruin the unprepared. You may think winning the lottery would solve your problems, but it might just expose, deepen, and escalate them.

Have you noticed? Most of us are much better able to handle success *after* we have tasted failure. The hard lessons learned through the tough times ready us to deal with better days by building into our lives needed virtues such as grace, dependence, and perspective. Bad times produce good things in us that mold us into the type of people God can trust to handle more good things.

Preparation for Greater Ministry Impact

Charles Spurgeon is considered "the prince of preachers." He was the first to regularly speak to crowds of multiple thousands Sunday after Sunday at his Metropolitan Tabernacle in London in the nineteenth century. He authored two hundred books. Yet during his adult life he battled painful gout and deep seasons of depression. He felt his hardship kept him humble and dependent on the Lord. With great insight he wrote:

> Uninterrupted success and unfading joy in it would be more than our weak heads
> could bear. . . . My witness is, that those who are honored by their Lord in public have
> usually to endure a secret chastening, or to carry a peculiar cross, lest by any means
> they exalt themselves, and fall into the snare of the devil.[4]

His experience was that misery was often the precursor to prosperity, buffeting the bridge to blessing. Given his familiarity with the formula, Spurgeon wrote:

> Depression comes over me whenever the Lord is preparing a larger blessing for my
> ministry. It has now become to me a prophet in rough clothing. . . . Before any great
> achievement, some measure of the same depression is very usual.[5]

Twice as Much without Prior Pain

A funny thing happens when a human suddenly experiences great wealth without the preparation that comes through prior pain. It does not make them any happier and often makes things worse. "Though buying power has more than doubled since the 1950s, the average American's reported happiness has remained almost unchanged," concluded Hope College professor David G. Meyers after analyzing data from National Opinion Research Center surveys and income data from *Historical Statistics of the United States* and *Economic Indicators*. He further states:

> The average American, though certainly richer, is not a bit happier. In 1957, some
> 35 percent said they were "very happy," as did slightly fewer—30 percent—in 2002.
> Indeed, if we can judge from statistics—a doubled divorce rate, more-than-doubled
> teen suicide, and mushrooming depression—contemporary Americans seem to be more
> often miserable.[6]

Losing by Winning

Job lost much, but he ultimately won more. Often, however, people who win much will lose even more. Few of us are really ready to receive greater blessing. Without the process of pain, we are unprepared for prosperity.

For example, a surprisingly high number of lottery winners end up worse off financially than they were before they won. Nearly one-third of multimillion-dollar lottery winners are bankrupt within a few years.[7]

Money alone can't buy happiness, and winning the lottery does not make people happier. One famous study measured the happiness of lottery winners against people who were recently paralyzed. The study found no measurable difference in happiness between the two groups.[8]

Many think that winning the lottery could solve their problems. Guess again. The evidence clearly indicates that gaining prosperity without developing the necessary value and character that come through hardship and suffering can be devastating.

Ask "Bud" Post, who won $16.2 million in a 1988 lottery. He now lives on his Social Security. "I wish it never happened. It was totally a nightmare," says Post. His former girlfriend successfully sued him for a share of his winnings. A brother was arrested for hiring a hit man to kill him, hoping to inherit a share of Post's winnings. His other siblings pestered him until he agreed to invest in ventures that made no money and further strained his relationship with them. Eventually, Post spent time in jail. Within a year, he was $1 million in debt. Today he lives on food stamps.[9]

Ask Evelyn Adams. She won the New Jersey lottery not just once, but twice (1985, 1986). Her total winnings numbered $5.4 million. Today, all her money is gone and she lives in a trailer. "Winning the lottery isn't always what it's cracked up to be," she said. "I won the American dream but I lost it, too. It was a very hard fall. It's called rock bottom."[10]

Receiving huge amounts of money often compounds problems for some people. Ask Jack Whittaker. He won the largest undivided lottery jackpot in U.S. history, $113 million. When he won, newspapers carried pictures of Jack, the boisterous, happy-go-lucky, respected contractor. Two years later they carried his mug shot as a haggard, somber man who had been arrested twice on drunken driving charges within a year and had been ordered into rehab. He also went to court for charges that he attacked a bar manager, and he was accused in two lawsuits of making trouble at a nightclub and a racetrack.[11]

God knows that the vast majority of us could never handle the sudden receipt of a large amount of money. We need to experience pain prior to being prepared for prosperity. He also knows that few can handle great ministry blessings without growing self-sufficient and proud. He develops our character and our humble dependency on Him through hardship. Buffeting prepares us for blessing.

Why?

Why would a good God allow His children to experience bad things? It might be to prepare us to receive greater blessings. Maybe the suffering you are enduring is part of God's plan to prepare you for greater blessings.

NOTES

[1]Bruce Wilkinson, *The Dream Giver* (Sisters, OR: Multnomah, 2003), 114.

[2]Ibid., 115.

[3]http://www.brucewilkinson.com/meetbruce.html (accessed February 18, 2007).

[4]As quoted in Helmut Thielicke, John Doberstein, trans., *Encounter with Spurgeon* (Grand Rapids: Baker, 1975), 214.

[5]Richard E. Day, *The Shadow of the Broad Brim* (Philadelphia: Judson, 1934), 175.

[6]David G. Meyers, "Happiness," http://www.davidmyers.org/Brix?pageID=48 (accessed October 21, 2006).

[7]Sherri Granato, "Winning the Lottery: Curse or Blessing?" http://www.associatedcontent.com /article/70165/winning_the_lottery_curse_or_a_blessing.html (accessed October 21, 2006).

[8]Philip Brickman, Dan D. Coates, and Ronnie J. Janoff-Bulman, "Lottery Winners and Accident Victims: Is Happiness Relative?", http://www.ncbi.nlm.nih.gov/entrez/query.gcgi?cmd+Retrieve&db+PubMed&list_uids=690806&dopt=Abstract (accessed October 21, 2006).

[9]Ellen Goodstein, "8 Lottery Winners Who Lost Their Millions," Bankrate.com, http://articles.moneycentral.msn.com/SavingandDebt/SaveMoney/8lotteryWinnersWhoLost TheirMillions.aspx (accessed October 21, 2006).

[10]Ibid.

[11]Kelley Schoonover, "For Lottery Winner 113m Hasn't Brought Happiness," Associated Press, December 14, 2004, http://www.boston.com/news/nation/articles/2004/12/14/lottery_winner_113m_hasnt_bought_happiness/.

7

To Position Us for Higher Promotion
GENESIS 50:20

How on earth could a Hebrew shepherd, the eleventh-ranked brother in his own family, possibly become prime minister of a mighty world power? Humanly speaking it would be absolutely, undeniably, irrevocably impossible. But there is a God who can use very bad things to accomplish very good things, even impossibly good things—and that is exactly what happened to a boy named Joe. This is his story.

Bad Things

A somewhat precocious teenager, seventeen-year-old Joseph awoke one morning thrilled yet fearful. That night he had dreamed a very clear dream of becoming a leader. He was convinced that God had pulled back the veil and had given him a glimpse of his destiny. God was calling him to a life of leadership.

Excitedly, Joseph shared with his already jealous older brothers his dream of eventually being leader of the family. This was not wise. Their envy turned to bitter hatred, and they waited for a chance to punish him. Bad things were about to happen to a good person.

Opportunity soon presented itself. Joseph was doing what his father had asked when he went to get a report on how his brothers were getting along grazing the flocks fifty miles away from the family compound. Unsuspectingly, Joseph walked into a trap. His jealous brothers grabbed him, threw him into an empty well, and were planning to leave him for dead. Eventually, Joseph's eldest brother convinced the others to sell him to a caravan of slave traders.

Just like that, his wonderful dream turned to a horrible nightmare. Betrayed and abused by his own brothers, he was left for dead, then sold into slavery. Why did a good God allow such a bad thing to happen to a good boy?

Son Becomes a Slave

What an awful event to occur, especially at the hands of his own brothers! One day Joseph had been the favored son of a wealthy shepherd; the next he was a slave. All his possessions, rights, and privileges were taken. He was nothing more than a commodity, a piece of property, in the hands of evil men. Where was God?

Eventually, the caravan stopped in Egypt, a bizarre land on the Nile River. Potiphar, the captain of Pharaoh's guard, bought Joseph and put him to work serving his large household.

Joseph's life began to look up. He refused to become bitter toward God. He worked hard. Soon he began to display leadership skills. Little by little he gained Potiphar's trust, and his role expanded until he was put in charge of managing the household. Far from home in a strange place, in the lowly position of slave, Joseph was learning how to lead. Good things were starting to happen.

Then everything came crashing down.

More Bad Things

Joseph was an attractive young man, and he caught the eye of Potiphar's wife. The lustful woman tried to seduce Joseph. In his loyalty to God and his master, he repeatedly rebuffed her advances. He did the right thing. You might expect God to bless him with good things because of his faithful obedience in the face of stiff testing, yet it was not to be. More very bad things happened to a very good person.

Scorned and vengeful, the awful woman accused Joseph of attempting to rape her. It was the word of the Egyptian wife of a high-ranking official against that of a foreign slave. Joseph stood no chance. The next thing he knew, Joseph found himself in prison. Sorrow was heaped on sorrow. If it had not been bad enough to be a slave, now he was a convict. Why was God allowing such bad things to happen to such a good man?

Bad Becomes Worse

Initially, Joseph's predicament contained a thread of promise. His work ethic and leadership were put to good use, and he was given opportunity to develop as a servant leader. Joseph was privileged to associate with a few of Pharaoh's formerly high-ranking political prisoners. They discussed life in the palace and the challenges of leading the nation. Good things were starting to happen.

Joseph's position in prison afforded him the usual opportunity of predicting that the king's ex-cupbearer would be restored to his former position. In making the prediction, Joseph hoped that the cupbearer would champion Joseph's unfair plight and plead his case on the outside. Maybe he would be freed from the prison.

But days turned to weeks. Weeks stretched into years. The cupbearer forgot him. Joseph's dream of freedom died.

How bad could it get? He was unfairly rejected by his family, unsuspectingly sold into slavery, and unjustly thrown into prison. Now he was forgotten, left to rot behind bars. Ever since he had been given that cursed dream, Joseph had known one terrible event after another.

Where was God? Why did God allow such extremely awful things to happen to Joseph? What had Joseph done to deserve such severe suffering and sorrow? Didn't God care? What was God doing?

As it turned out, God had it under control every step of the way.

Dream becomes Destiny

One fateful night, Pharaoh sat up in bed soaked in sweat, unable to escape the dreams that had haunted his sleep. He called in his advisers, but they were dumbfounded by his odd dreams. Lacking an interpreter for Pharaoh's dream, suddenly the cupbearer remembered what Joseph had done in interpreting his dream. So the cupbearer told Pharaoh about Joseph.

Immediately, Pharaoh called Joseph in and recounted his bizarre dream. Patiently Joseph listened, quietly asking God for direction. With God-given skill, Joseph interpreted Pharaoh's dream as a prediction from God of imminent years of extreme famine.

Astutely, Joseph also laid out a simple plan for avoiding the deadly destruction of the famine by stockpiling provisions. Deeply impressed by Joseph's ability not only to interpret the dreams, but also to detail a solution, Pharaoh acted.

With his authority as emperor of Egypt, Pharaoh stunned the world by proclaiming Joseph the prime minister of the entire nation. Talk about an unlikely and unbelievable promotion! A Hebrew slave and imprisoned alleged rapist was made the second most powerful ruler of the most powerful nation on the planet in one moment!

In his new role, Joseph carefully stockpiled provisions. Of all the nations of the Middle East, only Egypt was prepared when the horrible famine hit. Joseph fed his people, made a rich profit selling grain to the nations, and saved the lives of many people, including his family. He saw thirteen years of truly terrible experiences swept away by the dizzying good that God accomplished in, for, and through him—good that never would have occurred without the help of the bad.

Good Things Out of the Bad

I love this story. Like a wise master patiently placing together pieces of a puzzle to form a stunningly beautiful picture, God used every bit of bad that Joseph experienced to position him for the highest possible promotion and greatest possible good. Wow! Only God could use the awful, ugly pain of kidnapping, slavery, and prison to so providentially prepare and position a boy to fulfill his wildest dreams *and* save many people's lives *and* save the Hebrew race from starving.

Why does God allow bad things to happen to good people? Sometimes it is to position them for greater promotion. God is big enough to accomplish incredibly good results from very bad events. Think back through Joseph's life.

- By serving as a slave managing Potiphar's house and as a prisoner running a prison, Joseph learned more about leadership than he would have back home.
- It was only by being in prison that Joseph was able to meet some former cabinet officials and was thus strategically placed to be available to explain Pharaoh's dream.
- As a result of being sold into slavery to a caravan who took him to Egypt, Joseph was divinely positioned to ultimately serve as prime minister of Egypt, the most influential nation on earth at that time.

None of the positive things in Joseph's life would have or could have happened without the negative. Why had God allowed those bad things to happen to a good man?

Skillfully, like a master weaver, using widely diverse pieces, ugly events, evil people, unjust treatment, and long periods of obscurity, God had woven all these things into a very beautiful tapestry. Like an elite chef, He cooked up a delicious stew out of the old vegetables, overlooked spices, and forgotten leftovers languishing in the pantry of Joseph's life. God turned very bad things into great good.[1]

Redirection

During my junior year in high school I had a very successful wrestling season. Several colleges began pursuing me with the potential of scholarship offers. I had totally committed my life to God and hoped to use my athletic ability to bring glory to His name.

Yet, in my senior year I tore up my knee midseason. My big dreams were rudely shattered. Not only was my injury painful and frustrating, but it brought an abrupt end to the potential scholarships. I was bummed out by my misfortune but tried to maintain faith that God would work the situation for good.

Why did God allow a bad thing to happen to me when I was trying so hard to do life right? Now I can see that at least one reason was to redirect my path. I ended up wrestling at a Christian college, something I was not considering prior to my injury. While there I met Cathy, the girl who would become my wife, and I was called and trained for a life of ministry, as well.

God brought good out of bad. He used my injury to redirect me to a different college and a different career than I would have discovered otherwise. I now see that God used my injury, and the resulting disappointment, to place me where I needed to be for what He had ahead.

Why does God allow bad things to happen to good people? Sometimes it is to better position them for a promotion. Many businesspeople have told me of being unfairly passed over for promotions, or even being unjustly fired, only to later realize that God had used that trial to strategically place them in a much better job.

Why?

Why would God allow negative events to overtake His own people? He might do so to position them for a greater promotion.

NOTE

[1]Dave Earley, *The 21 Most Encouraging Promises in the Bible* (Uhrichsville, OH: Barbour, 2005), 50.

8

To Prepare Us for the Miraculous
2 Chronicles 20

"How do you define a miracle?" my friend asked in a very soft voice.

"I have heard it defined as the unusual intervention of God by which the ordinary laws, course, and operation of nature are overruled, suspended, or modified. Why?"

In a reverent voice and with teary eyes, he gulped and answered, "Because I believe I have experienced one."

Two months prior to that conversation, my good friend Dr. Daniel Mitchell had been diagnosed with pancreatic cancer. Since pancreatic cancer is almost always lethal, the news of the cancer had been quite a shock to Dan, his family, and everyone who knew him. The thought of losing the beloved theology professor and academic dean for the seminary was heartbreaking, and we prayed for a miracle. Many wept, prayed, and feebly tried to encourage his wife, Nancy. Dan, however, was amazingly calm. After a few weeks of initial struggle, Dan was remarkably confident in the fact that God would do what was best.

That week he had endured a daunting battery of strenuous tests the doctors had ordered and awaited the results. Amazed at what the physicians had seen, his doctor gave him the verdict. What was thought to be a cancerous tumor on his X-rays was now only a shadow on the scan.

Dan was given a completely clean bill of health by his doctors. His story proves that God is still in the miracle-working business![1]

No Messes, No Miracles

> When God is going to do something wonderful, He begins with a difficulty. If He is going to do something very wonderful, He begins with a mess.[2]

Would you like God to do an amazing, jaw-dropping, inexplicable, stand up and holler miracle in your life? Who wouldn't want to see sickness instantaneously healed? Who wouldn't want to see a healthy child placed in a barren womb? What about a dead man made alive? How about walking on top of a stormy sea? How about clean, bubbling torrents of water in the desert? Think before you answer.

One day, as I was studying the miracles in the Bible, I had a profound insight. To you it is probably obvious, but to me it was a new understanding and a big deal. My big brainstorm was this: *There are no miracles without messes.*

Walk through the scriptures. Every miracle followed closely on the heels of a giant mess. For example:

- Sarah endured ninety years of the frustrating humiliation of barrenness *before* her miracle baby, Isaac, was born.
- Moses was leading a million slaves to their slaughter at the hands of Pharaoh and his chariots *before* the Red Sea opened, allowing them to pass through on dry land.
- Thousands of people had to grow tired and hungry *before* Jesus multiplied fish

and bread enough for all to feast.

- The widow and her son had to be starving *ahead of* the unlimited bin of flour and unending jar of oil. Yet the flour and oil both ran out when no longer needed.
- Daniel had to be thrown into the lions' den *before* he could be spared from even a scratch.
- Shadrach, Meshach, and Abednego were thrown into the furnace *prior to* being protected so completely by the Son of God that no one could even smell smoke on them.
- Bartimaeus had to experience a lifetime of blindness *prior to* experiencing the Great Physician's healing touch.
- Jesus never would have had to free the man in the tombs from a legion of demons if the man had not been demonized in the first place.
- The ten lepers had to experience leprosy *before* experiencing the miracle of their healing.
- Peter had to go prison *before* the angel could unlock his chains and set him free.
- *Prior* to the amazing earthquake that opened the heart of the Philippian jailer, Paul and Silas had to go to jail.
- Lazarus had to die *before* he could rise from the dead! So did Jesus.

The biblical record is quite clear. There are no miracles without previous messes. The need for a miracle is necessitated by the presence of an impossible situation, usually unbearable suffering.

One Man's Miracle

Maybe you have been there. You were doing everything right. You were living as good and godly as you knew how. Yet suddenly, a heavy, sinister cloud darkened the sky. It blocked all hope from view. The odds were much too steep, the situation seemed impossible. You found yourself helplessly adrift in a huge mess. The only way out was a miracle.

King Jehoshaphat and his nation, Judah, were there. He had worked diligently to turn his people back to God. He was a good and godly man. Yet suddenly, three big, bloodthirsty armies allied themselves against him and breathed down the skinny neck of his lone army. A sea of evil invaders had amassed to sweep into Jerusalem like a terrible tide. He had a massive, ugly mess.

What could he do? Surrender meant certain slavery. Fighting meant definite defeat and death. What he needed was an undeniable, jaw-dropping, almost unbelievable, flat-out miracle.

When we experience the imminent threat of great pain and total loss, we always face a choice: We can run to God and trust Him or turn from Him and run away.

Take Your Problems to the Lord

Jehoshaphat ran to God. He turned his problems into prayer. I don't know if he prayed because he was a giant in the faith or just a coward with nowhere else to turn. It doesn't matter. What does matter is that he turned his greatest problem into his greatest prayer and added fasting. Wisely, he invited all of Judah to join him. Recognizing the desperate enormity of their plight, people came from all over Judah to join the prayer (2 Chronicles 20:3–13).

Jehoshaphat came to God with raw honesty, abject hopelessness, and naked humility in his request. In essence he said to God, "We are powerless. We don't know what to do. But we are looking to You!"

God is tenderhearted and is attracted to bare-boned brokenness. Such requests may not always get us what we want, but they put us on the path to getting what God wants.

I am a journal keeper. When I reread my journals, I find that the one prayer I pray most often consists of but three short, simple sentences. "I can't. You can. Please do." It is a good thing to give your problems to the Problem Solver. He can handle them.

The Battle Belongs to the Lord

Sometimes when we ask for miracles, God's wise response is silence. God sees that for us, at that time, deliverance is not best. But happily this is not always the case, and it wasn't the case for Jehoshaphat and Judah. In response to their desperate prayer, God gave them a speedy and amazingly encouraging reply.

> *"The battle is not yours but God's. . . . You will not have to fight this battle. Take up your positions; stand firm and see the deliverance the Lord will give you. . .and the Lord will be with you."*
>
> 2 CHRONICLES 20:15, 17

Praise Warfare

God had promised them a miracle, but they had to actively believe Him. So Jehoshaphat unveiled his Praise Warfare battle plan. It would be a symbol of their active faith in their living God.

> *Early in the morning they left for the Desert of Tekoa. As they set out, Jehoshaphat stood and said, "Listen to me, Judah and people of Jerusalem! Have faith in the Lord your God and you will be upheld; have faith in his prophets and you will be successful." After consulting the people, Jehoshaphat appointed men to sing to the Lord and to praise him for the splendor of his holiness as they went out at the head of the army, saying: "Give thanks to the Lord, for his love endures forever."*
>
> 2 CHRONICLES 20:20–21

The Real Battle

I wish I had been there that morning. I can only imagine being one of the musicians or singers, who usually watched battles from a safe distance in the rear. But now they were to line up in the front row of the army. Imagine the wild thoughts and reckless fear that must have brewed just below the surface of their minds. *This is insane. Unless God comes through, we are marching out like sheep to be slaughtered. We'll be singing, "Give thanks to the Lord," and they'll by cutting off our heads.*

Consider what thoughts must have been knocking at the doors of the minds of the Judean soldiers. *This is crazy. Those dumb singers are just going to be in the way. The only good thing is that maybe after killing all of them, the bad guys will be tired. But we still won't have a chance.*

We can guess what Jehoshaphat's cabinet members were thinking. *The old man has finally flipped out. March into battle singing praises? This plan stands no chance. I hope they will just make us slaves instead of examples.*

The biggest battle the Judeans faced was not fighting their foes, but fighting their fears. It was really a battle to believe. Often it is much tougher to fight invisible fear than visible enemies. Why did God allow them to get in this situation in the first place? One reason was that He wanted to test and strengthen their faith.

Fortunately, faith faced down fears. They lined up and marched out, singing praises to their Warrior God—and it worked!

God Wins!

> As they began to sing and praise, the Lord set ambushes against the men of Ammon and Moab and Mount Seir who were invading Judah, and they were defeated. The men of Ammon and Moab rose up against the men from Mount Seir to destroy and annihilate them. After they finished slaughtering the men from Seir, they helped to destroy one another.
>
> 2 CHRONICLES 20:22–23

I love this story. It was only *as* they began to sing and praise that God got busy ambushing the evil invaders. And ambush them He did. The enemy became so confused that they turned on one another. The next thing you know they had destroyed each other.

It probably took but a few hours at most for the men of Judea to gather together, line up, and march to the place overlooking the desert where the invaders had camped. Yet it took them three days to gather the plunder (2 Chronicles 20:25)!

But there is more. In one morning, God had not merely blessed and grown the Judeans' faith, He had not only given them a huge amount of free goodies, but He also so totally defeated Judea's nearest enemies that other potential enemies decided to stay away, as well (2 Chronicles 20:29–30). The nation enjoyed an extended period of peace.

But beyond all that, this sensational story of a miraculous victory has been recorded in our Bibles and has been the source of immense encouragement for an untold number of believers for thousands of years.

Don't miss the most glaring fact in this true story. The glorious miracle and these great by-products would never have, could never have, occurred without the enemy invaders breathing invincibly down their necks in the first place. Why did God allow a good king like Jehoshaphat to face such a bad thing as a bloody invasion and pending destruction? Why did an all-loving, all-powerful God allow such a massive mess in the first place? Because He knows there are no miracles without messes.

Why?

Everyone wants miracles, but we must never forget that miracles do not come without messes. People cannot be healed unless they are first sick or broken. Bills cannot be paid unless there are bills needing to be paid. There is no need for miracles until people find themselves in impossibly painful messes.

Why does God allow bad things to happen to good people? Sometimes it is in preparation for a miracle.

NOTES

[1] Daniel Mitchell's story is used by permission.
[2] Dewey Cass, quoted in Tim Hansel, *Through the Wilderness of Loneliness* (Elgin, IL: Cook, 1991), 18.

9

To Increase the Testimony of God
DANIEL 6

Daniel was an amazingly good and godly person who was an excellent administrator. His boss, King Darius, was so impressed with Daniel that he intended to appoint Daniel as prime minister, his right-hand man. Daniel would be in charge of the entire massive kingdom of the Medes and Persians.

But the other administrators were jealous of Daniel, and they began to plot a way to get rid of him. However, he was so competent and his record was so clean that the only accusation they could think of to use against him was his faith in the living God. So they came up with a devious scheme. They would play to the king's ego and trap Daniel at the same time. Brilliant! Read what they did:

> So the administrators and the satraps went as a group to the king and said: "O King Darius, live forever! The royal administrators, prefects, satraps, advisers and governors have all agreed that the king should issue an edict and enforce the decree that anyone who prays to any god or man during the next thirty days, except to you, O king, shall be thrown into the lions' den. Now, O king, issue the decree and put it in writing so that it cannot be altered—in accordance with the laws of the Medes and Persians, which cannot be repealed." So King Darius put the decree in writing.
>
> DANIEL 6:6–9

They did not underestimate Daniel or his faithfulness to God. When he learned of the decree, Daniel did exactly as he had done before, continuing to pray three times a day to his God. Together, his enemies came to find him praying, and they gleefully took the news to the king. Their evil plan was falling into place very nicely.

> So they went to the king and spoke to him about his royal decree: "Did you not publish a decree that during the next thirty days anyone who prays to any god or man except to you, O king, would be thrown into the lions' den?"
>
> The king answered, "The decree stands—in accordance with the laws of the Medes and Persians, which cannot be repealed."
>
> DANIEL 6:12

Understandably, the king was upset that Daniel was caught in the wicked web. Yet the decrees of the king of the Medes and Persians could not be repealed by anyone, including the king himself. He had no choice. He had to send Daniel to his death.

> So the king gave the order, and they brought Daniel and threw him into the lions' den. The king said to Daniel, "May your God, whom you serve continually, rescue you!"
>
> A stone was brought and placed over the mouth of the den, and the king sealed it with his own signet ring and with the rings of his nobles, so that Daniel's situation might not be changed.
>
> DANIEL 6:16–17

The Rest of the Story

Stop. Think about what happened. Daniel was a good man who was sentenced to death for doing a good thing, faithfully standing for God and praying to Him no matter what. Why did a good and almighty God permit this horrible event to happen to such a truly good person? Let's find out.

> At the first light of dawn, the king got up and hurried to the lions' den. When he came near the den, he called to Daniel in an anguished voice, "Daniel, servant of the living God, has your God, whom you serve continually, been able to rescue you from the lions?"
>
> Daniel answered, "O king, live forever! My God sent his angel, and he shut the mouths of the lions. They have not hurt me, because I was found innocent in his sight. Nor have I ever done any wrong before you, O king."
>
> The king was overjoyed and gave orders to lift Daniel out of the den. And when Daniel was lifted from the den, no wound was found on him, because he had trusted in his God.
>
> DANIEL 6:19–23

Wow! God allowed such a big mess so He could do such a great miracle. No one lived through a night in the lions' den, but Daniel did. No one could hope to survive even a minute or two in the lions' den without being hopelessly maimed and mangled, if not severely cut and injured, but Daniel did. His God had delivered him.

But that is not the end of the story. Read on.

> At the king's command, the men who had falsely accused Daniel were brought in and thrown into the lions' den, along with their wives and children. And before they reached the floor of the den, the lions overpowered them and crushed all their bones.
>
> DANIEL 6:24

I love it when the bad guys get it in the end. But there is more. It gets better. Darius issued a new decree that trumped the old one.

> Then King Darius wrote to all the peoples, nations and men of every language throughout the land:
>
> "May you prosper greatly! I issue a decree that in every part of my kingdom people must fear and reverence the God of Daniel. For he is the living God and he endures forever; his kingdom will not be destroyed, his dominion will never end. He rescues and he saves; he performs signs and wonders in the heavens and on the earth. He has rescued Daniel from the power of the lions."
>
> So Daniel prospered during the reign of Darius and the reign of Cyrus the Persian.
>
> DANIEL 6:25–28

The Big Picture

A big, ugly, evil thing happened to Daniel. He was unjustly plotted against and, as a result, was thrown into the lions' den for being faithful to his God. Yet God turned this one great evil into many greater goods.

- Daniel was spared.
- Daniel's enemies were destroyed.
- Daniel was securely set up for the rest of his life.
- The king received a mighty witness of the power of God and His love for His children.
- Religious freedom for all of the Jews was greatly expanded.
- And best of all, the entire nation was told that they needed to fear and reverence the God of Daniel!

Why did God allow a good and godly man, Daniel, to experience such a horrible incident? The reasons were manifold and the blessings abundant. Yeah, God!

The Bigger Picture

God's ultimate plan behind all of His activities on this planet is to present humanity with a clear testimony of who He truly is and what He does. While Daniel's situation impacted his life and future, it went well beyond that. An entire generation of pagans and Jews living in the most powerful kingdom on earth received a strong witness of the immense glory of the living God. Who knows how many of those people turned to God or were better able to live for Him because Daniel went to the lions' den? Beyond that, how many of us, through the past thousands of years, have had our faith strengthened by reading the true story of Daniel and the lions' den?

The Same Story Acted Out with Different Actors

What happened to Daniel is not unique. Several years prior, when the Babylonian king Nebuchadnezzar was on the throne, three of Daniel's Hebrew friends—you know their names: Shadrach, Meshach, and Abednego—faced a similar situation. They could either bow down to an idol made in the likeness of the king or be executed. Like Daniel, they refused to bow to anyone other than the living God. As a result, they were thrown into a red-hot furnace, heated hotter than ever before.

Again, a bad thing happened to good people because they were faithful to God. Again, God miraculously intervened.

> Then King Nebuchadnezzar leaped to his feet in amazement and asked his advisers, "Weren't there three men that we tied up and threw into the fire?"
>
> They replied, "Certainly, O king."
>
> He said, "Look! I see four men walking around in the fire, unbound and unharmed, and the fourth looks like a son of the gods."
>
> Nebuchadnezzar then approached the opening of the blazing furnace and shouted, "Shadrach, Meshach and Abednego, servants of the Most High God, come out! Come here!"
>
> So Shadrach, Meshach and Abednego came out of the fire, and the satraps, prefects, governors and royal advisers crowded around them. They saw that the fire had not harmed their bodies, nor was a hair of their heads singed; their robes were not scorched, and there was no smell of fire on them.
>
> DANIEL 3:24–27

Again, God used His turning of evil into good to provide a clear and powerful testimony of His glory. Again, laws were changed to advance His worship. And again, His people ended up with greater prosperity and promotion than they would have otherwise experienced! Yeah, God!

> *Then Nebuchadnezzar said, "Praise be to the God of Shadrach, Meshach and Abednego, who has sent his angel and rescued his servants! They trusted in him and defied the king's command and were willing to give up their lives rather than serve or worship any god except their own God. Therefore I decree that the people of any nation or language who say anything against the God of Shadrach, Meshach and Abednego be cut into pieces and their houses be turned into piles of rubble, for no other god can save in this way."*
>
> *Then the king promoted Shadrach, Meshach and Abednego in the province of Babylon.*

Daniel 3:28–30

Bad to Good in the Twenty-first Century

Matt, my good friend and a young man I have mentored, was called to start a new church across the city from our church. He saw firsthand how God could turn a potentially devastating situation into a blessing for the entire community.

His brand-new church, New Life Church, began meeting in a privately owned banquet facility. One month later, Matt received a "cease and desist" letter from city zoning officials requiring the church to immediately cease meeting at their current location. The reason given was that they were in violation of zoning code, and if they did not comply, they would be criminally charged for every meeting.

The church believed it had a constitutional right to assemble together, so they did not cease worshiping on Sundays. Matt sought counsel from the Bible and claimed the truth found in Acts 5:38–39.

> *"Therefore, in the present case I advise you: Leave these men alone! Let them go! For if their purpose or activity is of human origin, it will fail. But if it is from God, you will not be able to stop these men; you will only find yourselves fighting against God."*

In the weeks following, things got worse. The owner of the banquet hall faced criminal charges for allowing the church to meet in his facilities. The city's law director even publicly compared the church to an organization renting the place to sell illegal drugs. The unrelenting oppression forced the church and banquet hall to file a joint federal lawsuit against the city in order to retain the right for the church to assemble together.

That's when God stepped in to turn the tables and bless many. When the church had begun, zoning legislation did not allow for *any* new church buildings. Consequently, no new church buildings had been built in the city for more than twenty-five years. However, when the lawsuit wrapped up (out of court), the city had modified its zoning code. Today, church gatherings and church buildings are allowed in nearly every part of the city![1]

Why?

So why would God allow very good people to go through very trying times and stifling situations? Sometimes He uses it to accomplish much greater good and spread His testimony farther than it would have spread otherwise.

NOTE

[1]Story used by permission of Matt Chittum, pastor of New Life Church, Hilliard, Ohio (http://www.newlife.us/).

10

To Bring Us to Himself
Acts 16

He dreamed of a good life, a good job, and a good family. He was just a few months from retirement. Things had fallen into place and were going his way—until the night all his dreams were shaken and shattered.

Earlier in the day, he had taken into custody two political prisoners. Religious zealots, they had incited a riot. He did not know all the details, but somehow these terrible two claimed to have cast a demon out of a slave girl in the name of Jesus. They had been dragged before the authorities and severely whipped and beaten. That's when they were turned over to him.

He locked them into the inner cell and fastened their feet in stocks. He would sleep soundly tonight. No one could get out of there. Or so he thought.

Unlike most prisoners, moaning and crying, these crazy men started praying and singing praises to Jesus. They weren't great singers, but their singing was interesting and did sound pretty nice. . .and harmless—he thought. So he went to sleep.

Suddenly, the ground started pitching and the walls began shaking. An earthquake was taking place right under the cell of those two religious men. Miraculously, all the prison doors flew open and all the chains came loose. No one was hurt.

How had this happened? What had he done wrong? All his hopes and dreams were gone, completely gone.

Trembling, the jailer knew what he had to do. Allowing prisoners to escape was unacceptable. When he accepted the job, he knew the policy. For a jailer to lose a prisoner was to lose his life. So resolutely he grabbed his sword and drew it out before his stomach. One quick plunge and it would be over.

Good-bye wife, good-bye kids, good-bye world.

"Stop!" a voice broke his concentration.

"Don't harm yourself. We are all here." It was those two men.

Stunned, amazed, relieved, overjoyed, afraid—the man called for a light. Running into their cell, he found the two men concerned, calm, unhurt, and smiling. Happily, he led these miracle producers out into the room where his family was eagerly gathered. They were confused and relieved. They had assumed that the jailer would have killed himself by now. But there he was, standing before them with the two smiling men.

"Sirs," he asked the men through trembling lips, "what must I do to be saved?"

"Believe on the Lord Jesus, and you will be saved," one answered. Then gesturing to the man's family, he added, "You and your family."

They did believe on the Lord Jesus and proved it by being baptized (for the full account, read Acts 16:16–40). One reason these good men, Paul and Silas, suffered was so that they could be in a position to bring the Philippian jailer to faith in Jesus Christ. One reason the jailer lost his dream of sound sleep and a secure jail was so he could have an opportunity to express faith in Jesus Christ.

God turned shattered dreams into something better, an encounter with Himself. Why does God allow bad things? Sometimes it is so He can do what He knows is best, blessing us with Himself.

A Shattered Marriage

Like every other young woman, Melanie got married with high hopes and big dreams. Yet her dreams of a happy life with Jim quickly unraveled, and too quickly they lay tattered in the dust of her tears.

Melanie found herself in the place she never imagined she would be, a lawyer's office seeking a divorce. Hurt, angry, fed up, brokenhearted, and scared, Melanie sat down in front of the big desk. From the other side, the lawyer calmly listened to her story of lost love. When she finished, the lawyer calmly placed his notes in a big manila folder. With a confident smile, the lawyer looked Melanie in the eye.

"You do not need a divorce. You need Jesus."

The moment he said those words, a knife cut her heart and she knew he was right. For the next half hour, the lawyer shared with her the good news of the death, burial, and resurrection of Jesus Christ for her sins. With tears dropping off her cheeks, she bowed her head and gave her life to Christ. Her shattered dream led to her greatest joy. She met Jesus.

But that's not all. This story gets better. She went back to Jim and told him what had happened. He also gave his life to Christ.

Hold on. There's more. Jim and Melanie got involved in a good church. Soon Jim was called into full-time Christian ministry. Melanie's drunken, wayward husband became a loving man of God and a pastor. God used Melanie's shattered dreams to bring her to God, and then He gave her more than she had ever dreamed.

The Glorious Shattering of a Very Proud Man

At the age of thirty-eight, Chuck Colson arrogantly thought he had arrived. He had it all and didn't need God. As the chief counsel to the president of the United States, he wielded incredible power and had an ego to match. Thinking they could do no wrong, Richard Nixon's "hatchet man," Colson, among others, hatched a plan to steal secrets from their party's opposition.

Colson's big balloon burst as he and his cronies found themselves in a terrifying nightmare. Played out daily in the media was the sickening news of the dishonesty and petty political dirty tricks played by the Watergate Seven. Caught in the ugly web of the Watergate political scandal, his world crashed down around him as he found himself facing public scorn and ridicule, the loss of his lofty position, and a prison term.

This was the unbearably deepest, darkest time of his life. His dreams were shattered. His immense pride was broken. He was at the bottom and had nowhere else to look but up.

For the first time in his life, Colson thought seriously about a relationship with God. A concerned Christian pointed him to Christ. His failure and brokenness pointed out his need. Late one night he broke.

> I was crying so hard it was like I was swimming underwater. . .then I prayed my first
> real prayer. "God, I don't know how to find You, but I'm going to try! I'm not much
> the way I am, but somehow I want to give myself to You." I didn't know how to say it,
> so I repeated over and over the words: Take me.[1]

When news of Colson's conversion to Christianity leaked to the press in 1973, the *Boston Globe* reported, "If Mr. Colson can repent of his sins, there just has to be hope for everybody."

Colson would agree. He admitted he was guilty of political "dirty tricks" and was blindly willing to do almost anything for the cause of his president and his party. Colson entered a guilty plea to Watergate-related charges. He entered prison as a new Christian and as the first member of the Nixon administration to be incarcerated for Watergate-related charges. He served seven months of a one- to three-year sentence.

Shortly after Colson was sentenced to prison, he wrote his testimony of coming to God in the bestselling book *Born Again*. After his release from jail, he founded Prison Fellowship Ministries to help meet the needs of the kind of men he had met in prison.

Colson experienced great pain and heartache that ultimately led to greater good for many, many others. Best of all, his hurt brought him to God.

Susan's Story

It began the morning after I defended my master's thesis, when I woke up with a pounding migraine, the stomach flu, and a cold. . . . It never went away. And for the next eight months, frustration grew as I battled chronic illness and fatigue. I had some good days, but mostly I was exhausted. I always seemed to have the flu, and my weight plunged from 125 to 92 pounds. Not long after, I was diagnosed with chronic fatigue syndrome (CFS), namely, permanent fatigue and a depressed immune system. . . .

When I couldn't work effectively, my self-esteem plummeted and depression soared. My relationships deteriorated because I was too tired to do anything and too angry to be near anyone—especially people who had the energy to lead a productive life. I could not function at the level I was accustomed to, and in my mind, if I couldn't do it all, I didn't want to live.

As a result, my heart became very dark. And my spirit screamed out to God— WHY? Why was I in such torment? If God had abandoned me to death, then let me die. But if I was meant to live, then heal me and let me function like a normal person.

For the first time in my life, I was unable to control my circumstances. And as I reached the end of my own strength, my only hope was to look outside myself for help— or something or someone who was much bigger than me.

Author and scholar C. S. Lewis says that pain is God's "megaphone to rouse a deaf world." It's true. I never looked to God much when I was healthy, successful, busy. . .able. I knew He was there, but it was only as I was stripped of all my resources that I really began to seek God and to cry out to Him from the depths of my heart.[2]

Shattered Dreams: Doorway to the Best Dream, God

As a counselor, Larry Crabb has spent a lifetime giving direction to good people trying to make sense of their shattered dreams. As a man, Larry has had to battle the brokenness that comes through losing a brother in a plane wreck, coping with cancer, and having a granddaughter with a life-threatening infection. Out of his experiences, he has learned some deep truths about shattered dreams.

Our shattered dreams never are random. They are always a piece of a larger puzzle, a chapter in a longer story. . .a necessary mile on the long journey of joy. . . .

The suffering of shattered dreams must not be thought of as something to relieve if we can or endure if we must. It's an opportunity to be embraced, a chance to discover our desire for the highest blessing God wants to give us, an encounter with Himself.[3]

In other words, one of the major reasons God allows suffering in our lives is to bless us with the greatest blessing He can give us—more of Himself. God allows our dreams to shatter so He can guide us to our unspoken but ultimate dream—a deeper, higher, more comprehensive, more pervasive experience of Himself. Crabb states, "Only when we want Him as we want nothing else will there develop in our hearts a space large enough for Him to fill."[4]

According to Crabb, our shattered dreams are God's unexpected path to joy and the school where we are forced to abandon every dream but the dream of truly knowing God. It is then that we experience the presence of God moving through every detail of our lives, both good and bad.

Why?

So why does God seem to stand idly by and allow His children to suffer? Because it is in the depths of sorrow that we finally look up and see. . .God.

Maybe you are broken by sorrow. Maybe you are suffering in pain. If nothing else, allow your brokenness to bring you to God. Do as Melanie or the Philippian jailer or Chuck Colson did. Believe on the Lord Jesus Christ and be saved. Cry out to Him. Ask Him to take your life.

If you already know God, maybe the reason you are suffering is to bring you to a deeper awareness of, appreciation of, and experience with God. Use your shattered dreams to draw more closely to Him than ever before.

NOTES

[1]Charles W. Colson, *Born Again* (Old Tappan, NJ: Revell, 1976), 116–17, emphasis his.
[2]Susan Martinuk, "Why Me, God?" http://www.christianwomentoday.com/growth/susanmart.html (accessed November 11, 2006).
[3]Larry Crabb, *Shattered Dreams: God's Unexpected Pathway to Joy* (Colorado Springs: WaterBrook, 2001), 4.
[4]Ibid., 121.

11

To Stretch Us for Greater Growth
ROMANS 5:3–4

Are you suffering? Does affliction seem to come in waves that won't go away? Do you feel like it comes at you from all directions? Take hope. You are not alone. And you are not the first.

A devoted Christian man named Paul endured his own dizzying list of adversities. In fact, his sorrows are so numerous that he views himself as possibly the undisputed champion of pain. Read his testimony slowly, imagining how deeply these things must have hurt.

> I've worked much harder, been jailed more often, beaten up more times than I can count, and at death's door time after time. I've been flogged five times with the Jews' thirty-nine lashes, beaten by Roman rods three times, pummeled with rocks once. I've been shipwrecked three times, and immersed in the open sea for a night and a day. In hard traveling year in and year out, I've had to ford rivers, fend off robbers, struggle with friends, struggle with foes. I've been at risk in the city, at risk in the country, endangered by desert sun and sea storm, and betrayed by those I thought were my brothers. I've known drudgery and hard labor, many a long and lonely night without sleep, many a missed meal, blasted by the cold, naked to the weather.
>
> 2 CORINTHIANS 11:23–27 THE MESSAGE

Why would God allow such a good man to suffer so many bad things? In letters to his friends, Paul describes several benefits of suffering that we will discuss in coming chapters. One reason that especially stands out is his dogged insistence that in the hands of God, bad is good for us *because* it helps us grow. In fact, it is so good that Paul said he even shouted praises when he was surrounded by troubles!

> There's more to come: We continue to shout our praise even when we're hemmed in with troubles, because we know how troubles can develop passionate patience in us, and how that patience in turn forges the tempered steel of virtue, keeping us alert for whatever God will do next. In alert expectancy such as this, we're never left feeling shortchanged. Quite the contrary—we can't round up enough containers to hold everything God generously pours into our lives through the Holy Spirit!
>
> ROMANS 5:3–5 THE MESSAGE

Look at the benefits: "passionate patience," "the tempered steel of virtue," and "alert expectancy." Those three add up to personal spiritual growth.

Why do bad things happen to good people? Because in the hands of God, pain can help us grow and forge our character.

"What We Are Made Of"

It was Sunday morning, and thirteen-year-old Donald was getting dressed for church along with his father and his brothers. His mother was expected home any day from the hospital where she had successfully undergone surgery.

Feeling good and happy about life, Donald plopped a chocolate into his mouth. Then the telephone rang, and Donald heard his aunt tell his father the hospital wanted them to come right away. Somehow Donald knew what that meant: His mother was dead—from an embolism, he later learned.

Feeling sick, he rushed to the open window, lifted the screen, and let the chocolate fall from his mouth to the ground. Suddenly, his world was coming apart.[1]

After returning home from the hospital and facing the fact that his mother was gone, Donald gathered with his father and brothers in the dining room.

> As we stood there with our arms around one another, crying our eyes out, my older brother, then in college, said, "Now we'll see what we are made of!" To this day, those words stand out as some of the most important words I have ever heard. When life comes apart, we have a lifetime opportunity to discover our inner qualities, our true strengths—"what we are made of," as my older brother put it—to let them come forth and allow them to grow.[2]

What Donald discovered is that in the hand of God, difficulties become revealers of our character and aid in our development. He found that the path of progress runs through the valley of pain.

No Pain, No Pearl

As you know, pearls are some of the world's most beautiful jewels. They are naturally hard, yet incredibly smooth and perfectly round. As you may not know, they are the products of pain. Chuck Swindoll explains:

> For an unknown reason the shell of the oyster gets cracked and an alien substance—a grain of sand—slips inside. On the entry of that foreign irritant, all the resources within the tiny, sensitive oyster rush to the spot and begin to release healing fluids that otherwise would have remained dormant. By and by the irritant is covered and the wound is healed—by a pearl.[3]

A perfect, precious pearl is the product of a healed wound. That is what makes a pearl so precious. Swindoll observed that the tiny jewel was "conceived through irritation, born of adversity, and nursed by adjustments."[4] Pearls can only be created by suffering. Had there been no pain, there would be no pearl. No wonder our heavenly home will have gates made of pearl.

No Wind, No Strength

A few months ago Cathy and I were shopping at an Amish furniture shop. All the wooden pieces were wonderfully crafted and beautiful. I noticed that most of the wood used was either oak or pine. The oak was my first choice, until I looked at the price tag. The oak was much more expensive than the pine. Why?

Both oak and pine trees can grow very large in size. Yet oak is more coveted for furniture, floors, and outdoor use because oak is harder, stronger, and more durable than pine. Because it is much stronger, it allows header logs and floor beams to span greater lengths.

Why is oak such strong wood? Oaks are noted for their deep root systems. This allows them to face stiffer winds than pines, which have a much shallower root system. When a big storm comes along, the pines are vulnerable to being uprooted and falling over, especially when they stand alone. However, the deeper roots of the oak give it the ability to lean into the wind and get stronger.

As we sink the roots of our spiritual lives deep into God and His Word, God enables us to handle the storms of life. As we withstand the winds of adversity, they serve to make us stronger.

No Wilderness, No Promised Land

> *There is no shortcut to wholeness: if you want to reach the Promised Land you must first go through the wilderness.*[5]

God promised a wonderful land to His chosen people, the freed Hebrew slaves who escaped the tyranny of Egypt and Pharaoh. But they could not simply leave Egypt and be in the Promised Land. No. Instead, they had to first travel through the rugged wilderness.

So it is with us. God promises us rich blessings, such as greater power (2 Corinthians 12:7–10), deeper holiness (Hebrews 12:5–11), and more fruit (John 15:1–8), but only after we have gone through the wilderness of suffering. The wilderness is often dark, frequently scary, and always difficult. But as Tim Hansel says, "The only way out is through. It takes courage, tenacity, stamina, patience, God's immense grace, and time. . .there is no such thing as an up without a down."[6]

I don't know what wilderness you are facing, but I encourage you to keep going through it, because the promised land waits on the other side.

No Pain, No Gain

As that great weight lifter Benjamin Franklin once remarked, "There is no gain without pain." Ronald Mehl, a pastor who battled through cancer, wrote these words regarding the painful times in our lives:

> *[They] always leave us with a list of things to clean up and fix up. They are when God restores to us the things we lose through negligence, ignorance, rebellion, or sin. For the Christian, [times of pain] are no-lose propositions. They help us see and acknowledge the loose shutters, missing shingles, and rotten fence posts in our lives while returning us back to the One who can make the necessary repairs.*[7]

We must not forget that God is a lot more interested in our character than He is our comfort. He is willing to allow us to experience difficulties in order to realize development. Our heavenly Father is willing to let us fall down and skin our knees a few times in order for us to learn to walk. He will let us go through some pains so we can make some gains. Pastor, author, and cancer survivor David Jeremiah has written:

> *We live in a skin-deep world. Our culture glorifies clothing, fashion, makeup, tummy tucks, and nose jobs. There is nothing wrong with any of those, but in the end they are only cosmetic. Character and substance are shaped in the crucible of adversity. Show me someone who lives a carefree life with no problems or trials or dark nights of the soul, and I'll show you a shallow person.*[8]

No Brokenness, No Wholeness

In pain, failure, and brokenness, God does His finest work in the lives of people.[9]

God has an amazing way of using jagged, ugly, crushing brokenness to develop deep and beautiful wholeness in the lives of His people. I am not adequate to explain it, but I have seen it spread through the pages of scripture and in the lives of twenty-first-century people. We could start in Genesis with the seemingly impossible dreams of Abraham and Joseph, go through the wilderness with Moses, visit brokenhearted Hannah, run for our lives with David, be taken captive with Daniel, and cry our eyes out with Jeremiah. We could weep bitterly with Peter and be knocked on our face with Paul. Alongside Mary, we could witness the nightmare of the execution of her son Jesus.

Again and again, in every case, we would see the skillful hand of the Master Craftsman somehow using the worst of agonies to create amazing courage and character. Clay that cooperates with the potter is crafted into beautiful, useful pots.

Why?

So why does God allow bad things to happen to good people? One reason is that God will use the bad and the bitter to make us much better people.

NOTES

[1]Donald Morgan, *How to Get It Together When Your World Is Coming Apart* (Grand Rapids: Revell, 1988), 14.

[2]Ibid., 17.

[3]Charles Swindoll, *Growing Strong in the Seasons of Life* (Portland, OR: Multnomah, 1983), 164.

[4]Ibid.

[5]Clifton Burke, quoted in Tim Hansel, *Through the Wilderness of Loneliness* (Elgin, IL: Cook, 1991), 17.

[6]Ibid., 17–18.

[7]Ron Mehl, *Surprise Endings* (Portland, OR: Multnomah, 1993), 60.

[8]David Jeremiah, *A Bend in the Road* (Nashville: W, 2000), 21.

[9]Gordon MacDonald, *Rebuilding Your Broken World* (Nashville: Oliver Nelson, 1988), 28.

12

To Remind Us That We Are Not Home Yet
ROMANS 8

Slam!

My ear hurts. I just had an unethical tow truck driver call me a liar and hang up on me. This is the same man who charged me four hundred dollars more than he promised, yelled like a maniac at my wife and me, took my son's truck to his lot and impounded it without authorization, and then lied about the whole thing. I hate it when that happens.

Bad thoughts were starting to flood my mind. You know what I mean. First are the angry, crazy, *How can I blow up his office without getting caught?* type of thoughts. Then comes self-pity: *Why is this happening to me? What on earth did I do to deserve such unfair, unscrupulous, unrighteous treatment?*

Then I was struck with the profound thought: *Dave, you are writing a book called* 21 Reasons Bad Things Happen to Good People. *Which of the twenty-one reasons could this be?*

I thought of nearly a dozen possible, positive, probable products of this mess, but the one that best fit this situation is that bad stuff always reminds us that we are not home yet.

I recently had the joy of researching and writing a book on heaven. One of the plenteous reasons heaven is so heavenly is because there will be no irritations, injustice, price gouging, dishonesty, frustration, or need of tow trucks in heaven. Amen!

We make a grave mistake when we expect earth to be perfect and think of earth as our home. Neither is true. Life on earth is irritating, infuriating, frustrating, unfair, painful, and confusing.

Earth is a muddled mess; heaven is perfect. Earth is not our final forwarding address. Heaven is. We aren't home yet.

Life on the Cursed Planet

At the time of its creation, the earth was a lush, glorious, tropical garden paradise. All of creation—plants, animals, and humans—existed in perfect harmony under the rule of God. But because of the disobedience of Adam and Eve, planet Earth was placed under a curse. It has been groaning ever since.

> To Adam he said, "Because you listened to your wife and ate from the tree about which I commanded you, 'You must not eat of it,' cursed is the ground because of you; through painful toil you will eat of it all the days of your life. It will produce thorns and thistles for you, and you will eat the plants of the field. By the sweat of your brow you will eat your food until you return to the ground, since from it you were taken; for dust you are and to dust you will return."
>
> GENESIS 3:17–19

At that moment, a dark shadow was cast over our planet. Thorns and other weeds began to grow (Genesis 3:18). Viruses were born. Plagues were hatched. Mosquitoes became bloodsuckers. Snakes became poisonous, as did some types of ivy. The table was set for the rise of killer storms, hurricanes, tornadoes, earthquakes, and droughts.

Since that fateful day in the Garden of Eden, creation has been groaning under the curse as it awaits the coming day of redemption. Paul writes:

I consider that our present sufferings are not worth comparing with the glory that will be revealed in us. The creation waits in eager expectation for the sons of God to be revealed. For the creation was subjected to frustration, not by its own choice, but by the will of the one who subjected it, in hope that the creation itself will be liberated from its bondage to decay and brought into the glorious freedom of the children of God. We know that the whole creation has been groaning as in the pains of childbirth right up to the present time.

ROMANS 8:18–22

Notice some of the ugly descriptions Paul chose to depict earth at this time: *sufferings*, *subjected*, *frustration*, *decay*, *groaning*, *pains*. But a better day, a brighter day is approaching. It will be a great day of *glory*, *liberation*, and *glorious freedom*.

Make no mistake. Sickness, sorrow, pain, problems, trouble, and turmoil have been commonplace on this planet since the curse. Sometimes we look for deep and complex reasons why bad things happen, when the easiest answer is that bad things happen because we live on a planet that is no longer truly good. Everything on earth is now stained and strained by imperfection. Even though earth is not as bad as it could be, it is no longer as good as it once was. When bad things happen, they remind us that we are not home yet.

Heaven, on Its Worst Day, Is Far Better Than Earth on Its Best Day

One of the most comforting truths I discovered when I studied heaven—there are twenty-one amazing truths about heaven, by the way—is that heaven on its very worst day will be infinitely better than earth on its very best day.[1] This is true for many reasons. Consider this descriptive promise about heaven:

"He will wipe every tear from their eyes. There will be no more death or mourning or crying or pain, for the old order of things has passed away."

REVELATION 21:4

God will ultimately wipe away every tear. Death will be eradicated. There will be no more grieving. Having served its purpose, pain will be no more.

There Is No Sin in Heaven

In heaven there will be no sin or contamination created by sin's curse. This will make heaven so. . .heavenly. It will make it an amazingly wonderful home.

In heaven the transformational power of Jesus' death, burial, and resurrection for our sin will be experienced on a much greater level than we can now comprehend. Sin's power will be crushed, and its presence completely removed.

One definition of sin is breaking the law. In heaven no one will sin by breaking the law. In other words, there will be no bad people creating suffering for themselves or others in heaven (Revelation 21:8; 22:15). No one will rob, rape, or murder. No one will abuse, molest, assault, mug, or kidnap. You won't have to lock the doors. Security systems and fences will be unnecessary. Guns will be unnecessary, as will mace and pepper spray. In heaven, you won't be able to find courtrooms, jails, dungeons, or prisons, because there will be no criminals.

Sin is also defined as moral crookedness. Because sin will be absent in heaven, there will be no suffering caused by perversion, moral filth, or corruption. Pornography, prostitution, drug dealing, and sexual abuse will not exist there.

Because our sinful natures will not make the trip to heaven with us, we will not be the source of our own suffering. We won't ever put ourselves in pain because of our own sins, addictions, fears, guilt, shame, and regret.

There Is No Curse in Heaven

No longer will there be any curse.

REVELATION 22:3

Just as sin will be removed in heaven, its consequences will be absolutely absent (Revelation 22:3). The curse will be lifted. Imagine a world without any of the hardships caused as a result of natural disasters. Floods, storms, gales, tempests, tornadoes, typhoons, twisters, tsunamis, cyclones, whirlwinds, squalls, hurricanes, blizzards, whiteouts, blackouts, and monsoons will not exist. The land, air, and water will be perfectly pure. There will be absolutely no trace of pollution, smog, contamination, toxic waste, or trash. Cancer, famine, and drought will be forever gone. The environment will be pleasantly perfect in heaven. There will be no frostbite or sunburn.

In heaven, the human, plant, and animal kingdoms will live together in absolute harmony. Snakes won't tempt us to sin or be poisonous. Poison ivy won't itch, mosquitoes won't bite, and raccoons won't get in the trash (there won't be any). Termites won't eat your house. Bees won't sting. Dogs won't bite.

There will be no germs or viruses. You can cross all types of disease, illness, sickness, infirmity, infection, ailment, disorder, malady, and affliction off the list of potential sources of sorrow. No one will need a hospital, sanatorium, nursing home, rehab center, or clinic in heaven. Neither will there be morgues, funeral homes, or cemeteries. Heaven is all about life. Therefore, death, grief, and mourning will not exist (Revelation 21:4).

Why?

The joy of the Christmas season of 2004 was cruelly crushed under the giant waves of a killer tsunami, known by the scientific community as the Sumatra-Andaman earthquake. The devastating natural disaster began as an undersea quake that triggered a series of deadly tsunamis that spread throughout the Indian Ocean. Large numbers of people were killed and coastal communities across South and Southeast Asia, including parts of Indonesia, Sri Lanka, India, and Thailand, were inundated. The gruesome final tally lists more than 180,000 dead.

The response of Matthew Goh, a Malaysian architect and inventor, to the overwhelming devastation was like that of many others. He wrote on his Web site:

> *When the tsunami struck during Christmastime in the year 2004, I thought, Where was God? I was confused, sad, and even doubted if He existed, or if He really cared. Why, why, why. . .flooded my mind.*[2]

I know that there will be no tsunamis in heaven. We won't even need to ask, "Why?" again.

Heaven Is God's Final Answer to Pain and Suffering

While years, decades, or even a lifetime of suffering on earth may seem like an immense problem, such stands as a minute issue compared to the yawning length of eternity and the vast glory of heaven. Combine all the suffering of all the people on all of the planet through all of history, and it will register as less than a blip on the radar screen of eternal bliss. The bad times will be nothing compared to the good times. The pain will be forgotten because of the pleasure.

Because he understood this better than most, Paul was able to endure more suffering than most. No wonder he said:

> *I consider that our present sufferings are not worth comparing with the glory that will be revealed in us.*
>
> ROMANS 8:18

> *Therefore we do not lose heart. . . . For our light and momentary troubles are achieving for us an eternal glory that far outweighs them all. So we fix our eyes not on what is seen, but on what is unseen. For what is seen is temporary, but what is unseen is eternal.*
>
> 2 CORINTHIANS 4:16–18

We Are Not Home Yet

The familiar story is told of an elderly missionary couple coming home from years of faithful service on the mission field. They had served loyally, worked diligently, and sacrificed mightily. When they arrived back in the United States, their ship was greeted by a huge "Welcome Home" celebration. A band played, photographers jostled for pictures, dignitaries stood to offer an official welcome, brightly colored banners blew in the breeze.

The old missionary, Henry C. Morrison, smiled to himself as he thought, *Well, I guess it was not all unnoticed. This is beyond our wildest expectations.*

But when he and his wife disembarked from the ship, they were pushed aside in the rush to greet the real returning hero, Theodore Roosevelt, the president of the United States.

No one was there to greet the old couple. There was no banner with their name. No band to play a song. No dignitaries. Not a friendly smile, a hug, or even a welcoming word. Morrison gulped back the tears of his disappointment. Sadly he said, "I guess no one came to greet us."

"Don't be upset," he heard the Lord reply. "After all, you aren't home yet."[3]

Why?

So why do bad things happen to good people? One reason is to remind us that we aren't home yet.

NOTES

1. If you are interested in heaven, you will want to read Dave Earley's *The 21 Most Amazing Truths About Heaven* (Uhrichsville, OH: Barbour, 2006).

2. Matthew Goh Kok Soon, *Asian Tsunami 2004,* http://www.matthewgoh.com/index.html October 28, 2006).

3. R. Kent Hughes, *1001 Great Stories and Quotes* (Wheaton, IL: Tyndale House Publishers, 1998), 401.

13

To Shape Us More Like Jesus
ROMANS 8:28–29

Have you ever hurt so intensely that the pain was too deep for words? If so, you are certainly not alone. Most of us have been to that painful place where all we have is an awful, anguished inner groaning that reaches out to God for the tiniest ray of relief. Such is life on planet Earth. Such is life in the family of God.

The Christians who lived in Rome in the early years after the resurrection of Jesus were battling that type of cavernous brokenness. Historians tell us that to the general populous, Christians were viewed with suspicion, as *malefica* (the bringer of evil). Because they refused to give up their Christian identity and be swallowed by the pagan Roman culture, they were feared by Rome as dissidents who might upset Rome's hard-earned security. Under Claudius, emperor from AD 41 to 54, the Roman senate, in an official decree, declared Christians to be rebels and instigators. As such, they were considered as dangerous as an invasion by the barbarians. Since Rome's "universal peace" had been established by the ferocious efficiency of its army, Rome was willing to maintain it by whatever means deemed necessary, be it forced labor, exile, or even execution.[1]

This was the world Paul addressed in his letter to the Roman Christians. A catalog of their situation would include material suffering, physical affliction, vocational tribulation, family abandonment, and personal calamity. You can add persecution, hunger, homelessness, threats, backstabbing, other dangers, and even death.

These were good people. They loved God, followed Jesus, and kept the faith no matter what. Why would a good God allow such very bad things to happen to such good people? The answer is found in a familiar passage and an overlooked truth.

Familiar Passage, Overlooked Truth

And we know that in all things God works for the good of those who love him, who have been called according to his purpose.

ROMANS 8:28

Most of us can quote Romans 8:28 by heart. It is one of the most encouraging promises ever pledged. The almighty God of the universe reassures His people that no matter what things happen, He works every single one of them for our good and His glory. Knowing and believing this enables Christians to live as "super victors" (Romans 8:37, my paraphrase). It binds us irrevocably to the love of Christ no matter what we face. No amount of trouble, trials, or tribulations; no hard times, hunger, homelessness, harshness, or hatred; no type of pain, pressure, or problem is so strong as to separate us from the love of God. Nothing is too complex, overwhelming, pervasive, or powerful to keep God from using it for good. God works all things for the good of those who are called according to His purpose. Wow!

Therefore, the question that must be answered when we are suffering is, "What is God's purpose?" Fortunately, we don't have to guess. The answer is in the very next verse.

For those God foreknew he also predestined to be conformed to the likeness of his Son.

ROMANS 8:29

In other words, God has known what He was doing all along. From the beginning, He decided to shape the character of those who love Him along the same lines as the character of His Son. God knows exactly what He is doing, and He uses all the circumstances in the lives of His people, including the bad ones, to make us more like Jesus.

As I have already described, the apostle Paul was a veteran sufferer. Physical pain, emotional anguish, and spiritual torment were not foreign to his experience. While he learned many benefits of adversity, one of the greatest was that suffering is a familiar shaping tool in the hand of the Master.

The Master Sculptor

You must understand. It was not always a masterpiece. It was nothing more than a huge block of stone. Eventually, a sculptor named Agostino was contracted to turn it into a statue of the Old Testament hero David. He began preliminary efforts at shaping the legs, feet, and chest of the figure yet grew discouraged and ceased work. Then a man named Antonio was commissioned to take up where Agostino had left off. However, he botched the job and was soon terminated. The massive block of Tuscan marble looked worse than before as it remained forgotten and neglected for twenty-five years.

"The Giant," as the forsaken rock was churlishly called, lay exposed to the elements in the weeds outside the cathedral workshop. But a young artist named Michelangelo saw potential in it that no one else saw and begged for the commission. Receiving it, he spent the next three years hammering and chiseling away at the massive marble slab.

To Michelangelo, sculpture was the art of the "making of men." His approach to sculpture was to chip away the unnecessary pieces of stone in order to liberate the human body that was encased in the cold marble.[2]

Today his masterpiece, the *David*, stands alone as the most recognizable statue in the history of art. The sensational statue portrays the young man, David, at the moment he determined to go out and fight Goliath. Because of the masterful combination of size, shape, elegance, power, and motion, the *David* has become regarded as a symbol of both strength and youthful human beauty. The seventeen-foot marble statue stands as tall as a double-decker bus and weighs a staggering six tons. It is viewed by millions of visitors to Florence each year.

Stone turned to masterpiece. It took three years of the purposeful blows of a determined and gifted master to make marble take on the image of man. In a similar way, it takes a lifetime of enduring the hammer and chisel of God for Him to shape us into the image of His Son. Affliction is often painful and frequently confusing, but it is the way of the Master.

> *To be fanciful; if the hunk of stone out of which Michelangelo was hammering and chiseling his David could have spoken, it would no doubt have said it did not know what shape it was going to end up; it only knew that what was currently happening was painful. And to be realistic, that is often all we can say when God is using griefs and pains to sculpt our souls.*[3]

The story is told of a young boy who asked the master sculptor how he knew what parts of the stone to chisel off. The artist answered, "I take off everything that does not look like David."

What does God chisel from our lives through suffering? The short answer is that through our hardships He chisels off anything that keeps us from being like Jesus. What characteristics keep us from Christlikeness? They would include self-centeredness, selfishness, self-righteousness, and self-sufficiency, and self-pity. There is also pride, arrogance, lust, greed, jealousy, envy, insensitivity, harshness, cruelty, apathy, and laziness. We could add dishonesty, deceitfulness, rebellion, idolatry, immorality, ignorance, bitterness, resentment, doubt, and fear. I left some off, but I think you get the idea. God's goal is for us to be more Christlike.

The Master Potter

This is the word that came to Jeremiah from the Lord: "Go down to the potter's house, and there I will give you my message." So I went down to the potter's house, and I saw him working at the wheel. But the pot he was shaping from the clay was marred in his hands; so the potter formed it into another pot, shaping it as seemed best to him.

Then the word of the Lord came to me: "O house of Israel, can I not do with you as this potter does?" declares the Lord. "Like clay in the hand of the potter, so are you in my hand, O house of Israel."

JEREMIAH 18:1–6

I enjoy art. I remember when one of my art teachers brought a potter's wheel to class. It was a big, round, flat wheel that spun around, powered by a small motor. If I close my eyes, I can smell the fresh clay. I feel the soft, smooth, wet clay in my hands. In my memory, I see the ugly, shapeless clay slowly taking shape as I mold it on the spinning wheel. I feel it spinning in my hands, gently rising under the pressure I put on it.

Clay has lumps in it. Those lumps don't just go away. They have to be worked out by the hands of the potter. This takes time. The more lumps the potter leaves, the less valuable the pot and the greater the odds of the pot cracking, or even blowing up, when it is fired in the furnace.

Spiritual clay has lumps. Those lumps don't just go away. They have to be worked out by the hands of the Potter. This takes time. The more lumps the Potter leaves, the less beautiful we become and the greater the odds of our cracking, or even blowing up, when we get fired by the intensity of extreme affliction.

After the potter has worked the clay, he or she fires it by placing it in a very hot kiln. The heat turns soft clay into a strong, useful pot.

The Potter lovingly works us in His hands as we spin on the wheel of life. He also fires us in the kiln of affliction. Thus, He makes us strong and beautiful. Thus, He makes us like His Son.

When in God's providence believers are exposed to the pressures of being isolated, opposed, tempted, humbled, disappointed, and hurt, the divine purpose is that these things should further our transformation into the likeness of our Savior.[4]

God Shone All Over Her Face

Aunt Florence knew pain and restriction. She also radiated what it means to be transformed into the image of Jesus Christ. She is in heaven now, but a few years ago I described her with these words:

There she sat, day after day, tiny and crumpled, a prisoner to her wheelchair. Her limbs were withered and crooked, her joints gnarled and knotted by crippling rheumatoid arthritis. The joys and freedoms of daily life had long been taken from her. She could no longer take a walk across a field. She was unable to bend down and scoop up a wiggling grandchild in her arms. She could not cook her family a big meal. She could not even get up and clean her little farmhouse.

Yet God shone all over her face.

Even though she ached in continual pain, you would never know it by measuring her smile. If the frustrations of bondage to the chair or the bed bothered her, she never complained of it. Her heart was not filled with self-pity nor her countenance with sorrow. Resentment held no place in her heart. Instead, she sparkled with attractive depth of joy.

She would literally light up when she spoke to me of the wonderful preachers she saw on TV. She peppered me with questions about the church that was born in our basement. When she told me that she prayed for me, I could tell she meant it and she had and she did. Her Bible had that wonderful worn look. Her clear blue eyes shone with that deep warmth of someone who knew a secret.

God gave her the desire of her heart. All four of her children grew up to live as committed Christians. Her son became a minister and her daughters married pastors. Her husband was a good and honest man, rough through years of hard work, but he was always so tender with her.

As I look back, it is so obvious now. Aunt Florence had the Immanuel Factor. Her relationship with God turned the potential prison of her wheelchair into a sweet sanctuary of solitude. In spite of and in the midst of her suffering, the glorious golden glow of God shone all over her face and her life.[5]

God used her suffering to shape her character and transform her life. As she basked in His presence, the glory of His Son shone from her life.

Why?

Why does a good God allow His children to experience bad things? One of His primary purposes for pain is to shape us into the image of His Son.

NOTES

[1] Teresio Bosco, "Persecutions of the Christians," http://www.catacombe.roma.it/en/ricerche/ricerca2.html (accessed November 17, 2006).

[2] Floria Parmiani, "Michelangelo's David," http://www.floria-publications.com/italy/italian_culture/michelangelo_david.html (November 17, 2006).

[3] J. I. Packer, "Formed in the Wilderness," in *The Desert Experience: Personal Reflections on Finding God's Presence and Promise in Hard Times* (Nashville: Nelson, 2001), 112–13.

[4] Ibid., 111–12.

[5] Dave Earley, *Living in His Presence: The Immanuel Factor* (Minneapolis: Bethany House, 2005), 41–42.

14

To Remind Us That We Are the Body of Christ
1 CORINTHIANS 12:12–14

On January 9, 2004, my good friend Joan Angus and her family experienced a horrible nightmare. Joan was pulling out in her minivan from a grocery store parking lot when her vehicle was hit by a semi that was going about thirty-five miles per hour. Joan was crushed by the heavy truck. Although Joan has no memory of her, a nurse passing the scene opened her airway so she could breathe.

> I was. . .taken to Grant Medical Center. I had a broken hip and pelvis. I was suffering internal bleeding, so my spleen had to be removed. I was put in traction until I stabilized enough to have the hip and pelvis operated on. A few days later that was done. My hip has a plate that looks like a flattened chain that is screwed into the bone. It is at least ten inches long. I have another on the pelvis that is smaller.

Joan also had a fractured skull and a traumatic brain injury, or TBI. Because of the TBI, she was unable to swallow properly, so a tube was put directly into her stomach to prevent aspiration—getting food, liquid, or medication into her lungs. Joan still has some symptoms caused by the TBI.

She has no memories of anything between the date of the accident and the middle of February. Once Joan was accepted into the Grant Rehabilitation program, twice a day she received physical, occupational, recreational, and speech therapy. In all, she spent sixty-three days in the hospital.

> It has been almost three years. I am as healed as I will ever be. It is good enough. I am still somewhat numb on my right side. I know I will never be the same again. It makes me look forward to heaven even more than I had before. I am going to run, skip, and jump (which I can't do on earth anymore) to Jesus and thank Him for all He has done for me. I can't wait!

I will never forget going to the hospital on the night of Joan's accident. When I arrived, there were already about two dozen members of our church outside Joan's door praying and talking in small groups. Joan's teenage daughters, Bethany and Jessica, were repeatedly hugged and encouraged. We were afraid Joan could not survive being crushed by the semi, and our hearts ached for her stunned family.

When I was finally allowed to see her, I couldn't remember ever seeing a human look less human. Blood, swelling, bandages, tubes, and machines combined to create the macabre scene. As I recall that night and try to write this chapter, I cannot help choking back tears. As a pastor I have seen numerous people lying in intensive care units, but Joan was probably the worst. I did not see how she would live through it, and if she did, I was sure her disabilities would ensure that she would never have a very high quality of life.

Over the next few years, we saw God do many amazing things for Joan and her family. I could use them as illustrations for many of the principles discussed in this book. Her quiet husband, Mark, rose to the occasion unlike few men I have ever known. His confident faith in God and tender care for Joan and the girls was a huge encouragement to me. He is not a public speaker and never will be, but his e-mail updates on Joan's progress were truly some of the greatest sermons I have ever experienced.

Joan was incredibly restored to health, yet not fully. But her faith-filled acceptance of the entire gruesome ordeal overwhelmed me. She has often told me that she was glad she went into it knowing that sometimes bad things happen because we live in a no-longer-good world. I never heard her blame God or ask why. She continued to keep her wonderful sense of humor and to fight on.

But one of the most important benefits of the horribly bad things that happened to Joan and her family was not for them. It was for us. What was unbelievably bad for her was incredibly good for us. The body of Christ got to be just that for the Angus family.

> *My church acted as the hands and feet of Christ. My family received meals each night from January until my kids got out of school in June. My house was cleaned each week by teams of women from the church until I could manage it myself. I also had two women a day who sat with me once I came home. I could not be left alone because of the swallowing problem. This was such a huge amount of volunteerism, but I was never, ever made to feel like anybody minded the extra work.*[1]

The hospital chaplain was completely overwhelmed by the number of church members who came to the hospital to be with the family the night of Joan's accident. Other patients and their families were curious about a church that was so responsive to the needs of a hurting member.

I remember the first Sunday after the accident that Mark was able to come to church. People applauded him. I remember the first Sunday Joan was wheeled into church. People cheered, cried, and were incredibly happy to see her.

Christians who had been struggling with their faith were drawn back to Christ through the example of the Angus family. Church members who had never experienced the joy of selflessly serving others were blessed to help out. People beaten down by their problems were given new hope through the Angus family's valiant fight. I was going through a very dark season in my personal life, yet every time I got to speak with Joan, I was uplifted.

Such an awful, ugly, painfully bad event produced such deeply beautiful good things. Thank God!

The Beauty of the Body

The apostle Paul's most cherished description of the church is as the metaphor of the body of Christ. He was amazed by the potential unity of the body of Christ, saying, "The body is a unit, though it is made up of many parts; and though all its parts are many, they form one body. So it is with Christ" (1 Corinthians 12:12).

He loved the diversity of the body of Christ, writing, "Now the body is not made up of one part but of many" (1 Corinthians 12:14). He especially reveled in the value of each member:

> *If the foot should say, "Because I am not a hand, I do not belong to the body," it would not for that reason cease to be part of the body. And if the ear should say, "Because I am not an eye, I do not belong to the body," it would not for that reason cease to be part of the body. If the whole body were an eye, where would the sense of hearing be? If the whole body were an ear, where would the sense of smell be? But in fact God has*

arranged the parts in the body, every one of them, just as he wanted them to be. If they were all one part, where would the body be? As it is, there are many parts, but one body.

1 CORINTHIANS 12:15–20

Of all the glorious similarities between the human body and the church of Jesus Christ, Paul stressed none more than the mutual dependency of each member of the body on every other part.

The eye cannot say to the hand, "I don't need you!" And the head cannot say to the feet, "I don't need you!" On the contrary, those parts of the body that seem to be weaker are indispensable, and the parts that we think are less honorable we treat with special honor. . . . But God has combined the members of the body and has given greater honor to the parts that lacked it, so that there should be no division in the body, but that its parts should have equal concern for each other. If one part suffers, every part suffers with it; if one part is honored, every part rejoices with it.

1 CORINTHIANS 12:21–26

The eye needs the hand. The head cannot get along without the feet. Every part is interdependent on the others.

To summarize Paul's teaching: (1) We all are one, (2) we all are different, (3) we all are valuable, and (4) we all need each other. In a culture of individualism and increasing isolation, we need to be reminded that we need each other.

One thing that was flushed to the surface by Joan's accident was that Joan, Mark, and the girls needed each of us in very evident ways. Yet we needed them in possibly more important ways, as well.

We hurt when they hurt. We were thrilled when they made progress, because we are family, the family of God and the body of Christ.

Going It Alone Is Deadly

As a pastor for many years, I have seen numerous believers pull back from the church when trouble hits their lives. Some are embarrassed, some are distracted, and some are easily disappointed. The reason they don't participate in the body of Christ is not as important as that they decide to separate themselves. They feel hurt and choose to stay on the fringe "just until I heal."

But it doesn't work. Isolating oneself when hurt is exactly the wrong way of thinking and responding. As a member of the body, we must be connected to the body to be fully healed. Let me explain.

Let's say that you had a chain saw get out of hand and accidentally cut off your finger. At this point you have two choices: Put the finger in your pocket and hope it heals, or speed to a surgeon and have it reattached as soon as possible. Which would you choose?

As you know, putting the finger in your pocket would condemn it to death. The life of the body flows from member to member through the bloodstream. If a finger is not connected to the life-giving blood flowing through the hand, it will turn black, rot, and die. However, if the finger can be reconnected, the body is amazingly equipped to heal the injured member in a miraculously small amount of time.

Healing in the Company of Friends

According to Dr. Nancy Burkhart, numerous medical and psychological studies show the healing power of going through suffering in the company of others.

> *Shearn et al. (1985) conducted a randomized study of men and women with rheumatoid arthritis and found that patients who participated in a mutual support group showed greater improvement in joint tenderness than a similar group of nonparticipants. This is also true for women with breast cancer who participated in a weekly support group. Spiegel et al. (1981) found that women with metastasis of breast cancer who participated in a weekly support group had significantly lower mood disturbances, fewer maladaptive coping responses, and fewer phobias than a similar control group. . . . Researchers have reported that just having one "significant" confidant can improve overall health and well-being (Brown 1975, et al., and Broadhead 1983, et al.).*[2]

Those in mutual support groups "showed greater improvement." One significant confidant "improves health and well-being." We need each other. Adversity is often the necessary reminder that we are the body of Christ.

The first Christians faced incredible hardships, such as ridicule, threats, losing property, beatings, and imprisonment. Yet they endured these things because they went through them together.

More Healing in the Company of Friends

One dark winter night, a drunken woman dressed in black stepped out into the middle of the highway in front of Russ Robinson's motor home, hoping to commit suicide. She lived, but her bizarre act nearly killed Ron.

Yet he wrote that his connection to the body of Christ through Christian friends saved him.

> *Their prayer support helped me begin the road to emotional recovery. . . . When I wrestled with God—seeking to make sense of the experience—people offered reassurance and other help. I needed people to pray with and for me, and I came to know what it was to have someone "weep with those who weep" (Romans 12:15 NRSV). I experienced how the body of Christ can extend real personal hands to someone in pain.*[3]

You can heal from any hurt and withstand immense pain if you don't try to face it alone. You need a friend. You need a family. You need a small group. You need a church.

Why?

Why does God allow suffering? One reason is that it often sparks His body, the church, into action and reminds us that we need each other.

NOTES

[1] Joan Angus's story is used by permission.

[2] Nancy Burkhart, "The Value of Support Groups," Texas A&M University, University System Health Science Center, http://www.tambcd.edu/lichen/lifestyles/valuegroups/valuegroups.html (accessed March 28, 2007).

[3] Bill Donahue and Russ Robinson, *Building a Church of Small Groups* (Grand Rapids: Zondervan, 2001), 39.

15

To Equip Us for Further Ministry
2 CORINTHIANS 1:3–4

Think of me as a fellow-patient in the same hospital who, having been admitted a little earlier, could give some advice.[1]

The year I turned sixteen I had my summer well planned. I was going to take my driver's education courses, get my driver's license, and chase girls the rest of the summer. Just as summer began, however, I found myself doubled over with a severe stomachache. It kept getting worse, and I ended up in the hospital having my ruptured appendix removed. Because of the severity of the situation, I was in the hospital recovering for nearly a week and then was limited for several more weeks. While not totally torpedoing my plans, it was a severe setback.

As an immature teen, I wondered why God had let it happen at that time. Several years later, I got an answer.

I was a young pastor visiting a church member in the hospital. He was coming out of surgery and, after a short visit, went to sleep. The room he was in had two beds. In the other bed, lying uncomfortably, was a fifteen-year-old young man. I introduced myself and tried to chat with him. He seemed rather disinterested. Then I looked him in the eye and said, "I bet I can guess why you are in here."

"No, you can't," he replied, looking at me skeptically.

"Give me one guess," I said. He agreed.

"You just had an operation, and I am guessing that you had your appendix removed."

"How did you know that?" he asked.

"Easy," I said, "I can tell by the way you are lying in the bed." Then I lifted up my shirt to show him my appendectomy scar and the scar from when I had my spleen removed. "I got this scar when I was sixteen and this one when I was thirteen." He was impressed.

"So," he said and nodded, "you know just what I am feeling."

From then on, I had his attention. He opened up and told me all about himself. We had a great talk. Before I left, I had led him to Christ.

When I got in my car to leave the hospital parking garage, the thought hit me: So this is one good reason why I had appendicitis when I was sixteen.

The God of All Comfort

Called by many the greatest Christian of us all, Paul was a very good and godly man who was the veteran of extreme hardship. Persecuted for his faith, few have suffered as much. He faced frequent imprisonments, skin-shredding whippings, bloody beatings, shipwreck, betrayal, sleeplessness, hunger, cold, nakedness, and the awful stresses of leadership (2 Corinthians 11:23–29).

Why so much affliction for such a good and godly man? According to Paul, one of the lessons he learned in the school of severe sufferings was that the best person to help a sufferer is a veteran sufferer. Note what he said to some of his friends.

> *Praise be to the God and Father of our Lord Jesus Christ, the Father of compassion*
> *and the God of all comfort, who comforts us in all our troubles, so that we can*
> *comfort those in any trouble with the comfort we ourselves have received from God.*
>
> 2 CORINTHIANS 1:3–4

Notice carefully what Paul wrote. We can paraphrase his words into three primary statements.

1. Our God is the Father of compassion and the God of all comfort.
2. When we suffer, our God comforts us.
3. God comforts us in our suffering *so that* we can comfort others in theirs.

When we suffer and learn to position ourselves to receive the comfort of God in our sorrow, we gain a priceless key that enables us to unlock hearts and minister to them more effectively. In a very real sense, suffering is a primary education and qualification for effective ministry. In commenting on this principle, one pastor wrote,

> *When a person has mastered the full curriculum of suffering—completed the course in*
> *dungeons and chains, in whips and scourgings, in shipwrecks and persecutions—then*
> *that person has received a master's degree in tribulation and is thoroughly qualified for*
> *the ministry of compassion.*[2]

Why did God allow such a good man as Paul to experience such horrible suffering? Why does God allow bad things to happen to good people? One reason is *so that* we will be better equipped to minister to others.

A Burden for Addicts

Recently, I was the guest speaker at a church in Pennsylvania. After the service, a woman named Bonnie told me her story. She had started smoking pot and drinking alcohol at the age of ten. She soon advanced to harder, intravenous drugs. For twenty years she had been bound by the painful, unrelenting chains of drug addiction, prostitution, and poverty.

Some caring Christian people had reached down, pulled her out of the gutter, and set her on the right path. They helped her discover real freedom in Christ. Clean for eight years, she now has a vibrant ministry to others who are breaking the chains of addiction.

"My heart is for the lowest of the low, the dregs of society, the hopeless and the helpless, because that's what I was," she said. "I want to help them just like someone else helped me. After all, who better to help an addict than an addict?" We could also ask, who better to help a sufferer than a sufferer?

Praying for Prodigals

You probably know of the world's most famous evangelist, Billy Graham. What you probably don't know is that two of his five children were spiritual wanderers and they broke their parents' hearts. Billy's wife, Ruth Bell Graham, used the pain she experienced as she prayed, watched, and waited for them to return to the fold to minister to others by writing a book titled *Prodigals and Those Who Love Them*.

Ruth's writing shows deep understanding of the confusion and fear of the ones who wait for their prodigals to return. The power of the book is the fact that she was writing from brokenhearted experience and practice, not theory. Because she had suffered the heartache of raising two prodigal children, she has the hard-earned credentials to minister to others with prodigals in their lives.

The Desert School of Ministry Training

Often we have a mistaken view of what qualifies us to minister effectively to others. Education is certainly helpful. Training is always good. Gifts are important. But we too often overlook the fact that it is in the loneliness of the wilderness and the difficulties of the desert that God truly prepares us to minister to others.

After enjoying the thrill of successful ministry, cohosting a popular television show, writing books, and speaking and singing to large audiences, Sheila Walsh fell apart and checked into a psychiatric hospital. She thought she checked in alone, but Jesus checked in with her. As she deeply experienced the love of God in her place of brokenness, He prepared her for much more effective ministry.

With deep understanding she writes, "You do not come out of the desert empty-handed but with a pocket full of gifts to share." One of the gifts she discovered in the desert was that she had a deeper, broader ministry than before. She says, "The amazing thing was my brokenness was a far greater bridge to others than my apparent wholeness had ever been."[3]

Looking back on the burdens and benefits of brokenheartedness, she wisely concludes, "I now believe that God delights to use those of us who have had our hearts and wills broken in the desert, who understand that if we stood in front of the Red Sea and it parted, we should get on our faces and worship, not call a press conference."[4]

"I Have Cerebral Palsy—What's Your Problem?"

The odds were cruelly stacked against young David. He was born with cerebral palsy, an incurable set of neurological disorders that permanently affect body movement and muscle coordination. When he was nine, his father died. The family home burned to the ground a few years later. His mother died from cancer when he was only fourteen.

Orphaned and shuffled from family to family, David had nowhere definite to call home. He lived with continual humiliation and ridicule from other kids. But he met Christ as a teenager. Through Christ, David triumphed over his tremendous hardships. In Christ, he discovered that he could be a victor instead of a victim.

Miraculously, God called him into a full-time ministry of evangelism, and in his early twenties, David began to hold nearly fifty revival crusades a year. Today he speaks to an average of one hundred thousand people a year in a variety of venues. He is married with four children.

I first heard him speak over twenty years ago and have never forgotten his message. At first, his slurred speech was irritating and difficult to understand. But like the rest of the audience, I was quickly captivated by his amazing story, positive attitude, and wonderful self-deprecating sense of humor. He skillfully told his incredible story of overcoming such stiff odds. Then he looked at the audience and said, "I have cerebral palsy—what's your problem?"

All of our excuses for not serving God and all of our griping at our difficulties paled in comparison to what he had endured and still battles every day. His example of relying on Christ to rise above his overwhelming obstacles was an inspiration to all of us to rise above ours.[5]

A Broken Heart in Every Pew

"I know what it's like to sit in the pew with a broken heart," writes Ruth Graham, daughter of the famous evangelist Billy and his wife, Ruth Bell Graham.[6] With genuine candor and compassion, she tells her story in the book *In Every Pew Sits a Broken Heart*.

> *My own story is not tidy. Nor is it simple. My story is messy and complicated and still being written. I have known betrayal, divorce, depression, and the consequences of bad judgment. I have struggled to parent my children through crisis pregnancy, drug use, and an eating disorder. I have known heartbreak, desperation, fear, shame, and a profound sense of inadequacy. This is not the life I envisioned. Far from it.[7]*

Out of her pain, Ruth developed a deep desire to help others. With wisdom only gleaned in the classroom of suffering and sorrow, she discovered a ministry in helping the hurting.

> *My own plans for my life had been wrecked many times over, but it was not too late to join in on what God was doing. I knew I could serve others with compassion. . . . I was willing to touch hurting and broken people with the same grace God had shown me when I was hurting and broken.[8]*

Wounded Healers

In *The Wounded Healer*, Henri Nouwen argues that we heal from our wounds. He asks a profound question:

> *Who can take away suffering without entering into it? The great illusion of leadership is to think that others can be led out of the desert by someone who has never been there.[9]*

Through the empathy that comes from having been down the same road of suffering as another, we can minister more effectively than otherwise possible. Others can tell that we truly understand their pain and feel their hurt. A connection can be made. Trust can be built. Then real ministry can occur.

In describing the power of wounded healers, a young mother whose daughter died of sudden infant death syndrome shared:

> *It's as though people who have lost someone precious speak a different language. I don't have to explain things. There is a clear understanding that is so comforting.[10]*

Why?

So why does God allow bad things to happen to good people? One reason is that the very best person to help someone who is suffering is someone who has suffered. Let me encourage you to use your pain to more effectively minister to others.

Notes

[1] In a letter from C. S. Lewis's to Sheldon Vanauken, April 22, 1953, quoted in *A Severe Mercy* (reprint, San Francisco, HarperSanFrancisco: 1987), 134.

[2] D. James Kennedy, *Turn It into Gold* (Ann Arbor, MI: Vine, 1991), 34.

[3] Sheila Walsh, "A Winter's Tale," in *The Desert Experience: Personal Reflections on Finding God's Presence and Promise in Hard Times* Nashville: Nelson, 2001), 181.

[4] Ibid., 179.

[5] David Ring's full story is available on his Web site, http://www.davidring.org/biography.html (accessed March 28, 2007).

[6] Ruth Bell Graham, *In Every Pew Sits a Broken Heart* (Grand Rapids: Zondervan, 2004), 12.

[7] Ibid., 12–13.

[8] Ibid., 168.

[9] Henri Nouwen, *The Wounded Healer* (New York: Doubleday, 1979), 40.

[10] Marcia Lattanzi-Licht, "Living with Loss: Bereaved Swim against Tide of Grief," 2001, Partnership for Caring, Inc., distributed by Knight Ridder/Tribune Information Services, http://itrs.scu.edu/fow/pages/Course/C-14.html (accessed March 28, 2007).

16

To Remove Our Self-Sufficiency
2 CORINTHIANS 12:5–10

Death by Fire

Converted at the age of eighteen, Dwight flung himself into Christian work a few years later. Highly energetic and fearless, the next decade became a whirlwind of spiritual progress and effective ministry. His Sunday school grew to a previously unprecedented size of fifteen hundred boys and girls, all from off the street, most coming to a life-changing relationship with Christ. When the nation went to Civil War, Dwight, as a leader of the Young Men's Christian Association, went to work as an evangelist, winning huge numbers of soldiers to Christ. Then he launched a Chicago church that rapidly grew in impact and size. He raised the funds and oversaw the creation of the first large, multipurpose YMCA building in America. He also helped develop unified Sunday school lessons that were soon taught by Sunday schools everywhere. All this time, he was out speaking around the country three or four days a week in large conferences and churches.

Outwardly, Dwight was a picture of spiritual power, yet he knew all of the activity was mostly the result of his own energy and zeal. He was financially broke, emotionally burned out, and spiritually bankrupt. He became deeply discouraged. Exhausted by his ministry treadmill, Dwight began to cry out to God for help. Once in a prayer meeting, he even broke down, rolling on the floor and groaning to God for spiritual power.[1] Days later an answer came to Dwight in an unexpected form. Sunday night, October 8, as he finished preaching in his church, a fire alarm rang out. Droughtlike conditions and a strong wind quickly spread the fire across the city. Within minutes, flames engulfed huge sections of the town. The next morning a brokenhearted Dwight surveyed the damage. Four square miles of city were totally consumed, eighteen thousand buildings destroyed, one hundred thousand people left homeless, and over one thousand people dead. Destroyed in the fire was the new YMCA building, Dwight's church building, and his house. Later he stood with his wife and children, staring at the ashes that had once been their home. Ironically, nothing was salvageable except a tiny toy oven. Everything he had spent his life building was gone.

Insurance had not been held on any of the buildings, leaving nothing with which to rebuild. Dwight had to begin an exhausting campaign to raise funds to try and rebuild. He hated it, admitting, "My heart was not in the work of begging. I could not appeal. I was crying all the time that God would fill me with His Spirit."[2]

For Dwight, the anguish of his incredible loss stretched into an agonizing season of honest evaluation and numbing introspection. The purpose of the cross he was bearing is always one thing, and that is death, death to self. Dwight confessed:

> *God seemed to just be showing me myself. I found I was ambitious; I was not preaching for Christ, I was preaching for ambition. I found everything in my heart that ought not be there. For four months the wrestling went on within me. I was a miserable man.*[3]

Why did a good God allow such bad things to happen to such a good man and tireless servant? Sometimes God permits pain and suffering to strip us of our self-sufficiency. It is only then that we can realize His all-sufficiency.

A New Man

For Dwight, his incredible loss led to a rebirth of true spiritual power and truly effective ministry. Later he wrote, "After four months the anointing came." Describing it, he said, "Ah, what a day!—I cannot describe it, I seldom refer to it, it is almost too sacred an experience to name—Paul had an experience he never spoke of for fourteen years—I can only say God revealed Himself to me, and I had such an experience of His love that I had to ask Him to stay His hand."[4]

Dwight explained his experience to his friend D.W., who recorded it in his diary.

> *God blessed him with a conscious incoming to his soul of a presence and power of His Spirit such as he had never known before. His heart was broken by it. He spent much time just weeping before God, so overpowering was the sense of His goodness and love.*[5]

The change in Dwight was profound. In describing the new Dwight, one of his biographers wrote: "The quality of his relationship with God and his discernment of the difference between God's call and man's was so sharpened, and his power in ministry so enlarged that it sometimes seemed to him as if he had scarcely been—let alone useful—until this blessed time."[6] Such is the power of the resurrected life.

A New Power

Soon after this event, Dwight could not escape the sense that the Lord wanted him to spend some time in England resting, studying, and praying about his future. So he went and tried to hide on the sidelines. Eventually, however, he was recognized, and a pastor asked him to preach. Revival broke out in the church, and four hundred people made professions of faith during the ten days of impromptu meetings. Later he made the amazing discovery that Marianne Adlard, a bedridden girl, had literally prayed him over to England to be the tool of revival in her church. As a result, Dwight was given opportunity to be the tool of revival in many other English churches.

Dwight manifested the power of the resurrection in every association. A decade and a half before becoming president of the United States, Woodrow Wilson mentioned an unusual encounter in a barbershop when describing Dwight.

> *I became aware that a personality had entered the room and sat in the chair next to me. . . . I purposely lingered in the room after he left and noted the singular effect his visit had upon the barbers in that shop. They talked in undertones. They did not know his name, but they knew something had elevated their thought. And I felt that I left that place as I should have left a house of worship.*[7]

Dwight L. Moody returned home to Chicago a new man, and new ministry resulted. Orphanages, schools, ministry opportunities for women, and large crusades resulted. Most of his efforts still live and thrive today, 125 years later. They include Moody Press, the Moody Bible Institute, and Moody Church. Scholars estimate that in the pretelevision age, Moody preached the gospel to more than one hundred million people, and more than one million made professions of faith in Jesus Christ.

Why did a good God allow such bad things to happen to such a good man and tireless servant? Suffering removed his self-sufficiency and enabled Moody to experience what he truly wanted, the power of God's all-sufficiency.

Same Song, Second Verse

Dwight was not the first or last person who drank of the deep waters of devastating difficulties only to find a wellspring of real life and power. The apostle Paul gave this testimony:

> *I will not boast about myself, except about my weaknesses. . . . To keep me from becoming conceited because of these surpassingly great revelations, there was given me a thorn in my flesh, a messenger of Satan, to torment me. Three times I pleaded with the Lord to take it away from me. But he said to me, "My grace is sufficient for you, for my power is made perfect in weakness." Therefore I will boast all the more gladly about my weaknesses, so that Christ's power may rest on me. That is why, for Christ's sake, I delight in weaknesses, in insults, in hardships, in persecutions, in difficulties. For when I am weak, then I am strong.*
>
> 2 Corinthians 12:5, 7–10

Paul was a high-octane guy. Prior to his encounter with Christ, he was a respected scholar, an influential, up-and-coming leader of Judaism, and a Roman citizen, as well. After meeting Christ, he became the voice of Christianity, a great church planter, a mighty missionary, and a powerful minister. Beyond that, his letters were considered the very words of God and were collected as scripture. Moreover, he was given amazing revelations of heaven and the future, unlike anyone before him.

Through it all, Paul was a scholar in the school of severe suffering. He faced hunger, homelessness, cruel criticisms, frequent imprisonments, physical beatings, spiritual attacks, and more. In suffering he learned many priceless lessons, including this: "When I am weak, then I am strong." His pain and weakness removed his pride and self-sufficiency so he could more fully experience God's strength.

In this passage, Paul mentions a source of frustration and torment neglected in his other catalogs of personal sufferings: "a thorn in my flesh, a messenger of Satan." For two millennia, scholars have debated the exact nature of this thorn in the flesh. Some think it was physical, in the form of chronic maladies, such as eye problems caused by a severe form of ophthalmia (Galatians 4:15), earaches, malaria, migraine headaches, epilepsy, or a speech disability. Others see it as an internal struggle coming in the form of incessant temptation. There are those who view the thorn as human in nature, caused by persistent persecutors or constant Christian critics. Some view the thorn as an emotional burden, such as depression. Some say it was spiritual assault, an actual messenger of Satan in demonic form.

So who's right? What was Paul's thorn?

We don't know.

I think it is intentionally unclear. Why? So no matter what your "thorn" is—physical, emotional, relational, spiritual, demonic, or whatever—you can still apply the principle that God's strength is made perfect in your weakness.

Paul considered this thorn a hindrance to wider or more effective ministry (Galatians 4:14–16), and he repeatedly petitioned God for its removal (2 Corinthians 12:8). Paul's language here suggests that this was probably the most intensive prayer struggle he ever faced.

And yet God said no three times.

Why?

It was through the continual torment of the constraining thorn that Paul was constantly reminded of the critical lesson anyone eager to be used of God must learn: "My grace is sufficient for you, for my power is made perfect in weakness."

As I study the lives of dozens of servants of God who were greatly used by Him, one common denominator links each: All have endured severe suffering. They all testify that their thorns were used to strip away their self-sufficiency and to bring them to a much deeper place of dependency on God.

Why?

So why does God allow bad things to happen to good people? Sometimes He wants to remove our self-sufficiency so we can really live His sufficiency; He reminds us of our abject weakness so we will fully rely on His amazing strength.

NOTES

[1] Sarah Cooke, *Wayside Sketches* (Grand Rapids: Shaw, 1895), 363.

[2] D. L. Moody to C. H. McCormick, April 15, 1868, Moody Bible Institute archives.

[3] Lyle W. Dorsett, *A Passion for Souls* (Chicago: Moody, 1997), 156.

[4] A. P. Fitt, *The Life of D. L. Moody* (Chicago: Moody, n.d.), 65.

[5] D. W. Whittle diary, quoted in James F. Findlay Jr., *Dwight L. Moody: American Evangelist, 1837–1899* (Chicago: University of Chicago Press, 1969), 132.

[6] Dorsett, *Passion for Souls*, 159.

[7] Woodrow Wilson, quoted in John McDowell, *What D. L. Moody Means to Me* (Northfield MA: Northfield Schools, 1937), 23.

17

To Expand Our Evangelistic Efforts
PHILIPPIANS 1:12–18

September 11, 2001

My friend Sujo John was born in Calcutta, India. He and his wife, Mary, arrived in the United States in February 2001. Only a few months after their arrival, Sujo and Mary secured employment in offices inside the World Trade Center. Wrestling with the call of God on his life, Sujo was at work on the eighty-first floor of the North Tower, or Tower 1, of the World Trade Center on September 11, 2001.

Sujo knew God was calling him to greater ministry, but he wasn't doing anything about it. He sent an e-mail to a friend at 8:05 a.m. from his office, telling him how he felt. At about 8:45 he heard a tremendous explosion, and the building shook and tilted. People were screaming.

American Airlines Flight 11, bound from Boston to Los Angeles with a full tank of fuel, had hit the floors directly above them. Debris from the aircraft flew into the office and flames erupted, consuming everything. Sujo and his coworkers looked down nearly ten floors through the huge crater in the floor.

Sujo's heart sank. He had no idea whether the plane had hit just their tower or the second tower, as well—the one where his wife worked. She was four months' pregnant with their son.

I cannot imagine the thoughts that must have been running through his head and the fear that must have been gathering in his soul as they were evacuated through the stairway. His cell phone wasn't working, so he couldn't reach his wife.

When he looked out into the courtyard, he saw complete destruction. The fuselage of the plane, burning material, shattered glass, and bodies were strewn all over the courtyard. To Sujo, it looked like a war zone.

People were being led through different exits of the World Trade Center. Sujo decided to walk toward Tower 2 in hopes he might see his wife there. As he reached Tower 2, he heard a loud explosion, then all 110 stories of Tower 2 collapsed on those standing near the foot of the building—including Sujo.

> *Huge boulders and steel and mortar were tumbling down around us. We huddled at one end of the building, and I started praying for the blood of Jesus and asking God to give His strength. As I stared death in its face, I started having peace about this place called heaven. I told the people around me that all of us were going to die and if there was anyone who did not yet know Christ that they should call upon His name. At that point, everyone around me started crying: "Jesus!"*

Even in the midst of extreme tragedy, God was drawing people to Himself. Often, the most unlikely places and most inopportune times can be used of God to get out the message of the good news of Jesus.

Sujo's story continues: The whole building had collapsed, yet not a single piece of heavy debris had fallen on him.

I found myself in three feet of white soot. I got to my feet and was surrounded by silence. I could see dead bodies all around me. God directed me to a man on the ground who had a flashlight on him. I told him that only Jesus could save us and that we had to live.

[When the man] stood up, I saw that the jacket he was wearing had "FBI" written on it. We held hands and started walking through the rubble. It was like a blizzard, one caused by all the concrete and ash that had been stirred up into the atmosphere.

The Holy Spirit then showed me a light flashing on top of an ambulance, so I told the man from the FBI that we had to head to that flashing light, since the ambulance was on the street. We somehow made it to the ambulance, which had been badly hit by flying debris. God kept the flashing light on top of the ambulance working to show me the way. From that point, it was relatively easy for us to make our way out.

In the midst of one of the greatest tragedies in American history, God was right there. He protected Sujo every step along the way. He joined the crowds that began running away from the skyscrapers to safer places. They ran and walked for an hour, and Sujo's cell phone still didn't work. Finally, at noon it rang. His wife was alive! Her subway train had reached its stop at the World Trade Center just five minutes after the first plane crashed, so Mary hadn't made it to work yet.

She told Sujo she had seen people jumping out of the burning buildings and that she had been hysterical, thinking he was dead. Eventually, they met at 39th Street in Manhattan near the ferry.

We looked back and could see both our buildings now only a pile of smoking rubble and ashes.

It is impossible to explain the sense of relief that flowed through us when we saw each other. Both of us had been so close to believing that we would never see each other again. When the explosion took place and the building was crumbling around me, images of my wife, parents, grandmother, and other loved ones flashed through my mind. The relief that we were alive was almost more than I could bear.

This story of ours is almost too good to be true. In spite of 110 floors of one of the tallest buildings in the world falling around me, I had not one single scratch on my body. For me this is proof that not only is God good, but that He knows the number of every single hair on our head. God never sleeps or dozes. This event proved to me that He is coming soon and that it is fundamentally important that we live every day as if He will be coming that very day.

I am reminded, however, that thousands died on this fateful day. We will all have to go one day. It was not our time to go that day. It is appointed for all men to die once. We are here to challenge the world with the question "Do you know where you are going?"[1]

Why did God allow Sujo to experience such a horrific nightmare? First, it gave him an opportunity to share Jesus with dying coworkers who desperately needed Him. Beyond that, it showed Sujo the miraculous power of God who delivered both he and his wife from death. But the most important outcome was that by looking death in the face and seeing people die all around him, Sujo recognized the call of God on his life. He was given an unquenchable burden and a flaming passion to go to the world with the question, "Do you know where you are going?"

Immediately following the tragic terrorist attacks of September 11, 2001, media from all over the world took interest in the powerful story of Sujo's miraculous deliverance. His story was featured in the *New York Times, Times-London*, CBC, *National Post*, BBC, "The 700 Club, Billy Graham Special," and TBN. Speaking opportunities poured in from all over North America. Because of experiencing the horrors of September 11, 2001, Sujo John was launched into full-time proclamation evangelism that has taken him to over four hundred cities in North America, Asia, and Europe and has resulted in the salvation of thousands.

Why do bad things happen to good people? Sometimes it is to expand the kingdom of God by creating greater evangelistic opportunities.

The Jailhouse Revival

The apostle Paul was imprisoned in Rome for his faith. Awaiting possible execution, he wrote a letter to his friends at a church in Greece.

> *Now I want you to know, brothers, that what has happened to me has really served to advance the gospel. As a result, it has become clear throughout the whole palace guard and to everyone else that I am in chains for Christ. Because of my chains, most of the brothers in the Lord have been encouraged to speak the word of God more courageously and fearlessly.*

PHILIPPIANS 1:12–14

Paul used his suffering as a means of sharing his faith. God knows that the best way to get the attention of a seeker is not necessarily by having His children live pain-free lives. One of the best ways to get the attention of sincere spiritual seekers is for them to see a Christian suffering triumphantly. Trials create the opportunity for testimony.

There were three groups of people who were evangelistically helped because Paul was in prison. Probably none of them would have been helped if he hadn't been imprisoned.

The first people who benefited from Paul's imprisonment were his guards. Paul was a major political prisoner. In the past, God had miraculously opened prison doors to set him free. The Romans were taking no chances, so Paul was in chains, probably chained to a Roman guard.

Picture this. When one guard would come on duty, Paul would tell him about Jesus and the guy might get saved. That guard would go off duty and another one would be chained to Paul. Paul would tell this guard about Jesus, and he might be converted. One by one the guards who were chained to Paul would end up giving their lives to Christ. Roman guards who never would have been exposed to the gospel any other way were converted to Christ because Paul was chained in prison. One man called it a spiritual chain reaction.

A second set of people positively impacted by Paul's imprisonment included the other Christian leaders. Because of the fierce persecution, most Christians were not as bold as Paul. But when they saw what Paul had the courage to do inside the prison, they got on board outside the prison. They became bold in telling others about Jesus outside the prison because Paul was bold inside the prison.

A third, and by far largest, group has benefited from Paul's prison suffering. You see, while Paul was in prison, the Philippians sent him a care package. He sent them a lengthy thank-you note that we now call the letter to the Philippians. They were blessed by Paul's prison epistle, and so have been millions of others across the centuries. This letter, Philippians, is one he might not have had reason or time to write if he had not been suffering in prison.

Much good came from the bad. The message of Christ was spread throughout the prison, around the area, and down through history. Wow!

Why?

So why do bad things happen to good people? What good can come from the bad? Maybe the reason you are suffering is to open up doors of testimony that would have been otherwise closed. Maybe your suffering will allow you to reach someone for Christ who might not be reached otherwise.

NOTE

[1] Sujo John's story is used by permission. He is available for speaking opportunities and can be reached via his Web site, www.sujojohn.com, http://www.sujojohn.com/about_sujo_sept11.html (accessed March 28, 2007).

18

To Promote Us to Greater Glory
PHILIPPIANS 1:21; PSALM 116:15

"Why? Why? Why did God allow this to happen?" the teenage girl sobbed, brokenhearted by her grandmother's death after a long, painful battle with cancer.

"Think of it this way," replied her wise pastor. "Look back to that last week of her life when she was suffering so severely. What if you had the power to take away all of her pain? If you had that power, would you use it?"

"Of course I would remove her pain," the young lady said.

"What if you also had the resources to send her on a deluxe vacation in a beautiful place with her close friends? Would you send her?"

"Yes," she replied.

"Let's also say that you could give her a brand-new body that would be much better than her old one ever was. Would you give it to her?"

"Yes."

"What if you could move her out of her little house in the bad neighborhood and set her up in a new house in a great neighborhood? Would you do it?"

"Yes," the girl said. "But you know I can't do all those things for her."

"That's true," the pastor replied. "But God can, and He did when He took your grandmother to heaven." He continued, "Your grandmother is on an eternal vacation. God has a brand-new body for her. She is in a place with no suffering or death. She is seeing friends and family members she hasn't seen in years. She lives in a place especially designed for her, and it's in the best neighborhood on the planet."

"I see," she said. "So that's why God let Grandmother die."

"That's right," he said. "The death of someone we love is hard for us, but going to heaven is certainly good for them."

"But I'll miss her," she said.

"I know," he replied gently. "But remember, the years on earth in which we will miss our loved ones who have gone to heaven will go by quickly. They are next to nothing compared with eternity."

Graduation Day!

What is often seen as the very worst thing that can happen to a person—death—is actually a very, very good thing for God's people. For the Christian, death is not a termination, but rather a graduation to glory and a promotion to pure pleasure.

The first followers of Jesus believed the Bible taught that heaven is a genuine, literal, physical place. They always described heaven in concrete terms as a beautiful, wonderful, joyful, literal eternal home. Their confidence was obvious. For example, in AD 125 a non-Christian named Aristides wrote to a friend attempting to explain why the new religion called "Christianity" was so successful.

> *If any righteous man among the Christians passes from this world, they rejoice and offer thanks to God, and they escort his body with songs and thanksgiving as if he were setting from one place to another nearby.*[1]

For Christians, death is merely the door to the ultimate fulfillment of our dreams and destiny. When Christians die, they do not cease to live; rather, they start to live on a much higher level than any of us can possibly imagine.

Think about it. When Christians die, they don't pass away; they go on ahead. They don't leave home; they go home. They don't pass on; they are promoted up. They do not leave the land of the living to enter the land of the dying. No. They leave the land of the dying to enter the land of the living.

I recently had the opportunity to study everything the Bible teaches about heaven.[2] I came away from that study thrilled with the glorious joy awaiting us in heaven. Some of the amazing truths I discovered about heaven include:

1. Heaven is a literal place, more real than anywhere you have ever been.
2. Heaven is the home you always wanted.
3. Heaven is the place of the best parties ever.
4. Heaven is the most exciting place in the universe.
5. Heaven, on its worst day, is better than earth on its best day.
6. Heaven is the home of the most, the biggest, and the best reunions imaginable.
7. Heaven is a world far greater than this one but far less than the one to come.
8. Paradise, or heaven, is a restored, purified, and perfected Garden of Eden.
9. Heaven will be the site of a wonderful awards banquet.
10. You can increase your capacity to enjoy heaven tomorrow by the choices you make today.
11. In heaven we will get a total body makeover.
12. Heaven will host the greatest wedding of them all.
13. Heaven will be a glorious kingdom ruled by King Jesus.
14. One day, heaven will have a glorious capital city.
15. Heaven is God's home.
16. Heaven will ultimately be a God-filled, pleasure-packed, fresh, thirst-quenching inheritance available to all who truly want to be there.
17. In heaven we will associate with amazing creatures called angels.
18. We will enjoy animals in heaven.
19. Heaven is a mind-expanding experience.
20. Heaven is the place where dreams come true.
21. Heaven is accessible from anywhere on earth through faith in Jesus Christ.

I Can't Lose!

Paul had lived a life full of thrilling adventure as he followed Jesus. Now he was old, tired, and ready for relief. His body ached from the beatings and hardships he had endured for Christ. Now locked in a prison because of his faith, he was smart enough to know that if he pushed the right buttons, he would be executed. That would end the persecution and the pain. He would get to go to a much better place.

Yet there were people on earth who still counted on him. They needed his leadership and teaching. So a dilemma developed. He was confident that with enough prayer support he could get out so he could help more people. But should he? Or should he press his point and find his neck on the executioner's block? Then he could go to enjoy heaven. In a letter to his friends, he described his dilemma and why he chose deliverance over death.

And I'm going to keep that celebration going because I know how it's going to turn out. Through your faithful prayers and the generous response of the Spirit of Jesus Christ, everything he wants to do in and through me will be done. I can hardly wait to continue on my course. I don't expect to be embarrassed in the least. On the contrary, everything happening to me in this jail only serves to make Christ more accurately known, regardless of whether I live or die. They didn't shut me up; they gave me a pulpit! Alive, I'm Christ's messenger; dead, I'm his bounty. Life versus even more life! I can't lose.

As long as I'm alive in this body, there is good work for me to do. If I had to choose right now, I hardly know which I'd choose. Hard choice! The desire to break camp here and be with Christ is powerful. Some days I can think of nothing better. But most days, because of what you are going through, I am sure that it's better for me to stick it out here. So I plan to be around awhile, companion to you as your growth and joy in this life of trusting God continues.

PHILIPPIANS 1:19–26 THE MESSAGE

Notice the sentence at the end of that first paragraph: "Alive, I'm Christ's messenger; dead, I'm his bounty. Life versus even more life! I can't lose." What an unbeatable outlook on life. To continue to live was life. But to die was more life, eternal life, a higher quality of life. He could not lose!

Paul understood that for the believer, physical death is merely a step into eternal life. The "bad" of death is nullified by the "better" of heaven.

Saint Bert

My mom was a saint. I know that theologically all who have been born again are "saints" (see Philippians 1:1). At salvation we are "sainted" or "separated out" from this world to our God through faith in Jesus Christ. But my mom's sainthood was special. I am not saying that just because she was my mom. I am saying that because in the later years of her life, she so radiated the love of God that her pastor began to call her *Saint Bert*, and the nickname stuck.

Not long ago, after years of battling heavy physical afflictions, she quietly traded this life for the next. In preparing to speak at her memorial service, one verse quickly came to mind.

Precious in the sight of the Lord is the death of his saints.

PSALM 116:15

Mom's death was precious in the eyes of her Lord. This is because she, like all of us, was very valuable to Him because of the steep price He paid to redeem her. Her death was also precious because through her prayers, generosity, and loving acceptance of hurting people, she had become such a sweet and beloved person.

As a pastor, I have attended and participated in hundreds of funerals. There are but a handful I will never forget because it was obvious to me that the host of heaven had left heaven to join us in attendance. There seemed to be a golden glow in the room and the hint of angel music dancing in the air. The funeral was a glorious celebration of a wonderful, Christ-centered life and an anticipated arrival in heaven.

Why?

So why does God allow His people to experience the negative of death? Because He knows that death is the door to higher, greater, eternal life. It is a gift of blessed relief from pain and rest from labor. Even though we miss our loved ones who have gone ahead of us, we rejoice in the joy they have entered into.

NOTES

[1]Aristides, *The Apology of Aristides the Philosopher*, 15, http://www.earlychristianwritings.com/text/aristides-kay.html (accessed September 20, 2006).

[2]See Dave Earley, *The 21 Most Amazing Truths about Heaven* (Uhrichsville, OH: Barbour, 2006).

19

To Give Us Further Instruction
Hebrews 12; Psalm 119:67, 71

When C. S. Lewis was between the tender ages of six and eight, his mother suffered and died. As a young man, Lewis fought in World War I, where he faced the horrors of seeing friends grotesquely wounded and killed. As an adult, he pursued a relationship with his emotionally distant father, to no avail. Later in life, he fell hopelessly in love with an unlikely woman. She was a divorced, former communist atheist, who had recently become a Christian. Her name was Joy. She became the joy of his life. A popular movie was made of their courtship and marriage called *Shadowlands*.

Early in their marriage, Joy developed cancer. A few years later, she died. Out of his sorrow, Lewis developed a deeper appreciation of some of the costly benefits of pain and grief. One was the ability of agony to get our attention. With deep wisdom he wrote, "Pain is God's megaphone to rouse a deaf world."[1]

Why does God allow bad things to crowd into the lives of good people? One reason is that in pain we learn to hear God's voice. As one observed, "It is where we are wounded that God speaks to us."[2]

In Pain We Learn to Hear God's Voice

Steve was a good father, husband, and Christian. He also was a highly successful commercial Realtor who lost his company when the economy went south. Out of work and out of options, he heard God's voice through the megaphone of his pain. Adversity taught Steve many valuable lessons.

> *I began to see that my walk with Him had gradually eroded during years of fruitfulness. With the blinder removed from my eyes, I began to see myself in an unattractive new light; God was showing me hard truths about myself that I didn't want to see. Such things as my reputation, the esteem of my colleagues, and my net worth and assets had become pagan idols in my life. . . .*
>
> *These things all came as a shock because I thought I had it all together. God was "lovingly beating me up". . . . These were difficult lessons to learn, but I sat at His feet and listened to His Word. And in the midst of the discipline, I came to love Him more than I had in the past—much more.*[3]

Nancie also was a student in the school of suffering. Her story is that she was the model pastor's wife, publisher, mother, and church member. Yet bad things began to pile up on her. Nancie found herself numbly enduring the loss of her parents, the challenges of raising five children, one of whom had special needs, chronic pain, exhausting fatigue, paralyzing depression, and a dizzying schedule. She felt completely incapable of managing the overdesigned, overbusy, draining life she had created for herself.

When breakdown forced her to confront her pain, she learned many lessons. One of the most important was to listen to God. She writes, "I learned that the desert is not a tragedy. The tragedy is to fail to hear what God was saying to me there."[4]

In Pain We Learn Lessons in the School of Suffering

The first-century Roman world was a faith-draining world for a Jewish Christian. Read slowly from Hebrews 10:32–34; 11:35–38 the roll call of pain the Hebrew Christians had to endure that could only be called "a great contest and conflict of sufferings."

- Being made a public spectacle through reproaches and tribulations
- Seeing friends and loved ones endure the same
- Enduring the seizure of property
- Being tortured and refusing to be released
- Facing jeers and flogging
- Being chained and put in prison
- Being destitute, persecuted, and mistreated
- Finding shelter only in deserts, mountains, caves, and holes in the ground
- Facing death by stoning, being sawed in two, or being beheaded by the sword
- Having nothing to wear but sheepskins and goatskins

My hardships seem small compared to what they endured. It was to these people who were living in the school of suffering that God said, don't throw away your faith (Hebrews 10:35), keep running the marathon of faith (12:1), and focus your eyes on Jesus (vv. 2–3).

I often need to be reminded that most of life is education, not destination. One of the primary agents of instruction is adversity. There is much to be learned in the academy of agony. Sometimes the purpose is teaching us a truth, an attitude, or even a skill that we did not previously know. Often the objective is to correct our thinking, attitudes, or behavior.

Chapter 12 of the letter to the Hebrews addresses the matter of education through adversity. The author reminds us of several lessons we can learn when the storms of life grow intense.

1. *Don't feel sorry for yourself. You are not the only one who is suffering.*

   In this all-out match against sin, others have suffered far worse than you, to say nothing of what Jesus went through—all that bloodshed! So don't feel sorry for yourselves.

   HEBREWS 12:4 THE MESSAGE

Suffering has a way of isolating us from contact with others. We often feel as if we are the only one or that the extent of our suffering is much greater than others. Not true. Every human faces hardship. Adversity is the atmosphere of humanity.

2. *Don't blow off the lessons or, on the other hand, be crushed by suffering. Parental discipline is part of family life. The fact that God brings discipline into our lives proves that we are His children.*

   Or have you forgotten how good parents treat children, and that God regards you as his children? "My dear child, don't shrug off God's discipline, but don't be crushed by it either. It's the child he loves that he disciplines; the child he embraces, he also corrects."

   HEBREWS 12:5–6 THE MESSAGE

When my boys were small, they occasionally (okay, frequently) needed some discipline. We jokingly referred to administering the "board of education to the seat of understanding."

Our neighbor boys loved to be at our house and feel like part of the family. One day I caught them all in the backyard hiding behind the shed gambling with cards and poker chips.

As I gathered up my sons to discipline them, the neighbor boys asked, "What about us?"

"I only discipline my sons," I said. "It's up to your father to discipline you."

One reason I know I am the child of God is because He does not let me get away with much. If He did not love me so much, He would not discipline me so severely. Suffering is not a sign that my heavenly Father does not love me; it is evidence that He does.

3. Don't quit. Discipline is part of God's parenting process.

God is educating you; that's why you must never drop out. He's treating you as dear children.

HEBREWS 12:7 THE MESSAGE

Once, when my son Andrew got in trouble I found him in his room packing up his bags to run away. He was about four or five years old at the time. I asked him why he was leaving, and he told me it was because I was too mean. Today both he and I are glad he didn't run away. After a few years of going through the struggles of growing up, he has become a wonderful Christian young man, and we have a very close relationship.

I am coming to understand that most of my years on earth will be spent in the school of suffering. This is not because God does not love me, but because He does and He is preparing me for a close relationship with Him throughout eternity.

4. Don't view what you are experiencing as punishment. It is training.

God is educating you. . . . This trouble you're in isn't punishment; it's training, the normal experience of children.

HEBREWS 12:7–8 THE MESSAGE

One of the encouragements I have gained in researching and writing this book is that I have been reminded that every Christian goes through periods of discipline and difficulty. No believer is immune. No one is beyond the need of the Father's loving instruction.

5. Embrace God's training.

Only irresponsible parents leave children to fend for themselves. Would you prefer an irresponsible God? We respect our own parents for training and not spoiling us, so why not embrace God's training so we can truly live?

HEBREWS 12:9 THE MESSAGE

Real growth occurs when we move beyond numbly enduring suffering to the point of actually embracing it. I have to confess that even when I do try to welcome hardship, I struggle to maintain that outlook. But, as we have seen throughout this book, God produces many positive blessings in our life through affliction. As long as we remember that, we can embrace His training process.

6. ***Don't get discouraged. Maintain the big perspective.***

> *While we were children, our parents did what seemed best to them. But God is doing what is best for us, training us to live God's holy best. At the time, discipline isn't much fun. It always feels like it's going against the grain. Later, of course, it pays off handsomely, for it's the well-trained who find themselves mature in their relationship with God.*
>
> HEBREWS 12:10–11 THE MESSAGE

If we look at our current difficulty, it can be discouraging. But present pain plays an important role in a larger, longer process of producing maturity in our lives. Look at the ultimate rewards instead of the existing sorrows.

7. ***Don't go it alone.***

> *So don't sit around on your hands! No more dragging your feet! Clear the path for long-distance runners so no one will trip and fall, so no one will step in a hole and sprain an ankle. Help each other out. And run for it!*
>
> HEBREWS 12:12–13 THE MESSAGE

Suffering will shrink your world. The drudgery of dealing with daily difficulty and suffering can cause you to circle the wagons too tightly and focus on you and yours completely. One day you will wake up on a tiny, lonely island. Paradoxically, often the best way to lighten your load is to help carry someone else's burdens for a while.

My mom battled persistent respiratory challenges, tremors, macular degeneration, and arthritis, along with depression and other issues. Yet she was able to go on and remain contagiously positive in spite of it all. One of her secrets was that she found tremendous joy and relief in helping others. Visiting people in the hospital, taking flowers to shut-ins, and giving money to struggling young couples were some of her keys to being a victor over her difficulties.

In Pain We Learn to Live God's Word

One of the greatest Bible scholars and teachers in history, Martin Luther, said, "Affliction is the best book in my library."[5] Another, Charles Spurgeon, said, "Very little is to be learned without affliction. If we would be scholars, we must be sufferers."[6]

We all have a tendency to get off track, especially when it comes to the ways of God.

> *Before I was afflicted I went astray, but now I obey your word.*
>
> PSALM 119:67
>
> *It was good for me to be afflicted so that I might learn your decrees.*
>
> PSALM 119:71

Corrie ten Boom was thrown into a horrendous German concentration camp because of her faith in Christ. With an aching body, an empty stomach, and freezing hands, she wrote these words from her lice-infested bed: "We are in God's training school and learning much."[7]

My friend John Thomas writes, "The real truths of scripture cannot be completely grasped in a classroom setting. They are discovered and only fully understood in the laboratory of life."[8] He's right.

Why?

So why does God allow bad things to storm the gates of good people? Often it is merely part of the parenting process, designed to teach us how to practically live out the truths of God's Word.

NOTES

[1]C. S. Lewis, *The Problem of Pain* (New York: Macmillan, 1940), 93.

[2]W. H. Auden, quoted in *The Desert Experience: Personal Reflections on Finding God's Presence and Promise in Hard Times* (Nashville: Nelson, 2001), 72.

[3]Quoted in David Jeremiah, *A Bend in the Road* (Nashville: W, 2000), 128–29.

[4]Nancie Carmichael, "The Gift of the Desert," in *The Desert Experience: Personal Reflections on Finding God's Presence and Promise in Hard Times* (Nashville: Nelson, 2001), 78.

[5]Martin Luther, quoted by Elizabeth Skoglund, *Coping* (Ventura, CA: Regal, 1971), 23.

[6]Charles Haddon Spurgeon, *The Treasury of David*, vol. 6, Psalms 119–124 (Grand Rapids: Baker, 1981), 166.

[7]Corrie ten Boom, *Clippings from My Notebook* (Minneapolis: World Wide, 1982), 56.

[8]John Thomas and Gary Habermas, *Why Me?* unpublished manuscript, 112.

20

To Call Us to Increased Prayer
JAMES 1:5

I am a dad. I have three sons named Luke (sixteen), Andrew (eighteen), and Daniel (twenty). The older ones are in college. I think each of them would tell you that I have a very good relationship with them, but. . .when everything is going great, they don't call me much. If I call them, they are happy to talk. But they are busy, and they don't need me.

However, let them face some adversity they think I can help them with, and they are quick to call. Why?

They call because they need me.

I am happy to hear from them and glad to help.

It's not that they're bad guys. They aren't. Actually, they are great young men. It's not that they are selfish, unloving, uncaring brats—not at all. It's just that they are normal young men.

Let me ask you a question.

When do you talk to your heavenly Father most frequently?

Many of us would argue that prayer is a very important activity. Yet the vast majority of us would admit that we don't pray as much as we would like.

When do you pray most often?

Do you pray more when everything is going great or when everything is going wrong?

I thought so.

We usually pray most when times are tough.

Why? Because it is when times are tough that we realize how desperately we need God.

Why does a good God allow His children to face bad things? One reason is that privation, pressure, pain, and problems can prompt us closer to Him through prayer. We seek Him for provision, direction, and help.

Who Ya Gonna Call?

The pastor of the first church in the world, Pastor James, and his congregation of Hebrew Christians were good people who faced a plethora of problems. They dealt with severe opposition and persecution (Hebrews 10:32–34). Many were publicly exposed to insult and persecution. Some had their property confiscated. Others were imprisoned. Some of their leaders were killed for their faith (Acts 8, 12). In his profound statement about the benefits of facing trials, James recommended that his readers add increased prayer to the list.

> *Consider it pure joy, my brothers, whenever you face trials of many kinds, because you know that the testing of your faith develops perseverance. Perseverance must finish its work so that you may be mature and complete, not lacking anything. If any of you lacks wisdom, he should ask God, who gives generously to all without finding fault, and it will be given to him.*
>
> JAMES 1:2–5

"He should ask God." Suffering can be confusing. We wonder: *Why me? Why now? When will it get better? What do I do now? Which way do we turn? Who do we tell what? Who can help me through this?*

James tells us that when we are suffering and are not sure what to do, we need to call on God. God wants to help us. He will give us the wisdom we need.

David: A Prayer for Every Problem

David's life was both thrilling and excruciating. He knew lofty highs, but he also experienced devastating lows. Falsely accused, nearly murdered, hunted like a fugitive, hiding for his life in a desert wilderness, he experienced his share of problems. Plus, he had numerous battles with the barbaric Philistine armies. Added to those adversities were the agonies caused by his sins. Public ridicule, the death of a child, and bone-aching guilt and shame were heartbreaks he brought on himself. Family problems nearly destroyed him. One of his daughters was raped by his son. Another son grew resentful and rebellious, launched a successful political coup that kicked David off his throne, and was later tragically killed. What a massive, miserable mess!

Out of the volume of his life and sorrows, David wrote more than seventy-five songs. Many are biographical, reading like journal entries. A significant number were prayers, or better, pleadings with God written from the depths of his difficulties. David was called "a man after God's own heart" in part because he persistently turned his problems into prayer. His psalms teach us there is a prayer for every problem. For example, when he began to run for his life from crazed King Saul and his troops, David turned to God and prayed.

> *Save me, O God, by your name; vindicate me by your might. Hear my prayer, O God; listen to the words of my mouth. Strangers are attacking me; ruthless men seek my life—men without regard for God. Surely God is my help; the Lord is the one who sustains me.*
>
> PSALM 54:1–4

> *O my Strength, I watch for you; you, O God, are my fortress.*
>
> PSALM 59:9

In a humiliating turn of events while running from Saul, David had to fake insanity to keep from being killed by the Philistines. The great warrior had to become the drooling village idiot. This problem was turned into prayer. Later he wrote of his deliverance.

> *I sought the Lord, and he answered me; he delivered me from all my fears. Those who look to him are radiant; their faces are never covered with shame. This poor man called, and the Lord heard him; he saved him out of all his troubles. . . . The eyes of the Lord are on the righteous and his ears are attentive to their cry. . . . A righteous man may have many troubles, but the Lord delivers him from them all.*
>
> PSALM 34:4–6, 15, 19

Cries from the Cave

At one point, with Saul and his army breathing down David's neck, he was forced to hide out in a cave. That's right—a dark, dank, dirty cave. Maybe you feel as though you are in a cave of hardship. Noted English author and preacher Charles Spurgeon observed, "Caves make good closets for prayer."[1] Turn your cave into your prayer closet. David did.

David did not come to God with polite, memorized words or impressive eloquence. David's despair and dire circumstances invoked in him a deep inner wailing. He *cried ou* to God. It has been said that the best style of prayer is that which cannot be called anything else but a cry.

I figure that if the pain is so severe that I'm going to cry anyway, I may as well cry out to God. David knew what it meant to cry out to God. Listen to the confident cries and pleading prayers for help he offered God from the cave.

> *I cry out to God Most High, to God, who fulfills his purpose for me. He sends from heaven and saves me, rebuking those who hotly pursue me; God sends his love and his faithfulness.*
>
> PSALM 57:2–3

> *I cry aloud to the Lord; I lift up my voice to the Lord for mercy. I pour out my complaint before him; before him I tell my trouble. . . . I cry to you, O Lord; I say, "You are my refuge, my portion in the land of the living." Listen to my cry, for I am in desperate need.*
>
> PSALM 142:1–2; 5–6

His hard times were not immediately relieved. David lived the lonely life of a fugitive for many difficult desert years. His career was shot, his reputation marred, his family removed. He was homeless and, at times, hopeless. The sad emptiness of the sparse wilderness must have evoked images of better days and bred a deep longing in his soul. In his pain, at night, alone in the desert wilderness, he cried out to God. Hear the anguish in his prayers.

> *O God, you are my God, earnestly I seek you; my soul thirsts for you, my body longs for you, in a dry and weary land where there is no water.*
>
> PSALM 63:1

When the ugly ordeal with Saul was finally finished, David gazed back on his years of hardship and marveled at God's response to his prayers. Triumphantly he testified of God's rescue. Read carefully his powerfully poetic imagery.

> *I love you, O Lord, my strength. The Lord is my rock, my fortress and my deliverer; my God is my rock, in whom I take refuge. He is my shield and the horn of my salvation, my stronghold. I call to the Lord, who is worthy of praise, and I am saved from my enemies.*
>
> PSALM 18:1–3

> *The cords of death entangled me; the torrents of destruction overwhelmed me. The cords of the grave coiled around me; the snares of death confronted me. In my distress I called to the Lord; I cried to my God for help. From his temple he heard my voice; my cry came before him, into his ears.*
>
> PSALM 18:4–6

> *He reached down from on high and took hold of me; he drew me out of deep waters. He rescued me from my powerful enemy, from my foes, who were too strong for me. They confronted me in the day of my disaster, but the Lord was my support. He brought me out into a spacious place; he rescued me because he delighted in me.*
>
> PSALM 18:16–19

Never Far from the Need to Pray

After David finally became king, his problems did not disappear; they merely took different forms. Again he turned his problems into prayer. For example, when confronted about his adulterous sin, he longingly pleaded for cleansing. Out of a broken and repentant heart he wrote the classic Fifty-first Psalm.

> *Have mercy on me, O God, according to your unfailing love; according to your great compassion blot out my transgressions. Wash away all my iniquity and cleanse me from my sin. . . . Cleanse me with hyssop, and I will be clean; wash me, and I will be whiter than snow. Let me hear joy and gladness; let the bones you have crushed rejoice. Hide your face from my sins and blot out all my iniquity.*
>
> PSALM 51:1–2, 7–9

One of the most heartbreaking seasons of David's life was when his son Absalom turned against him and took the throne from him. It was an ugly, nasty, vile affair. I can't imagine how deeply it must have hurt him to have his own son repudiate everything about him and rebel so cunningly and violently. I can only guess at the pain he felt when he had to flee his throne because his people had turned against him. Yet confidently David prayed.

> *O Lord, how many are my foes! How many rise up against me! Many are saying of me, "God will not deliver him." But you are a shield around me, O Lord; you bestow glory on me and lift up my head. To the Lord I cry aloud, and he answers me from his holy hill.*
>
> PSALM 3:1–4

> *I lie down and sleep; I wake again, because the Lord sustains me. I will not fear the tens of thousands drawn up against me on every side.*
>
> PSALM 3:5–6

Turn Your Problems into Prayer

David was not the only one who allowed pain to press him to God in prayer. The secret to the success of people like Moses, Hannah, Asa, Hezekiah, Elijah, Nehemiah, Mary, Peter, Daniel, and Paul was that they learned to turn problems into prayer. We must do the same. Maybe you want to read back through the prayers of David highlighted in this chapter and make some of them your prayers. Use them to cry out to God.

Why?

What good can come from the bad things that we face? Our problems prompt us to draw closer to our heavenly Father in prayer.

NOTE

[1]Charles Haddon Spurgeon, *The Treasury of David*, vol. 7 (Byron Center, MI: Associated Publishers and Authors, 1970), 7:293.

21

To Refine Our Faith
1 PETER 1:6–9

Tested by Fire

When he awoke on that Thanksgiving Day morning, Merrill Womach was a handsome, vibrant man actively engaged in his expanding Christian music business and singing career. Yet by early afternoon, his life took on a devastating new direction as his plane crashed in a sea of flames. Amazingly, as the EMTs were pulling him from the fiery wreck and loading him onto a stretcher, he began singing praise to God!

Graciously, God spared his eyesight and vocal cords through the horrible fire and the numerous surgeries. Miraculously, his voice actually grew richer and fuller than before.

But Merrill's hands and head had been charred black and bloody by the furious flames of the fateful plane crash. His once handsome face was horribly disfigured and scarred. All his features had been consumed by the flames. His physical pain was drawn out, intense, and agonizing. But his emotional pain was much greater. Imagine how crushed he felt when he overheard his nurse say to an orderly, "Have you seen that horrible-looking creature? I can hardly touch him."[1] Think of how his wife, Virginia, must have felt to see nothing but a black charcoal blob where her husband's face had been.

Over the next fourteen years, Merrill somehow endured more than fifty excruciating skin-graft operations. Skin was taken from the non-charred parts of his body and sown onto the burned sections. Recovery from such operations was long, frustrating, and intensely painful.

By day there were painful treatments. At night he faced frightening nightmares of burning alive or being thrown into an oven or having his skin cut off with a machete. Understandably, he feared drug addiction to painkillers, and he battled severe seasons of loneliness, fear, and depression.

When he could finally go out in public, he was greeted by stares, laughs, fear, and insults. One woman actually yelled, "Hey, clown, take off your mask. It isn't Halloween yet."[2] Obviously, the fire severely tested Merrill's and Virginia's faith. Resolutely, they persevered, believing God had put them through the ordeal for a purpose. Virginia wrote:

> *Although it sounds strange, I feel it is an honor that God chose us. God had a purpose in all our suffering, and I believe it is to share the strength we have gained from it with others who have suffered or who will suffer tragedy in their lives.*[3]

Merrill said:

> *"God has tested us through the fire. And out of the suffering He was making something beautiful in our lives."*[4]

Why did God allow that good man to go through that awful fire? Why did his wife have to face such a trying ordeal? Often God uses the fire of affliction to mold character, refine faith, and make something more beautiful of our lives.

The Night of Regret!

I imagine it to be a night Peter would never forget and always regret. Unusually warm in Jerusalem for the spring, the heat was soon turned up on high. After an emotional meal, Jesus had led His disciples into the garden at Gethsemane for a time of rest and prayer. Jesus seemed strangely and unnecessarily energized, intense, serious, and agitated. But Peter had a hard time staying awake.

Then the reason for Jesus' mood became abundantly clear. Loud, angry voices and bright torchlights jolted him from drowsiness. The next thing Peter knew, Jesus was arrested and dragged off.

With hot adrenaline heightening his senses, Peter followed at a distance to find out what was going on—big mistake. The Sanhedrin was hot. Jesus had gone too far. Obviously Jesus was deep in very hot water, and a firestorm was coming down that had the power to engulf them all.

Fear began to pump through his veins and flow down his spine like boiling water. He was sweating. Thoughts floated through his head like angry bursts of steam.

What was going to happen to Jesus? These people wanted to kill Him.

What was to become of their movement of radical truth and love? The authorities wanted it squelched.

What about him? What was going to happen to him, Jesus' right-hand man, the one with the big sword and the big mouth? If they were going to kill Jesus, what were they going to do to him?

Fear gave way to doubt.

Was Jesus really the Messiah? Was He really the only way to God?

Was following Jesus worth the suffering Peter was about to face? What did he really believe about Jesus and about God?

Before he realized what had happened, he heard himself denying Jesus Christ not just once, but *three* times.

Immediately, he could not fathom what he had done. The fearless follower had given in to fear and had lost his faith. How could he have done it? He knew Jesus was real. This was one of the few times Jesus had ever needed him, and he had failed. Boy, had he failed.

Why did Peter give up and give in? He was so ashamed—excruciatingly shamed. He could never look at himself in the mirror again. The pain of regret was overwhelming. Brokenhearted, he put his head in his hands and sobbed.

The Day of Rejoicing!

Then came a day Peter would never forget and always rejoice over. Thousands of people were gathered in the temple courts because of the Pentecost celebration. With unusual boldness and fearless faith, Peter proudly, passionately, powerfully proclaimed the glories of the resurrected Lord Jesus Christ. They could stone him; they could crucify him. It did not matter. His faith was greater than anything they could do. Jesus was alive! He had risen from the dead! He would tell the world, no matter what it cost.

The crowd was inspired and deeply impressed by Peter's faith-filled words. They had the authoritative weight of the Word of God. The multitude accepted Peter's words, they believed them, and they were willing to obey. It was amazing. Three thousand people were willing to throw in with Jesus and be baptized in water—because of Peter and his words.

The Refining of Your Faith

It was with a clear eye and deep experience that thirty years later Peter was able to pen more faith-building words. His words were designed to encourage and educate people who were facing severe sufferings and painful persecutions because of their faith in Jesus Christ. They were good people who were trying to survive in a life full of trouble. Why were they experiencing such tough times?

Peter addressed that question. He did not sugarcoat the trials, but he did applaud their benefits. Read Peter's words carefully.

> *In this you greatly rejoice, though now for a little while you may have had to suffer grief in all kinds of trials. These have come so that your faith—of greater worth than gold, which perishes even though refined by fire—may be proved genuine and may result in praise, glory and honor when Jesus Christ is revealed. Though you have not seen him, you love him; and even though you do not see him now, you believe in him and are filled with an inexpressible and glorious joy, for you are receiving the goal of your faith, the salvation of your souls.*
>
> 1 PETER 1:6–9

Rejoicing in trials? A faith more valuable than gold? Refined by fire? What was Peter talking about?

Refined by Fire

Gold is a very precious metal. Its sparkling character, beautiful hue, malleable makeup, and unique metallurgical properties—including resistance to tarnishing and corrosion and virtual indestructibility—have made gold one of the world's most coveted precious metals since early history. Ancient Egyptian, Minoan, Assyrian, and Etruscan artists produced elaborate gold artifacts as early as 3000 BC. As increasingly complex economic systems developed, gold was used as a high-denomination currency and eventually as a backing for paper currency systems.

Yet when it is mined, gold is not in a pure state. Naturally occurring gold is dispersed throughout the earth's crust and is usually combined with other elements, such as silver, copper, platinum, and palladium. In order to isolate pure gold, a refining process must occur.

Gold is smelted by skilled craftsmen using intense heat. Fire separates the gold and silver from the dross impurities. The furnace is heated to extremely high temperatures. Gold melts at 1,062 degrees Celsius or 1,943 degrees Fahrenheit; therefore, it is smelted at temperatures above that. Refining is a practice that must be done precisely and methodically to ensure the full recovery of gold and to produce an end product that is free of impurities.

Goldsmiths heat the gold ore in a furnace. As they do, the impurities separate from the gold, and they skim them off. This takes time, as not all of the impurities were dislodged at once; different ones are only revealed as the temperature increases. After the appropriate amount of heat and subsequent removal of impurities, the final product is beautiful, pure gold.

What Peter is saying in his first letter is that he has learned that we can actually find joy in our trials *because* they can be used by God to refine our faith. While pure gold is highly valuable in this life, pure faith is much more valuable in both this life and especially in the next. Such faith can be refined only in the furnace of affliction.

The intense heat of severe suffering separates our pure faith in God from the dross of our trust in other things. Trust in material things, other people, and ourselves proves insufficient in the heat of intense trials. Only pure faith in God will get us through.

The Refiner, the Crucible, the Fire, and the Gold

Amy Carmichael lived a challenging life of selfless dedication and total abandonment to the Savior. She had one purpose: to make God's love known to those trapped in utter darkness. As a young woman, she obeyed the call of God and went to Dohnavur, India, where she served fifty-six years as a missionary, never taking a furlough.

Amy knew hardship. Living as a single female missionary in India at the end of the nineteenth century was very difficult. This was compounded by her calling to save children who had been sold into slavery by their families to be used as Hindu temple prostitutes. Once rescued, these children needed to be cared for, fed, housed, and educated. Her organization, Dohnavur Fellowship, ministered to hundreds of these children at a time.

Later in life, Amy experienced a horrific fall that left her an invalid for the remaining twenty years of her life. Amy, a gifted author, spent the time of her confinement writing many of her thirty-five beautiful books, including *Candles in the Dark*; *Edges of His Ways*; *God's Missionary*; *His Thoughts Said. . .His Father Said*; *Thou Givest. . .They Gather*; *If*; and *Toward Jerusalem*. In *Gold by Moonlight* she tells of her experience with the refiner's fire.

> *One day we took the children to see a goldsmith refine gold after the ancient manner of the East. He was sitting beside his little charcoal-fire. . .the goldsmith never leaves his crucible once it is on the fire. . . .*
>
> *In [the crucible] was the medicine made of salt, tamarind fruit, and burnt brick-dust, and embedded in it was the gold. The medicine does its appointed work on the gold, "then the fire eats it," and the goldsmith lifts the gold out with a pair of tongs, lets it cool, rubs it between his fingers, and if not satisfied puts it back again in fresh medicine.*
>
> *This time he blows the fire hotter than it was before, and each time he puts the gold into the crucible the heat of the fire is increased: "It could not bear it so hot at first, but it can bear it now; what would have destroyed it then helps it now."*
>
> *"How do you know when the gold is purified?" we asked him, and he answered, "When I can see my face in it, then it is pure."*[5]

God the Goldsmith

God is the Master Goldsmith of our faith. He wisely uses the heat of affliction to produce the pure gold of genuine trust in Him. Carefully He heats the furnace, allowing impurities in our faith to be separated from the real thing. These are skimmed off, revealing a pure faith. Beloved Bible teacher Warren Wiersbe wisely observed:

> *When God permits His children to go through the furnace, He keeps His eye on the clock and His hand on the thermostat. His loving heart knows how much and how long (1 Peter 1:6–7).*[6]

God the Goldsmith knows just the right amount of the heat of suffering He will allow in order to purify our faith. He knows exactly how long to allow our hardship to continue to make our faith more than "as good as gold." He will continue the process until He can see

His reflection in the purity of our faith.

Why?

So why does a good God allow bad things to happen to good people? Sometimes the intense heat of suffering is a refiner's fire, purifying the gold of godly faith, forging the steel of godly character.

NOTES

[1] Merrill and Virginia Womach with Mel and Lyla White, *Tested by Fire* (Grand Rapids: Revell, 1976), 29.

[2] Ibid., 104.

[3] Ibid., 123.

[4] Ibid., dustcover.

[5] Amy Carmichael, *Gold by Moonlight* (Fort Washington, PA: Christian Literature Crusade, n.d.), 36, emphasis added.

[6] Warren Wiersbe, quoted in David Jeremiah, *A Bend in the Road* (Nashville: W, 2000). 5.

What to Do When Bad Things Happen to You

Bad things will happen to good people. But God is powerful, wise, loving, and gracious, and He can use negatives to produce plenty of positives.

One of the central lessons of Christianity is this: *The real issue is not what happens to me so much as what happens in me.* Bad things will happen to you. The big question is: How will you respond to them?

As we have seen, one of the most profound stories of bad things happening to a good person is the story of Job. Job was one of the most moral, righteous, loving men on earth, yet in a rapid series of events, he lost everything—his wealth, his health, and his children. We can learn several valuable lessons from Job concerning how a good person should respond to bad things.

Job Faced His Affliction. . .

1. **With the choice to worship—Job 1:20–21**

    > At this, [the news that all his flocks, herds, servants, and his ten children had been killed] Job got up and tore his robe and shaved his head. Then he fell to the ground in worship and said: "Naked I came from my mother's womb, and naked I will depart. The Lord gave and the Lord has taken away; may the name of the Lord be praised."
    >
    > Job 1:20–21

Job faced his affliction with worship. The word here translated as "worship" means he put his face on the ground in humble submission to God. He said, "The Lord gives, the Lord takes away." He worshiped Jehovah as the One ordering his life, who is ever worthy of praise whether in His infinite wisdom He gives or takes away. Then he said, "The name of the Lord be praised." The word *praise* means to "speak highly of." Even though things were not going well for Job, God had not changed. He was still worthy of praise.

Let's learn a priceless lesson from Job: *Our response is always our choice.* We cannot control what happens to us, but we can control *how we respond to* what happens to us. We make the choice. When bad things come, how will you choose to respond? With praise and worship? Or with pouting and whining? Will you be God-focused or self-focused?

Job made his choice. He decided to praise and worship God. He got on his face and said, "The name of the Lord be praised." God is worthy even when life is rotten. God is worth it, even when life hurts badly. Real worship can be painful and costly.

2. **Without a sense of entitlement—Job 1:21; 2:9–10**

    > His wife said to him, "Are you still holding on to your integrity? Curse God and die!" He replied, "You are talking like a foolish woman. Shall we accept good from God, and not trouble?" In all this, Job did not sin in what he said.
    >
    > Job 2:9–10

Soon after losing everything, poor Job woke up covered from head to toe with painful, oozing, angry, red boils. His not-so-encouraging wife said, "Why don't you curse God and die?" But Job refused.

Job faced his affliction without a sense of entitlement. His attitude was, *I came with nothing. I will leave with nothing. What I have in between is up to God. It's God's choice. Sometimes He chooses to give, and He has given me much. Sometimes He chooses to take away. What right do I have to complain?*

Notice that he did not say what we so often are tempted to say. He did not say, "It's not fair. I have my rights. I deserve better than this. I am entitled to a pain-free, problem-free life."

No, he looked at his grief-stricken wife and said, "Shall we accept good and not trouble?" Job did not expect to live a pain-free, trouble-free life. He understood that life is not easy. It's not comfortable. It's hard. It's painful. Sometimes it really hurts. He accepted the reality without a sense of entitlement.

3. *Without sinning, losing his integrity, or cursing God—Job 1:22; 2:3, 9*

In all this, Job did not sin *by charging God with wrongdoing.*

JOB 1:22 (EMPHASIS ADDED)

Sometimes we see suffering as justification for sin. We think it is not fair; it is not right, so we have a perfectly good excuse to sin. Yet Job faced tremendous affliction without sinning. He did not allow anything, even the worst of things, to become an excuse to sin.

Then the Lord said to Satan, "Have you considered my servant Job? There is no one on earth like him; he is blameless and upright, a man who fears God and shuns evil. And he still maintains his integrity, though you incited me against him to ruin him without any reason."

JOB 2:3

His wife said to him, "Are you still holding on to your integrity?"

JOB 2:9

What is integrity? The Hebrew word speaks of wholeness, entireness, uprightness, innocence, sincerity. In Genesis 20:5 it is rendered as "a clear conscience and clean hands." It is used in Psalms as a synonym for righteousness and blamelessness.

Job was blameless before the disasters happened, and he was blameless afterward. Trials did not change him for the worse. He did not get bitter. If anything, he got better.

Satan had hoped he would curse God to His face (Job 1:11). But Job gave him no such satisfaction. To Job, God was worthy of following even when his life was in ruins. Think about it. Which God is better? A God who allows only good things or a God worth trusting even when bad things happen?

4. *Refusing to give up on life or on God—Job 2:9–10; 13:15*

Though he slay me, yet will I hope in him.

JOB 13:15

The suicide rate in the United States has skyrocketed. While twenty thousand Americans are murdered each year, thirty-one thousand take their own lives.[1] Part of this, no doubt, is the result of being a culture that does not know how to deal with pain. From our earliest years, we hear commercials telling us that we have a right to have our pain relieved. So when the type of pain hits that will not go away with a pill, we have a hard time dealing with it. When affliction hits, it is natural to want to give up.

Pain can cause us to want to quit on life. But Job did not follow his wife's advice to give up and die.

He wished he had not been born, but he did not wish himself dead or try to kill himself. He had several "good excuses" to take his life. He had lost all his wealth. All his kids had died. He was in excruciating pain. His wife encouraged him to die. Later in the book of Job, his friends tell him that all his suffering is his own fault. No one on earth gives him any encouragement to go on. On top of that, God is purposely silent. Yet Job refuses to quit on life. That is how good people are to face bad things—with a refusal to quit on life.

Even more impressively, Job did not quit on God. He did not follow the intent of Satan, which was to press him to get bitter toward God. He refused to give up on God. He had a faith that went beyond the good things and carried him through the bad. He did not believe *because of* circumstances. He believed *in spite of* circumstances. As we saw in chapter 2, this type of faith can shut Satan's mouth.

Think about it. He believed with a lot less information than we have. He had no Bible to read; it had not been written. He could not gain comfort from the book of Job. And the church did not exist then. Nevertheless, he stayed faithful. Do you realize what this shouts to us? If he could do it, so can we! We can be faithful. We can hang in there. We can go on.

5. *With questions—Job 3:11; 7:20; 21:7*

> *"Why did I not perish at birth, and die as I came from the womb?"*
>
> JOB 3:11

> *"If I have sinned, what have I done to you, O watcher of men? Why have you made me your target? Have I become a burden to you?"*
>
> JOB 7:20

> *"Why do the wicked live on, growing old and increasing in power?"*
>
> JOB 21:7

A myth running through Christianity says that good Christians don't question God. Not so. The presence or absence of questions does not reveal the level of our faith. Real faith wrestles through questions. And in the face of pain, it is normal to ask questions. If we asked no questions, we would not be human. We would be mere robots. God does not mind us asking questions. His person and past history can stand up to our questions.

6. *With genuine grief—Job 3:1; 6:1–3*

> *Then Job replied: "If only my anguish could be weighed and all my misery be placed on the scales! It would surely outweigh the sand of the seas—no wonder my words have been impetuous."*
>
> JOB 6:1–3

The reason Job's response to affliction is so compelling is because he was no robot. He was flesh and blood, a human being with feelings and emotions. This man lost his wealth, his career, his employees, and his businesses. His children were killed. His health was gone. He was in constant physical pain. So what did he do? He did what any human being must do—he grieved.

Job suffered victoriously, but he did not suffer without grief. This is another of those hurtful Christian myths: Strong Christians do not grieve. That is untrue, as grief is a natural expression of humanity. *Being a Christian does not make me less of a human. It makes me more of one.* Failing to grieve is a mistake.

When I counsel with families who have lost loved ones, I encourage them to grieve. They should go ahead and allow themselves to feel common emotions that come from loss. They need to work through the inevitable sense of shock and denial and the feelings of anger and guilt. They need to acknowledge the numbing sensation of loss.

7. *With prayer for others—Job 42:10*

I have read several books about Job, and they miss what I consider to be one of the biggest keys to this book. When you read Job, you read of his loss of wealth, health, and family. You read of his grief and questions, his meeting with God, and finally, of his release from the flames of affliction. When you read that section, be sure that you do not overlook verse 10.

> *After Job had prayed for his friends, the Lord made him prosperous again and gave him twice as much as he had before.*
>
> Job 42:10

God did not free Job from his pain and bless him with twice as much *until* he changed his focus from himself to others and prayed for his friends. Suffering has an ugly way of making us extremely self-centered. Life keeps closing in until all we can see is our problems and our pain. This must not be allowed to continue. Yes, we need to vent our frustrations, and yes, we need to grieve. But before too long, we need to get our eyes off ourselves and on the needs of others. This will lessen our pain even if it does not alleviate it completely.

When our affliction makes us self-oriented, it wins. But when we use it to be others-oriented, we win. We all win. If you are suffering, use it as motivation to minister to someone else.

8. *With desire for a mediator—Job 9:33*

> *"If only there were someone to arbitrate between us, to lay his hand upon us both."*
>
> Job 9:33

"Guess what? I'm a meditator," my oldest son proudly proclaimed one day when he came home from elementary school.

Cathy and I looked at each other. *Oh no*, we thought. *That guidance counselor at school must be teaching some bizarre New Age stuff.*

"What will you do as a meditator?" Cathy asked him.

He smiled. "I'll help kids who get in arguments at recess fix their problem and get along."

Cathy looked at me and said, "He doesn't mean *meditator*; he means *mediator*."

"That's right," he said. "I'm supposed to help kids who get in arguments at recess. I have to understand both points of view and help them get together."

What Job came to realize in his afflicted condition was that all of us need a mediator between us and our holy God. We have sinned; God is not happy. We have questions about how He is running the universe. And in one sense, He is far from us. We need a mediator, someone who can understand both points of view and bring us together.

Job was written thousands of years before Jesus came to earth. What we know now in the twenty-first century that Job did not know is that the perfect Mediator has come.

> *For there is one God and one mediator between God and men, the man Christ Jesus.*
> 1 TIMOTHY 2:5

When you are hurting, you don't need a new *explanation* about God as much as you need a new *experience* with God. You do not need more information; you need more of God. Job struggled to get to God, but we have access to the Father through the Son, Jesus (Ephesians 2:18). His life, death, burial, and resurrection are the door from your pain to God's heart.

God loves you more than you can imagine.

Take your sorrow to Him.

Allow His grace to comfort.

Be encouraged by the many blessings God can bring into your life through your suffering, especially the blessing of a closer relationship with Him.

NOTE

[1]National Center for Health Statistics, Data Warehouse, "LCWK9: Deaths, Percent of Total Deaths, and Death Rates for the 15 Leading Causes of Death: United States and Each State, 1999–2003," http://www.cdc.gov/nchs/datawh/statab/unpubd/mortabs/lcwk9_10.htm.

The 21 Most Amazing Truths about Heaven

Dedication

In loving memory of Bert and Bob Earley, and Carl Smith. Your presence in heaven makes me long to join you there.

Acknowledgments

Many thanks to the team of people who made this project a reality:

- Cathy, for twenty-five wonderful years of very happy marriage. You make Earth more heavenly for me.
- Daniel, Andrew, and Luke. I am very proud of you guys.
- "Szechwan Chicken." You "proofread pretty."
- Rod Bradley and the Mighty Men, for your prayers.
- Paul Muckley, for contacting me about this book, and Tim Martins, president of Barbour Publishing, for suggesting the idea. May our great adventure continue.
- Kelly McIntosh, for managing the in-house process, and Yolanda Chumney, for handling the typesetting.
- Elmer Towns, for your great example and sponsorship.
- Norm Rohrer, for your helpful advice.
- Carol Ann, you are my favorite sister.
- Steve, you are my favorite brother.
- Sandy, you are such a blessing to us.

Contents

Introduction

I am embarrassed to admit this, but for a long time I did not think much about Heaven. To be honest, I wasn't all that interested in Heaven. I had plenty to do and experience down here on Earth. Besides, what I knew about Heaven made it sound distant, overly vague, and frankly too boring to hold my interest.

Yet over the last few years that has all begun to change. Let me explain.

On January 12, 2002, after an exhausting war with illness, my mom went into the emergency room. We all knew she would never leave. Two days later, after silently saying good-bye to her family, she quietly slipped into eternity. Her departure planted a seed of curiosity in my heart about Heaven. I found myself daydreaming about what might be going on in Heaven.

> *I wonder what Mom is doing right now.*
> *I wonder what she looks like in Heaven.*
> *Is she singing and dancing?*
> *Is heaven as beautiful as they say?*
> *Can she see me right now?*
> *Does she miss me as much as I miss her?*

Three years later, Dad was worn out after a long battle with cancer. As one who was gifted at living and making the most of the here and now, he began to ask me questions about Heaven. He was lonesome for Mom, tired of pain, and wanted to see Jesus. He said he wanted to go home. On the night of January 6, 2005, he got his wish—and crossed over into eternity.

For the next few weeks, as I'd watch the winter sun setting in its magnificent display of gold, tracing the edges of pink and purple clouds, I seriously pondered what life was like beyond those clouds. Heaven crowded its way into more and more of my thoughts. Questions kept popping up:

> *How "old" will Mom and Dad be in Heaven?*
> *Will they live together as a married couple?*
> *What do they eat and drink?*
> *What work will Dad be doing?*
> *What are they doing for fun?*

I knew the Bible had much to say about Heaven, but I had never taken the time to thoroughly study it. I told myself, "Someday I'll do a detailed study of Heaven."

Exactly a year after my dad went to Heaven, my friend and editor, Paul Muckley, asked me to consider writing a book about Heaven. I jumped at the chance. What a perfect excuse to get my questions about Heaven answered.

In researching the subject, I was pleasantly surprised to discover that the Bible contains 582 references to Heaven in 550 verses. I learned that the Bible teaches amazingly big truths about Heaven. You might say it is the Garden of Eden, home, the Magic Kingdom, and Fantasy Island all combined and improved. I discovered that Heaven is anything but boring, and so much more.

I found that the first Christians had a rich preoccupation with Heaven based on the clear teachings of the Bible. Having a healthy, holy obsession with Heaven gave them hope and encouragement to face fierce trials and painful persecution. It provided resilient joy and supernatural strength. Studying the amazing truths about Heaven did the same for me. It also impacted my priorities down here in the present.

I believe that reading this book and gaining a better grasp of Heaven will not only satisfy your curiosity, but will undoubtedly give you authentic comfort, resounding peace, and tenacious energy as well. Plus, it will help prepare you to fully experience and enjoy your final forwarding address. . .Heaven.

Suggestions for getting the most out of this book:

1. *Study each chapter with a sanctified imagination and a prayerful heart.*

2. *Share what you are learning with someone else. Better yet, study this book with a friend or a small group.*

3. *Reread chapters as they apply to the needs of your life.*

4. *Start living for eternity now so you will be prepared to enjoy and experience all of Heaven when you get there.*

1

Don't Cut Your Feet!

One of my all-time favorite books is *The Great Divorce* by C. S. Lewis. This novella was Lewis's version of *The Divine Comedy*. In Lewis's story, a busload of people from Hell are driven to the outskirts of Heaven and given the opportunity to stay there, if they so chose. Sadly, all but one prefer to return to the dirty, congested, urban fog of Hell rather than live in the brilliant morning light of Heaven.

I love Lewis's imagery of Hell as mere shadow compared to the firm substance of Heaven. He vividly portrays the people from Hell as shadows, ghosts, and man-shaped stains unfit for the crystal-clear reality of Heaven.

There is a scene in the book I cannot erase from my mind. The phantoms from Hell have just arrived in the golden light shining on the lush beauty of the perpetual morning of Heaven. Gingerly, they step off the bus only to find that the reality of Heaven is so intense it literally hurts their feet. Lewis writes,

> It was the light, the grass, the trees, that were different; made of some different substance, so much solider than things in our country, that men were ghosts by comparison. . . . Reality is harsh to the feet of shadows.[1]

"Reality is harsh to the feet of shadows." Make no mistake. Heaven exists. It is more real than anywhere you have ever been. In fact, Earth is mere shadow compared to the dense substance of Heaven. Heaven is reality. It is so real that it would cut the feet of the unprepared.

Wired for Eternity

As a pastor, I have had the privilege and responsibility of officiating at numerous funerals. There is always something awkward, foreign, unwanted, and extremely painful about the death of someone we love. Even if the person was very old and ill, the cold reality of death never fails to knock the wind out of those left behind. This is because we innately sense that we were made for something more than a casket.

Author Randy Alcorn notes that, worldwide, 3 people die every second, 180 every minute, almost 11,000 per hour, and over 250,000 every day.[2] Yet death still stuns us. It just doesn't seem right. Why? We have an instinctive awareness that we are destined for life beyond the grave.

This nagging sense that we are to live forever *somewhere* is the universal dream of mankind. It is so integrated into the human psyche that nearly every religion has been built upon its expectation. While opinions, philosophies, and religions may differ, few people accept death as the end of life. Elaborate rituals and quaint customs permeate the cultures of all peoples from all time. From the native warriors of the American plains, to the primitive tribesmen of the jungles, to the sophisticated mystics of the East, virtually every tradition has some system of belief regarding the afterlife. Every current poll shows that an overwhelming majority of Americans believe in life after death. Why? Our Creator has endowed each of us with an inherent knowledge of an afterlife.

Wise King Solomon told us why we have a built-in hunger for Heaven when he spoke of God having "set eternity in the hearts of men" (Ecclesiastes 3:11). It only makes sense that if God placed this desire for eternity in our hearts, then it must be real. It is also logical that if eternity is real, God would give us some indication of what it will be like. So it should come as no surprise that He did. In 582 references in 550 verses, the Bible gives dozens of amazing truths about the eternal home of believers. This book will explore twenty-one of the major realities of Heaven.

One of the amazing truths about Heaven is that it is more than a wish, an analogy, a state of mind, or an ethereal realm. Heaven is an intensely real, acutely authentic, undeniably factual, literal place.

Heaven is a literal place, more real than anywhere you have ever been.

One major reason I struggled to get overly excited about Heaven was that I had a hard time finding comfort in the notion of being a disembodied spirit, dwelling in a vague state of nonphysical existence, somehow hovering in a mystical, ethereal realm totally unlike anything I had ever seen, known, or imagined. Thinking of Heaven as a really swell state of mind simply could not sustain my attention.

Fortunately, the more I studied the Bible on the subject of Heaven, the more it became obvious that Heaven is a real place, every bit as tangible, actual, literal, and concrete as the chair you are sitting in today. Granted, it is a much, much better, higher, sweeter place than Earth as we know it, but Heaven is undoubtedly a physical place. It is just as real as the place where you were born and the place you live today. In fact, Heaven should be capitalized just like Columbus, or Virginia, or France because it is an actual place, more real than any place we have ever been.[3]

The First Christians Believed in Heaven as a Literal Place

The first followers of Jesus believed the Bible taught that Heaven is a genuine, literal, physical place. They always described Heaven in concrete terms as a beautiful, wonderful, joyful, literal, eternal home. Their confidence was obvious. For example, in AD 125, a non-Christian named Aristides wrote to a friend attempting to explain why the new religion called "Christianity" was so successful.

> *If any righteous man among the Christians passes from this world, they rejoice and offer thanks to God, and they escort his body with songs and thanksgiving as if he were setting from one place to another nearby.*[4]

This belief in Heaven as a literal place continued throughout church history. For example, in the third century a church leader named Cyprian wrote,

> *Who that has been placed in foreign lands would not hasten to return to his own country? . . . We regard paradise as our country.*[5]

Throughout the scriptures, Heaven is portrayed as a genuine, actual place. Those who followed the God of the Bible believed in Heaven as real and literal.

Abraham Looked Forward to Living in a Solid City

> *By faith Abraham, when called to go to a place he would later receive as his inheritance, obeyed and went, even though he did not know where he was going. By faith he made his home in the promised land like a stranger in a foreign country; he lived in tents, as*

*did Isaac and Jacob, who were heirs with him of the same promise. For he was looking
forward to the city with foundations, whose architect and builder is God.*

HEBREWS 11:8–10

Abraham was called by God to leave his homeland and travel to a *place* he had never been
(Genesis 12:1). It was a *land* that was promised, but which he did not yet possess. He traveled
there by faith and lived there in tents. As he did, he anticipated one day living in another *place,* his
heavenly home, a *city* with firm *foundations*, whose architect and builder is God Himself. Abraham
viewed Heaven as a literal place, a celestial city. Unlike flimsy, temporary tents, it would have solid,
permanent foundations.

The Apostle John Saw Heaven as a Physical Reality

*Then I saw a new heaven and a new earth, for the first heaven and the first earth had passed
away, and there was no longer any sea. I saw the Holy City, the new Jerusalem, coming down
out of heaven from God, prepared as a bride beautifully dressed for her husband.*

REVELATION 21:1–2

In the book of the Revelation, God gave the apostle John a series of marvelous visions
into the future. When John saw into Heaven, he always saw it as a tangible place. In his most
extensive vision of Heaven, what John saw was a new Heaven, a new Earth, and a new city—
the new Jerusalem. He did not see a *non*-heaven, a *non*-earth, or a *non*-city.

John described Heaven in such detail that what he was seeing had to be more than a
ghostly, foggy, ethereal state of being. John depicted a city with literal walls and tangible gates
that were able to be measured (Revelation 21:12–21). It had real streets (21:21). Flowing
through the city was a genuine river (22:1–2), bordered with actual trees (22:2). This vision of a
literal Heaven was what John was told to write down for us to study, learn, and long for (21:5).

Jesus Promised His Disciples that Heaven Was a Literal Place

*"Do not let your hearts be troubled. Trust in God; trust also in me. In my Father's house are
many rooms; if it were not so, I would have told you. I am going there to prepare a place for
you. And if I go and prepare a place for you, I will come back and take you to be with me
that you also may be where I am. You know the way to the place where I am going."*

JOHN 14:1–4

Jesus promised His disciples that there would be a literal gathering in an actual place.
He deliberately chose clear material terms such as "house," "rooms," and "place." It was a *place*
that could be prepared. It was a *place* from which He would go and return. It was a *place* He
would take them to so they could be together. It was a *place* to which they had been told the
way. Clearly, Jesus wanted His disciples to understand Heaven as being a tangible place.

Jesus Promised the Thief That He Would Join Jesus in Paradise

*One of the criminals who hung there hurled insults at him: "Aren't you the Christ?
Save yourself and us!" But the other criminal rebuked him. "Don't you fear God," he
said, "since you are under the same sentence? We are punished justly, for we are getting*

what our deeds deserve. But this man has done nothing wrong." Then he said, "Jesus, remember me when you come into your kingdom." Jesus answered him, "I tell you the truth, today you will be with me in paradise."

LUKE 23:39–43

As Jesus hung on the cross, the crowd and the soldiers mocked Him. So did one of the criminals being killed alongside Him that day. But the other thief acknowledged God's justice, his own guilt, and Jesus' righteous innocence. Jesus heard the man's statement as a confession of faith and rewarded him with that wonderful promise: "Today you will be with me in paradise."

The word "paradise" describes a beautiful, tangible place. Early Christians understood Paradise as more than mere allegory, but rather as an actual physical place where God lives with His people.

Later, Jesus promised to the overcomers that He would "give the right to eat from the tree of life, which is in the paradise of God" (Revelation 2:7). The tree of life was seen by the apostle John standing by the banks of the river flowing through the city of New Jerusalem (Revelation 22:2). When Jesus told the thief He could join Him in Paradise, He was telling the man about a literal place.

The Resurrection of Jesus Proves That Heaven Is a Physical Reality

The central truth of Christianity is that Jesus rose from the dead with a unique, spiritual body that also had physical dimensions. He was able to be seen, heard, and touched. He ate literal food. More than a ghost, the resurrected Jesus had a visible, tangible, audible, recognizable body. It was a body designed to occupy a literal place, a place not so radically different from Earth as we know it.

Jesus' literal resurrection from the dead not only proved that His death on the cross was sufficient to pay for our sins, but also guaranteed our hope of experiencing eternal life. As the resurrected death destroyer, Jesus is the pioneer, the first one all the way through to the mountain pass. His resurrected body tells us a tremendous amount about the literal nature of Heaven. Although His new, improved body had increased abilities and heightened sensitivities, it was still an actual body. One day all of Jesus' followers will also have similar resurrected bodies. These new, improved bodies are designed for a literal Heaven.

So What?

Heaven is a literal place, so real that everything else we know is mere shadow to its substance. It is a Paradise awaiting those who really want to be there. The rest of this book will describe this glorious place. I pray that as you read of Heaven, it will not only satisfy your curiosity, but feed and fuel your soul to make sure that you will spend eternity there.

NOTES

[1] C. S. Lewis, *The Great Divorce* (New York: Harper Collins, 1946), 21.

[2] Randy C. Alcorn, *Heaven* (Carol Stream, Illinois: Tyndale House Publishers, 2004), xxi.

[3] I agree with Peter Kreeft, "What Will Heaven Be Like? Thirty-five frequently asked questions about eternity," Christianity Today (June 6, 2003), http://www.christianitytoday.com/ct/2003/122/51.0.html, that because Heaven is a literal place, it should be capitalized just as we capitalize Boston.

[4] Aristides, *The Apology of Aristides the Philosopher*, 15, http://www.early-christianwritings.com/text/aristides-kay.html.

[5] Cyprian, *On the Mortality*, 26, http://www.newadvent.org/fathers/050707.htm.

2

"There's No Place Like Home"

In 1939 an MGM movie swept American moviegoers away. Shown annually on television during holidays, the movie became a classic institution and a rite of passage for most of us. Interestingly, it is not a bloody war epic, an intrigue-laced detective story, or the tale of a passionate affair. It was the fantastic tale of a girl who ran away—only to find that "there's no place like home."

Kansas farm girl Dorothy Gale felt unnoticed, underappreciated, and lonely. When a nasty neighbor tried to have her little black dog, Toto, put to sleep, young Dorothy scooped Toto into her arms and ran away. A tornado swept up Dorothy, her house, and her dog, depositing them in the magical Land of Oz. She immediately realized that she and Toto weren't in Kansas anymore. Dorothy, in her newly acquired, enchanted, sequined ruby slippers, set out on an adventure down the Yellow Brick Road on a quest to see the only one with the power to help her return home, the wonderful Wizard of Oz.

On her way to the Emerald City, the home of the Wizard, she met a Scarecrow who wanted a brain, a Tin Man who hoped for a heart, and a Cowardly Lion who desperately desired courage. Each hoped to get to the city so the Wizard would help them before the Wicked Witch of the West could catch them.

After an avalanche of adventures, Dorothy discovered that the key to getting home was with her all along. She needed only to close her eyes and tap her heels together three times while thinking, "There's no place like home." When she did, the magic slippers transported her to the place she had so longed to be.

Awakening in her own bed, in her own house, surrounded by the anxious faces of her family and friends, Dorothy made a resolution. She declared, "I will never leave here ever, ever again because. . .there's *no* place like *home*."

Homesick for Heaven

As they say where I grew up, "Homesick is a bad kind of sick to be." There is no pill you can take to relieve its symptoms. No surgery removes its awful ache. There are temporary distractions, but at best they are still only temporary. The only and ultimate cure for homesickness is going home.

God's children, living life on a groaning planet, live with a gnawing tension and hungry ache for home. There are amazingly good moments in the here and now. Yet, often, life is oddly awkward and uncomfortable. We feel out of step and not quite in sync with "down here." There is holy discontent and persistent inner dissatisfaction. Why? Etched deep into the heart of the Christian is the hunger for Heaven, which is the home we have always longed for.

Heaven is the home you always wanted.

For the Christian, there exists a constant tension between "the here and now" and the "then and there." Even though we have never been there, our spiritual DNA instinctively tells us that our true home is a place we have not yet visited. Our heart is with our treasure, Christ in heaven (Matthew 6:21; 2 Corinthians 5:8). Heaven is described in the Bible as the home we inwardly desire. To the people of faith described by the author of Hebrews, it was a distant homeland, a country of their own, a better country, a heavenly home.

All these people were still living by faith when they died. They did not receive the things promised; they only saw them and welcomed them from a distance. And they admitted that they were aliens and strangers on earth. People who say such things show that they are looking for a country of their own. If they had been thinking of the country they had left, they would have had opportunity to return. Instead, they were longing for a better country—a heavenly one. Therefore God is not ashamed to be called their God, for he has prepared a city for them.

HEBREWS 11:13–16

To the first Christians, the concept of Heaven as the home God's people really desire was so strong that the apostle Peter addressed his first letter "To God's elect, *strangers* in the world . . ." (1 Peter 1:1, emphasis added). In that letter, he encouraged the readers to "live your lives as *strangers* here in reverent fear" (1:17, emphasis added). He used their status as pilgrims on this planet to motivate them to godly living by saying, "Dear friends, I urge you, as *aliens* and *strangers* in the world, to abstain from sinful desires, which war against your soul" (2:11, emphasis added).

"It's Good to Be Home"

Because of the nature of my ministry, I am out of state several times a month, living from a suitcase, speaking at churches or training pastors. I usually fly back into town late at night. Looking out of the window as the plane is drawing down on the airport, there is always a warm sense of the familiar. I can tell I am getting close to where I long to be. Soon Cathy, my wife, is pulling up to the curb and smiling at me as I pile in. After a quick kiss she says, "It's nice to have you home."

Driving down customary streets, time drags until we pull into the driveway. Quickly, I am inside. Rocky, our little dog, dives into me with a flurry of delighted barks. My sons yell out, "Hey, Dad, glad you're home," and come by to give me a hug.

Soon, I am lying in my own bed, with my wonderful wife, in my own room, in my own house, with my kids down the hall, on my own street, and all feels well with the world. I give a happy sigh and think, "It's awfully nice to be home."

One day, all of God's children will have that same feeling, multiplied. We will awake and breathe the rich, fresh air of Heaven and sigh, "It is so nice to finally be home."

All the Comforts of Home, Only Better

Think of everything we enjoy about home and realize those elements will be in Heaven, only better, much better. For example, my wife, Cathy, is an outstanding mother. Since our children were born, she has made it a mission that, if nothing else, home was a place of unconditional love and acceptance. The world may give you a rough time, but you can always walk in the door of home and feel received, expected, acknowledged, listened to, and recognized as being valuable.

It will be the same in Heaven, only more so. Rejection, denunciation, and abuse will be unwelcome in Heaven. Genuine affection, fond friendship, and close companionship will reign supreme, and it won't only be in a few rooms with family members. Acceptance and love will be given everywhere you go.

Make Yourself at Home

When you visit good friends, they often encourage you to "make yourself at home." Of course, you never fully do because you are afraid they might never let you come back if you did. But you understand that what they mean is "relax and feel free to be yourself, just as you would at home."

Home is the one place where you can be yourself. You don't have to dress up in uncomfortable clothes and try to impress somebody you really don't know. You can wear a beat-up old sweatshirt if you want (I usually do). You can sing badly in the shower (I am guilty of that one as well). You don't have to comb your hair (I would gladly comb my hair if I had enough to comb).

In Heaven you can kick off your shoes and relax. You can drink right out of the pitcher if you feel like it. You will feel free to be the true you. You will finally be home.

Home-Cooked Meals

We have three teenage sons. One of their favorite things about home is that there is always good food there. Cathy makes the extra effort to bring home their favorite foods and preferred snacks from the grocery store. She is a master at making their best-loved meals and most desired desserts. Yet as good a job as Cathy does with the food in our house, in Heaven we will enjoy even finer food together, as God Himself will be our cook.

> On this mountain the LORD Almighty will prepare a feast of rich food for all peoples, a banquet of aged wine—the best of meats and the finest of wines.
>
> ISAIAH 25:6

FFGs

Every few months our family holds an FFG ("Festive Family Gathering"). We come together to celebrate birthdays, graduations, or homecomings from mission trips. My wife and boys are there. Cathy's sister is always there. My sister and her husband never miss. My brother and his wife make it when they can. My parents used to come.

The agenda is simple. We eat and then usually eat a little more. After that we gather in a large room and do a variety of activities. We may sing (usually badly), pray (we are much better at that), and my sister loves to give out goofy "door prizes" (don't even ask). We often give out brutally funny birthday cards. We may look at pictures from someone's mission trip or a video of one of our boy's school events or discuss family business. We always laugh a lot. Our family loves FFGs because they are an excuse to get together and be a family.

Our heavenly home will be filled with FFGs. We will gather with our spiritual brothers and sisters and our heavenly Father, for glorious times of family fun.

Family Feasts

One of the favorite times in our home is family mealtime around the kitchen table. We especially love those rare and wonderful times when Cathy has found steaks on sale at the grocery store and marinated them all day. I grill them outside while she makes salads, vegetables, and all the rest of the fixings. The boys set the table and get the drinks. Someone says grace and we all dig in. Loud laughing punctuates conversations that cover a wide gamut of topics. Everyone is happy because it is good to be home with family.

Don't think this pleasure will be missing in Heaven. Our heavenly home is described as a place of enjoying fantastic feasts together with the ones we love (Matthew 8:11). Jesus promised a rich feast fit for a king for all in Heaven.

And I confer on you a kingdom, just as my Father conferred one on me, so that you
may eat and drink at my table in my kingdom.

LUKE 22:29–30

Family Is What Makes a House a Home

I grew up in a small yellow house in a small Midwestern town. My folks lived in that same house for over forty years. After I had gone to college and had not been back in months, I will never forget how excited I was to be driving home. When the car turned onto the street and I spotted the tiny yellow house, my heart skipped a beat in anticipation. I was eager to be somewhere familiar. But most of all, I wanted to see the two people that made home "home" for me—Mom and Dad.

Oh, don't get me wrong. Having a room to myself, being done with exams, and having twenty-four-hour access to a refrigerator was deeply appreciated. But that was not what I had missed most. It was Mom and Dad. Yes, eating Mom's homemade apple pie, dining on her special scalloped potatoes, having her do my laundry, and having Dad hand me a twenty-dollar bill was glorious. But I mostly liked being there with them.

A funny thing happened a few months after Dad followed Mom to Heaven. I drove by their old house and, strangely, I felt nothing. What had previously always produced a warm feeling evoked nothing but an eerie void. Their old house was just another house on just another street. Why? My family did not live there anymore. Being together with loved ones is what makes a house a home.

One of the great aspects of our heavenly home is being reunited with loved ones. Yet this reunion will be even better than any family gathering we have ever experienced. Our loved ones will be perfected, and we will be together with them and with the Lord forever.

Brothers, we do not want you to be ignorant about those who fall asleep, or to grieve
like the rest of men, who have no hope. We believe that Jesus died and rose again and
so we believe that God will bring with Jesus those who have fallen asleep in him. . . .
And so we will be with the Lord forever.

1 THESSALONIANS 4:13–14, 17

So What?

Maybe you did not have a pleasant home life, or possibly yours was wonderful. Either way, remember that Heaven is the home you always longed for. It will have all the comforts of home and much more. Heaven on its worst day will be better than your home ever was on its best day. Don't get too tied to this Earth, and don't get too frustrated when it fails to meet your expectations. Heaven is the home you have always longed for.

3

Partying in Paradise

If you are not allowed to laugh in Heaven,
I don't want to go there.

Martin Luther[1]

Never Underestimate the Power of a Good Party

We all love parties. From little kids getting excited about a birthday party, to teenage boys who finally bathe and use deodorant before going to a party where girls will be attending, to young ladies all atwitter at bridal showers, people love parties. From wedding receptions and anniversaries, to tailgates, getting together with good friends and tasty food is a can't-miss recipe for fun.

Never underestimate the power of a party. My family hosts a weekly Bible study for teens. We have found that we can double our attendance and get unchurched students to come to our house if the kids invite them to a "party." We have found if we have a theme ("Squirt Gun Wars," "I Hate Winter," "Halloween Bonfire," and "Fifties Night" are always hits), grill some hot dogs, and play a few corny games, we'll have a crowd. They will have a blast and will listen intently to a few of their friends share their story of how they came to a personal relationship with Jesus. We have had as many as eighty-nine kids show up and as many as a dozen make salvation decisions for Christ—all because we had a party.

"No, I Don't Want to Go to Heaven. Heaven Is Boring, and I Love to Party."

Several years ago I was talking with a young man. In the course of our conversation, I asked him if he would like to know how to go to Heaven. "No!" he said, shaking his head. "I don't want to go to Heaven. Heaven is so boring and I just love to party."

Some of the saddest misconceptions the devil has spread about God and Heaven are that "God hates fun" and "Heaven is boring." Nothing could be further from the truth! God is the absolutely, positively most exciting Being in the universe. Where God is, parties break out. If you *like* parties, you will *love* Heaven.

Heaven is the home of the best parties ever.

God Loves a Good Party

In the Bible, God went out of His way to tell His people that He wanted them to have parties on Earth. These parties certainly weren't drunken, but they were fun gatherings with great amounts of good food, good friends, and good times. For example, in the seemingly unlikely, widely viewed as "dull as dust" book of Deuteronomy, God commands His people to have an annual national celebration.

> *Be sure to set aside a tenth of all that your fields produce each year. Eat the tithe of your grain, new wine and oil, and the firstborn of your herds and flocks in the presence of the LORD your God at the place he will choose as a dwelling for his Name, so that you may learn to revere the LORD your God always. But if that place is too distant and you have been blessed by the LORD your God and cannot carry your tithe*

*(because the place where the L*ORD* will choose to put his Name is so far away), then exchange your tithe for silver, and take the silver with you and go to the place the L*ORD* your God will choose. Use the silver to buy whatever you like: cattle, sheep, wine or other fermented drink, or anything you wish. Then you and your household shall eat there in the presence of the L*ORD* your God and rejoice.*

DEUTERONOMY 14:22–26

The first time I read that passage I thought, "This is the very best tithing text I have ever heard! Why didn't anyone tell me this was in the Bible?"

Note carefully what it is saying. The Jewish law stated that every year all Jewish families were to gather up one-tenth of their crops from that year and bring them to Jerusalem. What were they to do with all of that? Were they to feed the poor, clothe the naked, or possibly add a family life center onto the temple? No, they were to use it to have a humongous party!

This was to be an amazing celebration. Everyone would be there. Farmers, merchants, family leaders, large families, soldiers, priests, grandmas, and little kids, widows, orphans, lame people, the blind—everyone was welcome. No one was excluded. There would be plenty of food, singing, and lots of fun. And it would all be done to honor God.

The Lord was honored by their party! Our God is a God who loves celebration. He is a God whose very presence breathes joy into living. God loves a good party.

God loves parties so much that He commanded His children to take time off work and to faithfully enjoy parties together. He even ordained that the entire Jewish religious calendar be based on national parties, or "feasts." If God prescribed parties such as the following for inclusion in the Jewish calendar, don't you think He'll have them in Heaven?

1. The Feast of Dedication was held in the winter month of Chisleu (John 10:22).

2. The Feast of Jubilee was proclaimed by trumpets every fiftieth year (Leviticus 25:8–12).

3. The Feast of the New Moon was to be observed the first day of every month with trumpets (Numbers 10:10) and entertainment (1 Samuel 20:5, 18).

4. The Feast of Pentecost (also called the Feast of Harvest or the Feast of Weeks) was to be kept fifty days after the barley harvest with great rejoicing (Leviticus 23:15–16; Deuteronomy 16:9–12).

5. The Feast of Purim or Lots was commemorated on the fourteenth and fifteenth days of the twelfth month with feasting, gladness, and the sharing of gifts (Esther 9:17–22).

6. The Feast of the Sabbatical Year was to be celebrated every seventh year (Leviticus 25:2–7; Exodus 23:11).

7. The Feast of Tabernacles was a joyous, weeklong annual feast of singing and camping out (Exodus 23:16–17; Leviticus 23:34–41; Deuteronomy 16:13–15).

8. The Feast of the Passover (or Feast of Unleavened Bread) was also an annual weeklong feast (Exodus 12:6–18; Leviticus 23:5–6).

9. The Feast of Trumpets was held the first day of the seventh month (Leviticus 23:24–25; Numbers 29:1–6).

10. The Anniversary Feasts (Exodus 23:14–16) were to be times of gratitude, joy, gladness, and entertainment (Psalm 122:4; 42:4; 1 Samuel 1:4–9).

Jesus Loves a Good Party

Q: Where did Jesus do His first miracle?
A: At a wedding party (John 2:1–10)

Q: Where was Jesus anointed for His burial?
A: At a dinner party (Luke 7:36–50)

Q: Where did Jesus eat His last meal with His disciples?
A: At a supper party (Matthew 26:17–30)

Q: What did Jesus say happens in the presence of God when a sinner repents?
A: The Father throws a party (Luke 15:5–7, 9–10, 22–24).

"When he finds [his lost sheep], he joyfully puts it on his shoulders and goes home. Then he calls his friends and neighbors together and says, 'Rejoice with me; I have found my lost sheep.' I tell you that in the same way there will be more rejoicing in heaven over one sinner who repents than over ninety-nine righteous persons who do not need to repent."

LUKE 15:5–7

"When she finds [her lost coin], she calls her friends and neighbors together and says, 'Rejoice with me; I have found my lost coin.' In the same way, I tell you, there is rejoicing in the presence of the angels of God over one sinner who repents."

LUKE 15:9–10

"'Quick! Bring the best robe and put it on him. Put a ring on his finger and sandals on his feet. Bring the fattened calf and kill it. Let's have a feast and celebrate. For this son of mine was dead and is alive again; he was lost and is found.' So they began to celebrate. Meanwhile, the older son was in the field. When he came near the house, he heard music and dancing."

LUKE 15:22–25

I absolutely love this. When I lead people to Jesus, I tell them that they cannot possibly fathom the profound, life-changing importance of the commitment they made. "It is so significant," I say, "that this very moment the Father, the Son, and the Holy Spirit, the angels, and a whole bunch of people like your godly great-grandma are 'high-fiving,' dancing, and laughing. They are having a party in your honor, in the honor of one day having you join them in Heaven, and in the honor of Jesus Christ, who died to make it possible!"

In our church, we celebrate baptism once a month. Those who have trusted Christ as Savior the previous month have their testimonies read out loud before they are baptized. When they come up out of the water, everyone in the audience breaks into clapping and cheering. It's a mini-party.

Q: Why did the Pharisees get so upset with Jesus?
A: He was too interested in parties (Luke 7:34).

"The Son of Man came eating and drinking, and you say, 'Here is a glutton and a drunkard, a friend of tax collectors and "sinners."'

LUKE 7:34

Pharisees were the "no-fun" bunch in Jesus' day. They consistently valued man-made rules over eternal relationships. They loved their policies more than people. Jesus gave them fits. He refused to make religion a dull, dry, rigid, sober, stupefying act. He was obviously a very holy person who connected with people and knew how to have fun with them. He frequented the parties of "sinners," prostitutes, and tax collectors in order to bring light into their darkness.

Q: To what did Jesus compare the kingdom of Heaven?
A: A big-time banquet (Luke 14:15–24)

Jesus was the master storyteller. He told simple stories with profound meaning. In one He compares Heaven with a great banquet.

When one of those at the table with him heard this, he said to Jesus, "Blessed is the man who will eat at the feast in the kingdom of God."

Jesus replied: "A certain man was preparing a great banquet and invited many guests. At the time of the banquet he sent his servant to tell those who had been invited, 'Come, for everything is now ready.'

"But they all alike began to make excuses. The first said, 'I have just bought a field, and I must go and see it. Please excuse me.'

"Another said, 'I have just bought five yoke of oxen, and I'm on my way to try them out. Please excuse me.'

"Still another said, 'I just got married, so I can't come.'

"The servant came back and reported this to his master. Then the owner of the house became angry and ordered his servant, 'Go out quickly into the streets and alleys of the town and bring in the poor, the crippled, the blind and the lame.'"

"'Sir,' the servant said, 'what you ordered has been done, but there is still room.'

"Then the master told his servant, 'Go out to the roads and country lanes and make them come in, so that my house will be full. I tell you, not one of those men who were invited will get a taste of my banquet.'"

LUKE 14:15–24

Jesus told this tale to teach us about God's huge heart of love for hurting, helpless people and something of His nature as the heavenly host with the most. In this story, Jesus teaches five truths about Heaven.

 Heaven will host a feast of fulfillment and happiness: *Blessed is the man who will eat at the feast in the kingdom of God* (Luke 14:15).

2. Heaven is being prepared as a great banquet: *A certain man was preparing a great banquet* (Luke 14:16).

3. Heaven is a celebration where misplaced priorities may prohibit entrance: *But they all alike began to make excuses. The first said, "I have just bought a field, and I must go and see it. Please excuse me." Another said, "I have just bought five yoke of oxen, and I'm on my way to try them out. Please excuse me." Still another said, "I just got married, so I can't come."... Then the master told his servant, "I tell you, not one of those men who were invited will get a taste of my banquet"* (Luke 14:18–20, 23–24).

4. Heaven is a blessed bash where supposed liabilities are overlooked: *Go out quickly into the streets and alleys of the town and bring in the poor, the crippled, the blind and the lame* (Luke 14:21).

5. Heaven is large enough to accommodate all who really want to be there: *Go out to the roads and country lanes and make them come in, so that my house will be full* (Luke 14:23).

So What?

This very moment God is preparing a party in Heaven. An invitation has been sent to you. I hope you will accept. We could have a great time together in Heaven.

NOTE

1. Martin Luther Quotes, Brainy Quotes, http://www.brainyquote.com/quotes/authors/ m/martin_luther.html.

4
Not Even Close to Boring

I was an active little boy who was easily bored. During my days in elementary school, I spent many hours standing in the corner or visiting with our principal, Mr. Crabtree, not because I was "bad" as much as because I was too "busy" and easily bored.

I remember leaving Sunday school one morning in a real dilemma. I knew I should want to go to Heaven, but it sounded so b–o–r–i–n–g. The thought of playing harps and singing hymns all day, every day, forever did nothing to capture my attention. It sounded like choir practice, which was fine once a week, but having it all the time, every week, year after year, century after century—boring!

No Yawns Allowed

Q: What happens in hell?
A: Nothing
Q: What happens in Heaven?
A: Everything[1]

Studying what the Bible says about Heaven has produced the definite resolution of my dilemma regarding the supposedly dull nature of Heaven. I no longer wonder about being restless in Heaven, because Heaven is the most exciting place in the universe. Being in Heaven is called eternal *life*, not endless boredom. Heaven will pulsate with life and vibrancy. It is an active, fun, peaceful, positive, adventurous place.

Heaven is the most exciting place in the universe.

God Is the Most Exhilarating Person in the Universe

God has many characteristics, but none of them are boring. God is unparalleled regarding creativity, unrivaled regarding riches, and untouched in terms of power. He is the inventor of miracles and the fulfiller of dreams. He is the Author of *life*, for crying out loud!

No accurate description of God can contain any words like *dead, dry, dull, dreary, lackluster, lethargic,* or *lifeless*. *Electrifying, exciting, exhilarating, stirring, thrilling, dynamic, lively, active, vigorous,* and *vibrant* are just a few adjectives that anyone who truly knows God would use to describe Him. The people who have lived the most adventuresome and adrenaline-laced lives are the ones who have lived closest to Him.

Remember David, the shepherd boy? By being associated with God, he got to bring down a real giant, chase Philistines, avoid an entire army, rule a kingdom, and dance before the Lord in unbridled, uninhibited joy. His closest companions were fearless warriors called "Mighty Men," not "Boring Boys." Nobody could call them, or their life experiences, dull.

What about Daniel? He served on the cabinet of several world rulers, was miraculously delivered from death by lions, and was privileged to see a vision of the future equaled only by one other man, John the apostle.

How about Elijah? He and God single-handedly caused a three-year drought, miraculously fed a widow and her son, and defeated 850 false prophets. He called down real fire from Heaven and took a ride to Heaven in a flaming chariot chauffeured by angels.

Boring? You have to be kidding.

Ponder the exciting perils of Paul. His introduction to Jesus began when he was knocked off his horse by a blinding light. Knowing Jesus forced him to flee for his life over a wall in a basket. Being close to God led Paul in and out of jail, before adoring and lethally angry crowds, into the presence of kings, through earthquakes and shipwrecks, and to travel around the known world. Because of God, Paul healed the sick and raised the dead. There was nothing routine and monotonous about his life.

Talk to the original disciples. They will tell you that by hanging around with Jesus they saw the lame walk, the blind see, the dead live, storms stop, and thousands of hungry people fed with a handful of food, twice.

Any view of God that contains the notion of boredom is an absolute lie. Such lies are exploded the moment people experience the thrilling nature of His home, Heaven.

God Created Us to Live Anything but Boring Lives

I often tell audiences, "If you are living a boring Christian life, don't blame God!" I have found that truly following Jesus is anything but dull. It is definitely not easy, but it is also never boring. Following Jesus will force us out of our comfort zone.

Convenience and complacency flee in the face of the courage and creativity required to pursue and obey Christ. Following Jesus will push us out of the security of the boat to walk on water and out onto the battlefield to face giants. People who think Christianity is boring ought to try it the way it was meant to be lived. And people who think that Heaven is dull ought to read the Bible.

Daily Life in Heaven

Daily life in Heaven will be similar to daily life on Earth, only much more fun and fulfilling. God created humans with an immense capacity to experience pleasure, adventure, fun, and joy. In Heaven this capacity will not only be greatly expanded, it will also be powerfully purified and gloriously satisfied.

Remember, the curse will be lifted (Revelation 22:3). Therefore, everything good, pleasant, and truly fun about Heaven will be better than it ever could be here on Earth.

Dining Will Be Delightful

We will eat better-tasting, more exotic, much healthier, and more delicious foods than are available on Earth now under the curse (Isaiah 25:6). I see creative chefs, remarkable recipes, and awe-inspiring menus. We will be able to dine with good people who love us, as well as with fascinating people we have always wanted to meet.

Travel Will Be Tremendous

Travel will be incredible in Heaven. Ultimately, the new Earth will be every bit as beautiful as Earth is now, and even better. We will have all of eternity to explore mountains, nations, islands, and other places we have never had the time or money to see. We can discover marvelous museums, glorious art galleries, and look at extraordinary architecture. Beyond that, why won't we be able to visit the sights on other planets, stars, galaxies, and solar systems? There will be practically no end to where we can go and what we can see.

Work Will Be Wonderful

Although it is not necessarily the case on Earth now under the curse, work will be a great joy in Heaven. Everyone in Heaven will serve in positions they thoroughly enjoy, doing work that is meaningful and deeply fulfilling. It will stretch us and we will love it. We will work alongside great companions and serve a wonderful Boss (Revelation 22:3).

Worship Won't Put You to Sleep

One of the great misconceptions about Heaven is that it will be one infinitely long, dreadfully brain-numbing, boring church service. According to the Bible, there will be a lot of worship in Heaven, but don't worry. It will be better than anything you have ever been a part of. I can guarantee you, it will be vastly superior to the shot made at the buzzer of the championship game, bigger than the best concert, and a cut above the most peaceful sunset.

Unlike too much of what some call worship on Earth, in Heaven there will be absolutely no lifeless singing, no dry prayers, no passionless preaching, and no looking at the clock and wondering what is for lunch. Worship in Heaven will be so thoroughly captivating it will be unlike any worship you have ever experienced down here under the curse.

Heavenly worship will elevate you out of yourself and shake you down to your core. It will drain you and flood you, lift you up, and drop you to your knees. It will strike every emotional chord you have ever felt and many you did not even know you had. You will cry, laugh, cheer, and shudder. Every negative emotion inside you will be swept aside in tidal waves of raw joy, holy happiness, deep awe, extreme peace, and outrageous love. It will fully engage all five senses and possibly enliven new senses that did not exist previously. Boring? No way!

For example, the book of Revelation is more than an amazing book of prophecy telling us of coming events. It is also a glorious glimpse into a few of the wonderful worship events in Heaven. The word *throne* appears over forty times in Revelation, often in the context of the staggering events God's people will experience worshiping around His throne. From looking at just a few of them, I can tell you that when you worship in Heaven it will be anything but boring.

Imagine every color in the rainbow ignited and exploding before your eyes (Revelation 4:2–3). Feel rocked to your core by the thunder, lightning, and sea of voices roaring in perfect syncopation and symphony around the throne (4:5). Drink in stunning splendor and spectacular beauty (4:6), and witness astounding angelic creatures (4:7–9). By worshiping directly at the throne of the Author of life, you become more alive than you ever imagined possible (4:9–11).

As you worship in Heaven, you will cry like a baby (5:4) and be comforted by astounding truth (5:5). Your breath will be swept away as you see Jesus as He has never been seen before (5:6–7) and find within your heart a river of gratitude beyond what you conceived possible. Such experiences will pull the very best out of your entire life and present it to Him (5:8).

At the throne, you will sing in tune and perfect pitch in a choir of millions of voices, including people from every epoch in history, every nation on earth, and every station of life, each tuned perfectly to one another and to the Lord (5:9–10). Billions of angels will join you at the throne in celestial crescendos that defy description (5:11–12). Ultimately, every animal, every fish, and every bird will join you in jubilant praise and worship of their creator King (5:13–14). Think about it: You may be standing behind a regal Ethiopian warrior and in front of a Polish grandma, together proclaiming God's worth, with an enormous glowing angel on one side and a happy polar bear on the other.

But if all of that is not enough, imagine the righteous pride exploding in your chest for Jesus as every evil, dirty, slithering demon and the dark prince himself, Satan, bow down before Jesus. Hear them sheepishly acknowledge the truth they have lived to deny, as they finally proclaim, "Jesus is Lord!" (Revelation 5:13–14; Philippians 2:9–11).

Friend, if that does not send shivers down your spine and cause goose bumps to spread down your arms, call 911. For all practical purposes, you are dead.

So What?

After studying the enthralling adventure of Heaven, I no longer fear that anyone will be bored. Actually, my greatest concern is that many Christians I know who are in the habit of going through the motions will be so energized, keyed up, and enthused by the thrilling atmosphere of Heaven that they will not survive, unless God performs a major miracle.

My goal is to live the adventure now. I want to have my heart, mind, and soul stretched so far by loving God and serving Him that Heaven won't be such a big shock to my system. I want to be well prepared to completely comprehend it and entirely enjoy it all when I get there.

NOTE

1.   Peter Kreeft, "What Will Heaven Be Like? *Thirty-five frequently asked questions about eternity,*" *Christianity Today* (06/06/2003), http://www.christianitytoday.com/ct/2003/122/51.0.html.

5
A MUCH BETTER PLACE

When I was a very young boy, my grandfather passed away. He had a habit of telling the same jokes over and over again, so we called him "Granddaddy Joke." My brother and I considered Granddaddy Joke our favorite grandfather, because he gave us big bowls of pink peppermint ice cream when we visited him and tickled us with his stubbly face. (Our other grandfather always put us to work when we visited him.)

As we were riding in the hearse from the funeral service to the cemetery, everyone in my family was silent except for sniffles and sobs. Finally, I could not take it anymore.

"Why are we all crying?" I asked, as my childish mind grappled with the weighty issue of mortality and the puzzling nature of grief.

"We should be happy. Granddaddy Joke's in Heaven, and Heaven is a much better place, right?"

My appreciation for the pain of grief was obviously underdeveloped, but my theology was quite good. Heaven is a much better place than Earth as we now know it.

Heaven on its worst day is better than Earth on its best day.

> *Then I saw a new heaven and a new earth. . . . And I heard a loud voice from the throne saying, "Now the dwelling of God is with men, and he will live with them. They will be his people, and God himself will be with them and be their God. He will wipe every tear from their eyes. There will be no more death or mourning or crying or pain, for the old order of things has passed away." He who was seated on the throne said, "I am making everything new!"*
>
> REVELATION 21:1, 3–5

Heaven will be a much better place than Earth for many reasons. It will ultimately be a new and vastly improved version (Revelation 21:1). God will ultimately wipe away every tear (21:4). Death will be eradicated (21:4). Heaven is vastly superior to the Earth we now inhabit. In Heaven everything good about Earth will be refreshed, expanded, and enhanced (21:5). Everything bad about it will be absent.

There Is No Sin in Heaven

One major element that will make Heaven "heavenly" is that the curse of sin will be left far behind (Revelation 22:3). The transformational power of Jesus' death, burial, and resurrection for our sin will be experienced on a much greater level than we can now comprehend. Sin's penalty will be paid, its power broken, and its presence completely removed. There is no sin in Heaven.

Sin is breaking God's law. In Heaven there is no sin (Romans 6:14). Therefore, no one will break the law. In other words, there will be no bad people in Heaven (Revelation 21:8; 22:15). No one will steal, rob, rape, or murder. You will not need to fear being abused, molested, assaulted, mugged, or kidnapped. You won't have to lock the doors when you leave. Security systems and fences will be unnecessary. No one will need to carry a gun. Mace and pepper spray will be missing.

In Heaven there will be no need for courtrooms, jails, dungeons, or prisons, because there will be no criminals. The role of judges, lawyers, and police officers will be unnecessary or will radically change.

I am not sure about the role, if any, for policemen in Heaven. During the Welsh Revival of 1904, God's presence was incredibly thick in Wales for a period of months. In twelve months on that tiny land, one hundred thousand people were saved and many others' spirits were revived. As a result, crime all but ceased. The courts and jails were deserted, and the police found themselves without any work to do. The story is told of policemen who closed their station and formed a choir to sing at the revival meetings.

Sin is moral crookedness. There will be no perversion, moral filth, or corruption in Heaven. Pornography, prostitution, drug dealing, and sexual abuse will have no role in Heaven. The media, if there is need for one, will be pure, positive, and powerfully encouraging. There will be no bad news to report. Nothing will fly out over the airwaves or appear on a printed page that would dishonor God or offend His people.

Sin is rebellion. In the new Heaven, there will be no need of a military presence to put down uprisings. Soldiers will have no one to fight. Peace will rule.

Sin is straying off God's course and following the wrong path. Satan worshipers, false teachers, fortune tellers, witches, and psychics will have no home in Heaven (Revelation 22:15).

Sin is missing God's mark. In Heaven moral, spiritual, mental, emotional, and physical potential will be realized. Instead of focusing on illness and disease, heath care persons can help us maximize health and nutrition. There will be no disease. There are no negatives in Heaven.

There Will Be No Untransformed "Sinners" in Heaven

I am quite certain that there will be "sinners" in Heaven—after all, I plan on being there. In fact, Heaven will be full of "sinners," or, more accurately, "*ex*-sinners." Former thieves, liars, murderers, and adulterers will abound. Didn't Jesus tell the thief on the cross he would join Jesus in Paradise (Luke 23:43)? Didn't Paul describe himself as the worst of sinners (1 Timothy 1:15)?

The human luminaries in Heaven will be a "who's who" of people with a past. Moses *was* a murderer. So *was* David. Joshua *had been* cowardly and initially lacked faith. So *did* Gideon, Moses, and Thomas. Rahab *was* a harlot. Bathsheba *was* an adulteress. Judah and David *were* adulterers. Mary Magdalene *had been* a very "loose woman." Solomon *had* three hundred concubines. He also *had* married hundreds of pagan women who turned his heart from the Lord.

Abraham and Jacob *had* terrible troubles with lying. Noah *had* a drinking problem. Miriam *was* a gossip. Jonah *ran* from God. Martha *was* a work-addicted worrier. Mary *might have been* a bit lazy. James and John *wrestled* with selfish ambition. Peter *denied* Jesus. The disciples *hid*. Mark *was* a quitter.

Every human in Heaven will have a past as a "sinner." All will be an ex-something (replace *something* with words like "liar," "drunk," "thief," "cheat," "gossip," "doubter," "glutton"). But, unlike people now on Earth, that sinful part of our personality will be gone, washed away forever by the power of the crucified blood of the Lord Jesus Christ. Our personalities will be transformed into what they were originally intended to be before the world, the flesh, and the devil twisted them into something hideous and grotesquely evil. They will be a glorious reflection of the character of the Lord Jesus. So, even though there will be "sinners" in Heaven, we will become gloriously transformed saints.

Heaven will be a much better place. You will like yourself and others much better because all our sinful tendencies will be gone.

You Will Like Yourself Much Better in Heaven

One of the big reasons I committed my life completely to following Jesus Christ is because a long time ago I realized that I could never escape "me." I have to be with "me" 24/7. There is no place I can go on this planet to flee from myself. Therefore, I had better enjoy the person I am becoming. Other people will not always like me, but I had better be able to appreciate and respect the person I am.

One of the aspects of Heaven I am most thrilled about is I'll be the very best "me" I can be. Self-centeredness, selfish ambition, and selfishness will no longer be enemies I must constantly fight. Fear, doubt, dread, worry, and anxiety will not limit me. Bitterness, resentment, and anger will not have to be continually rooted out of my heart. Greed, lust, jealousy, and envy won't try to capture my heart.

You Will Enjoy People Much More in Heaven

I have to confess, I have a hard time loving, or even liking, some Christian people. Some are hard to like because they have chosen to become so incredibly dull or dreary. There are those who are far too narrow-minded and others who are too open-minded. Some I struggle to love because they rub me the wrong way, their battles with sin correspond too closely with my own. Others have hurts, hang-ups, or habits that have so tainted their lives they are very hard to love.

However, I am sure I won't have any trouble enjoying the company of every single person in Heaven. Pride, arrogance, pettiness, jealousy, and self-righteousness will be gloriously absent from their personalities. . .and mine. The deep wounds that turned them into hurtful people will be gloriously healed in Heaven.

There Is No Curse in Heaven

Just as sin will be removed, its consequences will be eradicated from Heaven (Revelation 22:3). Prior to sin staining Earth, it was a paradise of perfect peace, ideal innocence, and complete community. Since sin entered the world, our universe has lived under the curse of the consequences of sin. Everything has been tainted, stained, twisted, and cheapened.

Prior to sin, in the Garden of Eden the perfect atmosphere produced wonderful weather. There were no natural disasters. Floods, storms, gales, tempests, tornadoes, cyclones, typhoons, whirlwinds, twisters, squalls, hurricanes, blizzards, whiteouts, blackouts, and monsoons did not exist. Heaven will be like that, but even better. The land, air, and water will be perfectly pure. There will be absolutely no trace of pollution, smog, contamination, toxic waste, or trash.

In Heaven the human, plant, and animal kingdoms will live together in absolute harmony. Snakes will not be poisonous. (They also won't tempt us to sin.) If there are any mosquitoes, they will not bite humans. Raccoons won't tip over garbage cans. Termites won't eat the porch. Bees won't sting. Dogs won't bite. I am guessing that even cats will be nice, that is if cats make it to Heaven (just kidding!).

The environment will be pleasantly perfect in Heaven. There will be no frostbite. My balding head won't get sunburned. The disturbing nightmares that often come on full-moon nights won't happen in Heaven.

No germs or viruses will exist in Heaven. *Disease, illness, sickness, infirmity,* and *infection* will drop out of our dictionaries. So will terms such as *ailment, disorder, malady*, and *affliction*.

What will scientists, doctors, dentists, pharmacists, opticians, nurses, and surgeons do in Heaven? My guess is that they will focus on studying health and helping us maximize the potential of our new bodies. What about psychologists, psychiatrists, and counselors? If those jobs exist in any form, I assume that they will help us maximize our mental and emotional potential.

Don't plan on seeing hospitals, sanatoriums, nursing homes, rehab centers, or clinics in Heaven. There definitely will be no morgues, funeral homes, or cemeteries. Heaven is all about life, and death will not exist (Revelation 21:4).

So What?

Knowing that Heaven is a much better place than Earth makes me long for Heaven. It also gives me patience with the imperfections of Earth, knowing that they will largely be forgotten in the superior perfections of Heaven.

6

THE WORLD'S GREATEST FAMILY REUNION

None of those earthly family reunions, however, prepared me for the sublime gathering of saints I experienced at the gates of heaven.

DON PIPER[1]

"I Will See Them on the Other Side"

In January 2006 the tiny town of Tallmansville, West Virginia, was rocked when an explosion in the Sago Mine left twelve miners trapped underground to die of toxic gases. Some of the twelve scrawled farewell notes to their loved ones. One, Martin Toler, Jr., known as "JR," wrote these words, "Tell them all I will see them on the other side. . .I love you."[2]

"I will see them on the other side." One of the most anticipated aspects of Heaven is the assurance of being reunited with friends and family who have gone on before us. Heaven hosts a happy and continual series of fantastic family reunions.

Heaven is the home of the most, the biggest, and the best reunions imaginable.

"The World's Largest Family Reunion"

One of the most notorious family feuds in history was finally put to rest in the summer of 2000. The rivalries between the Hatfields and the McCoys began boiling in 1863 and continued off and on for nearly thirty years. The true origin of the feud between these two families is lost in the mists of history, but legend has it that bitter feelings became violent in 1878 when Randolph McCoy accused Floyd Hatfield of stealing one of his hogs. In total, the feud claimed the lives of twelve men.

Descendants of these famous families saw lingering effects disappear at the first ever Hatfield and McCoy national reunion held in June 2000 in Pikeville, Kentucky, and Matewan, West Virginia. The "truce signing" ceremony was aired on national television.

Today, the reunion claims to be "The World's Largest Family Reunion." It has grown into a full-blown festival spread across three counties and into two states (Kentucky and West Virginia) complete with corporate sponsors and news media in attendance. It features heated "rematches" between the Hatfields and the McCoys in a "friendly" game of softball and a tug-of-war across the appropriately named Tug River. The festival covers several busy days and includes free concerts, a live dramatic reenactment of the feud, a golf tournament, a street fair, a carnival, an ATV ride, and a marathon.

The Hatfield and McCoy reunion has become quite elaborate, very large, and a great deal of fun—but it is nothing compared to the family reunions to be staged in Heaven. It's estimated that twenty million family members gather at some four hundred thousand reunion events each year. But they will not compare with the intensity and joy of the family reunions in Heaven. In Heaven the food will be better, the fun purer, the joy deeper, and the good times endless.

Heaven, God's Forever Family Reunion

God's family reunion is open to all who have been born again by faith in Jesus Christ. God loves us and deeply desires to have us in His family. He loves us so much that He gave His Son to die on the cross to pay for our sins. His death provides us with the gift of eternal life. When we place faith in Jesus Christ, we are born again into God's forever family.

Yet to all who received him, to those who believed in his name, he gave the right to become children of God—children born not of natural descent, nor of human decision or a husband's will, but born of God.

JOHN 1:12–13

As God's children, we relate to Him as our Father (Matthew 6:9; Romans 8:15; Galatians 4:6), to Jesus as our brother (Romans 8:17; Hebrews 2:11), and to one another as siblings (Galatians 6:10). In one sense, we will relate to everyone in Heaven as family.

Ninety Minutes in Heaven

Don Piper's car was crushed by a semi-truck that crossed into his lane. Medical personnel said he died instantly. While his body lay lifeless inside the ruins of his car, Piper experienced the glories of Heaven, awed by its beauty and music. Ninety minutes after the wreck, while a minister prayed for him, Piper miraculously returned to life on earth with only the memory of inexpressible heavenly bliss.[3]

Piper's memory of his ninety minutes in Heaven was of intense joy created by indescribably beautiful music, warm wonderful light, an immense shimmering gate, and a welcoming committee. The heavenly welcome wagon was made up of all the people who had played a role in Piper's spiritual journey. They displayed extreme delight that he was joining them. One by one they hugged him and touched him with the profoundest level of pure affection and love Don had ever experienced. He never felt more welcome and at home.

There are many tales of near-death experiences that I do not accept as true because they don't correspond with what the Bible says about death and Heaven—but not so Piper's. His story of ninety minutes in Heaven rings true when compared to the Bible. I am not sure everyone will have exactly the same experience as his, but I do believe we will be graciously greeted by our spiritual brothers and sisters who have gone on before us.

United with the Father

In one sense, just arriving in Heaven will create a festive family union. We will be united with our heavenly family as the prodigal son was with his family (Luke 15:11–24). I think that every time one of us arrives in Heaven, the Father, seeing us coming from a long way off, will run to us, hug our necks, and kiss us (Luke 15:20). We will be delighted not to see His face *again,* but to see it for the very first time. While we are broken by His uninhibited expression of unconditional love to undeserving sinners, He will brush our apologies aside and call for a celebration.

Joy will burst out like the sun. First, He will tell the angels (possibly our guardian angels) to bring the best robe and put it on our shoulders, place the family ring on our finger, and put sandals on our feet (Luke 15:22). Then Father will have the fatted calf slaughtered and call our brothers and sisters to eat with us, be merry, and celebrate our arrival (Luke 15:23). Being a very wealthy Father, our arrival party could last days, or even weeks. Yet not one will want to leave because of the joy of having us there finally at home.

The celebration in Heaven will not be because we have *returned* home, but because we have finally *arrived* home. We will share the family name, likeness, and history with everyone in Heaven. If not a family *re*-union, it will be a family union. It will surpass any earthly family reunion ever held, in terms of ebullient joy, extreme love, and expressive celebration.

Spiritual Family Reunions

Paul told the believers in Thessalonica and Philippi he was eager to join together with them before Jesus in Heaven.

> *For what is our hope, our joy, or the crown in which we will glory in the presence of our Lord Jesus when he comes? Is it not you?*
>
> 1 THESSALONIANS 2:19

> *Therefore, my brothers, you whom I love and long for, my joy and crown, that is how you should stand firm in the Lord, dear friends!*
>
> PHILIPPIANS 4:1

In Heaven we will be reunited with *spiritual* family members. As an adult, I would love to be able to sufficiently thank the three men who pastored my church when I was growing up. Only now am I able to truly appreciate their sacrifices and hard work.

I have had the privilege of leading people to Christ in distant states and other countries, whom I have never seen again. In Heaven we will have time and opportunity for them to tell me of their spiritual journeys. As a pastor, many of my sheep moved on to other states, and I have not seen them since. It will be a treat to catch up with them in Heaven. I will have great joy as I hear how my children walked in truth (3 John 4).

Heavenly Family Reunions

Last year our family went on a cruise. We were surprised by the number of families celebrating reunions on the cruise. They wore brightly colored T-shirts emblazoned with messages such as "Smith Family Reunion 2005."

While earthly family reunions can be big and fun, heavenly ones will be even bigger and better. In Heaven we will be reunited with biological family members who have gone on before us. As I have mentioned previously, I deeply long to see my mom and dad again. Cathy and I look forward to seeing her father again. My grandparents and most of my aunts and uncles are already there; it will be interesting to see them again. It will also be fascinating to meet family members who knew the Lord and went to Heaven hundreds and even thousands of years ago.

Maybe the thought of a family reunion gives you the creeps. Maybe you have some odd, ornery, or annoying family members whom you would rather not spend eternity with. Let me remind you, our sin natures stay behind when we go to Heaven. All of us will be our very best selves. We will be more patient and loving, and our family members will be more like Christ as well. Family reunions in Heaven will be heavenly.

Maybe your family has been fractured by divorce, division, or distance. Those who are Christians will lay aside every difference and be reunited in Heaven to sign a permanent truce. They may enjoy a "friendly game of softball" or a low-key tug-of-war.

Possibly you are the only Christian in your family. May the notion of heavenly family reunions motivate you to continue to pray for and witness to your loved ones. You have nothing to lose and everything to gain. Cathy and I have worked hard to make sure our children have a growing, personal relationship with Jesus. We want to be sure we can share Heaven together as a family.

The 65th Troop Carrier

One of the highlights of my parents' later years was the semiannual reunion of the 65th Troop Carrier Squadron of the U.S. Army Air Force. Dad and his cronies who served together in the Philippines in World War II, along with their wives, loved to gather in various parts of the country for a weekend of food, fun, and the retelling of old stories. Every six months a different veteran hosted the group in his hometown. Group size ranged from twenty to nearly a hundred.

They shared a special bond, having endured the Great Depression as a generation and, especially, because they had endured the hardships of war as a unit. The more they met together, the deeper their love for each other grew.

In Heaven there will be reunions of spiritual soldiers. I can picture David's Mighty Men manhandling a massive meal and reliving their exciting exploits (2 Samuel 23:8–39). Shadrach, Meshach, and Abednego could get together to celebrate the annual anniversary of the fiery furnace affair (Daniel 3). The disciples may meet to celebrate the anniversary of the Last Supper, or the Resurrection, or the day of Pentecost, or maybe all three. All those martyred for their faith could meet to recount the awesome privilege of giving their lives for the Master.

I think that Heaven could host huge conventions of those who served as Sunday school teachers, choir members, or deacons. There may be massive meetings of missionaries, great gatherings of pastors, or events held for evangelists. Why won't church planters convene, worship leaders unite, and small group leaders cluster?

So What?

Knowing that Heaven will be a huge family reunion comforts me with the assurance that I will see Mom and Dad again. It humbles me with the thought of having the opportunity to thank those who helped me get on, and stay on, the path to Heaven. It also motivates me to keep helping others get there, so we can enjoy eternity together.

NOTES

[1] Don Piper with Cecil B. Murphey, *90 Minutes in Heaven: A True Story of Death and Life* (Grand Rapids: Baker, 2004), 25.

[2] "A Miner's Last Words," Columbus *Dispatch* (January 6, 2006), 1.

[3] Piper, 21–28.

7
You Ain't Seen Nothin' Yet

The very first word man was ever given regarding God is that He is the Good Creator. In the beginning, God created humans and a vast variety of amazing plants and animals. His inventive genius produced an astounding array of stars and planets. He made the breathtaking beauty of the sunset. When He was finished, even He was impressed with His work and described it as "very good" (Genesis 1:1–31).

Elsewhere, scripture makes it clear that the primary player in the creation of the universe was God the Son, Jesus Christ.

> *Through him all things were made; without him nothing was made that has been made.*
>
> John 1:3

> *For by him all things were created: things in heaven and on earth, visible and invisible, whether thrones or powers or rulers or authorities; all things were created by him and for him.*
>
> Colossians 1:16

> *In these last days he has spoken to us by his Son, whom he appointed heir of all things, and through whom he made the universe.*
>
> Hebrews 1:2

When God became man (Jesus), He became a carpenter (Mark 6:3). Carpenters are creators. Good carpenters will look at a lifeless piece of wood and see something valuable and beautiful. Carefully and skillfully, they will craft it to detailed specifications. They will lovingly polish it, and when it is ready they will proudly show it to others. Creating beautiful things is what excellent carpenters do.

Jesus wanted to encourage His disciples in the wake of His nearing departure. He gave them a powerful promise that He was going to take on a massive renovation and building project—Heaven.

> *"Do not let your hearts be troubled. Trust in God; trust also in me. In my Father's house are many rooms; if it were not so, I would have told you. I am going there to prepare a place for you. And if I go and prepare a place for you, I will come back and take you to be with me that you also may be where I am."*
>
> John 14:1–3

Jesus was telling them that Heaven, although perfect in its present state at that time, was not yet fully prepared. He wanted to continue modifying and expanding it to suit its coming inhabitants. This means that ever since Jesus spoke those words in the first century, Heaven has been under renovation, being remodeled, enlarged, and enhanced by the Magnificent Creator, Marvelous Carpenter, and Master Craftsman, Jesus Christ. Wow!

Heaven is a world far greater than this one, but far less than the one to come.

Change in Heaven

My family began when Cathy and I were married in 1981. Over the past twenty-five years, three boys have come into our family and much has occurred. Yet the essence of our family has not changed much. We try to put God first, be church-centered, grow as individuals, and make a difference in our world. Although our family dynamics have changed through the years as children have been added and progressed through various stages, and it will undoubtedly change in the future as daughters-in-law and grandbabies are added, it will still be our family. It is currently not all it will one day be.

Heaven is similar in that it has and will continue to undergo some changes, additions, expansions, and renovations while maintaining its core distinctive. In any of its stages, Heaven is the place of blessed reward for God's faithful children. It is God's home and man's hope. Yet much of what the Bible says about Heaven can become confusing until we understand that Heaven, as it is, is not yet all it will ultimately become.

The Phases of Heaven

Heaven past, Heaven present, and Heaven future should all be understood as Heaven, but must not be viewed as being exactly the same. The Bible describes at least five phases of Heaven. Each stage is still Heaven, yet is slightly different from the others.

1. Early Heaven

Early Heaven is the Heaven that existed until the time Satan led a mutiny against God (Isaiah 14:12–15; Ezekiel 28:12–17). Joining Satan were up to a third of the angels (Revelation 12:4, 9). This is nearly all we know about Early Heaven. Was there a stage of Heaven prior to this? We don't know.

2. Abraham's Side

After the fall of Satan and prior to the resurrection of Jesus, Heaven was one side of two compartments of one place called "Sheol" in Hebrew, or "Hades" in Greek. The two compartments were divided by an uncrossable chasm (Luke 16:26). Jesus called the heavenly side "Abraham's side" (Luke 16:22). The other compartment was an earlier version of hell (Luke 16:23). Those on Abraham's side experienced the pleasure of God's presence (Psalm 16:11). Those on the other side were in misery (Luke 16:23).

3. Paradise or the Third Heaven

On the cross, Jesus promised the repentant thief that he would soon join Jesus in "paradise" (Luke 23:43). Seemingly, Jesus was planning on relocating the heavenly compartment of Sheol. The scriptures teach that Paradise is where believers now ascend directly into the Lord's presence at the time of physical death (Ephesians 4:8–10; 2 Corinthians 5:8). It is the place to which Jesus ascended in a cloud and the place from which He will one day return.

> *After he said this, he was taken up before their very eyes, and a cloud hid him from their sight. They were looking intently up into the sky as he was going, when suddenly two men dressed in white stood beside them. "Men of Galilee," they said, "why do you stand here looking into the sky? This same Jesus, who has been taken from you into heaven, will come back in the same way you have seen him go into heaven."*
>
> ACTS 1:9–11

Paradise is the "far better" place Paul was privileged to see and, thereafter, longed for. He called it "the third heaven" (2 Corinthians 12:1–4). The first heaven is the domain of birds and clouds, the second heaven is what we call outer space. For Paul, being in Paradise was "gain" (i.e., "more life") compared to life on Earth, primarily because Christ is there (Philippians 1:21–23).

> *For to me, to live is Christ and to die is gain. If I am to go on living in the body, this will mean fruitful labor for me. Yet what shall I choose? I do not know! I am torn between the two: I desire to depart and be with Christ, which is better by far.*
> PHILIPPIANS 1:21–23

> *I must go on boasting. Although there is nothing to be gained, I will go on to visions and revelations from the Lord. I know a man in Christ who fourteen years ago was caught up to the third heaven. . .[he] was caught up to paradise.*
> 2 CORINTHIANS 12:1– 2, 4

John also was honored to see visions of Paradise (Revelation 2:7). Fortunately, he was encouraged to write down what he saw (Revelation 1:19). And we are deeply indebted to John for much of our knowledge about Heaven.

Paradise is the present stage of Heaven. It is the heavenly place my mom and dad now call home. Every believer who has died since Jesus' resurrection has gone directly to Paradise. Paradise is where I am confidently preparing to go when I die. It is the place where I hope to meet you face-to-face.

Some believe Paradise exists as a different dimension alongside our visible universe. Others feel it may be a distinct universe with portals to ours. We don't know for sure. We do know that this present realm of Paradise is an angelic realm. It is distinct from the Earth. Except in rare, isolated incidents, it is invisible to our current human eyes. It is a spiritual dimension with physical elements. Occasionally people could see into it or see beings from Paradise (Acts 7:55–59; 2 Kings 6:17). People in it have or assume some sort of visible bodies (Matthew 17:3).

Paradise will undergo a transition of its own during the time of Tribulation on Earth. The amazing prophetic books of Daniel and Revelation and some of Jesus' final teachings tell us much about the future happenings on planet Earth. After a departure of the Christians in an event known as the Rapture, Earth will experience seven dreadful years of pain and suffering known as the Tribulation. The Antichrist will assume a season of power and will use it to persecute and execute many of God's people. Great numbers of Jewish people will return to faith in Jesus as their Messiah. At the end of these seven years of tribulation, King Jesus will return to Earth to establish His kingdom.

While the Bible is clear about many earthly events and even much of the timing of these events during the seven years of the Tribulation, it is not as specific about the timing of the happenings in Heaven during this time. As I link the pieces of the puzzle together, I see several major events that believers in Heaven will experience as they transition from Paradise to the millennial Kingdom. These include the resurrection of the dead and rapture of the living (1 Thessalonians 4:13–18), the judgment seat of Christ (2 Corinthians 5:10), and the wedding supper of the Lamb (Revelation 19:6–9).

4. The Millennial Kingdom

The Bible describes a glorious time when Jesus Christ will return to reign as King on Earth for one thousand years (Revelation 20:1–10). There is much we do not currently understand about the millennial Kingdom. However, we do know that Jesus will bring a season of tremendous tranquility to this planet. This will be an unprecedented, glorious time of prosperity and peace on Earth.

> *"The wolf and the lamb will feed together, and the lion will eat straw like the ox, but dust will be the serpent's food. They will neither harm nor destroy on all my holy mountain," says the* LORD.
>
> ISAIAH 65:25

5. The New Heaven and the New Earth

Heaven is not yet all it will be. When John saw into the future, he saw "a *new* heaven and a *new* earth" (Revelation 21:1, emphasis added). Following the millennial Kingdom, sin, suffering, and sorrow will be completely removed from this earth. Earth will be reborn, resurrected, and remade into something wonderfully new, and even better than paradise is right now.

> *Then I saw a new heaven and a new earth. . . . And I heard a loud voice from the throne saying, "Now the dwelling of God is with men, and he will live with them. They will be his people, and God himself will be with them and be their God. He will wipe every tear from their eyes. There will be no more death or mourning or crying or pain, for the old order of things has passed away." He who was seated on the throne said, "I am making everything new!"*
>
> REVELATION 21:1, 3–5

Many view the new Heaven and new Earth of Revelation 21 and 22 as Heaven the way it ultimately will be. This may or may not be the case. There may be further phases of Heaven following this one; the Bible does not say. Since Heaven is an eternal place, I would not be surprised if the Master Builder continued to renovate Heaven, each phase being yet more glorious than the one before.

So What?

The size, scope, quality, beauty, functionality, and value of any construction project are limited by its location and the skills, resources, and imagination of its designer and builder. Remember, the Designer and Builder of Heaven is our unlimited God. Although we do not currently know all there is to know about it, we do know the One who created the wonders we call our universe has been working on preparing Heaven for nearly two thousand years. Therefore, it will be truly amazing and will only get better.

8

Paradise, Heaven

My friend and writing mentor, Norm Rohrer, grew up in Paradise. . .that's Paradise, Pennsylvania. Paradise, PA, is a beautiful little town tucked in the heart of Pennsylvania Dutch country in Lancaster County. This picturesque place is known for peaceful living, rich fruit farms, and the nationally acclaimed cornfield maze, "The Amazing Maize Maze."

Norm tells me that it was a great place to grow up. He says that he smiles when he thinks of Heaven, because if Paradise, Pennsylvania, was such a fantastic hometown, then how much *more* wonderful life will be in *the* Paradise we call Heaven. In other words, as great as it is, Paradise, Pennsylvania, will not compare to Paradise, Heaven.

Paradise, Heaven

Since my mom and dad have already departed from Earth and taken the trip to Paradise, Heaven, I often wonder what Paradise must be like and what their lives are like now. A quick look at the Bible tells me the word *paradise* is found three times. By looking up those verses I discover that my parents, like the thief Jesus comforted on the cross, are with the Lord in Paradise (Luke 23:43; 2 Corinthians 5:8). I find that Paul saw a glimpse of Paradise and deeply desired to return there as opposed to staying on Earth (2 Corinthians 12:1–4; Philippians 1:21–23). Based on Paul's words, I believe my parents are definitely somewhere more desirable than Earth.

I also notice that in John's revelation, Jesus told him that spiritual overcomers would eat from the tree of life found in Paradise (Revelation 2:7). Therefore, Mom and Dad must now be in a literal place graced by access to the extremely powerful tree of life.

But what is life like in Paradise? The Bible gives us many clues.

Clues from the Garden of Eden

The word *Paradise* comes from an Iranian word meaning "enclosed park or garden."[1] It also is used to refer to the Garden of Eden in the Greek version of the Old Testament (Genesis 2:8; Ezekiel 28:13). This makes sense, as it will be the domain of the tree of life that adorned the original Garden of Eden (Revelation 2:7; Genesis 3:24). Ancient Jews felt that Heaven was a restored Eden. The best way to understand Heaven as it is today is to think of it as a restored and perfected Garden of Eden.

Paradise, Heaven, is a restored, purified, and perfected Garden of Eden.

God called Eden "very good" (Genesis 1:31). In Eden, Adam and Eve had brand-new bodies that had the appearance of age and maturity (they were man and woman, not newborns). The garden was filled with fantastic fruit trees (2:9). Rivers flowed through the garden (2:10–14). Adam was given the responsibility of working and protecting the garden (2:15). Humans had a good relationship with the animals (2:19–20). Adam and Eve were married in Eden (2:24). They lived in innocence (2:25). They communicated with each other (3:6), with at least some of the animals (3:1–2), and directly with God (3:9–10).

So I assume that, quite possibly, Paradise, Heaven, is quite similar to what the Garden of Eden was before sin. Like Eden, it is an extremely pleasant garden, carefully cultivated, lush, and filled with gorgeous exotic plants and animals. Paradise is totally free of any form of pollution, contamination, corruption, perversion, and sin. It is a place of boundless beauty, profound rest, and tremendous tranquility. God Himself walks there and is accessible for conversations. No wonder it's called Heaven!

The residents in Paradise will probably have wonderful, prime bodies; amazing and healthy meals; and meaningful work. Like the Garden of Eden, there are animals, and Mom and Dad may be able to talk with them! No doubt they are waiting for the ultimate and perfect union with Christ at the marriage supper of the Lamb. They are undoubtedly enjoying an incredibly delightful time in a wonderfully pleasant place.

Clues from the Mount of Transfiguration

There are a couple of men who were permanently relocated to Heaven, yet returned to Earth briefly. Their names are Moses and Elijah. Observing how they were described can give us some clue as to what people are like in Paradise right now.

> Jesus. . .took Peter, John and James with him and went up onto a mountain to pray. As he was praying, the appearance of his face changed, and his clothes became as bright as a flash of lightning. Two men, Moses and Elijah, appeared in glorious splendor, talking with Jesus. They spoke about his departure, which he was about to bring to fulfillment at Jerusalem. Peter and his companions . . .saw his glory and the two men standing with him.
>
> Luke 9:28–32

The above passage about Moses and Elijah tells us several important facts about people in Paradise. First, they were recognizable for who they really were. Peter and John had never seen them before but immediately knew their names and identities. Second, they had some sort of perceivable, physical bodies. Third, the bodies they had carried a remarkable, incandescent radiance. This splendor either came from the bodies themselves or was reflected glory from the place they had recently departed, Paradise. Fourth, they were able to speak with one another. Fifth, they spoke with Jesus face-to-face. Sixth, they were aware of what was happening with Jesus on Earth. Seventh, they had some knowledge of the future as it was about to unfold in the life of Jesus.

From this account, I assume Mom and Dad will be immediately recognizable to themselves and others. They have some sort of nifty radiant bodies. They can talk to each other and others. They can talk to Jesus! They probably have some idea of what is happening on Earth involving events relating to God's Kingdom. They may even have some knowledge of other events, like what is occurring in the lives of their children and grandchildren. They also may have a good understanding of what is about to happen in the future.

Clues from Lazarus the Beggar

Jesus told a fascinating story about a rich man who went to hell and a beggar named Lazarus who inhabited an early phase of Heaven. As previously stated, after the fall of Satan and prior to the resurrection of Jesus, Heaven was one of two compartments of what was referred to as "Sheol" in Hebrew. Jesus called the heavenly side "Abraham's side" (Luke 16:22). The other compartment is an earlier version of hell (Luke 16:23). The bulk of this story is about the man in hell. We can conclude that much of what was true of Lazarus in Abraham's side will be true of people in the updated version of Heaven, called Paradise.

> *"There was a rich man who was dressed in purple and fine linen and lived in luxury*
> *every day. At his gate was laid a beggar named Lazarus. . . . The time came when the*
> *beggar died and the angels carried him to Abraham's side. The rich man also died and*
> *was buried. In hell, where he was in torment, he looked up and saw Abraham far*
> *away, with Lazarus by his side. So he called to him, 'Father Abraham, have pity on*
> *me and send Lazarus to dip the tip of his finger in water and cool my tongue, because*
> *I am in agony in this fire.'"*
>
> LUKE 16:19, 22–24

In Jesus' story, Lazarus was carried to Heaven by angels. This is also probably what happens to Christians who die today. Lazarus was recognizable, just as Elijah and Moses were recognizable. People in Paradise won't be shapeless, formless, ethereal ghosts.

> *"But Abraham replied, 'Son, remember that in your lifetime you received your good*
> *things, while Lazarus received bad things, but now he is comforted here and you are*
> *in agony. And besides all this, between us and you a great chasm has been fixed, so*
> *that those who want to go from here to you cannot, nor can anyone cross over from*
> *there to us.'"*
>
> LUKE 16:25–26

Lazarus was receiving comfort in Heaven. My parents both suffered at the end of their earthly lives. It is encouraging to know that they are now in a place of comfort. Lazarus's destiny was fixed. My parents both loved God. It is good to know that their place in Paradise is secure.

> *"He answered, 'Then I beg you, father, send Lazarus to my father's house, for I have*
> *five brothers. Let him warn them, so that they will not also come to this place of*
> *torment.' Abraham replied, 'They have Moses and the Prophets; let them listen to*
> *them.' 'No, father Abraham,' he said, 'but if someone from the dead goes to them, they*
> *will repent.' He said to him, 'If they do not listen to Moses and the Prophets, they will*
> *not be convinced even if someone rises from the dead.'"*
>
> LUKE 16:27–31

Lazarus was not allowed to leave Heaven to intervene in the affairs of people on Earth. They were to work on their own destinies based on the guidance of the scriptures. I assume this is also true of my parents and others in Paradise. They may see what we are experiencing, but they probably are not permitted to interfere with it.

Other Clues

There are a few other scriptures that shed light on the goings-on in Paradise. Although these scriptures are not conclusive, they leave some interesting clues.

> *Therefore, since we are surrounded by such a great cloud of witnesses, let us throw*
> *off everything that hinders and the sin that so easily entangles, and let us run with*
> *perseverance the race marked out for us.*
>
> HEBREWS 12:1

Scholars debate the identity of these witnesses who surround us, but it is entirely possible that the believers in Paradise somehow can see our efforts to follow God and cheer us on.

In Luke chapter 15, Jesus tells the stories of the lost sheep, the lost coin, and the lost son. In each case the result of the successful pursuit was a joyous party. What is interesting is that He also says that a party is thrown in Heaven when a sinner repents.

> *"I tell you that in the same way there will be more rejoicing in heaven over one sinner who repents than over ninety-nine righteous persons who do not need to repent."*
>
> LUKE 15:7

It is probable that the ones described as "rejoicing" in this verse are not only the members of the holy Trinity or just the holy angels. Friends and relatives, pastors and missionaries will also join in the joyous occasion. People on the other side understand the supreme significance of salvation more deeply than we do (Luke 16:27–28). It only makes sense that one of the greatest sources of delight and happiness for believers in Heaven will be to observe the marvelous miracle of regeneration in the lives of those with whom they have shared and love.

The apostle Peter makes an offhand but extremely insightful comment about God's relationship to time in his last letter.

> *But do not forget this one thing, dear friends: With the Lord a day is like a thousand years, and a thousand years are like a day.*
>
> 2 PETER 3:8

Peter's point is that God lives outside of the realm of time. I assume that once we leave our earthly lives and enter Paradise we also will enter a world that operates largely outside the realm of time. Time will have no meaning in Heaven as it does on Earth.

So What?

Based on what we have studied about Paradise, we can conclude that Paradise, Heaven, is not totally unlike Earth at its very best. It is simply much, much better. It is like a restored, purified, and perfected Garden of Eden.

Writing this chapter has given me peace. Instead of wondering if my parents are some sort of mystical, disembodied spirits, I can picture my parents younger, stronger, and more vibrant then ever, but still themselves—their very best selves. They live in the most delightful, wonderful, lovely place ever created or imagined. Harmony and deep happiness rule the day. They are living in a place of vibrant rest. And they are communing with God.

I am also reminded of the incredible importance of inspiring others to put their faith in Jesus Christ as their Savior. Their eventual turning to God will bring great joy to untold others in Paradise.

NOTE

1. *Webster's Ninth Collegiate Dictionary* (Springfield MA: Merriman-Webster Inc. Publishers, 1987), 853.

9

Heaven's Awards Banquet

I'll never forget my first real awards banquet. It was early evening in the spring of my sophomore year. We wore suits and our parents joined us for the Winter Sports Awards Banquet. The cafeteria of Chillicothe High School was the same as usual, except for two things: the walls were decorated with blue and white streamers, and sitting on a long table was a stunning array of big blue and silver trophies.

Excitedly, we chewed the mandatory rubbery chicken dinner with the artificial mashed potatoes, plastic-tasting green beans, and white rolls. After we washed down the stale cake with a couple of glasses of overly sweetened iced tea, the school officials began to honor the athletes of the various teams. I quickly noticed that the athletes fit into three categories and received three types of awards based on their category.

First were the people who had made the team. They received a paper certificate for being on the team. Every athlete got one of those. No negative comments were made about any of the team members. Everything shared that night was the positive observation of the person's performance and effort.

Next to be honored were the varsity athletes who had played on the varsity team. Those select individuals got big, fluffy, white letter Cs with blue trim. They were the lettermen. I was pretty excited because I was earning a varsity letter as a sophomore.

But it was the last, select group that caught my attention. They were given the few big, beautiful silver trophies. They were the top varsity athletes, who got trophies for leading the team in scoring, being the most dedicated, or being the most valuable. They were the ones selected all-league, all-district, or even all-state.

Several years later I was reading in my Bible about the great awards banquet that will be attended by everyone who goes to Heaven. I had come to understand that at the judgment seat of Christ we would be rewarded for the sacrifice and the sweat we had put forth for God down here on Earth. I was impressed by how similar and also by how much different, more important, and better the heavenly awards presentation would be, compared to the Winter Sports Banquet at Chillicothe High School.

At the heavenly awards banquet, only those who are on Jesus' "team" by faith in Christ as Savior will be invited. Everyone on the team will be recognized. No negative comments will made about any of the team members. Everything shared will be the positive observation of the person's performance and effort spent serving Christ. Some will receive special recognition for their extra efforts and achievements by receiving crowns, commendations, and commissions.

Heaven will be the site of a wonderful awards banquet.

Judgment Day

> *Just as man is destined to die once, and after that to face judgment.*
>
> Hebrews 9:27

The Bible does not teach reincarnation. After death, we face judgment. This begins as a judgment of faith. Those who have placed their faith in Jesus Christ are ushered immediately into Paradise. Those without faith in Christ are not. Those with names recorded in the Lamb's book of life are escorted to Paradise. Those whose names have not been written there face an eternity without God.

Sometime subsequent to death everyone will face a second judgment. This judgment is focused on how they have lived and what they have done. Nonfollowers of Jesus Christ will face the terrifying great white throne judgment (Revelation 20:11–13). However, followers of Christ attend the tremendously encouraging judgment seat of Christ.

Judgment Seat of Christ	Great White Throne of Judgment
2 Corinthians 5:10	Revelation 20:11–13
Believers only	Non-Christians
Awards Banquet	Courtroom
Rewards given	Punishment doled out
Positive	Negative

The judgment seat of Christ is an awards ceremony. The great white throne judgment is a courtroom. The judgment seat of Christ is a positive event we should prepare for and anticipate. The great white throne judgment must be avoided and can be, by placing your faith in Jesus Christ's death, burial, and resurrection for your sins.

Not an Entrance Exam

Contrary to many very funny jokes, Saint Peter is not at the gates of Heaven with a clipboard, checking off those who get in and those who don't based on the judgment seat of Christ. That will already have been decided. Everyone at the judgment seat of Christ will be a follower of Jesus. They are the ones already on His team through faith. Everyone being evaluated will be already in Heaven.

The judgment seat of Christ will not be a place of punishing people for poor performance. No punishment is given out, only rewards. If you are a true Christian, the Bible states very clearly, "There is therefore now *no condemnation* for those who are in Christ Jesus" (Romans 8:1 NASB, emphasis added).

Jesus took all the punishment for our sins when He died on the cross. He didn't just die for *some* of our sins. He died to pay for *all* of our sins. His sacrifice was sufficient to cover the full debt of our sins. Note Hebrews 8:12 (NKJV), which states, "For I will be merciful to their unrighteousness, and *their sins and their lawless deeds I will remember no more*"(emphasis added). When we are saved, our sins are forgiven and functionally forgotten by God forever! There will be no punishment for sins handed out at the judgment seat of Christ. It is the heavenly awards banquet.

The Heavenly Awards Stand

For we must all appear before the judgment seat of Christ, that each one may receive the things done in the body, according to what he has done, whether good or bad.

2 CORINTHIANS 5:10 NKJV

When you read the words "judgment seat," do not think courtroom; rather think of an awards stand. To us the concept of judgment sounds rather negative, but this is an unquestionably positive event. In the first century BC, in the city of Corinth, there were some games that were actually more popular than the Olympic games held in Athens. They were called the Isthmian games and were held every two years in the Greek city. In these games, the winner of each event would be led in front of the judge's stand where the judge, usually the highest dignitary in attendance (the mayor or the governor), would put a laurel crown on the victor's head.

The concept of the judgment seat of Christ is not so much a judicial one as an athletic one. Don't picture a courtroom—picture an Olympic stadium, an awards stand, or, even better, an awards banquet. Don't think of punishment being doled out by a judge—instead, picture awards given out by the greatest dignitary and head coach of them all—the King of kings, the Lord of lords, Jesus Christ.

"And behold, I am coming quickly, and My reward is with Me, to give to every one according to his work."

REVELATION 22:12 NKJV

Judge Jesus

When we are evaluated at the judgment seat of Christ, who will evaluate us? The scripture says, "For we must all appear before the judgment seat of *Christ*" (2 Corinthians 5:10 NKJV, emphasis added). This is also seen in John 5:22 (NKJV): "For the Father judges no one, but has committed all judgment to *the Son*" (emphasis added). Speaking of Jesus, the apostle Peter said, "He is the one whom God appointed as judge of the living and the dead" (Acts 10:42). The apostle Paul said in 2 Timothy 4:8 (NKJV), "Finally, there is laid up for me the crown of righteousness, which *the Lord, the righteous Judge*, will give to me on that Day, and not to me only but also to all who have loved His appearing" (emphasis added).

A perfect evaluator should know all the facts, be just and righteous, and have empathy for the one evaluated. Jesus is the perfect evaluator-judge. As the Son of God, He knows absolutely every detail about you. He also is perfectly just and righteous. Beyond that, two thousand years ago He stepped down out of Heaven and came to Earth, not as a spectator of human life, but as a full participant. Jesus was born in a barn. He had to learn to walk and talk. He was a teenager. He was tempted. He had friends and enemies. He got hungry, thirsty, and tired. He died. Therefore, He can fully empathize with everything we have gone through, making Him the perfect judge (Hebrews 2:14–18).

Some people find the thought of this detailed examination a little unnerving. If you are the type of person who puts on a good front but has some nasty secrets, let me remind you Jesus knows those secrets, and He is not fooled. Now is the time to make whatever adjustments are necessary.

However, there is also great comfort in the fact that Jesus is our only judge. People's evaluations of us can be inaccurate. Jesus won't make any mistake, and He won't miss any of the good we have done, even if no one else takes notice. Ultimately, there is only one person we have to please: our judge, the Lord Jesus.

Refined by Fire

When the apostle John saw the resurrected Jesus in Heaven, he was deeply impressed that Jesus' eyes were like flames of fire (Revelation 1:14). Fire is a powerful purifier. It is used to burn the impurities out of precious metals. Heaven is a perfect place, and before we fully enter into it, our lives down here on Earth will need to be purified and refined. Paul described the judgment seat of Christ as an examination by fire.

> *For no other foundation can anyone lay than that which is laid, which is Jesus Christ. Now if anyone builds on this foundation with gold, silver, precious stones, wood, hay, straw, each one's work will become clear; for the Day will declare it, because it will be revealed by fire; and the fire will test each one's work, of what sort it is. If anyone's work which he has built on it endures, he will receive a reward. If anyone's work is burned, he will suffer loss; but he himself will be saved, yet so as through fire.*
>
> 1 CORINTHIANS 3:11–15 NKJV

Jesus, the Evaluator, will examine our lives. As His eyes of fire see the positives, described here as gold, silver, or precious stones, they will be refined and made more evident, more beautiful. The negatives, described as wood, hay, or straw, will be burned up. The good works we have done in our lives will be refined and rewarded. Based on how we lived and what we did for God down on Earth, we will receive rewards such as crowns, commendations, and commissions.

Casting Crowns

The purpose of winning crowns is not selfish. In fact, it is the exact opposite. The purpose of winning crowns is to have as many as possible to cast at Jesus' feet (Revelation 4:9–11). This will be our way of telling Him "thank You" for all He has done for us.

Temporary Trophy

After attending the awards banquet my sophomore year in high school, I decided I'd go all-out to win a trophy my next year. Every day for the next year, I made sacrifices in order to achieve my goal. I worked out more often, lifted more weights, and ran more miles. I lived on a Spartan diet. It paid off. In fact, one year later, I earned the Most Valuable Player award for my team.

A couple of years after that, I was home from college. I looked at my MVP trophy and found that my nameplate had fallen off. Then it hit me: Earthly trophies won't last, but heavenly trophies will last forever.

So What?

Heaven will have an awesome awards banquet where we can receive eternal rewards; but first, we need to be certain that we will be there by making sure we are on the team. If you have not done so already, you can join this team by making Jesus your personal Lord and Savior. Second, we all need to earn our "varsity letter" by not just coasting, but fully engaging in His service. Third, we must start living for eternity and go all-out to win trophies that we can give back to Jesus.

10
Prepare Yourself

I have a recurring dream—well, actually it's more of a nightmare. I bet many of you have had it as well. The essence of the dream is this: It is the day of final exams. I am walking through my high school on my way to take a final exam. As I am scurrying down the hall, terror is slowly rising in my heart, as I realize that I have not prepared for this final. I have not studied. I have not even read the books that were assigned.

I begin to sweat when I realize it has been weeks since I even attended the class. In fact, my attendance was so infrequent I am not sure where the room is. Terror takes over. Frantically, I dash around unfamiliar hallways. Time is running out and I not only don't have time to prepare, I can't even find the room to take the test. I am engulfed in dread knowing I am completely unprepared. Just as I think things could not get any worse, I look down and notice. . .that I am not wearing pants!

Prepare Yourself!

Having two sons in college and being a college professor, I find some enjoyment in the following tale about a college freshman who really enjoyed his first semester away from Mom and Dad. In fact, he enjoyed it so much, he hadn't done any studying. Just prior to Parents' Weekend, he e-mailed his mom:

> *Having a great time.*
> *Send money.*
> *Flunking all my classes.*
> *Prepare Pop.*

Mom e-mailed back:

> *Pop prepared.*
> *Prepare yourself!*

The most life-changing truth about Heaven is that life on Earth is merely the preparation for eternity in Heaven. We can increase our capacity to enjoy Heaven tomorrow by the choices we make today. The eternal investments we make now will determine where we start there.

> **You can increase your capacity to enjoy Heaven tomorrow by the choices you make today.**

Two thousand years ago, God gave the warning "man is destined to die once, and after that to face examination" (Hebrews 9:27, author's paraphrase). At the heavenly awards banquet, we will undergo the most comprehensive final exam ever administered. Theologians call this exam the judgment seat of Christ. He will evaluate us, looking to reward everything He can in our lives. We will be given crowns, commendations, and commissions as awards. There will be so much to experience and enjoy in Heaven. How we live on earth will directly influence our capacity to fully take pleasure in Heaven.

A study of the Bible reveals many areas of life that the Lord will evaluate. I found the top nine areas of evaluation that you and I need to be prepared for on that day of our final exam. We need to get out our syllabus, the Bible, to see what is coming and to start getting ready for it now.

The Top Areas of Examination

1. Our Motives, Thoughts, and Deeds

> *"I, the LORD, search the heart, I test the mind, even to give every man according to his ways, according to the fruit of his doings."*
>
> JEREMIAH 17:10 NKJV

The Lord will examine us from the inside out. This will include our affections, our thoughts, and our deeds since becoming a Christian. Every selfless, unnoticed act we have ever done will be rewarded. Our private thoughts of God will be recognized.

2. Our Words

> *"But I say to you that for every idle word men may speak, they will give account of it in the day of judgment."*
>
> MATTHEW 12:36 NKJV

The verse is quite clear. The Lord will examine our words. Every time we shared Jesus with a coworker, prayed for someone else, or uttered words of praise to God, Jesus will acknowledge and reward it. However, our ungodly, unwholesome, unkind words will be burned up.

3. Our Treatment of Others

> *For God is not unjust to forget your work and labor of love which you have shown toward His name, in that you have ministered to the saints, and do minister.*
>
> HEBREWS 6:10 NKJV

> *"He who receives a prophet in the name of a prophet shall receive a prophet's reward. And he who receives a righteous man in the name of a righteous man shall receive a righteous man's reward. And whoever gives one of these little ones only a cup of cold water in the name of a disciple, assuredly, I say to you, he shall by no means lose his reward."*
>
> MATTHEW 10:41–42 NKJV

> *"And whoever welcomes a little child like this in my name welcomes me."*
>
> MATTHEW 18:5

These verses point out that God is very concerned with the way we treat others. Sometimes I forget that the Lord may have put that needy person or that difficult person in my life on purpose. He is giving me a chance to show them love and serve them, in part, so He can give me a reward. Sometimes I forget that the way I view and treat others is, in one way, a microcosm of how I view the Lord.

4. Our Use of and/or Response to Spiritual Authority

Obey those who rule over you, and be submissive, for they watch out for your souls, as those who must give account. Let them do so with joy and not with grief, for that would be unprofitable for you.

HEBREWS 13:17 NKJV

This verse tells us to watch how we respond to the spiritual authorities in our lives, because they must give an account for our souls. The context here is talking about pastors. But I believe the principle applies in a broader sense. I will give an account of how I acted not merely as a pastor, but also as a husband, a father, and an employer. Also, I think that if persons in authority are accountable for how they use it, those under authority will also be accountable for how they respond to spiritual authority. How did they treat a father, husband, pastor, or church leader?

5. Our Evangelistic Efforts

For what is our hope, our joy, or the crown in which we will glory in the presence of our Lord Jesus when he comes? Is it not you? Indeed, you are our glory and joy.

1 THESSALONIANS 2:19

Everybody we help get to Heaven will become a crown for us. They may be in Heaven as a result of our inviting them to church, sharing our testimony, praying for them, or giving to outreach projects. I anticipate being warmly welcomed into Heaven by everyone I helped to get there. The joy in their faces will be an incredible reward for whatever role I had in their decision to trust Christ.

6. Our Use of Money

Jesus talked about giving an account of how we use our money more than any other topic. He mentioned it in about half of the parables He told. He knew there is often no clearer picture of our spiritual condition than how we handle and give our money. Paul built on the teachings of Jesus when he wrote,

Command those who are rich in this present age not to be haughty, nor to trust in uncertain riches but in the living God, who gives us richly all things to enjoy. Let them do good, that they be rich in good works, ready to give, willing to share, storing up for themselves a good foundation for the time to come, that they may lay hold on eternal life.

1 TIMOTHY 6:17–19 NKJV
(SEE ALSO MATTHEW 25:14–23, LUKE 12:21; 16:9–14)

7. Our Willingness to Suffer for Christ

> *"Blessed are you when they revile and persecute you, and say all kinds of evil against you falsely for My sake. Rejoice and be exceedingly glad, for great is your reward in heaven, for so they persecuted the prophets who were before you."*
>
> MATTHEW 5:11–12 NKJV
>
> *"Do not be afraid of what you are about to suffer. I tell you, the devil will put some of you in prison to test you, and you will suffer persecution for ten days. Be faithful, even to the point of death, and I will give you the crown of life."*
>
> REVELATION 2:10

There are many thousands of faithful Christians in other parts of the world who truly suffer for their faith. Many even die for Jesus. I am so happy that on the day of evaluation they will be recognized and richly rewarded for their sufferings and sacrifices. They will be receiving "most valuable" awards and lengthy standing ovations.

8. Our Service

One of the chief reasons for the judgment seat is to reward our service for Jesus Christ. The New Testament simply assumes that every Christian will actively serve Christ. When you find a place of service in your church, you are preparing for the coming of Jesus. He desires every member to minister. Whether your place is setting up the chairs on Saturday, working in the nursery, working the lights, teaching a Sunday school class, helping get cars parked, greeting people on their way in, leading a small group, working with teenagers, or singing in the choir, every member needs to be a minister.

The Bible gives several significant criteria with which Jesus will evaluate our service.

The Criteria for Evaluating Our Works
1. Content: Good or bad? Worthwhile or worthless? 2 Corinthians 5:10
2. Motive: To please people or God? Matthew 6:1
3. Source: His strength or ours? John 15:5
4. Faithfulness: Convenient or costly? 1 Corinthians 4:2
5. Quality: Heavenly or earthly? Matthew 6:19–20
6. Proportion: All-out or partial? Luke 12:48

9. Our Level of Church Participation

> *Let us not give up meeting together, as some are in the habit of doing, but let us encourage one another—and all the more as you see the Day approaching.*
>
> HEBREWS 10:25

The author of Hebrews wrote to people who were experiencing persecution because of their church involvement. As a result of the persecution, some wanted to stop drawing attention to themselves and had stopped worshiping together. He encouraged them to "go to church!"

I doubt that many of us miss church because we are trying to avoid persecution. Some people think they can be good Christians but not be involved in a church. The New Testament does not assume that anyone can be a Christian without being actively involved in a local church. It is a nonnegotiable. God will evaluate your level of involvement in His beloved institution—the church.

So What?

For me, the difference between high school and college was the difference between night and day. Of course, college was much harder and had much more homework than high school. But interestingly, I got much better grades in college than in high school.

Did I get smarter in college? No and yes. No, my IQ did not go up. Yes, I got smarter, in that I always made sure I was prepared. In high school I tried to cram and it was never enough. My grades showed it.

In college I started preparing for my finals the first day of class and almost every day in between. On a few occasions, I got some of the highest grades my professors had given. The tests were not something I dreaded; I actually enjoyed them because I was well prepared. I also learned and retained much more than I had in high school.

Shortly after arriving in Heaven, you will be taking your final exam. How you do on your exam will determine how much you will enjoy Heaven. You have all you need in order to be prepared because you have a syllabus, the Bible. So prepare yourself.

11
Total Body Makeover

The body of B. Franklin, printer,
(Like the Cover of an Old Book,
Its Contents torn Out
And Stript of its Lettering and Gilding)
Lies Here, Food for Worms.
But the Work shall not be Lost;
For it will (as he Believ'd) Appear once More
In a New and More Elegant edition,
Revised and Corrected
By the Author.

Franklin's self-written epitaph

Every year at the end of winter, downtown Columbus, Ohio, is the home of the Arnold Sports Festival. Over a three-day period thirty events are held, including fifteen Olympic sports. Everything from arm wrestling, to weightlifting, to figure skating, to volleyball, to archery, to martial arts, to gymnastics is contested. The main events, however, are the bodybuilding competitions for men and women. Considered the most lucrative competition in bodybuilding, winners may leave with such prizes as one hundred thousand dollars' cash, a huge Hummer vehicle, or a Rolex watch. The event is billed as the ultimate celebration of the human body.

I must admit that I fail to see the big appeal of bronzed, bulging, super-sized, steroid-enhanced, chiseled muscles. The winners have obviously worked extremely hard to gain such muscle size and sculpture, but I just don't get it. So much time, expense, and energy spent building up a body that will age, sag, bag, and wear out in just a few decades.

Total Body Makeover

What I do want is a total body makeover, and I don't mean just losing some weight. I mean getting a whole new body—one that will last.

Please, don't get me wrong. I am very thankful for my body. I don't know where I'd be without it. I try to be a good steward of my body through careful diet, wise rest, and regular exercise. But it wouldn't upset me one tiny bit to trade it in on an entirely brand-new model. My old version has over four decades of scars, breaks, and cavities. Frankly, "it ain't what it used to be," and for that matter, "it ain't never been all it could be." A much faster, stronger, sleeker, tanner, more attractive model would be just fine with me. One with keener eyesight and thicker hair would be nice. It would also help my basketball game if I was several inches taller.

No total body makeover on this side of eternity will last very long. Eventually, the strain of living on a sin-cursed planet wears our bodies out. One day, however, we will be given a new, improved version of our body, designed especially for eternity, honed for Heaven.

In Heaven we will get a total body makeover.

One of the best deals about Heaven is that at the resurrection of the redeemed, we will get amazing new bodies. When Jesus rose from the dead, He not only proved His deity and secured our salvation, He also guaranteed our resurrection (1 Corinthians 15:14–20). These better bodies will be issued on that "Great Gettin' Up Morning."

"Oh, That Great Gettin' Up Morning"

Pastor and writer Tony Campolo tells the story of an African American pastor preaching a funeral sermon for a man named Clarence. After a glowing eulogy of some twenty minutes, the pastor concluded, "That's it, Clarence. There is nothing else to say. So if there is nothing else to say, I'm going to say this—'Good night!' "

Closing the lid of the casket, the preacher turned to the congregation and boomed, "And I know that God is going to give him a good morning!"

On cue the choir rose to sing, "Oh, That Great Gettin' Up Morning, We Shall Rise, We Shall Rise." Everyone jumped to their feet, clapping and singing, anticipating the glories of their resurrection.[1]

Resurrection Bodies

God gave the apostle Paul special insight into the type of bodies we would have at our resurrection. In the fifteenth chapter of his letter to the Corinthians, he described several aspects of our new bodies.

1. Perfected

Our new bodies will be perfected versions of the bodies we now have. We know from the apostle John that others will be able to recognize us (John 21:4–7). Sexual identities will remain. Racial identities will continue (Revelation 5:9; 7:9). You will still be yourself, but only much improved.

In speaking of the nature of our resurrection bodies, Paul argues that just as a seed is a precursor and smaller indication of the plant to follow, our earthly bodies are unfulfilled versions of the bodies we will receive at the resurrection. Our new bodies will be completed editions of the bodies we now wear.

> But someone may ask, . . . "With what kind of body will they come?" How foolish! What you sow does not come to life unless it dies. When you sow, you do not plant the body that will be, but just a seed, perhaps of wheat or of something else. But God gives it a body as he has determined, and to each kind of seed he gives its own body
>
> 1 CORINTHIANS 15:35–38

In Heaven you will still look like you, only much, much healthier and whole. Your new body will be what it *should* have been, had Adam and Eve never sinned, only better. It will be what *could* have been if you lived on a perfect diet, breathed only pure air, exercised properly, rested well, and never had a mismanaged emotion, yet even finer. Your new body will be an improved version of all it *can* be without scars, blemishes, fat, cancers, or broken bones. It will reflect no genetic defects. Every single person in Heaven will look breathtaking and incredibly better than the most healthy and attractive person to ever walk the Earth.

2. Human

When we get our new bodies, they will be improved versions of *human* bodies. In speaking of our resurrection bodies, Paul wrote,

All flesh is not the same: Men have one kind of flesh, animals have another, birds another and fish another.

1 CORINTHIANS 15:39

What He is saying is that in Heaven humans will have human bodies; animals will have animal bodies; and birds will have bird bodies. When I was a little boy, I loved to watch birds fly. In fact I still do. I hoped that in Heaven I might be a bird. I won't. I won't be a panther, lion, shark, or angel, either. I will be a man with a man's body, only a much improved version of the one I have now.

3. Imperishable

In terms of age, I am north of forty. The last few years my hair has been rapidly fleeing the top of my head. The hair that still remains has become silver. Several years ago, my bottom teeth moved out of line, throwing off my bite so badly I had to wear braces (just like my youngest son—talk about a humbling experience). For the first time in my life, I have to watch my calories. I now need bifocals to read. The hair on my back, in my nose, and on my eyebrows has been growing like it is fertilized. And if that is not enough, my joints ache on rainy days. In other words, as my sons love to tell me, "Dad, you are really getting old!"

Human bodies that have not experienced the resurrection are destined to wear out, break down, and fall apart. That's bad news and a frustrating reality. But the good news is our resurrection bodies are imperishable (1 Corinthians 15:42). They won't spoil, rot, or decay. No sags or bags. No bunions, bifocals, baldness, or big bellies. Hallelujah!

4. Glorious

No one has ever accused my body of being glorious. But not only will our resurrected bodies be healthier and perpetually young, they will be downright glorious. That's right. In Heaven you will be able to look in the mirror and say, "My, my. You look glorious!" In speaking of these bodies Paul said, "It is sown in dishonor, it is raised in glory" (1 Corinthians 15:43). In Heaven Jesus won't be the only one with a royal radiance. You and I will also have a golden glow.

"Then the righteous will shine like the sun in the kingdom of their Father. He who has ears, let him hear."

MATTHEW 13:43

"Those who are wise will shine like the brightness of the heavens, and those who lead many to righteousness, like the stars for ever and ever."

DANIEL 12:3

On the Mount of Transfiguration, Peter and John got a sample of what people in Heaven will look like when they saw Jesus. The Bible says, "As he was praying, the appearance of his face changed, and his clothes became as bright as a flash of lightning" (Luke 9:29). As Moses and Elijah spoke with Him, they "appeared in glorious splendor" (Luke 9:31).

5. Powerful

In discussing the nature of a resurrection body, Paul wrote, "It is sown in weakness, it is raised in power" (1 Corinthians 15:43). One aspect of my new body I anticipate most is having new abilities.

The Bible repeatedly tells us that when Jesus appears for our resurrection, "We shall be like him, for we shall see him as he is" (1 John 3:2; see also 1 Corinthians 15:44–49). Therefore, our new bodies will be like the body the disciples saw after Jesus rose from the dead. It could appear suddenly, apparently walking through a locked door (John 20:19). It could disappear from sight (Luke 24:31). It was able to defy gravity and rise up into the clouds (Acts 1:9). Amazing!

Another of my recurring dreams is that I am flying. I never get very high in my dreams, only about as high as the tops of the trees. I can't fly very far, but I am still flying. One day in Heaven, I may really be able to fly. My dream might come true. Wow!

6. Changed

Listen, I tell you a mystery: We will not all sleep, but we will all be changed—in a flash, in the twinkling of an eye, at the last trumpet. For the trumpet will sound, the dead will be raised imperishable, and we will be changed.

1 CORINTHIANS 15:51–52

Paul was very clear. At the return of Jesus, the bodies of deceased believers will be instantly transformed. This instantaneous alteration will change us into people with wonderful resurrection bodies perfectly suited for fully accessing God and experiencing the wonders of Heaven, His home, in every dimension.

7. Immortal

As a pastor, I have learned to help grieving family members focus on eternity. We talk of the funeral service being the graduation of the deceased from Earth to Heaven. Yet, while the funeral of a saint is sweet, it is also bitter. It is so hard to say good-bye to someone we have loved.

In Heaven there will be no good-byes. There will be no morgues, funeral parlors, or cemeteries. Our amazing new bodies will never, ever die. Death will be forever left behind. The victory over death that Jesus set in process by His resurrection will be consummated at ours.

For the perishable must clothe itself with the imperishable, and the mortal with immortality. When the perishable has been clothed with the imperishable, and the mortal with immortality, then the saying that is written will come true: "Death has been swallowed up in victory."

"Where, O death, is your victory? Where, O death, is your sting?" The sting of death is sin, and the power of sin is the law. But thanks be to God! He gives us the victory through our Lord Jesus Christ.

1 CORINTHIANS 15:53–57

So What?

We can look forward to heavenly bodies similar to the ones we have now, but oh, so much better. They will not age or die. They will be radiant in perfect health and with special abilities. So how should knowing this impact our lives today? Paul answered that question for us when he concluded his lengthy discussion of the nature of our resurrection bodies with these words.

Therefore, my dear brothers, stand firm. Let nothing move you. Always give yourselves fully to the work of the Lord, because you know that your labor in the Lord is not in vain.

1 CORINTHIANS 15:58

NOTE

¹Tony Campolo, "The Kingdom Is a Party," program #3315. January 14,1990, http://www.csec.org/csec/sermon/campolo 3315.htm.

12
The Royal Wedding

On July 29, 1981, the most elegant, most talked about, most watched wedding in the history of planet Earth occurred. The fairy-tale romance of Lady Diana Spencer and Prince Charles raised worldwide interest in Britain's royal family. The heir to Britain's ancient throne and his beautiful princess-to-be obliged their admirers by holding a glittering storybook wedding with all the royal trappings imaginable. No one was disappointed.

Crowds of six hundred thousand people filled the streets of London, eager to catch even a glimpse of Prince Charles and Lady Diana on their wedding day. The couple were married at St. Paul's Cathedral before an invited congregation of thirty-five hundred and an estimated global television audience of 750 million—making it the most popular program ever broadcast. The entire nation of England enjoyed a national holiday to mark the occasion. Most people felt this was the wedding to beat all weddings, and would never be surpassed in its size, scope, and splendor.

They were wrong.

The Greatest Wedding of Them All

One day, in the not-so-distant future, Heaven will host a royal wedding that will cause the royal wedding of 1981 to be quickly forgotten. The wedding in Heaven will involve grander participants, a superior officiator, a much larger audience, and the best feast of all time. It will be called the marriage supper of the Lamb, and it is described in the book of Revelation.

> *I heard what sounded like a great multitude, like the roar of rushing waters and like loud peals of thunder, shouting: "Hallelujah! For our Lord God Almighty reigns. Let us rejoice and be glad and give him glory! For the wedding of the Lamb has come, and his bride has made herself ready. Fine linen, bright and clean, was given her to wear." (Fine linen stands for the righteous acts of the saints.) Then the angel said to me, "Write: 'Blessed are those who are invited to the wedding supper of the Lamb!'" And he added, "These are the true words of God."*
>
> REVELATION 19:6–9

Heaven will host the greatest wedding of them all.

One day the streets of Heaven will resound with the joyous bells of the marriage supper of the Lamb. Using Revelation chapter 19 as the foundation, we can glean many insights into Heaven, the home of the greatest royal wedding of them all.

The Royal Bridegroom Is Jesus

This event is called the wedding *of the Lamb*. The Lamb is the Bridegroom. So who's the Lamb? Fortunately, we need not speculate. John the Baptizer told us that the Lamb is Jesus.

> *The next day John saw Jesus coming toward him, and said, "Behold! The Lamb of God who takes away the sin of the world!"*
>
> JOHN 1:29 NKJV

John wanted to clearly explain to the Jews that he was not the Messiah. He was the *forerunner* of the Messiah, the path preparer for the Messiah. John said that he was the friend of the Bridegroom, but Jesus was the Bridegroom.

> *John answered and said, "A man can receive nothing unless it has been given to him from heaven. You yourselves bear me witness, that I said, 'I am not the Christ,' but, 'I have been sent before Him.' He who has the bride is the bridegroom; but the friend of the bridegroom, who stands and hears him, rejoices greatly because of the bridegroom's voice. Therefore this joy of mine is fulfilled. He must increase, but I must decrease."*
>
> JOHN 3:27–30 NKJV

John was not the only one who knew Jesus was the Royal Bridegroom. Jesus Himself referred to Himself as the Bridegroom.

> *Then they said to Him, "Why do the disciples of John fast often and make prayers, and likewise those of the Pharisees, but Yours eat and drink?" And He said to them, "Can you make the friends of the bridegroom fast while the bridegroom is with them? But the days will come when the bridegroom will be taken away from them; then they will fast in those days."*
>
> LUKE 5:33–35 NKJV

Many thought Prince Charles made an extremely regal and handsome groom in the full dress uniform of a British naval commander. However, the majesty of every human prince in history will pale in the splendor and glory of Prince Jesus arrayed for His wedding day.

The Bride Is the Church

In understanding the Bible, it is vital to know that when the Bible speaks of the church, it is always speaking of a designation of people, and it is never referring to a building. In fact, there were no church buildings for one hundred or more years after the birth of the church. The church has many local assemblies (I used to pastor the New Life *Church* of Gahanna, Ohio), but *the* church is one united entity made up of redeemed people of every tribe, tongue, and nation.

Just as a bride pledges supreme love and unparalleled loyalty to her husband forever, members of the church, the Bride of Christ, are those who have pledged priority love and utmost devotion to Jesus forever. It is our natural response to the sacrificial love He has already shown us. Paul wrote, "Husbands, love your wives [your brides], just as Christ also loved the church [his bride] and gave Himself for her" (Ephesians 5:25 NKJV). He also wrote, "I have betrothed you to one husband that I may present you as a chaste virgin to Christ" (2 Corinthians 11:2 NKJV).

Lady Diana made a beautiful bride. People gasped at the way her elaborate and costly dress adorned her beautiful figure. In a similar yet vastly superior way, the Bride of Jesus will be a glorious virgin, simply, yet majestically, dressed in the pure white linen of those whose sins have been washed by the blood of Jesus Christ and who show their gratitude by living righteous lives.

> *"Fine linen, bright and clean, was given her to wear."* (Fine linen stands for the righteous acts of the saints.)
>
> REVELATION 19:8

No one is exactly sure how the huge number of believers from the church era can "wed" Jesus Christ. We can assume there will be an unprecedented level of uninhibited, undisguised, unadorned unity of souls between Bride and Groom. We will enjoy complete exposure and joyous knowledge without a hint of promiscuity. We will drink deeply of pure intimacy that will not only draw us deeply to Christ, but also to each other as well.

The Guest List Will Be Impressive in Size

Lady Di and Prince Charles had thirty-five hundred invited guests. The marriage of the Lamb will have a much, much larger number in attendance. John said that he "heard what sounded like a great multitude, like the roar of rushing waters and like loud peals of thunder, shouting: 'Hallelujah!' . . . For the wedding of the Lamb has come" (Revelation 19:6–7). The guest list will include all the angels. Scripture tells us they number more than humans can count. The believers from the Old Testament era will also be glad guests at the wonderful wedding party.

God the Father Will Be the Gracious Host

Although not stated in Revelation 19, other scriptures tell us that in a unique and wonderful way, at the marriage supper of the Lamb, God the Father will serve as both the Father of the Bride and the Father of the Groom (He is *our* Father—Matthew 6:9). Because God is easily the wealthiest being in the universe, absolutely no expense will be spared. Everyone who wants to attend is welcome. There will be enough sumptuous food to last a thousand years!

Luke recorded a story Jesus told that serves as a portrait of how eager the Father is to have multitudes attend His Son's wedding. God wants everyone to be there.

> *"Then He said to him, 'A certain man gave a great supper and invited many, and sent his servant at supper time to say to those who were invited, "Come, for all things are now ready." But they all with one accord began to make excuses. . . . So that servant came and reported these things to his master. Then the master of the house, being angry, said to his servant, 'Go out quickly into the streets and lanes of the city, and bring in here the poor and the maimed and the lame and the blind.'. . .' Go out into the highways and hedges, and compel them to come in, that my house may be filled.'"*
>
> LUKE 14:16–18, 21, 23 NKJV

Ancient Hebrew Wedding Customs

History tells of three common elements of a Jewish wedding during the time of Christ. A look at these three elements gives us insight into the incredible celebration that will occur in Heaven.

1. The Betrothal Stage

According to the custom, during this stage in the relationship between a bride and groom, three things occur: First, the parents select a bride for the son. Second, a contract is signed. Third, the bride's father is paid a dowry. As you may recall, this was the stage Joseph and Mary were in when he found out she was pregnant. It required a divorce to break a betrothal. Fortunately, the angel told him the baby she was carrying was one miraculously conceived by God, so Joseph didn't divorce her. The rest is history.

On a spiritual level, God the Father selected a bride for His Son before the annals of time (Ephesians 1:3–4). Jesus and the Father created a contract of commitment called the new covenant (Luke 22:20; 1 Corinthians 11:25; Hebrews 9:15). The Father gave His Son, and Jesus gave His life to pay the price for His bride (1 Corinthians 6:19–20; Ephesians 5:25). The betrothal has been fulfilled.

2. The Presentation Stage

In an ancient Hebrew wedding, the bride was fetched to the house of the groom's father for a private ceremony. One day soon, Jesus will come to get His Bride to join Him in His Father's house. Spiritually, this event has been called the Rapture of the church. Many consider it to be the next event on the prophetic calendar.

> "In My Father's house are many mansions; if it were not so, I would have told you. I go to prepare a place for you. And if I go and prepare a place for you, I will come again and receive you to Myself; that where I am, there you may be also."
>
> JOHN 14:2–3 NKJV

> For the Lord Himself will descend from heaven with a shout, with the voice of an archangel, and with the trumpet of God. And the dead in Christ will rise first. Then we who are alive and remain shall be caught up together with them in the clouds to meet the Lord in the air. And thus we shall always be with the Lord.
>
> 1 THESSALONIANS 4:16–17 NKJV

3. The Celebration Stage

In an ancient Hebrew wedding, a public party was held to celebrate the wedding. All of the friends and family were invited. These parties were huge celebrations. It was said that in those days, the party presented by a poor man would last all day; the wedding supper of the son of an average man would last close to a week; and the celebration given by a rich man would last up to a month. But the party provided by a king for his son could last for one year!

Well, friends, as they say, "you ain't seen nothin' yet." The Bible tells us that the party thrown in Heaven by God the Father for His Son, Jesus Christ, the King of kings and Lord of lords, will not be a one-day affair. It won't last a mere week or month; it will not last a year. No, there is a strong possibility that the marriage of the Lamb, given by God the Father for His Son, King Jesus, and His daughter, the Bride of Christ, will last one thousand years (Revelation 20:1–6)!

So What?

What good does knowing this do us now? It certainly gives us something marvelous to look forward to. It gives us hope. Sometimes Christians look at people in the world who are godless and who seem to party their lives away, and we feel a twinge of envy. We ponder, "Why do the ungodly get to have all the fun?"

Friend, if you miss a few decades' worth of parties down here, don't worry. God is going to throw us a thousand-year party up there!

13
THE ROYAL KINGDOM

Do you ever get tired of living on a rebel planet? I do.

Let me explain.

When Adam and Eve introduced sin and rebellion to Earth way back in the Garden of Eden, they unwittingly handed Satan the title deed to the planet. Since then, Satan, the usurper prince, has lived as god of this world and prince of the power of the air. Under his wicked reign, sickness, sorrow, sadness, disease, destruction, debauchery, and death have polluted the planet and enslaved its citizens. His reign of terror has been building in these last days, and it will reach a horrible zenith during the seven years of tribulation. But fear not: Lucifer, the pretender prince, is on a short lease. His downfall is certain and soon.

For thousands of years, King Jesus has lived as a monarch in exile (John 18:36–37). He briefly visited His planet to shed His royal blood to free an army of loyal subjects (Revelation 5:9). One day very soon, in the climactic battle of Armageddon, He will return to Earth to claim His throne and restore His kingdom (Revelation 19:11–21; Psalm 2; Zechariah 14:3–5). At this time Heaven will, in a sense, be relocated to Earth as a glorious kingdom.

Heaven will be a glorious kingdom ruled by King Jesus.

King of Kings and Lord of Lords

When Jesus returns to Earth to establish His kingdom, it will not be a quiet, political, on-paper transfer of power. No way! Satan will not let go easily and will fight Jesus with every weapon at his disposal, including all the armies of Earth. Jesus left Earth as a Lamb slain for our sins, but He will return as the Lion of the tribe of Judah, dressed in full battle array, to put down the enemy insurrection.

> *I saw heaven standing open and there before me was a white horse, whose rider is called Faithful and True. With justice he judges and makes war. His eyes are like blazing fire, and on his head are many crowns. He has a name written on him that no one knows but he himself. He is dressed in a robe dipped in blood, and his name is the Word of God. The armies of heaven were following him, riding on white horses and dressed in fine linen, white and clean. Out of his mouth comes a sharp sword with which to strike down the nations. He will rule them with an iron scepter. He treads the winepress of the fury of the wrath of God Almighty. On his robe and on his thigh he has this name written: KING OF KINGS AND LORD OF LORDS.*
>
> REVELATION 19:11–16

After Satan and his cohorts-in-crime are defeated, they will be punished for all of the pain they wreaked on the innocent. The devil will be sentenced to one thousand years of hard time. During that millennium, King Jesus will reign on Earth.

> *And I saw an angel coming down out of heaven, having the key to the Abyss and holding in his hand a great chain. He seized the dragon, that ancient serpent, who is the devil, or Satan, and bound him for a thousand years. He threw him into the*

Abyss, and locked and sealed it over him, to keep him from deceiving the nations anymore until the thousand years were ended.

REVELATION 20:1–3

A Kingdom of Prosperity and Peace

I have never been overly impressed with earthly governments. As long as sinful humans are in control, ignorance and incompetence can and will occur. Power, corruption, and greed have decayed and destroyed countless earthly kingdoms. As a result, rank-and-file citizens suffer. But one day King Jesus will establish an excellent, everlasting kingdom on earth (2 Samuel 7:16; Micah 4:7–8).

The LORD will be king over the whole earth. On that day there will be one LORD, and his name the only name.

ZECHARIAH 14:9

Israel will be renewed as the center of world power. Jerusalem will serve as the home base of His glorious kingdom.

For the LORD Almighty will reign on Mount Zion and in Jerusalem, and before its elders, gloriously.

ISAIAH 24:23

The kingdom of Jesus will be unlike any other kingdom. It will have a perfect, supremely sinless, radically righteous, just, wise, kind, benevolent leader—Jesus Christ the Lord. Those ruling under Him will be perfected saints who left their sinful natures behind when they stepped into eternity.

It will be wonderful to be a citizen of the kingdom ruled by Jesus. Imagine how nice it will be to live in a beautiful country that is amazingly absent of illogical, unreasonable, needless layers of red tape. What a joy it will be to live in a place devoid of divisive, partisan politics and the bribery of special interest groups. Imagine a government completely lacking power-hungry politicians and out-of-touch, uncaring bureaucrats.

Jesus' kingdom will be marked by unprecedented peace and prosperity in every area of life. Previously inconceivable animal, civil, political, military, and social tranquility will rule the day. It will be heavenly.

The wolf will live with the lamb, the leopard will lie down with the goat, the calf and the lion and the yearling together; and a little child will lead them. The cow will feed with the bear, their young will lie down together, and the lion will eat straw like the ox. The infant will play near the hole of the cobra, and the young child put his hand into the viper's nest. They will neither harm nor destroy on all my holy mountain, for the earth will be full of the knowledge of the LORD as the waters cover the sea. In that day the Root of Jesse will stand as a banner for the peoples; the nations will rally to him, and his place of rest will be glorious.

ISAIAH 11:6–10

He will judge between many peoples and will settle disputes for strong nations far and wide. They will beat their swords into plowshares and their spears into pruning hooks.

Nation will not take up sword against nation, nor will they train for war anymore.
Every man will sit under his own vine and under his own fig tree, and no one will
make them afraid, for the LORD Almighty has spoken.

MICAH 4:3–4

During this season, Israelis will return to their Messiah and experience unprecedented prosperity in their land.

Sing, O Daughter of Zion; shout aloud, O Israel! Be glad and rejoice with all your
heart, O Daughter of Jerusalem! The LORD has taken away your punishment, he has
turned back your enemy. The LORD, the King of Israel, is with you; never again will
you fear any harm. . . . . At that time I will deal with all who oppressed you; I will
rescue the lame and gather those who have been scattered. I will give them praise and
honor in every land where they were put to shame.

ZEPHANIAH 3:14–15, 19

We Will Reign with Him

Jesus will receive wonderful worship in Heaven because He is genuinely worth it. He not only purchased us out of the slave market of sin by His blood, but He also made it possible for us one day to rule with Him on the Earth.

And they sang a new song: "You are worthy to take the scroll and to open its seals,
because you were slain, and with your blood you purchased men for God from every
tribe and language and people and nation. You have made them to be a kingdom and
priests to serve our God, and they will reign on the earth."

REVELATION 5:9–10

John heard them singing that those purchased by the blood of the Lamb would one day "reign on the earth" (Revelation 5:9). Paul reminded his readers, "If we endure, we will also reign with him" (2 Timothy 2:12). Jesus told a story indicating that those who handled their God-given responsibilities and resources wisely would one day "take charge" of cities (Luke 19:11–27).

It seems that I have been leading one group of people or another all of my adult life. There are several aspects or situations of leadership that make it extremely draining and discouraging. One, for example, is trying to lead while serving under an incompetent, corrupt, or uncaring boss. This problem will be removed in the kingdom of the Lord Jesus, as He will be the perfect superior, completely capable, incredibly incorruptible, and having the greatest heart for humanity in the universe.

Another frustrating aspect of governance is seldom having enough resources to do the job right. Again, this will not be a difficulty in Heaven, as our kingdom will have every resource on the renewed planet at our disposal.

I also find leading imperfect people can be one of the most infuriating tasks one can undertake. Leading self-oriented people can be like herding cats—nearly impossible and often frustrating. But in the kingdom of the Son, we will have the opportunity to lead perfected, glorified people, who have left their egos and agendas behind. Their problem-causing baggage of hurts, hang-ups, and nasty habits will be long gone.

Responsibility Is Earned

During the last week of Jesus' earthly life, many people thought He was going to establish His kingdom on earth very soon (Luke 19:11). In trying to adjust their expectations, Jesus told a story related to His coming kingdom.

> *"A man of noble birth went to a distant country to have himself appointed king and then to return. So he called ten of his servants and gave them ten minas. 'Put this money to work,' he said, 'until I come back.' "*
>
> LUKE 19:12–13

A *mina* was worth a lot of money—about three months' worth of salary. If you make fifty thousand dollars a year, three months of salary would be $12,500. Each of these servants received *ten* times that amount to invest for their master.

> *"He was made king. . .and returned home. Then he sent for the servants to whom he had given the money, in order to find out what they had gained with it. The first one came and said, 'Sir, your mina has earned ten more.'*
>
> *" 'Well done, my good servant!' his master replied. 'Because you have been trustworthy in a very small matter, take charge of ten cities.'*
>
> *"The second came and said, 'Sir, your mina has earned five more.' His master answered, 'You take charge of five cities.' "*
>
> LUKE 19:15–19

Jesus makes it clear that the key to future kingdom responsibility is wise use of what He has already given us here on Earth. If we maximize and use our time, treasures, and talents for Him and His kingdom, then we will have a better role in the royal kingdom. But if we don't, we won't.

> *"Then another servant came and said, 'Sir, here is your mina; I have kept it laid away in a piece of cloth. I was afraid of you, because you are a hard man. You take out what you did not put in and reap what you did not sow.'*
>
> *"His master replied, 'I will judge you by your own words, you wicked servant! You knew, did you, that I am a hard man, taking out what I did not put in, and reaping what I did not sow? Why then didn't you put my money on deposit, so that when I came back, I could have collected it with interest?'*
>
> *Then he said to those standing by, 'Take his mina away from him and give it to the one who has ten minas.'*
>
> *" 'Sir,' they said, 'he already has ten!'*
>
> *"He replied, 'I tell you that to everyone who has, more will be given, but as for the one who has nothing, even what he has will be taken away.' "*
>
> LUKE 19:20–26

So What?

Having a lousy job is. . .well. . .lousy. It is a daily frustration. I know because I have had a few, and most likely so have you. While there will be no miserable jobs in the royal kingdom, some positions will be better than others. If I want to guarantee myself the best possible role in the royal kingdom, I must try to live my life wisely and well, using everything God has put at my disposal responsibly for Him.

14
The Royal City

Cities display humanity at its very best and its absolute worst. Cities have the greatest highways but also the nastiest traffic. In a city, you can be treated by the finest medical specialists yet sit for hours in the waiting rooms of the most impersonal physicians. Cities offer museums filled with breathtaking, amazing pieces of art and also galleries cluttered with outrageously offensive objects.

Only in cities can you choose between dozens of outstanding restaurants as you drive by projects where children go to bed hungry. Only in cities can you walk by homeless men begging on the street as you enter a five-star hotel.

Per capita, cities employ the most police to protect the citizens, but that is because they have the most criminals. You will find the irony of stately old church buildings with working prostitutes outside on the sidewalk, soliciting clients on Friday nights.

Cities have mass transit and mass hysteria, remarkable affluence and marked apathy. Only in cities can you see hundreds of thousands of people, but often no one to lend a hand. The loneliest people on Earth often live in the most populated cities. In cities, we look up and gasp as we witness the fruit of man scaling the heights of his architectural and constructive achievement, only to trip over a broken-down bum stumbling around drunk or sleeping in the stench of his own vomit.

Can the potential good of the city ever be harnessed for God? Certainly, but there is only who can pull it off: His name is Jesus. Following the millennial kingdom, He will reveal the grandest, greatest, most glorious city that anyone has ever seen or imagined. It is called New Jerusalem and it will be the capital of New Heaven.

One day Heaven will have a glorious capital city.

The Holy City
The apostle John had the incomparable privilege of seeing into the future of both Earth and Heaven. Those two futures will one day gloriously collide in a realm known as New Heaven, New Earth, and New Jerusalem.

> *Then I saw a new heaven and a new earth, for the first heaven and the first earth had passed away, and there was no longer any sea. I saw the Holy City, the new Jerusalem, coming down out of heaven from God.*
>
> REVELATION 21:1–2

> *"He who overcomes will inherit all this, and I will be his God and he will be my son. But the cowardly, the unbelieving, the vile, the murderers, the sexually immoral, those who practice magic arts, the idolaters and all liars—their place will be in the fiery lake of burning sulfur. This is the second death."*
>
> REVELATION 21:7–8

> *Nothing impure will ever enter it, nor will anyone who does what is shameful or deceitful, but only those whose names are written in the Lamb's book of life.*
>
> REVELATION 21:27

The word *holy* in the Greek language means "separate from sin." New Jerusalem will be the first truly *holy* city to ever exist on Earth. It will be a place without sin. As such, it will have every single good thing about large cities, but absolutely none of the bad. There will be culture without crime and people without pollution. There will be decency with dignity, purity with power, and greatness with goodness. Happiness and harmony will flood each heart, fill the air, and flow down every street.

New Jerusalem will have no active muggers, burglars, thieves, con artists, pornographers, pimps, drug dealers, rapists, arsonists, or murderers. It will, of course, have former felons who have been forgiven by Jesus. New Jerusalem will be gloriously void of jails, prisons, and courtrooms. Lawyers, district attorneys, judges, bailiffs, police officers, and detectives will either have different roles to play or will find entirely different lines of work.

Imagine living in a city where you won't have to lock your doors when you go out or deadbolt them when you stay in. Imagine being able to walk down any street, any time, without fear of urban predators. Imagine great quantities of good food, good fun, and good times enjoyed in the company of very good people. New Jerusalem will be all of that and so much more.

The Perpetually New City

Many, if not all, of the major metropolitan cities in America have crumbling sections of their inner city. Once-regal buildings slowly rot and deteriorate. Plumbing is bad and often ineffective. Wiring is outdated and unsafe. Roaches and rats thrive in the revolting filth and repulsive stench that crowd the alleys and flood the basements.

But New Jerusalem will have none of these depressing and dangerous divisions of downtown. God will make "everything new!" (Revelation 21:5). Every wire and window, fiber and floor, of every single building and block, will be entirely fresh, clean, bright, and brand spanking new! And I believe Jesus has the creative ability and knack of making it perpetually new, throughout eternity. Imagine being in a place that is always familiar, yet fresh—that will be New Jerusalem.

The Beautiful New City

Twenty years ago, if you walked down the streets of Moscow, the capital of the former Soviet Union, you would have discovered that decades of godless tyranny had literally drained color out of the skyline. Apart from the brightly colored spheres of the domes of the Kremlin, every building sagged in depressing shades of gray and brown. Hunched-over citizens dragged down the dreary streets draped in dull, tired clothes. Drab clouds hung in the air, straining out the life and brightness of the sun. Happiness was hard to find, as though joy had been outlawed.

Yet, by the mid-nineties, the positive impact of perestroika was beginning to be visible. Here and there a radiant red scarf or an effervescent blue tie would sprinkle the otherwise bland backdrop. Girls' dresses of vivacious greens and vibrant yellows began to break the otherwise monotonous gray of the city. It is amazing what a little freedom did for the face of that city. Imagine what true freedom will do to the city of God.

New Jerusalem was described by John as undoubtedly the most stunning city anyone has ever seen. Rising majestically on a lofty mountain, it will radiate in the golden glow of the glory of God. Color and light will commingle to create an awesome, inspiring, delightful feast for the eyes. Every color of the rainbow will be stretched, massaged, and empowered to levels man has never witnessed. Using a palette of pure gold, clear crystal, and precious stones, Jesus will paint His city into a massive masterpiece.

I saw the Holy City, the new Jerusalem, coming down out of heaven from God,
prepared as a bride beautifully dressed for her husband.

REVELATION 21:2

One of the seven angels who had the seven bowls full of the seven last plagues came
and said to me, "Come, I will show you the bride, the wife of the Lamb." And he
carried me away in the Spirit to a mountain great and high, and showed me the Holy
City, Jerusalem, coming down out of heaven from God. It shone with the glory of God,
and its brilliance was like that of a very precious jewel, like a jasper, clear as crystal.

REVELATION 21:9–11

The wall was made of jasper, and the city of pure gold, as pure as glass. The
foundations of the city walls were decorated with every kind of precious stone. The first
foundation was jasper, the second sapphire, the third chalcedony, the fourth emerald,
the fifth sardonyx, the sixth carnelian, the seventh chrysolite, the eighth beryl, the
ninth topaz, the tenth chrysoprase, the eleventh jacinth, and the twelfth amethyst. The
twelve gates were twelve pearls, each gate made of a single pearl. The great street of the
city was of pure gold, like transparent glass.

REVELATION 21:18–21

The City of Life

The downtowns of many large cities are dying. Abandoned stores, empty restaurants, and
collapsing buildings dot the landscape. Jobs are scarce and business is disappearing. But New
Jerusalem will be full of life and prosperity.

Most cities were born because of their prime location along either seaboards or water
routes. Even today, the geography of many cities is defined by a river. Even though it stands on
a mountain, New Jerusalem will pulsate with the crystal-clear river of life. The banks of the river
will be graced by the tree of life. This miraculous tree yields perpetual wonder fruit that will
give all who eat it continual youth and life. Its leaves will somehow have the capacity to bring
health and healing.

Then the angel showed me the river of the water of life, as clear as crystal, flowing
from the throne of God and of the Lamb down the middle of the great street of the
city. On each side of the river stood the tree of life, bearing twelve crops of fruit,
yielding its fruit every month. And the leaves of the tree are for the healing of the
nations. No longer will there be any curse.

REVELATION 22:1–3

The City of Light

The city does not need the sun or the moon to shine on it, for the glory of God gives it
light, and the Lamb is its lamp. The nations will walk by its light, and the kings of the
earth will bring their splendor into it. On no day will its gates ever be shut, for there will
be no night there. The glory and honor of the nations will be brought into it.

REVELATION 21:23–26

There will be no more night. They will not need the light of a lamp or the light of the sun, for the Lord God will give them light.

REVELATION 22:5

Picture a place without darkness. Imagine a city that needs no streetlights, lamps, house lights, headlights, flashlights, night-lights, or chandeliers. Envision a municipality that is wonderfully warmed and lit without the aid of the sun. New Jerusalem will be such a place. Because God makes His residence there and manifests His presence in an unhindered, uninhibited, unlimited way, His very being will give Heaven an ongoing, glorious, golden glow. It will be a city lit by the light of the Lamb. There will be nothing to fear and nothing to hide.

The Gigantic City

John was not only struck by the beauty of the glorious city of God. He also was told to carefully note its immense and unique dimensions.

The angel who talked with me had a measuring rod of gold to measure the city, its gates and its walls. The city was laid out like a square, as long as it was wide. He measured the city with the rod and found it to be 12,000 stadia in length, and as wide and high as it is long. He measured its wall and it was 144 cubits thick, by man's measurement, which the angel was using.

REVELATION 21:15–17

John measured a city that was 12,000 stadia (1,400 miles) long and wide, making New Jerusalem 1.96 million square miles! Such an immense city would surpass any city man has ever known. It will be larger than most countries. New Jerusalem will be nearly *nine thousand* times the size of Chicago. It will be over *six thousand* times the size of New York City. It will be nearly *four hundred* times the size of the state of Texas, nearly ten times the size of France, and over half the size of China. That is one huge city. But that's not all John saw.

The city John saw was also 1,400 *miles* high! The tallest building in America is the Sears Tower in downtown Chicago. It is 1,450 *feet* tall, 110 stories high. There are 5,280 feet in a mile, making New Jerusalem 7.39 million feet high and over 5,000 times taller than the Sears Tower! It could theoretically house more than half a million stories, nearly two million square miles each.

Some say that New Jerusalem will be a colossal cube, others a giant pyramid. Either way, it will certainly be big enough to spaciously house and feed a mammoth population. None of the numbers discussed even addresses the new Heaven and the new Earth. There is definitely plenty of room for all who want to be in Heaven to live comfortably and well.

So What?

New Jerusalem will be a gorgeous, gigantic, holy city full of life and light. It will have everything good any city in history has ever had, plus much more, while at the same time having none of the bad. It will be *the* place to spend eternity. You will not want to miss it.

15

God's House

There is little we need other than God Himself.
A. W. Tozer[1]

We Need God

Every person who lives on this planet now, lived on this planet in the past, or will live on this planet in the future has one common characteristic. The unanimous, universal denominator linking us all is a gaping, God-shaped void in our hearts. When He made us, He made us to have a holy hunger for Him.

This sacred space has been violated and twisted by the curse of sin. As a result, instead of seeking to fill our yawning emptiness with God, we easily settle for substitutes. Some of these surrogate gods are decidedly negative and dangerously addictive. Everyone knows dependency on drugs, alcohol, gambling, pornography, or illicit sex can never satisfy. Other alternatives are neutral entities. Money, work, career, achievement, hobbies, food, and material things are only evil when we expect them to take the place of God. Then they fall pathetically short.

Most of us suffer from the continual temptation to put very good entities in our God void. We all attest to the intrinsic value of family, friends, church, and ministry. Yet when we try to place even these good entities into the God-shaped space in our hearts, inevitable emptiness comes. Why? Nothing or no one can replace God. Only God can fill the holy hole in our hearts. Everything else is, at best, a square peg in a round hole or, better yet, a tiny pebble in an infinite chasm.

We need God. One 100 percent pure God is our deepest need and greatest fulfillment. Clearly, nothing else can compare with infinite perfection. The very best of all things is *God*. With God you have all things. Without God you have nothing.[2]

The great appeal of Heaven is more than the incredible beauty, astounding wealth, or fantastic fun we will experience there. It is the infinite God. The bottom line is that Heaven is about *God*. Maybe you want to go to Heaven because you were looking for something that seems to be missing. Let me tell you, that something is a *Someone*—God! What you really crave is found by experiencing more of Him—more often, more deeply, more intimately, and more powerfully—than you imagined possible. We experience tiny tastes of Him on Earth, but heaping spoonfuls in Heaven. That is why it is Heaven.

In this book, we learn twenty-one of the best truths about Heaven. But absolutely, undeniably, and unquestionably the most significant truth anyone can grasp about Heaven is this: God will be there. Heaven is God's home, and we will see Him face-to-face.

Heaven is God's home.

Jesus encouraged His disciples by telling them about His Father's house.

"In my Father's house are many rooms; if it were not so, I would have told you. I am going there to prepare a place for you."

John 14:2

When the apostle John saw into Heaven, the central feature was not the tree of life or the crystal sea. It was God.

> *I saw the Holy City, the new Jerusalem, coming down out of heaven from God. . . . And I heard a loud voice from the throne saying, "Now the dwelling of God is with men, and he will live with them. They will be his people, and God himself will be with them and be their God."*
>
> REVELATION 21:2–3

> *I did not see a temple in the city, because the Lord God Almighty and the Lamb are its temple.*
>
> REVELATION 21:22

> *The throne of God and of the Lamb will be in the city.*
>
> REVELATION 22:3

Heaven Is God's Home

The beat drumming throughout the Bible is that Heaven is the dwelling place of God. Moses prayed, "Look down from *heaven, your holy dwelling place*, and bless your people Israel" (Deuteronomy 26:15, emphasis added). Jesus told us to pray to "Our Father *in heaven*" (Matthew 6:9, emphasis added). John saw the Father sitting on His throne (Revelation 4:2–9). Jesus claimed that as the Son of God, He "came down from heaven" (John 6:42). Forty days after His resurrection, He ascended visibly back to Heaven (Acts 1:9–11). He will one day return to Earth from Heaven (Revelation 19:11–16). Heaven is the dwelling place of God.

One of the very best aspects of having a home is being in a place where you can be yourself. You can relax. You do not have to hold back. You can fully express yourself.

Heaven will be astoundingly amazing because, as His home, it is the only place in the universe where God is free to fully express Himself. In Heaven God holds nothing in reserve. Nothing is limited by the presence of sin. God can be Himself. All of His goodness, all of His grandeur, all of His greatness, all of His generosity, and all of His magnificent glory can be let out. Everything His infinite heart has held in check since the creation of the universe can be conveyed.

In their own home, people reveal their true selves. Their hobbies, humor, personalities, passions, and pursuits are unveiled. At home, in Heaven, the Lord's personality, humor, dreams, and desires will be evident.

We Will See Him Face-to-Face

Moses begged God for a glimpse of His glory. Knowing that a direct look at His glory would be much more than Moses could safely comprehend, God suggested a plan.

> *Then Moses said, "Now show me your glory."*
>
> *And the LORD said, "I will cause all my goodness to pass in front of you, and I will proclaim my name, the LORD, in your presence. . . . But," he said, "you cannot see my face, for no one may see me and live."*
>
> *Then the LORD said, "There is a place near me where you may stand on a rock. When my glory passes by, I will put you in a cleft in the rock and cover you with my hand until I have passed by. Then I will remove my hand and you will see my back."*
>
> EXODUS 33:18–23

Moses was given a privilege no one else in his day could ever hope for. He received an unprecedented look at God's back. But every single person in Heaven will get to see God face-to-face (Revelation 22:3–4).

For those of us who proudly line up in the company of God seekers, the mere whisper of seeing our God face-to-face sends shivers down our spines. For so many years, we have worshiped a God we have never seen. As His children, we have often heard the comfort of our Father's voice, but we have never been allowed to sit in His lap, look into His eyes, or touch His face. We have tried to be loyal servants, faithfully fulfilling the wishes of a Master we have yet to see. As dutiful soldiers, we have gladly laid down our lives for our King, yet our eyes have yet to see His throne. As His betrothed Bride we have received many gifts from His hands and letters of love from His pen, yet what we long for is our wedding day. Then we will dance in His arms, be consumed by His love, and gaze into His eyes.

It's the Person Who Makes the Place

What makes Heaven so amazing is not merely the stunning streets of gold, the gates of pearl, the radiant light, the crystal river of life, or the everyday association with angels. It is not merely receiving a great new body, enjoying the absence of sickness and death, experiencing the reunion with loved ones, or basking in the majestic magnificence of the Master's throne—although each is amazingly impressive. What makes Heaven heavenly is not the *place,* it is the *person.* Heaven is heavenly because the Lord lives there.

Heaven is the only place where God's presence is revealed in an unlimited fashion. In Heaven God's presence is unhindered and unrestricted. Heaven is all God, all the time. That is what makes it so heavenly.

The Bible clearly tells us that God is love (1 John 4:8, 16). Since Heaven is the only place where God's presence is fully expressed, the very atmosphere of Heaven will be swimming in the pure, good, deep, rich, wonderful love of God. Just breathing the oxygen of God's love in the air will heal our deepest hurts and soothe our greatest fears.

God is also light (1 John 1:5). Because Heaven is the place where God dwells unhindered and unrestricted, Heaven will radiate in the brilliant, perpetual light of His glory. Sun, moon, and stars will be unnecessary there.

> *The city does not need the sun or the moon to shine on it, for the glory of God gives it light, and the Lamb is its lamp. The nations will walk by its light, and the kings of the earth will bring their splendor into it. On no day will its gates ever be shut, for there will be no night there.*
>
> REVELATION 21:23–25

> *There will be no more night. They will not need the light of a lamp or the light of the sun, for the Lord God will give them light.*
>
> REVELATION 22:5

As God is creative, excellent, loving, joyful, encouraging, faithful, true, good, and holy, so is Heaven a marvelously holy place, overflowing with all that is beautiful and truly excellent, running over with love, joy, encouragement, truth, and peace. Heaven is the sphere where the heavenly presence of God is unleashed.

So What?

The insightful twentieth-century prophet A. W. Tozer said, "The man who has God for his treasure has all through One."[3] Everyone in Heaven will be astoundingly rich because the Lord will be our treasure. Our capacity to enjoy and appreciate this privilege will be expanded and enhanced to the extent that we make God our primary passion now.

NOTES

[1] A. W. Tozer, *The Pursuit of God* (Camp Hill, Pennsylvania: Christian Publications, 1982), 7

[2] Dave Earley, *Living in His Presence*, (Minneapolis: Bethany House, 2005), 9

[3] Tozer, 19.

16
Your Final Forwarding Address

Heaven is better than anything we can imagine, and it will get even better. From Paradise to the Royal Kingdom, Heaven will be renovated, re-created, expanded, and improved. The last phase of Heaven described in the Bible is the new Heaven and new Earth. After the millennium will come the final purging of Earth. This will birth the re-creation and the wedding of Heaven and Earth. The capital will be New Jerusalem. We have already talked about the giant royal city, New Jerusalem. In this chapter, we want to discuss what the rest of New Heaven will be like.

As I read what the scriptures say about New Heaven and meditate on it through the lens of a sanctified imagination, several adjectives crystallize and summarize what it will be like to be in New Heaven.

Heaven will ultimately be a God-filled, pleasure-packed, fresh, thirst-quenching inheritance, available to all who truly want to be there.

God Filled

As we said in the previous chapter, New Heaven will be marvelously enhanced by the manifest presence of God. God will set up shop right in the middle of town (Revelation 21:1, 3; 22:3–4). What makes Heaven heavenly? It is God. It is having easy access, close proximity, and refreshing closeness to God. Everything else we can say, think, or feel about Heaven will pale compared to seeing His face, looking in His eyes, and hearing His voice. Imagine sitting down and talking to Jesus, opening your eyes, finding Him right there looking at you, and drinking in every word. Imagine being able to finally ask Him every question that has plagued your thoughts.

New Heaven is where God's creative, excellent, living, loving, joyful, encouraging, faithful, true, good, and holy presence flows. New Heaven will be adorned by the distinctive aura of God punctuating and permeating everything about it.

Pleasure Packed

> *"He will wipe every tear from their eyes. There will be no more death or mourning or crying or pain, for the old order of things has passed away."*
> REVELATION 21:4

Imagine never having your heart broken again. Consider what it will be like to never have to say good-bye to a loved one again. Imagine no more bitter, angry tears. Picture a life without pain. How wonderful it will be never to have to stand aside helplessly while someone else suffers.

New Heaven will be a continual celebration of the ultimate and absolute amputation of every evil or painful aspect of life that accompanied the curse of sin. The spoils of Jesus' victory over the grave will be on continual display. Death will be decisively defeated and deleted. Grief and guilt will be gloriously gone, all gone. Fear will be forbidden. Mourning will permanently turn to dancing, sorrow to joy, pain to pleasure, and misery to celebration. Love will reign supreme. Peace will flow like water.

In New Heaven suffering must say, "So long, farewell," gloom, "Good-bye," and shame, "See you later." There will be no more anxiety, no more anguish, no more tears. Heartache, misery, sadness, and depression will be eternally ejected. In Heaven contentment will consume your emotions and satisfy your soul.

Fresh

One man was upset to find that his death was mistakenly noted in the local paper. He hastened to the editor to protest. "I'm awfully sorry," said the editor, "and it's too late to do much about it. The best thing I can do for you is to put you in tomorrow's birth column and give you a brand-new start."

New Heaven will be an everlasting morning and perpetually brand-new start.

> *He who was seated on the throne said, "I am making everything new!" Then he said,*
> *"Write this down, for these words are trustworthy and true."*
>
> REVELATION 21:5

If you live above the Mason-Dixon line, the coming of spring has mysterious power. Magically, the dormant earth awakens to new life. Grass begins to grow again, flowers poke their heads out of clean-smelling dirt, and buds boldly sprout on the trees. Birds sing before sunup like there is no tomorrow. New moms proudly push their new babies down the street in brand-new strollers.

The air is fresh, the colors ignited, the earth reborn. Everyone is in a good mood. Everything smells fresh and clean. Everywhere there is new hope. Winter is over. Cold, cloudy skies have been conquered by clear, sunny, warm days. The aroma of honeysuckle graces the air. Ahh—I love spring.

But, amazingly, in a way that will never get old, New Heaven will be an eternal spring. The vibrant, fresh feeling that permeates the atmosphere at spring will saturate Heaven. Forgotten dreams will be reborn. Old, broken relationships will be restored. Deep passions will be rekindled. Everything will be made new.

Thirst Quenching

We all live with a cavernous craving for something we cannot quite comprehend. No matter how intensely we strive, somewhere just beyond our grasp is something we long for. This gnawing yearning, this profound passion, this deep desire drives the sensitive among us to distraction or despair. What is this vague something that we know we have tasted, but realize we never have enough of? What is this mysterious motivation and terrible thirst?

Is it love? Or maybe truth? How about peace? Maybe what we really want is true happiness? Do we yearn for rest, or affirmation, or stability, or security? Or is it intimacy, or maybe acclaim, or attention? Could our hearts be longing after adventure, excitement, or thrill? What about life, eternal life, the fountain of youth? Is that it?

The answer is yes. . .and no. What we really crave, yet so often fail to recognize and always fail to satisfy, is a hunger for Heaven. It is God and all that comes from being close to Him. It is the life, real life, the eternal life that He gives. It is only fulfilled in Heaven.

One of the very best things about Heaven is that the annoying, frustrating, inner thirst that will never be fully quenched down here and now will be fully quenched in New Heaven. Jesus promised:

"To him who is thirsty I will give to drink without cost from the spring of the water of life."

REVELATION 21:6

Inheritance

According to *Forbes* magazine, the richest person on Earth is Bill Gates, the founder of Microsoft. His net worth is fifty billion dollars—that is a five plus ten zeroes! Gates is a self-made man who dropped out of college to start a computer company thirty years ago. If he were to divide his wealth among his three children, they would each be among the richest people on Earth.[1]

Sam Walton began as a JCPenney clerk but opened his first discount store in Rogers, Arkansas, in 1962. His little store, Walmart, has become the world's largest retailer, with more than 5,100 stores serving 138 million customers per week. At his death in 1992, each of his four children received over five billion dollars. They are now worth over three times that amount.[2]

The Bible is very clear that we are the heirs of God. In Heaven we have an inheritance waiting for us. We will be the heirs of God Himself, who has promised,

"He who overcomes will inherit all this, and I will be his God and he will be my son."

REVELATION 21:7

Now if we are children, then we are heirs—heirs of God and co-heirs with Christ.

ROMANS 8:17

Praise be to the God and Father of our Lord Jesus Christ! In his great mercy he has given us new birth into a living hope through the resurrection of Jesus Christ from the dead, and into an inheritance that can never perish, spoil or fade—kept in heaven for you.

1 PETER 1:3–4

Our inheritance could easily dwarf anything anyone on Earth has ever received. How much will we inherit in Heaven? The answer is easy. We will inherit exactly the amount that is best for us and exactly the amount we deserve. If we were generous in making eternal investments in Heaven, God will be generous in giving us our inheritance in Heaven (Matthew 6:19–21).

According to *Forbes,* Updown Court, Windlesham, England, is currently the most expensive residence on the market in the world with an asking price of $122 million. The brand-new property is totally over the top, with 103 rooms, five swimming pools, and 24-carat-gold leafing on the study's mosaic floor. There's a squash court, bowling alley, tennis court, 50-seat screening room, heated marble driveway, and helipad. All eight of your limousines will fit in the underground garage. The neighbors include the Queen of England at Windsor Castle.[3]

Jesus promised us special dwellings connected to the Father's house.

"In My Father's house are many dwelling places; if it were not so, I would have told you; for I go to prepare a place for you."

JOHN 14:2 NASB

We don't know much more about these residences, but we can be sure that they will be exactly the best size, style, shape, and location for us. In our heavenly homes, we will enjoy being neighbors with the King—that is King Jesus, the King of kings and the Lord of lords!

Available

> *The Spirit and the bride say, "Come!" And let him who hears say, "Come!" Whoever is thirsty, let him come; and whoever wishes, let him take the free gift of the water of life.*
> REVELATION 22:17

Apart from God being there, one of the greatest points about Heaven is its amazing availability to all who truly want in. Granted, I realize that some people don't want 100 percent of God 100 percent of the time. Some people have no stomach for good, clean fun. Some are repulsed by the thought of endless morning, perpetual beauty, and never-ending spring. Some hate worship, mock truth, and discount or deny Jesus. The bottom line is they simply don't want to be in Heaven.

Don't worry.

God won't make them go. Heaven is only available to those who really *want* to be there. It is *free* to those who will receive the free gift of the water of life, by expressed faith in Jesus Christ the Lord.

So What?

The new Heaven will be a God-filled, pleasure-packed, new, thirst-quenching inheritance available to all who truly want to be there. The big question for us to ask ourselves is this: Do we love God enough to want to spend eternity with Him? If so, we can. You can come to Him right now in prayer. Tell Him that you want to spend eternity with Him. Tell Him you want to drink deeply of the free gift of the water of life. If you really mean it, reservations will be made for you in Heaven.

NOTES

[1]Luisa Kroll and Allison Fass, ed. "The World's Billionaires" (March 9, 2006), http://www.forbes.com/billionaires.

[2]"Freeze and Squeeze," http://gift-estate.com/article/Freeze.htm.

[3]Sara Clemence, "The Most Expensive Homes in the World," http://www.forbes.com/2005/07/26/cx_sc_0729home_eu.html?thisSpeed=6000.

17
ANGEL ASSOCIATES

You are not alone. I would guess that this very moment invisible visitors are viewing your every movement. Even though you cannot see them, they are definitely there. Who are these unseen onlookers who accompany us every second of our lives, witnessing our words, deeds, and possibly even our thoughts? They are angels.

You may be surprised to know that the Bible contains more than three hundred direct references to angels. What the Bible says about angels is stirring, eye-opening, awe inspiring, comforting, and challenging. It whets our appetite for Heaven, for in Heaven we will be allowed to associate more directly with these marvelous creations called angels than we do down here and now.

In Heaven we will associate with amazing creatures called angels.

Angel Myths

Because there is so much misinformation floating around about angels, it is helpful to examine some of the most common myths. Let's look briefly at several of the legends of angels and compare them with what the Bible clearly teaches.

1. Angels are adorable chubby babies with wings and/or pale females.

Walking into many gift shops, one might imagine that the primary role of angels is purely decorative. Holiday angels are soft, luscious creatures, all ruffles and fluff. They are sweet, beautiful ladies wearing kind, nonjudgmental smiles. Valentine angels are pink, plump, dimpled, whimsical, cute, baby cupids carrying little bows. Neither representation is anything anyone would take seriously.

The Bible paints a drastically different portrait of angels. Every angel described in the Bible is an awe-inducing adult male. (For examples, see Daniel 10:8; Luke 1:12–13, 30; 2:9–10; Matthew 28:2–5). Repeatedly, when you read of an angel appearing to a human, the first words out of the angel's mouth are "Fear not." Why? Because seeing a real angel would easily scare you out of your wits. Even the fearless man of God, Daniel, described his encounter with an angel this way, "I had no strength, my face turned deathly pale and I was helpless" (Daniel 10:8). When angels appeared to the shepherds, announcing the birth of Messiah, the Bible says those poor shepherds were terrified. Words like *cute* and *cuddly* don't go with any of the angels described in the Bible.

2. Angels must earn their wings.

The cute concept that angels must earn their wings by doing good deeds comes from the mild angel character "Clarence" in the classic holiday movie *It's a Wonderful Life*. It makes for a great story, but it has no basis in truth. The fact is that such a notion is never mentioned in the Bible. When God created angels, they already had their wings and seem to be able to hide them when they take a human form.

3. Angels lounge in Heaven playing harps.

I think this myth comes from a misunderstanding of Revelation 5. A close reading of that passage makes it clear that the only persons said to be playing harps in Heaven are the twenty-four elders, who are redeemed *humans,* not angels (Revelation 5:8–14).

4. Angels reproduce.

I hate to break it to you, but you cannot marry an angel. Oh, she may be a cute girl, but technically she can't be an angel. Also, note that angels don't make babies. I know the old song says it's angels who create really special people, mixing sunlight and star dust to make a "dream come true." It makes for a nice song, but not a true one. The fact is, Jesus Himself stated clearly that angels do not marry or reproduce (Mark 12:25).

5. Angels are former humans.

A common myth is that when a nice person dies, he or she goes to Heaven and becomes an angel. According to the Bible, humans and angels are two entirely and eternally different classes of beings. We are different species. Humans do not graduate to "angelhood" at death. Instead, we will ultimately receive heavenly *human* bodies similar to the one Jesus had after His resurrection.

Angel Facts

I hope that some of the truths about angel myths did not upset you. If so, don't worry. The rest of the story of angels will enrich and excite you. It will also give you a greater longing for Heaven.

1. Angels are real.

Angels really exist. As we said, there are over three hundred direct references to angels in the Bible. You cannot believe the Bible without believing in angels.

2. Angels are spirit beings.

The writer of the biblical book of Hebrews asks an important rhetorical question when he says, "Are not all angels ministering *spirits* sent to serve those who will inherit salvation?"(Hebrews 1:14, emphasis added). The answer of course is yes, angels are spirits sent to serve us. Humans have a spirit, but we are dominated by our bodies. Angels *are* spirits who can take a bodily form, but most of the time they don't. Therefore, to us they are invisible.

However, in Heaven angels will be visible. We will see them and interact with them. When the apostle John looked into Heaven in the future, he repeatedly saw and spoke with angels (Revelation 5:2; 7:2; 8:3–12; 9:1,13–14; 10:1, 5–9; 11:15; 14:6–9,15–19; 16:2–17; 17:3, 7, 15; 18:1, 21; 19:9, 17; 21:15, 17; 22:1, 6, 8, 16). Hanging out with angels is a major attraction of Heaven.

3. Angels exist to obey God and serve the saved.

Angels are "sent to *serve* those who will inherit salvation" (Hebrews 1:14, emphasis added). David wrote, "Praise the LORD, you his angels, you mighty ones who do his bidding" (Psalm 103:20).

Angels, good and bad, live to obey the will of their superior. Good angels exist to serve those who are born again. If you are a Christian, God's angels exist to aid you. There is no reason to believe that their service will diminish in Heaven. In fact, it will probably be enhanced.

4. Angels were created by God.

God is the only uncreated being in the universe. Angels are not on the same level as God. They are created *by* God (Colossians 1:16; Job 38:4, 7; Psalm 104:4–5). Angels have not always existed. Unlike God, they are not self-existent or self-sufficient.

5. Angels are highly organized in a governmental/military structure.

The Bible speaks of thrones, powers, rulers, and authorities in the current heavenly realm (Colossians 1:16; Ephesians 3:10). Although it is not the focus of this book, we should mention the great unseen war going on in the spirit world right now. Every angel is a part of this war effort. They aren't isolated, wandering souls. They are on-purpose beings whose manner is strictly business. They realize the severity of the spiritual war being waged between God and Satan for your soul. They recognize their position in either the army of light or the army of darkness. They have a tight hierarchy with positions of rank and order.

6. Angels are mighty creatures.

Angels are not cuddly babies or soft ladies. They are called "mighty ones" (Psalm 103:20). One angel had the strength to lift and carry the huge stone in front of Jesus' tomb up the hill (Matthew 28:2). In the future, four angels will have the power to hold back the wind (Revelation 7:1). Later, a single angel will throw into the sea a boulder so large that the wave will drown an entire city (Revelation 18:21). Angels are currently far superior to humans in terms of speed, strength, and intelligence.

7. Angels are immortal.

Jesus says that after the resurrection, humans will be as angels already are, in that we will no longer die (Luke 20:36). You cannot kill an angel. At this time in history, good angels fight with demons in spiritual warfare. Eventually, all evil angels will be imprisoned.

8. When not taking a humanlike form, angels are described as wind, fire, and stars.

Angels are spirits. Frequently, the Bible writers describe them in a way we could identify with—flames of fire, bursts of wind, shining stars (Judges 5:20; Job 38:7; Psalm 18:10–14; Hebrews 1:7; Revelation 9:1–2). Even when they do appear in human form, they are bright, shining, brilliantly lit beings.

9. Angels are only visible when God opens our eyes to see them.

I love one particular story in 2 Kings. Aram was at war with Israel. The Arameans were mad at God's man, Elisha. Every time they planned an attack, Elisha informed Israel's army as to exactly what the Arameans were going to do. The Arameans got so angry that when they discovered Elisha's location, they sent an entire army to get him. Elisha's servant woke him up in the morning to tell him that the enemy had surrounded the entire town with their army. The servant was terrified, exclaiming, "What'll we do? What'll we do?"

Elisha confidently calmed his consternated servant.

> "Don't be afraid," the prophet answered. "Those who are with us are more than those who are with them." And Elisha prayed, "O LORD, open his eyes so he may see." Then the LORD opened the servant's eyes, and he looked and saw the hills full of horses and chariots of fire all around Elisha.
>
> 2 KINGS 6:16–17

God opened the servant's eyes to give him a little glimpse behind the scenes. What did he see? He saw an awesome army of angels surrounding the army of Aram. Elisha prayed and the angels blinded the enemy soldiers. Then Elisha led the enemy army back to his capital. There the king served them lunch and sent them home. Not surprisingly, we never read about them bothering Israel or Elisha ever again.

10. Angels do not compare with Jesus Christ.

The primary point of the book of Hebrews is that Jesus is better than anything else out there. No one or no thing compares to Him, not even angels. He is supreme. Jesus' person and His name are superior to the angels (Hebrews 1:4). Jesus is worthy of worship from angels (1:6). He will sit at the right hand of the Father; they are simply servants (1:8–14). Jesus will ultimately rule the world (2:5).

In Philippians 2 we read that because Jesus left the glories of Heaven to become a man, died on the cross to pay for our sins, and rose from the dead, one day in Heaven every knee will bow and every tongue will confess that He is Lord. It is very clear which knees will bow— *every* knee on earth and in Heaven (Philippians 2:9–11). That means that every knee of every human *and* every knee of every angel will one day bow down and claim Jesus is Lord. He is superior to all, including angels.

11. Angels are not to be worshiped, but were created to lead us to worship God.

Paul warned against the futility of worshiping angels and getting overly caught up in angel sightings (Colossians 2:18). The saddest aspect about the current "angel mania" is that people are choosing angels to be their spiritual touch point, in place of Jesus Christ. People who choke on the hard truths of the Bible and the holiness side of God often substitute angels as a handy compromise of sweet, gooey, nonjudgmental fluff. Yet angels are inadequate spiritual touch points. We all need a genuine relationship with God through the Lord Jesus Christ. We were created to worship God, not His servants.

Granted, angels are amazing beings. They are smarter, faster, stronger, and more beautiful than any of us. They are so impressive that twice even the apostle John tried to worship them. But, in both cases, the angel said the same thing.

> At this I fell at his feet to worship him. But he said to me, "Do not do it! I am a fellow servant with you and with your brothers who hold to the testimony of Jesus. Worship God!"
>
> REVELATION 19:10

> But he said to me, "Do not do it! I am a fellow servant with you and with your brothers the prophets and of all who keep the words of this book. Worship God!"
>
> REVELATION 22:9

Worship God!

So What?

In Heaven we will have unparalleled access to and association with awe-inspiring beings called angels. They will do for us then what they desire to do for us now—serve us and help us worship God.

Why not pause right now and worship the One who is superior to the angels? Worship Jesus Christ.

18
Do All Dogs Go to Heaven?

A young mother was trying to comfort her daughter when her pet kitten died. The mother stroked the little girl's hair and said, "Remember, dear, Fluffball is up in Heaven right now with God."

"But Mommy," the little girl sobbed, "what in the world does God want with a dead cat?" There will be no dead cats in Heaven.

However, the questions often raised are, "Will there be living animals in Heaven? If so, which animals? How do we know?"

Before I answer those questions, consider the following. Someone observed that a dog thinks: "Hey, these people I live with feed me, love me, provide me with a nice warm, dry house, pet me, and take good care of me. . . . They must be gods!" On the other hand, a cat thinks: "Hey, these people I live with feed me, love me, provide me with a nice warm, dry house, pet me, and take good care of me. . . . I must be a god!"

The above facts and my own careful study of the Bible lead me to conclude: There will be animals in Heaven, but probably no cats. (Just kidding about the cats. . .)

We will enjoy animals in Heaven.

Earth has had three heads. Adam was the head of the first Earth. Noah was the head of the Earth cleansed by the flood. And thirdly, Jesus is coming to be the King of a renewed Earth. God surrounded Adam with *animals* in the Garden of Eden. God instructed Noah to fill a huge boat with *animals* to save them from the flood. When Jesus was born, He was surrounded by *animals* in a barn. God created and loves animals. We should expect God to surround those in Heaven with animals.[1]

Edenizing

Several years ago the concept of Edenizing was introduced to some retirement and long-term nursing facilities. The concept was developed to combat three primary challenges facing seniors in long-term care facilities: loneliness, helplessness, and boredom. The key principle is that the environments need to be seen as habitats for human beings, rather than facilities for the frail and elderly. The major means of making environments more human-friendly is providing "close and continuing contact with plants, *animals,* and children, as these relationships offer a pathway to a life worth living." Companion animals (usually dogs, not cats by the way) are introduced to their environments to provide the opportunity to give meaningful care to other living creatures. Proponents claim amazing results.[2]

Edenizing has been successfully proving that people feel more human, and are therefore happier and healthier, when they are around animals, plants, and children. Heaven right now is a restored Garden of Eden, called Paradise. The original Garden of Eden was a festival of plant and animal life. God created *animals* to live in the garden and called them "good" (Genesis 1:20–25). He created man and gave him the primary responsibility for ruling the *animals* (Genesis 1:28). When Adam was created, God surrounded him with animals, so we should expect that there will be animals in Paradise, the restored Garden of Eden.

Noah's Ark

You remember the story. God was brokenhearted by the unrelenting wickedness and corruption of early man, and planned to cleanse the earth (Genesis 6:5–7, 11–13). Noah was the righteous exception, and God decided to spare him and his family (Genesis 6:8–10). God instructed Noah to build a huge boat, or ark, to protect them from the coming flood (Genesis 6:14–17). But that was not all God wanted to spare from destruction. Noah was to fill the huge boat with *animals*, keep them with him, and feed them in order to save them from the flood.

> *You are to bring into the ark two of all living creatures, male and female, to keep them alive with you. Two of every kind of bird, of every kind of animal and of every kind of creature that moves along the ground will come to you to be kept alive. You are to take every kind of food that is to be eaten and store it away as food for you and for them.*
>
> GENESIS 6:19–21

God was so concerned about the animals that He supernaturally sent them to Noah so he could load them onto the ark (Genesis 7:8–9, 15). After the flood subsided, "God remembered Noah *and* all the wild animals and the livestock that were with him in the ark" (Genesis 8:1, emphasis added). God instructed Noah that when he exited the ark, he was to bring all of the animals with him (Genesis 8:17). God promised, "Never again will I destroy all living creatures, as I have done" (Genesis 8:21). God's promise was established in a covenant between God, Noah, *and* the animals.

> *"I now establish my covenant with you and with your descendants after you and with every living creature that was with you—the birds, the livestock and all the wild animals, all those that came out of the ark with you—every living creature on earth. . . . I will remember my covenant between me and you and all living creatures of every kind. Never again will the waters become a flood to destroy all life. Whenever the rainbow appears in the clouds, I will see it and remember the everlasting covenant between God and all living creatures of every kind on the earth."*
>
> GENESIS 9:9–10, 15–16

When Noah was spared, God showed how much He valued animals, and how much He thought man needed animals by making certain the animals were delivered with him. When He promised not to destroy Earth again by flood, God was careful to include animals in His covenant. Therefore, we should expect that God surrounds man with animals in Heaven.

The Peaceable Kingdom of Heaven

Edward Hicks was a Quaker preacher in Bucks County, Pennsylvania, in the early 1800s. His artistic endeavors provided modest support for his church activities. In 1833 Hicks created an American masterpiece entitled *Peaceable Kingdom*. In the work, Hicks gives a pleasant, pastoral portrayal of a lion, tiger, wolf, bear, and leopard happily lounging with an ox, calf, goat, and several children. In the background, Quaker statesman William Penn is seen making peace with the Indians. The painting is a visual sermon based on Isaiah 11:6–9, which describes peaceful animals coexisting with small children on the renewed Earth after the coming of Christ.

The wolf will live with the lamb, the leopard will lie down with the goat, the calf and the lion and the yearling together; and a little child will lead them. The cow will feed with the bear, their young will lie down together, and the lion will eat straw like the ox. The infant will play near the hole of the cobra, and the young child put his hand into the viper's nest. They will neither harm nor destroy on all my holy mountain, for the earth will be full of the knowledge of the LORD as the waters cover the sea.

ISAIAH 11:6–9

Isaiah repeats the Lord's prophecy of peaceful animals on renewed Earth later in his book:

"The wolf and the lamb will feed together, and the lion will eat straw like the ox, but dust will be the serpent's food. They will neither harm nor destroy on all my holy mountain," says the LORD.

ISAIAH 65:25

From the above two passages we know there will be some, if not all, animals in Heaven. Wolves, lambs, lions, oxen, leopards, calves, yearlings, cows, and even serpents are mentioned.

Horses in Heaven

I love to ride horses. Those big, powerful animals have a strong appeal to humans. When John saw into Heaven, he saw horses. On two separate occasions he saw horses ridden by those in Heaven.

I looked, and there before me was a white horse! . . . Then another horse came out, a fiery red one. . . . I looked, and there before me was a black horse! . . . I looked, and there before me was a pale horse!

REVELATION 6:2, 4–5, 8

I saw heaven standing open and there before me was a white horse, whose rider is called Faithful and True. . . . The armies of heaven were following him, riding on white horses and dressed in fine linen, white and clean.

REVELATION 19:11, 14

Talk to the Animals

Dr. Dolittle is the central character of a series of children's books by British author Hugh Lofting. Dolittle is a doctor who shuns human patients in favor of animals, with whom he can speak in their own languages. He later becomes a naturalist, using his abilities to speak with animals to better understand nature and the history of the world. Dr. Dolittle has become a classic and much-loved character of children's literature. But Dr. Dolittle was not the first to talk to an animal.

Over three thousand years ago, a man named Balaam had an interesting conversation with his donkey. The seemingly "dumb" donkey showed itself to be much wiser than the prophet for hire. Notice the superior intelligence of the animal.

> *Balaam got up in the morning, saddled his donkey and went with the princes of Moab. But God was very angry when he went, and the angel of the LORD stood in the road to oppose him. Balaam was riding on his donkey, and his two servants were with him. When the donkey saw the angel of the LORD standing in the road with a drawn sword in his hand, she turned off the road into a field. Balaam beat her to get her back on the road. Then the angel of the LORD stood in a narrow path between two vineyards, with walls on both sides. When the donkey saw the angel of the LORD, she pressed close to the wall, crushing Balaam's foot against it. So he beat her again.*
>
> NUMBERS 22:21–25

The donkey had greater spiritual insight than Balaam. She could see the angels when he couldn't.

> *Then the angel of the LORD moved on ahead and stood in a narrow place where there was no room to turn, either to the right or to the left. When the donkey saw the angel of the LORD, she lay down under Balaam, and he was angry and beat her with his staff. Then the LORD opened the donkey's mouth, and she said to Balaam, "What have I done to you to make you beat me these three times?"*
>
> NUMBERS 22:26–28

God gave the donkey the ability to speak Balaam's language.

> *Balaam answered the donkey, "You have made a fool of me! If I had a sword in my hand, I would kill you right now."*
> *The donkey said to Balaam, "Am I not your own donkey, which you have always ridden, to this day? Have I been in the habit of doing this to you?" "No," he said.*
>
> NUMBERS 22:29–30

The donkey showed greater reasoning ability than Balaam.

> *Then the LORD opened Balaam's eyes, and he saw the angel of the LORD standing in the road with his sword drawn. So he bowed low and fell facedown. The angel of the LORD asked him, "Why have you beaten your donkey these three times? I have come here to oppose you because your path is a reckless one before me."*
>
> NUMBERS 22:31–32

What does this have to do with Heaven? God gave an animal the ability to talk to a human on Earth, so why shouldn't He also give them the ability to talk to us in Heaven? The serpent could speak in the Garden of Eden (Genesis 3:1–2). Humans are going to get new bodies with enhanced abilities and maybe animals will, as well. If "wild" animals will be changed enough to peacefully coexist with each other and young children (Isaiah 11:6–9), couldn't they be changed enough to speak in our language?

Like all of God's creations, animals were created to praise Him. Praise is a verbal expression of appreciation and adoration. Some feel that animals will verbally join in when we praise God in Heaven.[3]

Praise the LORD. . . . Praise the LORD from the earth, you great sea creatures. . . wild animals and all cattle, small creatures and flying birds, kings of the earth and all nations, you princes and all rulers on earth, young men and maidens, old men and children. Let them praise the name of the LORD, for his name alone is exalted; his splendor is above the earth and the heavens.

PSALM 148:1, 7, 10–13

Then I heard every creature in heaven and on earth and under the earth and on the sea, and all that is in them, singing: "To him who sits on the throne and to the Lamb be praise and honor and glory and power, for ever and ever!"

REVELATION 5:13

So What?

There will definitely be animals in Heaven. I love my own dog and hope he'll join us in Heaven, though I am not positive that he will. (He does makes a mess in the garbage frequently.) But I am confident animals, including dogs, will be there. (Of course, I'm not so sure about cats.)

This knowledge should give those of us who love pets comfort. Knowing that even wild animals will be tamed should give non animal lovers comfort as well. It should also remind us that humans were originally charged with caring for animals. We must be careful how we treat animals, for they may one day tell us off in Heaven.

NOTES

[1]Randy Alcorn, *Heaven,* 381.
[2]"The Eden Alternative," Data and Resources, http://www.edenalt.com/data/htm#Elm
[3]Alcorn, *Heaven,* 378–379.

19

It'll Blow Your Mind

"What sort of day was it? A day like all days, filled with those events that alter and illuminate our times. . .and you were there."

When the narrator spoke those words in his deep, dramatic voice, they always captured my attention. For over five seasons, noted broadcaster Walter Cronkite hosted reenactments of historical events in the television series *You Were There*. Shows included "The Landing of the Hindenburg," "The Salem Witchcraft Trials," "The Gettysburg Address," and "The Fall of Troy." The charm of the program was picturing yourself embedded into the most fascinating events of human history.

Unfortunately, the black-and-white footage, the mediocre acting, and the inexpensive sets did not live up to the promise of the premise. But that will not be the case in Heaven. I believe Heaven will have its own sort of *You Were There* theater that will not only insert you into some of the most amazing events in history, but will also depict the key events in your life. By being there, you will gain a level of understanding otherwise impossible to attain.

When picturing the *You Were There* theater, envision a redbrick, 1950s-style theater on a quaint main street in small-town USA. Inside, you smell popcorn in the lobby and hear the seats creak when you sit down.

However, once you sit down and the movie begins, it will be unlike any show you have ever experienced. Miraculously, you will be transported through time and space as an up-close-and-personal unseen spectator of such incredibly amazing events as the creation of the universe, Moses parting the Red Sea, David bringing down Goliath, and Elijah facing down the prophets of Baal. The Bible will no longer be words of black typed on white pages. It will become a living theater, and you will be on stage in every scene you want and need to see.

Imagine being there with Peter, with the spray of the sea in his face, as he walks toward Jesus on the water or tasting the bread Jesus has just broken to feed the five thousand. Picture yourself gasping in awe and then elation when Lazarus walks out of the tomb, newly alive. Listen to the fear in the voices of the disciples just before Jesus walks into the upper room on the night of His resurrection.

You'll feel the heat and hear the voice of God radiating from Moses' burning bush. You'll see the mysterious handwriting on the wall at Belshazzar's party. You'll be stunned with the shepherds as the heavenly host erupts in the sky proclaiming the birth of the Messiah.

I believe you will get to see the role of angels, God's unseen secret agents, played in key proceedings. You will be there with Elisha and his servant when God opens his eyes and he sees the hills full of the angelic army. You will be there when God's angels rout three armies as Jehoshaphat leads his people out in praise and thanks. You'll see Gabriel delivering the prophecy of the seventy weeks to the aged Daniel. You'll see the angels knocking down the walls of Jericho.

Yet, maybe even more importantly, I believe Heaven will give you the opportunity to relive and review the key events of *your* life. You'll have the opportunity to see the joy in Jesus' face as you accepted Him as your Savior. You'll "be there" the first time you tried to share your faith and the Holy Spirit graciously put the right words in your mouth. From a new vantage point, you'll relive those times you fought through bitter tears to a position of resolved faith and you'll see the Father quietly stroking your hair.

You'll also be there for the crushing, brutal episodes of your life that you never understood before. Now, for the first time, you'll get the rest of the story. You'll receive answers to the gnawing *what, how,* and especially *why* questions in your life. You'll see a clearer, larger, deeper picture. . .and healing, profound healing, will occur.

But enough of what I think or believe we will come to understand once we are in Heaven. Let's look at what we *know* about what we will know in Heaven.

What We Know About What We'll Know in Heaven

Now we see but a poor reflection as in a mirror; then we shall see face to face. Now I know in part; then I shall know fully, even as I am fully known.

1 CORINTHIANS 13:12

When the apostle Paul wrote the words recorded in the letter to the Corinthians, mirrors were not what they are today. They gave a distorted image. There was a big difference between seeing your face in a mirror and seeing it live, face-to-face. This verse tells us we will see more clearly and understand more fully in Heaven than we can now.

Heaven is a mind-expanding experience.

We Won't Know Everything

We will know much more in Heaven than we do now, but we will not know everything. Only God is infinite; therefore, only God knows everything. We will know more fully, but not exhaustively.

We don't *need* to know everything there is to know. I doubt that I'll *need* to know how many grains of salt are in my salt shaker, or the total number of words ever printed on every book, typewriter, and computer screen in history, or even the batting average of Mickey Mantle in 1961. (It's .317, by the way.)

There are also many things I don't think I will ever *want* to know. I don't wish to know how many earthworms have ever lived. I have no desire to know the intricate details of the life of maggots. There are many things I just don't want to know.

We'll Know Much More Than We Know Now

While it is true we won't know everything in Heaven, we will know much more, much more fully, and much more accurately than we do now. One scholar writes,

1 Corinthians 13:12. . .rightly translated, simply says that we will know in a fuller or more intensive way, "even as we have been known, that is without error or misconceptions in our knowledge."[1]

Many life issues that have always been murky will become crystal-clear in the golden light of Heaven. Pieces of the puzzle will come together. Confusing matters will make sense.

We Will Continue to Learn in Heaven

Learning and growing are what keep life from becoming mundane. Contrary to popular opinion, life in Heaven will be anything but mundane. One reason Heaven will be such a vibrant place is because we will continue to learn in Heaven. We will have the time and opportunity to be taught more than we could even imagine on Earth.

Among other things, we will know more about God, the Bible, the mystery of salvation, the complexities of the universe, the history of the world, and more about ourselves than we could possibly know now. In Heaven our capacity for knowing and understanding will be greatly expanded. Also, our opportunity for knowing and understanding will be wildly enhanced. We will have the greatest guides imaginable.

Guided Tours

Growing up, my favorite family vacation was a week spent crawling through the caves of Carter Caves State Park in beautiful Kentucky. My dad, brother, and I spelunked with a fascinating guide named John. John knew the major facts, the offbeat details, and the tantalizing legends. He had a way of sharing them that was absolutely riveting and delightful. His love for the caves was contagious.

Years later, my dad and I took my boys back through the caves, hoping they would enjoy it as much as we had. They didn't and neither did we. Why? John had moved on. Our guides were dry, bland, busy sorts who seemed rather businesslike and bored by it all.

Maybe you have never been much of a fan of science, archaeology, astronomy, biology, botany, ecology, entomology, geology, hydrology, meteorology, or zoology. I think you will be in Heaven, simply because you will be given a guided tour by some of the greatest guides and most amazing scientists who ever lived. But even better, you will have access to the One who made it all! Imagine having an eternity to study the vast complexity of creation at the feet of the Creator!

Great Books

In Heaven we will have time and opportunity to read the greatest books ever written. We know that these books will be there:

1. The Bible (Matthew 24:35; Psalm 119:89). Just think, we can discuss the books at length with each of the thirty-nine or so human writers.

2. The scroll of remembrance, recounting times of fellowship shared by those who feared the Lord (Malachi 3:16). It's possible to have your name written in that book repeatedly.

3. The books containing documentation of every single deed done by every person of all time (Revelation 20:12). Noble deeds, seemingly unnoticed by history, will be recorded for all who look in the books.

4. The book of life, containing information about every one of God's people (Revelation 3:5; 13:8; 17:8; 20:12, 15; 21:27). Your name and mine can be in that book.

5. A record of David's tears (Psalm 56:8). I would guess the tears of others may also be written there, as God has also saved "the prayers of the saints" (Revelation 5:8).

Beyond these heavenly books, there will probably be no shortage of other outstanding reading material. With some of the greatest authors in history having unlimited time and expanded intellect, we can imagine they will author some truly incredible books while they are in Heaven. In Heaven you will have the time to read the book you never had time for and write that book you have always wanted to write.

Adult Education

In Heaven we will have the opportunity to learn skills that we did not have the time or ability to acquire on earth. I hope to draw and paint the pictures I have mentally recorded during my lifetime. I also anticipate painting heavenly sights that can only be imagined on Earth. I hope to learn to play the piano and the guitar really well. I want to understand the nuances of music well enough to write a symphony. I want to write songs. Why not? I will have access to wonderful teachers and all of eternity to practice.

We'll Know and Understand Ourselves Better Than We Do Now

In Heaven we will not only have more information, we'll have a better context for that information. We'll see facts through the 20/20 vision of eternity. We'll see the events of life as they are reflected in the eyes of the Master, especially the events of our lives.

The point of Mitch Albom's bestselling fictional story *The Five People You Meet in Heaven* is that the first five people you meet in Heaven will illuminate the unseen or misunderstood connections of our earthly lives.

> *"People think of heaven as a paradise garden, a place where they float on clouds and laze in rivers and mountains. But scenery without solace is meaningless. This is the greatest gift God can give you: to understand what happened in your life. To have it explained. It is the peace you have been searching for."[2]*

While I don't fully accept Albom's view of Heaven, I do think he is right about one thing. From the vantage point of Heaven, we will accurately be able to understand our lives and the meaning of the events of our lives. We will finally have answers to the "why?" questions that taint our joy and plague our minds down here on Earth. Missing pieces of the puzzle will be supplied.

So What?

Don't be frustrated by all you can't and don't understand now. In Heaven you will be continually learning and growing as a person. The day is coming when you will know and understand much more than you ever imagined possible. All of the various events of your life will finally make sense.

NOTES

[1] Wayne Gruden, *Systematic Theology: An Introduction to Biblical Doctrine* (Grand Rapids: Zondervan, 1994), endnote on 1162.

[2] Mitch Albom, *The Five People You Meet In Heaven* (Hyperion, NY: 2003), 35

20
WHERE DREAMS COME TRUE

"De plane! De plane!"

So began the wildly popular early 1980s television show *Fantasy Island*. Each week two guests came to Fantasy Island to have their fantasy fulfilled. Their mysterious host, the suave, white-suited Mr. Roarke, would sometimes do the impossible in order to grant their wishes. Somehow, the magical island could accommodate every dream, even if it meant visiting another time period, meeting a special person, or getting William Shakespeare to write a play. But there was always a twist to the fulfillment of the fantasy, giving the guests greater insight into themselves. The one constant from week to week was that at the sight of incoming visitors, Mr. Roarke's midget assistant, Tattoo, would scurry up to the bell tower, ring the bell, and shout, "De plane! De plane!"

Fantasy Island was a mediocre television show, but a very appealing idea. Wouldn't you love to go someplace where dreams come true? You can.

The Real Fantasy Island

The last several months, as I have pored over all that the Bible said about Heaven and eternity, I have discovered dozens of tremendous truths about Heaven. Some of my favorites include learning that Mom and Dad are having a splendid time in Paradise, the best parties in the universe are held in Heaven, and Heaven is anything but boring. I also look forward to enjoying my awesome new body, hanging out with angels, and having pets, maybe even all the perpetual puppies I want. I am especially thrilled to know that I might be able to fly. I am deeply challenged to prepare for Heaven now by living for eternity. Most important, I am eager to see God face-to-face in Heaven. But if I had to sum Heaven up with one epitaph, it might be this:

Heaven is the place where dreams come true.

God Is the Giver of Dreams

The story of the Bible is the story of God planting big dreams deep in human hearts. God gave a childless pagan, Abram (meaning "exalted father"), the calling of being the father of nations and changed his name to Abra*ham* (meaning "father of many," Genesis 12:1–2). God gave a boy named Joseph the dream of becoming a great leader (Genesis 37:5–10). Moses was given the desire to deliver his people (Exodus 2:11–12). Hannah's longing was for motherhood (1 Samuel 1:11).

We all have a dream or dreams etched deep into our DNA. On Earth, most never recognize their dreams. Many fewer ever see their fantasies fulfilled. Some scheme and sweat to chase a dream. Others deny their unfulfilled desires, hoping the dull ache will go away. But it never really goes away, does it?

God Is the Fulfiller of Dreams

We know the names of Abraham, Joseph, Moses, and Hannah because their dreams came true. Abraham saw his fantasy of fatherhood fulfilled as he fathered two entire nations of people—the Hebrews and the Arabs (Genesis 12:1–3, 6–7; 16:1–12; 17:20–21, 26). Joseph was promoted to a position in charge of one of the strongest nations on Earth (Genesis 41:39–41). Moses led God's people out of four hundred years of bondage (Exodus 12:33–42). Hannah got pregnant, delivered a son, and dedicated him to the Lord. Her son, Samuel, ended up leading a nation back to God (1 Samuel 2:19–20, 24–28; 3:19–21). No doubt, God is the fulfiller of dreams.

David, whose dream of becoming king was gloriously fulfilled, wrote a verse that acknowledges God to be the giver and fulfiller of dreams. "Delight yourself in the LORD, and he will give you the desires of your heart" (Psalm 37:4).

God Is the Rewarder of Faith

Hebrews 11 is one of the greatest chapters in the Bible. It could be called "The Faith Chapter," "The Hall of Faith," or my favorite, "Heaven's Heroes." In the first thirty-four verses, we see joyous examples of God's faithful people being rewarded on Earth for their faith. He tells of the rewarded faith of Enoch, Noah, Abraham, Moses' parents, and Moses himself. The writer builds a great crescendo of testimony to the power of faith.

> *By an act of faith, Israel walked through the Red Sea on dry ground. The Egyptians tried it and drowned. By faith, the Israelites marched around the walls of Jericho for seven days, and the walls fell flat. . . .*
>
> *I could go on and on, but I've run out of time. There are so many more— Gideon, Barak, Samson, Jephthah, David, Samuel, the prophets. . . . Through acts of faith, they toppled kingdoms, made justice work, took the promises for themselves. They were protected from lions, fires, and sword thrusts, turned disadvantage to advantage, won battles, routed alien armies. Women received their loved ones back from the dead.*
>
> HEBREWS 11:29–30, 32–35 THE MESSAGE

Did you catch that? God did not "just kinda, sorta" reward their faith. He did major-league miracles. Walking through the Red Sea on dry ground and watching the massive walls of Jericho falling down flat were major miracles. God indeed rewards faith. Hebrews said faithful people conquered kingdoms, shut the mouth of lions, routed foreign armies, even saw their dead raised to life again! Wow, it truly can't get any better than that.

But then the mood of Hebrews 11 suddenly darkens.

> *Others were tortured and refused to be released, so that they might gain a better resurrection. Some faced jeers and flogging, while still others were chained and put in prison. They were stoned; they were sawed in two; they were put to death by the sword. They went about in sheepskins and goatskins, destitute, persecuted and mistreated— the world was not worthy of them. They wandered in deserts and mountains, and in caves and holes in the ground. These were all commended for their faith, yet none of them received what had been promised.*
>
> HEBREWS 11:35–39

What happened? Being tortured, flogged, chained and put in prison, stoned, and sawn in two is no health, wealth, and happiness reward for faith. Neither is being destitute, persecuted, and mistreated. Trusting in God did not cause these good people to reach their destinies on Earth. In fact, just the opposite occurred—faith led to horrible results. None of these people ever saw the fulfillment of their faith. Their dreams were not reached on Earth. Their faith was unrewarded. Why? God had planned something better (Hebrews 11:40). In other words, Earth is not the end of the line or the final chapter. Rewards will come in

Heaven. Earth has no reward big enough for this type of faith (Hebrews 11:38).

How do we deal with the disappointments of unfulfilled fantasies, unrewarded faith, and unattained dreams? We remember that Heaven is the only place where some dreams come true.

Misplaced Priorities

Occasionally, in the place where I exercise, the television is on. One day the show that was being broadcast was about an incredibly attractive and talented family that had left behind most of their Christian roots and integrity to intently pursue big-time fame and fortune in Hollywood. Beating the odds, they quickly succeeded in reaching their dreams of world-renowned celebrity status.

As I watched the story of their lives, I felt a profound sense of sadness. They had systematically sold out in order to reach earthly dreams. One gave away her reputation, another sacrificed her virginity, a third walked away from his ministry. . .all to reach shallow, temporal dreams. They left God behind to chase dreams which, when viewed through the lens of Heaven, will be nothing more than a tiny blip on the radar screen of eternity. They had given up so much in order to gain what they will one day understand to be so very little.

I wonder how often I have been guilty of also chasing my self-centered, earthly dreams. How often have I found the profound sting of disappointment when they are unfulfilled or worse, the hollow emptiness when they are?

True Dream Catchers

One of the rich privileges of Heaven will be meeting people who, while on Earth, made incredible sacrifices for the gospel. They certainly weren't wealthy on Earth. They were not famous. No one down here even remembers their names. Pain, persecution, suffering, sorrow, misery, and, for some, martyrdom described their lives.

Don't feel sorry for them. They weren't pursuing earthly dreams. They had eternity in view all along. In Heaven they will be incredibly rewarded.

> *"I tell you the truth," Jesus replied, "no one who has left home or brothers or sisters or mother or father or children or fields for me and the gospel will fail to receive a hundred times as much in this present age (homes, brothers, sisters, mothers, children and fields—and with them, persecutions) and in the age to come, eternal life."*
>
> MARK 10:29–30

So What?

Maybe living for God has caused you to put some of your dreams on hold. Maybe there are deep desires and ardent longings that cannot, or will not, ever be fulfilled on Earth. Your unfulfilled dream involves holding a child or having a true friendship. It could involve taking a trip or attaining a level of accomplishment. Take hope. In Heaven there will be time and opportunity to reach for dreams unimagined on Earth. Friends, don't ever forget: If your dreams are from God, Heaven—not Earth—is the place where real dreams come true.

21
You Can Get There from Here

My friend Dave Watson is the pastor of a fine church on Staten Island in New York City. Recently, he sent me a video his church had produced entitled, "How to Get to Heaven from New York City." The video had some music, a few testimonies, and a brief talk by Pastor Dave.

In his talk, Dave told the wonderful story of how God sent His Son, Jesus, to Earth to die for our sins. He said that by trusting Jesus as Savior, a person would not only have a life wonderfully changed now, but would also have a place reserved in Heaven. Then he gave watchers the opportunity to pray a prayer expressing their faith in Jesus Christ.

As I viewed the video, I was reminded that the way to get to Heaven is the same from any place. However, all roads won't get you there. Jesus is the only way.

Many Ways to the Post Office?
Years ago I spent a summer doing street evangelism in England. I was on a team of young people who shared Jesus in schools, prisons, churches, and on street corners. During our street meetings, we usually sang several songs to draw a crowd. Then one of us would briefly tell the audience how much Jesus loved them. Our American accents never failed to get and keep their attention.

We would share how Jesus lived a sinless life, yet undeservedly died in our place as a sacrifice for our sin. We told how He rose from the dead to prove that He was God, and that God was satisfied with His payment for our sin. After a prayer, we would spread out through the crowd and try to engage them in conversation. Then we would discuss their response to the message of Jesus' death and resurrection for their sins.

Often near the beginning of the conversations we would ask them, "If you died today are you sure that you would go to Heaven?" This simple question usually gave us the opportunity to share how Jesus had changed our lives and why we had confidence that we were on our way to Heaven.

One day a nicely dressed gentleman who looked to be somewhere in his early sixties gave me a very condescending smile. "Young man," he said, "I am happy that your religion gives you such bold confidence about your eternal destiny. But I believe that Jesus is just one of many ways to Heaven. Every religion and philosophy is just a different way to the same place."

When I gave him a frown, he continued, "You see, right now we are sitting in a park. The post office is on the other side of town. From here there is more than one way to the post office. In the same way, there is more than one way to Heaven."

I looked at him and said, "But sir, we aren't talking about getting to the post office, we are talking about something infinitely more important—getting to Heaven."

He frowned as I continued. "Jesus claimed to be the only way to Heaven. In John 14:6 He emphatically said, 'I am the way and the truth and the life. No one comes to the Father except through me.'

"So, sir, you have to decide if Jesus was a liar, or a lunatic, or if He really is the Lord God. If there are many ways to Heaven and Jesus knew there were other ways, then He was a liar, and not a good man like you say. Following Him wouldn't be one of the ways to Heaven. Sir, do you really think Jesus was a liar?"

He shook his head no.

I continued, "If there truly are many ways to Heaven and Jesus sincerely believed that He is the only way, then He must have been a lunatic. Certainly trusting in a lunatic would never get anyone to Heaven. Sir, do you really believe that Jesus was a lunatic? Do you think I am a nut for following Him?"

Again he slowly shook his head no.

"Then your only other option is that He knew exactly what He was saying and what it meant. He really is *the way*, the truth, and the life. No one does go to the Father in Heaven *except through Him*. Jesus really was the Son of God. He did live a sinless life. He did die for our sins and He rose from the dead. He is the Lord of life. No one else did all of that for you, no one else could. But Jesus did because He loves you. He is the way to get to Heaven."

He rose to leave. "Son, you have given me much to think about. I will definitely read your pamphlet tonight."

"Where are you going?" I asked.

Sheepishly he said, "You are not going to believe this, but I've got to go to the post office."

How to Get to Heaven from Anywhere on Planet Earth

No matter where you live, the route to Heaven is the same for everyone. Whether you live in Russia, China, or West Virginia, there is one way that will get you to Heaven—faith in Jesus Christ.

Salvation is a faith process leading to an event. This process consists of several necessary steps. Maybe you have heard people speak of being "saved." Let me show you the seven biblical steps of faith that a person takes to be saved. A person needs to believe the following facts:

1. There is a God.

The Bible assumes the existence of God. It starts with these words, "In the beginning God. . ." (Genesis 1:1). His creation verifies His reality.

For since the creation of the world God's invisible qualities—his eternal power and divine nature—have been clearly seen, being understood from what has been made, so that men are without excuse.

ROMANS 1:20

Do you believe there is a God? If so, you have enough faith to go to step 2.

2. I am responsible to God.

The Bible says, "So then, each of us will give an account of himself to God" (Romans 14:12). It also says, "Just as man is destined to die once, and after that to face judgment" (Hebrews 9:27). One day each of us must stand before God and give an account of our lives to Him.

Do you accept the fact that you are accountable to God? If so, go to step 3.

3. I have failed my responsibility; I have not lived up to God's standard; I have broken God's laws. In other words, I have sinned.

It is as though God demands that our lives hit the bull's-eye on the target of moral righteousness before we can enter Heaven. Some of us may get closer than others, but all of us have missed the bull's-eye, because we are not perfect. Failing to hit this bull's-eye is sin. The Bible says, "All have sinned and fall short of the glory of God" (Romans 3:23). There are no perfect people. The Bible is quite clear, "There is no one righteous, not even one" (Romans 3:10). It also says, "If we claim to be without sin, we deceive ourselves and the truth is not in us" (1 John 1:8).

Have you perfectly kept all of the Ten Commandments? (See Exodus 20.) Can you even name all ten? Do you deem it to be true that you have sinned by failing to perfectly keep God's commands? If so, go to step 4.

4. My sin has alienated/separated me from my God.

Every sin we commit is like a brick in a wall of separation between us and God, because He is holy. The Bible says, "Your iniquities [sins] have separated you from your God" (Isaiah 59:2).

This separation from God, when carried to its logical conclusion, leads to death. The Bible says, "For the wages of sin is death" (Romans 6:23). Sin has the awful price tag of death. Death, as used in the Bible, speaks of separation. Physical death is the separation of the soul from the body when you stop breathing. Spiritual death is the separation of the soul from God. Eternal death is the separation of the soul from God, forever. The Bible says that we deserve death on all three levels because we have sinned against God.

Do you believe this? If so, go to step 5.

5. Jesus never sinned.

Jesus, the Son of God, was like mankind in every way except one. He never sinned. His sinless nature is seen throughout the Bible. For example, the Bible says He "has been tempted in every way, just as we are—yet *was without sin*" (Hebrews 4:15, emphasis added). By being sinless, He alone could take away our sin. As John wrote, "But you know that he appeared so that he might take away our sins. And *in Him is no sin*" (1 John 3:5, emphasis added).

It is as though God has an accounting book in Heaven. On the first page is the ugly record of all our sins and the fact that they add up to death and separation from God. But on the second page is the sinless record of Jesus Christ. So, instead of deserving death, He deserved life and union with God.

GOD'S ACCOUNTING BOOK

BAD NEWS	GOOD NEWS
US	JESUS
+SIN	-SIN
DEATH	LIFE
Page 1	Page 2

Do you believe that Jesus, the Son of God, never sinned? If so, go to step 6.

6. I can only be reconciled to God through Jesus Christ.

The third page of God's accounting book has the sad news that Jesus died on the cross two thousand years ago for our sins. He died in our place. He took our penalty. He did this in order to pay for our sins and to bring us to God.

That is why Jesus is the only way to God. Everyone human has sinned. None of us are perfect. Only Jesus Christ is the sinless Son of God, capable of paying for all of our sins.

If we place our faith in Him, and only Him, we can receive the gift of eternal life in Heaven. Read these verses carefully:

> *God made him who had no sin to be sin for us, so that in him we might become the righteousness of God.*
>
> 2 CORINTHIANS 5:21

> *For Christ died for sins once for all, the righteous for the unrighteous, to bring you to God.*
>
> 1 PETER 3:18

> *The wages of sin is death, but the gift of God is eternal life in Christ Jesus our Lord.*
>
> ROMANS 6:23

> *For it is by grace you have been saved, through faith—and this not from yourselves, it is the gift of God—not by works, so that no one can boast.*
>
> EPHESIANS 2:8–9

SAD NEWS	GLAD NEWS
JESUS	US
+OUR SIN	+FAITH IN JESUS
DEATH IN OUR PLACE	ETERNAL LIFE
Page 3	Page 4

Do you believe that Jesus died to pay for all of your sins? Do you believe eternal life is a free gift to be received by faith in Christ? If so, go to step 7. You have enough faith to be saved and to go to Heaven.

7. I am willing to receive the gift of eternal life.

Are you willing to be saved from your sin and receive God's free gift of eternal life? Receiving the gift of eternal life is an act of simple faith. It is as simple as ABC: Admit you need to be saved. Believe completely on Christ as the only one who can save you. Call upon Him to take control of your life and save you.

God promises, "Everyone who calls on the name of the Lord will be saved" (Romans 10:13). You can do that right now. If that is your desire, read this prayer and pray it to God as you do.

Dear God,

I admit that I am not perfect. I have sinned. Please forgive me.

I do not deserve eternal life. I have come short of Your standard of righteousness. I admit I need a Savior.

I believe that Jesus took my place and died for my sin. I believe that He rose from the dead to prove He can offer eternal life.

Now I call upon You to be my Lord and Savior. I personally commit myself completely to You.

So What?

Congratulations! If you have sincerely expressed your faith in the Lord Jesus as your Savior by calling out to Him through this prayer, the Bible says that you are saved (Romans 10:13). I will look you up when we all get to Heaven.

Final Thoughts

Q: How long is eternity?

A: Eternity is a very *long* time.

John Ankerberg illustrates eternity by comparing it to the efforts of a parakeet to pick up a single grain of sand in its beak, fly to the moon, drop it off, and return to Earth. If each round trip took a million years, and you commanded him to transport all the sand from all the beaches and deserts on Earth until there was no more sand, all the millions of years it took him to accomplish the task would just begin eternity. Eternity is a very long time.[1]

Where we spend eternity will be determined by whether or not we have trusted Jesus Christ as our Savior. Knowing this motivates us to be certain that we've been born into God's forever family through faith in Jesus Christ. I pray that reading this book did not merely give you good information about Heaven, but more importantly provided you with firm resolution to make certain you will be there by faith in Jesus.

How we spend eternity will be determined by how we live on Earth today. Our ability and capacity to enjoy and experience all that will be Heaven is established by how we live on Earth. Knowing this should motivate us to live for God now. I pray that reading this book has fueled an unrelenting passion to go all out for God in every area of your life, every day of your life, no matter what. You will never regret it.

Eternity is long. Live for God.

The author of Hebrews used this truth to motivate his readers who were suffering persecution.

> *Remember those earlier days after you had received the light, when you stood your ground in a great contest in the face of suffering. Sometimes you were publicly exposed to insult and persecution; at other times you stood side by side with those who were so treated. You sympathized with those in prison and joyfully accepted the confiscation of your property, because you knew that you yourselves had better and lasting possessions. So do not throw away your confidence; it will be richly rewarded.*
>
> Hebrews 10:32–35

Note

[1] John Ankerberg, "How Long Is Eternity?" Ankerberg Theological Research Institute, http://www.ankerberg.org/Articles/practical-christianity/PC0101W1.htm (May 15, 2006)

About the Author

Dave Earley is pastor of Grace City Church in Las Vegas, Nevada (www.gracecityvegas.com). He is the author of 18 books and serves as online professor for Pastoral Leadership and Evangelism for Liberty University. More importantly, he is the husband of Cathy and the father of Daniel, Andrew, and Luke.

Notes

288 Hell song